10/12

W9-CXZ-433

Directory
A–Z

Accommodation
Across the North Island, you
can bed down in historic
guesthouses, facility-laden
guesthouses, uniform motel units,
beautifully situated campsites and hostels that range
in character from clean-living
to YHA-prone.
For online listings

ing facilities and up-to-date
prices; many can also make
bookings on your behalf.
For online listings, visit
Automobile Association
(AA; www.aa.co.nz) and
Jasons (www.jasons.com).

B&Bs
Bed and breakfast
accommodation
industry

DISCARDED

THIS

Sarah Be

Charles

welcome to the North Island

Volcanic Thrills

Welcome to one of the planet's youngest countries, at least in geological terms. Ascend the volcanic cones surrounding Auckland for super city views, before heading south to Rotorua for hot mud spa treatments and helicopter journeys to the jagged volcanic summit of Mt Tarawera. Head due south to Lake Taupo, the legacy of one of the planet's biggest-ever volcanic eruptions, and now gateway to Tongariro National Park. Ski or snowboard on Mt Ruapehu's still-active slopes, or negotiate a steady path past Mt Ngauruhoe's brooding volcanic cone on the Tongariro Alpine Crossing.

Outdoor Experiences

New Zealand's South Island usually gets the kudos, but the oft-overlooked North Island also features a sublime combination of forests, mountains and beaches. Tackle one of the North Island's 'Great Walks' – one even offers a river journey by canoe or kayak – or spend a few hours wandering through the accessible wilderness of the Coromandel Peninsula. Day trips from vibrant Auckland can include kayaking to dormant volcanoes or canyoning and abseiling down forested waterfalls.

Food, Wine & Beer

Kiwi food was once a bland echo of a British Sunday dinner, but these days NZ chefs

Packing in cosmopolitan cities, authentic opportunities to experience NZ's indigenous Maori culture, and the country's bubbling and boiling volcanic heart, the North Island is an exceedingly versatile destination.

(left) Trampers on the Tongariro Alpine Crossing, Tongariro National Park
(below) The *hongi* is a traditional Maori greeting

dip into New World culinary oceans for inspiration, especially the Pacific with its abundant seafood and encircling cuisines. Don't go home without trying some Maori faves: *paua* (abalone), *kina* (sea urchin) and *kumara* (sweet potato). Thirsty? NZ's cool-climate wineries have been collecting award trophies for decades now, and the vineyard restaurants of the Hawke's Bay region are seriously good, too. The North Island's booming craft-beer scene also deserves serious scrutiny – keep an eye out for brews from Hallertau or Crouchers. And with a firmly entrenched coffee culture, you can always slake your craving for a decent double-shot.

Maori Culture

If you're even remotely interested in rugby, you'll have heard of the all-conquering All Blacks, New Zealand's national team, who would never have become world-beaters without their awesome Maori players. This is just one example of how Maori culture impresses itself on contemporary Kiwi life: across the North Island you can hear Maori language, watch Maori TV, see main street *marae* (meeting houses), join in a *hangi* (Maori feast), or catch a cultural performance with traditional Maori song, dance and usually a blood-curdling *haka* (war dance). Venture to the North Island's East Cape for the most authentic Maori experiences.

› New Zealand – North Island

Top Experiences ›

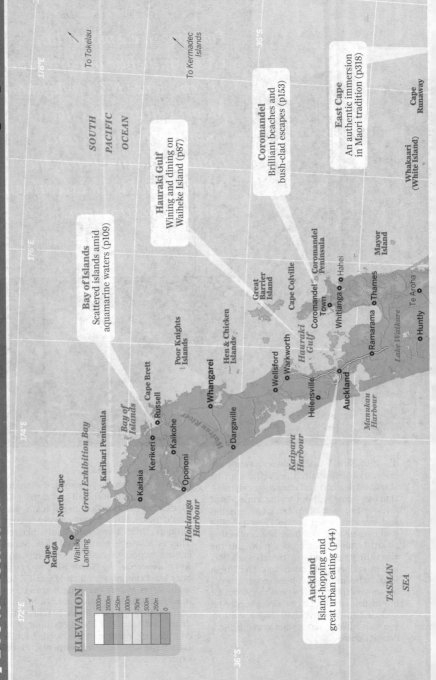

Bay of Islands
Scattered islands amid aquamarine waters (p109)

Hauraki Gulf
Wining and dining on Waiheke Island (p87)

Coromandel
Brilliant beaches and bush-clad escapes (p153)

East Cape
An authentic immersion in Maori tradition (p318)

Auckland
Island-hopping and great urban eating (p44)

ELEVATION
2000m
1500m
1250m
1000m
750m
500m
250m
0

SOUTH
PACIFIC
OCEAN

To Tokelau

To Kermadec
Islands

Cape Runaway

Whakaari
(White Island)

Mayor
Island

Te Aroha
Huntly
Thames
Ramarama
Whitianga ○ Hahei
Coromandel
Town
Coromandel
Peninsula
Cape Colville
Great
Barrier
Island
Hauraki
Gulf
Lake Waikare

Auckland
Helensville
Manukau
Harbour
Wellsford
Warkworth
Kaipara
Harbour

Hen & Chicken
Islands
Poor Knights
Islands
Whangarei
Cape Brett
Russell
Kerikeri
Bay of
Islands
Kaikohe
Opononi
Dargaville
Wairoa River
Hokianga
Harbour

Kaitaia
Karikari Peninsula
Great Exhibition Bay
North Cape
Cape
Reinga
Waitiki
Landing

TASMAN
SEA

172°E 174°E 176°E 178°E

34°S

36°S

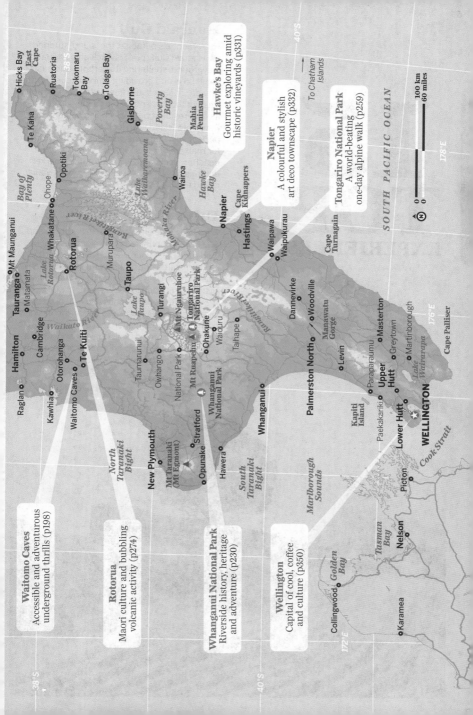

Waitomo Caves
Accessible and adventurous underground thrills (p198)

Rotorua
Maori culture and bubbling volcanic activity (p274)

Whanganui National Park
Riverside history, heritage and adventure (p230)

Wellington
Capital of cool, coffee and culture (p350)

Hawke's Bay
Gourmet exploring amid historic vineyards (p331)

Napier
A colourful and stylish art deco townscape (p332)

Tongariro National Park
A world-beating one-day alpine walk (p259)

SOUTH PACIFIC OCEAN

0   100 km
0   60 miles

To Chatham Islands

Hicks Bay
East Cape
Ruatoria
Te Kaha
Tokomaru Bay
Tolaga Bay
Gisborne
Poverty Bay
Mahia Peninsula
Opotiki
Ohope
Bay of Plenty
Whakatane
Lake Waikaremoana
Wairoa
Hawke Bay
Cape Kidnappers
Mt Maunganui
Tauranga
Matamata
Lake Rotorua
Rotorua
Murupara
Rangitaiki River
Mohaka River
Napier
Hastings
Waipawa
Waipukurau
Cape Turnagain
Hamilton
Cambridge
Otorohanga
Raglan
Kawhia
Waitomo Caves
Te Kuiti
Taupo
Lake Taupo
Turangi
Mt Ngauruhoe
Tongariro National Park
Mt Ruapehu
Ohakune
Waiouru
Taihape
Danevirke
Woodville
Manawatu Gorge
Waikato River
Taumarunui
Owhango
National Park
Whanganui National Park
Whanganui River
Rangitikei River
Palmerston North
Levin
Masterton
Greytown
Martinborough
New Plymouth
Mt Taranaki (Mt Egmont)
Stratford
Opunake
Hawera
North Taranaki Bight
South Taranaki Bight
Whanganui
Kapiti Island
Paraparaumu
Upper Hutt
Paekakariki
Lower Hutt
WELLINGTON
Lake Wairarapa
Cape Palliser
Marlborough Sounds
Cook Strait
Picton
Tasman Bay
Golden Bay
Nelson
Collingwood
Karamea

15 TOP
EXPERIENCES

Hauraki Gulf

1 A yachtie's paradise, the island-studded Hauraki Gulf (p84) is Auckland's aquatic playground, sheltering its harbour and east coast bays and providing ample excuse for the City of Sails' pleasure fleet to breeze into action. Despite the busy maritime traffic, the gulf has its own resident pods of whales and dolphins. Rangitoto Island is an icon of the city, its near-perfect volcanic cone provides the backdrop for many a tourist snapshot. With beautiful beaches, acclaimed wineries and upmarket eateries, Waiheke is Auckland's most popular island escape. Waiheke Island (p87)

Urban Auckland

2 Held in the embrace of two harbours and liberally sprinkled with volcanoes, Auckland (p44) isn't your average metropolis. It's regularly rated one of the world's most liveable cities, and while it's never going to challenge Sydney or London in the excitement stakes, it's blessed with good beaches and is flanked by wine regions. Auckland also has an increasingly cosmopolitan population that's large enough to support a thriving dining, drinking and live music scene boosted by new entertainment precincts developed for the Rugby World Cup in 2011.

Waitomo Caves

3 Waitomo (p198) is a must-see – an astonishing maze of subterranean caves, canyons and rivers perforating the northern King Country limestone. Blackwater rafting is the big lure here (similar to white-water rafting, but through a dark cave), plus glowworm grottos, underground abseiling and more stalactites and stalagmites than you'll ever see in one place again. Above ground, Waitomo township is a quaint collaboration of businesses: a pub, a cafe, a holiday park and some decent B&Bs.

Geothermal Rotorua

4 The first thing you'll notice about Rotorua (p274) is the smell of sulphur, meaning this geothermal hot-spot is a tad whiffy. But volcanic activity is what everyone comes to see, with gushing geysers, bubbling mud, steaming cracks in the ground, and boiling pools of mineral-rich water. Rotorua is definitely unique, a fact exploited by some commercially savvy local businesses. But you don't have to spend a fortune, and there are plenty of affordable (and free) volcanic encounters to be had in parks, Maori villages, or just along the roadside.

Bay of Islands

5 Turquoise waters lapping in pretty bays, dolphins frolicking at the bows of boats, pods of orcas gliding gracefully by: chances are these are the kind of images that drew you to New Zealand in the first place, and these are exactly the kind of experiences that the Bay of Islands (p122) delivers so well. Whether you're a hardened sea dog or a confirmed landlubber, there are myriad options to tempt you out on the water to explore the 150-odd islands that dot this beautiful bay. Urupukapuka Island (p134)

Tongariro Alpine Crossing

6 At the centre of the North Island, Tongariro National Park (p259) presents an alien landscape of alpine desert punctuated by three smoking and smouldering volcanoes. The Tongariro Alpine Crossing offers the perfect taste of what the park has to offer, skirting the bases of two of the mountains and providing views of craters, brightly coloured lakes, and the vast Central Plateau stretching out beyond. It's for these reasons that it's often rated as one of the world's best single-day wilderness walks.

Rugby

7 Rugby Union is New Zealand's national game and governing sporting pre-occupation. If your timing's good you might catch the revered national team (and reigning world champions), the All Blacks, in action. The 'ABs' are resident gods – mention Richie McCaw or Dan Carter in any conversation and you'll win friends for life. Watch some kids chasing a ball around a suburban field on a Saturday morning, or yell along with the locals in a small-town pub as the big men collide on the big screen.

Wellington

8 Voted the 'coolest little capital in the world' by Lonely Planet in 2011, windy Wellington (p350) lives up to the mantle by keeping things fresh and dynamic. Long famed for a vibrant arts and music scene, fuelled by excellent espresso and more restaurants per head than New York, Wellington has a host of craft-beer bars that have now elbowed in on the action. Edgy yet sociable, colourful yet often dressed in black, Wellington is big on the unexpected and unconventional. Erratic weather only adds to the excitement. Enjoy!

Maori Culture

9 New Zealand's indigenous Maori culture is both accessible and engaging: join in a *haka* (war dance); chow down at a traditional *hangi* (Maori feast cooked in the ground), carve a pendant from bone or *pounamu* (jade), learn some Maori language, or check out an authentic cultural performance with song, dance, legends, arts and crafts. Big-city and regional museums around the North Island are crammed with Maori artefacts and historical items, but this is a living culture: vibrant, potent and contemporary.

10

PAUL KENNEDY / LONELY PLANET IMAGES ©

Auckland's Pacific Island Culture

10 Welcome to 'The Big Taro', where around 180,000 residents of Polynesian descent make Auckland the capital of the South Pacific. The influence of Pacific Islanders from Samoa, the Cook Islands, Tonga, Niue, Fiji, Tokelau and Tuvalu is evident throughout Auckland. On the sports field, the city's professional teams showcase the best of Polynesian power, especially the NZ Warriors Rugby League team. Immerse yourself in Pacific Island culture at the weekly Otara market, or time your visit for March's annual Pasifika Festival. Performers at the Pasifika Festival (p65)

Coromandel Peninsula

11 A stunning peninsula combining sweeping beaches, quirky and idiosyncratic coastal landscapes, and rugged bush-clad mountains, the Coromandel region (p153) is a perfect and relaxing escape from the energy and verve of Auckland. The area's hippie and alternative lifestyle roots linger, with organic farms, New Age retreats and well-marked, and sometimes challenging, trails crisscrossing the peninsula's inland spine. Other options for active adventure include sea kayaking around Cathedral Cove, followed by a DIY natural spa pool at nearby Hot Water Beach. Cathedral Cove (p167)

Napier Art Deco

12 Volcanically active NZ is known as the 'Shaky Isles', and seven decades before the Christchurch earthquakes of 2010 and 2011, the country was impacted by a significant seismic event. When a magnitude 7.8 earthquake struck the North Island's east coast in 1931, many brick buildings in the cities of Napier (p332) and Hastings (p340) collapsed. Reconstruction harnessed the art deco and Spanish mission architectural fashions of the day, and now Napier especially is a showcase of art deco design. Visit during February's annual art deco weekend for the full 1930s experience.

ELLISON & DUNCAN LTD

Hawke's Bay Wine Country

13 Wine has been crafted in the Hawke's Bay region (p331) since 1851, with many more recent vineyards now joining established and iconic local wineries such as Mission Estate and Church Road. The emphasis is on excellent Bordeaux-style reds and chardonnay, and many wineries also incorporate good vineyard restaurants. Farmers markets and a tasty menu of other gourmet and artisan producers make it easy for foodie travellers to craft a DIY exploration of the region, and smart lodge and B&B accommodation often celebrate stunning rural and coastal locations.

East Cape

14 Get right off the beaten track around NZ's easternmost region, a twisting and turning coastal procession of isolated bays and coves, many punctuated during summer with the crimson blooms of the pohutukawa tree. Nowhere else in NZ is everyday Maori culture and society quite so evident, with quiet villages and *marae* (Maori meeting places) tucked into sleepy bays. Several East Cape (p318) tour operations are run by members of the local Ngati Porou *iwi* (tribe), providing the opportunity for authentic and heartfelt interaction with travellers.
Tolaga Bay (p321)

Whanganui National Park

15 After frantic jetboating or river rafting in other parts of the North Island, slow right down with a canoe or kayak trip down the history-rich Whanganui River (p230) in the gloriously isolated Whanganui National Park. Snaking 329km from its source on Mt Tongariro to the Tasman Sea, it's the country's longest navigable river, and tracks carefully through brooding native bush scattered with the remains of historical villages and trading stops. If you're more keen on a driving holiday, the spidery Whanganui River Road is equally spectacular.

need to know

When to Go

Paihia
GO Feb–Apr

Auckland
GO Feb–Apr

Rotorua
GO Oct–Dec

Taupo
GO Jul–Oct (skiing) or Feb–Apr

Wellington
GO Dec–Feb

High Season
(Dec–Feb)

» Summer with busy beaches, outdoor explorations, festivals and sporting events.

» Pay more for big-city accommodation.

» It's school holiday time with local families hitting popular beaches.

Shoulder Season
(Mar–Apr)

» Fine weather, short queues, kids in school and warm(ish) ocean.

» Evenings supping Kiwi wines and beers.

» Spring (Sep–Nov) is also shoulder season: local business isn't stressed by summer crowds yet.

Low Season
(May–Aug)

» Head for the slopes of Mt Ruapehu for brilliant southern hemisphere skiing.

» No crowds, good accommodation deals and a seat in any restaurant.

» Watch the All Blacks rugby team in welcoming local pubs.

Your Daily Budget

Budget less than
$130

» Dorm beds or campsites: $25–35 per night

» Big-city food markets for self-catering bargains

» Explore NZ with a money-saving bus pass

Midrange
$130–250

» Double room in a midrange hotel/motel: $100–180

» Midrange restaurant, a movie or a live band, a few beers at a pub

» Hire a car and explore further

Top end over
$250

» Double room in top-end hotel: from $180

» Three-course meal in a classy restaurant: $70

» Take a guided tour, go shopping or hit some ritzy bars

Money

» ATMs are widely available, especially in larger cities and towns. Credit cards accepted in most hotels and restaurants.

Visas

» Citizens of Australia, UK and 56 other countries don't need visas for NZ (length of stay allowances vary). Other countries' citizens require visas. See www.immigration.govt.nz.

Mobile Phones

» Australian and European phones will work on NZ's networks, but not most American or Japanese phones. Use global roaming or a local SIM card on prepay.

Driving

» Driving is on the left, with the steering wheel on the right-hand side of the car.

Websites

» **100% Pure New Zealand** (www.newzealand.com) Official tourism site.

» **Department of Conservation** (www.doc.govt.nz) DOC parks and camping info.

» **Destination New Zealand** (www.destination-nz.com) Resourceful tourism site.

» **Lonely Planet** (www.lonelyplanet.com/new-zealand) Advice from travellers who've actually been there.

» **Living Landscapes** (www.livinglandscapes.co.nz) Maori tourism operators.

» **DineOut** (www.dineout.co.nz) Restaurant reviews.

Exchange Rates

Australia	A$1	NZ$1.30
Canada	C$1	NZ$1.23
China	Y10	NZ$1.98
Euro zone	€1	NZ$1.59
Japan	¥100	NZ$1.62
Singapore	S$1	NZ$0.97
UK	UK£1	NZ$1.92
US	US$1	NZ$1.25

For current exchange rates see www.xe.com

Important Numbers

Regular NZ phone numbers have a two-digit area code followed by a seven-digit number. When dialling within a region, the area code is still required. Drop the initial 0 if dialling from abroad.

NZ country code	✓64
International access code from NZ	✓00
Emergency (ambulance, fire, police)	✓111
Directory assistance	✓018
International directory	✓0172

Arriving

» **Auckland International Airport**
Bus – 24-hour Airbus Express at least every 30 minutes
Shuttle Bus – Pre-booked, 24-hour door-to-door services
Taxi – Around $70; 45 minutes to the city

» **Wellington Airport**
Bus – Airport Flyer every 15 minutes 5.50am to 9.30pm
Shuttle Bus – Pre-booked, 24-hour door-to-door services
Taxi – Around $30; 20 minutes to the city

Driving Around the North Island

There are extensive bus networks and a couple of handy train lines crisscrossing the North Island, but for the best scenery, flexibility and pure freedom it's hard to beat piling into a campervan or rent-a-car and hitting the open road. Scanning the map you might think that driving from A to B won't take long, but remember that many of the roads here are two-lane country byways, traversing hilly landscape in curves, crests and convolutions: always allow plenty of time to get wherever you're going. And who's in a hurry anyway? Slow down and see more of the country: explore little end-of-the-line towns, stop for a swim/surf/beer, and pack a Swiss Army knife for impromptu picnics at roadside produce stalls.

if you like...

Cities

New Zealand is urbanised: 72% of Kiwis reside in the 16 biggest towns, and one in three New Zealanders lives in Auckland. It follows that cities here are great fun! Coffee shops, restaurants, bars, boutiques, bookshops, museums, galleries... You're never far from a live gig or an espresso.

Auckland Sydney for beginners? We prefer 'Seattle minus the rain', infused with vibrant South Pacific culture (p46)

Wellington All the lures you'd expect in a capital city, packed into what is really just a very big town. Is San Francisco this pretty? (p350)

Hamilton NZ's fourth-biggest town doesn't raise much of a blip on the tourist radar, but the bar scene, restaurants, museum and Waikato River deserve a second look (p179)

New Plymouth First appearances can definitely be deceiving. Beyond New Plymouth's laidback provincial charm is a winning selection of cosmopolitan museums and galleries, great cafes and restaurants (p210)

Beaches

New Zealand has a helluva lot of coastline with plenty of sun, surf and sand (much of which is volcanic, coloured black or brown). Top tip: book your trip for summer, or you might find the water a little cooler than you bargained for...

Karekare Classic black sand beach west of Auckland with wild surf (Eddie Vedder nearly drowned here), so be careful (p99)

Hahei Iconic Kiwi beach experience on the Coromandel, with mandatory side trips to Cathedral Cove and Hot Water Beach (p167)

Wainui Beach On the North Island's East Coast, with surfing, sandcastles, sunshine... The quintessential Kiwi beach for all travelling beach bums. BYO Jack Johnson tunes (p324)

Manu Bay NZ's most famous surf break (seen *Endless Summer*?) peels ashore south of Raglan. There's not much sand, but the left-hand point break is what you're here for (p188)

History

New Zealand's European history goes back just a couple of hundred years, but Maori have lived here since at least AD 1200. Across the country you'll uncover places where the two cultures have met to forge a modern nation.

Waitangi Treaty Grounds In the Bay of Islands, where the contentious Treaty of Waitangi was first signed by Maori chiefs and the British Crown (p130)

Te Papa Wellington's vibrant treasure-trove museum, where history, both Maori and Pakeha, speaks, sparkles, shakes (p358)

Whanganui River Road Drive alongside the slow-curling Whanganui River past Maori towns and groves of deciduous trees, remnants of failed Pakeha farms (p231)

Russell New Zealand's first capital used to be a rambunctious and rowdy haven for boozing sailors, but now it's a pretty harbourside village with historic sites aplenty (p126)

» Te Papa (p358), Wellington, designed by Jasmax Architects

Maori Culture

After you touch down in New Zealand it won't take long to notice how prominent, potent and accessible indigenous Maori culture is in contemporary society: language, music, arts and crafts, performance, tattoos, and of course, rugby.

Auckland The country's biggest city is renowned for having the planet's biggest Pacific Island population, but a handful of excellent Maori tour operators also showcase Auckland's indigenous culture and history (p63)

Rotorua Catch a cultural performance at one of several venues: experience a *haka* (war dance) and a *hangi* (Maori feast), with traditional song, dance, folklore and storytelling (p278)

Footprints Waipoua Explore the staggeringly beautiful Waipoua Kauri Forest on Northland's West Coast with a Maori guide (p148)

Taiami Tours Heritage Journeys Help paddle a *waka* (Maori canoe) along the sleepy Waitangi River to Haruru Falls. Tours include being welcomed onto a *marae* (meeting place) by the passionate Mihaka family (p125)

Museums

Take time out from the wineries, beaches and bars to spend a few hours meandering through a museum: it's good for the soul!

Auckland Museum A classical Greek-temple design housing a superb collection of Maori and Pacific Islander artefacts, with wonderful guided tours (p51)

New Zealand Maritime Museum From the earliest Maori migrations to the yachting heroics of the America's Cup, seafaring and sailing has been important to the city of Auckland (p49)

Te Papa The country's biggest and best museum is in Wellington – brilliant by any measure and a much-loved national showcase of the history, culture and geography of NZ (p358)

Puke Ariki New Plymouth's snazzy waterfront museum is dappled with Maori, colonial and wildlife exhibits...and a great cafe! (p210)

Rotorua Museum Learn about Rotorua's volcanic and spa town history before exploring the art and culture of the local Te Arawa Maori people at this recently renovated museum (p276)

Tramping

NZ has a world-wide rep for hiking, with nine epic 'Great Walks' managed by the Department of Conservation. But you needn't be Sir Edmund Hillary: short walks can also deliver you a taste of wilderness.

Cape Reinga Coastal Walkway A 53km Northland long-haul, which can be easily bitten off as a series of short, scenic strolls (p142)

Mt Taranaki short walks You can loop around the mountain or bag the summit, but a couple of hours spent strolling on its photogenic flanks is equally rewarding (p218)

Hillary Trail Invest an active four days tackling this recently opened coastal trail named after 'Sir Ed'. There are good campsites along the way and regular access to Auckland's West Coast surf beaches (p98)

Tongariro Alpine Crossing Strike out on what is reputedly NZ's best one-day walk, featuring spectacular alpine and volcanic scenery. Spend a few extra days and incorporate interesting summit diversions up Mts Ngauruhoe and Tongariro (p262)

» Cathedral Cove (p167), Coromandel Peninsula

Pubs, Bars & Beer

Sometimes it's the simple things you encounter on holiday that stay with you: a sunset, a conversation, a splash in the sea, a cold beer at the end of a long day on the road...

Wellington craft-beer scene Malthouse and Hashigo Zake are just two of nearly a dozen craft-beer bars in the capital (something to do with thirsty politicians?) (p367)

Hood St precinct Hamilton's Hood and Victoria Sts offer up more pubs, beer barns and bars than you have nights left on your holiday (p183)

Auckland While Wellington and Nelson argue over where the country's craft-beer capital really is, the country's biggest city is becoming a hoppy hub in itself. Head to Galbraith's Alehouse, Hallertau or Golden Dawn for Auckland micro-brewed goodness (p76)

Rotorua The crafty team at Rotorua's Croucher Brewing Co create some of the country's best brews. Check them out at Rotorua's Brew bar (p286)

Foodie Experiences

New Zealand is no longer the land of meat-and-three-veg: eating here these days can be as simple or sophisticated as you like, with the emphasis squarely on fresh regional produce (without a boiled turnip in sight).

Eating out in Auckland When it comes to fine dining, cafes and delicatessens, Auckland takes the cake (and the bouillabaisse, the lamb rack, the fish pie...) (p96)

Bay of Plenty kiwifruit Pick up a dozen fuzzy, ripe and delicious kiwifruit from roadside stalls for as little as $1-a-dozen (p304)

Wellington Everyone accepts the nation's capital is a hotspot for craft beer and coffee, but classy fine dining, casual cafes, and authentic ethnic eateries also line Wellington's streets (p363)

Hawke's Bay Combine dining in the vineyard restaurants of Hawke's Bay with exploring farmers markets and roadside stalls in this fertile and productive region (p331)

Wine Regions

If you haven't been down to your local liquor store in the last decade, you might have missed the phenomenon that is New Zealand wine: a pristine environment, abundant sunshine, volcanic soils and passionate wine-makers have been busy bottling world-beating cool-climate drops.

Martinborough A small-but-sweet wine region a day-trip from Wellington: easy cycling and easy-drinking pinot noir (p378)

Waiheke Island Auckland's favourite weekend playground has a hot, dry microclimate: perfect for Bordeaux-style reds and rosés (p87)

Hawke's Bay One of NZ's oldest and most established wine areas is still one of the country's best. Combine history and wine-tasting at the iconic Church Road or Mission Estate wineries (p331)

Matakana From NZ's oldest wine areas to one of its newest. Around an area north of Auckland, Matakana combines an expanding boutique vineyard scene, brilliant beaches, and a great weekly farmers market (p106)

If you like...mountain biking, don't miss a rampaging ride through the superb Redwoods Whakarewarewa Forest, just outside Rotorua (p289)
If you like...surfing, wax your longboard and head for Surf Hwy 45, south of New Plymouth (p222)

Markets

Weekend markets are big business in NZ and the national appetite for organic, locally grown and artisan produce is seemingly bottomless. They're also great places to eat breakfast, drink coffee, watch buskers, meet friends and generally unwind.

Otara Market Multicultural and edgy, Auckland's Saturday-morning Otara Market brims with buskers, arts and crafts, fashions and food. The city's Polynesian community is particularly present (p81)

River Traders Market Whanganui's riverside market is a Saturday-morning fixture: up to 100 stalls, with a particularly good farmers market section (p229)

Harbourside Market Wellington's obligatory fruit and veg pit stop, complimented by fancy artisan produce in the adjacent City Market (p363)

La Cigale The profound French influence of this weekend Auckland farmers market is joined by a tasty array of other stallholders to reflect the increasingly cosmopolitan population of Auckland. Three nights a week the space is converted to house a quirkily informal bistro (p75)

Extreme Activities

We're not sure if it's something that has evolved to lure tourists, or if it's something innate in the Kiwi psyche, but extreme activities (skydiving, bungy jumping, jetboating, zorbing, white-water rafting etc) are part and parcel of today's NZ experience.

SkyWalk & SkyJump, Auckland Sky Tower New Zealand's adrenaline-pumping extreme scene permeates even downtown Auckland (p59)

Waitomo black-water rafting Don a wetsuit, a life vest and a helmet with a torch attached, and rampage along an underground river (p199)

Zorbing Go on – you've always wanted to bounce down a Rotorua hillside ensconced in a giant inflatable globe. And no, it's not true there's a secret office in Wellington dreaming up new extreme sports (p278)

Skydiving Old school thrills maybe, in the land of weird and wonderful activities, but skydiving above Taupo is one of the world's best spots to leap from a perfectly safe aircraft (p250)

Festivals

Music? Wine? Food? A combination of all three? You'll find plenty of reasons to join the locals for festive celebrations across the North Island. Bring your dancing shoes and an appetite for great tastes.

Pasifika Every March, Auckland's Western Springs is transformed into a slice of the tropical South Pacific. Dine on Polynesian food, learn the finer points of Pacific dance, and experience authentic island culture without booking a flight to Fiji or Samoa (p65)

WOMAD Is New Plymouth's Bowl of Brooklands one of NZ's best outdoor concert venues? When the world music fiesta of WOMAD comes to town in March, there's simply no debate (p213)

Pohutukawa Named after the scarlet-bloomed tree that punctuates the North Island coastline during summer, the Pohutukawa Festival brightens the entire Coromandel Peninsula with art, music, food and wine every November (p153)

month by month

Top Events

1	**National Jazz Festival**, April
2	**New Zealand International Sevens**, February
3	**WOMAD**, March
4	**World of WearableArt Award Show**, September

January

New Zealand peels its eyes open after New Year's Eve, gathers its wits and gets set for another year. Great weather, cricket season in full swing and happy holidays for the locals.

★ Festival of Lights

New Plymouth's Pukekura Park is regularly dubbed a 'jewel', but the gardens really sparkle during this festival. It's a magical scene: pathways glow and trees are impressively lit with thousands of lights. Live music, dance and kids' performances too.

February

The sun is shining, the nights are long, and the sav blanc and pale ale are chillin' in the fridge: this is prime party time across NZ. Book your festival tickets (and beds) in advance!

★ Waitangi Day

On 6 February 1840, the Treaty of Waitangi was first signed between Maori and the British Crown. The day remains a public holiday across NZ, and in Waitangi itself (the Bay of Islands) there are guided tours, concerts, market stalls and family entertainment.

★ New Zealand International Arts Festival

This month-long spectacular happens in Wellington in February to March every even-numbered year, and is sure to spark your imagination. NZ's cultural capital exudes artistic enthusiasm with theatre, dance, music and visual arts, and there are international acts aplenty.

★ Te Matatini National Kapa Haka Festival

This engrossing Maori *haka* (war dance) competition happens in February in odd-numbered years. Venues vary: 2011 was Gisborne, 2013 will be Rotorua. And it's not just the *haka*: expect traditional song, dance, storytelling and other performing arts.

★ Fringe NZ

More music, theatre, comedy, dance and visual arts in Wellington, but not the mainstream stuff from the New Zealand International Arts Festival. This festival highlights the more unusual, emerging, controversial, low-budget and/or downright weird acts.

★ Splore

Explore Splore, a cutting-edge outdoor summer fest in Tapapakanga Regional Park, southeast of Auckland. Contemporary live music, performance and visual arts, safe swimming, pohutukawa trees, and the company of very laid-back locals. Come here to chill out.

New Zealand International Sevens

Yeah, we know, it's not rugby season, but February sees the world's top seven-a-side rugby teams crack heads in Wellington: everyone from heavyweights such as Australia and South Africa, to minnows like the Cook Islands and Kenya. A great excuse for a party.

March

March brings a hint of autumn, with harvest time in the vineyards and orchards and long, dusky evenings with plenty of festivals plumping out the calendar. Locals unwind post-tourist season.

WOMAD

Local and international music, arts and dance performances fill New Plymouth's Brooklands Bowl to overflowing. An evolution of the original world-music festival dreamed up by Peter Gabriel, who launched the inaugural UK concert in 1990. Perfect for families (usually not too loud).

Auckland International Boat Show

Auckland harbour blooms with sails and churns with outboard motors. It doesn't command the instant nautical recognition of Sydney or San Diego, but Auckland really is one of the world's great sailing cities.

Pasifika Festival

With around 140,000 Maori and notable communities of Tongans, Samoans, Cook Islanders, Niueans, Fijians and other South Pacific Islanders, Auckland has the largest Polynesian community in the world. These vibrant island cultures come together at this annual fiesta in Western Springs Park.

April

April is when canny travellers hit NZ: the ocean is still swimmable and the weather still mild, with nary a tourist or queue in sight. Easter means pricey accommodation everywhere.

National Jazz Festival

Every Easter Tauranga hosts the longest-running jazz fest in the southern hemisphere. The line up is invariably impressive (Kurt Elling, Keb Mo), and there's plenty of fine NZ food and wine to accompany the finger-snappin' sonics.

May

The nostalgia of autumn runs deep: party-nights are long gone and another chilly Kiwi winter beckons. Thank goodness for the Comedy Festival! Farmers markets overflow with good value and organic eating.

New Zealand International Comedy Festival

Three-week laugh-fest in May with venues across Auckland, Wellington and various regional centres: Whangarei to Invercargill with all the mid-sized cities in between. International gag-merchants (such as Arj Barker, Danny Bhoy) line up next to home-grown talent.

June

It's the beginning of the ski season, so time to head to Mt Ruapehu. For everyone else, head north: the Bay of Plenty is always sunny, and is it just us, or is Northland underrated?

Matariki

Maori New Year is heralded by the rise of Matariki (aka Pleiades star cluster) in May and the sighting of the new moon in June.

Remembrance, education, music, film, community days and tree planting take place, mainly around Auckland and Northland.

July

Wellington's good citizens clutch collars, shiver and hang out in bookshops and cafes. The All Blacks kick off the international rugby season, so find a pub and get cheering. Yes, even you Aussies.

NZ International Film Festival

After separate film festivals in both Auckland and Wellington, a selection of flicks hits the road for screenings in regional North Island towns from July to November. Movie buffs in Masterton and Palmerston North get very excited – understandably so.

Russell Birdman

Birdman rallies are just so '80s... But they sure are funny! This one in Russell features the usual cast of costumed contenders propelling themselves off a jetty in pursuit of weightlessness. Bonus points if your name is Russell.

August

Land a good deal on accommodation pretty much anywhere except around Mt Ruapehu's ski scene. Winter is almost spent, but there's still not much happening outside. Music, great pubs and art are your saviours.

Taranaki International Arts Festival

Beneath the snowy slopes of Mt Taranaki, August used to be a time of quiet repose. Not any more: this whizz-bang arts festival in New Plymouth now shakes the winter from the city with music, theatre, dance, visual arts and parades.

Jazz & Blues Festival

You might think that the Bay of Islands is all about sunning yourself on a yacht while dolphins splash salt-water on your stomach. In the depths of winter, this jazzy little festival will give you something else to do.

September

Spring has sprung! The amazing and surprising World of WearableArt Award Show is always a hit. And will someone please beat Canterbury in the annual ITM rugby cup final?

World of WearableArt Award Show

A bizarre (in the best pos-sible way) two-week long Wellington event featuring amazing hand-crafted gar-ments. Entries from the show are displayed at the World of WearableArt & Classic Cars Museum across Cook Strait in Nelson after the event.

October

This post-rugby and pre-cricket season leaves sports fans twiddling their

(above) Maori women perform the *kapa haka* (cultural dance) at Waitangi Day celebrations
(below) Members of a Polynesian group representing Tonga at the Pasifika Festival

thumbs. Maybe it's time to head east to Gisborne? October is shoulder season, with reasonable accommodation rates, minimal crowds and no competition for the good campsites.

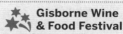

Gisborne Wine & Food Festival

Around Labour Weekend – in the back half of the month – Gisborne's proud winemakers pair with local foodies and artisan producers to showcase the region's tasty goodies. There's lots of great music too.

November

Across Northland, the Coromandel Peninsula, Bay of Plenty and the East Coast, NZ's iconic pohutukawa trees erupt with brilliant crimson blooms. The weather is picking up, and a few tourists are starting to arrive.

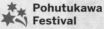

Pohutukawa Festival

Coromandel comes alive with markets, picnics, live music, kiteflying, snorkelling, and poetry. It's all very clean-living and above-board, but not everything has to be about drinking, dancing and decadence. And just look at those pohutukawa trees!

BikeFest & Lake Taupo Cycle Challenge

Feeling fit? Try cycling 160km around Lake Taupo and then come and talk to us. In the week prior to the big race, BikeFest celebrates all things bicycular from BMX and mountain bikes, to unicycles and tandems.

December

Summer! The crack of leather-on-willow resounds across the nation's cricket pitches and office workers surge towards the finish line. Everyone gears up for Christmas: avoid shopping centres like the plague.

Rhythm & Vines

Wine, music and song (all the good things) in sunny east coast Gisborne on New Year's Eve. Top DJs, hip-hop acts, bands and singer-songwriters compete for your attentions. Or maybe you'd rather just drink some chardonnay and kiss someone on the beach?

itineraries

Whether you've got one week or two, these itineraries provide a starting point for the trip of a lifetime. Want more inspiration? Head online to lonelyplanet. com/thorntree to chat with other travellers.

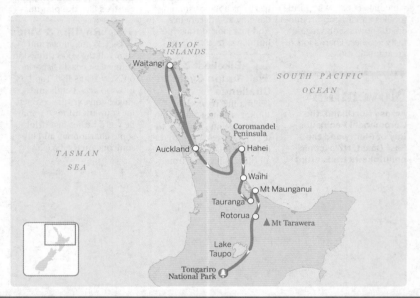

10 Days to Two Weeks
Northern Highlights

Discover the harbours, beaches and Pacific culture of **Auckland**, before heading north to the **Bay of Islands**. At **Waitangi**, explore colonial history and New Zealand's indigenous Maori culture, before hitting the water to swim with dolphins.

Return to Auckland and detour east to the rugged **Coromandel Peninsula** for bushwalking and sea kayaking. Stay overnight in the sleepy beach community of **Hahei**. Then follow looping SH25 around the peninsula to the historic mining town of **Waihi**, before continuing to **Tauranga**, gateway to beachy **Mt Maunganui**.

Head south to **Rotorua** for the classic combo of bubbling thermal activity and vibrant Maori culture. Splash out on a helicopter ride for stunning views of **Mt Tarawera** and the surrounding lakes. Continue south to **Lake Taupo** for jetboating thrills or the more relaxed appeal of trout fishing. If you're feeling brave, bungy jump from 47m above the Waikato River.

Follow the coves of the lake's picturesque eastern shore to **Tongariro National Park**. where there's good winter skiing and the Tongariro Alpine Crossing, judged one of the world's best one-day walks.

» (above) Bungy jumping over the Waikato River
» (left) Hot springs, Rotorua

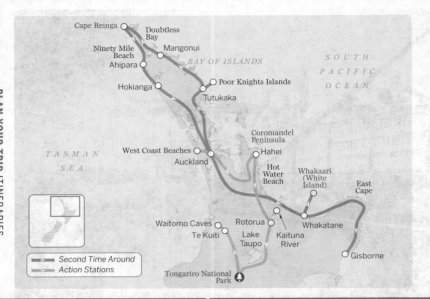

Second Time Around
Action Stations

One Week to 10 Days
Second Time Around

From energetic and cosmopolitan **Auckland**, head north to sleepy **Tutukaka** for diving around **Poor Knights Islands**. Kayaking, paddleboarding and snorkelling are also available. Further north combine sailing and dolphin swimming trips at **Doubtless Bay** with possibly the world's best fish and chips at **Mangonui**. Continue to windswept **Cape Reinga**, the end of the road for NZ's SH1.

Venture south, skirting the windswept expanses of **Ninety Mile Beach**, before hitting **Ahipara** and traversing massive sand dunes on sand yachts or quad bikes. Continue to **Hokianga** for a taste of colonial history, before heading south through Auckland to **Whakatane**. Take a boat or helicopter out to **Whakaari** (White Island), NZ's most active volcano.

Meander on the SH35 around the **East Cape**, a procession of hidden coves and bays. Here locally owned tourism operators showcase NZ's indigenous Maori culture. Maybe go horse riding on the beach or try a *hangi* (Maori feast). Continue to **Gisborne** for excellent wines and craft beers. NZ's iconic combination of active adventure and stunning scenery is definitely not restricted to the country's South Island.

One Week to 10 Days
Action Stations

Kick off in **Auckland** with the vertiginous combination of SkyWalk and SkyJump. Slow down with a twilight sea kayaking trip across the harbour, before heading to the **West Coast Beaches** for canyoning down bush-clad waterfalls.

Take the long way round to the **Coromandel Peninsula** for the legendary beach town of **Hahei** and more kayaking around stunning Cathedral Cave. Finish the day – if the tides are in your favour – by digging a natural spa pool at nearby **Hot Water Beach**.

Back on the road, head to **Rotorua**, where action options include zorbing, jetboating, mountain biking and a downhill luge. White-water rafting and river sledging on the nearby Grade V **Kaituna River** are exciting, especially the 7m drop over the Okere Falls.

Continue south to **Lake Taupo** for skydiving with mountain views and bungy jumping above the Waikato River, before completing the superb Tongariro Alpine Crossing, a stunning one-day tramp in **Tongariro National Park**.

Saving the best for last, head back north to `Te Kuiti` and black-water rafting at **Waitomo Caves**.

Active North Island

Top Short Tramps

Tongariro Alpine Crossing, Tongariro National Park (p262)
)Kohi Point Walkway, Whakatane (p306)
Mangawhai Walk, Northland (p113)
Pinnacles, Coromandel Peninsula (p161)

Top Anti-Gravity Activities

Bungy jumping There are many locations to take the plunge, but in Auckland you can make the leap of faith from the Sky Tower (p47)
Zorbing The downhill thrills of zorbing takes place south in Rotorua (p278)
Swoop There's the sweep and swoosh of the Swoop and Shweeb also in Rotorua (p278)

Top White-Water Rafting Trips

Tongariro River, Taupo (p257)
Kaituna River, Rotorua (p280)

Top Mountain-Biking Tracks

Makara Peak Mountain Bike Park, Wellington (p357)
Redwoods Whakarewarewa Forest, Rotorua (p289)
42 Traverse, Central Plateau (p262)

Top Surf Spots

Manu Bay, Raglan (p188)
Waikanae Beach, Gisborne (p324)
Mount Beach, Mt Maunganui (p299)

Trekking in the North Island

Trekking (aka bushwalking, hiking, or tramping as Kiwis call it) is the perfect vehicle for a close encounter with the North Island's natural beauty. There are thousands of kilometres of tracks here – some well marked (including three of New Zealand's celebrated 'Great Walks'), some barely a line on a map –plus an excellent network of huts enabling trampers to avoid lugging tents and (in some cases) cooking gear. Before plodding off into the forest, get up-to-date information from the appropriate authority – usually the Department of Conservation (DOC; see p433) or regional i-SITE visitor information centres.

Planning Your Tramp
When to Go

» **Mid-December–late January** Tramping high season is during the school summer holidays, starting a couple of weeks before Christmas – avoid it if you can.

» **January–March** The summer weather lingers into March: wait until February if you can, when tracks are less crowded.

» **June–August** Winter is not the time to be out in the wild, especially at altitude – some paths close in winter because of snow and there are correspondingly lower levels of facilities and services.

RESPONSIBLE TRAMPING

If you went straight from the cradle into a pair of hiking boots, some of these tramping tips will seem ridiculously obvious; others you mightn't have considered. Online, the 'leave no trace' website (www.lnt.org) is a great resource for low-impact hiking, and the DOC site (www.camping.org.nz) has plenty more responsible camping tips. When in doubt, ask DOC or i-SITE staff.

The ridiculously obvious:

» Time your tramp to avoid peak season: less people equals less stress on the environment and fewer snorers in the huts.

» Carry out *all* your rubbish. Burying rubbish disturbs soil and vegetation, encourages erosion, and animals will probably dig it up anyway.

» Don't use detergents, shampoo or toothpaste in or near watercourses (even if they're biodegradable).

» Use lightweight kerosene, alcohol or Shellite (white gas) stoves for cooking; avoid disposable butane gas canisters.

» Where there's a toilet, use it. Where there isn't one, dig a hole and bury your by-product (at least 15cm deep, 100m from any watercourse).

» If a track passes through a muddy patch, just plough straight on through – skirting around the outside increases the size of the bog.

You mightn't have considered:

» Wash your dishes 50m from watercourses; use a scourer, sand or snow instead of detergent.

» If you *really* need to scrub your bod, use biodegradable soap and a bucket, at least 50m from any watercourse. Spread the waste water around widely to help the soil filter it.

» If open fires are allowed, use only dead, fallen wood in existing fireplaces. Leave any extra wood for the next happy camper.

» Keep food-storage bags out of reach of scavengers by tying them to rafters or trees.

» Feeding wildlife can lead to unbalanced populations, diseases and animals becoming dependent on handouts. Keep your dried apricots to yourself.

What to Bring

Primary considerations: your feet and your shoulders. Make sure your footwear is as tough as old boots and that your pack isn't too heavy. If you're camping or staying in huts without stoves, bring a camping stove. Also bring insect repellent to keep sandflies away, and don't forget your scroggin – a mixture of dried fruit and nuts (and sometimes chocolate) for munching en route.

Books

DOC publishes detailed books on the flora and fauna, geology and history of NZ's national parks, plus leaflets (50c to $2) detailing hundreds of NZ walking tracks.

Lonely Planet's *Tramping in New Zealand* describes around 50 walks of various lengths and degrees of difficulty. Mark Pick-

ering and Rodney Smith's *101 Great Tramps* has suggestions for two- to six-day tramps around the country. The companion guide, *202 Great Walks: the Best Day Walks in New Zealand,* by Mark Pickering, is handy for shorter, family-friendly excursions. New trampers should check out *Don't Forget Your Scroggin* by Sarah Bennett and Lee Slater – all about being safe and happy on the track. The *Birdseye Tramping Guides* from Craig Potton Publishing have fab topographical maps, and there are countless books covering tramps and short urban walks around NZ – scan the bookshops.

Maps

The topographical maps produced by Land Information New Zealand (LINZ; see p430) are a safe bet. Bookshops don't often have a good selection of these, but LINZ has map sales offices in major cities and towns, and DOC offices often sell LINZ maps for local tracks. Outdoor stores also stock them. The LINZ map series includes park maps (national, state and forest), dedicated walking-track maps, and detailed 'Topo50' maps (you may need two or three of these per track).

Online Resources

» **www.trampingtracks.co.nz** Descriptions, maps and photos of long and short tramps all over NZ.

» **www.tramper.co.nz** Articles, photos, forums and excellent track and hut information.

» **www.trampingnz.com** Region-by-region track info with readable trip reports.

» **www.peakbagging.org.nz** Find a summit and get up on top of it.

» **www.topomap.co.nz** Online topographic maps of the whole country.

Track Classification

Tracks in NZ are classified according to various features, including level of difficulty. We loosely refer to the level of difficulty as easy, medium, hard or difficult. The widely used track classification system is as follows:

» **Short Walk** Well formed; allows for wheelchair access or constructed to 'shoe' standard (ie walking boots not required). Suitable for people of all ages and fitness levels.

» **Walking Track** Easy and well-formed longer walks; constructed to 'shoe' standard. Suitable for people of most ages and fitness levels.

» **Easy Tramping Track** or **Great Walk** Well formed; major water crossings have bridges and track junctions have signs. Light walking boots required.

» **Tramping Track** Requires skill and experience; constructed to 'boot' standard. Suitable for people of average physical fitness. Water crossings may not have bridges.

» **Route** Requires a high degree of skill, experience and navigation skills. Well-equipped trampers only.

Great Walks

Three of NZ's nine official 'Great Walks' are on the North Island, and one is actually a highly-regarded river trip. Natural beauty abounds, but prepare yourself for crowds, especially during summer.

All three of the North Island's Great Walks are described in Lonely Planet's *Tramping in New Zealand,* and are detailed in pamphlets provided by DOC visitor centres.

To tramp these tracks you'll need to buy **Great Walk Tickets** before setting out. These track-specific tickets cover you for hut accommodation (from $10 to $51.10 per adult per night, depending on the track and season) and/or camping ($5 to $20.40 per adult per night). You can camp only at designated camping grounds; note there's no camping on the Milford Track. In the off-peak season (May to September), you can use **Backcountry Hut Passes** ($92 per adult, valid for six months) or pay-as-you-go **Backcountry Hut Tickets** (huts $10 to $15, camping $5) instead of Great Walk tickets on Great Walks except for the Lake Waikaremoana Track. Kids under 18 stay in huts and camp for free on all Great Walks.

There's a booking system in place for Great Walk huts and campsites. Trampers must book their chosen accommodation and specify dates when they purchase Great Walk tickets. Bookings are required year-round for the Lake Waikaremoana Track. For the Tongariro Northern Circuit and the Whanganui Journey, bookings are required for the peak season only (October to April).

Bookings and ticket purchases can be made online (www.doc.govt.nz), by email (greatwalksbooking@doc.govt.nz), or via

---

TRACK SAFETY

Thousands of people tramp across NZ without incident, but every year a few folks meet their maker in the mountains. Some trails are only for the experienced, fit and well-equipped – don't attempt these if you don't fit the bill. Ensure you are healthy and feel comfortable walking for sustained periods.

NZ's climatic changeability subjects high-altitude walks to snow and ice, even in summer: always check weather and track conditions before setting off, and be ready for conditions to change rapidly. Consult a DOC visitor centre and leave your intentions with a responsible person before starting longer walks.

Also see www.mountainsafety.org.nz and www.metservice.co.nz for weather updates.

Great Walks

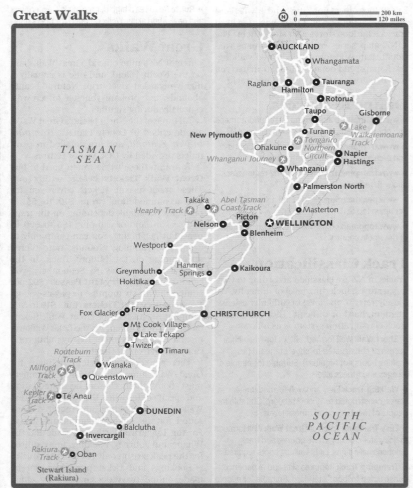

DOC offices close to the tracks. Bookings open mid-July each year.

Other Tracks

Of course, there are a lot more walks in NZ than just the great ones! Try these selections on for size:

» **Cape Reinga Coastal Walkway** A 50km, three-day, easy beach tramp (camping only) in Northland. A 132km six- to eight-day route is also possible.

» **Mt Holdsworth–Jumbo Circuit** A medium-to-hard, three-day tramp in Holdsworth Forest Park, scaling alpine Mt Holdsworth.

» **Pouakai Circuit** A 25km, two- to three-day loop in the lowland rainforest, cliffs and subalpine forest at the foot of Mt Taranaki in Egmont National Park.

» **Tongariro Alpine Crossing** A brilliant 18km, one-day, medium tramp through Tongariro National Park.

Backcountry Huts & Conservation Campsites

Huts

DOC maintains more than 950 backcountry huts in NZ's national and forest parks. Hut categories comprise:

THE NORTH ISLAND'S THREE 'GREAT WALKS'

WALK	DISTANCE	DURATION	DIFFICULTY	DESCRIPTION
Lake Waikaremo-ana Track	46km	3–4 days	Easy to medium	Lake views, bush-clad slopes and swimming in Te Urewera National Park
Tongariro Northern Circuit	41km	3–4 days	Medium to hard	Through the active volcanic landscape of Tongariro National Park; see also Tongariro Alpine Crossing
Whanganui Journey	145km	5 days	Easy	Canoe or kayak down the Whanganui River in Whanganui National Park

» **Basic huts** Just a shed!

» **Standard huts** No cooking equipment and sometimes no heating, but mattresses, water supply and toilets.

» **Serviced huts** Mattress-equipped bunks or sleeping platforms, water supply, heating, toilets and sometimes cooking facilities.

Details about the hut services can be found on the DOC website. Backcountry hut fees per adult, per night range from free to $52, with tickets bought in advance at DOC visitor centres (some huts can also be booked online: visit www.doc.govt.nz). Children under 10 can use huts for free; 11- to 17-year-olds are charged half-price. If you do a lot of tramping DOC sells a six-month Backcountry Hut Pass applicable to most huts except Great Walk huts in peak season (October to April, during which time you'll need Great Walk tickets). In the low season (May to September), backcountry hut tickets and passes can also be used to procure a bunk or campsite on some Great Walks.

Depending on the hut category, a night's stay may use one or two tickets. Date your tickets and put them in the boxes provided at huts. Accommodation is on a first-come, first-served basis.

Campsites

DOC also manages 250 'Conservation Campsites' (usually vehicle accessible) with categories as follows:

» **Basic campsites** Basic toilets and water; free and unbookable.

» **Standard campsites** Toilets and water supply, and perhaps barbecues and picnic tables; $5 to $16; unbookable.

» **Serviced campsites** Full facilities: flush toilets, tap water, showers and picnic tables. They may

also have barbecues, a kitchen and laundry; $7 to $19; bookable via DOC visitor centres.

See the Great Walks section in this chapter for information on Great Walks campsites. Children aged five to 17 pay half-price for Conservation Campsites; those four and under stay free.

Guided Walks

If you're new to tramping or just want a more comfortable experience than the DIY alternative, several companies can escort you through the wilds, usually staying in comfortable huts (showers!), with meals cooked and equipment carried for you.

Places on the North Island where you can sign up for a guided walk include Mt Taranaki, Lake Waikaremoana and Tongariro National Park. Prices for a four-night guided walk start at around $1500, and rise towards $2000 for deluxe guided experiences.

Getting There & Away

Getting to and from trailheads can be problematic, except for popular trails serviced by public and dedicated trampers' transport. Having a vehicle only helps with getting to one end of the track (you still have to collect your car afterwards). If the track starts or ends down a dead-end road, hitching will be difficult.

Of course, tracks accessible by public transport are also the most crowded. An alternative is to arrange private transport, either with a friend or by chartering a vehicle to drop you at one end, then pick you up at the other. If you intend to leave a vehicle at a trailhead, don't leave anything valuable inside – theft from cars in isolated areas is a significant problem.

TE ARAROA

After a lengthy planning and construction period, **Te Araroa** (The Long Pathway; www.teararoa.org.nz) finally opened in December 2011. A 3000km tramping trail from Cape Reinga in NZ's north to Bluff in the south (or the other way around), the route links existing tracks with new sections. Built over a decade, mostly by volunteers, it's one of the longest hikes in the world: check the website for maps and track notes, plus blogs and videos from hardy types who have completed the end-to-end epic.

Skiing & Snowboarding on the North Island

Global warming is triggering a worldwide melt, but NZ remains an essential southern hemisphere destination for snow bunnies, with downhill skiing, cross-country (Nordic) skiing and snowboarding all passionately pursued. Heliskiing, where choppers lift skiers to the top of long, isolated stretches of virgin snow, also has its fans. The North Island ski season is generally June to October, though it can vary depending on annual weather conditions.

Planning Your Snow Session
Where to Go

On the North Island, the volcanic landscape of Mt Ruapehu in Tongariro National Park showcases the Whakapapa and Turoa resorts, while club areas such as Tongariro's Tukino and Taranaki's Manganui are publicly accessible and usually less crowded and cheaper than the commercial fields.

Practicalities

NZ's commercial ski areas aren't generally set up as 'resorts' with chalets, lodges or hotels. Rather, accommodation and après-ski carousing are often in surrounding towns, connected with the slopes via daily shuttles. Many club areas have lodges you can stay at, subject to availability.

Visitor information centres in NZ and international Tourism New Zealand offices (p433) have info on the various ski areas and can make bookings and organise packages. Lift passes cost anywhere from $40 to $95 per adult per day (half-price for kids). Lesson and lift packages are available in most areas. Ski/snowboard equipment rental starts at around $40 per day (cheaper for multiday hire).

Online Resources

» **www.brownbear.co.nz/ski** Brilliant reference detailing all of NZ's ski areas.

» **www.mtruapehu.com** The go-to website for information on Whakapapa and Turoa.

» **www.snow.co.nz** Reports, cams and ski info across the country.

» **www.newzealandsnowtours.com** Snowboarding and skiing tours, north and south.

North Island Ski Areas
Tongariro National Park

» **Whakapapa & Turoa** (p260) On either side of Mt Ruapehu, these well-run twin resorts comprise NZ's largest ski area. Whakapapa has 30 intermediate groomed runs, plus snowboarding, cross-country, downhill, a terrain park and the highest lift access in NZ. Drive from Whakapapa Village (6km; free parking), or shuttle-bus in from National Park Village, Taupo, Turangi or Whakapapa Village. Smaller Turoa has a beginners' lift, plus snowboarding, downhill and cross-country skiing. There's free parking or shuttle-bus transport from Ohakune 17km away, which has the North Island's liveliest post-ski scene.

» **Tukino** (p262) Club-operated Tukino is on Mt Ruapehu's east, 46km from Turangi. It's quite remote, 14km down a gravel road from the sealed Desert Rd (SH1), and you need a 4WD vehicle to get in. Uncrowded, with mostly beginner and intermediate runs.

Taranaki

» **Manganui** (p219) Offers volcano-slope, club-run skiing on the eastern slopes of spectacular Mt Taranaki in the Egmont National Park, 22km from Stratford (and a 20-minute walk from the car park). Ski off the summit when conditions permit: it's a sweaty two-hour climb to the crater, but the exhilarating 1300m descent compensates.

ANDERS BLOMQVIST / LONELY PLANET IMAGES ©

MICAH WRIGHT / LONELY PLANET IMAGES ©

» (above) Tramping in Tongariro
   National Park (p259)
» (left) Surf instruction at Raglan
   (p185)

Extreme North Island

The North Island's astounding natural assets encourage even the laziest lounge lizards to drag themselves outside and get active. 'Extreme' sports are abundant and supremely well organised here. Mountaineering is part of the national psyche; skydiving, mountain biking, jetboating and rock climbing are well established; and pant-wetting, illogical activities like bungy jumping have become everyday pursuits. While adrenaline-pumping activities obviously have an element of risk, the perception of danger is part of the thrill. (Just make sure you have travel insurance anyway.)

Bungy Jumping

Bungy jumping was made famous by Kiwi AJ Hackett's 1986 plunge from the Eiffel Tower, after which he teamed up with champion NZ skier Henry van Asch to turn the endeavour into a profitable enterprise. The South Island resort town of Queenstown is the spiritual home of bungy, but Taupo, Taihape, Auckland and Rotorua on the North Island all offer the opportunity to leap bravely into the void on a giant rubber band.

Caving

Caving (aka spelunking) opportunities abound in NZ's honeycombed karst (limestone) regions. In the North Island, you'll find local clubs and organised tours around Auckland, Waitomo, and Whangarei.

Useful resources:

» **Wellington Caving Group** (www.caving. wellington.net.nz)

» **Auckland Speleo Group** (www.asg.org.nz)

» **New Zealand Speleological Society** (www.caves.org.nz)

Horse Trekking

Unlike some other parts of the world where beginners get led by the nose around a paddock, horse trekking in NZ lets you really get out into the countryside – on a farm, forest or beach. Rides range from one-hour jaunts (from around $50) to week-long, fully catered treks.

On the North Island Taupo, the Coromandel Peninsula, Waitomo, Pakiri, Ninety Mile Beach, Rotorua, the Bay of Plenty and East Cape are top places for an equine encounter.

For info and operator listings:

» **100% Pure New Zealand** (www.new zealand.com)

» **True NZ Horse Trekking** (www.truenz. co.nz/horsetrekking)

» **Auckland SPCA Horse Welfare Auxiliary Inc** (www.horsetalk.co.nz)

Jetboating

Hold onto your breakfast: passenger-drenching 360-degree spins ahoy!

On the North Island the Whanganui, Motu, Rangitaiki and Waikato Rivers are excellent for jetboating, and there are sprint jets at the Agrodome in Rotorua. Jetboating around the Bay of Islands in Northland is also de rigueur.

Parasailing & Kiteboarding

Parasailing (dangling from a modified parachute that glides over the water, whilst being pulled along by a speed-boat/jetski) is perhaps the easiest way for humans to achieve assisted flight. After a half-day of instruction you should be able to do limited solo flights. Tandem flights in the North Island happen at Te Mata Peak in Hawke's Bay.

Kiteboarding (aka kitesurfing), where a mini parachute drags you across the ocean on a mini surfboard, can be attempted at Paihia, Tauranga, Mt Maunganui, Raglan and Wellington. You can tee up lessons at most of these places, too. Karikari Peninsula near Cape Reinga on NZ's northern tip is a kiteboarding mecca.

Mountain Biking

The North Island is laced with quality mountain-biking opportunities. Mountain bikes can be hired in Taupo and Rotorua, and both cities have bicycle repair shops.

Companies will take you up to the summit of Mt Ruapehu, so you can hurtle down without the grunt-work of getting to the top first. Rotorua's Redwoods Whakarewarewa Forest offers famously good mountain biking, as does the 42 Traverse near the township of National Park (close to Tongariro National Park). Other North Island options include Woodhill Forest, Waihi, Te Aroha, Te Mata Peak and Makara Peak in Wellington.

Some traditional tramping tracks are open to mountain bikes, but DOC has restricted access in many cases due to track damage and the inconvenience to walkers,

CYCLE TOURING

OK, so cruising around the country on a bicycle isn't necessarily 'extreme', but it is super-popular in NZ, especially during summer. Most towns offer bike hire at either backpacker hostels or specialist bike shops, with bike repair shops in bigger towns.

The $50-million **Nga Haerenga, New Zealand Cycle Trail** (www.nzcycletrail.com) is a national network of bike trails from Kaitaia to Bluff, featuring 18 'Great Rides', a similar concept to tramping's 'Great Walks'. Some sections/trails are still in the developmental stages, but some stages are open: see the website for updates.

Online resources:

» **Independent Cycle Tours** (www.cyclehire.co.nz)

» **Paradise Press** (www.paradise-press.co.nz) produces *Pedallers' Paradise* booklets by Nigel Rushton.

especially at busy times. Never cycle on walking tracks in national parks unless it's permissible (check with DOC), or you risk heavy fines and the unfathomable ire of hikers.

Resources include:

» **Classic New Zealand Mountain Bike Rides** (www.kennett.co.nz) Details short and long rides all over NZ.

» **New Zealand Mountain Biker** (www.nzmtbr.com.nz) A magazine which comes out every two months.

Rock Climbing

Time to chalk up your fingers and don some natty little rubber shoes. On the North Island, popular rock-climbing areas include Auckland's Mt Eden Quarry; Whanganui Bay, Kinloch, Kawakawa Bay and Motuoapa near Lake Taupo; Mangatepopo Valley and Whakapapa Gorge on the Central Plateau; Humphries Castle and Warwick Castle on Mt Taranaki; and Piarere and Wharepapa South in the Waikato.

Climb New Zealand (www.climb.co.nz) has the low-down on the gnarliest overhangs around NZ, plus access and instruction info.

Sea Kayaking

Sea kayaking is a fantastic way to see the coast and get close to wildlife you'd otherwise never see.

Highly rated sea kayaking areas around the North Island include the Hauraki Gulf (particularly off Waiheke and Great Barrier Islands), the Bay of Islands and Coromandel Peninsula. Other North Island kayaking locations include Auckland's Waitemata Harbour, Hahei, Raglan and East Cape. Useful resources:

» **Kiwi Association of Sea Kayakers** (www.kask.org.nz)

» **Sea Kayak Operators Association of New Zealand** (www.skoanz.org.nz)

Scuba Diving

NZ is prime scuba territory, with warm waters up north, brilliant sea-life and plenty of interesting sites.

Around the North Island, get wet at the Bay of Islands Maritime and Historic Park, the Hauraki Gulf Maritime Park, the Bay of Plenty, Great Barrier Island, Goat Island Marine Reserve, the Alderman Islands, Te Tapuwae o Rongokako Marine Reserve near Gisborne, and Sugar Loaf Islands Marine Park near New Plymouth. The Poor Knights Islands near Whangarei are reputed to have the best diving in NZ (with the diveable wreck of the Greenpeace flagship *Rainbow Warrior* nearby). Stay tuned to see whether the MV *Rena,* grounded off Tauranga in 2011, will become a dive site.

Expect to pay anywhere from $180 for a short, introductory, pool-based scuba course; and around $600 for a four-day, PADI-approved, ocean dive course. One-off organised boat- and land-based dives start at around $170.

Resources include:

» **New Zealand Underwater Association** (www.nzunderwater.org.nz)

» **Dive New Zealand** (www.divenewzealand.com)

Skydiving

Feeling confident? For most first-time skydivers, a tandem skydive will help you make the leap, even if common sense starts to get the

SURFING IN NEW ZEALAND: JOSH KRONFELD

As a surfer I feel particularly guilty in letting the reader in on a local secret – NZ has a sensational mix of quality waves perfect for beginners and experienced surfers. As long as you're willing to travel off the beaten track, you can score some great, uncrowded waves. The islands of NZ are hit with swells from all points of the compass throughout the year. So, with a little weather knowledge and a little effort, numerous options present themselves. Point breaks, reefs, rocky shelves and hollow sandy beach breaks can all be found – take your pick!

Surfing has become increasingly popular in NZ and today there are surf schools up and running at most premier surf beaches. It's worth doing a bit of research before you arrive: **Surfing New Zealand** (www.surfingnz.co.nz) recommends a number of surf schools on its website. If you're on a surf holiday in NZ, consider purchasing a copy of the *New Zealand Surfing Guide*, by Mike Bhana.

Surf.co.nz (www.surf.co.nz) provides information on many great surf spots, but most NZ beaches hold good rideable breaks. Here are some of the ones I particularly enjoy on the North Island:

» **Waikato** Raglan, NZ's most famous surf break and usually the first stop for overseas surfies

» **Coromandel** Whangamata

» **Bay of Plenty** Mt Maunganui, now with a 250m artificial reef that creates huge waves, and Matakana Island

» **Taranaki** Fitzroy Beach, Stent Rd and Greenmeadows Point all lie along the 'Surf Highway'

» **East Coast** Hicks Bay, Gisborne city beaches and Mahia Peninsula

» **Wellington Region** Beaches such as Lyall Bay, Castlepoint and Tora

NZ water temperatures and climate vary greatly from north to south. For comfort while surfing, wear a wetsuit. In summer on the North Island you can get away with a spring suit and boardies, while in winter you'll need to use a 2–3mm steamer.

Josh Kronfeld, surfer and former All Black

better of you. Tandem jumps involve training with a qualified instructor, then experiencing up to 45 seconds of free fall before your chute opens. The thrill is worth every dollar (around $250/300/350 for a 8000/10,000/12,000ft jump, extra for a DVD/photograph). The **New Zealand Parachute Federation** (www. nzpf.org) is the governing body.

At the time of writing safety concerns had sparked a review of skydiving in NZ, with operators having to comply with stringent new Civil Aviation Authority (CAA) regulations. Ask your operator if it has CAA accreditation before you take the plunge.

White-Water Rafting, Kayaking & Canoeing

There are almost as many white-water rafting and kayaking possibilities as there are rivers in NZ, with no shortage of companies to get you into the rapids. Rivers are graded from I to VI, with VI meaning 'unraftable'. On the rougher stretches there's usually a minimum age limit of 12 or 13 years.

Popular North Island rafting rivers include the Rangitaiki, Wairoa, Motu, Mokau, Mohaka, Waitomo, Tongariro and Rangitikei. There is also the Kaituna Cascades near Rotorua, with its 7m drop at Okere Falls.

Canoeing is so popular on the North Island's Whanganui River that it's been designated one of NZ's 'Great Walks'. You can also dip your paddle into Lake Taupo and Lake Rotorua. Some backpacker hostels close to canoe-friendly waters have Canadian canoes and kayaks for hire (or for free), and loads of commercial operators run guided trips

Resources include:

» **New Zealand Rafting Association** (www.nz-rafting.co.nz)

» **Whitewater NZ** (www.rivers.org.nz)

» **New Zealand Kayak** (www.canoeandkayak. co.nz) NZ's premier kayaking magazine.

regions at a glance

Experience Auckland's confident and cosmopolitan Pacific buzz, before heading north for the Bay of Islands' combination of colonial history, Maori heritage, and sweeping beaches amid isolated coves. The Coromandel Peninsula features yet more bush-clad beaches, and New Zealand's indigenous Maori culture bubbles away proudly in volcanic Rotorua and around the remote East Cape, quite probably the North Island's most quintessentially laid-back region. Further inland, the country's violent volcanic past produced the wonders of Lake Taupo and Tongariro National Park, now a haven for skiers, trampers, and travellers looking to lure a plump rainbow trout. Wine and foodie treats abound in Hawke's Bay and Gisborne, and Wellington is arty and caffeine-fuelled proof that capital cities definitely don't have to be boring.

Auckland

Beaches
Food & Drink
Volcanoes

Beaches
From the calm, child-friendly bays facing the Hauraki Gulf, to the black sand, surf beaches of the west coast, Auckland's water-lovers really are spoilt for choice.

Food & Drink
Auckland has some of the nation's best restaurants, a lively cafe and bar scene, and wine regions on three of its flanks. Coffee culture is definitely booming here too – just don't tell anyone from Wellington.

Volcanoes
Auckland is, quite literally, a global hot spot, with more than 50 separate volcanoes forming a unique topography. Take a hike up one of the landscape's dormant cones for a high, wide and handsome city panorama.

p44

Bay of Islands & Northland

Beaches
Forests
History

Beaches
Bay after beautiful bay lines Northland's east coast, making it a favourite destination for families, surfers and fishing enthusiasts. To the west, long windswept beaches stretch for dozens of kilometres, in places forming towering sand dunes.

Forests
Kauri forests once blanketed the entire north, and in the pockets where these giants remain, particularly in the Waipoua Forest, they're an imposing sight.

History
New Zealand was settled top down by both Maori and Europeans, with missionaries erecting the country's oldest surviving buildings in Kerikeri. In nearby Waitangi, the treaty that fo⸱ the moder⸱ was fir⸱

p109

Coromandel Peninsula

Beaches
Forests
Mining Towns

Beaches
Some of the country's most beautiful beaches are dotted around this compact peninsula, and while they're extremely popular in summer, splendid isolation can still be found.

Forests
Dense bush shrouds the ranges at the heart of the peninsula, much of which is protected by the Coromandel Forest Park and is accessible via well-maintained walking tracks.

Mining Towns
The gold rush roots of Thames and Coromandel Town are displayed through cutesy streets lined with historic wooden buildings, while at the base of the peninsula, Waihi teeters on the edge of a giant opencast mine.

153

Waikato & the King Country

Caves
Beaches
Small Towns

Caves
Don't miss Waitomo Caves, NZ's most staggering cave site. Rafting along underground rivers (blackwater rafting) is popular, or you can just float through amazing grottos of glowworms.

Beaches
Near Raglan you'll find safe swimming and world-class surf beaches, including Manu Bay. Further south are wild, isolated Tasman Sea beaches where sea spray whips across your face and your footprints are the only ones within miles.

Small Towns
Hamilton is a big city here, but more charming are towns such as Te Aroha, Cambridge, Matamata, Raglan and Waitomo: great pubs, cafes, restaurants and friendly locals.

p175

Taranaki & Whanganui

National Parks
Underrated Cities
Beaches

National Parks
Whanganui National Park offers canoeing and kayaking on the Whanganui River. Near New Plymouth, Mt Taranaki (Egmont National Park) is a picture-perfect peak with fabulous tramping.

Underrated Cities
New Plymouth, Whanganui and Palmerston North are mid-sized cities often overlooked by travellers. Visit and you'll find fantastic restaurants and bars, great coffee, wonderful museums and friendly folk.

Beaches
South of New Plymouth are black sand beaches and gnarly breaks. Whanganui offers remote, buffeted beaches, while south of Palmerston North, Horowhenua District has acres of empty brown sand.

p207

Taupo & the Central Plateau

Lake & Rivers
Mountains
Adrenaline

Lake & Rivers
New Zealand's mightiest river is borne from New Zealand's greatest lake: aquatic pursuits in picturesque settings abound (kayaking, sailing, fishing). The water is famously chilly, but hot springs bubble up on the lakeside and riverbank.

Mountains
The three steaming, smoking, occasionally erupting volcanoes at the heart of the North Island are an imposing sight, with the focus of skiing in winter and tramping at other times.

Adrenaline
Skydiving, bungy jumping, white-water rafting, jetboating, mountain biking, wakeboarding, parasailing, skiing – if you want thrills, there's an entire souvenir DVD of Kiwi action waiting to be compiled.

p242

Rotorua & the Bay of Plenty

Thermal Activity
Maori Culture
Outdoor Action

Thermal Activity
The Rotorua landscape is littered with geysers, steaming thermal vents, hot mineral springs and boiling mud pools. NZ's most active volcano, Whakaari (White Island), is 48km off the coast of Whakatane.

Maori Culture
Engage with Maori culture in Rotorua: a slew of companies offer cultural experiences for travellers, most involving traditional dance and musical performance, a *haka* (war dance) and a *hangi* (Maori feast).

Outdoor Action
Fun in the sun: try paragliding, surfing, skydiving, zorbing, jetboating, blokarting, white-water rafting, mountain biking, kayaking... Or just have a swim at the beach.

p272

The East Coast

Coastal Scenery
Wine & Food
Architecture

Coastal Scenery
Follow in the footsteps (or rather wake) of early Maori and James Cook along this stretch of coastline, home to the East Cape Lighthouse and Cape Kidnappers' gaggling gannet colony.

Wine & Food
Sip your way through Gisborne's bright chardonnays, or head to Hawke's Bay for seriously good Bordeaux-style reds and excellent winery dining at some of New Zealand's most historic vineyards.

Architecture
Napier's art deco town centre is a magnet for architecture lovers, the keenest of whom time their visit for the annual art deco weekend, an extravaganza of music, wine, cars and costumes.

p315

Wellington Region

Museums
Cafe Culture
Nightlife

Museums
Crowbarred into the city centre are a significant collection of quality display spaces, including the highly interactive Te Papa museum and internationally flavoured City Gallery.

Cafe Culture
With more than a dozen roasters and scores of hip cafes, Wellington remains the coffee capital of New Zealand. Get a hit from one of the best: Midnight Espresso or Caffe L'affare.

Nightlife
Between the boho bars around Cuba St and Courtenay Pl's glitzy drinking dens, you should find enough to keep you entertained until sun-up. Don't leave town without sampling Wellington's brilliant craft-beer scene.

p348

> Every listing is recommended by our authors, and their favourite places are listed first

> Look out for these icons:

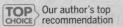 Our author's top recommendation

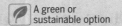 A green or sustainable option

 No payment required

On the Road

Auckland

POPULATION: 1.4 MILLION

Best Places to Eat

» Grove (p72)

» La Cigale market (p75)

» Depot (p72)

» Clooney (p73)

» MooChowChow (p73)

Best Places to Stay

» Hotel de Brett (p67)

» Auckland Takapuna Oaks (p71)

» Verandahs (p68)

» 23 Hepburn (p68)

» Waldorf Celestion (p67)

Why Go?

Paris may be the city of love, but Auckland is the city of many lovers, according to its Maori name, Tamaki Makaurau. Those lovers so desired this place that they fought over it for centuries.

It's hard to imagine a more geographically blessed city. Its two harbours frame a narrow isthmus punctuated by volcanic cones and surrounded by fertile farmland. From any of its numerous vantage points you'll be astounded by how close the Tasman Sea and Pacific Ocean come to kissing and forming a new island.

As a result, water's never far away – whether it's the ruggedly beautiful west-coast surf beaches or the glistening Hauraki Gulf with its myriad islands. And within an hour's drive from the high-rise heart of the city there are dense tracts of rainforest, thermal springs, wineries and wildlife reserves. No wonder Auckland's rated as offering the third-best quality of life of any major city.

When to Go

Auckland has a mild climate, with the occasional frost in winter and high humidity in summer. Summer months have an average of eight days of rain, but the weather is famously fickle, with 'four seasons in one day' possible at any time of the year. If you're after a big-city buzz, don't come between Christmas and New Year, when Aucklanders desert the city for the beach en masse. The sights remain open but many cafes and restaurants close, some not surfacing again until well into January.

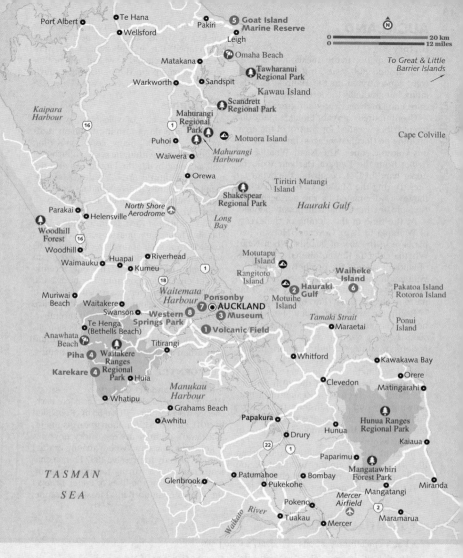

Auckland Highlights

1 Going with the flows, exploring Auckland's fascinating **volcanic field** (p55)

2 Getting back to nature on the island sanctuaries of the beautiful **Hauraki Gulf** (p84)

3 Being awed by the Maori *taonga* (treasures) of the **Auckland Museum** (p51)

4 Going west to the mystical and treacherous black sands of **Karekare** and **Piha** (p99)

5 Swimming with the fishes at **Goat Island Marine Reserve** (p107)

6 Schlepping around world-class wineries and beaches on **Waiheke Island** (p87)

7 Buzzing around the cafes, restaurants and bars of **Ponsonby** (p73)

8 Soaking up the Polynesian vibe at the **Pasifika Festival** (p65), held in March at Western Springs Park

AUCKLAND

History

Maori occupation in the Auckland area dates back around 800 years. Initial settlements were concentrated on the Hauraki Gulf islands, but gradually the fertile isthmus beckoned and land was cleared for growing food.

Over hundreds of years Tamaki's many different tribes wrestled for control of the area, building *pa* (fortified villages) on the numerous volcanic cones. The Ngati Whatua *iwi* (tribe) from the Kaipara Harbour took the upper hand in 1741, occupying the major *pa* sites. During the Musket Wars of the 1820s they were decimated by the northern tribe Ngapuhi, leaving the land all but abandoned.

At the time of the signing of the Treaty of Waitangi in 1840, Governor Hobson had his base in the Bay of Islands. When Ngati Whatua chief Te Kawau offered 3000 acres of land for sale on the northern edge of the Waitemata Harbour, Hobson decided to create a new capital, naming it after one of his patrons, George Eden (Earl of Auckland).

Beginning with just a few tents on a beach, the settlement grew quickly, and soon the port was kept busy exporting the region's produce, including kauri timber. However, it lost its capital status to centrally located Wellington after just 25 years.

Since the beginning of the 20th century Auckland has been New Zealand's fastest-growing city and its main industrial centre. Political deals may be done in Wellington, but Auckland is the big smoke in the land of the long white cloud.

In 2010 the municipalities and urban districts that made up the Auckland Region were merged into one 'super city', and in 2011 the newly minted metropolis was given a buff and shine to prepare it for hosting the Rugby World Cup. The waterfront was redeveloped, the art gallery and zoo were given a makeover, and a swag of new restaurants and bars popped up – leaving a much more vibrant city in the cup's wake.

◎ Sights

Auckland is a city of volcanoes, with the ridges of lava flows forming its main thoroughfares and its many cones providing islands of green within the sea of suburbs. As well as being by far the largest, it's also the most multicultural of NZ's cities. A sizable Asian community rubs shoulders with the biggest Polynesian population of any city in the world.

The traditional Kiwi aspiration for a free-standing house on a quarter-acre section has resulted in a vast, sprawling city. The CBD was long ago abandoned to commerce, and inner-city apartment living has only recently caught on. While geography has been kind, city planning has been less so. Unbridled and ill-conceived development has left the centre of the city with plenty of architectural embarrassments. To get under Auckland's skin it's best to head to the streets of Victorian and Edwardian villas in its hip inner-city suburbs.

CITY CENTRE

TOP CHOICE **Auckland Art Gallery**   GALLERY
(Map p52; www.aucklandartgallery.com; cnr Kitchener & Wellesley Sts; ◎10am-5pm) Reopened in 2011 after a $121-million refurbishment, Auckland's premier art repository now has a gorgeous glass-and-wood atrium grafted onto its already impressive 1887 French chateau frame. It's a worthy receptacle for important works by the likes of Pieter Bruegel the Younger, Guido Reni, Picasso, Cezanne,

---

ESSENTIAL AUCKLAND

» **Eat** Multiculturally, at one of the city's food halls

» **Drink** Cold Waiheke Island rosé on a hot summer's day

» **Read** *Under the Mountain* (1979) – Maurice Gee's teenage tale of slimy things lurking under Auckland's volcanoes

» **Listen to** *One Tree Hill* (1987) – U2's elegy to their Kiwi roadie is no less poignant now that the tree is gone

» **Watch** *Sione's Wedding* (2006) – comedy set in Grey Lynn and central Auckland

» **Festival** Pasifika

» **Online** www.aucklandnz.com; www.aucklandcouncil.govt.nz; www.lonelyplanet.com/new-zealand/auckland

» **Area code** ☑09

AUCKLAND IN...

Two Days

Start by acquainting yourself with the inner city. Take our walking tour from Karangahape Rd (K Rd) to the Wynyard Quarter, stopping along the way to have at least a quick whiz around the NZ section of the Auckland Art Gallery. Catch a ferry to **Devonport**, head up North Head and cool down at **Cheltenham Beach** (weather and tide permitting), before ferrying back to the city for dinner.

On day two, head up **One Tree Hill**, wander around **Cornwall Park** and then visit the **Auckland Museum** and **Domain**. Take a trip along **Tamaki Drive**, stopping at **Bastion** or **Achilles Point** to enjoy the harbour views. Spend the evening dining and bar hopping in **Ponsonby**.

Four Days

On the third day, get out on the **Hauraki Gulf**. Catch the ferry to **Waiheke Island** and divide your time between the beaches and the wineries.

For your final day, head west. Grab breakfast in **Titirangi** before exploring the **Waitakere Ranges Regional Park**, **Karekare** and **Piha**. Freshen up for a night on the town on **K Rd** or **Britomart**.

Gauguin and Matisse. It also showcases the best of NZ art, from the intimate 19th-century portraits of tattooed Maori subjects by Charles Goldie, to the text-scrawled canvases of Colin McCahon, and beyond.

Free tours depart from the main entrance at 11.30am, 12.30pm and 1.30pm.

Albert Park &
Auckland University   PARK, UNIVERSITY

(Map p52) Hugging the hill on the city's eastern flank, Albert Park is a charming Victorian formal garden overrun by students during term time, the more radical of whom have been known to deface the statues of Governor Grey and Queen Victoria. Auckland University's campus stretches over several streets and incorporates a row of stately Victorian merchant houses (Princes St) and **Old Government House** (Waterloo Quadrant). The latter was the colony's seat of power from 1856 until 1865, when Wellington became the capital.

The **University Clock Tower** (22 Princes St) is Auckland's architectural triumph. The stately 'ivory tower' (1926) tips its hat towards art nouveau (the incorporation of NZ flora and fauna into the decoration) and the Chicago School (the way it's rooted into the earth). It's usually open, so wander inside.

At the centre of the campus is a wall of the **Albert Barracks** (1847), a fortification that enclosed 9 hectares, including Albert Park, during the New Zealand Wars.

Sky Tower   LANDMARK

(Map p52; www.skycityauckland.co.nz; cnr Federal & Victoria Sts; adult/child $25/8; ☺8.30am-10.30pm) The impossible-to-miss Sky Tower looks like a giant hypodermic giving a fix to the heavens. Spectacular lighting renders it space-age at night and the colours change for special events. At 328m it is the tallest structure in the southern hemisphere. A lift takes you up to the observation decks in 40 stomach-lurching seconds; look down through the glass floor panels if you're after an extra kick. It costs $3 extra to catch the skyway lift to the ultimate viewing level. Late afternoon is a good time to go up: you can sip a beverage in the Sky Lounge as the sun sets. Sky Tower is also home to the SkyWalk (p59) and SkyJump (p59). The tower is the best part of the SkyCity complex, a tacky 24-hour casino with ritzy restaurants, cafes, bars, theatres and hotels.

Civic Theatre   ARCHITECTURE

(Map p52; www.civictheatre.co.nz; cnr Queen & Wellesley Sts) The 'mighty Civic' (1929) is one of seven 'atmospheric theatres' remaining in the world and a fine survivor from cinema's Golden Age. The auditorium has lavish Moorish decoration and a starlit southern-hemisphere sky in the ceiling, complete with cloud projections. The foyer is an Indian indulgence, with elephants and monkeys hanging from every conceivable fixture. Buddhas were planned to decorate the street frontage but were considered too

Central Auckland

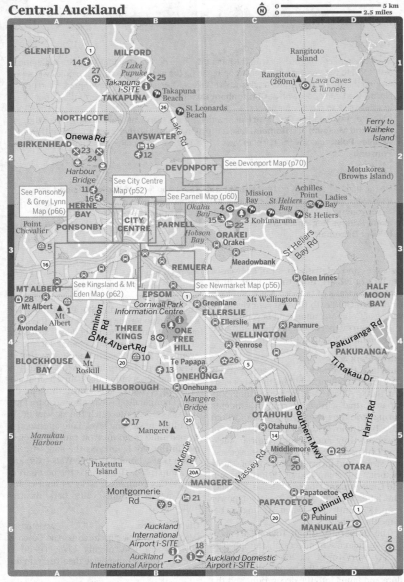

risqué at the time – they chose neoclassical naked boys instead!

If at all possible, try to attend a performance here. It's mainly used for touring musicals, big premieres and Film Festival (p65) screenings.

St Patrick's Cathedral CHURCH
(Map p52; www.stpatricks.org.nz; 43 Wyndham St; ⊙7am-7pm) Auckland's Catholic cathedral is one of its loveliest buildings. Polished wood and Belgian stained glass lend warmth to the interior of this majestic Gothic Revival

Central Auckland

church (1907). There's a historical display in the old confessional on the left-hand side.

BRITOMART, VIADUCT HARBOUR & WYNYARD QUARTER

Stretching for only a small grid of blocks above the train station, Britomart is a tiny enclave of historic buildings and new developments that has been transformed into one of the city's best eating, drinking and, increasingly, shopping precincts.

Once a busy commercial port, the Viaduct Harbour was given a major makeover for the 1999/2000 and 2003 America's Cup tournaments. It's now a fancy dining and boozing precinct, and guaranteed to have at least a slight buzz any night of the week. Historical plaques, public sculpture and the chance to gawk at millionaires' yachts make it a diverting place for a stroll.

Connected to the Viaduct by a raiseable bridge, Wynyard Quarter opened in advance of another sporting tournament, 2011's Rugby World Cup. With its public plazas, waterfront cafes, events centre, fish market and children's playground, it has quickly become Auckland's favourite new place to promenade.

The precinct is something of a work-in-progress, with plans to tart up the scrappy surrounds. Still, things have gotten off to a good start and we hope that the free outdoor movies and night markets become summertime institutions.

Voyager – New Zealand Maritime Museum MUSEUM
(Map p52; ☎09-373 0800; www.maritimemuseum. co.nz; 149-159 Quay St; adult/child $17/9; ☺9am-5pm) This well-presented museum traces NZ's seafaring history from Maori voyaging canoes to the America's Cup. Recreations include a tilting 19th-century steerage-class cabin and a fab 1950s beach store and bach (holiday home). The *Blue Water Black Magic* exhibition is a tribute to Sir Peter Blake, the Whitbread-Round-the-World and America's Cup–winning yachtsman who was murdered in 2001 while on an environmental monitoring trip on the Amazon.

Check the website for details of regular historic steam-tug and sailing-ship cruises.

HAVE YOUR SAY

Found a fantastic restaurant that you're longing to share with the world? Disagree with our recommendations? Or just want to talk about your most recent trip?

Whatever your reason, head to lonelyplanet.com, where you can post a review, ask or answer a question on the Thorntree forum, comment on a blog, or share your photos and tips on Groups. Or you can simply spend time chatting with like-minded travellers. So go on, have your say.

START ST KEVIN'S AR-
CADE, KARANGAHAPE RD
FINISH WYNYARD
QUARTER
DISTANCE 4.5KM
DURATION AROUND
THREE HOURS

Walking Tour
City Centre Ramble

❯ Auckland's CBD can seem scrappy, so this walk aims to show you some hidden nooks and architectural treats.

Start among the second hand boutiques of ① **St Kevin's Arcade** and take the stairs down to Myers Park. Look out for the reproduction of ② **Michelangelo's Moses** at the bottom of the stairs. Continue through the park, taking the stairs on the right just before the overpass to head up to street level.

Heading down Queen St, you'll pass the ③ **Auckland Town Hall** and ④ **Aotea Sq**, the civic heart of the city. On the next corner is the wonderful ⑤ **Civic Theatre**. Turn right on Wellesley St and then left onto Lorne St. Immediately to your right is ⑥ **Khartoum Pl**, a pretty little square with tiling celebrating the suffragettes; NZ women were the first in the world to win the vote. Head up the stairs to the ⑦ **Auckland Art Gallery**.

Behind the gallery is ⑧ **Albert Park**. Cross through it and turn left into Princes St, where a row of ⑨ **Victorian merchants' houses** faces the ⑩ **University Clock Tower**. Cut around behind the clock tower to ⑪ **Old Government House** and then follow the diagonal path back to Princes St. The attractive building on the corner of Princes St and Bowen Ave was once the city's main ⑫ **synagogue**.

Head down Bowen Ave and cut through the park to the ⑮ **Chancery precinct**, an upmarket area of designer stores and cafes. A small square connects it to ⑭ **High St**, Auckland's main fashion strip. Take a left onto ⑮ **Vulcan Lane**, lined with historic pubs. Turn right onto Queen St and follow down to the ⑯ **Britomart Train Station**, housed in the former central post office. You're now standing on reclaimed land – the original shoreline was at Fort St.

Turn left on Quay St and head to ⑰ **Viaduct Harbour**, bustling with bars and cafes, and then continue over the bridge to the rejuvenated ⑱ **Wynyard Quarter**.

Auckland Fish Market MARKET
(Map p52; www.aucklandfishmarket.co.nz; 22-32 Jellicoe St; ⊗6am-7pm) No self-respecting city with a position like this should be without a fish market. Auckland's has a boisterous early-morning auction, retail fish shops, eateries and a seafood-cooking school.

Dockline Tram TRAM
(www.aucklandtram.co.nz; adult/child $5/1; ⊗9am-7.30pm Dec-Feb, 10am-5pm Mar-Nov) A dose of nostalgia is offered by this heritage tram, but the 15-minute loop won't take you anywhere very interesting.

MT EDEN
Mt Eden (Maungawhau) VOLCANO
(Map p62; ⊗road access 7am-11pm) From the top of Auckland's highest volcanic cone (196m) the entire isthmus and both harbours are laid bare. The symmetrical crater (50m deep) is known as *Te Ipu Kai a Mataaho* (the Food Bowl of Mataaho, the god of things hidden in the ground) and is highly *tapu* (sacred); do not enter it, but feel free to explore the remainder of the mountain. The remains of *pa* terraces and storage pits are clearly visible.

You can drive to the very top or you can join the legions of fitness freaks jogging or trudging up. Tour buses are banned from the summit, but shuttles will transport infirm passengers to the top from the car park on the lower slopes.

Eden Garden GARDENS
(Map p56; www.edengarden.co.nz; 24 Omana Ave; adult/child $8/6; ⊗9am-4pm) On the eastern slopes of Mt Eden, this horticultural showpiece is noted for its collections of camellias, rhododendrons and azaleas.

PARNELL & NEWMARKET
Parnell likes to think of itself as a village, although the only tractors to be seen here are the SUVs driven by the affluent suburb's soccer mums. This is one of Auckland's oldest areas and has retained several heritage buildings. Inexplicably, it also has an excellent selection of budget accommodation, although it's doubtful that backpackers will be frequenting the pricey eateries of the main strip. Neighbouring Newmarket is a busy shopping precinct known for its boutiques.

[TOP CHOICE] **Auckland Museum** MUSEUM
(Map p60; ☎09-309 0443; www.aucklandmuseum.com; adult/child $10/free; ⊗10am-5pm) Domi-

WANT MORE?
For in-depth information, reviews and recommendations at your fingertips, head to the Apple App Store to purchase Lonely Planet's Auckland City Guide 1.2.2 iPhone app.

nating the Domain is this imposing neoclassical temple (1929), capped with an impressive copper-and-glass dome (2007). Its comprehensive display of Pacific Island and Maori artefacts on the ground floor deserves to be on your 'must see' list. Highlights include a 25m war canoe and an extant carved meeting house (remove your shoes before entering). There's also an Egyptian mummy (a sure-fire hit with the kids) and a fascinating display on the volcanic field, including an eruption simulation.

The upper floors are given over to military displays, fulfilling the building's dual role as a war memorial. Auckland's main ANZAC commemorations take place at dawn on 25 April at the cenotaph in the museum's forecourt.

Hour-long museum highlights tours (adult/child $20/8) are held daily at 10.30am, 12.30pm and 2pm. Half-hour Maori cultural performances (adult/child $25/13) take place at 11am and 1.30pm, with Maori gallery tours (adult/child $10/5) departing immediately afterwards.

Auckland Domain PARK
(Map p60) Covering about 80 hectares, this green swathe contains sports fields, interesting sculpture, formal gardens, wild corners and the **Wintergarden** (admission free; ⊗9am-5.30pm Mon-Sat, 9am-7.30pm Sun Nov-Mar, 9am-4.30pm Apr-Oct), with its fernery, tropical house, cool house, cute cat statue and neighbouring cafe. The mound in the centre of the park is all that remains of Pukekaroa, one of Auckland's volcanoes. At its humble peak, a totara surrounded by a palisade honours the first Maori king.

Holy Trinity Cathedral CHURCH
(Map p60; www.holy-trinity.org.nz; Parnell Rd; ⊗10am-3pm) Auckland's Anglican cathedral is a hodgepodge of architectural styles, especially compared to **St Mary's** (1886) next door, a wonderful wooden Gothic Revival church with a burnished interior and interesting stained-glass windows. The cathedral's windows are also notable, especially

AUCKLAND

City Centre

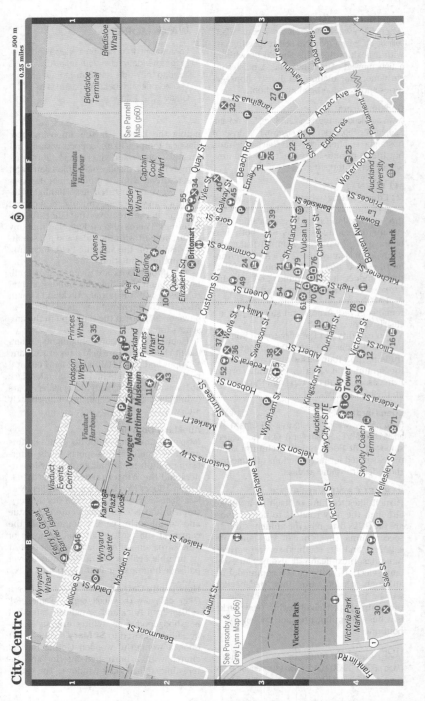

N

0 0
0 0

500 m
0.25 miles

Bledisloe Wharf

Bledisloe Terminal

Waitemata Harbour

See Parnell Map (p60)

27

32

Captain Cook Wharf

Marsden Wharf

Queens Wharf

Beach Rd

Tangihua St

Emily Pl

26

22

Marutuhu Cres

Te Taoa Cres

Anzac Ave

Eden Cres

Short St

Parliament St

Waterloo Qd

25

Auckland University

4

Pier 2

Ferry Building

9

Quay St

Tyler St

34

55

Galway St

40

45

Gore St

Fort St

39

53

Britomart

Commerce St

Shortland St

Bankside St

Princes La

Bowen Ave

Albert Park

Kitchener St

Bowen St

Queen Elizabeth Sq

10

Customs St

Queen St

24

49

21

79

76

Vulcan La

Chancery St

73

High St

74

78

Hobson Wharf

Princes Wharf

35

8

51

Auckland Princes Wharf i-SITE

7

Wolfe St

Mills La

54

77

61

70

Victoria St

19

12

Elliot St

16

11

43

37

36

Swanson St

Albert St

Durham St

Federal St

52

38

5

Sturdee St

Market Pl

Hobson St

Wyndham St

Kingston St

Victoria St

33

Federal St

71

Viaduct Events Centre

Viaduct Harbour

Voyager – New Zealand Maritime Museum

Karanga Plaza Kiosk

Customs St W

Nelson St

Fanshawe St

Sky Tower

Auckland SkyCity i-SITE

13

SkyCity Coach Terminal

Wellesley St

Wynyard Wharf

Ferry to Great Barrier Island

46

Wynyard Quarter

2

Jellicoe St

Daldy St

Madden St

Halsey St

Beaumont St

Gaunt St

See Ponsonby & Grey Lynn Map (p66)

Victoria Park

Victoria Park Market

47

Sale St

30

Frank Lin Rd

1

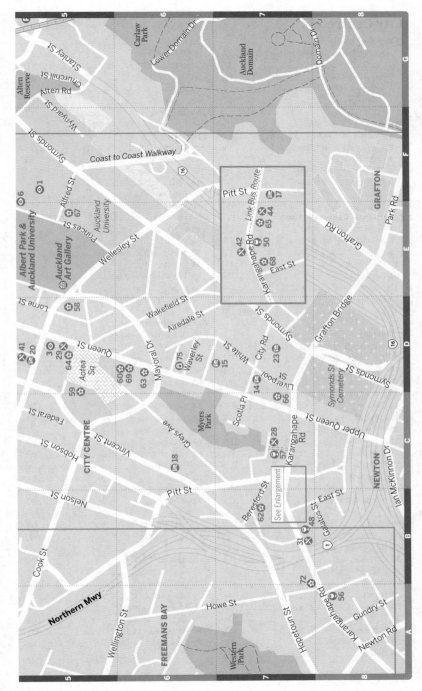

GRAFTON

NEWTON

CITY CENTRE

FREEMANS BAY

Auckland Domain

Carlaw Park

Lower Domain Dr

Domain Dr

Park Rd

Grafton Rd

Coast to Coast Walkway

(16)

Stanley St

Churchill St

Alten Reserve

Alten Rd

Wynyard St

Symonds St

Alfred St

Princes St

Auckland University

1

6

67

Auckland University

Pitt St

Link Bus Route

17

65 44

42

50

68 East St

Karangahape Rd

Wellesley St

Auckland Art Gallery

Albert Park & Auckland University

Lorne St

58

Wakefield St

Airedale St

Symonds St

Gratton Bridge

(16)

41

20

3

29

64

59

60

69

63

Queen St

Aotea Sq

Mayoral Dr

Waverley St

75

White St

15

City Rd

23

Symonds St Cemetery

Symonds St

Federal St

Vincent St

Greys Ave

Myers Park

Scotia Pl

Liverpool St

14

66

Upper Queen St

Ian McKinnon Dr

Hobson St

Nelson St

Pitt St

18

Karangahape Rd

28

57

See Enlargement

Beresford St

62

East St

48

Galatos St

31

1

Cook St

Northern Mwy

Wellington St

Howe St

Hobson St

Karangahape Rd

72

56

Gundry St

Newton Rd

Western Park

City Centre

AUCKLAND VOLCANIC FIELD

Some cities think they're tough just by living in the shadow of a volcano. Auckland's built on 50 of them and, no, they're not all extinct. The last one to erupt was Rangitoto about 600 years ago and no one can predict when the next eruption will occur. Auckland's quite literally a hot spot – with a reservoir of magma 100km below, waiting to bubble to the surface. But relax: this has only happened 19 times in the last 20,000 years.

Some of Auckland's volcanoes are cones, some are filled with water and some have been completely quarried away. Moves are afoot to register the field as a World Heritage site and protect what remains. Most of the surviving cones show evidence of terracing from when they formed a formidable series of Maori *pa*. The most interesting to explore are Mt Eden (p67), One Tree Hill (p74) and Rangitoto, but Mt Wellington (Maungarei), Mt Albert (Owairaka), Mt Roskill (Puketapapa), Lake Pupuke, Mt Mangere and Mt Hobson (Remuwera) are all worth a visit.

the rose window by English artist Carl Edwards, which is particularly striking above the simple kauri altar.

Parnell Rose Gardens   GARDENS
(Map p60; 85-87 Gladstone Rd; ⊙7am-7pm) These formal gardens are blooming excellent from November to March. A stroll through the park leads to peaceful **Judges Bay** and tiny **St Stephen's Chapel** (Judge St), built for the signing of the constitution of NZ's Anglican Church (1857).

Highwic   HISTORIC BUILDING
(Map p56; www.historic.org.nz; 40 Gillies Ave; adult/child $9/free; ⊙10.30am-4.30pm Wed-Sun) A marvellous example of a Carpenter Gothic house (1862), sitting amid lush, landscaped grounds.

Kinder House   HISTORIC BUILDING
(Map p60; www.kinder.org.nz; 2 Ayr St; entry by donation; ⊙noon-3pm Wed-Sun; 🛈) Built of volcanic stone, this 1857 home displays the subtle but skilful watercolours and memorabilia of the Reverend Dr John Kinder (1819–1903), who was the headmaster of the Church of England Grammar School.

Ewelme Cottage   HISTORIC BUILDING
(Map p60; www.historic.org.nz; 14 Ayr St; adult/child $8.50/free; ⊙10.30am-4.30pm Sun) Built in 1864 for a clergyman who clearly didn't throw wild parties, this storybook cottage has been left in exceptionally good condition.

TAMAKI DRIVE

This scenic, pohutukawa-lined road heads east from the city, hugging the waterfront. In summer it's a jogging/cycling/rollerblading blur.

A succession of child-friendly, peaceful swimming beaches starts at Ohaku Bay. Around the headland is Mission Bay, a popular beach with an iconic art deco fountain, historic mission house, restaurants and bars. Safe swimming beaches Kohimarama and St Heliers follow. Further east along Cliff Rd, the Achilles Point lookout offers panoramic views. At its base is Ladies Bay, where nudists put up with mud and shells for the sake of relative seclusion.

Buses 745 to 769 from Britomart follow this route.

Kelly Tarlton's   AQUARIUM
(Map p48; ☎09-531 5065; www.kellytarltons.co.nz; 23 Tamaki Dr; adult/child $34/17; ⊙9.30am-5.30pm) In the **Underwater World**, sharks and stingrays swim around and over you as you're shunted on a conveyor belt through transparent tunnels in what were once stormwater and sewage holding tanks. If you want to get even closer, you can enter the tanks in a shark cage ($79; 12.30pm, 1.30pm and 3pm), and if that doesn't sound terrifying enough, you can dive directly into the tanks ($129; 10am).

In a post-*Happy Feet* world, Kelly Tarlton's biggest attraction is the permanent winter wonderland known as **Antarctic Encounter**. It includes a walk through a replica of Robert Falcon Scott's 1911 Antarctic hut, and a ride aboard a heated snowcat through a frozen environment where a colony of king and Gentoo penguins lives. New owners with big plans took over the aquarium in March 2012, so there may be some new attractions in place by the time you visit.

Book online for a shorter wait (queues can be horrendous) and a 10% discount. There's

Newmarket

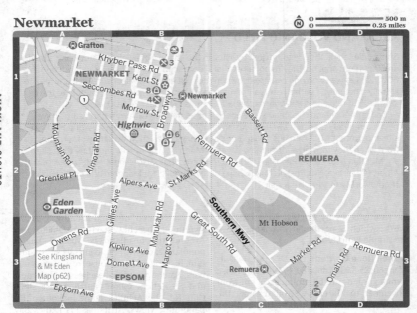

Newmarket

a free shark-shaped shuttle bus that departs from 172 Quay St (opposite the ferry terminal) on the hour between 9am and 4pm.

Bastion Point PARK
(Map p48; Hapimana St) Politics, harbour views and lush lawns combine on this pretty headland with a chequered history. An elaborate cliff-top garden mausoleum honours Michael Joseph Savage (1872–1940), the country's first Labour prime minister, whose socialist reforms left him adored by the populace. Follow the lawn to a WWII gun embankment – one of many that line the harbour.

DEVONPORT
Nestling at the bottom of the North Shore, Devonport is a short ferry trip from the city. Quaint without being sickeningly twee, it retains a village atmosphere, with many well-preserved Victorian and Edwardian buildings and loads of cafes. If your interests are less genteel, there are two volcanic cones and easy access to the first of the North Shore's beaches.

For a self-guided tour of historic buildings, pick up the *Old Devonport Walk* pamphlet from the i-SITE. Bikes can be hired from the ferry terminal, making a pedal-powered exploration of the lower North Shore beaches an enticing possibility.

Ferries to Devonport (adult/child return $11/5.80, 12 minutes) depart from the Auckland Ferry Building every 30 minutes (hourly after 8pm) from 6.15am to 11.15pm Monday to Thursday (until 1am Friday and Saturday), and from 7.15am to 10pm on Sundays and public holidays. Some Waiheke Island and Rangitoto ferries also stop here.

Mt Victoria & North Head VOLCANO

Mt Victoria (Takarunga; Map p70; Victoria Rd) and **North Head** (Maungauika; Map p70; Takarunga Rd; ⊙6am-10pm) were Maori *pa* and they remain fortresses of sorts, with the navy maintaining a presence. Both have gun embankments and North Head is riddled with tunnels, dug at the end of the 19th century in response to the Russian threat, and extended during WWI and WWII. The gates are locked at night, but that's never stopped teenagers from jumping the fence and terrifying themselves on subterranean explorations. Between the two, **Cambria Reserve** stands on the remains of a third volcanic cone that was largely quarried away.

FREE Navy Museum MUSEUM

(Map p70; www.navymuseum.mil.nz; Torpedo Bay; ⊙10am-5pm) The navy has been in Devonport since the earliest days of the colony. Its history is on display at this well-presented and often moving museum, focussing on the stories of the sailors themselves.

WESTERN SPRINGS

Auckland Zoo ZOO

(Map p62; www.aucklandzoo.co.nz; Motions Rd; adult/child $21/11; ⊙9.30am-5pm, last entry 4.15pm) At this modern, spacious zoo, the big foreigners tend to steal the attention from the timid natives, but if you can wrestle the kids away from the tigers and orang-utans, there's a well-presented NZ

section. Called *Te Wao Nui*, it's divided into six ecological zones: Coast (seals, penguins), Islands (mainly lizards, including NZ's pint-sized dinosaur, the tuatara), Wetlands (ducks, herons, eels), Night (kiwi, naturally, along with frogs, native owls and weta), Forest (birds) and High Country (cheekier birds and lizards).

Western Springs PARK

(Map p62; Great North Rd) Parents bring their children to this picturesque park to be traumatised by pushy, bread-fattened geese and to partake of the popular adventure playground. It's a great spot for a picnic and to get acquainted with playful pukeko (swamp hens). Formed by a confluence of lava flows, more than 4 million litres bubble up into the central lake daily. Until 1902 this was Auckland's main water supply.

From the city, catch any bus heading west via Great North Rd (adult/child $3.40/2). By car, take the Western Springs exit from the North Western Motorway.

MOTAT MUSEUM

(Museum of Transport & Technology; Map p62; www.motat.org.nz; 805 Great North Rd; adult/child $14/8; ⊙10am-5pm) This trainspotter's and technology boffin's paradise is spread over two sites and 19 hectares. In **MOTAT 1** look out for Helen Clark's Honda 50 motorbike and the cutesy pioneer village. **MOTAT 2** (Map p48) is an aircraft graveyard, featuring rare military and commercial planes. The two sites are linked by a vintage tram (free with admission, $1 otherwise), which passes the park and zoo. It's a fun kids' ride whether you visit MOTAT or not.

WHAT BECAME OF NGATI WHATUA?

By the end of the 1840s Maori were already a minority in the Auckland area, and eventually the Ngati Whatua o Orakei *hapu* (subtribe) was reduced to a small block of land in the vicinity of Okahu Bay and Bastion Point. In 1886 Bastion Point was confiscated by the government for military use, and then in 1908 more land was taken to build a sewage pipe that pumped raw effluent into the water in front of the *hapu*'s last remaining village at Okahu Bay. All but the cemetery was confiscated in 1951, with the people removed from their homes and the village destroyed to 'clean up' the area before the royal visit of Queen Elizabeth II.

When the government decided to sell the prime real estate on Bastion Point in 1977, the *hapu* staged a peaceful occupation that lasted for 507 days before they were once again taken into custody. It was a seminal moment in the Maori protest movement. During the next decade the government apologised and returned the land where the *marae* now stands. At the time of research, further negotiations between the government and *hapu* were progressing, with several of the volcanic cones likely to be part of the final settlement. The former railway land on which the Vector Arena now sits has already been returned.

DON'T MISS

NORTH SHORE BEACHES

A succession of fine swimming beaches stretches from North Head to Long Bay. The gulf islands provide a picturesque backdrop and shelter them from strong surf, making them safe for supervised children. Aim for high tide unless you fancy a lengthy walk to waist-deep water. **Cheltenham Beach** is a short walk from Devonport. **Takapuna Beach**, closest to the Harbour Bridge, is Auckland's answer to Bondi and the most built up. Nearby **St Leonards Beach**, popular with gay men, requires clambering over rocks at high tide.

OTHER SUBURBS

One Tree Hill PARK

(Maungakiekie; Map p48; www.cornwallpark.co.nz) This volcanic cone was the isthmus' key *pa* and the greatest fortress in the country. It's easy to see why: a drive or walk to the top (182m) offers 360-degree views. At the summit is the grave of John Logan Campbell, who when gifting the land to the city in 1901 requested that a memorial (the imposing obelisk and statue above the grave) be built to the Maori people. Nearby is the stump of the last 'one tree'.

Allow plenty of time to explore the craters and surrounding **Cornwall Park**, with its impressive mature trees and **Acacia Cottage** (1841), Auckland's oldest wooden building. The information centre (p81) has fascinating interactive displays illustrating what the *pa* would have looked like when 5000 people lived here.

Near the excellent **children's playground**, the **Stardome Observatory** (☎09-624 1246; www.stardome.org.nz; 670 Manukau Rd; exhibits free, shows adult/child $10/8; ⊙10am-3pm Mon, 9.30am-4.30pm & 6.30-9.30pm Tue-Fri) offers stargazing and planetarium shows that aren't dependent on Auckland's fickle weather (usually 8pm Wednesday to Saturday; phone ahead).

To get here from the city, take a train to Greenlane and walk 1km along Green Lane West. By car, take the Greenlane exit of the Southern Motorway and turn right into Green Lane West.

FREE **Wallace Arts Centre** GALLERY

(Map p48; www.tsbbankwallaceartscentre.org.nz; Pah Homestead, 72 Hillsborough Rd, Hillsborough; ⊙10am-3pm Tue-Fri, 10am-5pm Sat & Sun) Housed in a gorgeous 1879 mansion with views to One Tree Hill and the Manakau Harbour, the Wallace Arts Centre is lavishly endowed with contemporary NZ art from a private collection, generously offered for free public viewing. The collection is so extensive that the works are changed every four to six weeks. Even if you're not much of a culture vulture, it's worth the trip to explore the house, pick which room you'd have as your bedroom, have lunch on the veranda and wander among the magnificent trees in the park (collect a map from the homestead's reception). And the art is very accessible, ranging from a life-size skeletal rugby ruck to a vibrant Ziggy Stardust painted on glass.

Bus 299 (Lynfield) departs every 15 minutes from Wellesley St in the city (near the Civic Theatre) and heads to Hillsborough Rd ($4.50, about 40 minutes).

FREE **Auckland Botanic Gardens** GARDENS

(Map p48; www.aucklandbotanicgardens.co.nz; 102 Hill Rd, Manurewa; ⊙8am-6pm mid-Mar–mid-Oct, 8am-8pm mid-Oct–mid-Mar) This 64-hectare park has over 10,000 plants (including threatened species), dozens of themed gardens and an infestation of wedding parties. By car, take the Southern Motorway, exit at Manurewa and follow the signs. Otherwise take the train to Manurewa ($5.70, 40 minutes) and then walk along Hill Rd (1.5km).

Alberton HISTORIC BUILDING

(Map p48; www.historic.org.nz; 100 Mt Albert Rd; adult/child $9/free; ⊙10.30am-4.30pm Wed-Sun) A classic colonial mansion (1863), Alberton featured as a backdrop for some scenes in *The Piano*. It's a 1km walk from Mt Albert train station.

Spookers AMUSEMENT PARK

(☎09-291 9002; www.spookers.co.nz; 833 Kingseat Rd, Karaka; 1/2 attractions $20/35; ⊙8pm-late Fri & Sat) If walking around an old mental hospital in the dark wasn't scary enough, try it with freaks dripping blood and wielding chainsaws chasing you. Attractions include the *Haunted House*, the *Freaky Forest of Fear*, *Disturbia* and, perhaps freakiest of all, the summer-only *Cornevil* set in a real corn maze. It's rated R16, but there are some R8 daytime *Creepers* shows.

Take the Southern Motorway to the Papakura off-ramp (about 32km), turn left and drive 14km towards impending doom.

Rainbow's End
AMUSEMENT PARK

(Map p48; www.rainbowsend.co.nz; 2 Clist Cres; superpass adult/child $49/39; ⊙10am-5pm) It's a bit lame by international standards but Rainbow's End has enough rides (including a corkscrew rollercoaster) to keep the kids happy all day, plus plenty of sugary snacks to fuel it all. Admission includes unlimited rides.

Activities

Hey, this is the 'City of Sails' and nothing gets you closer to the heart and soul of Auckland than sailing on the gulf. If you can't afford a yacht cruise, catch a ferry instead.

Visitors centres and public libraries stock the city council's *Auckland City's Walkways* pamphlet, which has a good selection of urban walks, including the Coast to Coast Walkway (p61).

Trading on the country's action-packed reputation, Auckland has sprouted its own set of insanely frightening activities. Look around for backpacker reductions or special offers before booking anything.

Sailing

Sail NZ
SAILING

(Map p52; ☎0800 397 567; www.explorenz.co.nz; Viaduct Harbour) Shoot the breeze on a genuine America's Cup yacht (adult/child $160/115) or head out on a Whale & Dolphin Safari (adult/child $160/105); dolphins are spotted 90% of the time and whales 75%. The *Pride of Auckland* fleet of glamorous large yachts offers 90-minute Harbour Sailing Cruises (adult/child $75/55), 2½-hour Dinner Cruises ($120/85) and full-day Sailing Adventures ($165/125).

CharterLink
SAILING

(Map p48; ☎09-445 7114; www.charterlink.co.nz; Bayswater Marina; per day $345-1125) Charters a fleet of well-maintained older yachts, luxury yachts and catamarans.

Gulfwind
SAILING

(Map p48; ☎09-521 1564; www.gulfwind.co.nz; Westhaven Marina) Offers charters (half-/full day $395/795) and small-group sailing courses; a two-day Start Yachting course costs $595.

Penny Whiting Sailing School
SAILING

(Map p48; ☎09-376 1322; www.pennywhiting.com; Westhaven Marina; course $700) Runs 15-hour learners' courses either as five afternoon lessons or over two weekends.

Extreme Sports

SkyWalk
EXTREME SPORTS

(Map p52; ☎0800 759 925; www.skywalk.co.nz; Sky Tower, cnr Federal & Victoria Sts; adult/child $145/115; ⊙10am-4.30pm) The Sky Tower offers an ever-expanding selection of pant-wetting activities. If you thought the observation deck was for pussies, SkyWalk involves circling the 192m-high, 1.2m-wide outside halo of the tower without rails or a balcony – but with a safety harness (they're not completely crazy).

SkyJump
EXTREME SPORTS

(Map p52; ☎0800 759 586; www.skyjump.co.nz; Sky Tower, cnr Federal & Victoria Sts; adult/child $225/175; ⊙10am-5pm) This 11-second, 85km/h base wire leap from the observation deck of the Sky Tower is more like a parachute jump than a bungy and it's a rush and a half. Combine it with the SkyWalk in the Look 'n' Leap package ($290).

Auckland Bridge Climb & Bungy
BUNGY

(Map p48; ☎09-360 7748; www.bungy.co.nz; Curran St, Herne Bay; climb adult/child $120/80, bungy $150/120) Bungy originators, AJ Hackett, offer the chance to climb up or jump off the Auckland Harbour Bridge.

ONE TREE TO RULE THEM ALL

Looking at One Tree Hill, your first thought will probably be 'Where's the bloody tree?'. Good question. Up until 2000 a Monterey pine stood at the top of the hill. This was a replacement for a sacred totara that was chopped down by British settlers in 1852. Maori activists first attacked the foreign usurper in 1994, finishing the job in 2000. It's unlikely that another tree will be planted until local land claims have moved closer to resolution, but you can bet your boots that this time around it'll be a native.

Auckland's most beloved landmark achieved international recognition in 1987 when U2 released the song 'One Tree Hill' on their acclaimed *The Joshua Tree* album. It was only released as a single in NZ, where it went to number one.

Parrnell

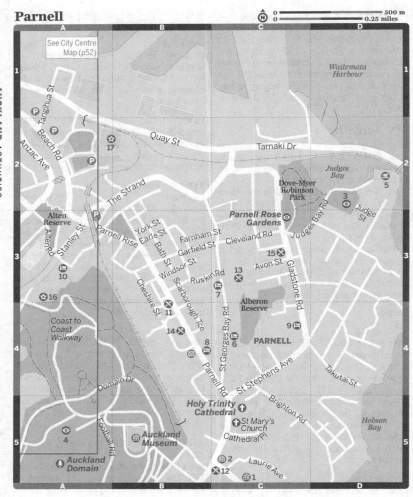

0 ────── 500 m
0 ────── 0.25 miles

Waitemata Harbour

Quay St

Tamaki Dr

Judges Bay

Dove-Myer Robinson Park

Parnell Rose Gardens

The Strand

Alten Reserve

York St
Earle St
Farnham St
Cleveland Rd
Garfield St
Windsor St
Ruskin Rd
Avon St
Scarborough Tce
Cheshire St
Bath St
Parnell Rise

Alberon Reserve

PARNELL

Gladstone Rd

St Georges Bay Rd

Parnell Rd

St Stephens Ave

Brighton Rd

Takutai St

Hobson Bay

Coast to Coast Walkway

Domain Dr

Footbath Rd

Holy Trinity Cathedral

St Mary's Church

Cathedral Pl

Auckland Museum

Laurie Ave

Auckland Domain

Tangihua St
Beach Rd
Anzac Ave
Stanley St
Allen Rd

See City Centre Map (p52)

Judge St

NZ Skydive

SKYDIVING

(☎0800 865 867; www.nzskydive.co.nz; 9000/ 12,000ft $245/295) Offers tandem skydives from Mercer airfield, 55km south of Auckland; capture your excitement/terror on DVD for $165.

Sky Screamer

BUNGY

(Map p52; ☎09-377 1328; www.skyscreamer.co.nz; cnr Albert & Victoria Sts; ride $40; ☉9am-10pm Sun-Thu, 10am-2am Fri & Sat) Imagine a giant slingshot with yourself as the projectile. Rest assured, once you're strapped in and reverse-bungyed 60m up in the air, the whole city will hear you scream.

Diving

Dive Centre

DIVING

(Map p48; ☎09-444 7698; www.divecentre.co.nz; 97 Wairau Rd, Takapuna; PADI Open Water $599) Runs PADI courses and books diving charters.

Kayaking

Fergs Kayaks

KAYAKING

(Map p48; ☎09-529 2230; www.fergskayaks.co.nz; 12 Tamaki Dr, Okahu Bay; ☉10am-5pm) Hires out kayaks and paddleboards (per hour/ day from $15/50), bikes ($20/120) and inline skates $15/30). Day and night guided kayak trips are available to Devonport (three

Parnell

◎ Top Sights

Auckland Domain	A5
Auckland Museum	B5
Holy Trinity Cathedral	C5
Parnell Rose Gardens	C3

◎ Sights

1	Ewelme Cottage	C5
2	Kinder House	C5
3	St Stephen's Chapel	D2
4	Wintergarden	A5

◉ Activities, Courses & Tours

5	Parnell Baths	D2

◉ Sleeping

6	City Garden Lodge	C4
7	Lantana Lodge	C3
8	Parnell Inn	B4
9	Quality Hotel Barrycourt	C4
10	Quest Carlaw Park	A3

✖ Eating

11	Burgerfuel	B4
12	Domain & Ayr	C5
13	La Cigale	C3
14	Non Solo Pizza	B4
15	Rosehip Cafe	C3

◎ Entertainment

16	ASB Tennis Centre	A3
	Ticketmaster	(see 17)
17	Vector Arena	A2

hours, 8km, $95) or Rangitoto Island (six hours, 13km, $120).

Auckland Sea Kayaks KAYAKING
(☎0800 999 089; www.aucklandseakayaks.co.nz) Takes guided trips (including lunch) to Rangitoto ($225, 10 hours) and Browns Island/Motukorea ($175, six hours). Multiday excursions also available.

Other Water Activities

Auckland Jet Boat Tours JETBOATING
(Map p52; ☎0508 255 382; www.aucklandjetboattours.co.nz; Princes Wharf; adult/child incl museum $65/45) Take a 40-minute blast around the harbour and then peruse the Maritime Museum at a more leisurely pace.

New Zealand Surf'n'Snow Tours SURFING
(☎09-828 0426; www.newzealandsurftours.com; 5-/12-day tour $799/1699) Runs day-long surfing courses that include transport, gear and two two-hour lessons ($120). Day tours

usually head to Piha (with/without own gear $50/99; year-round), while five- and twelve-day tours include accommodation in Ahipara (October to May only).

Parnell Baths SWIMMING
(Map p60; www.parnellbaths.co.nz; Judges Bay Rd; adult/child $6.30/4.20; ◷6am-8pm Mon-Fri, 8am-8pm Sat & Sun Nov-Apr) Outdoor saltwater pools with an awesome 1950s mural.

Olympic Pools & Fitness Centre SWIMMING
(Map p56; www.theolympic.co.nz; 77 Broadway; adult/child $7.50/5; ◷5.30am-9.30pm Mon-Fri, 7am-8pm Sat & Sun) Pools, gym, sauna, steam room and crèche.

Ballooning

Balloon Expeditions BALLOONING
(☎09-416 8590; www.balloonexpeditions.co.nz; flight $340) Offers hour-long flights in a hot-air balloon at sunrise, including breakfast and a bottle of bubbles.

Balloon Safaris BALLOONING
(☎09-415 8289; www.balloonsafaris.co.nz; flight $345) Allow four hours for these early morning flights (including one hour in the air), which include snacks and sparkling wine.

Tramping

Coast to Coast Walkway WALKING
(Map p48; www.aucklandcity.govt.nz) Heading clear across the country from the Tasman to the Pacific (actually, that's only 16km), this walk encompasses One Tree Hill, Mt Eden, the Domain and the University, keeping as much as possible to reserves rather than city streets. You can do it in either direction: starting from the Viaduct Basin and heading south, it's marked by yellow markers and milestones; heading north from Onehunga there are blue markers. We recommend catching the train to Onehunga, the least

---

AUCKLAND FOR CHILDREN

All of the east coast beaches (St Heliers, Kohimarama, Mission Bay, Okahu Bay, Cheltenham, Narrow Neck, Takapuna, Milford, Long Bay) are safe for supervised kids, while sights such as Rainbow's End, Kelly Tarlton's, Auckland Museum and Auckland Zoo are all firm favourites. Parnell Baths has a children's pool, but on wintry days, head to the thermal pools at Parakai or Waiwera.

Kingsland & Mt Eden

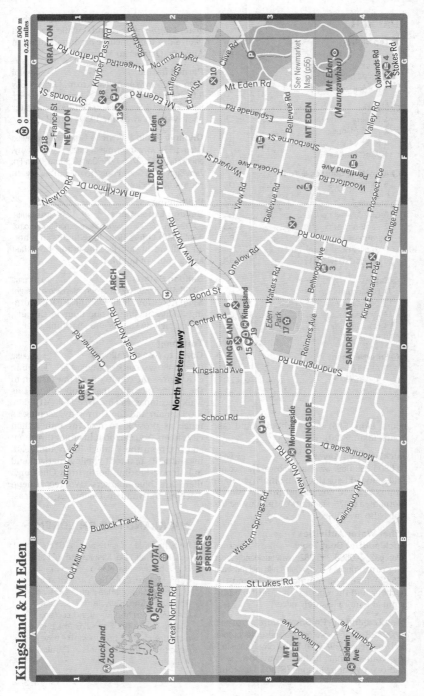

500 m
0.25 miles

See Newmarket
Map (p56)

Kingsland & Mt Eden

impressive trailhead, and finishing up at one of the Viaduct's bars. From Onehunga Station, take Onehunga Mall up to Princes St, turn left and pick up the track at the inauspicious park by the motorway.

☞ Tours

Cultural Tours

🚩 TIME Unlimited CULTURAL TOUR
(☎09-446 6677; www.newzealandtours.travel) To Integrate Maori Experiences (TIME) is the motto. A hefty set of cultural, fishing, kayaking, trekking and sightseeing tours are outlined on their website, including excellent kayak-fishing excursions (full day $295)

Toru Tours CULTURAL TOUR
(☎027 457 0011; www.torutours.com; with/without performance $213/178) Maori cultural tours stopping in at a *marae*, Auckland Museum (with an optional cultural show), the native critter section of the zoo, Mt Eden, One Tree Hill and Bastion Point. Three-hour Express Tours ($69) are also available.

Tamaki Hikoi CULTURAL TOUR
(☎0800 282 552; www.tamakihikoi.co.nz; 1/3 hr $40/95) Ngati Whatua guides lead these Maori cultural tours, including an hour's walk around the Domain; a three-hour tour including a walk and a cultural performance; and a three-hour walking tour from Mt Eden (Maungawhau) to the Domain (transfers from the city included).

Wineries

NZ Winepro WINE TASTING
(☎09-575 1958; www.nzwinepro.co.nz; tours $119-325) Offers a range of highly rated tours to all of Auckland's wine regions, combining tastings with sightseeing.

Wine Trail Tours WINE TASTING
(☎09-630 1540; www.winetrailtours.co.nz) Small-group tours around West Auckland wineries and the Waitakere Ranges (half-/full day $115/245); further afield to Matakana ($255); or a combo of the two ($255).

Fine Wine Tours WINE TASTING
(☎0800 023 111; www.insidertouring.co.nz) Tours of Kumeu, Matakana and Waiheke wineries including four-hour Kumeu tour ($169), with cheese ($189); six-hour tour including Muriwai Beach ($245); food-and-wine tour with stops at city providores ($245).

Walking

Waitakere Tours TRAMPING
(☎0800 492 482; www.waitakeretours.co.nz; per day $150) Lifelong Westies (West Aucklanders) offering guided tours of the west coast beaches, as well as guided walks in the Waitakeres.

🚩 Bush & Beach TRAMPING, WINE TASTING
(☎09-837 4130; www.bushandbeach.co.nz) Guided walks in the Waitakere Ranges and along west coast beaches (half-/full day $140/225, including transfers); half-day city minibus

64

AUCKLAND FESTIVALS & EVENTS

tours ($140); and food, wine and art tours in either Matakana or Kumeu (half-/full day $179/295).

Auckland Ghost Tours
WALKING TOUR

(☎09-630 5721; www.aucklandghosttours.com; adult/child $50/25) Stories of Auckland's scary side – and we don't just mean the architecture – shared on a two-hour walking tour of the central city.

Hiking NZ
TRAMPING

(☎0800 697 232; www.hikingnewzealand.com) Runs 'hiking safaris' leaving from Auckland, including Far North ($995, six days); and Volcanoes & Rainforest ($1880, 10 days).

Bus Tours

Explorer Bus
BUS TOUR

(☎0800 439 756; www.explorerbus.co.nz; adult/child $40/20) This hop-on, hop-off service departs from the Ferry Building every hour from 10am to 3pm (more frequently in summer), heading to 14 tourist sites around the central city.

Gray Line
BUS TOUR

(☎0800 698 687; www.graylinetours.co.nz; tour $74; ⊙9.15am) Three-hour bus tour taking in the Harbour Bridge, Wynyard Quarter, Queen St, university, museum, Domain and Tamaki Dr.

GreatSights
BUS TOUR

(Map p52; ☎0800 744 487; www.greatsights.co.nz; adult/child $74/37; ⊙8.45am) Three-hour bus tours, including the Harbour Bridge, Viaduct, Queen St, Domain, Parnell and Tamaki Dr.

Cruises

Riverhead Ferry
CRUISE

(☎09-376 0819; www.riverheadferry.co.nz; adult/child $38/20) Offers harbour and gulf cruises including a 90-minute jaunt up the inner harbour to Riverhead (p101), returning after two hours' pub time.

Fullers
CRUISE

(Map p52; ☎09-367 9111; www.fullers.co.nz; Ferry Building, 99 Quay St; adult/child $38/19; ⊙10.30am &1.30pm) As well as ferry services, Fullers has daily 1½-hour harbour cruises which include a stop on Rangitoto, a complimentary cuppa and a free return ticket to Devonport.

360 Discovery
CRUISE

(Map p52; ☎0800 360 3472; www.360discovery.co.nz; Pier 4, 139 Quay St; cruise adult/child $27/17, 3-day pass $35/21; ⊙10am, noon & 2.30pm) Apart from their regular ferries, 360 has an Auckland Harbour cruise that stops at Devonport's Torpedo Bay, Rangitoto, Motuihe and Orakei Wharf (for Kelly Tarlton's). You can either stay onboard for the full 1½ hours or hop on and off as many times as you like over the course of three days.

Other Tours

Paradise Motorcycle Tours
MOTORCYCLE TOUR

(☎09-473 9404; www.paradisemotorcycletours.co.nz) See the sights on a guided motorcycle tour or hire a bike for a self-guided trip. Tours range from a two-hour pillion ride around the city ($199) to a 21-day guided ride on a 1200cc BMW bike ($19,904).

Red Carpet Tours
MOVIE LOCATIONS

(☎09-410 6561; www.redcarpet-tours.com) This brave fellowship will run a gauntlet of orcs to get you safely there (to Hobbiton/Matamata) and back again in one day ($245), or show you all of Middle Earth over 12 days ($6320).

★ Festivals & Events

Check www.aucklandnz.com for full details of what's on in the city.

Auckland Anniversary Day Regatta
SPORTS

(www.regatta.org.nz) The 'City of Sails' lives up to its name; Monday of last weekend in January.

MAORI NZ: AUCKLAND

Evidence of Maori occupation is literally carved into Auckland's volcanic cones. The dominant *iwi* (tribe) of the isthmus was Ngati Whatua, but these days there are Maori from almost all of NZ's *iwi* living here.

For an initial taste of Maori culture, start at Auckland Museum (p51), where there's a wonderful Maori collection and a culture show. For a more personalised experience, take a tour with TIME Unlimited (p63), Toru Tours (p63) or Ngati Whatua's Tamaki Hikoi (p63), or visit the *marae* and recreated village at Te Hana (p106).

LOCAL KNOWLEDGE

URBAN PASIFIKA *SHIMPAL LELISI*

To try Pacific Island food in Auckland, head to the markets at Otara, Avondale or Mangere, or to a festival day put on by the community – Pasifika and Polyfest are always good. Polyfest is in March, and it's the biggest PI cultural festival in the world. It's been going on since the early '70s and it's enormous, with thousands of people coming through. I was in the Niuean group when I was at school, and it was when I first got the buzz for performing. It's amazing now watching the calibre of the performances.

The students take it really seriously, and there are new moves every year - it's like *Strictly Ballroom*! At its core Polyfest is still about teaching the young people all of the old songs, but it's really exciting to see change.'

Shimpal Lelisi, actor (bro'Town, Sione's Wedding)

Laneway Festival MUSIC
(www.lanewayfestival.com.au) Presents the latest batch of international indie wunderkinds to an adoring crowd in a one-day festival on Anniversary Day.

Music In Parks MUSIC
(www.musicinparks.co.nz) A series of free gigs in parks around the city; runs from January until March.

Movies In Parks FILM
(www.moviesinparks.co.nz) Just like it sounds: free movies in parks in February and March.

Lantern Festival CULTURAL
(www.asianz.org.nz) Three days of Asian food and culture in Albert Park to welcome the lunar New Year (usually held in early February).

Devonport Food & Wine Festival FOOD & WINE
(www.devonportwinefestival.co.nz; admission $30) Sip and sup with the smart set at this two-day festival in mid-February.

Big Gay Out GAY & LESBIAN
(www.biggayout.co.nz) The big event on the gay and lesbian calendar; 12,000 people descend on Coyle Park, Pt Chevalier on a Sunday afternoon in mid-February.

Splore MUSIC
(www.splore.net; Tapapakanga Regional Park) Three days of camping and music (generally of the dancy and soulful variety), held by the beach in mid-February. The headliners always include big-name international acts.

Auckland Cup Week SPORTS
(www.ellerslie.co.nz; Ellerslie Racecourse) Back a winner at the biggest horse race of the year; early March.

Auckland Arts Festival ARTS
(www.aucklandfestival.co.nz) Held over three weeks in March in odd-numbered years, this is Auckland's biggest celebration of the arts.

Pasifika Festival CULTURAL
(www.aucklandcouncil.govt.nz) Western Springs Park hosts this giant Polynesian party with cultural performances, food and craft stalls; held early to mid-March.

Polyfest CULTURAL
(www.asbpolyfest.co.nz; Sports Bowl, Manukau) Massive Auckland secondary schools' Maori and Pacific Islands cultural festival.

Royal Easter Show AGRICULTURAL
(www.royaleastershow.co.nz; ASB Showgrounds, 217 Green Lane West) It's supposedly agricultural but people descend in their droves for the funfair rides.

NZ International Comedy Festival COMEDY
(www.comedyfestival.co.nz) Three-week laughfest with local and international comedians; held late April to early May.

Out Takes FILM, GAY & LESBIAN
(www.outtakes.org.nz; Rialto Cinemas) Gay and lesbian film festival, running from late May to early June.

NZ International Film Festival FILM
(www.nzff.co.nz) Auckland goes crazy for arthouse films from mid-July.

Auckland Art Fair ARTS
(www.artfair.co.nz; Viaduct Events Centre) Art for sale (lots of it), in August in odd-numbered years.

NZ Fashion Week FASHION
(www.nzfashionweek.com) Is any country better qualified to show what you can do with me-

Ponsonby & Grey Lynn

rino wool and a sense of imagination? Held in early September.

Auckland International Boat Show SPORTS
(www.auckland-boatshow.com) It doesn't command the instant nautical recognition of Sydney or San Diego, but Auckland really is one of the world's great sailing cities. And here's proof; held in September.

Heritage Festival CULTURAL
(www.aucklandcouncil.govt.nz) Two weeks of fabulous (mainly free) tours of Auckland's neighbourhoods and historic buildings; mid-September.

Diwali Festival of Lights CULTURAL
(www.asianz.org.nz) Auckland's Indian community lights up the city with an explosion of colour, music and dance; held in mid-October.

Grey Lynn Park Festival CULTURAL
(www.greylynnparkfestival.org) Join Grey Lynn's students, Pacific Islanders, lesbians, urban bohemians, hipsters and hippies in the park on the third Saturday in November for a free festival of craft and food stalls, and live music.

Santa Parade PARADE
(www.santaparade.co.nz) Santa gets an early start proceeding with his minions along Queen St before partying in Aotea Sq on the last Sunday of November.

Christmas in the Park FAMILY
(www.christmasinthepark.co.nz) A party so big it has to be held in the Auckland Domain.

🛏 Sleeping
CITY CENTRE
Auckland has plenty of luxury hotels, with many of the international chains taking up

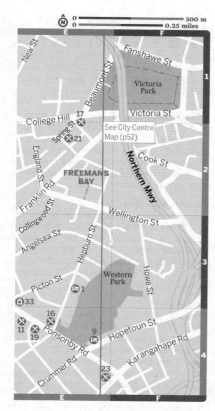

Ponsonby & Grey Lynn

Sleeping
1 23 Hepburn	E3
2 Abaco on Jervois	C1
3 Brown Kiwi	D1
4 Great Ponsonby Arthotel	C2
5 Henry's	A4
6 Ponsonby Backpackers	D3
7 Red Monkey	D4
8 Uenuku Lodge	D2
9 Verandahs	E4

Eating
10 Agnes Curran	D3
11 Burgerfuel	E4
12 Cocoro	D3
13 Delicious	B4
14 Dizengoff	D2
15 Landreth & Co	D2
16 MooChowChow	E4
17 New World	E1
18 Ponsonby Road Bistro	D3
19 Ponsonby Village International Food Court	E4
20 Prego	D3
21 Queenie's Lunchroom	E2
22 Richmond Rd Cafe	A3
23 Satya	E4
24 Soto	D1
25 SPQR	D3

Drinking
26 Dida's Wine Lounge & Tapas Bar	D1
27 Golden Dawn	D4
28 Gypsy Tea Room	A4
29 Lolabar	D3
30 Mea Culpa	D3
31 Ponsonby Social Club	D3

Shopping
Karen Walker	(see 30)
32 Marvel	D3
33 Texan Art Schools	E3
34 Women's Bookshop	D3
Zambesi	(see 18)

inner-city real estate. At the other extreme, any backpackers who leave with a bad impression of Auckland have invariably stayed in crummy, noisy digs in the city centre. Not all of the cheap city accommodation is bad but you'll generally find better in the inner suburbs.

Hotel de Brett TOP CHOICE BOUTIQUE HOTEL **$$$**
(Map p52; ☎09-925 9000; www.hoteldebrett .com; 2 High St; r $300-600; @☎) Supremely hip, this lavishly refurbished historic hotel has been zooshed up with stripy carpets and clever designer touches in every nook of the extremely comfortable rooms. Prices include breakfast, free broadband and a pre-dinner drink.

Waldorf Celestion APARTMENT **$$**
(Map p52; ☎09-280 2200; www.celestion-waldorf. co.nz; 19-23 Anzac Ave; apt $137-239) A rash of Waldorfs have opened in recent years, all presenting a similar set of symptoms: affordable, modern, inner-city apartments in city fringe locations. We prefer the Waldorf Celestioin for its stylish red, black and grey colour palate, and the sumptuous velvet curtains in reception.

Elliott Hotel
APARTMENT $$

(Map p52; ☑09-308 9334; www.theelliotthotel. com; cnr Elliott & Wellesley Sts; apt $139-219; P) Housed in a grand historic building (1880s), this apartment-style hotel is much plusher than the price implies. Rooms may not be huge but the high ceilings let your spirits rise.

Quadrant
HOTEL $$

(Map p52; ☑09-984 6000; www.thequadrant.com; 10 Waterloo Quadrant; apt $165-600; ☜) Slick, central and full of all the whiz-bang gadgets, this apartment-style complex is an excellent option. The only catch is that the units are tiny and the bathrooms beyond small.

Waldorf Stadium
APARTMENT

(Map p52; ☑09-337 5300; www.stadium-apartments-hotel.co.nz; 40 Beach Rd; apt $162-357) Another of the Waldorf chain, this large newish block has spacious (if generic) family-friendly apartments with double-glazing to keep out the road noise.

CityLife
HOTEL $$

(Map p52; ☑09-379 9222; www.heritagehotels. co.nz/citylife-auckland; Durham St; apt $169-850; P@☜⊠) A worthy tower-block hotel offering numerous apartments over dozens of floors, ranging from studios to three-bedroom suites. Facilities include a heated lap pool, gym, valet parking and a babysitting service.

Jucy Hotel
HOTEL $

(Map p52; ☑09-379 6633; www.jucyhotel.com; 62 Emily Pl; hostel s/d $49/69, hotel r $99; P@☜) The Jucy car-rental company has taken over this long-standing hostel, repainted everything in their trademark lurid green and purple, and converted it into a zippy budget hotel. Rooms in the main section have en suites, and there's a hostel wing for those who don't mind bunks and shared bathrooms.

City Lodge
HOTEL $

(Map p52; ☑09-379 6183; www.citylodge.co.nz; 150 Vincent St; s $75, d $99-115; @☜) City Lodge is a YMCA-run, purpose-built tower for the budget market. The tiny rooms and stamp-sized bathrooms may be plain, but they make a clean and secure resting place. There's a fantastic industrial-style kitchen and a comfy lounge.

Auckland International YHA
HOSTEL $

(Map p52; ☑09-302 8200; www.yha.co.nz; 5 Turner St; dm $32-36, r $98-110; P@☜) Clean and brightly painted, this 170-bed YHA has a friendly vibe, good security, a games room and lots of lockers. In short, it's your typical, well-run YHA.

Auckland City YHA
HOSTEL $

(Map p52; ☑09-309 2802; www.yha.co.nz; 18 Liverpool St; dm $29-49, s/d $76/92; @☜) Struggle up one of the city's steepest streets to this big, impersonal tower block near the K Rd party strip. The rooms are clean and well kept, and some have views and terraces.

Nomads Auckland
HOSTEL $

(Map p52; ☑09-300 9999; www.nomadsauckland. com; 16 Fort St; dm $24-36, r $91-111; @☜) Bustling is an understatement for this large backpackers with a cafe, bar, travel agency, female-only floor and a roof deck with sauna and spa. The private rooms have TVs but not all have windows.

Base Auckland
HOSTEL $

(Map p52; ☑09-358 4877; www.stayatbase.com; Level 3, 229 Queen St; dm $27-32, r $65-93; @☜) With more than 500 beds, this is the place where many young visitors get their bearings. If you don't like a hive of activity (or stained carpets), then you'll need to go elsewhere, as this place hums with questions about who's got work where, whether bungy jumping's worth it and where the cute guys/girls are. There's a bar to aid this last quest.

FREEMAN'S BAY

Verandahs
HOSTEL $

(Map p66; ☑09-360 4180; www.verandahs.co.nz; 6 Hopetoun St; dm $27-31, s $55, d $72-88, tr $92; P@☜) Ponsonby Rd, K Rd and the city are an easy walk from this grand hostel, housed in two neighbouring villas overlooking the mature trees of Western Park. It's easily Auckland's best backpackers.

23 Hepburn
B&B $$$

(Map p66; ☑09-376 0622; www.23hepburn.co.nz; 23 Hepburn St; r $210-250; P☜) The three boutique rooms are a symphony in muted whites and creams, inducing the pleasant sensation of waking up inside an extremely chic pavlova. Continental breakfast is left in your fridge the previous evening to enjoy at your leisure.

PONSONBY & GREY LYNN

Henry's
B&B $$$

(Map p66; ☑09-360 2700; www.henrysonpeel.
co.nz; 33 Peel St; r/apt $220/275; @��) These
beautiful wooden villas are what Auckland's
inner suburbs are all about. Henry's has
been stylishly renovated, adding en suites to
the downstairs rooms and a self-contained
harbour-view apartment above.

Great Ponsonby Arthotel
B&B $$$

(Map p66; ☑09-376 5989; www.greatpons.co.nz;
30 Ponsonby Tce; r $245-400; P@) This decep-
tively spacious Victorian villa has gregarious
hosts, impressive sustainability practices,
great breakfasts and it's located a stone's
throw from Ponsonby Rd in a quiet cul-de-
sac. Studio apartments open onto an attractive rear courtyard.

Abaco on Jervois
MOTEL $$

(Map p66; ☑09-360 6850; www.abaco.co.nz;
57 Jervois Rd; r $125-165, ste $184-205; P) A
neutral-toned motel, with a contempo-
rary fit-out, including slick stainless-steel
kitchenettes (with dish drawers and prop-
er ovens) and fluffy white towels for use in
the spa. The darker rooms downstairs are
priced accordingly.

Red Monkey
GUESTHOUSE $

(Map p66; ☑09-360 7977; www.theredmonkey.
co.nz; 49 Richmond Rd; weekly s $240-280, d $360-
480; @) If you're planning to stay for a week
or longer, make one of these two renovated
villas your home away from home. There
are lamps, bedside tables and built-in ward-
robes in all the smartly decorated rooms,
most of which share bathrooms. Book well
ahead.

Brown Kiwi
HOSTEL $

(Map p66; ☑09-378 0191; www.brownkiwi.co.nz;
7 Prosford St; dm $27-30, r $72; @�) As unas-
suming as its namesake, this gay-friendly
hostel is tucked away in a busy-by-day com-
mercial strip, a stone's throw from all the
good shopping and grazing opportunities.
The garden courtyard is made for mooching.

Uenuku Lodge
HOSTEL $

(Map p66; ☑09-378 8990; www.uenukulodge.
co.nz; 217 Ponsonby Rd; dm $26-33, s $48, d $62-
80; P@�) It could do with a freshen up,
but this hostel is well located and some of
the rooms afford city views. There's a decent
lounge, a large kitchen, good security and a
courtyard.

Ponsonby Backpackers
HOSTEL $

(Map p66; ☑09-360 1311; www.ponsonby-back
packers.co.nz; 2 Franklin Rd; dm $26-28, s/d
$45/62; P@�) The interiors don't live up
to the imposing exterior of this turreted
wooden villa, commanding a corner site on
tree-lined Franklin Rd. Yet it's kept reason-
ably clean and is superbly located.

NEWTON

Langham
HOTEL $$$

(Map p52; ☑09-379 5132; www.auckland.langham
hotels.co.nz; 83 Symonds St; r $220-390, ste $510-
2430; P@��) The glamour of the giant
chandelier in reception dissipates somewhat once you reach the low-ceilinged guest
floors. Still, the Langham's service is typically faultless, the beds are heavenly, and its
day spa is reputedly the best in Auckland.

BK Hostel
HOSTEL $

(Map p52; ☑09-307 0052; www.bkhostel.co.nz;
3 Mercury Lane; s $45-49, d $58-66; @��) Prices
are cheaper for windowless rooms, but if
you're planning to be partying in the neighbourhood's all-night clubs, that might be an
advantage. The hostel is housed in a 1910
building with high ceilings and good security.

MT EDEN

Eden Park B&B
B&B $$$

(Map p62; ☑09-630 5721; www.bedandbreakfastnz.
com; 20 Bellwood Ave; s $135-150, d $235-250; �)
If you know any rugby fans who require
chandeliers in their bathrooms, send them
here. The hallowed turf of Auckland's legen-
dary rugby ground is only a block away and
while the rooms aren't overly large for the
prices, they mirror the Edwardian elegance
of this fine wooden villa.

Bamber House
HOSTEL $

(Map p62; ☑09-623 4267; www.hostelbackpacker.
com; 22 View Rd; dm $28-30, d $70-90; P@�)
The original house here is a mansion of
sorts, with some nicely maintained period
trimmings and large grounds. The new pre-
fab cabins have less character but come with
en suites.

Pentlands
HOSTEL $

(Map p62; ☑09-638 7031; www.pentlands.co.nz;
22 Pentland Ave; dm $25-28, s/d $46/68; P@�)
Set down a peaceful tree-lined cul-de-sac,
this powder-blue villa offers recently reno-
vated rooms, a sunny deck with a BBQ, and
quiet tables on the lawn. It's an altogether
chilled-out environment.

AUCKLAND SLEEPING

Devonport

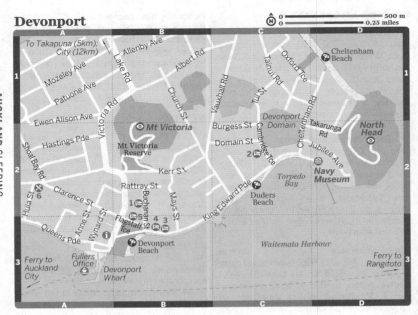

Devonport

◉ Top Sights

🛏 Sleeping

✕ Eating

Oaklands Lodge HOSTEL $
(Map p62; ☎09-638 6545; www.oaklands.co.nz; 5a Oaklands Rd; dm $25-27, s $48, d $64-74; @☎) At the foot of the mountain in a leafy cul-de-sac, this bright, well-kept hostel is close to Mt Eden village and city buses. The communal facilities are in good nick.

Bavaria GUESTHOUSE $$
(Map p62; ☎09-638 9641; www.bavariabandbhotel. co.nz; 83 Valley Rd; s $95-110, d $145-175; P@☎) Sitting somewhere between a B&B and a small hotel, this spacious villa offers large,

airy rooms and a buffet breakfast. The communal TV lounge, dining room and deck all encourage mixing and mingling.

PARNELL & NEWMARKET

City Garden Lodge HOSTEL $
(Map p60; ☎09-302 0880; www.citygardenlodge. co.nz; 25 St Georges Bay Rd; dm $30-32, s/d $54/70; P@☎) Occupying a character-filled, two-storey house built for Tongan royalty, this friendly and well-run backpackers has a lovely garden and high-ceilinged rooms. If you need to unwind, there's yoga on the front lawn.

Quest Carlaw Park APARTMENT $$
(Map p60; ☎09-304 0521; www.questcarlawpark. co.nz; 15 Nicholls Lane; apt $130-320; @☎) It's in an odd spot but this set of smart, modern apartments is handy for Parnell, the city and the Domain, and if you've got a car you're practically on the motorway.

Parnell Inn MOTEL $$
(Map p60; ☎09-358 0642; www.parnellinn.co.nz; 320 Parnell Rd; r $105-140; P@☎) You'll get a chipper welcome from the friendly folks at this good-looking, revamped motel with local photography on the walls. Rooms 3 and 4 have great harbour views and some rooms have kitchenettes.

Quality Hotel Barrycourt HOTEL **$$**
(Map p60; ☑09-303 3789; www.barrycourt.co.nz; 20 Gladstone Rd; units $113-283, r $131-179, ste $188-283; P❄) A mixed bag of more than 100 motel rooms and units are available in this large, well-maintained complex with friendly multilingual staff. The newer north wing has some fantastic harbour views.

Lantana Lodge HOSTEL **$**
(Map p60; ☑09-373 4546; www.lantanalodge.co.nz; 60 St Georges Bay Rd; dm $27-30, s/d $59/70; P❄) There are only eight rooms available in this cosy villa on a quiet street with an instantly welcoming, social vibe. It's not flash by any means, but it's clean enough to be homely.

DEVONPORT
Devonport has masses of beautiful Edwardian B&Bs within a relaxing ferry ride of the city.

Peace & Plenty Inn B&B **$$$**
(Map p70; ☑09-445 2925; www.peaceandplenty. co.nz; 6 Flagstaff Tce; s $195-265, d $265-465; P❄) This perfectly located, five-star Victorian house is stocked with antique furnishings and a thousand conversation pieces. The romantic, luxurious rooms have en suites, TVs, flowers, free sherry/port and local chocolates.

Hampton Beach House B&B **$$$**
(Map p70; ☑09-445 1358; www.hamptonbeach house.co.nz; 4 King Edward Pde; s $195, r $235-305; @❄) One of a fine strip of waterside mansions, this upmarket, gay-friendly, Edwardian B&B has rooms opening onto the rear garden. It's all very tastefully done; expect quality linen and gourmet breakfasts.

Devonport Motel MOTEL **$$**
(Map p70; ☑09-445 1010; www.devonportmotel. co.nz; 11 Buchanan St; r $150; ❄) This minimotel has just two units in the tidy back garden. They're modern, clean, self-contained and in a nice quiet location that's still close to Devonport's action (such as it may be).

Parituhu B&B **$$**
(Map p70; ☑09-445 6559; www.parituhu.co.nz; 3 King Edward Pde; r $125-185; ❄) There's only one double bedroom (with its own adjoining bathroom) available in this cute Edwardian waterfront bungalow. It's a relaxing and welcoming place, and gay- and lesbian-friendly too.

Devonport Sea Cottage COTTAGE **$$**
(Map p70; ☑09-445 7117; www.devonportseacottage nz.com; 3a Cambridge Tce; s/d $110/130; ❄) Head up the garden path to your own self-contained cottage, which has everything you'll need for a relaxing stay near the sea. Excellent weekly rates are available in summer.

OTHER AREAS

TOP CHOICE **Auckland Takapuna Oaks** HOTEL **$$**
(Map p48; ☑09-445 7100; www.aucklandtakapuna oaks.co.nz; 1 Beresford St, Bayswater; apt $129-349; P@❄) It sounds almost too good to be true: affordable spacious apartments (with full kitchens and laundry facilities) situated at the end of a peaceful peninsula that's close to beaches and a short ferry ride from the city. But wait, there's more: harbour and city views, breakfast included and ample parking... There may not be a free set of steak knives but they do chuck in a return ferry ticket each day.

Omahu Lodge B&B **$$$**
(Map p56; ☑09-524 5648; www.omahulodge.co.nz; 33 Omahu Rd, Remuera; s $170-200, d $230-325; ❄) Art and family photos cover the walls at this cheerful, deluxe B&B. The three en-suite rooms in the main house all have neighbourhood views, but the spacious suite opens straight onto the solar-heated pool.

Jet Park HOTEL **$$**
(Map p48; ☑09-275 4100; www.jetpark.co.nz; 63 Westney Rd, Mangere; r $153-310, ste $220-430; @❄☀) Friendly Jet Park has comfortable rooms, a decent vibe (unusual for an airport hotel), and a pool straight out of *Hawaii 5-0*. Departure screens in the lobby and free airport shuttles mean there's no excuse for missing your flight.

Grange Lodge MOTEL **$$**
(Map p48; ☑09-277 8280; www.grangelodge.co.nz; cnr Grange & Great South Rds, Papatoetoe; units $115-190; ❄) If you've driven up from the south and can't face crossing the city, consider staying at this friendly little suburban motel, offering reasonable rates, free wi-fi and a teddy bear in every room. It's hardly a salubrious location but it is handy for the airport. From the Southern Motorway, take the East Tamaki Rd exit, turn right and right again onto Great South Rd.

Nautical Nook
B&B **$$**

(Map p48; ☑09-521 2544; www.nauticalnook. com; 23b Watene Cres, Orakei; s/d $108/162; ☎) If you're a sailing buff you'll find a kindred spirit in Keith, who runs this cosy homestay with his wife Trish. The lounge and terrace have views over the harbour, and the beach is close at hand.

Auckland Airport
Campervan Park
CAMPERVAN PARK

(Map p48; ☑09-256 8527; www.aucklandairport. co.nz; Jimmy Ward Crescent, Mangere; sites from $29; ☎) The world's first airport-run campervan park offers 54 powered spaces with toilets and showers, all within 1km of the terminals. It's a great option for those wanting to park-up after a long flight before hitting the road.

Ambury Regional Park
CAMPSITE **$**

(Map p48; ☑09-366 2000; www.arc.govt.nz; Ambury Rd, Mangere; sites per adult/child $10/5) A slice of country in the middle of suburbia, this regional park is also a working farm. Facilities are limited (a vault toilet, warm showers and not much shade) but it's handy to the airport, right on the water and dirt cheap.

✗ Eating

Because of its size and ethnic diversity, Auckland tops the country when it comes to dining options and quality. Lively eateries have sprung up to cater to the numerous Asian students, offering inexpensive Japanese, Chinese and Korean staples. If you're on a budget, you'll fall in love with the city's food halls.

Aucklanders demand good coffee, so you never have to walk too far to find a decent cafe. Suburbs such as Ponsonby, Grey Lynn and Kingsland are teeming with them. Some double as wine bars or have gourmet aspirations, while others are content to fill their counters with fresh, reasonably priced snacks.

The 2011 Rugby World Cup brought with it a flurry of restaurant and bar openings, shifting the locus of gastronomic activity back to the city centre. Nowadays the hippest new foodie enclaves are Britomart (the blocks above the train station) and Federal St (under the Sky Tower) – although Ponsonby still stands out for the quality and variety of its eateries.

You'll find large supermarkets in most neighbourhoods; there's a particularly handy **Countdown** (Map p52; www.countdown.

co.nz; 76 Quay St; ⏰24hr) at the bottom of town and a **New World** (Map p66; www.new world.co.nz; 2 College Hill, Freemans Bay; ⏰7am-midnight) by Victoria Park. Self-caterers should consider the Otara Market (p81) and Avondale Sunday Market (p81) for cheap, fresh vegetables and La Cigale (p75) for fancier fare.

CITY CENTRE

🔺 TOP CHOICE Grove
MODERN NZ **$$$**

(Map p52; ☑09-368 4129; www.thegroverestaurant .co.nz; St Patrick's Sq, Wyndham St; mains $43; ⏰lunch Mon-Fri, dinner Mon-Sat) Romantic fine dining at its best: the room is cosy and moodily lit, the menu encourages sensual experimentation and the service is effortless. If you can't find anything to break the ice from the extensive wine list, give it up mate – it's never going to happen.

Depot
MODERN NZ **$$**

(Map p52; www.eatatdepot.co.nz; 86 Federal St; dishes $14-32; ⏰7am-late) Opened to instant acclaim in 2011, TV chef Al Brown's first Auckland eatery offers first-rate comfort food in informal surrounds (communal tables, butcher tiles and a constant buzz). Dishes are divided into 'small' and 'a little bigger' and are designed to be shared. A pair of clever shuckers are kept busy serving up the city's freshest oysters.

Food Alley
FOOD HALL **$**

(Map p52; 9 Albert St; mains $7-13; ⏰10.30am-10pm) There's Chinese, Indian, Thai, Vietnamese, Turkish, Malaysian, Korean and Japanese on offer at this large, no-frills (but plenty of thrills) food hall. Our pick of the bunch is Wardani, hidden in the back corner, serving first-rate Indonesian fare.

O'Connell Street Bistro
FRENCH **$$$**

(Map p52; ☑09-377 1884; www.oconnellstbistro. com; 3 O'Connell St; lunch $28-38, dinner $34-45; ⏰lunch Mon-Fri, dinner Mon-Sat) O'Connell St is a grown-up treat, with elegant decor and truly wonderful food and wine, satisfying lunchtime powerbrokers and dinnertime daters alike. If you're dining before 7.30pm, a fixed-price menu is available (two-/three-courses $33/40).

🍴 Federal & Wolfe
CAFE **$$**

(Map p52; 10 Federal St; mains $12-21; ⏰7am-3pm Mon-Sat; ☎) Packing crates and mismatched chairs (some seemingly liberated from a high school) lend an air of recycled chic to this corner cafe. Yet the be-suited swarm here for the first-rate coffee, delicious food (much of it organic and free range) and a quick dose of cool to get them through their working day.

Ima
MIDDLE EASTERN **$$**

(Map p52; ☑09-300 7252; www.imacuisine.co.nz; 57 Fort St; lunch $15-23, dinner $26-34; ☺lunch Mon-Fri, dinner Tue-Sat) Named after the Hebrew word for mother, the menu is a harmonious blend of Israeli, Palestinian, Yemenite and Lebanese dishes. Excellent coffee, too.

Reslau
CAFE **$**

(Map p52; 39 Elliott St; mains $7.50-11; ☺7.30am-7.30pm Mon-Wed, 7.30am-9.30pm Thu-Sat) Spilling into the Elliott Stables laneway, this tiny cafe–wine bar literally has a trolley-load of delicious snacks and light meals, not to mention excellent coffee.

BRITOMART, VIADUCT HARBOUR & WYNYARD QUARTER

Soul Bar
MODERN NZ **$$**

(Map p52; ☑09-356 7249; www.soulbar.co.nz; Viaduct Harbour; mains $20-42; ☺11am-late) Eating seafood by the water is a must in Auckland and this modernist gastrodome boasts an unbeatable see-and-be-seen location (Jay-Z and Beyoncé dined not-at-all-inconspicuously on the deck) and some of the best seafood in town.

Euro
MODERN NZ **$$**

(Map p52; ☑09-309 9866; www.eurobar.co.nz; Shed 22, Princes Wharf; mains $28-45; ☺lunch & dinner) Euro is a thoroughly slick package of imaginative cuisine, good-looking wait staff and sexy surrounds. The dishes are always as pretty as a picture and the relaxed atmosphere gets decidedly more bar-like as the night progresses.

Ebisu
JAPANESE **$$**

(Map p52; www.ebisu.co.nz; 116-118 Quay St; large plates $28-35; ☺lunch Mon-Fri, dinner daily) Auckland's food-lovers are in the midst of a minicraze for *izakaya*, a style of drinking and eating that eschews Japanese formality, yet doesn't involve food being flung around the room or chugging along on a conveyor belt. This large bar gets it exactly right, serving exquisite plates, large and small, designed to be shared.

L'Assiette
FRENCH **$$**

(Map p52; www.lassiette.co.nz; 9 Britomart Pl, Britomart; breakfast & lunch $10-19, dinner $28-33;

☺breakfast & lunch daily, dinner Thu-Sat) Fresh and bright, this little cafe is a popular coffee-and-pastry stop for harried office workers. By night it morphs into a fully fledged bistro, serving a delicious but limited menu of French classics at reasonable prices.

FREEMANS BAY

Clooney
MODERN NZ **$$$**

(Map p52; ☑09-358 1702; www.clooney.co.nz; 33 Sale St; mains $42-45; ☺dinner) Like the Hollywood actor of the same name, Clooney is suave, stylish and extremely sophisticated, suited up in basic black. While the taste combinations are complex, the results are faultless – which coupled with impeccable service puts Clooney firmly in the pricy-but-worth-it category.

Queenie's Lunchroom
CAFE **$$**

(Map p66; www.queenieslunchroom.co.nz; 24a Spring St; mains $11-22; ☺8am-3.30pm) Kiwiana reigns supreme at this eccentric corner cafe with one wall devoted to a 1950s paint-by-numbers Maori maiden mural. The food is a step up from standard cafe fare, with an adventurous menu justifying the prices.

PONSONBY & GREY LYNN

Auckland's busiest restaurant-cafe-bar strip is so damn cool it has its own website (www.ponsonbyroad.co.nz).

⌐TOP CHOICE⌐ MooChowChow
THAI **$$**

(Map p66; ☑09-360 6262; www.moochowchow.co.nz; 23 Ponsonby Rd; dishes $18-30; ☺lunch Tue-Fri, dinner Tue-Sat) It's Thai, Nahm Jim, but not as we know it. Bangkok's street food has been channelled into this supremely Ponsonby mooching spot without missing a piquant note. We haven't had a bad dish here, and we've sampled most of the menu.

SPQR
ITALIAN **$$**

(Map p66; www.spqrnz.co.nz; 150 Ponsonby Rd; mains $25-39; ☺noon-late) This Ponsonby Rd hot spot is well known for Roman-style, thin, crusty pizzas and excellent Italian-influenced mains. The surrounds are a stylish blend of the industrial and the chic, the lights are *low* (bring your reading glasses!), the buzz constant and the smooth staff aren't beyond camping it up.

Cocoro
JAPANESE **$$$**

(Map p66; ☑09-360 0927; www.cocoro.co.nz; 56a Brown St; dishes $5-25, degustation $80; ☺lunch & dinner Tue-Sat) Japanese elegance infuses everything about this excellent restaurant, from the soft lighting and chic decor, to the professional staff and the delicate flavours of the artistically arranged food. Dishes are designed to be shared, tapas-style – or more correctly *izakaya*-style.

Richmond Rd Cafe   CAFE $$
(Map p66; www.richmondrdcafe.co.nz; 318 Richmond Rd; mains $14-25; ⊙7am-4pm) The location is a little odd – anchored to a small island of industry in a sea of suburbia – but this is one of Auckland's 'it' cafes regardless. If you're suffering from breakfast boredom, you're bound to find the antidote within its creative menu.

Ponsonby Road Bistro   INTERNATIONAL $$
(Map p66; ☎09-360 1611; www.ponsonbyroadbistro.co.nz; 165 Ponsonby Rd; mains $23-36; ⊙lunch Mon-Fri, dinner Mon-Sat) Portions are large at this modern, upmarket restaurant with an Italian/French sensibility and first-rate service. Imported cheese and wine are a highlight, and the crispy-based pizzas make a delicious shared snack.

Ponsonby Village International Food Court   FOOD HALL $
(Map p66; www.ponsonbyfoodcourt.co.nz; 106 Ponsonby Rd; mains $8-20; ⊙10am-10pm; ☎) The city's best food hall, only partly due to its location at the heart of the Ponsonby strip. There's Italian, Japanese, Malaysian, Chinese, Turkish, Thai, Lao and Indian on offer but we rarely go past the excellent Vietnamese and Indonesian.

Prego   ITALIAN $$
(Map p66; ☎09-376 3095; www.prego.co.nz; 226 Ponsonby Rd; mains $23-37; ⊙noon-midnight) This friendly and stylish Italian restaurant covers all the bases, with a fireplace in winter and a courtyard in summer. And on the subject of bases, the pizza is pretty damn fine, as are the inventive Italian mains.

Dizengoff   CAFE $
(Map p66; 256 Ponsonby Rd; mains $7-19; ⊙6.30am-5pm) This stylish shoebox crams in a mixed crowd of corporate and fashion types, gay guys, Jewish families and Ponsonby denizens, as well as travellers. Mouth-watering scrambled eggs, tempting counter food and heart-starting coffee are on offer, plus a great stack of reading material if you tire of eavesdropping and people-watching.

Burgerfuel   BURGERS $
(www.burgerfuel.com; burgers $6-13; ☎) Ponsonby (Map p83; 114 Ponsonby Rd); City (Map p52; 291 Queen St); Parnell (Map p60; 187 Parnell Rd); Mt Eden (Map p62; 214 Dominion Rd) Kiwis love their gourmet burgers, so much that they've taken the concept to the world; you can find Kiwi-run chains from Auckland to Edinburgh, by way of Oman and Athens. Burgerfuel are exemplars of the art, filling their buns with high-quality, fresh ingredients and giving them petrolhead names like Studnut Stilton and V8 Vegan.

Landreth & Co   CAFE $$
(Map p66; www.landrethandco.co.nz; 272 Ponsonby Rd; mains $14-25; ⊙6.30am-4pm; ☎) A popular brunch spot with a sunny rear courtyard and free wi-fi. It's fully licensed, just in case you feel the urge for a beer with your truffled eggs.

Soto   JAPANESE $$
(Map p66; ☎09-360 0021; www.soto.co.nz; 13 St Marys Rd; mains $29-33; ⊙lunch Tue-Fri, dinner Tue-Sat) Auckland has a surfeit of excellent Japanese restaurants but this is one of the best. The staff glide by efficiently, leaving a trail of exquisitely presented dishes in their wake – including sushi, sashimi and *zensai* (Japanese tapas).

Agnes Curran   CAFE $
(Map p66; 181 Ponsonby Rd (enter Franklin Rd); snacks $7-9) It may sound like someone's maiden aunt but this cute little cafe is much more hipster than spinster. Still Aunt Agnes would appreciate the cake selection and fresh baguettes, although the super-strong coffee might set her heart aflutter.

Delicious   ITALIAN $$
(Map p66; www.delicious.co.nz; 472 Richmond Rd; mains $28-34; ⊙lunch Wed-Fri, dinner Tue-Sat) The name doesn't lie. Foodies flock to this neighbourhood eatery for simple but first-rate pasta, risotto and gnocchi. They don't take bookings so expect to wait – it's usually busy.

Satya   INDIAN $$
(www.satya.co.nz; mains $11-26; ☎); 17 Great North Rd (Map p66; ☎09-361 3612; ⊙lunch Mon-Sat, dinner daily); 271 Karangahape Rd (Map p52; ☎09-377 0027; ⊙lunch & dinner) Hugely popular, this humble-looking and humbly priced eatery has the best *dahi puri* (chickpea, potato and yoghurt on a pappadam) and masala dosa (crêpe filled with potato-and-onion curry) in town.

75

AUCKLAND EATING

NEWTON

K Rd is known for its late-night clubs, but cafes and plenty of inexpensive ethnic restaurants are mixed in with the second hand boutiques, tattooists and adult shops.

French Cafe FRENCH $$$
(Map p62; ☎09-377 1911; www.thefrenchcafe.co.nz; 210 Symonds St; mains $45; ☺lunch Fri, dinner Tue-Sat) The legendary French Cafe has been rated as one of Auckland's top restaurants for around 20 years now and it still continues to excel. The cuisine is (unsurprisingly) French, but chef Simon Wright sneaks in some Pacific Rim touches.

Coco's Cantina ITALIAN $$
(Map p52; www.cocoscantina.co.nz; 376 Karangahape Rd; mains $27-31; ☺5pm-late Tue-Sat) Rub shoulders with Auckland's hipsters and foodsters at this bustling cantina where the wait for a table is part of the experience. Propping up the bar is hardly a hardship: the ambience and drinks list see to that. The rustic menu is narrowly focussed, seasonal and invariably delicious.

Alleluya CAFE $
(Map p52; St Kevin's Arcade, Karangahape Rd; mains $10-19; ☺8am-3pm; ☎🎤) To the bohemian denizens of K Rd, Alleluya means good coffee, moreish cakes and lots of vegetarian options. It's situated at the end of the city's hippest arcade, with windows offering a wonderful snapshot of the city skyline.

Theatre CAFE $
(Map p52; www.theatrecoffee.co.nz; 256 Karangahape Rd; ☺7am-3pm) Once the grand entrance to a long-gone theatre, this narrow vaulted corridor has been transformed into a supremely cool licensed cafe serving excellent coffee, cooked breakfasts and made-to-order sandwiches and bagels.

O'Sarracino ITALIAN $$
(Map p62; ☎09-309 3740; www.osarracino.co.nz; 3 Mt Eden Rd; mains $22-38; ☺dinner Tue-Sat) A delicious reminder that Neapolitan cuisine offers so much more than pizza, this excellent restaurant serves generous antipasti, light and simple pasta, and delectable seafood *secondi*. The somewhat grand surroundings were once the chapel of a funeral parlour.

KINGSLAND

Atomic Roastery CAFE $
(Map p62; www.atomiccoffee.co.nz; 420c New North Rd; snacks $9-10; ☺8am-3pm) Coffee hounds should follow their noses to this, one of the country's best-known coffee roasters. Tasty accompaniments include pies served in mini-frypans, rolls, salads and cakes.

Shaky Isles CAFE $
(Map p62; 492 New North Rd; mains $10-21; ☺8am-4pm; 🎤) Kingsland's coolest cafe has cute cartoons on the wall, free wi-fi and serves delicious cooked breakfasts and super-food salads.

Fridge CAFE $
(Map p62; 507 New North Rd; mains $8-20; ☺breakfast & lunch) Serves excellent coffee, gourmet pies, healthy salads and wraps, and drool-inducing cakes.

MT EDEN

Merediths MODERN NZ $$$
(Map p62; ☎09-623 3140; www.merediths.co.nz; 365 Dominion Rd; 6-9 course degustation $90-130; ☺lunch Fri, dinner Tue-Sat) Dining at Merediths is the culinary equivalent of blackwater rafting – tastes surprise you at every turn, you never know what's coming next and you're left with a sense of breathless exhilaration.

Molten MODERN NZ $$$
(Map p62; ☎09-638 7236; www.molten.co.nz; 422 Mt Eden Rd; mains $32-35; ☺lunch Tue-Sat, dinner Mon-Sat) Under the volcano's shadow, Molten oozes neighbourhood charm and erupts with flavour. The consistently excellent menu is extremely well crafted, taking advantage of the latest seasonal produce to create innovative, beautifully presented meals.

Gala CAFE $
(Map p62; www.galacafe.co.nz; Zone 23, 23 Edwin St; mains $11-20; ☺breakfast & lunch) Mixing modern architecture and antique silver tea services, this bright cafe brings sophistication to the prison precinct. The whiteboard menu is crammed with interesting options: try My Mother-in-law's North Indian Eggs for a fragrant version of eggs on toast.

PARNELL & NEWMARKET

TOP CHOICE La Cigale FRENCH $$
(Map p60; ☎09-366 9361; www.lacigale.co.nz; 69 St Georges Bay Rd; cafe $8-18, bistro $30; ☺cafe 9am-4pm Mon-Fri, bistro dinner Wed-Fri, market 9am-1.30pm Sat & Sun) Catering to Francophiles, foodies and homesick Gauls, this warehouse stocks French imports (wine, cheese, tinned snails etc) and has a patisserie-laden cafe.

Yet it's during the weekend farmers markets that this *cigale* (cicada) really chirps, with stalls laden with produce and all manner of tasty eats. Three nights a week the space is converted into a quirky bistro, where mains are ordered three days in advance and served in large communal bowls.

Basque Kitchen Bar
TAPAS **$$**

(Map p56; ☎09-523 1057; 61 Davies Cres; tapas $7-15; ☺4pm-late Mon-Thu & Sat, noon-late Fri) It doesn't look like much but this dark little bar serves delectable tapas accompanied by a large range of Spanish wine and sherry. The stuffed squid is sublime.

Teed St Larder
CAFE **$**

(Map p56; www.teedstreetlarder.co.nz; 7 Teed St; ☺8am-4pm) Polished concrete floors, beer crate tables and colourful oversized lampshades set the scene at Newmarket's best cafe. There are plenty of enticing cooked items on the menu but it's hard to go past the delicious sandwiches and tarts beckoning from the counter.

Roseship Cafe
CAFE **$$**

(Map p60; 82 Gladstone Rd; mains $15-27; ☺7am-4pm) The name fits: it's near the Rose Gardens and it's pretty darn hip. The cooked meals are a tad pricey but the food is delicious.

Domain & Ayr
CAFE **$**

(Map p60; 492 Parnell Rd; mains $9-19; ☺8am-3.30pm; ✐) Fair-trade and organic delights that won't unduly strain the bank balance await in this light-filled cafe. There's a good selection of counter food as well as delicious cooked breakfasts, salads and plenty of options for vegetarians.

Non Solo Pizza
ITALIAN **$$**

(Map p60; ☎09-379 5358; www.nonsolopizza.co.nz; 259 Parnell Rd; mains $23-39; ☺lunch & dinner) Like the name says, there's not only pizza on offer here – delicious though it is. NSP has a large menu of classic Italian antipasti, pasta and grills and a cool street-facing bar with a chandelier made of Peroni bottles.

DEVONPORT

Calliope Road Cafe
CAFE **$**

(Map p70; 33 Calliope Rd; mains $6-17; ☺8am-3pm) Devonport's best cafe is at a short remove from the main tourist strip, serving a tasty mix of cafe classics and Southeast Asian dishes to locals in the know.

OTHER AREAS

TOP CHOICE Takapuna Beach Cafe
CAFE **$$**

(Map p48; www.takapunabeachcafe.co.nz; 22 The Promenade; mains $15-25; ☺7am-5pm) With a menu that reads like a travel magazine (Moroccan eggs, Berkshire pork, Central Otago muesli) and absolute beach views, it's no wonder this cafe is constantly buzzing. If you can't snaffle a table you can always grab an award-winning ice cream or snack from the attached shop.

Engine Room
MODERN NZ **$$$**

(Map p48; ☎09-480 9502; www.engineroom.net.nz; 115 Queen St, Northcote; meals $32-35; ☺dinner Tue-Sat) One of Auckland's best restaurants, this informal eatery serves up lighter-than-air goat's cheese soufflés, inventive whiteboard mains and oh-my-God chocolate truffles. It's worth booking ahead and catching the ferry.

Eight.Two
MODERN NZ **$$$**

(Map p48; ☎09-419 9082; www.eightpointtwo.co.nz; 82 Hinemoa St, Birkenhead; mains $34-35; ☺dinner Mon-Sat) Hollowed out of an old villa, this dazzlingly white dining room offers a similarly breezy menu and a great wine list. Catch the Birkenhead ferry from the city for a memorable night out.

🍷 Drinking

Auckland's nightlife tends to be quiet during the week – if you're looking for some vital signs, head to Ponsonby Rd, Britomart or the Viaduct. K Rd wakes up late on Friday and Saturday; don't even bother staggering this way before 11pm.

CITY CENTRE

Hotel de Brett
BAR

(Map p52; www.hoteldebrett.com; 2 High St; ☺noon-late) Grab a beer in the cornerbar, a cocktail in the chic art deco housebar or nab a spot by the fire in the atrium, an interesting covered space fashioned from the alleyway between the old buildings.

Mo's
BAR

(Map p52; www.mosbar.co.nz; cnr Wolfe & Federal Sts; ☺4pm-3am Mon-Fri, 6pm-3am Sat) There is something about this tiny corner bar that makes you want to invent problems just so the barperson can solve them with soothing words and an expertly poured martini. It's just that kind of place.

GAY & LESBIAN AUCKLAND

The Queen City (as it's known for completely coincidental reasons) has by far the country's biggest gay population. While the bright lights attract gays and lesbians from all over the country, the even brighter lights of Sydney eventually steal many of the 30- to 40-somethings, leaving a gap in the demographic. There are a handful of gay venues but they only really kick off on the weekends.

To find out what's going on, grab a copy of the fortnightly newspaper *Express* (available from gay venues) or log on to www.gaynz.com. The big events on the calendar are the Big Gay Out (p65) and the Out Takes (p65) film festival.

Venues change with alarming regularity, but these ones, along with straight-friendly SPQR, were the stayers at the time of research:

Family (Map p52; www.familybar.co.nz; 270 Karangahape Rd, Newton) Trashy, brash and young, this bar can be a lot of fun, with dancing into the wee hours.

Urge (Map p52; www.urgebar.co.nz; 490 Karangahape Rd, Newton; ☺9pm-late Thu-Sat) Older and hairier than Family, this black-painted pocket-sized venue has DJs on Friday and Saturday nights.

Lolabar (Map p66; www.lolabar.co.nz; 212 Ponsonby Rd, Ponsonby; ☺5pm-late Tue-Sat) Upmarket cocktail-style bar with regular drag shows.

Centurian (Map p52; www.centuriansauna.co.nz; 18 Beresford St, Newton; before/after 3pm $23/28; ☺11am-2am Sun-Thu, 11am-6am Fri & Sat) Gay men's sauna.

Everybody's
BAR

(Map p52; www.everybodys.co.nz; 44 Queen St) Part of the transformation of a forgotten cinema complex, Everybody's sprawls through various stylish spaces, including a mezzanine with couches and discreet banquettes.

Occidental
PUB

(Map p52; www.occidentalbar.co.nz; 6 Vulcan Lane; ☺7.30am-late Mon-Fri, 9am-late Sat & Sun) Belgian beer, Belgian food (plenty of *moules* and *frites* – mussels and chips) and live music are on offer at this historic 1870 pub.

BRITOMART, VIADUCT HARBOUR & WYNYARD QUARTER

Tyler Street Garage
BAR

(Map p52; www.tylerstreetgarage.co.nz; 120 Quay St; ☺11.30am-late) Just in case you were in any doubt that this was actually a garage, they've left the parking lines painted on the concrete floor. It's still an excellent place to get well lubricated, with on-to-it staff and a little roof terrace facing over the wharves.

Agents & Merchants/Racket
BAR

(Map p52; www.agentsandmerchants.co.nz; Roukai Lane, 50 Customs St; ☺11am-late Mon-Sat) Tucked into their own covered lane with an outdoor fireplace and sofas, this duo conjures an old-world yet thoroughly modern atmosphere. A&M serves excellent tapas and wine while Racket makes one well into the morning once the DJs kick in.

Northern Steamship Co.
PUB

(Map p52; www.northernsteamship.co.nz; 122 Quay St) Standard lamps hang upside down from the ceiling while the mural behind the bar dreams of NZ summer holidays in this good-looking large pub by the train station.

Conservatory
BAR

(Map p52; www.theconservatory.co.nz; North Wharf, 1-17 Jellicoe St) The coolest of the new Wynyard Quarter hang-outs is this liquored up greenhouse sprouting a living wall of greenery and a profusion of cocktails.

Ice House
THEME BAR

(Map p52; Princes Wharf; before/after 6pm $25/30; ☺noon-midnight Sun-Thu, noon-2am Fri & Sat) Put on special clothing and sip a complimentary vodka-based cocktail in this gimmicky bar where everything from the seats to your glass is made of ice. You can only stay inside the shimmering ice world for 30 minutes, making it a quick way to blow your cold hard cash.

PONSONBY & GREY LYNN

Along Ponsonby Rd, the line between cafe, restaurant, bar and club gets blurred. A lot of eateries also have live music or become clubs later on.

Golden Dawn
BAR

(Map p66; http://thegoldendawntavernofpower.blog spot.com/; 134b Ponsonby Rd (enter Richmond Rd);

⊙4pm-late Tue-Sun) Here be where Ponsonby's hipsters hide. Occupying an old shopfront and an inviting stables yard, this late-night drinking den regularly hosts random happenings: live bands, burlesque, drag and the like.

Gypsy Tea Room
COCKTAIL BAR

(Map p66; www.gypsytearoom.co.nz; 455 Richmond Rd; ⊙4-11.30pm Sun-Thu, 3pm-2am Fri & Sat) No one comes here for tea. This cute wine/cocktail bar has dishevelled charm in bucketloads.

Mea Culpa
COCKTAIL BAR

(Map p66; 3/175 Ponsonby Rd; ⊙5pm-1am Sun-Wed, Thu-Sat 5pm-3am) If you can't find a cocktail to your taste at this small but perfectly formed bar, it's nobody's fault but your own.

Ponsonby Social Club
BAR

(Map p66; www.ponsonbysocialclub.com; 152 Ponsonby Rd; ⊙5pm-late) Half-and-half alleyway and bar, the back end of this long, narrow space heaves on the weekends when the DJs crank out classic funk and hip-hop.

Dida's Wine Lounge & Tapas Bar
WINE BAR

(Map p66; www.glengarrywines.co.nz; 54 Jervois Rd; ⊙11.30am-midnight) Great food and an even better wine list attract a grown-up crowd. There's an associated wine store, providore and cafe next door and another, more food-focussed branch in **Freemans Bay** (Map p52; cnr Sale & Wellesley Sts; tapas $7-12; ⊙8am-6pm Sun & Mon, 7am-8pm Tue-Sat).

NEWTON

Wine Cellar & Whammy Bar
BAR

(Map p52; St Kevin's Arcade, Karangahape Rd; ⊙5pm-midnight Mon-Thu, 5.30pm-2am Fri & Sat) Secreted down some stairs in an arcade, this is the kind of bar that Buffy the Vampire Slayer would have hung out in on Auckland-based assignments. It's dark, grungy and very cool, with regular live music in the neighbouring Whammy Bar.

DOC
BAR

(Map p52; 352 Karangahape Rd; ⊙5pm-late) This little bar's endemic critters are indie kids who have been known to dance on tables to sugary pop later in the night. The only endangered species here are healthy livers, so we doubt it's got anything whatsoever to do with the Department of Conservation.

Galbraith's Alehouse
BREWERY, PUB

(Map p62; www.alehouse.co.nz; 2 Mt Eden Rd; ⊙noon-11pm) Brewing up real ales and lagers on-site, this English-style pub offers bliss on

tap. The back-door beer garden trumps the brightly lit bar.

KINGSLAND

Winehot
WINE BAR

(Map p62; www.winehot.co.nz; 605 New North Rd, Morningside; ⊙5pm-late Tue-Sat) Behind an unlikely-looking doorway, this tiny black-painted and chandelier-festooned hideaway serves an impressive selection of both beer and wine along with delicious platters of French goodies (terrines, pâtés, baguettes).

Neighbourhood
BAR

(Map p62; www.neighbourhood.co.nz; 498 New North Rd; 🐱) With picture windows overlooking Eden Park and a front terrace that's pick-up central after dark, this upmarket pub is the place to be either side of rugby fixtures. DJs play on weekends.

☆ Entertainment

The *NZ Herald* has an in-depth rundown of the coming week's happenings in its *Time Out* magazine on Thursday and again in its Saturday edition. If you're planning a big night along K Rd, then visit www.kroad.co.nz for a detailed list of bars and clubs.

Tickets for most major events can be bought from the following:

Ticketek
TICKETING AGENCY

(📞0800 842 538; www.ticketek.co.nz) Outlets include Real Groovy (p80) and **SkyCity Theatre** (Map p52; 📞09-363 6000; www.skycity.co.nz; cnr Victoria & Federal Sts).

Ticketmaster
TICKETING AGENCY

(📞09-970 9700; www.ticketmaster.co.nz) Outlets at Real Groovy (p80), **Vector Arena** (Map p60; 📞09-358 1250; www.vectorarena.co.nz; Mahuhu Cres), Aotea Centre (p79) and Britomart Train Station (p83).

Live Music & Nightclubs

The Viaduct, Britomart and K Rd are the main late-night hang-outs, but some of the Ponsonby Rd bars continue into the wee smalls. Cover charges vary depending on the night and the event. See also Whammy Bar (above) for live indie music and Ponsonby Social Club (above) for a boogie.

TOP CHOICE Rakinos
DJ

(Map p52; www.rakinos.com; Level 1, 35 High St) By day it's a cafe but we only head here after dark, when the DJs are spinning old-school hip-hop, funk, Motown and R'n'B like it's, well, anytime between 1968 and the present.

When the mood takes, it's hands-down our favourite place to bust a move.

Cassette Nine   CLUB
(Map p52; www.cassettenine.com; 9 Vulcan Lane, City; ⊙noon-late Tue-Sat) Auckland's most out-there hipsters gravitate to this eccentric bar/club where swishy boys rub shoulders with beardy dudes and girls in very short dresses, and the music ranges from live indie to international DJ sets.

Kings Arms Tavern   LIVE MUSIC
(Map p62; www.kingsarms.co.nz; 59 France St, Newton) Auckland's leading small venue for local and international bands, which play four or five nights per week. It's a rite of passage if you want to get your band noticed.

Ink & Coherent   CLUB
(Map p52; www.inkcoherent.co.nz; 268 & 262 Karangahape Rd, Newton) Neighbouring venues for serious dance aficionados, sometimes hosting big-name DJs.

Khuja Lounge   DJ
(Map p52; www.khuja.co.nz; 536 Queen St, Newton; ⊙8pm-late Wed-Sat) Above the Westpac building, this laid-back bar has a lively roster of DJs and jazz/soul/hip-hop bands.

Thirsty Dog   LIVE MUSIC
(Map p52; www.thirstydog.co.nz; 469 Karangahape Rd, Newton) This dog's both thirsty and noisy, with a booming sound system and a regular roster of local musos.

AUCKLAND TOP 10 PLAYLIST

Download these Auckland songs to your MP3 player for cruising the city's streets:

» 'Grey Lynn Park' – The Veils (2011)

» 'Auckland CBD Part Two' – Lawrence Arabia (2009)

» 'Forever Thursday' – Tim Finn (2008)

» 'Riverhead' – Goldenhorse (2004)

» 'A Brief Reflection' – Nesian Mystik (2002)

» 'Hopetown Bridge' – Dave Dobbyn (2000)

» 'New Tattoo' – Hello Sailor (1994)

» 'Dominion Road' – The Mutton Birds (1992)

» 'Andy' – The Front Lawn (1989)

» 'One Tree Hill' – U2 (1987)

Cinema
Most offer cheaper rates on weekdays before 5pm; Tuesday is usually bargain day.

Rialto   CINEMA
(Map p56; ☑09-369 2417; www.rialto.co.nz; 167 Broadway, Newmarket; adult/child $16.50/10) Screens art-house and international films, plus some of the better mainstream fare.

Academy Cinemas   CINEMA
(Map p52; ☑09-373 2761; www.academycinemas.co.nz; 44 Lorne St, City; adult/child $14/8) Screens independent foreign and art-house films in the basement of the Central Library.

Event Cinemas   CINEMA
(Map p52; ☑09-369 2400; www.eventcinemas.co.nz; Level 3, 297 Queen St, City; adult/child $16.50/10.50) Part of Aotea Sq's futuristic Metro mall, which also includes bars and a food court.

NZ Film Archives   CINEMA
(Map p52; ☑09-379 0688; www.filmarchive.org.nz; 300 Karangahape Rd, Newton; ⊙11am-5pm Mon-Sat) A wonderful resource of more than 150,000 Kiwi feature films, documentaries and TV shows, which you can watch for free on a TV screen.

Theatre, Classical Music & Comedy
Auckland's main arts and entertainment complex is grouped around Aotea Sq. Branded **The Edge** (☑09-357 3355; www.the-edge.co.nz), it comprises the Town Hall, Civic Theatre (p47) and Aotea Centre.

Auckland Town Hall   CLASSICAL MUSIC
(Map p52; 305 Queen St) This elegant Edwardian venue (1911) hosts concert performances by the likes of the NZ Symphony Orchestra (www.nzso.co.nz) and Auckland Philharmonia (www.apo.co.nz).

Aotea Centre   THEATRE
(Map p52; 50 Mayoral Dr) Auckland's largest venue for theatre, dance, ballet and opera, with two main stages: the cavernous ASB Auditorium and the tiny Herald Theatre. NZ Opera (www.nzopera.com) regularly performs here.

Q Theatre   THEATRE
(Map p52; ☑09-309 9771; www.qtheatre.co.nz; 305 Queen St) The city's newest theatre showcases works by various companies as well as intimate live music events. Silo Theatre (www.silotheatre.co.nz) often performs here.

Classic Comedy Club
COMEDY

(Map p52; ☎09-373 4321; www.comedy.co.nz; 321 Queen St; tickets $5-27) Auckland's top venue for comedy, with performances from Wednesday through to Saturday.

Maidment Theatre
THEATRE

(Map p52; ☎09-308 2383; www.maidment.auck land.ac.nz; 8 Alfred St) The University's theatre often stages Auckland Theatre Company (www.atc.co.nz) productions.

Sport

Eden Park
RUGBY, CRICKET

(Map p62; www.edenpark.co.nz; Reimers Ave, Kingsland) Fresh from its Rugby World Cup makeover, this is the stadium for top rugby (winter) and cricket (summer) tests by the All Blacks (www.allblacks.com) and the Black Caps (www.blackcaps.co.nz), as well as the home ground for Auckland Rugby (www.aucklandrugby.co.nz), the Blues Super Rugby team (www.theblues.co.nz), and Auckland Cricket (www.aucklandcricket. co.nz). To get here, take the train from Brito-mart to Kingsland Station.

Mt Smart Stadium
RUGBY, FOOTBALL

(Map p48; www.mtsmartstadium.co.nz; Maurice Rd, Penrose) The venue of choice for the Warri-ors rugby league team (www.warriors.co.nz), Auckland Football Federation (www.auck landfootball.org.nz), Athletics Auckland (www.athleticsauckland.co.nz) and *really* big concerts.

North Shore Events Centre
BASKETBALL

(Map p48; ☎09-443 8199; www.nseventscentre. co.nz; Argus Pl, Wairau Valley) The home ground of the NZ Breakers basketball team (www. nzbreakers.co.nz) and an occasional concert venue.

ASB Tennis Centre
TENNIS

(Map p60; www.aucklandtennis.co.nz; 1 Tennis Lane, Parnell) In January the women's ASB Clas-sic (www.asbclassic.co.nz) is held here, fol-lowed by the men's Heineken Open (www. heinekenopen.co.nz).

🔒 Shopping

Followers of fashion should head to High St in the city, Newmarket's Teed and Nuffield Sts, and Ponsonby Rd. For secondhand bou-tiques try K Rd or Ponsonby Rd.

CITY CENTRE

Real Groovy
MUSIC

(Map p52; www.realgroovy.co.nz; 438 Queen St; ⊙9am-7pm Sat-Wed, 9am-9pm Thu & Fri) A music-

lovers' nirvana, this huge store has masses of new, second hand and rare releases, as well as concert tickets, giant posters, DVDs, books, magazines and clothes.

Pauanesia
GIFTS

(Map p52; www.pauanesia.co.nz; 35 High St; ⊙9.30am-6.30pm Mon-Fri, 10am-4.30pm Sat & Sun) A treasure-trove of homewares and gifts with a pronounced Polynesian influence.

Unity Books
BOOKS

(Map p52; www.unitybooks.co.nz; 19 High St; ⊙8.30am-7pm Mon-Thu, 8.30am-9pm Fri, 9am-6pm Sat, 11am-6pm Sun) Excellent independent bookshop with knowledgeable staff.

Strangely Normal
CLOTHING

(Map p52; www.strangelynormal.com; 19 O'Connell St) Quality, NZ–made, men's tailored shirts straight out of *Blue Hawaii* sit alongside hipster hats, sharp shoes and cufflinks.

Karen Walker
CLOTHING

(www.karenwalker.com) City (Map p52; 15 O'Connell St); Ponsonby (Map p66; 171 Ponsonby Rd); New-market (Map p56; 6 Balm St) Join Madonna and Kirsten Dunst in wearing Walker's cool (but pricey) threads.

Zambesi
CLOTHING

(www.zambesi.co.nz) City (Map p52; cnr Vulcan Lane & O'Connell St); Ponsonby (Map p66; 169 Pon-sonby Rd); Newmarket (Map p56; 38 Osborne St) The most famous fashion label to come out of NZ, and much sought after by local and international celebs.

Whitcoulls
BOOKS

(Map p52; www.whitcoulls.co.nz; 210 Queen St) The mothership of the biggest local chain, with good travel and fiction sections.

PONSONBY & GREY LYNN

Women's Bookshop
BOOKS

(Map p66; www.womensbookshop.co.nz; 105 Pon-sonby Rd; ⊙10am-6pm) An excellent independ-ent bookshop that's a community resource in its own right.

Marvel
CLOTHING

(Map p66; www.marvelmenswear.co.nz; 143 Pon-sonby Rd) Smart, tailored shirts and trousers in interesting fabrics and quirky partywear are the mainstays of this local menswear designer.

Texan Art Schools
ARTS & CRAFTS

(www.texanartschools.co.nz; ⊙9.30am-5.30pm) Ponsonby (Map p66; 95 Ponsonby Rd); Newmarket (Map p56; 366 Broadway) Despite the name, it's

AUCKLAND, THE BIG TARO

There are nearly 180,000 Pacific Islanders (PI) living in Auckland, making it the world's principal Polynesian city. Samoans are by far the largest group, followed by Cook Islanders, Tongans, Niueans, Fijians, Tokelauans and Tuvaluans. The biggest PI communities can be found in South Auckland and pockets of West and Central Auckland.

Like the Maori renaissance of recent decades, Pasifika has become a hot commodity for Auckland hipsters. You'll find PI motifs everywhere: in art, architecture, fashion, homewares, movies and especially in music.

got nothing to do with the Lone Star State. A collective of 200 local artists sell their wares here.

KINGSLAND

Royal Jewellery Studio JEWELLERY
(Map p62; www.royaljewellerystudio.com; 486 New North Rd; ⌚10am-5pm) Displaying interesting work by local artisans, including some beautiful Maori designs, this is a great place to pick up authentic *pounamu* (greenstone) jewellery.

OTHER AREAS

Otara Market MARKET
(Map p48; Newbury St; ⌚6am-noon Sat) Held in the car park between the Manukau Polytech and the Otara town centre, this market has a palpable Polynesian atmosphere and is a good place to stock up on South Pacific food, music and fashions. Take bus 497 from Britomart ($6.80, 50 minutes).

Avondale Sunday Market MARKET
(Map p48; www.avondalesundaymarkets.co.nz; Avondale Racecourse, Ash St; ⌚6am-noon Sun) Easier to get to than the Otara Markets, Avondale also has a distinctly Polynesian atmosphere and is particularly good for fresh produce. Take the train to Avondale station.

ℹ Information

Internet Access

Auckland Council has set up free wi-fi in parts of the city centre, Newton, Ponsonby, Kingsland, Mt Eden and Parnell, but at the time of writing, its future was up in the air, pending sponsorship. Public libraries are a safe bet for computers with free internet access and, often, wi-fi. Internet cafes catering mainly to gaming junkies are scattered about the inner city.

Media

Metro Glossy monthly magazine covering Auckland issues in depth.

New Zealand Herald (www.nzherald.co.nz) The country's biggest daily newspaper.

Medical Services

Auckland City Hospital (☎09-367 0000; www.adhb.govt.nz; Park Rd, Grafton; ⌚24hr) The city's main hospital has a dedicated accident and emergency (A&E) service.

Auckland Metro Doctors & Travelcare (☎09-373 4621; www.aucklandmetrodoctors.co.nz; 17 Emily Pl, City; ⌚9am-5.30pm Mon-Fri, 10am-2pm Sat) Specialises in health care for travellers, such as vaccinations and travel consultations.

Starship Children's Hospital (☎09-367 0000; www.adhb.govt.nz; Park Rd, Grafton; ⌚24hr) Has its own A&E department.

Tourist Information

Auckland Domestic Airport i-SITE (☎09-256 8480; ⌚7am-9pm) In the Air New Zealand terminal.

Auckland International Airport i-SITE (☎09-275 6467; ⌚24hr) Located on your left as you exit the customs hall.

Auckland Princes Wharf i-SITE (☎09-307 0612; www.aucklandnz.com; 137 Quay St; ⌚9am-5.30pm)

Auckland SkyCity i-SITE (☎09-363 7182; www.aucklanμdnz.com; SkyCity Atrium, cnr Victoria & Federal Sts; ⌚8am-8pm)

Cornwall Park Information Centre (☎09-630 8485; www.cornwallpark.co.nz; Huia Lodge; ⌚10am-4pm)

Devonport i-SITE (☎09-446 0677; www.northshorenz.com; 3 Victoria Rd; ⌚8.30am-5pm; @📶)

DOC Information Centre (☎09-379 6476; www.doc.govt.nz; Auckland Princes Wharf i-SITE, 137 Quay St; ⌚9am-5pm Mon-Sat)

Karanga Plaza Kiosk (www.waterfrontauckland.co.nz; Wynyard Quarter; ⌚10am-5.30pm) What looks like a haphazardly stacked set of shipping containers is actually Wynyard Quarter's striking little visitor centre.

Takapuna i-SITE (☎09-486 8670; 34-36 Hurstmere Rd; ⌚8.30am-5pm Mon-Fri, 10am-3pm Sat & Sun)

PLANE DELAYED? TIME FOR A TIPPLE!

Clearly the roar of jets doesn't bother grapes, as NZ's most awarded winery is just 4km from the airport. The parklike grounds of **Villa Maria Estate** (Map p48; www.villamaria .co.nz; 118 Montgomerie Rd; ⊗9am-6pm Mon-Fri, 9am-4pm Sat & Sun) are a green oasis in the encircling industrial zone. A series of concerts is held here every January and February featuring big international artists popular with the 40- to 50-something wine-swilling demographic.

Short tours ($5) take place at 11am and 3pm. There's a charge for tastings ($5), but lingering over wine and cheese on the terrace sure beats hanging around the departure lounge.

❶ Getting There & Away

Air

Auckland is the main gateway to NZ (see the Transport chapter for flights into NZ), and a hub for domestic flights. **Auckland International Airport** (AKL; ☑09-275 0789; www.auckland airport.co.nz; Ray Emery Dr, Mangere) is 21km south of the city centre. It has separate international and domestic terminals, each with a tourist information centre. A free shuttle service operates every 15 minutes (5am to 10.30pm) between the terminals and there's also a sign-posted footpath (about a 10-minute walk). Both terminals have left-luggage facilities, ATMs and car-rental desks, although you may get better rates from companies in town.

For flights to Great Barrier Island, see Great Barrier Island's Getting There & Away information. The following are the other domestic airlines flying from Auckland and the destinations they serve:

Air New Zealand (☑09-357 3000; www. airnewzealand.co.nz) Flys to Kaitaia, Kerikeri, Whangarei, Hamilton, Tauranga, Whakatane, Gisborne, Rotorua, Taupo, New Plymouth, Napier, Whanganui, Palmerston North, Masterton, Wellington, Nelson, Blenheim, Christchurch, Queenstown and Dunedin.

Jetstar (☑0800 800 995; www.jetstar.com) Flies to Wellington, Christchurch, Queenstown and Dunedin.

Sunair (☑0800 786 847; www.sunair.co.nz; one way $160) Flies to Whitianga twice daily.

Bus

Coaches depart from 172 Quay St, opposite the Ferry Building, except for InterCity services, which depart from **SkyCity Coach Terminal** (☑09-913 6220; 102 Hobson St). Many south-bound services also stop at the airport.

Dalroy Express (☑0508 465 622; www.dalroy tours.co.nz) Operates a daily coach between Auckland and New Plymouth ($60, six hours).

Go Kiwi (☑07-866 0336; www.go-kiwi.co.nz) Has daily Auckland City–International Airport–Thames–Tairua–Whitianga shuttles.

InterCity (☑09-583 5780; www.intercity.co.nz)

Main Coachline (☑09-278 8070; www.main coachline.co.nz) Has a bus most days between Auckland and Dargaville (three hours) via Orewa, Warkworth and Matakohe.

Naked Bus (☑0900 62533; www.nakedbus. com) Naked Buses travel along SH1 as far north as Kerikeri (four hours) and as far south as Wellington (12 hours), as well as heading to Tauranga (3½ hours) and Napier (12 hours). The cost of calling their helpline is $1.99 per minute.

Car, Caravan & Campervan

HIRE Auckland has the biggest selection of hire agencies, with a swag of them conveniently grouped together along Beach Rd and Stanley St close to the city centre. The major companies have offices at the airport.

A2B (☑09-254 4670; www.a2b-car-rental. co.nz; 167 Beach Rd) Cheap older cars with no visible hire-car branding, making them less of a thief-magnet.

Apex Car Rentals (☑09-307 1063; www.apexrentals.co.nz; 156 Beach Rd)

Budget (☑09-976 2270; www.budget.co.nz; 163 Beach Rd)

Escape (☑0800 216 171; www.escaperentals. co.nz; 39 Beach Rd) Eccentrically painted campervans.

Explore More, Maui & Britz (☑09-255 3910; www.maui.co.nz; 36 Richard Pearse Dr, Mangere)

Gateway 2 NZ (☑0508 225 587; www. gateway2nz.co.nz; 50 Ascot Rd, Mangere)

Gateway Motor Home Hire (☑09-296 1652; www.motorhomehire.co.nz)

Go Rentals (☑09-257 5142; www.gorentals. co.nz; Auckland Airport)

Hertz (☑09-367 6350; www.hertz.co.nz; 154 Victoria St)

Jucy (☑0800 399 736; www.jucy.co.nz)

Kea Campers (☑09-448 8800; www. keacampers.com)

NZ Frontiers (☑09-299 6705; www.new zealandfrontiers.com) Campervans.

Omega (☑09-377 5573; www.omegarentals. com; 75 Beach Rd)

Quality Rentals (☑0800 680 123; www.quality rental.co.nz; 8 Andrew Baxter Dr, Mangere)

Thrifty (☑09-309 0111; www.thrifty.co.nz; 150 Khyber Pass Rd)

Wilderness Motorhomes (☑09-255 5300; www.wilderness.co.nz; 21 Rennie Drive, Mangere)

PURCHASE Mechanical inspection services are on hand at the following second hand car fairs, where sellers pay to display their cars:

Auckland Car Fair (☑09-529 2233; www. carfair.co.nz; Ellerslie Racecourse, Green Lane East; display fee $35; ☺9am-noon Sun) Auckland's largest car fair.

City Car Fair (☑09-837 7817; www.auckland citycarfair.co.nz; 27 Alten Rd; display fee $25; ☺8am-1pm Sat)

Motorcycle

See also Paradise Motorcycle Tours (p64).

NZ Motorcycle Rentals (☑09-486 2472; www. nzbike.com; 72 Barrys Point Rd, Takapuna; per day $145-360) Guided tours also available.

Train

Overlander (☑0800 872 467; www.tranz scenic.co.nz) trains depart from **Britomart station** (Queen St), the largest underground diesel train station in the world. They depart from Auckland at 7.25am (daily late September to April, Friday to Sunday otherwise) and arrive in Wellington at 7.25pm (the return train from Wellington departs and arrives at the same time). Useful stops include Hamilton (2½ hours), Otorohanga (three hours), Te Kuiti (3¼ hours), Taumarunui (4½ hours), National Park (5½ hours), Ohakune (6½ hours), Palmerston North (9½ hours) and Paraparaumu (11 hours). A standard fare to Wellington is $129, but a limited number of discounted seats are available for each journey at $79 and $99 (first in, first served).

❶ Getting Around

To & From the Airport

A taxi between the airport and the city usually costs between $60 and $80, more if you strike traffic snarls.

Airbus Express (☑09-366 6400; www. airbus.co.nz; one-way/return adult $16/26, child $6/12) Runs between the terminals and the city, every 10 minutes from 7am to 7pm and at least hourly through the night. Stops include Mt Eden Rd or Dominion Rd (on request), Symonds St, Queen St and the Ferry Building. Reservations are not required; buy a ticket from the driver or online. The trip usually takes less than an hour (longer during peak times).

Super Shuttle (☑0800 748 885; www.super shuttle.co.nz) This convenient door-to-door shuttle charges $28 for one person heading between the airport and a city hotel; the price increases for outlying suburbs. You'll save money if you share a shuttle.

Bicycle

Maxx Regional Transport (see below) publishes free cycle maps, available from public buildings such as stations, libraries and i-SITEs. Bikes can be taken on ferries (free) and trains ($1), but only folding bikes are allowed on buses.

Adventure Cycles (☑09-940 2453; www. adventure-auckland.co.nz/adventurecycles; 9 Premier Ave, Western Springs; per day $25-40, per week $100-150, per month $230-300; ☺7.30am-7pm Thu-Mon) Hires out road, mountain and long-term touring bikes, runs a buy-back scheme and does repairs.

Car & Motorcycle

Auckland's motorways jam up badly at peak times, particularly the Northern and Southern Motorways. It's best to avoid them between 7am and 9am, and from 4pm to 7pm. Things also get tight around 3pm during term time, which is the end of the school day.

Expect to pay for parking in central Auckland during the day, from Monday to Saturday. Most parking meters are pay-and-display; follow the instructions, collect your ticket and display it inside your windscreen. You usually don't have to pay between 6pm and 8am or on Sunday – check the meters and parking signs carefully.

Prices can be steep at parking buildings. Better value are the council-run open-air parks near the old train station on Beach Rd ($8 per day) and on Ngaoho Pl, off The Strand ($6 per day).

Public Transport

Due to rampant privatisation during the 1980s, Auckland's public transport system is run by a hodgepodge of different operators and as a result there are few integrated public transport passes. The Auckland Council is trying to sort out the mess with their HOP smartcard (www. myhop.co.nz), but until it's bedded down it's probably not worth your while. They also run the **Maxx** (☑09-366 6400; www.maxx.co.nz) information service, covering buses, trains and ferries, which has an excellent trip-planning feature. The Discovery Pass provides a day's transport on most trains and buses and on North Shore ferries ($15); buy it on the bus or train or at Fullers offices.

BUS Bus routes spread their tentacles throughout the city and you can purchase a ticket from the driver. Many services terminate around Britomart station. Some bus stops have electronic displays giving an estimate of waiting times; be warned: they lie.

Single-ride fares in the inner city are 50c for an adult and 30c for a child (free for HOP users). If you're travelling further afield there are fare stages from $1.80/1 (adult/child) to $10.30/6.10.

Perhaps the most useful services are the environmentally friendly Link Buses that loop in both directions around three routes (taking in many of the major sights) from 7am to 11pm:

» City Link (50c, every seven to 10 minutes) – Britomart, Queen St, Karangahape Rd, with some buses connecting to Wynyard Quarter.

» Inner Link (maximum $1.80, every 10 to 15 minutes) – Queen St, SkyCity, Victoria Park, Ponsonby Rd, Karangahape Rd, Museum, Newmarket, Parnell and Britomart.

» Outer Link (maximum $3.40, every 15 minutes) – Art Gallery, Ponsonby, Herne Bay, Westmere, MOTAT 2, Pt Chevalier, Mt Albert, St Lukes Mall, Mt Eden, Newmarket, Museum, Parnell, University.

FERRY Auckland's Edwardian baroque **Ferry Building** (Quay St) sits grandly at the end of Queen St. Fullers (p64) ferries (to Bayswater, Birkenhead, Devonport, Great Barrier Island, Half Moon Bay, Northcote, Motutapu, Rangitoto and Waiheke) leave direcly behind the building, while 360 Discovery (p64) ferries (to Coromandel, Gulf Harbour, Motuihe, Rotoroa and Tiritiri Matangi) leave from adjacent piers.

Sealink (p91) ferries to Great Barrier Island leave from Wynyard Wharf, along with some car ferries to Waiheke, but most of the ferries to Waiheke leave from Half Moon Bay which is in East Auckland.

TRAIN Auckland's train services are limited and infrequent but the trains are generally clean, cheap and on time – although any hiccup on the lines can bring down the entire network.

Impressive Britomart station (p83) has food retailers, foreign-exchange facilities and a ticket office. Downstairs are plush toilets and left-luggage lockers.

There are just four train routes: one runs west to Waitakere, one runs south to Onehunga, and two run south to Pukekohe. Services are at least hourly from around 6am to 8pm (later on the weekends). Pay the conductor on the train (one stage $1.70); they'll come to you. All trains have wheelchair ramps.

Taxi

Auckland's many taxis usually operate from ranks, but they also cruise popular areas. **Auckland Co-op Taxis** (☑ 09-300 3000; www.3003000.co.nz) is one of the biggest companies. There's a surcharge for transport to and from the airport and cruise ships, and for phone orders.

HAURAKI GULF ISLANDS

The Hauraki Gulf, stretching between Auckland and the Coromandel Peninsula, is dotted with *motu* (islands) and gives the Bay of Islands stiff competition in the beauty stakes. Some islands are only minutes from the city and make excellent day trips: wine-soaked Waiheke and volcanic Rangitoto really shouldn't be missed. Great Barrier requires more effort (and cash) to get to, but provides an idyllic escape from modern life.

There are 47 islands in the Hauraki Gulf Maritime Park, administered by DOC. Some are good-sized islands, others are no more than rocks jutting out of the sea. They're loosely put into two categories: recreation and conservation. The recreation islands can easily be visited and their harbours are dotted with yachts in summer. The conservation islands, however, have restricted access. Permits are required to visit some, while others are closed refuges for the preservation of rare plants and animals, especially birds.

The gulf is a busy highway for marine mammals. Sei, minke and Bryde's whales are regularly seen in its outer reaches, along with orcas and bottlenose dolphins. You might even spy a passing humpback.

Rangitoto & Motutapu Islands
POP 75

Sloping elegantly from the waters of the gulf, 259m **Rangitoto** (www.rangitoto.org), the largest and youngest of Auckland's volcanic cones, provides a picturesque backdrop to all of the city's activities. As recently as 600 years ago it erupted from the sea and was probably active for several years before settling down. Maori living on **Motutapu** (Sacred Island; www.motutapu.org.nz), to which Rangitoto is now joined by a causeway, certainly witnessed the eruptions, as footprints have been found embedded in ash and oral history details several generations living here before the eruption.

The island makes for a great day trip. Its harsh scoria slopes hold a surprising amount of flora (including the world's largest pohutukawa forest) and there are excellent walks, but you'll need sturdy shoes and plenty of water. Although it looks steep, up

BATTLE OF THE BACHES

During the 1920s a dinky set of simple baches started to sprout on Rangitoto on land leased from the council, forming a thriving community of holiday-makers. In the 1930s prison labour was used to construct roads, public toilets, tennis courts and a swimming pool out of the scoria. It was back-breaking work, but the men weren't locked up and by all accounts enjoyed island life. The threat of fire was a constant danger for the bach-holders, as it is today – the baking scoria keeps the leaf litter tinder-dry.

During the 1970s and '80s the bach community itself came under threat – a significant number of houses were removed when their leases expired, with the plan to remove them all. Following a public outcry, the remaining communities were listed as Historic Areas by the Historic Places Trust in 1997. Just left of the wharf, a 1929 bach has been fully restored and opened as a museum of sorts; the hours are sporadic but it's most likely to be open on summer weekends.

close it's shaped more like an egg sizzling in a pan. The walk to the summit only takes an hour and is rewarded with sublime views. At the top a loop walk goes around the crater's rim. A walk to lava caves branches off the summit walk and takes 30 min utes return. There's an information board with walk maps at the wharf.

Motutapu, in contrast to Rangitoto, is mainly covered in grassland, which is grazed by sheep and cattle. Archaeologically, this is a very significant island, with the traces of centuries of continuous human habitation etched into its landscape.

At Home Bay there's a **DOC campsite** (www.doc.govt.nz; adult/child $6/3) with only basic facilities (running water and a flush toilet). Bring cooking equipment, as open fires are forbidden, and book online. It's a three-hour walk from **Rangitoto wharf**; Fullers run a weekend-only service to Home Bay in the summer months.

In 2011 both islands were officially declared predator-free after an extensive eradication program. Endangered birds such as takahe and tieke (saddleback) have been released and others such as kakariki and bellbirds have returned of their own volition; listen for their chiming calls while you're exploring.

❶ Getting There & Around

Fullers (☑09-367 9111; www.fullers.co.nz; adult/child return $27/14) Has 20-minute ferry services to Rangitoto from Auckland's Ferry Building (three daily on weekdays, four on weekends) and Devonport (two daily). They also offer the Volcanic Explorer (adult/child $59/30), a guided tour around the island in a canopied 'road train'.

Motuihe Island

Between Rangitoto and Waiheke Islands, 176-hectare Motuihe has a lovely white-sand beach and a fascinating history. There are three *pa* sites, last occupied by the Ngati Paoa tribe. The island was sold in 1840 (for a heifer, blankets, frocks, garden tools, pots and pans) and from 1872 to 1941 served as a quarantine station. During WWI the dashing swashbuckler Count von Luckner launched a daring escape from the island (where he was interned with other German and Austrian nationals), making it 1000km to the Kermadec Islands before being recaptured.

Motuihe has been rendered pest-free and is now subject to a vigorous reforestation project by enthusiastic volunteers. As a result, endangered birds have returned, including the loquacious tieke. Contact the **Motuihe Trust** (☑0800 668 844; www.motuihe.org.nz) if you want to get involved. On weekends in January the trust runs heritage- and restoration-themed guided tours ($5); book through 360 Discovery.

Apart from the trust's headquarters, the only accommodation on the island is a basic **DOC campsite** (www.doc.govt.nz; adult/child $6/3); only toilets and water are provided. There are no permanent residents or shops, except for a lunchtime kiosk during January.

❶ Getting There & Away

360 Discovery (☑0800 360 3472; www.360discovery.co.nz; adult/child return $27/17) Three ferries make the hour-long journey from Auckland every day.

Waiheke Island

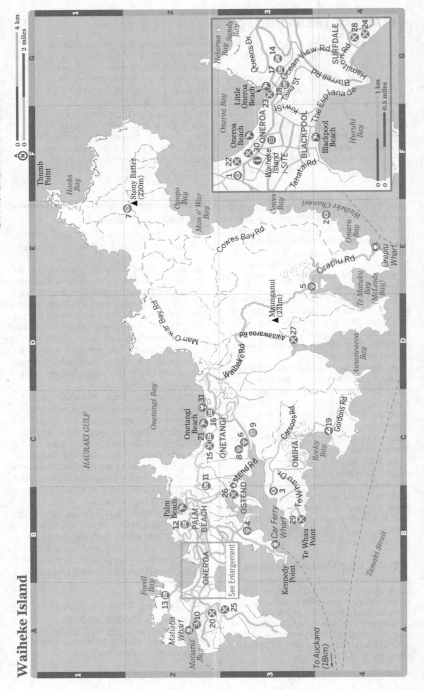

HAURAKI GULF

Thumb Point

Hooks Bay

Opopo Bay

Stony Batter (220m)

7

Man o' War Bay

Cowes Bay

Waiheke Channel

Cowes Bay Rd

2

Omaru Bay

Oraplu Rd

Oraplu Wharf

Te Matuku Bay (McLeods Bay)

5

Maunganui (231m)

Awaawaroa Rd

27

Man O' War Bay Rd

Waiheke Rd

Onetangi Bay

Onetangi Beach

31

21 16

15 ONETANGI

8 6

9

Avaawaroa Bay

Gordons Rd

19

Carsons Rd

Rocky Bay

OMIHA

Te Whau Dr

Ostend Rd

11

26 OSTEND

3

4

Car Ferry Wharf

29

Te Whau Point

Kennedy Point

Palm Beach

12 PALM BEACH

Fossil Bay

13

10

20

25

ONEROA

See Enlargement

Matiatia Wharf

Matiatia Bay

To Auckland (18km)

Tamaki Strait

Enlargement

Hekerua Bay

Helena Bay

Sandy Bay

Queens Dr

Ocean View Rd

17 14

18

Tawa St

SURFDALE

Hamilton Rd

28

24

Burrell Rd

Ianade

The Esp

Oneroa Bay

Little Oneroa Beach

23

Kiwi St

Oneroa Beach

ONEROA

22

1

20

Waiheke Island i-SITE

BLACKPOOL

Blackpool Beach

Huruhi Bay

Tahatai Rd

1 km
0.5 miles

0   2 km
0   1 mile... 4 km
2 miles

N

Waiheke Island

POP 7700

Waiheke is 93 sq km of island bliss only a 35-minute ferry ride from the CBD. Once they could hardly give land away here; nowadays multimillionaires rub shoulders with the old-time hippies and bohemian artists who gave the island its green repute. Auckland office workers fantasise about swapping the daily motorway crawl for a watery commute and a warm, dry microclimate.

On Waiheke's city side, emerald waters lap at rocky bays, while its ocean flank has some of the region's best sandy beaches. While beaches are the big drawcard, wine is a close second. There are 19 boutique wineries to visit, many with swanky restaurants and breathtaking city views. On top of that, the island boasts dozens of galleries and craft stores.

Waiheke has been inhabited since at least the 14th century, most recently by Ngati Paoa, and there are more than 40 *pa* sites scattered around the island. Europeans arrived with the missionary Samuel Marsden in the early 1800s and the island was soon stripped of its kauri forest.

There are petrol stations in Oneroa, Ostend and Onetangi, ATMs in Oneroa and Ostend, and a supermarket in Ostend.

◉ Sights & Activities

Beaches

Waiheke's two best beaches are **Onetangi**, a long stretch of white sand at the centre of the island, and **Palm Beach**, a pretty little horseshoe bay between Oneroa and Onetangi. Both have nudist sections; head west just past some rocks in both cases. **Oneroa** and neighbouring **Little Oneroa** are also excellent, but you'll be sharing the waters with moored yachts in summer.

Wineries

Waiheke's hot, dry microclimate has proved excellent for bordeaux reds, syrah and some superb rosés. Because of an emphasis on quality rather than quantity, the premium wine produced here is relatively expensive. And be warned: most of the wineries charge for tastings (from $3 to $10; sometimes refunded if you make a purchase). Some are spectacularly located and worth a visit for that reason alone. Over summer many extend their hours, some even sprouting temporary restaurants.

AUCKLAND WAIHEKE ISLAND

Waiheke Island

Pick up the *Waiheke Island of Wine* map for a complete list of vinyards on the island.

Goldie Vineyard
WINERY
(www.goldieroom.co.nz; 18 Causeway Rd; tastings $5-10, refundable with purchase; ☻noon-4pm Wed-Sun Mar-Nov, daily Dec-Feb) Founded as Goldwater Estate in 1978, this is Waiheke's pioneering vineyard. The tasting room sells well-stocked baskets for a picnic among the vines (for two people $55).

Passage Rock
WINERY
(☑09-372 7257; www.passagerockwines.co.nz; 438 Orapiu Rd; ☻noon-4pm Sat & Sun Aug-Dec, daily Jan, Wed-Sun Feb-Apr) Excellent pizza among the vines.

Saratoga Estate
WINERY, BREWERY
(☑09-372 6450; www.saratogaestate.com; 72 Onetangi Rd; ☻11am-4pm) Has a cafe and microbrewery on site.

⬘Stonyridge
WINERY
(☑09-372 8822; www.stonyridge.com; 80 Onetangi Rd; tastings per wine $3-15; ☻11.30am-5pm) Famous organic reds, an atmospheric cafe, tours ($10, 35 minutes, 11.30am Saturday and Sunday) and the occasional dance party.

Wild On Waiheke
WINERY, BREWERY
(☑09-372 3434; www.wildonwaiheke.co.nz; 82 Onetangi Rd; tastings per beer or wine $2; ☻11am-4pm Thu-Sun, daily in summer) If you like to shoot stuff after a few drinks, this winery and microbrewery offers tastings, archery, laser clay shooting, *pètanque*, a sandpit and a giant chess board.

Art & Culture
The *Waiheke Art Map* brochure, free from the i-SITE, lists 37 galleries and craft stores.

Artworks Complex
ARTS CENTRE
(2 Korora Rd; @🛜) The Artworks complex houses a **community theatre** (☑09-372 2941; www.artworkstheatre.org.nz), an **art-house cinema** (☑09-372 4240; www.wicc.co.nz; adult/child $14/7), an attention-grabbing **art gallery** (☑09-372 9907; www.waihekeartgallery.org.nz; admission free; ☻10am-4pm) and **Whittaker's Musical Museum** (☑09-372 5573; www.musical-museum.org; adult/child $5/free; ☻1-4pm), a collection of antique concert instruments. This is also the place for free internet access, either on a terminal at the **library** (☻9am-5.30pm Mon-Fri, 10am-4pm Sat; @) or in the allocated wi-fi room.

Stony Batter Historic Reserve
HISTORIC SITE
(www.fortstonybatter.org.nz; Stony Batter Rd; adult/child $8/5; ☻10am-3.30pm) At the bottom end of the island, Stony Batter has WWII tunnels and gun emplacements that were built in 1941 to defend Auckland's harbour. The walk leads through private farmland and derives its name from the boulder-strewn fields. Bring a torch and cash.

Waiheke Museum & Historic Village
MUSEUM
(www.waihekemuseum.org.nz; 165 Onetangi Rd; admission by donation; ☻noon-4pm Wed, Sat & Sun) Displays Islander artefacts in six restored buildings.

Dead Dog Bay
GARDENS
(www.deaddogbay.co.nz; Margaret Reeve Lane; adult/child $10/free; ☻10am-5pm) Wander steep pathways through rainforest, wetlands and gardens scattered with sculpture in this jealousy-inducing private property.

Connells Bay
GARDENS
(☑09-372 8957; www.connellsbay.co.nz; Cowes Bay Rd; adult/child $30/15; ☻by appointment, late Oct-late Apr) A pricey but excellent private sculpture park featuring a stellar roster of NZ artists. Admission is by way of a two-hour guided tour; book ahead.

Walks
Ask at the i-SITE about the island's beautiful coastal walks (ranging from one to three hours) and the 3km Cross Island Walkway (from Onetangi to Rocky Bay). Other tracks traverse **Whakanewha Regional Park**, a haven for rare coastal birds and geckos, and the Royal Forest & Bird Protection Society's three reserves: **Onetangi** (Waiheke Rd), **Te Haahi-Goodwin** (Orapiu Rd) and **Atawhai Whenua** (Ocean View Rd).

Kayaking
Ross Adventures
KAYAKING
(☑09-372 5550; www.kayakwaiheke.co.nz; Matiatia beach; half-/full-day trips $85/145, per hr hire from $25) It's the fervently held opinion of Ross that Waiheke offers kayaking every bit as good as the legendary Abel Tasman National Park. He should know – he's been offering guided kayak trips for over 20 years. Experienced sea kayakers can comfortably circumnavigate the island in four days, exploring hidden coves and sand spits inaccessible by land.

LOCAL KNOWLEDGE

WAIHEKE ISLAND *ZOË BELL*

Thirty years ago, Waiheke Island was home to an eclectic mix of outlaws who could not (or chose not to) live in 'normal' society: hippies and hermits, alternative healers and writers, potters and pot growers, and everything in between. Sometime in the late '80s, Waiheke was 'discovered', and it's quite a different place now. But even with all the changes – fine dining, vineyards and luxury holiday homes – Waiheke Island's identity and spirit are still undeniable. The beautiful weather remains the same, as do the phenomenal vistas, the lush bush and native birds, the chooks in your neighbours' backyards, the feeling that everything deserves to move a little slower (we call it 'Waiheke time'), the smell of honeysuckle, the crystal waters, the best fish and chips ever, the house I was born in and, probably, still a few pot growers. Waiheke was, and remains, like nowhere else on the planet.

Zoë Bell, stuntwoman & actor

 Tours

Ananda Tours   FOOD & WINE

(☑09-372 7530; www.ananda.co.nz) Offers a gourmet wine and food tour ($110) and a wine connoisseurs' tour ($210). Small-group, informal tours can be customised, including visits to artists' studios.

Fullers   FOOD & WINE

(☑09-367 9111; www.fullers.co.nz) Runs a Wine on Waiheke Tour (adult $115, 4½ hours, departs Auckland 1pm) that visits three of the island's top wineries and includes a platter of nibbles. Taste of Waiheke (adult $125, 5½ hours, departs Auckland 11am) also includes three wineries plus an olive grove and light lunch. There's also a 1½-hour Explorer Tour (adult/child $49/25, departs Auckland 10am, 11am and noon). All prices include the ferry and an all-day bus pass.

Waiheke Island Adventures   FOOD & WINE

(☑09-372 6127; www.waihekeislandadventures. com) Scenic tours ($25), vineyard tours ($25), or Stony Batter tours ($35) in a 15-seater bus. Art and beach tours also available.

Waiheke Executive Transport   WINE, CULTURAL

(☑0800 372 200; www.waiheketransport.co.nz) Highlights tours (from $15), wine tours (standard/premium $89/115) and art tours ($115).

🎎 **Festivals & Events**

Sculpture on the Gulf   ARTS

(www.sculptureonthegulf.co.nz) A wacky 2km cliff-top sculpture walk, held every January in odd-numbered years.

Waiheke Blues Festival   MUSIC

(www.waihekeblues.co.nz) Live blues played in various venues on the last weekend in August.

🛏 **Sleeping**

Waiheke is so popular in the summer holidays that many locals rent out their houses and bugger off elsewhere. You'll need to book ahead and even then there are very few bargains. Prices drop considerably in winter, especially midweek.

Tawa Lodge   GUESTHOUSE **$$**

(☑09-372 9434; www.pungalodge.co.nz; 15 Tawa St; r $120, apt $175-240; ☜) Between the self-contained cottage at the front and the apartment at the rear are three reasonably priced loft rooms sharing a small kitchen and bathroom. On a hot day there's a wonderfully languid vibe as guests spill out onto the deck.

Fossil Bay Lodge   CABIN **$**

(☑09-372 8371; www.fossilbay.webs.com; 58 Korora Rd; s $45, d $75-120; ☜) Three cutesy cabins open onto a courtyard facing the main building, which houses the toilets, a communal kitchen and living area and, on the other side, a Steiner kindergarten. Apart from the occasional squawking duck (or toddler), it's a peaceful place.

Punga Lodge   B&B **$$**

(☑09-372 6675; www.pungalodge.co.nz; 223 Ocean View Rd; r $145-165, apt $140-200; @☜) Both the colourful en-suite rooms in the house and the self-contained garden units have access to decks looking onto a lush tropical garden. There's a spa, and prices include home-made breakfast, afternoon tea and wharf transfers.

Enclosure Bay
B&B $$$

(☎09-372 8882; www.enclosurebay.co.nz; 9 Great Barrier Rd; r $325, ste $450) If you're going to shell out for a luxury B&B you're going to want something a little special, and that's certainly what's offered here. Each of the three guest rooms have sumptuous views and balconies, and the owners subscribe to the nothing's-too-much-trouble school of Kiwi hospitality.

Crescent Valley Eco Lodge
GUESTHOUSE $$

(☎09-372 4321; www.waihekeecolodge.co.nz; 50 Crescent Rd East; r $145; ☎) Surrounded by bush and peaceful gardens this little eco-retreat has only two tidy rooms, affable hosts and a spa pool under the stars. Bathrooms are private but not en suite.

Onetangi Beach Apartments
APARTMENT $$$

(☎09-372 0003; www.onetangi.co.nz; 27 The Strand; apt $189-410; ☎) Three different blocks of townhouses are clumped together, all offering modern, perfectly located, well-managed accommodation, along with a spa and sauna. Best (and priciest) are the Strand Apartments, with large decks overlooking the sea.

Hekerua Lodge
HOSTEL $

(☎09-372 8990; www.hekerualodge.co.nz; 11 Hekerua Rd; sites from $18, dm $32-36, s $55, d $86-120; @☎☎) This secluded hostel is surrounded by native bush and has a barbecue, stone-tiled pool, sunny deck, casual lounge area and its own walking track. It's far from luxurious, but it has a laid-back feel, no doubt assisted by the serene images of Buddha scattered about.

Kina
HOSTEL $

(☎09-372 8971; www.kinabackpackers.co.nz; 421 Seaview Rd; dm $27-31, s/tw $55/68, d $70-90; @☎) This old-style, well-positioned hostel has a large garden overlooking Onetangi Beach. The rooms are a little cell-like but the dorms have only two bunk beds and linen is provided.

Whakanewha Regional Park Campsite
CAMPSITE $

(☎09-366 2000; www.arc.govt.nz; Gordons Rd; sites per adult/child $10/5) A pretty but basic campsite with toilets, gas barbecues and drinking water. Self-contained campervans can park in the neighbouring car park for a single night only (per adult/child $5/3).

🍴 Eating

Priding itself on the finer things in life, Waiheke has some excellent eateries and, if you're lucky, the views will be enough to distract from the hole being bored into your hip pocket.

Te Whau
WINERY $$$

(☎09-372 7191; www.tewhau.com; 218 Te Whau Dr; mains $42-44; ☺lunch Fri-Sun, dinner Sat, extended summer) Perched on the end of Te Whau peninsula, this winery restaurant has exceptional views, food and service, and one of the finest wine lists you'll see in the country. Try its own impressive bordeaux blends, merlot, chardonnay and rosé for $3 per taste (11am to 5pm).

Dragonfired
PIZZERIA $

(Little Oneroa Beach; mains $8-12; ☺11am-8pm; ☎) Specialising in what they describe as 'artisan woodfired food', this black caravan by the beach serves the three Ps: pizza, polenta plates and pocket bread. It's easily the best place for cheap eats on the island.

Island Thyme & Thymes Tables
CAFE, RESTAURANT $

(☎09-372 3400; www.islandthyme.co.nz; 8 Miami Ave, Surfdale; Island Thyme light meals $9, Thymes Tables mains $36; ☺Island Thyme breakfast & lunch, Thymes Tables dinner Tue-Sat) For pre-packaged gourmet meals, deli goodies, tempting pastries and excellent coffee, clock in on Island Thyme, downstairs. Thymes Tables, upstairs, is an elegant 'plat du jour' restaurant offering only one or two dishes per evening, posted daily on the blackboard outside.

Wai Kitchen
CAFE $$

(www.waikitchen.co.nz; 1/149 Ocean View Rd, Oneroa; mains $17-23; ☺9am-4pm, extended summer) Why? Well firstly there's the lively menu abounding in Mediterranean and Asian flavours. Then there's the charming service and the breezy ambience of this glassed-in wedge, facing the wai (water).

Casita Miro
SPANISH $$

(☎09-372 7854; www.mirovineyard.co.nz; 3 Brown St, Onetangi; dishes $19-40; ☺lunch Wed-Sun, dinner Sat) A wrought-iron and glass pavilion backed with a Gaudi-esque mosaic garden is the stage for a very entertaining troupe of servers who will guide you through the menu of delectable *racion tapas* – dishes bigger than regular tapas, designed to be shared.

Cable Bay
WINERY $$$

(☎09-372 5889; www.cablebayvineyards.co.nz; 12 Nick Johnstone Dr; mains $42-45; ☺lunch daily, dinner Thu-Sun, extended summer) Impressive ubermodern architecture, sculpture and beautiful views set the scene for this acclaimed restaurant. The food is sublime but if the budget won't stretch to a meal, stop in for a wine tasting (from $8) or a snack on the terrace.

Poderi Crisci
ITALIAN $$$

(☎09-372 2148; www.podericrisci.co.nz; 205 Awaawaroa Rd; mains $32; ☺lunch Fri-Sun) Owned by the Italian-born patriarch behind Parnell's Non Solo Pizza, Poderi Crisci has quickly gained a sterling reputation for its food, particularly its four-hour Sunday long lunches. Italian varietals and olives have been planted alongside the existing vines.

Delight
TURKISH $$

(☎09-372 9035; www.delightcafe.co.nz; 29 Waikare Rd, Oneroa; mains $14-23, mezze $10-19; ☺8am-3pm daily year-round, dinner Fri-Sun Nov-Mar) If you're bored with eggs Benedict, try one of the piquant breakfast tagines at this stylish cafe/mezze bar. Paninis, wraps and salads are served along with more traditional mezze, and the views are just as delicious.

Mudbrick
WINERY $$$

(☎09-372 9050; www.mudbrick.co.nz; 126 Church Bay Rd; mains $41-49; ☺lunch & dinner) Auckland and the gulf are at their glistening best when viewed from Mudbrick's picturesque veranda. The winery also offers tours and tastings (from $10, 10am to 5pm).

Stefano's
PIZZERIA $$

(☎09-372 5309; www.stef.co.nz; 18 Hamilton Rd, Surfdale; mains $16-31; ☺5.30-9.30pm Tue-Sun, extended summer) The best-smelling joint on Waiheke, serving pasta and pizza in the presence of a dodgy mural. It also does takeaways.

Ostend Market
MARKET

(www.ostendmarketwaiheke.co.nz; War Memorial Hall, Belgium St; ☺7.30am-1pm Sat) Stock up on fresh local produce and peruse local craft and second hand knick-knacks.

Drinking

Apart from the wineries, you'll find bars in Oneroa and pubs in Surfdale and Ostend.

Charlie Farley's
BAR

(www.charliefarleys.co.nz; 21 The Strand, Onetangi; ☺8.30am-late) Supping on a Waiheke wine or beer under the pohutukawas on the beach-gazing deck, it's easy to see why the locals love this place.

Information

Waiheke Island i-SITE (☎09-372 1234; www.waihekenz.com; 118 Ocean View Rd; ☺9am-5pm) As well as the very helpful main office, there's a (usually unstaffed) counter in the ferry terminal at Matiatia Wharf.

Getting There & Away

Fullers (☎09-367 9111; www.fullers.co.nz; return adult/child $35/18; ☺5.20am-11.45pm Mon-Fri, 6.25am-11.45pm Sat, 7am-9.30pm Sun) Has frequent passenger ferries from Auckland to Matiatia Wharf (on the hour from 9am to 5pm), some via Devonport.

Sealink (☎09-300 5900; www.sealink.co.nz; adult/child/car/motorcycle return $30/17/130/48; ☺4.30am-6.30pm Mon-Thu, 4.30am-8pm Fri, 6am-6.30pm Sat & Sun) Runs car ferries to Kennedy Point, mainly from Half Moon Bay (east Auckland) but some leave from Wynyard Wharf in the city. The ferry runs at least every two hours and takes 45 minutes (booking essential).

360 Discovery (☎0800 360 3472; www.360discovery.co.nz) You can pick up the 360 Discovery tourist ferry at Orapiu on its journey between Auckland and Coromandel Town. However Orapiu is quite remote and not served by buses.

Getting Around
Bike

Various bicycle routes are outlined in the *Bike Waiheke!* brochure, available from the wharf and the i-SITE; be prepared for a lot of hills.

Waiheke Bike Hire (☎09-372 7937; Matiatia Wharf) Hires mountain bikes (half-/full day $25/35) from their base near the wharf and at the Oneroa i-SITE.

Bus

The island has regular bus services, starting from Matiatia Wharf and heading through Oneroa (adult/child $1.50/80c, five minutes) on their way to all the main settlements, as far west as Onetangi (adult/child $4.20/2.40, 30 minutes); see **MAXX** (☎09-366 6400; www.maxx.co.nz) for timetables. A day pass (adult/child $8.20/5) is available from the Fullers counter at Matiatia Wharf.

Car, Motorbike & Scooter

Fun Rentals (📞09-372 8001; www.funrentals. co.nz; 14a Belgium St, Ostend; per day car/ scooter/4WD from $59/49/59) If you're staying overnight, this company has the advantage of offering 24-hour rental periods (as opposed to a calendar day); transfers from the ferry are included. They offer unlimited kilometres and an insurance excess of $1500, falling to $1000 for over 25-year-olds.

Rent Me Waiheke (📞09-372 3339; www. rentmewaiheke.co.nz; 14 Ocean View Rd, Matiatia; per calendar day cars/scooters $59/49) Unlimited kilometres; excess $3000, dropping to $2500 for over 25s.

Waiheke Auto Rentals (📞09-372 8998; www. waiherekentals.co.nz; Matiatia Wharf; per calendar day car & scooter from $59, motorbike & 4WD from $79) Excess $1500, dropping to $1000 if you're over 25 years old. There's an additional charge of 65c per kilometre for cars or 4WDs.

Waiheke Rental Cars (📞09-372 8635; www. waihererentalcars.co.nz; Matiatia Wharf; per calendar day car/4WD from $59/79) Unlimited kilometres; excess $3000, dropping to $2500 for over 25s.

Taxi

Waiheke Independent Taxis (📞0800 300 372)
Waiheke Taxi Co-op (📞09-372 8038)
Waiheke Taxis (📞09-372 3000)

Rotoroa Island

From 1911 to 2005 the only people to have access to this blissful little island on the far side of Waiheke were the alcoholics and drug addicts who came (or were sentenced) here to dry out – and the Salvation Army staff who cared for them. In 2011, after 100 years, 82-hectare **Rotoroa** (📞0800 76 86 76; www.rotoroa.org.nz; access fee $5) opened to the public, giving visitors access to three sandy swimming beaches and the social history and art displays in the restored buildings of the former treatment centre. There are also three well-appointed, wildly retro holiday homes for rent ($250 to $500).

ℹ️ Getting There & Away

360 Discovery (📞0800 360 3472; www.360discovery.co.nz; adult/child from Auckland $55/30, from Orapiu $21/13) From Auckland the ferry takes 75 minutes, stopping at Orapiu on Waiheke Island en route. There are four boats per week from Labour Day to Easter (daily in January) and two boats per week over the cooler months.

Tiritiri Matangi Island

This magical, 220-hectare, predator-free **island** (www.tiritirimatangi.org.nz) is home to the tuatara (a prehistoric lizard) and lots of endangered native birds, including the very rare and colourful takahe. Other birds that can be seen here include the bellbird, stitchbird, saddleback, whitehead, kakariki, kokako, little spotted kiwi, brown teal, NZ robin, fernbird and penguins; 78 different species have been sighted in total. The saddleback was once close to extinction with just 150 left, but now there are more than 600 on Tiritiri alone. To experience the dawn chorus in full flight, stay overnight at the **DOC bunkhouse** (📞09-425 7812; www.doc.govt.nz; adult/child $30/20); book well ahead and ensure there's room on the ferry.

The island was sold to the Crown in 1841, deforested and farmed until the 1970s. Since 1984 hundreds of volunteers have planted 250,000 native trees and the forest cover has regenerated. An 1864 lighthouse stands on the eastern end of the island.

ℹ️ Getting There & Away

360 Discovery (📞0800 360 3472; www.360discovery.co.nz; return Auckland/Gulf Harbour $66/49; 🕐Wed-Sun) Book a guided walk ($5) with your ferry ticket; the guides know where all the really cool birds hang out.

Motuora Island

Halfway between Tiritiri Matangi and Kawau, Motuora has 80 predator-free hectares and is used as a kiwi 'crèche'. There's a wharf on the west coast of the island, but you'll need your own boat to get here. The **DOC campsite** (📞027-492 8586; www.doc.govt.nz; adult/child $6/3) requires bookings and provides toilets, cold showers and water. There's also a bach that sleeps five ($52); bring your own linen and food.

Kawau Island

POP 300

Kawau Island lies 50km north of Auckland off the Mahurangi Peninsula. There are few proper roads through the island, the residents relying mainly on boats. The main attraction is **Mansion House** (adult/child $4/2;

noon-2pm), an impressive wooden manor extended from an 1845 structure by Governor George Grey, who purchased the island in 1862. It houses a fine collection of Victoriana, including some of Grey's effects, and is surrounded by the original exotic gardens. A set of short walks (10 minutes to two hours) are signposted from Mansion House, leading to beaches, the old copper mine and a lookout; download DOC's *Kawau Island Historic Reserve map* (www.doc.govt.nz).

Sleeping & Eating

Kawau Lodge   B&B $$$
(09-422 8831; www.kawaulodge.co.nz; North Cove; s $160, d $210-245) This eco-conscious boutique hotel has its own jetty, wraparound decks and views. Meals ($10 to $60) can be arranged, as can excursions.

Mansion House Cafe Restaurant
(09-422 8903; lunch $12-18, dinner $18-28; hrs vary) If you haven't packed a picnic, this idyllically situated eatery will be a welcome relief, serving all-day breakfasts, sandwiches and hearty evening meals. It's also your only option for stocking up on bread, milk, ice and pre-ordered newspapers.

Getting There & Away

Kawau Water Taxis (0800 111 616; www.kawauwatertaxis.co.nz) Daily ferries from Sandspit to Kawau (adult/child return $50/26) and a water-taxi service (minimum charge $130). The Super Cruise (adult/child $68/30, barbecue lunch $22/11) departs Sandspit at 10.30am and circles the island, delivering the post to 75 different wharves.

Great Barrier Island

POP 860

Named Aotea (meaning cloud) by the Maori and Great Barrier (due to its position at the edge of the Hauraki Gulf) by James Cook, this rugged and exceptionally beautiful place falls in behind South, North and Stewart as NZ's fourth-largest island (285 sq km). It closely resembles the Coromandel Peninsula to which it was once joined, and like the Coromandel it was once a mining, logging and whaling centre. Those industries have long gone and today two-thirds of the island is publicly owned and managed by DOC.

Great Barrier has unspoilt beaches, hot springs, old kauri dams, a forest sanctuary and a network of tramping tracks. Because there are no possums on the island, the native bush is lush.

Although only 88km from Auckland, Great Barrier seems a world – and a good many years – away. The island has no supermarket, no electricity supply (only private solar, wind and diesel generators) and no main drainage (only septic tanks). Many roads are unsealed and petrol costs are high. Mobile-phone reception is very limited and there are no banks, ATMs or street lights.

From around mid-December to mid-January is the peak season, so make sure you book transport, accommodation and activities well in advance.

Tryphena is the main settlement, 4km from the ferry wharf at Shoal Bay. Strung out along several kilometres of coastal road, it consists of a few dozen houses and a handful of shops and accommodation places. From the wharf it's 3km to Mulberry Grove, and then another 1km over the headland to Pa Beach and the Stonewall Store.

The airport is at **Claris**, 12km north of Tryphena, a small settlement with a general store, bottle shop, laundrette, garage, pharmacy and cafe.

Whangaparapara is an old timber town and the site of the island's 19th-century whaling activities. **Port Fitzroy** is the other main harbour on the west coast, a one-hour drive from Tryphena. These four main settlements have fuel available.

Activities
Water Sports
The beaches on the west coast are safe, but care needs to be taken on the surf-pounded eastern beaches. **Medlands Beach**, with its wide sweep of white sand, is one of the most beautiful and accessible beaches on the island. Remote **Whangapoua**, in the northeast, requires more effort to get to, while **Kaitoke**, **Awana Bay** and **Haratāonga** on the east coast are also worth a visit.

Okiwi Bar has an excellent right-hand break, while Awana has both left- and right-hand breaks. Pohutukawa trees shelter the pretty bays around Tryphena.

Diving is excellent, with shipwrecks, pinnacles, lots of fish and more than 33m visibility at some times of the year.

Hooked on Barrier   DIVING, FISHING
(09-429 0740; www.hookedonbarrier.co.nz; 89 Hector-Sanderson Rd; half-/full-day charter $700/1200) Hooked on Barrier hires out diving, snorkelling, fishing, surfing and

Great Barrier Island

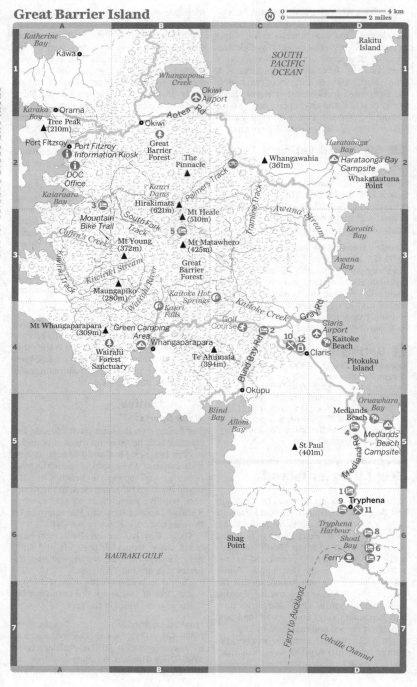

Katherine Bay

Kawa

SOUTH PACIFIC OCEAN

Rakitu Island

0   4 km
0   2 miles

Whangapoua Creek

Okiwi Airport

Karaka Bay

Orama

Tree Peak (210m)

Okiwi

Aotea Rd

Port Fitzroy

Port Fitzroy Information Kiosk

Great Barrier Forest

The Pinnacle

Whangawahia (361m)

Haratonga Bay

Haratonga Bay Campsite

DOC Office

Whakatautuna Point

Kaiaraara Bay

Kauri Dams

Hirakimata (621m)

Palmers Track

Mt Heale (510m)

Awana Stream

3

Mountain Bike Trail

South Fork Track

5

Mt Matawhero (425m)

Tramline Track

Korotiti Bay

Coffin's Creek

Mt Young (372m)

Great Barrier Forest

Awana Bay

Kiwiriki Track

Kiwiriki Stream

Waiuha River

Maungapiko (280m)

Kaitoke Hot Springs

Kauri Falls

Kaitoke Creek

Gray Rd

Claris Airport

Mt Whangaparapara (309m)

Green Camping Area

Golf Course

2

10 12

Kaitoke Beach

Whangaparapara

Blind Bay Rd

Claris

Pitokuku Island

Wairahi Forest Sanctuary

Te Ahumata (394m)

Okupu

Medlands Beach

Oruawharo Bay

Blind Bay

Allom Bay

4

Medlands Beach Campsite

St Paul (401m)

Medland Rd

HAURAKI GULF

Shag Point

1
9 Tryphena
11

Tryphena Harbour

8

Shoal Bay

6

Ferry

7

Ferry to Auckland

Colville Channel

Great Barrier Island

Activities, Courses & Tours
Hooked on Barrier .... (see 12)

Sleeping
1 Aotea Lodge D6
2 Crossroads Lodge C4
3 Kaiaraara Hut A2
4 Medlands Beach Backpackers
    & Villas...D5
5 Mt Heale Hut..B3
6 Pigeons Lodge.................................... D6
7 Shoal Bay Lodge D6
8 Sunset Waterfront Lodge.................. D6
9 Tipi & Bob's Waterfront Lodge D6

Eating
10 Claris Texas....................................... C4
Currach Irish Pub....................... (see 11)
Tipi & Bob's Waterfront Lodge ... (see 9)
11 Wild Rose D6

Shopping
12 Aotea Community Art Gallery............ C4

kayaking gear, as well as running fishing, diving and sightseeing charters.

Mountain Biking
With rugged scenery and relatively little traffic on the roads, mountain biking is a popular activity here. There's a designated 25km ride beginning on Blind Bay Rd, Okupu, winding beneath the Ahumata cliffs before crossing Whangaparapara Rd and beginning the 15km Forest Rd ride through beautiful forest to Port Fitzroy. Cycling on other DOC walking tracks is prohibited.

Tramping
The island's very popular walking tracks are outlined in DOC's free *Great Barrier Island (Aotea Island)* booklet. Before setting out, make sure you're properly equipped with water and food, and be prepared for both sunny and wet weather.

The most popular easy walk is the 45-minute **Kaitoke Hot Springs Track**, starting from Whangaparapara Rd and leading to natural hot springs in a bush stream. Check the temperature before getting in and don't put your head under the water.

Windy Canyon, which is only a 15-minute walk from Aotea Rd, has spectacular rock outcrops and affords great views of the island. From Windy Canyon, an excellent trail continues for another two to three hours through

scrubby forest to Hirakimata (Mt Hobson, 621m), the highest point on the island, with views across the Hauraki Gulf and Coromandel. Near the top of the mountain are lush forests and a few mature kauri trees that survived the logging days. From Hirakimata it is 40 minutes south to Mt Heale Hut or two hours west through forest and past a kauri driving dam to Kaiaraara Hut, where it's another 45 minutes on to Port Fitzroy.

A more challenging tramp is the hilly **Tramline Track** (five hours), which starts on Aotea Rd and follows old logging tramlines to Whangaparapara Harbour. The initial stages of this track are not maintained and in some parts the clay becomes slippery after rain.

Of a similar length, but flatter and easier walking, is the 11km **Haarataonga Coastal Walk** (five hours), which heads from Haraataonga Bay to Whangapoua.

Many other trails traverse the forest, taking between 30 minutes and five hours. The **Aotea Track** combines bits of other paths into a three-day walk, staying overnight in each of the huts.

See Great Barrier Island's Getting Around information for details of shuttle buses to and from the trailheads.

Sleeping
Unless you're camping, Great Barrier isn't a cheap place to stay. At pretty much every price point you'll pay more than you would for a similar place elsewhere. Rates drop considerably, however, in the off-season. **Island Accommodation** (09-429 0995; www.island accommodation.co.nz) offers a booking service, which is particularly handy for finding self-contained houses for longer stays.

Aotea Lodge   APARTMENT **$$**
(09-429 0628; www.aotealodge.com; 41 Medland Rd; units $120-210) A well-tended, sunny garden surrounds these reasonably priced units, perched on the hill just above Tryphena. They range from a two-bedroom house to an unusual mezzanine unit loaded with bunks, but each has its own cooking facilities.

Shoal Bay Lodge   APARTMENT **$$**
(09-429 0890; www.shoalbaylodge.co.nz; 145 Shoal Bay Rd; apt $150-240) Hidden among the trees these comfy self-contained apartments offer sea views, bird song, solar power and environmentally friendly cleaning products. Best is the three-bedroom lodge with its sunset-guzzling deck.

Sunset Waterfront Lodge   MOTEL $$$
(☎09-429 0051; www.sunsetlodge.co.nz; Mulberry Grove; apt $195-300) Gaze across the lawn to the sea from the attractive studio units, or fight over who's going to get the pointy room in the two-bedroom A-frame villas. There's a small shop and cafe next door.

Pigeons Lodge   APARTMENT $$
(☎09-429 0437; www.pigeonslodge.co.nz; 179 Shoal Bay Rd; apt $135) Above the water, south of Tryphena, Pigeons has two tidy self-contained units near the top of the drive, sharing a deck and a barbecue. The owners lead a double life as real-estate agents, which is handy if you fall in love with the island and fancy staying.

**Medlands Beach
Backpackers & Villas**   HOSTEL $
(☎09-429 0320; www.medlandsbeach.com; 9 Mason Rd; dm $35, d/units from $70/120) Chill out in the garden of this house on the hill, overlooking beautiful Medlands Beach. The backpackers' area is simple, with a little double cabin for romantic budgeteers at a slight remove from the rest. The self-contained houses sleep up to six.

Tipi & Bob's Waterfront Lodge   MOTEL $$$
(☎09-429 0550; www.waterfrontlodge.co.nz; 38 Puriri Bay Rd; units $195-350) West of Tryphena, these smart but overpriced motel-style units have some wonderful sea views and very helpful owners. The complex includes a restaurant and bar.

Crossroads Lodge   HOSTEL $
(☎09-429 0889; www.xroadslodge.com; 1 Blind Bay Rd; dm/s/d $30/50/75; @🛜) This low-key backpackers is 2km from the airfield and close to forest walks and hot springs. Mountain bikes can be hired, and golf clubs can be borrowed to play on the nearby nine-hole golf course.

Kaiaraara & Mt Heale Huts   HUT $
(www.doc.govt.nz; dm per adult/child $15/5) These DOC huts in the Great Barrier Forest have bunk beds, cold running water, chemical toilets and a kitchen/dining area. Bring your own sleeping bag and cooking/eating equipment and book online. Mt Heale Hut sleeps 20 people and has a gas cooker, but Kaiaraara Hut (which sleeps 28) doesn't.

DOC Campsites   CAMPSITE $
(☎09-379 6476; www.doc.govt.nz; site per adult/child $10/5) There are campsites at Harataonga Bay, Medlands Beach, Akapoua Bay, Whangapoua, The Green (Whangaparapara) and Awana Bay. All have basic facilities, including water, cold showers (none at The Green), toilets and a food preparation shelter. You need to bring your own gas cooking stove as open fires are prohibited. Book in advance online as the sites are not staffed.

🍴 Eating & Drinking

In summer, most places are open daily but for the rest of the year the hours can be sporadic. There's a monthly guide as to what's open when posted on www.thebarrier.co.nz but it still pays to call ahead for an evening meal.

Self-caterers will find small stores in Tryphena, Claris, Whangaparapara and Port Fitzroy.

Wild Rose   CAFE $
(☎09-429 0905; Blackwell Dr; mains $5-18; ⊘8.30am-4pm) Wild Rose does the best impersonation of an Auckland cafe on the island, albeit with the addition of local crowd-pleasers such as toasted sandwiches and burgers. It uses free-range, organic and local produce whenever possible.

Claris Texas   CAFE $
(129 Hector Sanderson Rd; mains $5-13; ⊘8am-4pm; @🛜) While it doesn't live up to the promise of its quirky name, this is the best gap-filler in the centre of the island, serving cooked breakfasts, nachos, salads and pies.

**Tipi & Bob's
Waterfront Lodge**   RESTAURANT $$$
(☎09-429 0550; www.waterfrontlodge.co.nz; 38 Puriri Bay Rd; mains $32-33; ⊘breakfast & dinner) Serving simple but satisfying meals in large portions, this popular haunt has an inviting deck overlooking the harbour. There's a cheaper pub menu in the bar.

Currach Irish Pub   PUB $$
(☎09-429 0211; Blackwell Dr; mains $14-28; ⊘from 4pm) This lively, child-friendly pub has a changing menu of seafood, steak and burgers, and is the island's social centre. Rub shoulders with local musos on jam nights.

🛍 Shopping

Aotea Community Art Gallery   ARTS & CRAFTS
(80 Hector Sanderson Rd; ⊘10.30am-3.30pm) Nothing if not eclectic, this showcase for

the island's artsy fraternity sells everything from paintings to handmade soap, to baby booties, to cross-stitched Virgin Marys.

ℹ Information

There's an information kiosk at the GBI Rent-A-Car office in Claris. Claris Texas cafe has internet access.

DOC Office (☑09-429 0044; www.doc.govt. nz; ⊙8am-4.30pm Mon-Fri) Call in for brochures, maps, weather information and to sign the intentions book for longer walks.

Great Barrier Island i-SITE (www.great barriernz.com; Claris Airport; ⊙11am-noon Mon, Wed & Fri, 8am-2.30pm Sat, extended in summer) Stocks brochures including their own *Great Barrier Island* pamphlet, which is full of useful information and has a handy map.

Port Fitzroy Information Kiosk (☑09-429 0848; www.thebarrier.co.nz; ⊙9.30am-3pm Mon-Sat) Privately run kiosk that publishes the *Great Barrier Island Visitor Information Guide*.

ℹ Getting There & Away

Air

Fly My Sky (☑09-256 7026; www.flymysky. co.nz; one way adult/child $104/79) Flies at least three times a day from Auckland. Cheaper flights are available if you travel to the island on a Sunday or leave on a Friday ($76), and there's a special return fare for flying one way and ferrying the other (adult/child $179/159).

Great Barrier Airlines (☑09-275 9120; www. greatbarrierairlines.co.nz; one way standard/ advance $124/99) Departs from Auckland Domestic Airport (at least twice daily) and North Shore Aerodrome (at least daily) for the 30-minute flight to Claris. In summer they also stop at Okiwi, as well as offering on-demand flights to Whangarei and Whitianga.

Sunair (☑0800 786 847; www.sunair.co.nz; one way $160) Flies from Whitianga twice daily.

Boat

Fullers (☑09-367 9111; www.fullers.co.nz; adult/child one way $75/45) Runs the fastest services (2½ hours) from Auckland's Ferry Building to Shoal Bay and Port Fitzroy from mid-December to the end of January, as well as on the Easter long weekend.

Sealink (☑09-300 5900; www.sealink. co.nz; return adult/child/car/motorcycle $120/79/370/100) The main provider, running car ferries from three to five days a week from Wynyard Wharf in Auckland to Tryphena's Shoal Bay (six hours).

ℹ Getting Around

Most roads are narrow and windy but even small hire cars can handle the unsealed sections. Many of the accommodation places will pick you up from the airport or wharf if notified in advance.

Aotea Car Rentals (☑0800 426 832; www. aoteacarrentals.co.nz; Mulberry Grove) Hires out cars (from $60), 4WDs (from $75) and vans (from $99). Rental clients get to use the associated Great Barrier Travel trampers' shuttles for free.

GBI Rent-A-Car (☑09-429 0062; www.great barrierisland.co.nz; 67 Hector Sanderson Rd) Has a somewhat battered fleet of cars starting at $55 and 4WDs from $85. They also operate shuttle services from Claris to Tryphena ($20), Medlands ($15), Whangaparapara ($20) and Port Fitzroy ($30, minimum four passengers), as well as trampers' shuttles. There's a $5 flagfall for solo passengers; call ahead to book.

Great Barrier Travel (☑09-429 0474; www. greatbarriertravel.co.nz; tickets from $10) Runs shuttles between Tryphena and Claris (timed to meet all the planes and boats), a daily shuttle from Claris to Port Fitzroy, and transfers to and from the walking tracks. Call ahead to confirm times and to book.

WEST AUCKLAND

West Auckland epitomises rugged: wild black-sand beaches, bush-shrouded ranges, and mullet-haired, black-T-shirt-wearing 'Westies'. The latter is just one of several stereotypes of the area's denizens. Others include the back-to-nature hippie, the eccentric bohemian artist and the dope-smoking surfer dude, all attracted to a simple life at the edge of the bush.

Add to the mix Croatian immigrants, earning the fertile fields at the base of the Waitakere Ranges the nickname 'Dallie Valley' after the Dalmatian coast where many hailed from. These pioneering families planted grapes and made wine, founding one of NZ's major industries.

Titirangi
POP 3200

This little village marks the end of Auckland's suburban sprawl and is a good place to spot all of the stereotypes mentioned above over a caffe latte, fine wine or cold beer. Once home to NZ's greatest modern painter, Colin McCahon, there remains an artsy feel to the place. Titirangi means

'Fringe of Heaven' – an apt name for the gateway to the Waitakere Ranges, or indeed a hair salon. This is the last stop for petrol and ATMs on your way west.

⊙ Sights

McCahon House   MUSEUM
(www.mccahonhouse.org.nz; 67 Otitori Bay Rd; admission $5; ⊙10am-2pm Wed, Sat & Sun) It's a mark of the esteem in which Colin McCahon is held that the house he lived and painted in during the 1950s has been opened to the public as a minimuseum. The swish pad next door is home to the artist lucky enough to win the McCahon Arts Residency. Look for the signposts pointing down Park Rd, just before you reach Titirangi village.

FREE Lopdell House Gallery   GALLERY
(www.lopdell.org.nz; 418 Titirangi Rd; ⊙10am-4.30pm) An excellent modern art gallery housed in the former Hotel Titirangi (1930), on the edge of the village, with a theatre and Italian bakehouse attached.

🛏 Sleeping & Eating

Fringe of Heaven   B&B $$$
(☎09-817 8682; www.fringeofheaven.com; 4 Otitori Bay Rd; r $225-265) Surrounded by native bush, this Frank Lloyd Wright–inspired house offers glorious views over Manukau Harbour, an outdoor bath, glowworms in the garden and a songbird choir – all within 20 minutes of the city centre.

Hardware Cafe   CAFE $$
(404 Titirangi Rd; brunch $10-18, dinner $22-28; ⊙6am-4.30pm Sun-Tue, 6am-late Wed-Sat) Great for Westie-watching, this popular licensed cafe serves delicious, reasonably priced cooked breakfasts and lunches along with a tempting array of counter food. More substantial evening meals start from $22.

Waitakere Ranges

This 160-sq-km wilderness was covered in kauri until the mid-19th century, when logging claimed most of the giant trees. A few stands of ancient kauri and other mature natives survive amid the dense bush of the regenerating rainforest, which is now protected inside the Waitakere Ranges Regional Park. Bordered to the west by wildly beautiful beaches on the Tasman Sea, the park's rugged terrain makes an excellent day trip from Auckland.

⊙ Sights & Activities

Arataki   VISITORS CENTRE
(☎09-817 0077; www.arc.govt.nz; Scenic Dr; ⊙9am-5pm) As well as providing information on the 250km of trails within the park, this impressive, child-friendly centre, with its Maori carvings (some prodigiously well hung) and spectacular views, is an attraction in its own right. The carvings that greet visitors at the entrance depict the ancestors of the Kawerau *iwi*. You can also book here for several basic campsites (adult/child $5/3) within the park – toilets are provided but nothing much else.

A 1.6km nature trail opposite the centre leads visitors past labelled native species, including mature kauri.

Hillary Trail & other tracks   TRAMPING
(www.arc.govt.nz/hillarytrail) Arataki Vistor Centre is the starting point for this 70km trail, opened in 2010 to honour NZ's most famous son, Everest-conqueror Sir Edmund Hillary. It can be tackled in stages or in its four-day entirety, staying at campsites along the way. Walkers head to the coast at Huia then tick off all the iconic Westie beaches: Whatipu, Karekare, Piha and, Sir Ed's favourite, remote Anawhata. From here you can continue up the coast through Te Henga to Muriwai or head through bush to the Cascades Kauri area to end at Swanson train station.

Other noted walks in the park include the **Kitekite Track** (1.8km, 30 minutes one way), the **Fairy Falls Track** (5.6km, 2½-hour loop) and the **Auckland City Walk** (1.5km, one-hour loop).

Rain Forest Express   NARROW-GAUGE RAILWAY
(☎09-302 8028; www.watercare.co.nz; 280 Scenic Dr; 2.5hr trip adult/child $25/12) Departs from Jacobsons' Depot and follows an old logging track through several tunnels deep into the bush. You'll need to book well ahead; check the website for the schedule. Less regular are the 3½-hour twilight trips (adult/child $28/14), offering glimpses of glowworms and cave weta.

Waitakere Tramline
Society   NARROW-GAUGE RAILWAY
(☎09-818 4946; www.waitakeretramline.org.nz; adult/child $15/5) Runs four scenic trips every Sunday that pass through a glowworm tunnel en route to the Waitakere Falls and Dam. Trips start from the end of Christian Rd, which runs south of Swanson station.

HILLARY TRAIL *PETER HILLARY*

My family grew up loving Auckland's wild west coast, where the Tasman Sea pounds the black-sand beaches and black-back gulls ride the westerlies. Our family has walked and explored and lived out here for nearly a century and this is also where we came to grieve after my mother and sister were killed in 1975, where the invigorating salty air and the marvellous wild vistas to the Tasman Sea worked like a balm for our broken hearts. My father would come here to dream up and then prepare for new expeditionary challenges. It seemed the right sort of environment for someone like him: not a passive coastline, but active and exciting, with huge cliffs, crashing waves, thick bush and a tantalising far-away horizon.

Peter Hillary, mountaineer & explorer

AWOL Canyoning Adventures CANYONING
(09-834 0501; www.awoladventures.co.nz; half-/full day $145/175) Offers plenty of slippery, slidey, wet fun in Piha Canyon, including glowworm-illuminated night trips ($165); transfers from Auckland are included.

Canyonz CANYONING
(0800 422 696; www.canyonz.co.nz; trips $195) Runs canyoning trips from Auckland to the Blue Canyon, which has a series of 18 waterfalls ranging from 2m to 25m in height.

Karekare

Few stretches of sand have more personality than Karekare. Those prone to metaphysical musings inevitably settle on descriptions such as 'spiritual' and 'brooding'. Perhaps history has left its imprint: in 1825 it was the site of a ruthless massacre of the local Kawerau *iwi* by Ngapuhi invaders. Wild and gorgeously undeveloped, this famous beach has been the setting for onscreen moments both high- and lowbrow, from Oscar-winner *The Piano* to *Xena, Warrior Princess*.

From the car park the quickest route to the black-sand beach involves wading through a stream. Karekare rates as one of the most dangerous beaches in the country, with strong surf and ever-present rips, so don't even think about swimming unless the beach is being patrolled by lifeguards (usually only in summer). Pearl Jam singer Eddie Vedder nearly drowned here while visiting Neil Finn's Karekare pad.

Follow the road over the bridge and up along Lone Kauri Rd for 100m, where a short track leads to the pretty **Karekare Falls**. This leafy picnic spot is the start of several walking tracks.

Karekare has no shops of any description and no public transport. To get here take Scenic Dr and Piha Rd until you reach the well-signposted turn-off to Karekare Rd.

Piha

If you notice an Auckland surfer dude with a faraway look, chances are they're daydreaming about Piha... or just stoned. This beautifully rugged, iron-sand beach has long been a favourite for refugees from the city's stresses – whether for day trips, weekend teenage parties or family holidays.

Although Piha is popular, it's also incredibly dangerous, with wild surf and strong undercurrents; so much so that it's spawned its own popular reality TV show, *Piha Rescue*. If you don't want to inadvertently star in it, always swim between the flags, where lifeguards can provide help if you get into trouble.

Piha may be bigger and more populated than Karekare, but there's still no supermarket, liquor shop, bank or petrol station, although there is a small general store that doubles as a cafe, takeaway shop and post office.

Sights & Activities

The view of the coast as you drive down Piha Rd is spectacular. Perched on its haunches near the centre of the beach is **Lion Rock** (101m), whose 'mane' glows golden in the evening light. It's actually the eroded core of an ancient volcano and a Maori *pa* site. A path at the south end of the beach takes you to some great lookouts. At low tide you can walk south along the beach and watch the surf shooting through a ravine in another large rock known as the **Camel**. A little further along, the waves crash through the **Gap** and form a safe swimming hole. A small colony of blue penguins nests at the beach's north end.

For surfboard hire, refer to the Piha Store and Piha Surf Shop listings.

🛏 Sleeping & Eating

TOP CHOICE **Piha Beachstay – Jandal Palace**   HOSTEL **$**
(📞09-812 8381; www.pihabeachstay.co.nz; 38 Glenesk Rd; dm $33, r $86-120; @🛜) Attractive and ecofriendly, just like the surf lifesaver who runs it, this wood-and-glass lodge has extremely smart facilities. It's 1km from the beach but there's a little stream at the bottom of the property and bushwalks nearby. In winter an open fire warms the large communal lounge.

Black Sands Lodge   APARTMENT **$$**
(📞021 969 924; www.pihabeach.co.nz/Black-Sands -Lodge.htm; Beach Valley Rd; cabin $130, apt $180-220; 🛜) These two modern conjoined apartments with private decks match their prime location with attractive touches such as stereos and DVD players. The cabin is kitted out in a 1950s Kiwiana bach style and shares a bathroom with the main house. Bikes and wi-fi are free for guests, and in-room massage and lavish dinners can be arranged on request. It's gay-friendly too.

Piha Domain Motor Camp   CAMPSITE **$**
(📞09-812 8815; www.pihabeach.co.nz; 21 Seaview Rd; sites from $15, s/d cabin $50/60; 🛜) Smack-bang on the beach, this well-kept campsite is great for those seeking an old-fashioned, cheap-as-chips, no-frills, family holiday. To keep unruly teens at bay, under 20s must be accompanied by parents. The cabins are tiny.

Piha Surf Accommodation   CABIN **$**
(📞09-812 8723; www.pihasurf.co.nz; 122 Seaview Rd; caravans & cabins $60-90) Each basic but charmingly tatty caravan has its own linen, TV, fridge, cooker and long-drop toilet, and they share a very simple shower. The private cabins have the same rudimentary bathroom arrangement but are a more comfortable option.

🍴 Piha Cafe   CAFE **$$**
(www.thepihacafe.co.nz; 20 Seaview Rd; mains $13-23; ⊘9am-4pm Wed & Thu, 9am-7pm Fri-Sun)

Big-city standards mesh seamlessly with sand-between-toes informality at this attractive ecofriendly cafe. Cooked breakfasts and crispy pizzas provide sustenance for a hard day's surfing – then afterwards, head back here for a cold beverage on the deck.

Piha Store   BAKERY **$**
(www.pihastore.co.nz; Seaview Rd; snacks $2-10) Call in for pies and other baked goods, groceries and ice creams. The attached Lion Rock Surf Shop rents surfboards (two hours/half-day/day $15/25/35) and body boards ($10/20/25).

🛍 Shopping

West Coast Gallery   ARTS & CRAFTS
(www.westcoastgallery.co.nz; Seaview Rd; ⊘10am-5pm Wed-Sun) The work of more than 180 local artists is sold from this small not-for-profit gallery next to the Piha fire station.

Piha Surf Shop   OUTDOOR EQUIPMENT
(www.pihasurf.co.nz; 122 Seaview Rd; ⊘8am-5pm) A family-run venture, with well-known surfboard designer Mike Jolly selling his wares and wife Pam selling a small range of crafts. Surfboards (three hours/day $25/35), wet suits ($8/15) and boogie boards ($15/25) can be hired and private surfing lessons can be arranged.

❶ Getting There & Away

There's no public transport to Piha, but **NZ Surf'n'Snow Tours** (📞09-828 0426; www. newzealandsurftours.com; one way $25, return trip incl surfing gear $99) provides shuttles when the surf's up.

Te Henga (Bethells Beach)

Breathtaking Bethells Beach is reached by taking Te Henga Rd at the northern end of Scenic Dr. It's another raw, black-sand beach with surf, windswept dunes and walks, such as the popular one over giant sand dunes to Lake Wainamu (starting near the bridge on the approach to the beach).

Kumeu & Around

West Auckland's main wine-producing area still has some vineyards owned by the original Croatian families who kick-started NZ's wine industry. The fancy eateries that have mushroomed in recent years have done little to dint the relaxed farmland feel to the region, but everything to encourage an afternoon's indulgence on the way back from the beach or the hot pools. And unlike Waiheke Island, most cellars here offer free tastings.

✕ Eating & Drinking

Tasting Room   TAPAS $$
(☏09-412 6454; www.thetastingshed.com; 609 SH16; dishes $5-24; ⊙4-9pm Wed & Thu, noon-10pm Fri-Sun) Complementing its rural aspect with rustic chic decor, this slick eatery conjures up delicious dishes designed to be shared. It's not exactly tapas as the menu strays from Spain, appropriating flavours from Asia, the Middle East, Croatia, Serbia, Italy and France.

Dante's   PIZZERIA $$
(www.dantespizza.co.nz; 316 Main Rd, Huapai; pizza $16-24; ⊙from 3.30pm Wed-Sun; ☞) Widely regarded as Auckland's best pizzeria, this tiny takeaway is the only one in NZ to carry an official accreditation with the True Neapolitan Pizza Association.

🐝 Bees Online   CAFE $$
(☏09-411 7953; www.beesonline.co.nz; 791 SH16, Waimauku; mains $19-32; ⊙10am-5pm Wed-Sun) At this architecturally impressive facility you can watch the busy bees at work, safely behind glass, and then taste the results in the store. The cafe showcases honey and native bush ingredients. Mum and dad might even get a coffee in peace while the kids play spot-the-queen in the hive.

Soljans Estate   WINERY
(www.soljans.co.nz; 366 SH16; mains $19-33; ⊙tastings 9am-5.30pm, cafe 9.30am-3pm) One of the pioneering Croat-Kiwi family vineyards, Soljans has a wonderful (albeit atmosphere-deficient) cafe offering brunch, Dalmatian-style squid and Vintner's platters crammed with Mediterranean treats.

Hallertau   BREWERY
(☏09-412 5555; www.hallertau.co.nz; 1171 Coatesville-Riverhead Hwy, Riverhead; mains $22-37; ⊙11am-midnight) If you'd rather hit the hops than Kumeu's wines, Hallertau offers tasting paddles of five of its microbrews ($14), served on a vine-covered terrace edging the restaurant.

Riverhead   PUB
(www.theriverhead.co.nz; cnr Queen & York Sts, Riverhead; mains $15-36; ⊙11am-late Mon-Sat, 9am-late Sun) A blissful terrace, shaded by oak trees and overlooking the river, makes this 1857 hotel a memorable drink stop, even if the menu doesn't quite live up to its gastropub ambitions. Make a day of it, with a boat cruise (p64) from the city to the pub's own jetty.

Kumeu River   WINERY
(www.kumeuriver.co.nz; 550 SH16; ⊙9am-5pm Mon-Fri, 11am-5pm Sat) Owned by the Brajkovich family, this winery produces one of NZ's best chardonnays, among other things.

Coopers Creek   WINERY
(www.cooperscreek.co.nz; 601 SH16, Huapai; ⊙10.30am-5.30pm) Buy a bottle, spread out a picnic in the attractive gardens and, from January to Easter, enjoy Sunday afternoon jazz sessions.

❶ Getting There & Away

From central Auckland, Kumeu is 25km up the Northwestern Motorway (SH16). Helensville-bound buses head here from Lower Albert St (adult/child $7.90/4.50, 50 minutes), but you'll really need a car or bike to get around.

Muriwai Beach

Yet another rugged black-sand surf beach, stretching 60km, Muriwai Beach's main claim to fame is the **Takapu Refuge gannet colony**, spread over the southern headland and outlying rock stacks. Viewing platforms get you close enough to watch (and smell) these fascinating seabirds. Every August hundreds of adult birds return to this spot to hook up with their regular partners and get busy – expect lots of outrageously cute neck-rubbing, bill-touching and general snuggling. The net result is a single chick per season; December and January are the best times to see the little fellas testing their wings before embarking on an impressive odyssey.

Nearby, a couple of short tracks will take you through beautiful native bush to a lookout that offers views along the length of the beach. Wild surf and treacherous rips mean that swimming is safe only when the beach is patrolled (and you must always swim between the flags). Apart from surfing, Muriwai Beach is a popular spot for hang gliding, parapunting, kiteboarding and horse riding. There are also tennis courts, a golf course and a cafe that doubles as a takeaway chippie.

THE GREAT GANNET OE

After honing their flying skills, young gannets get the ultimate chance to test them – a 2000km journey to Australia. They usually hang out there for several years before returning home, never to attempt the journey again. Once back in the homeland they spend a few years waiting for a piece of waterfront property to become available in the colony, before settling down with a regular partner to nest – returning to the same patch of dirt every year. In other words, they're your typical New Zealander on their OE (Overseas Experience). Why are they called Kiwis again?

Helensville

POP 2600

A smattering of heritage buildings, antique shops and cafes makes village-like Helensville a good whistle-stop for those taking SH16 north.

🏃 Activities

Parakai Springs　　　　THERMAL POOLS
(www.parakaisprings.co.nz; 150 Parkhurst Rd; adult/child $16/8; ⊙10am-9pm) Aucklanders bring their bored children to Parakai, 2km northwest of Helensville, on wet wintry days as a cheaper alternative to Waiwera. It has large thermally heated swimming pools, private spas ($8 per hour) and a couple of hydroslides.

**Woodhill Mountain
Bike Park**　　　　MOUNTAIN BIKING
(⌨027 278 0949; www.bikepark.co.nz; Restall Rd, Woodhill; adult/child $7/2, bike hire per hr $25-30; ⊙9am-4pm Thu-Tue, 10am-10pm Wed) Maintains many challenging tracks (including jumps and beams) within Woodhill Forest, 14km south of Helensville.

Tree Adventures　　　　ROPES COURSE
(⌨0800 827 926; www.treeadventures.co.nz; Restall Rd, Woodhill; 1/4/8/10 courses $16/34/38/40; ⊙9.30am-5.30pm) A set of high-ropes courses within Woodhill Forest, consisting of swinging logs, nets, balance beams, Tarzan swings and a flying fox.

4 Track Adventures　　　　QUAD BIKES
(⌨09-420 8104; www.4trackadventures.co.nz; Restall Rd, Woodhill; 1½/2½/3½hr tours $155/236/275) Rattle through Woodhill Forest (and along Muriwai Beach on the longer tours) on a quad bike. Pick up from Auckland is available at $50 per person.

🛏 Sleeping

Malolo House　　　　B&B $
(⌨09-420 7262; www.malolohouse.co.nz; 110 Commercial Rd; r $70-120) Housed in a beautifully refurbished kauri villa that served for a time as the town's hospital, Malolo offers a range of restful accommodation, including two luxury en-suite doubles and cheaper ones with shared bathrooms.

ℹ Information

Helensville Library (Commercial Rd; @)
Visitor Information Centre (⌨09-420 8060; www.helensville.co.nz; 87 Commercial Rd; ⊙10am-4pm Mon-Sat) Pick up free brochures detailing the *Helensville Heritage Trail* and *Helensville Riverside Walkway*.

ℹ Getting There & Away

Bus 60 heads from Lower Albert St (near Britomart) to Helensville ($10.30, 1½ hours).

NORTH AUCKLAND

The Auckland super-city sprawls 90km north of the CBD to just past the point where SH16 and SH1 converge at Wellsford. Beaches, regional parks, tramping trails, quaint villages, wine, kayaking and snorkelling are the main drawcards.

Long Bay Regional Park

The northernmost of Auckland's East Coast Bays, Long Bay is a popular family picnic and swimming spot, attracting over a million visitors a year. A three-hour-return coastal walk heads north from the sandy beach to the Okura River, taking in secluded Grannys Bay and Pohutukawa Bay (which attracts nude bathers).

Regular buses head to Long Bay from Albert St in the city (adult/child $6.80/4, one hour); the $10 day pass works out cheapest. If you're driving, leave the Northern Motorway at the Oteha Valley Rd exit, head towards Browns Bay and follow the signs.

Shakespear Regional Park

Shooting out eastward just before Orewa, the Whangaparaoa Peninsula is a heavily developed spit of land with a sizable South African expat community. At its tip is this gorgeous 376-hectare regional park, it's native wildlife protected by a 1.7km pest-proof fence.

Sheep, cows, peacocks and pukeko ramble over the grassy headland, while pohutukawa-lined **Te Haruhi Bay** provides great views of the gulf islands and the city. Walking tracks take between 40 minutes and two hours, exploring native forest, WWII gun embankments, Maori sites and lookouts. If you can't bear to leave, there's an idyllic beachfront **campsite** (☑09-301 0101; www.arc.govt.nz; adult/child $10/5) with flush toilets and cold showers.

It's possible to get here via a torturous two-hour bus trip from Albert St. The one-way fare is $10.30, so it's best to buy a $10 day pass. An alternative is to take the **360 Discovery** (☑0800 360 3472; www.360discovery. co.nz; adult/child $14/8.20) ferry service to **Gulf Harbour**, a Noddy-town development of matching townhouses, a marina, country club and golf course. Enquire at the ferry office about picking up a bus or taxi from here. Alternatively, walk or cycle the remaining 3km to the park. The ferry is a good option for cyclists wanting to skip the boring road trip out of Auckland; carry-on bikes are free.

Orewa

POP 7400

Locals have fears that Orewa is turning into NZ's equivalent of Queensland's Gold Coast, but until they start exporting retirees and replacing them with bikini-clad parking wardens that's unlikely to happen. It is, however, very built-up and high-rise apartment towers have begun to sprout.

◉ Sights & Activities

Orewa Beach BEACH
Orewa's 3km-long stretch of sand is its main drawcard. Being in the gulf, it's sheltered from the surf but is still patrolled by lifeguards in the peak season.

Alice Eaves Scenic Reserve FOREST
(Old North Rd) Ten hectares of native bush with labelled trees, a *pa* site, a lookout and easy short walks.

WHICH HIGHWAY?

From Auckland, the multilane Northern Motorway (SH1) bypasses Orewa and Waiwera on a **tolled section** (☑0800 40 20 20; www.tollroad.govt.nz; per car/motorbike $4/2). It will save you about 10 minutes, provided you pay online or by phone (in advance or within five days of your journey) rather than stopping to queue at the toll booths.

Between Christmas and New Year SH1 can be terribly gridlocked heading north between the toll road and Wellsford; SH16 through Kumeu and Helensville is a sensible alternative. The same is true if heading south in the first few days of the New Year.

Millennium Walkway WALKING
Starting from South Bridge this 8km route loops through various parks before returning along the beach; follow the blue route markers.

Snowplanet SNOW SPORTS
(www.snowplanet.co.nz; 91 Small Rd, Silverdale; day pass adult/child $59/39; ⊙10am-10pm Sat-Thu, 10am-midnight Fri) A winter wonderland that allows every day to be a snowy one, Snowplanet offers indoor skiing, tobogganing and snowboarding. It's just off SH1, 8km south of Orewa.

🛏 Sleeping

Waves APARTMENT $$$
(☑09-427 0888; www.waves.co.nz; cnr Hibiscus Coast Hwy & Kohu St; units $180-299; ⚛) Like a motel only much flasher, this complex offers spacious, self-contained apartments with double glazing and smart furnishings. The downstairs units have gardens and most have spa baths. Best of all, it's only a few metres from the beach.

Orewa Motor Lodge MOTEL $$
(☑09-426 4027; www.orewamotorlodge.co.nz; 290 Hibiscus Coast Hwy; units $155-195; ⚛) One of a string of motels that line Orewa's main road, this complex has scrupulously clean wooden units that are prettied up with hanging flower baskets. There's also a spa pool.

Orewa Beach Top 10 HOLIDAY PARK $
(☑09-426 5832; www.orewaholidaypark.co.nz; 265 Hibiscus Coast Hwy; sites from $19, units $57-142; ⚛) Taking up a large chunk of the beach's

south end, this well-kept park has excellent facilities but road noise can be a problem. The prefab 'tourist flats' even have art on the walls and bedside lamps.

Eating

Mozaik
CAFE $

(www.mozaik.co.nz; 350 Hibiscus Coast Hwy; mains $11-23; ⊘7am-5.30pm) Spilling out onto the pavement in the middle of the main drag, this licensed cafe offers an appealing array of counter food and a crowd-pleasing menu including pasta and burgers.

Asahi
JAPANESE

(6 Bakehouse Lane; mains $11-20; ⊘9am-3pm Mon, 9am-9pm Tue-Sat) A handy little option for a sushi fix, with excellent *bento* boxes ($21.50).

ℹ Information

Hibiscus Coast i-SITE (☑09-426 0076; www. orewabeach.co.nz; 214a Hibiscus Coast Hwy; ⊘9am-5pm Mon-Fri, 10am-4pm Sat & Sun)

ℹ Getting There & Away

Direct buses run between Orewa and Albert St in the city (adult/child $11/6.10, 1¼ hours), as well as Shakespear Regional Park (adult/child $3.40/2, 35 minutes) and Waiwera (adult/child $1.80/1, 10 minutes).

Waiwera

This pleasant river-mouth village has a great beach, but it's the *wai wera* (hot waters) that people come here for. Warm mineral water bubbles up from 1500m below the surface to fill the 19 pools of the **Waiwera Thermal Resort** (☑09-427 8800; www.waiwera.co.nz; 21 Main Rd; adult/child $26/15; ⊘9am-9pm). There's a movie pool, 10 big slides, barbecues, private tubs ($50) and a health spa. If you can't face driving afterwards, luxuriously appointed modern houses have been built nearby (doubles $250); enquire about indulgence packages.

Squeezed between the Waiwera and Puhoi Rivers, the exquisite 134-hectare **Wenderholm Regional Park** (☑accommodation 09-366 2000; www.arc.govt.nz; sites per adult/child $10/5, house $128-170) has a diverse ecology, abundant bird life, beaches and walks (30 minutes to 1½ hours). **Couldrey House** (adult/child $3/free; ⊘1-4pm Sat & Sun, daily Jan), the original homestead (1860s), is now a museum. The campsite provides only tap water and long-drop toilets, and the coun-

cil also rents two comfortable self-contained houses.

Bus 895 from Auckland's Albert St heads to Waiwera (adult/child $11/6.10, one hour) via Orewa.

Puhoi
POP 450

Forget dingy cafes and earnest poets – this quaint village is a slice of the real Bohemia. In 1863 around 200 immigrants from the present-day Czech Republic settled in what was then dense bush.

◉ Sights & Activities

Church of Sts Peter & Paul
CHURCH

(www.holyname.org.nz; Puhoi Rd) The village's pretty Catholic church dates from 1881 and has an interesting tabernacle painting (a copy of one in Bohemia), stained glass and statues.

Bohemian Museum
MUSEUM

(www.puhoihistoricalsociety.org.nz; Puhoi Rd; adult/child $3/free; ⊘1-4pm Sat & Sun, daily Christmas-Easter) Tells the story of the hardship and perseverance of the original Bohemian pioneers.

Puhoi River Canoe Hire
CANOEING

(☑09-422 0891; www.puhoirivercanoes.co.nz; 84 Puhoi Rd) Hires kayaks and Canadian canoes, either by the hour (kayak/canoe $25/50) or for an excellent 8km downstream journey from the village to Wenderholm Regional Park (single/double kayak $50/100, including return transport). Bookings are essential.

✗ Eating & Drinking

Puhoi Valley
CAFE $$

(www.puhoivalley.co.nz; 275 Ahuroa Rd; mains $13-22; ⊘10am-4pm) You'll find Puhoi Valley cheese in supermarkets nationwide but this blissful location is where it originates. It features heavily on the menu of their upmarket cheese-shop cafe, set alongside a lake, fountain and children's playground. In the summer there's music on the lawn.

Puhoi Hotel
PUB

(www.puhoipub.co.nz; cnr Saleyards & Puhoi Rds; ⊘10am-7pm) There's character and then some in this 1879 pub, with walls completely covered in old photos, animal heads and vintage household goods.

Puhoi Cottage   TEAHOUSE
(www.puhoicottage.co.nz; 50 Ahuroa Rd; ⊙10am-
4pm Thu-Tue) Drop in for a Devonshire cream
tea ($11).

❶ Getting There & Away

Puhoi is 1km west of SH1. The turn-off is 2km
past the Johnstone Hills tunnel.

Mahurangi & Scandrett Regional Parks

Straddling the head of Mahurangi Harbour,
Mahurangi Regional Park (☑09-366 2000;
www.arc.govt.nz; sites from $5, baches $106-
128) has three distinct fingers: Mahurangi
West, accessed from a turn-off 3km north
of Puhoi; Scott Point on the eastern side,
with road access 16km southeast of Warkworth; and isolated Mahurangi East, which
can only be reached by boat. This boaties'
paradise incorporates areas of coastal forest, *pa* sites and a historic homestead and
cemetery. Its sheltered beaches offer prime
sandy spots for a dip or picnic and there are
loop walks ranging from 1½ to 2½ hours.
Accommodation is available in four basic
campsites and four baches sleeping six to
eight.

On the way to Mahurangi West you'll pass
Zealandia Sculpture Garden (☑09-422
0099; www.zealandiasculpturegarden.co.nz; 138
Mahurangi West Rd; admission $10; ⊙by appoint-
ment Nov-Mar only), where the work of Terry
Stringer is showcased within impressive architecture and grounds.

On the ocean side of the Mahurangi Peninsula, **Scandrett Regional Park** (☑09-
366 2000; www.arc.govt.nz; bach $128) has a
sandy beach, walking tracks, patches of
regenerating forest, another historic homestead, more *pa* sites and great views towards
Kawau Island. Three baches (sleeping six to
eight) are available for rent.

Warkworth

POP 3300

River-hugging Warkworth makes a pleasant
pit stop, its dinky main street retaining a village atmosphere.

◉ Sights

Dome Forest   FOREST
(SH1) Two kilometres north of Warkworth,
a track leads through this regenerating for-

est to the Dome summit (336m). On a fine
day you can see the Sky Tower from a lookout near the top. The summit walk takes
about 1½ hours return, or you can continue
for a gruelling seven-hour one-way tramp
through the Totora Peak Scenic Reserve, ex-
iting on Govan Wilson Rd.

Sheepworld   FARM
(www.sheepworldfarm.co.nz; SH1; adult/child $15/8,
incl show $26/10; ⊙9am-5pm) The paddock of
florescent sheep says all you need to know
about this agricultural attraction, which offers farm experiences for little city slickers
(pony rides, lamb feeding) and the ubiquitous sheep and dog show, including a shear-
ing demonstration (showtimes 11am and
2pm).

Warkworth & District Museum   MUSEUM
(www.wwmuseum.orcon.net.nz; Tudor Collins Dr;
adult/child $8/2; ⊙9am-3pm) Pioneer-era de-
tritus is displayed at this small local museum. Of more interest is the surrounding
Parry Kauri Park, which harbours a couple
of giant kauri trees, including the 800-year-
old McKinney kauri (girth 7.6m).

FREE **Honey Centre**   STORE
(www.honeycentre.co.nz; cnr SH1 & Perry Rd;
⊙8.30am-5pm) About 5km south of Warkworth, the Honey Centre makes a diverting
pit stop, with its cafe, free honey tasting
and glass-fronted hives. The shop sells all
sorts of bee-related products, from candles
to mead.

🍴 Sleeping & Eating

Bridgehouse Lodge   MOTEL $$
(☑09-425 8351; www.bridgehouse.co.nz; 16 Eliza-
beth St; r $85-150; ⊙11am-late) Right by the riv-
er, this local institution has a mixed bag of
rooms – some newer and nicer than others.
The refurbished bar is downright swanky,
dishing up fancy pub grub including burg-
ers, pastas and pizzas (mains $15 to $30).

Ransom Wines   WINERY
(www.ransomwines.co.nz; Valerie Close; tasting with
purchase free, otherwise donation to Tawharanui
Open Sanctuary of $5; ⊙10am-5pm Tue-Sun) Well
signposted from SH1, about 3km south of
Warkworth, Ransom produces great food
wines and showcases them with matching
tapas ($17 for five) and tasting platters (per
person $17 to $19).

WORTH A TRIP

TE HANA TE AO MARAMA

You'll see the terraces of a lot of historic *pa* (fortified village) sites etched into hillsides all around NZ, but if you want to get an idea of how these fortified villages actually looked, take a guided tour of the re-created *pa* at **Te Hana Te Ao Marama** (www.tehana.co.nz; 307-308 SH1, Te Hana). Tours leave on the hour from 10am to 3pm daily (adult/child $25/13). The daytime tours can be combined with a *powhiri* (formal welcome) on to the very real *marae* (Maori temple) next door, with some packages including a meal and a cultural concert.

For the most atmospheric experience, take one of the Friday night *Starlight Tours* (adult/child $100/50, bus from Auckland $25 extra), where you'll be on the receiving end of a *powhiri*, have a meal within the *marae* complex and then proceed into the dramatically lit village for a guided tour and concert.

ℹ Information

Warkworth i-SITE (☑09-425 9081; www.warkworthnz.com; 1 Baxter St; ◷8.30am-5pm Mon-Fri, 9am-3pm Sat & Sun)

ℹ Getting There & Away

InterCity and Naked Bus services both pass through town, en route between Auckland and the Bay of Islands; see Northland's Getting There & Away section.

Matakana & Around

Matakana suffers from reverse alcoholism – the more wine gets poured into it, the more genteel it becomes. A decade ago it was a nondescript rural village with a handful of heritage buildings and an old-fashioned country pub. Now the locals watch bemused as Auckland's chattering classes idle away the hours in stylish wine bars and cafes. The most striking symbol of the transition is the fantastical **Matakana Cinemas** (☑09-422 9833; www.matakana cinemas.co.nz; 2 Matakana Valley Rd) complex, its domed roof reminiscent of an Ottoman bathhouse. The humble **Farmers Market** (www.matakanavillage.co.nz; ◷8am-1pm Sat) is held in its shadow – or should that be Farmers Upmarket?

The reason for this epicurean ecstasy is the success of the area's boutique wineries, which are developing a name for pinot gris, merlot, syrah and a host of obscure varietals. Local vineyards are detailed in the free *Matakana Coast Wine Country* (www.matakanacoast.com) and *Matakana Wine Trail* (www.matakanawine.com) brochures. Both are available from the Matakana Information Centre in the foyer of the cinema.

◉ Sights

Tawharanui Regional Park `TOP CHOICE` BEACH
(☑09-366 2000; www.arc.govt.nz; Takatu Rd) A partly unsealed road leads to this 588-hectare reserve at the end of a peninsula. This special place is an open sanctuary for native birds, protected by a pest-proof fence, while the northern coast is a marine park (bring a snorkel). There are plenty of walking tracks (1½ to four hours) but the main attraction is **Anchor Bay**, one of the region's finest white-sand beaches. Camping is allowed at a basic site near the beach (adult/child $10/5) and there's a six-person bach for hire ($128).

Omaha BEACH
The nearest swimming beach to Matakana, Omaha has a long stretch of white sand, good surf and plenty of ritzy holiday homes.

Brick Bay Sculpture Trail SCULPTURE PARK
(www.brickbaysculpture.co.nz; Arabella Lane, Snells Beach; adult/child $12/8; ◷10am-5pm) After taking an hour-long artistic ramble through the beautiful grounds of Brick Bay Wines, recuperate with a wine tasting at the architecturally impressive cafe.

`FREE` **Morris & James** STORE
(www.morrisandjames.co.nz; 48 Tongue Farm Rd; ◷9am-5pm) Watch the potters at work during the free daily tour (11.30am) or just call in to check out the colourful finished products and the courtyard cafe.

🛏 Sleeping

Sandspit Holiday Park PARK **$**
(☑09-425 8610; www.sandspitholidaypark.co.nz; 1334 Sandspit Rd; sites from $16, units $60-152; @ ?) A campsite masquerading as a pioneer village, this quirky place incorporates his-

toric buildings and faux shopfronts into its facilities. It's right by the water at Sandspit.

Matakana Country Lodge   B&B **$$$**
(📞09-422 3553; www.matakanacountry.co.nz; 149 Anderson Rd; r $275-375; 🛜🏊) It's only five minutes from Matakana by way of an unsealed road and a very long driveway, but this lodge offers tranquillity in bucketloads and expansive views over the countryside. The three guest rooms have the run of the entire villa, including the kitchen, pool and spa.

✗ Eating & Drinking

Plume   WINERY **$$**
(📞09-422 7915; www.plumerestaurant.co.nz; 49a Sharp Rd; mains $20-32; ⊘lunch Tue-Sun, dinner Fri & Sat) The best of the winery restaurants, Plume has rural views from its terrace and an adventurous menu that jumps from China to Spain by way of Thailand and India.

Vintry   WINE BAR
(📞09-423 0251; www.thevintry.co.nz; 2 Matakana Valley Rd; tastings from $8.50; ⊘10am-10pm) In the Matakana Cinemas complex, this wine bar serves as a one-stop cellar door for all the local producers.

Matakana House   PUB
(📞09-422 9770; 11 Matakana Valley Rd; ⊘3pm-late Mon-Fri, noon-late Sat & Sun) A real local pub, this 1903 wooden hotel has taxidermied animals everywhere, a beer garden out front and occasional live music and DJs. It's an affectation-free zone.

ℹ Information

Matakana Information Centre (📞09-422 7433; www.matakanainfo.org.nz; 2 Matakana Valley Rd; ⊘10am-1pm) In the foyer of the cinema complex.

ℹ Getting There & Away

Matakana village is a 10km drive northeast of Warkworth along Matakana Rd; there's no public transport. Ferries for Kawau Island leave from Sandspit, 8km east of Warkworth along Sandspit Rd.

Leigh
POP 390
Appealing little Leigh (www.leighbythesea.co.nz) has a picturesque harbour dotted with fishing boats, and a decent swimming beach at **Matheson Bay**. Longstanding **Goat Island Dive & Snorkel** (📞0800 348 369; www.goatislanddive.co.nz; 142a

Pakiri Rd; mask, snorkel & fin hire $18, dive trips incl equipment $100-260, PADI Open Water $600) offers PADI courses and boat dive trips in the Hauraki Gulf, throughout the year.

Apart from its proximity to Goat Island, the town's other claim to fame is the legendary **Leigh Sawmill** (📞09-422 6019; www.sawmillcafe.co.nz; 142 Pakiri Rd; mains $12-32; ⊘10am-late daily Jan–mid-Feb, noon-late Thu, 10am-late Fri-Sun mid-Feb–Dec), a spunky little pub and beer garden that's a regular stop on the summer rock circuit, sometimes attracting surprisingly big names. If you imbibe too much at the on-site **microbrewery** (⊘1.30-5pm Fri & Sat), there's accommodation inside the old sawmill shed, including basic backpacker rooms (from $25) and massive doubles with en suites (from $125). Alternatively, you can rent the Cosy Sawmill Family Cottage (from $300, sleeps 10).

Goat Island Marine Reserve

Only 3km from Leigh, this 547-hectare aquatic area was established in 1975 as the country's first marine reserve. In less than 40 years the sea has reverted to a giant aquarium, giving an impression of what the NZ coast must have been like before humans arrived. You only need step knee-deep into the water to see snapper (the big fish with blue dots and fins), blue maomao and stripy parore swimming around. There are dive areas all round Goat Island, which sits just offshore, or you can snorkel or dive directly from the beach.

Excellent interpretive panels explain the area's Maori significance (it was the landing place of one of the ancestral canoes) and provide pictures of the species you're likely to encounter. Colourful sponges, forests of seaweed, boarfish, crayfish and stingrays are common sights, and if you're very lucky you may see orcas and bottle-nosed dolphins. Visibility is claimed to be at least 10m, 75% of the time.

A **glass-bottomed boat** (📞09-422 6334; www.glassbottomboat.co.nz; adult/child $25/13) provides an opportunity to see the underwater life while staying dry. Trips last 45 minutes and run from the beach all year round, weather permitting; ring to check conditions and to book.

You can usually rent kayaks and snorkelling gear right from the beach. Snorkelling gear (from $15), wetsuits (from $18) and underwater cameras ($45) can also be hired at **Seafriends** (📞09-422 6212;

www.seafriends.org.nz; 7 Goat Island Rd; ⊙9am-7pm), further up the road, which also has saltwater aquariums and a cafe.

Pakiri

Blissful Pakiri Beach, 12km past Goat Island (4km of the road is unsealed), is an unspoilt expanse of white sand and rolling surf – a large chunk of which is protected as a regional park.

Right by the water, **Pakiri Beach Holiday Park** (✆09-422 6199; www.pakiriholidaypark. co.nz; 261 Pakiri River Rd; sites from $46, units $60-310) has a shop and tidy units of varying degrees of luxury in a secure setting under the shade of pohutukawas.

Just 6km on from Pakiri is **Pakiri Horse Riding** (✆09-422 6275; www.horseride-nz.co.nz; Rahuikiri Rd), which has more than 80 horses available for superb bush-and-beach rides, ranging from one hour ($65) to multiday 'safaris'. Accommodation is provided in basic but spectacularly situated beachside cabins (dorm/cabin $30/150) or in a comfortable four-bedroom house ($500) secluded among the dunes.

Bay of Islands & Northland

Best Places to Eat

» à Deco (p118)
» Acorn Bar & Bistro (p140)
» Bennetts (p113)
» Food at Wharepuke (p136)

Best Places
to Stay

» Kahoe Farms Hostel (p139)
» Endless Summer Lodge
(p145)
» Little Earth Lodge (p117)
» Tree House (p146)

Why Go?

For many New Zealanders, the phrase 'up north' conjures up sepia-toned images of family fun in the sun, pohutukawa in bloom and dolphins frolicking in pretty bays. From school playgrounds to work cafeterias, owning a bach (holiday house) 'up north' is a passport to popularity.

Beaches are the main drawcard and they're present in profusion. Visitors from more crowded countries are flummoxed to wander onto beaches without a scrap of development or another human being in sight. The west coast shelters the most spectacular remnants of the ancient kauri forests that once blanketed the top of the country. The remaining giant trees are an awe-inspiring sight and one of the nation's treasures.

It's not just natural attractions that are on offer: history hangs heavily here as well. The site of the earliest settlements of both Maori and Europeans, Northland is unquestionably the birthplace of the nation.

When to Go

The 'winterless north' boasts a subtropical climate, which is most noticeable from Kerikeri upwards. It averages seven rainy days per month in summer but 16 in winter. Temperatures are often a degree or two warmer than Auckland, especially on the east coast. Like all the nation's beach hotspots, Northland's beaches go crazy at New Year and remain busy throughout the January school holidays. Don't fret, as the long lazy days of summer usually continue into February and March. Even in winter the average highs hover around 16°C and the average lows around 7°C.

Bay of Islands & Northland Highlights

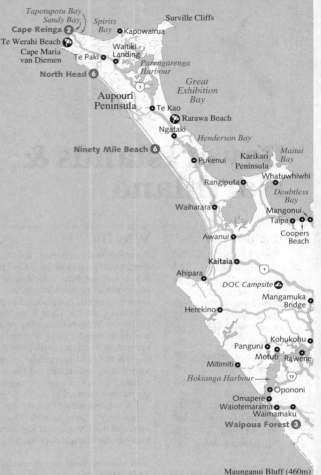

❶ Splashing about, body surfing, sunbathing and strolling at any of the abundant **beaches** on either coast

❷ Watching oceans collide while souls depart at **Cape Reinga** (p142)

❸ Paying homage to the ancient kauri giants of the **Waipoua Forest** (p149)

❹ Diving at one of the world's top spots, the **Poor Knights Islands** (p119)

❺ Frolicking with dolphins and claiming your own island paradise among the many in the **Bay of Islands** (p124)

❻ Surfing the sand dunes at **Ninety Mile Beach** (p142) or Hokianga's **North Head** (p146)

❼ Delving into history and culture at the **Waitangi Treaty Grounds** (p130)

Tapotupotu Bay
Sandy Bay
Cape Reinga ❷
Te Werahi Beach ❼
Cape Maria van Diemen
Te Paki
North Head ❻
Aupouri Peninsula
Spirits Bay
Surville Cliffs
Kapowairua
Waitiki Landing
Parengarenga Harbour
Great Exhibition Bay
Te Kao
Rarawa Beach ❼
Ngataki
Ninety Mile Beach ❻
Henderson Bay
Karikari Peninsula
Maitai Bay
Pukenui
Rangiputa
Whatuwhiwhi
Waiharara
Doubtless Bay
Mangonui
Taipa
Coopers Beach
Awanui
Kaitaia
Ahipara
DOC Campsite
Mangamuka Bridge
Herekino
Kohukohu
Panguru
Motuti
Rawene
Mitimiti
Omapere
Opononi
Hokianga Harbour
Waiotemarama
Waimamaku
Waipoua Forest ❸

Maunganui Bluff (460m)

TASMAN SEA

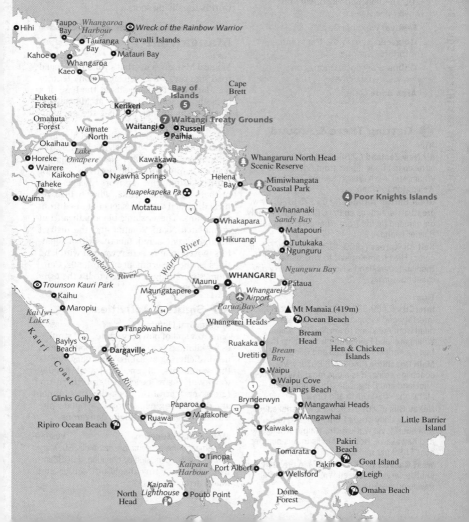

SOUTH
PACIFIC
OCEAN

Hihi
Taupo Bay
Whangaroa Harbour
Tauranga Bay
Wreck of the Rainbow Warrior
Cavalli Islands
Kahoe
Whangaroa
Matauri Bay
Kaeo
10
Puketi Forest
Omahuta Forest
Waimate North
Kerikeri
Bay of Islands
5
Cape Brett
Waitangi
7 Waitangi Treaty Grounds
Russell
Paihia
Okaihau
Lake Omapere
Horeke
Kawakawa
Wairere
Kaikohe
Ngawha Springs
Whangaruru North Head Scenic Reserve
Taheke
Helena Bay
Mimiwhangata Coastal Park
Waima
Ruapekapeka Pa
4 Poor Knights Islands
Motatau
1
Whananaki
Sandy Bay
Whakapara
Matapouri
Hikurangi
Tutukaka
Ngunguru
Mangakahia River
Wairua River
Ngunguru Bay
Trounson Kauri Park
Maunu
WHANGAREI
Pataua
Kaihu
Maungatapere
Whangarei Airport
Maropiu
Kai Iwi Lakes
14
Parua Bay
Tangowahine
▲ Mt Manaia (419m)
Whangarei Heads
Ocean Beach
Baylys Beach
12
Ruakaka
Bream Head
Dargaville
Uretiti
Bream Bay
Hen & Chicken Islands
Wairoa River
Waipu
Waipu Cove
Glinks Gully
Langs Beach
Paparoa
Brynderwyn
Mangawhai Heads
Ruawai
Matakohe
12
Mangawhai
Ripiro Ocean Beach
Kaiwaka
Little Barrier Island
Kauri Coast
Pakiri Beach
Tomarata
Tinopai
Pakiri
Goat Island
Kaipara Harbour
Port Albert
Wellsford
Leigh
North Head
Kaipara Lighthouse
Pouto Point
Dome Forest
Omaha Beach

0   50 km
0   30 miles

Getting There & Around

Air

Air New Zealand (✆0800 737 000; www.airnz.co.nz) Daily flights from Auckland to Whangarei, Kerikeri and Kaitaia, and from Wellington to Whangarei.

Great Barrier Airlines (✆09-275 9120; www.greatbarrierairlines.co.nz) Offers summer-only, on-demand flights from Whangarei to Great Barrier Island.

Salt Air Xpress (✆09-402 8338; www.saltair.co.nz) Flies from Kerikeri to Whangarei and then on to Auckland's North Shore, every day except Saturday.

Bus

InterCity (✆09-583 5780; www.intercity.co.nz) InterCity and associated Northliner services head from Auckland to Kerikeri via Waipu, Whangarei and Paihia; and from Paihia to Kaitaia via Kerikeri, Mangonui and Coopers Beach.

Main Coachline (✆09-278 8070; www.maincoachline.co.nz) Has a bus most days between Auckland and Dargaville (three hours) via Matakohe, Warkworth and Orewa.

Naked Bus (✆0900 625 33; www.nakedbus.com) Has daily buses from Auckland to Paihia (3¾ hours), via Warkworth, Waipu, Whangarei and Kawakawa. Note that calls to this number cost $1.99 per minute.

West Coaster (✆021 380 187) A privately run shuttle service between Whangarei and Dargaville on weekdays.

WHANGAREI DISTRICT

To truly experience this area you have to be prepared to get wet. Beach after clear-watered beach offers munificent opportunities for swimming, surfing, splashing about or just wading in the shallows. Consequently the hot spots heave with Kiwi holidaymakers at peak times, but even then it's possible to find isolated stretches of sand where your footprints are the only ones.

If you're reading this and you're a diving fanatic, drop everything and head to Tutukaka immediately. The neighbouring Poor Knights Islands are considered one of the world's top diving spots.

Mangawhai

POP 1670

Magical Mangawhai – that's what the official road sign says, and such signs don't tend to lie. Mangawhai Village sits at the base of a horseshoe harbour, but it's at Mangawhai Heads, 5km further on, that the enchantment really takes hold.

Various Maori tribes inhabited the area before the 1660s, when Ngati Whatua became dominant. In 1807 Ngati Whatua defeated Ngapuhi from the north in a major battle, letting the survivors escape. One of them was Hongi Hika, who in 1825 returned, armed with muskets obtained from Europeans. The ensuing bloodbath all but annihilated Ngati Whatua and the district became *tapu* (sacred, taboo). British squatters moved in and were rewarded with land titles by the government in the 1850s. Ceremonies were only performed to lift the *tapu* in the 1990s.

Sights & Activities

Mangawhai Heads BEACH
A narrow spit of powdery white sand stretches for kilometres to form the harbour's south head, sheltering a seabird sanctuary. Across the water sits an uncomplicated holiday town with a surf beach at its northern tip. Life-savers patrol on weekends in summer and daily during school holidays, but despite the rollers it's not especially dangerous.

Mangawhai Museum MUSEUM
(www.mangawhai-museum.org.nz; Moir St, Mangawhai Village; admission by donation; ⊙10.30am-1pm Sat) Has a tiny display of settler and Maori artefacts.

Mangawhai Cliff Top Walkway TRAMPING
Starting at Mangawhai Heads, this track
affords extensive views of sea and land. It
takes two to three hours, provided you time
it with a return down the beach at low tide.
This is part of Te Araroa, the national walking track.

🛏 Sleeping

Milestone Cottages COTTAGES $$
(☑09-431 4018; www.milestonecottages.co.nz; 27
Moir Pt Rd, Mangawhai Heads; cottages $125-260;
☒) A Pasifika paradise with lush tropical
gardens and five self-contained cottages
(sleeping up to five). At the time of research
the owners were planning to sell off the
front three cottages, including the pool;
check before booking.

🌿 Mangawhai Lodge B&B $$$
(☑09-431 5311; www.seaviewlodge.co.nz; 4 Heather
St, Mangawhai Heads; s $185, d $190-195, unit
$220-280; @🐾) The comfortable, smartly
furnished rooms have access to the picture-
perfect wraparound veranda at this boutique B&B, with a commanding position and
great views.

🍴 Eating

TOP CHOICE Bennetts CAFE $
(☑09-431 5072; www.bennettsofmangawhai.com;
52 Moir St, Mangawhai Village; mains $13-22; ⊙shop
9.30am-4pm, cafe breakfast & lunch, dinner season-
ally) Rural France comes to the village in the
form of this atmospheric chocolaterie, gelat-
eria and cafe, where you can sit by the fountain in the courtyard listening to Edith Piaf
while pigging out on delectable truffles and
sipping a glass of wine.

Sail Rock Cafe CAFE $
(12a Wood St, Mangawhai Heads; mains $13-32;
⊙9.30am-late) At the tail end of a day's surfing, this is the place to chat about the break
that got away over an ice-cold beer and a
serving of salt-and-pepper squid.

Smashed Pipi CAFE, BAR $
(www.smashedpipi.com; 40 Moir St, Mangawhai Village; mains $12-20) An eclectic combination,
with counter food and a blackboard menu
in the cafe, occasional live music in the bar,
and vibrant ceramics and glassware in the
neighbouring gallery.

Mangawhai Market MARKET $
(Moir St; ⊙9am-1pm Sat) Held in the library
hall in Mangawhai Village, this is a good
place to stock up on organic produce (including wine and olive oil) and peruse local craft.
Another market is held on Sunday mornings
in the Domain, Mangawhai Heads, from
mid-October to Easter.

ℹ Information

Visitor Information Centre (☑09-431 5090;
www.mangawhai.co.nz) It's only staffed sporadically (mainly on weekends and in high summer), but there are information boards outside.

Waipu & Bream Bay
POP 1491

Generations of Kiwi kids have giggled over
the name 'Waipu'; the makers of Imodium
missed a golden opportunity by failing to
adopt it as their product's brand name for
the NZ market. Be that as it may, Waipu and
neighbouring **Waipu Cove** are bonny wee
places.

MAORI NZ: NORTHLAND

Known to Maori as Te Tai Tokerau, this region has a long and proud Maori history and today has one of the country's highest percentages of Maori people. Along with East Cape,
it's a place where you might hear Maori being spoken. In mythology the region is known
as the tail of the fish of Maui.

Maori sites of particular significance include Cape Reinga, the Waitangi Treaty
Grounds, Ruapekapeka Pa Historic Reserve and, in the Waipoua Forest, Tane Mahuta.

Maori cultural experiences are offered by many local operators, including Footprints
Waipoua, Sandtrails Hokianga, Motuti Marae, Ahikaa Adventures, Sand Safaris, Terenga
Paraoa, Native Nature Tours, Taiamai Tours, Tiki Tours, Rewa's Village and Culture North.
Many businesses catering to travellers are owned or run by Maori individuals or *hapu*
(subtribal) groups. **Tai Tokerau Tourism** (www.taitokerau.co.nz) lists dozens of them on
its website.

The original 934 British settlers came from Scotland via Nova Scotia (Canada) between 1853 and 1860. These dour Scots at least had the good sense to eschew frigid Otago, where so many of their kindred settled, for sunnier northern climes. Their story comes to life through holograms, a short film and interactive displays at the **Waipu Museum** (36 The Centre; adult/child $8/3; ⊘9.30am-4.30pm; @).

Only 10% of current residents are direct descendants, but there's a big get-together on 1 January every year, when the **Highland Games** (www.waipugames.co.nz; adult/child $15/5), established in 1871, take place in Caledonian Park.

There are excellent walks in the area, including the **Waipu Coastal Trail**, which heads south from Waipu Cove to Langs Beach, passing the **Pancake Rocks** on the way. The 2km **Waipu Caves Walking Track** starts at Ormiston Rd and passes through farmland and a scenic reserve en route to a large cave containing glowworms and limestone formations; bring a torch, a compass and sturdy footwear to delve the depths.

Bream Bay has miles of blissfully deserted beach, blighted only slightly by a giant oil refinery at the north end. At **Uretiti**, a stretch of beach south of a **Department of Conservation (DOC) campsite** (www.doc.govt.nz; SH1; sites per adult/child $8/4) is unofficially considered 'clothing optional'. Over New Year the crowd is evenly split between Kiwi families, serious European nudists and gay guys.

🛏 Sleeping

Stonehouse GUESTHOUSE $
(☏09-432 0432; www.stonehousewaipu.co.nz; 641 Cove Rd; apt $80-220; 🛜) Nestled between the road to Waipu Cove and a saltwater lagoon, this unique Cornish-style house built of huge stone slabs offers three self-contained units decorated in bright, fresh colours. They range from the budget-orientated 'cutesy' (with a double sofa bed downstairs and six bunks above) to more comfortable rooms in the main house, which can be rented either individually or as a three-room apartment with a spacious living area.

Waipu Wanderers Backpackers HOSTEL $
(☏09-432 0532; waipu.wanderers@xtra.co.nz; 25 St Marys Rd; dm/s/d $30/45/66; 🛜) There are only three rooms at this bright and friendly backpackers in Waipu township – a real

home away from home – with free fruit in season.

Ruakaka Reserve Motor Camp HOLIDAY PARK $
(☏09-432 7590; www.motorcamp.co.nz; 21 Ruakaka Beach Rd; sites from $22, units $46-112; 🛜) Priced and positioned somewhere between a DOC campsite and a holiday park, this ginormous motor camp offers simple facilities on a grassy area fronting the beach and rivermouth at Ruakaka.

🍴 Eating

Cafe Deli CAFE $
(29 The Centre; mains $8-19; ⊘9am-4pm) Enticing salads, pasta, muffins and organic, fairtrade coffee are served at this attractive little cafe on the Waipu strip.

Pizza Barn ITALIAN $
(2 Cove Rd; mains $12-25; ⊘11.30am-late Wed-Sun Apr-Nov, daily Dec-Mar) In Waipu even the pizza place has a tartan logo (and a cool ladies' loo). Pizza Barn has popular platters, light fare and hunger-assuaging pizzas that go well with cold beer as this cool place morphs into a bar.

Beach House MODERN NZ $$
(891 Cove Rd; mains $20-35; ⊘5pm-late Wed-Sat, 9am-late Sun) Attached to the Waipu Cove Resort, this little restaurant offers hearty meals in a distinctive courtyard enclosed by *ponga* (tree fern) logs.

ℹ Information

Tourist brochures and internet access are available at the museum.

ℹ Getting There & Away

Waipu Cove can be reached by a particularly scenic route heading from Mangawhai Heads through Langs Beach. Otherwise turn off SH1 38km south of Whangarei.

InterCity (p112) and Naked Bus (p112) both operate bus services.

Whangarei

POP 52,200

Northland's only city is surrounded by natural beauty and its compact town centre offers plenty of rainy-day diversions. It's hardly NZ's most thrilling city but you may be pleasantly surprised by the thriving artistic community and the interesting selection of cafes and bars.

◉ Sights

TOWN BASIN

Whangarei's tourist centrepiece, this attractive riverside marina is home to museums, cafes, shops, interesting public art, an information centre and an ever-expanding fleet of flash yachts. It's a great place for a stroll, with a marked **Art Walk** and **Heritage Trail** to guide you on your way. An **artisans' market** is held on Saturdays from October to April under the shade of the spiky new canopy on the pedestrian bridge.

Whangarei Art Museum   GALLERY
(www.whangareiartmuseum.co.nz; The Hub, Town Basin; admission by donation; ◷10am-4pm) With its brand new home, accessed through the Hub information centre (p119), Whangarei's public gallery has an interesting permanent collection, the star of which is a 1904 portrait by Goldie.

Clapham's Clocks   MUSEUM
(www.claphamsclocks.com; Town Basin; adult/child $8/4; ◷9am-5pm) Far more interesting than it sounds, this collection of 1400 ticking, gonging and cuckoo-ing timepieces constitutes the National Clock Museum.

CITY CENTRE

FREE Old Library Arts Centre   GALLERY
(www.apt.org.nz; 7 Rust Ave; ◷10am-4pm Tue-Fri, 9am-noon Sat) Local artists are exhibited in this wonderful art deco building and a night market is held here on the last Friday of each month, selling art, craft, antiques and second-hand goods. Set between the old and new libraries is **Pou**, an intriguing sculpture consisting of 10 large poles carved with Maori, Polynesian, Celtic, Croatian and Korean motifs. Grab an interpretive pamphlet from the library.

FREE Botanica & Cafler Park   GARDENS
(First Ave & Water St; ◷10am-4pm) Native ferns, tropical plants and cacti are displayed in this little council-run fernery, set on the edge of cute Cafler Park. The park encloses the Waiarohia Stream and includes a rose garden and a scented garden.

SURROUNDS

FREE Abbey Caves   CAVES
(Abbey Caves Rd) The budget traveller's answer to Waitomo, Abbey Caves is an undeveloped network of three caverns full of glowworms and limestone formations, 4km east of town. Grab a torch, strong shoes and a mate (you wouldn't want to be stuck down here alone if things go pear-shaped) and prepare to get wet. The surrounding reserve is a forest of crazily shaped rock extrusions. If you're staying at neighbouring Little Earth Lodge, you can borrow helmets and hire head torches.

Kiwi North   MUSEUM, WILDLIFE
(www.kiwinorth.co.nz; 500 SH14, Maunu; adult/child $10/5; ◷10am-3pm) Five kilometres west of Whangarei, this complex includes a veritable village of 19th-century buildings and a museum displaying an impressive collection of Maori and colonial artefacts. A new gecko and kiwi house offers a rare chance to see the country's feathery fave in a darkened nocturnal house.

Native Bird Recovery Centre   WILDLIFE CENTRE
(www.whangareinativebirdrecovery.org.nz; 500 SH14, Maunu; admission free; ◷10.30am-4.30pm Mon-Fri) Next to Kiwi North, this avian hospital nurses sick and injured birds back to health. Say hi to the talking tuis.

Whangarei Falls   WATERFALL
(Otuihau; Ngunguru Rd) These 26m-high falls are the Kim Kardashian of NZ waterfalls – not the most impressive but reputedly the most photographed. Short walks provide views of the water cascading over the edge of an old basalt lava flow. The falls can be reached on the Tikipunga bus ($3, no service on Sundays), leaving from Rose St in the city.

SAH Reed Memorial Kauri Park   FOREST
(Whareora Rd) A grove of immense 500-year-old kauri trees has been preserved in this lush tract of native bush, where a cleverly designed boardwalk leads you effortlessly up into the canopy. To get here, head north on Bank St and turn right into Whareora Rd.

Quarry Gardens   GARDENS
(www.whangareiquarrygardens.org.nz; Russell Rd; admission by donation; ◷8am-5pm) Green-fingered volunteers have transformed this old quarry into a blissful park with a lake, waterfalls, pungent floral aromas, wild bits, orderly bits and lots of positive energy.

FREE Quarry Arts Centre   ARTS CENTRE
(www.quarryarts.org; 21 Selwyn Ave; ◷9.30am-4.30pm) An eccentric village of artists'

Whangarei

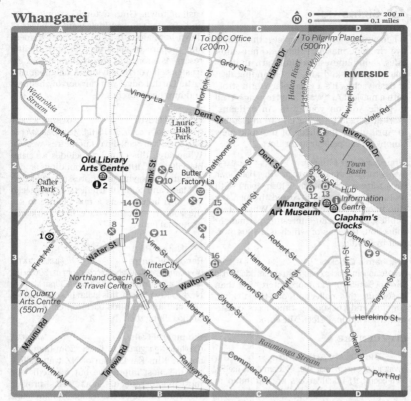

studios and co-operative galleries where you can often pick up well-priced art and craft. To get here, take Rust Ave, turn right into Western Hills Dr and then left into Russell Rd.

Activities

The free *Whangarei Walks* brochure, available from the i-SITE, has maps and detailed descriptions of some excellent local tracks. The **Hatea River Walk** follows the river from the Town Basin to the falls (three hours return). Longer tracks head through **Parihaka Reserve**, which is just east of the Hatea River and encompasses the remnants of a volcanic cone (241m) and a major *pa* (fortified village) site. The city is spread out for inspection from the lookout at the top, which is equally accessible by car. Other tracks head through **Coronation Scenic Reserve**, an expanse

of bush immediately west of the centre that includes two *pa* sites and abandoned quarries.

Skydive Ballistic Blondes SKYDIVING
(☎0800 695 867; www.skydiveballisticblondes. co.nz; 12,000ft tandem $340) Not only is this the oddest-named skydiving outfit in the country, it's also the only one licensed to land on the beach (Ocean Beach or Paihia).

Pacific Coast Kayaks KAYAKING
(☎09-436 1947; www.nzseakayaking.co.nz; kayak hire 2½/4/8hr $40/60/80, tours $40-120) Hires kayaks and offers a range of guided paddles to various locations in the vicinity and beyond.

Tours

Pupurangi Hire & Tour CULTURAL TOUR
(☎09-438 8117; www.hirentour.co.nz; Jetty 1, Riverside Dr; ⊙10.30am-5.30pm) Offers a suite of

Whangarei

hour-long tours of Whangarei, all with a Maori flavour, including *waka* (canoe) trips on the river ($35). It also hires kayaks (per hour $25), *waka* ($25), aquacycles ($17) and bikes ($15).

Terenga Paraoa　　　　　　CULTURAL TOUR
(☎09-430 3083; departs Town Basin; adult/child morning $55/30, afternoon $32/20; ◷9.30am & 1pm) Guided Maori cultural tours taking in Whangarei Harbour, Mt Manaia, the Kauri Park and, in the mornings, Parihaka *pa*. By the time you're reading this, *waka* (canoe) journeys should also be offered.

Tiki Tours　　　　　　　CULTURAL TOUR
(☎09-437 2955; Charmaine.tiki@xtra.co.nz; 2hr tour $35; ◷11am & 2pm Mon-Sat) Departing from the Hub, this well-priced tour takes in the Falls and Parihaka before heading to the Tikipunga Tavern for a traditional Maori meal.

🛏 Sleeping

TOP CHOICE Little Earth Lodge　　　HOSTEL $
(☎09-430 6562; www.littleearthlodge.co.nz; 85 Abbey Caves Rd; dm/s/d/tr $30/67/70/90; @🖅) Set on a farm 4km from town and right next to Abbey Caves, Little Earth's standards are so high that most other hostels look shabby in comparison. Forget dorm rooms crammed with nasty spongy bunks: settle down in a proper cosy bed with nice linen and a maximum of two roommates. Resident critters include miniature horses Tom and Jerry, and the lovable pooch Muttley.

Pilgrim Planet　　　　　GUESTHOUSE $$
(☎09-459 1099; www.pilgrimplanet.co.nz; 63 Hatea Dr; r $115-145; @🖅) Upmarket rooms open onto a shared kitchen and lounge, giving this smart place the sociability of a hostel but without the German teenagers living off rice and canned corn (not that there's anything wrong with that!).

Whangarei Views　　　　　　B&B $$
(☎09-437 6238; www.whangareiviews.co.nz; 5 Kensington Heights Rise; s/d $99/120, apt $169-229; @🖅) The name clearly articulates its prime proposition: views over the city and then some. Modern and peaceful, it has a self-contained two-bedroom flat downstairs and a B&B room in the main part of the house. To get here, follow the directions to Quarry Gardens. Kensington Heights Rise is off Russell Rd.

Lodge Bordeaux　　　　　　MOTEL $$$
(☎09-438 0404; www.lodgebordeaux.co.nz; 361 Western Hills Dr; apt $195-540; @🖅) Sitting somewhere between a super-schmick motel and an apartment hotel, Lodge Bordeaux has tasteful units with stellar kitchens and bathrooms (most with spa baths), private balconies and access to excellent wine. To get here, take Rust Ave and turn left into Western Hills Dr.

BK's Pohutukawa Lodge　　　　MOTEL $$
(☎09-430 8634; www.pohutukawalodge.co.nz; 362 Western Hills Dr; units $125-190; @🖅) Just west of town, this straightforward, nicely furnished motel has 14 units with well-kept facilities and ample parking. Thoughtful extras include plunger coffee and ironing equipment.

🏄 YHA Manaakitanga　　　　HOSTEL $
(☎09-438 8954; www.yha.co.nz; 52 Punga Grove Ave; dm/r $30/90; @🖅) This small hostel has

only a handful of rooms on a quiet hillside overlooking the river. It has a covered deck and barbecue area, and a short walk leads through the bush to glowworms. To get here, head east on Riverside Dr and look for Punga Grove Ave, heading uphill on the left.

Whangarei Top 10 HOLIDAY PARK $
(☑09-437 6856; www.whangareitop10.co.nz; 24 Mair St; sites from $20, units $67-253; @奈) This centrally located riverside holiday park has friendly owners, a better-than-average set of units and supershiny stainless-steel surfaces. Mair St is off Hatea Dr, north of the city centre.

✖ Eating

TOP CHOICE à Deco MODERN NZ $$$
(☑09-459 4957; 70 Kamo Rd; mains $37-39; ◷lunch Fri, dinner Tue-Sat) Northland's best restaurant offers an inventive menu that prominently features local produce, including plenty of seafood. Art deco fans will adore the setting – a wonderfully curvaceous marine-style villa with original fixtures. To get here, head north on Bank St and veer left into Kamo Rd.

Pimarn Thai THAI $$
(12 Rathbone St; mains $16-22; ◷lunch Mon-Sat, dinner daily; ✍) As gaudy as every good Thai restaurant should be (lots of gold and coloured glass), Pimarn has a lengthy menu featuring all of Thailand's blockbuster dishes, including a tasty pad thai.

Nectar CAFE $
(www.nectarcafe.co.nz; 88 Bank St; mains $10-18; ◷breakfast & lunch Mon-Sat) Nectar offers the winning combination of fair-trade coffee, generous serves from a menu full of Northland produce, friendly staff (some drawn from a youth development program) and urban views from the back windows.

Fresh CAFE $
(12 James St; mains $10-22; ◷7.30am-4pm Sat-Wed, 7.30am-7pm Thu & Fri) Fresh as a daisy, and with supersized flower photography on the walls, this chic cafe serves up great coffee and interesting breakfasts. It's open later for after-work drinkies on Thursday and Friday.

Mokaba CAFE $
(Town Basin; mains $8-18) The best of the Town Basin's cafes has outdoor tables overlooking the forest of yacht masts, and indoor seating

bleeding into a gallery. The usual cooked-breakfast suspects are on offer along with a fresh selection of counter food.

Stumpy's FISH & CHIPS $
(121 Riverside Dr; meals $4-20; ◷10am-7pm Mon-Thu, 10am-8pm Fri-Sun) A legendary chippie with a seafood basket ($14) that could leave you stumped.

Whangarei Growers' Market MARKET
(Water St; ◷6.30-10.30am Sat) Early birds get the best local produce at this long-standing farmers market.

🍷 Drinking & Entertainment

Brauhaus Frings BREWERY
(www.frings.co.nz; 104 Dent St; ◷10am-late) This popular microbrewery has a range of chemical-free beers, a terrace, board games and live music on Wednesday (jam night), Friday and every second Sunday. It's usually closed by 10pm earlier in the week but can push on to 3am.

Butterbank BAR
(www.butterfactory.co.nz; 84 Bank St; ◷4pm-late Tue-Sat) Occupying a converted bank building, this tapas and cocktail bar hosts live musicians on Fridays. As the hours dissolve, DJs kick in.

McMorrissey's IRISH PUB
(www.mcmorrisseys.co.nz; 7 Vine St; ◷noon-late) A better-than-average Irish pub with cosy old-world decor and live music (trad Irish, rock and jam sessions).

🛍 Shopping
See also Quarry Arts Centre (p115).

Tuatara ARTS & CRAFTS
(www.tuataradesignstore.co.nz; 29 Bank St) A primo spot for funky Maori and Pasifika design, art and craft.

Bach ARTS & CRAFTS
(www.thebach.org.nz; Town Basin) You'll often find well-priced gifts and souvenirs at this excellent co-op store representing over 100 Northland artisans.

Burning Issues ARTS & CRAFTS
(www.burningissuesgallery.co.nz; Town Basin; ◷10am-5pm) Exquisite high-end arty stuff, especially glasswear, ceramics and jewellery.

Market Books BOOKS
(www.marketbooks.co.nz; 85 Cameron St) Search the shelves for a rare collectable treasure or

grab something trashy and secondhand for the beach.

Classics GIFTS
(www.classics.net.nz; 41 Bank St) Interesting eclectica, from Rubik's cubes to literature.

Kathmandu OUTDOOR EQUIPMENT
(www.kathmandu.co.nz; 22 James St; ⊙9am-5.30pm Mon-Fri, 9am-4pm Sat, 10am-3pm Sun) A branch of the outdoor and travel supplies empire, selling everything from tents to plug adapters.

❶ Information

DOC Office (☑09-470 3300; www.doc.govt. nz; 149 Bank St; ⊙8.30am-4pm Mon-Fri)

Hub Information Centre (☑09-430 1188; Town Basin; ⊙9am-5.30pm; @☎) Branch of the i-SITE, in the foyer of the Art Museum.

Whangarei i-SITE (☑09-438 1079; www. whangareinz.com; 92 Otaika Rd (SH1); ⊙8.30am-5pm Mon-Fri, 9am-4pm Sat & Sun; @☎) Information, cafe, toilets and internet access.

❶ Getting There & Around

Air

Whangarei Airport (WRE; ☑09-436 0047; www.whangareiairport.co.nz; Handforth St) Whangarei Airport is at Onerahi, 6km southeast of the centre. Air New Zealand, Salt Air Xpress and Great Barrier Airlines flights (p112) all service Whangarei. Taxis into town cost around $25. A city bus stops 400m away on Church St ($3, 18 buses on weekdays, seven on Saturdays).

Bus

Bus services (p112) to Whangarei are run by InterCity, whose buses stop outside the **Northland Coach & Travel Centre** (☑09-438 3206; 3 Bank St; ⊙8am-5pm Mon-Fri, 8.30am-2.30pm Sat & Sun) and Naked Buses, whose buses stop at the Hub, in the Town Basin. West Coaster shuttles also service Whangarei.

Taxi
A1 Cabs (☑0800 438 3377)

Whangarei Heads

Whangarei Heads Rd winds 35km along the northern reaches of the harbour to its entrance, passing mangroves and picturesque pohutukawa-lined bays. Holiday homes, B&Bs and galleries are dotted around the water-hugging small settlements. There are great views from the top of **Mt Manaia** (419m), a sheer rock outcrop above McLeod Bay, but prepare for a lung- and leg-busting 1½-hour climb.

Bream Head caps off the craggy finger of land. A five-hour one-way walking track from **Urquharts Bay** to **Ocean Beach** passes through the **Bream Head Scenic Reserve** and lovely **Smugglers Bay** and **Peach Cove**.

Magnificent **Ocean Beach** stretches for miles on the other side of the headland. There's decent surfing to be had and lifeguards patrol the beach in summer. A detour from **Parua Bay** takes you to glorious **Pataua**, a small settlement that lies on a shallow inlet linked to a surf beach by a footbridge.

🛏 Sleeping & Eating

Kauri Villas B&B $$
(☑09-436 1797; www.kaurivillas.com; 73 Owhiwa Rd, Parua Bay; r $125-175; 🐾) Perched on a hill with views back over the harbour to Whangarei, this pretty blue-trimmed villa has an old world feel due in part to some very chintzy wallpaper. The decor's more restrained in the self-contained lodge and annex rooms.

Parua Bay Tavern PUB $$
(www.paruabaytavern.co.nz; 1034 Whangarei Heads Rd; meals $15-24; ⊙11.30am-late) A magical spot on a summer's day, this friendly pub is set on a thumb-shaped peninsula, with a sole pohutukawa blazing red against the green water. Grab a seat on the deck, a cold beverage and a decent pub meal.

Tutukaka Coast & the Poor Knights Islands

If Goat Island Marine Reserve whetted your appetite, diving at the Poor Knights is the feast followed by a wafer-thin mint that might cause your stomach to explode. Apart from the natural underwater scenery, two decommissioned navy ships have been sunk nearby for divers to explore.

Following the road northeast of Whangarei for 26km, you'll first come to the sweet village of **Ngunguru** near the mouth of a broad river. **Tutukaka** is 1km further on, its marina bustling with yachts, dive crews and game-fishing boats.

From Tutukaka the road heads slightly inland, popping out 10km later at the golden sands of **Matapouri**. A blissful 20-minute coastal walk leads from here to **Whale Bay**, fringed with giant pohutukawa trees.

MARINE RICHES AT THE POOR KNIGHTS

Established in 1981, this marine reserve is rated as one of the world's top-10 diving spots. The islands are bathed in a subtropical current from the Coral Sea, so varieties of tropical and subtropical fish not seen in other NZ waters can be observed here. The waters are clear, with no sediment or pollution problems. The 40m to 60m underwater cliffs drop steeply to the sandy bottom and are a labyrinth of archways, caves, tunnels and fissures that attract a wide variety of sponges and colourful underwater vegetation. Schooling fish, eels and rays are common (including manta rays in season).

The two main volcanic islands, Tawhiti Rahi and Aorangi, were home to the Ngai Wai tribe, but since a raiding-party massacre in the early 1800s the islands have been *tapu* (forbidden). Even today the public is barred from the islands, in order to protect their pristine environment. Not only do tuatara and Butler's shearwater breed here, but there are unique species of flora, such as the Poor Knights lily.

Continuing north from Matapouri, the wide expanse of **Sandy Bay**, one of Northland's premier surf beaches, comes into view. Long-boarding competitions are held here in summer. The road then loops back to join SH1 at Hikurangi. A branch leading off from this road doubles back north to the coast at **Whananaki**, where there are more glorious beaches and the **Otamure Bay DOC campsite** (☎09-433 8402; www.doc.govt.nz; sites per adult/child $8/4).

🏃 Activities

Dive trips leave from Tutukaka and cater for both first-timers and experts. There are some excellent walks along the coast. Pick up a copy of the *Tutukaka Coast Tracks & Walks* brochure from the Whangarei i-SITE (p119).

 Dive! Tutukaka   DIVING
(☎0800 288 882; www.diving.co.nz; Marina Rd; 2 dives with gear $249) Deservedly Tutukaka's main operator, Dive! has won an array of tourism, business and environmental awards. It offers a variety of dive courses and excursions, including a five-day PADI open-water course ($799). Perhaps the jewel in its crown is the much-raved-about Perfect Day Ocean Cruise ($149), which includes a commentary, lunch and snacks, snorkelling from a platform in the middle of the marine reserve, kayaking through caves and arches, paddleboarding, and sightings of dolphins (usually) and whales (occasionally). Cruises run from November to April, departing at 11am and returning at 4.15pm. In the off months, snorkellers can tag along on the dive boats.

Dive! Tutukaka has daily shuttles from Whangarei for its customers ($20).

Yukon Dive   DIVING
(☎09-434 4506; www.yukon.co.nz; 2 dives with full gear $235) An owner-operator offering dive trips for a maximum of 12 people at a time.

Tutukaka Surf Experience   SURFING
(☎09-434 4135; www.tutukakasurf.co.nz; Marina Rd; 2hr lesson $75) If you've got the bushy blond hair-do and baggy boardies but need credibility to pull off the look, these guys run regular surf lessons at 9am most days in summer and on the weekends otherwise, operating from whichever beach has the best beginner breaks that day. If you've already got the skills, you can buy or hire a board here (per day $45).

🛏 Sleeping

Lupton Lodge   B&B $$
(☎09-437 2989; www.luptonlodge.co.nz; 555 Ngunguru Rd; s $118-150, d $165-210; @🛜🏊) The rooms are spacious, luxurious and full of character in this historic homestead (1896), peacefully positioned in farmland halfway between Whangarei and Ngunguru. Wander the orchard, splash around the pool or shoot some snooker in the guest lounge.

Pacific Rendezvous   MOTEL $$
(☎09-434 3847; www.pacificrendezvous.co.nz; Motel Rd; apt $180-245) Perfectly situated for spectacular views on the south head of Tutukaka harbour, this is a great choice for families and small groups. Most of the units are 1960s duplexes with multiple bedrooms, but they're all individually owned and decorated. Some are smart and some are a little tired, but they're all kept shipshape by the friendly managers.

✖ Eating & Drinking

🗩 Schnappa Rock   CAFE, BAR $$

(www.schnapparock.co.nz; cnr Marina Rd & Marlin Pl; breakfast & lunch $10-22, dinner $26-35; ⊘breakfast, lunch & dinner) Filled with expectant divers in the morning and those capping off their Perfect Days in the evening, this cafe-restaurant-bar is often buzzing – not least because of the excellent coffee. Top NZ bands play on summer weekends.

Whangarei Deep Sea Anglers Club   PUB $

(www.sportfishing.co.nz; Tutukaka Marina; mains $9-23; ⊘from 4pm) The club plays host to the nicely named Moocha's, where standard eats (burgers, fish and chips, ham steaks) and a good children's menu mingle with mounted fish and garrulous locals.

Marina Pizzeria   PIZZERIA $$

(www.marinapizzeria.co.nz; Tutukaka Marina; pizzas $15-29; ⊘lunch & dinner Thu-Sun) Everything is homemade at this excellent takeaway joint and restaurant – the bread, the pasta, the pizza and the ice cream.

Russell Rd

The quickest route to Russell takes SH1 to Opua and then crosses by ferry. The old Russell Rd is a snaking scenic route that adds about half an hour to the trip.

The turn-off is easy to miss, 6km north of Hikurangi at Whakapara (look for the sign to Oakura). It's worth a stop after 13km at the Gallery & Cafe (www.galleryhelenabay. co.nz; mains $14-18; ⊘10am-5pm) high above Helena Bay for excellent organic fair-trade coffee, scrummy cake, amazing views and a gander at some interesting Kiwiana art and craft. Is there anything that corrugated iron can't do?

At Helena Bay an unsealed detour leads 8km to Mimiwhangata Coastal Park, a gorgeous part of the coastline with sand dunes, pohutukawa trees, jutting headlands and picturesque beaches. DOC manages a range of accommodation options in the reserve, including a well-appointed lodge (per week $512-2045 per week) and a simpler but comfortable cottage and beach house (per week $358-1534); each sleeps seven to eight people. Basic camping (per adult/child $8/4) is available at secluded Waikahoa Bay.

Back on Russell Rd, you'll find the Farm (☏09-433 6894; www.thefarm.co.nz; 3632 Russell Rd; sites from $13, dm/s $20/30, d $60-100), a rough-and-ready backpackers rambling through various buildings, including an old woolshed fitted out with a mirror ball. The rooms are basic and its popular with bikers during the summer holidays, but off-season it's a chilled-out rustic escape. Best of all, you can arrange a horse trek (2hr $50) or motorbike ride (1hr $60) through the 1000-acre working farm.

At an intersection shortly after the Farm, Russell Rd branches off to the left for an unsealed, winding section traversing the Ngaiotonga Scenic Reserve. Unless you're planning to explore the forest (there are two short walks: the 20-minute Kauri Grove Nature Walk and the 10-minute Twin Bole Kauri Walk), you're better off veering right onto the sealed Rawhiti Rd.

After 2.6km, a side road leads to the Whangaruru North Head Scenic Reserve, which has beaches, walking tracks and fine scenery. A loop route from DOC's Puriri Bay Campsite (☏09-433 6160; www. doc.govt.nz; sites per adult/child $7/4) leads up to a ridge, offering a remarkable coastal panorama.

If you want to head directly to Russell, continue along Rawhiti Rd for another 7km before veering left onto Manawaora Rd, which skirts a succession of tiny idyllic bays before reconnecting with Russell Rd.

Otherwise take a detour to isolated Rawhiti, a small Ngapuhi settlement where life still revolves around the *marae*. Rawhiti is the starting point for the tramp to Cape Brett, a tiring eight-hour, 16.3km walk to the top of the peninsula, where overnight stays are possible in DOC's Cape Brett Hut (dm $13). An access fee is charged for crossing private land (adult/child $30/15), which you can pay at the Paihia i-SITE (p133). Another option is to take a water taxi to Cape Brett lighthouse from Russell or Paihia and walk back.

A shorter one-hour walk leads through Maori land and the Whangamumu Scenic Reserve to Whangamumu Harbour. There are more than 40 ancient Maori sites on the peninsula and the remains of an unusual whaling station. A net fastened between the mainland and Net Rock was used to ensnare or slow down whales so the harpooners could get in an easy shot.

BAY OF ISLANDS

Undeniably pretty, the Bay of Islands ranks as one of NZ's top drawcards. The footage that made you want to come to NZ in the first place no doubt featured lingering shots of lazy, sun-filled days on a yacht floating atop these turquoise waters punctuated by around 150 undeveloped islands. The reality is that NZ has many beautiful spots and this bay, while wonderful, could be a teensy bit overhyped.

What sets it apart from the rest is its fascinating history and substantial tourist infrastructure. Paihia has one of the best selections of budget accommodation of anywhere in the country. After that the budget goes out the window as a bewildering array of boat trips clamour to wrestle money out of your wallet. There's no point coming here if you don't head out on the water, so be prepared to fork out.

The Bay of Islands is a place of enormous historical significance. Maori knew it as Pewhairangi and settled here early in their migrations. As the site of NZ's first permanent British settlement (at Russell), it is the birthplace of European colonisation. It was here that the Treaty of Waitangi was drawn up and first signed in 1840; the treaty remains the linchpin of race relations in NZ today.

 Activities

The Bay of Islands offers some fine subtropical diving, made even better by the sinking of the 113m navy frigate HMNZS *Canterbury* in Deep Water Cove near Cape Brett. Local operators also head to the wreck of the *Rainbow Warrior* off the Cavalli Islands, about an hour from Paihia by boat. Both offer a colourful feast of pink anemones, yellow sponges and abundant fish life.

There are plenty of opportunities for kayaking or sailing around the bay, either on a guided tour or by renting and going it alone. Cruises and dolphin-swimming are also available.

Dive North   DIVING
(☎09-402 5369; www.divenorth.co.nz; reef & wreck $220) Experienced operators based in Kerikeri but offering free pick-ups from Paihia. They cover all the local dive sites and offer PADI courses.

Paihia Dive   DIVING
(☎09-402 7551; www.divenz.com; Williams Rd, Paihia; reef & wreck $229) Offers combined reef and wreck trips to either the *Canterbury* or the *Rainbow Warrior*. Various PADI courses are available and gear can be hired.

Bay of Islands

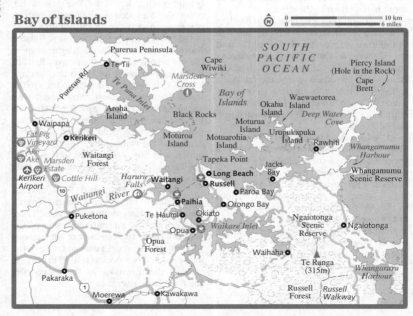

Dive Ops DIVING
(☑09-402 5454; www.diveops.co.nz; 2 dives incl equipment $230-280) Family-run diving operators, based out of Paihia.

**Island Kayaks &
Bay Beach Hire** KAYAKING, BOATING
(☑09-402 6078; www.baybeachhire.co.nz; Marsden Rd, Paihia; half-day kayaking tour $69; ☺9am-5.30pm) Hires kayaks (from $15 per hour), sailing catamarans ($50 first hour, $40 per additional), motor boats ($85 first hour, $25 per additional), mountain bikes ($35 per day), boogie boards ($25 per day), fishing rods ($10 per day), wetsuits and snorkelling gear (both $20 per day).

Coastal Kayakers KAYAKING
(☑0800 334 661; www.coastalkayakers.co.nz; Te Karuwha Pde, Paihia) Runs guided tours (half-/full day $75/95, minimum two people) and multiday adventures. Kayaks (per hour/half-/full day $15/40/50) and snorkelling gear (per day $15) can also be rented.

Skydive Zone SKYDIVING
(☑09-407 7057; www.skydivezoneboi.co.nz; Kerikeri Airport; tandem jump from 16,000/12,000/8000ft $395/325/265) At the time of research, this operator offered the highest tandem jump in the North Island and one of the most scenic.

Flying Kiwi Parasail PARASAILING
(☑09-402 6068; www.parasail-nz.co.nz; solo $99, tandem $89) Departs from both Paihia and Russell wharves for NZ's highest parasail (1200ft).

Great Escape Yacht Charters SAILING
(☑09-402 7143; www.greatescape.co.nz) Offers sailing lessons (two-day course $445) and yacht hire (per day $120 to $780).

Northland Paddleboarding PADDLEBOARDING
(☑027 777 1035; www.northlandpaddleboarding.co.nz; beginner lessons per hr $50) If you've been lured by all the talk of toning your tummy while blatting around on the water, these guys will get you standing up on a board and paddling around the bay in no time.

Horse Trek'n HORSE RIDING
(☑027 233 3490; www.horsetrekn.co.nz; 2hr ride $95) Offers treks through the Waitangi Forest.

Jet Ski Adventure Tours JET SKIING
(☑027 435 4497; www.jetskikayak.co.nz; Te Ti Bay, Paihia) While we must confess to finding jet skis incredibly annoying, they can be a really fun way of exploring the bay. These guys set

POU HERENGA TAI TWIN COAST CYCLE TRAIL

Eventually this cycle route will stretch from the Bay of Islands clear across the country to the Hokianga Harbour. OK, so that's only 84km, but as far as we're concerned that still gives you boasting rights when you get home. The final route will head from Opua to Kawakawa, Ngawha Springs, Kaikohe and finish up in Horeke.

At the time of research, the 13km section from **Kaikohe** to **Okaihau** had been completed, starting from a rest area immediately west of Kaikohe on SH12 and passing through an abandoned rail tunnel before skirting **Lake Omapere**. A 7km section from Kawakawa to Otiria has also opened, starting near the train station. For maps, tips and updates, visit www.nzcycletrail.com/twin-coast-cycle-trail-pou-herenga-tai.

themselves up on the beach during summer and take tours all the way out to the Hole in the Rock.

☞ Tours

Where do you start? First by praying for good weather, as torrential rain or choppy seas could literally put a dampener on some options. The Paihia i-SITE (p133) is extremely helpful and can book tours. Some of the hostels can arrange cheap deals and several of the main operators offer backpacker specials.

Boat

You can't leave the Bay of Islands without taking some sort of cruise, and there are plenty of vessels keen to get you onboard, including sailing boats, jetboats and large launches. Boats leave from either Paihia or Russell, calling into the other town as their first stop.

Of all the bay's islands, perhaps the most striking is **Piercy Island (Motukokako)** off Cape Brett, at the bay's eastern edge. This steep-walled rock fortress is rent by a vast natural arch – the famous **Hole in the Rock**. Provided the conditions are right, most boat tours will pass right through the heart of the island. En route it's likely you'll encounter

SWIMMING WITH DOLPHINS

Cruises offering the opportunity to interact with wild dolphins operate all year round and are one of the bay's big drawcards. They have a high success rate and you're generally offered a free trip if dolphins aren't sighted. Dolphin swims are subject to weather and sea conditions, with restrictions if calves are present.

It's totally up to the dolphins as to whether they chose to swim with you or not. There's no point timidly floating around the boat; you're more likely to attract cetacean attention if you're prepared to muck around, duck and dive, make dolphin noises and generally act like you're a good-time-human. You'll need to be a strong swimmer to keep abreast with them – even when they're humouring you by cruising along at half-speed.

Only three operators are licensed for dolphin-swimming: Explore NZ, Fullers and the yacht Carino. All pay a portion of the cost towards marine research, via DOC.

bottlenose and common dolphins, and you may see orcas, other whales and penguins.

The best way to explore the bay is under sail. In most cases you can either help crew the boat (no experience required), or just spend the afternoon island-hopping, sun-bathing, swimming, snorkelling, kayaking and fishing.

Explore NZ   CRUISES, SAILING
(☎09-402 8234; www.explorenz.co.nz; cnr Marsden & Williams Rds, Paihia) This was the first outfit to offer dolphin-swimming trips in the bay. Their Swim with the Dolphins Cruise (adult/child $89/45) is a four-hour trip departing at 8am and 12.30pm, with an additional $30 payable if you choose to swim. If you'd like to see dolphins but prefer to stay dry, the four-hour Discover the Bay Cruise (adult/child $95/48) departs at 9am and 1.30pm, heading to the Hole in the Rock and stopping at Urupukapuka Island. This cruise is combined with a trip to Kerikeri Basin in the seven-hour Day Discovery Cruise (adult/child $109/45).

Other options include a day sail on *Lion NZ* (adult/child $110/70), the 80ft maxi yacht used by the late Sir Peter Blake on two Whitbread round-the-world races and his winning Sydney-to-Hobart entry in 1984. If you've a taste for speed, Ocean Adventure (adult/child $95/48) is a 2½ hour blast on a rigid-hulled inflatable to the Hole in the Rock.

Fullers Great Sights   CRUISES
(☎0800 653 339; www.dolphincruises.co.nz; Paihia Wharf) The four-hour Dolphin Cruise (adult/child $95/48) departs daily at 9am and 1.30pm, actively seeking out dolphins and any other marine mammals en route to the Hole in the Rock, stopping at Urupukapuka Island on the way back.

You won't visit the Hole in the Rock on the four-hour Dolphin Eco Experience (adult/child $105/53, departs 8am and 12.30pm), rather the focus is finding pods of dolphins you can swim with.

The full-day Cream Trip (adult/child $109/55) follows the old supply and mail route around the whole of the bay and includes dolphin-swimming and boom-netting (where you can get close to the critters while being dragged through the water in a net).

A glamorous option for an overnight cruise is the launch **Ipipiri** (www.overnight cruise.co.nz; s/d $563/750). On this floating hotel the accommodation is by way of en-suite state rooms. All meals are included, and if you get sick of lazing around the bar on the sundeck, you can partake in kayaking, snorkelling or island walks.

R Tucker Thompson   SAILING
(☎09-402 8430; www.tucker.co.nz) There's sailing and then there's this... Run by a charitable trust with an education focus, the *Tucker* is a majestic tall ship offering day sails (adult/child $145/73, including a barbecue lunch) and late-afternoon cruises (adult/child $69/35). It also partners with the Historic Places Trust and DOC for special sailings. Talking like a pirate is optional.

Rock   OVERNIGHT CRUISE
(☎0800 762 527; www.rocktheboat.co.nz; dm/s/d $178/356/396) A former vehicle ferry that's now a floating hostel, the Rock has six-bed dorms, twin, double and family rooms, and (of course) a bar. The cruise departs at 5pm and includes a barbecue and seafood dinner with live music, then a full day spent island-hopping, fishing, kayaking, snorkelling and swimming.

Carino
SAILING, DOLPHIN-SWIMMING

(☑09-402 8040; www.sailingdolphins.co.nz; adult/child $114/69) This 50ft catamaran is the only yacht licensed for swimming with dolphins. A barbecue lunch is available for $6.

Ecocruz
SAILING

(☑0800 432 627; www.ecocruz.co.nz; dm/d $595/1350) A highly recommended three-day/two-night sailing cruise aboard the 72ft ocean-going yacht *Manawanui*, with an emphasis on the marine environment. Prices include accommodation, food, fishing, kayaking and snorkelling.

She's a Lady
SAILING

(☑0800 724 584; www.bay-of-islands.com; day sail $97) On the day sails you can try your hand at snorkelling or paddling about in a see-through-bottomed kayak. The operator also charters boats for longer trips and runs a sailing school.

Phantom
SAILING

(☑0800 224 421; www.yachtphantom.com; adult/child $110/60) A fast 50ft racing sloop, known for its wonderful food (10 people maximum, BYO allowed).

Gungha II
SAILING

(☑0800 478 900; www.bayofislandssailing.co.nz; day sail $90) A beautiful 65ft ocean yacht with a friendly crew; lunch included.

Mack Attack
JETBOATING

(☑0800 622 528; www.mackattack.co.nz; 9 Williams Rd, Paihia; adult/child $89/40) Fasten your seatbelt for a high-speed 1½-hour Hole in the Rock trip on board a jetboat – good fun and handy if you're short on time.

Bus

It's cheaper and quicker to take trips to Cape Reinga from Ahipara, Kaitaia or Doubtless Bay, but if you're short on time, several long day trips (10 to 12 hours) leave from the Bay of Islands. They all drive one way along Ninety Mile Beach, stopping to sandboard on the dunes.

Fullers (see opposite) runs regular bus tours and backpacker-oriented versions, both stopping at Puketi Forest. The standard, child-friendly version (adult/child $129/65) includes an optional lunch at Houhora (lunch $23). It also runs **Awesome NZ** (☑0800 653 339; www.awesomenz.com; tour $115) tours, with louder music, more time

sandboarding and stops to chuck a Frisbee around at Taputaputa Beach and devour fish and chips at Mangonui.

Explore NZ's Dune Rider (adult/child $145/110) also samples Mangonui's feted fish and chips and includes a stop at Gumdiggers Park.

Transport options to the Hokianga and Waipoua Forest are limited, so a day trip makes sense if you don't have your own car or if you're time starved. Fullers' Discover Hokianga (adult/child $105/61) takes in Tane Mahuta and Wairere Boulders in an eight-hour tour with local Maori guides.

Maori

Native Nature Tours
CULTURAL, TRAMPING

(☑0800 668 873; www.nativenaturetours.co.nz; 581 Tipene Rd, Motatau; day treks $185-195, overnight $375) A local couple formally welcome you to their *marae* (temple) and and lead you on treks into their ancestral lands, including visits to sacred sites and an introduction to Maori food and medicine. Overnight stays include a traditional *hangi* (earth-cooked meal) and glowworm spotting.

Taiamai Tours
Heritage Journeys
CULTURAL, CANOEING

(☑09-405 9990; www.taiamaitours.co.nz; 2½hr tour $135; ☉10am & 1pm Oct-Apr) For a hands-on experience of Maori culture, paddle a traditional 50ft carved *waka* from the Waitangi bridge to the Haruru Falls. The Ngapuhi hosts wear traditional garb and perform the proper *karakia* (incantations) and share stories.

Other

Salt Air
SCENIC FLIGHTS

(☑09-402 8338; www.saltair.co.nz; Marsden Rd, Paihia) Offers a range of scenic flights, including a five-hour light aircraft and 4WD tour to Cape Reinga and Ninety Mile Beach ($425) and helicopter flights out to the Hole in the Rock ($220).

Total Tours
FOOD & WINE

(☑0800 264 868; www.totaltours.co.nz) Head to the countryside around Kerikeri on a full-day Food, Wine and Craft tour ($99), half-day wine tour ($75) or an evening Wine & Dine tour ($120), departing from Paihia's Maritime Building.

WORTH A TRIP

HOLD ON UNTIL KAWAKAWA

Kawakawa is just an ordinary Kiwi town, located on SH1 south of Paihia, but the public toilets (60 Gillies St) are anything but. They were designed by Austrian-born artist and ecoarchitect Friedensreich Hundertwasser who lived near Kawakawa in an isolated house without electricity from 1973 until his death in 2000. The most photographed toilets in NZ are typical Hundertwasser – lots of wavy lines decorated with ceramic mosaics and brightly coloured bottles, and with grass and plants on the roof. Other examples of his work can be seen in Vienna and Osaka.

Kawakawa's other claim to fame is the railway line running through the centre of the main street, on which you can take a 45-minute spin pulled by **Gabriel the steam engine** (☑021 171 2697; www.bayofislandsvintagerailway.org.nz; adult/child $10/3; ⊗10.45am, noon, 1.15pm, 2.30pm Fri-Sun, daily school holidays).

South of town, a signpost from SH1 points to **Kawiti Glowworm Caves** (☑09-404 0583; 49 Waiomio Rd; adult/child $15/7.50; ⊗8.30am-4.30pm). Explore the insect-illuminated caverns with a 30-minute subterranean tour.

★★ Festivals & Events

Tall Ship Race   SPORTS
Held in Russell on the first Saturday after New Year's Day.

Waitangi Day   COMMEMORATION
Various ceremonial events at Waitangi on 6 February.

Country Rock Festival   MUSIC
(www.country-rock.co.nz; festival pass $50) Second weekend in May.

Russell Birdman   LUNACY
(www.russellbirdman.co.nz) Where a bunch of lunatics with flying contraptions jump off the wharf into the frigid (July) waters to the amusement of all.

Jazz & Blues Festival   MUSIC
(www.jazz-blues.co.nz; festival pass $50) Second weekend in August.

Weekend Coastal Classic   SPORTS
(www.coastalclassic.co.nz) NZ's largest yacht race, from Auckland to the Bay of Islands, held on Labour Weekend in October.

Russell

POP 820

Although it was once known prosaically as 'the hellhole of the Pacific', those coming to Russell for debauchery will be sadly disappointed: they've missed the orgies on the beach by 170 years. Instead they'll find a sweetly historic town that is a bastion of gift shops and B&Bs. In summer, you can often rent kayaks or dinghies from the water's edge along the Strand.

Before it was known as a hellhole, or even as Russell, it was Kororareka (Sweet Penguin), a fortified Ngapuhi village. In the early 19th century the tribe permitted it to become Aotearoa's first European settlement. It quickly became a magnet for rough elements such as fleeing convicts, whalers and drunken sailors. By the 1830s dozens of whaling ships at a time were anchored in the harbour. Charles Darwin described it in 1835 as full of 'the refuse of society'.

In 1830 the settlement was the scene of the so-called Girls' War, when two pairs of Maori women were vying for the attention of a whaling captain called Brind. A chance meeting between the rivals on the beach led to verbal abuse and fighting. This minor conflict quickly escalated as family members rallied around to avenge the insult and harm done to their respective relatives. Hundreds were killed and injured over a two-week period before missionaries managed to broker a peace agreement.

After the signing of the Treaty of Waitangi in 1840, Okiato (where the car ferry now leaves from) was the residence of the governor and the temporary capital. The capital was officially moved to Auckland in 1841 and Okiato, which was by then known as Russell, was eventually abandoned. The name Russell ultimately passed to Kororareka – a marginally better choice than Bruce or Barry.

⊙ Sights

Pompallier Mission   HISTORIC BUILDING
(www.pompallier.co.nz; The Strand; tours adult/child $10/free; ⊗10am-4pm) Built in 1842 to house the Catholic mission's printing press, this

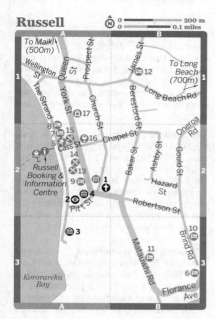

Russell

rammed earth building is the mission's last remaining building in the Western Pacific. A staggering 40,000 books were printed here in Maori. In the 1870s it was converted into a private home, but it has been restored to its original state, complete with tannery and printing workshop. On the excellent guided tour you get to play with the tools and learn how to 'skive off' and become a 'dab hand'.

ChristChurch   CHURCH
(Church St) Creationists may be surprised to learn that Charles Darwin made a donation towards the cost of the construction of this, the country's oldest church (1836). The biggest memorial in the graveyard commemorates Tamati Waka Nene, a powerful Ngapuhi chief from the Hokianga who sided against Hone Heke in the Northland War. If you look closely at the church's exterior, you'll see musket and cannonball holes dating from the 1845 battle.

Maiki   HILL
(Flagstaff Rd) Overlooking Russell, this is the hill where Hone Heke chopped down the flagpole four times. You can drive up but the view justifies a climb. Take the track west from the boat ramp along the beach at low tide, or up Wellington St otherwise.

Tapeka Point   LOOKOUT, BEACH
(www.tapeka.com) North of Russell, on the other side of Maiki hill, Tapeka Rd heads down to a quiet, sandy beach in the shadow of a craggy headland. A *pa* once stood at the top of the hill, and you need only follow the pathway to realise that the position was strategic as well as scenic, with views stretching to the far northern reaches of the Bay of Islands.

Long Beach   BEACH
(Long Beach Rd) About 1.5km behind Russell (an easy walk or cycle) is this placid, child-friendly beach. Turn left (facing the sea) to visit Donkey Bay, a small cove that is an unofficial nudist beach.

Russell Museum   MUSEUM
(www.russellmuseum.org.nz; 2 York St; adult/child $7.50/2; ⊙10am-4pm) This small, modern museum has a well-presented Maori section, a large 1:5-scale model of Captain Cook's *Endeavour* and a 10-minute video on the town's history.

Haratu
CULTURAL BUILDING

(www.kororarekanz.com; cnr The Strand & Pitt St; ⏰10am-5pm Tue-Sat Sep-Apr) Run by the local *marae* society, Haratu brings authentic Maori art and craft to the Russell waterfront, most of which is available for purchase. There are also audiovisual displays and information boards.

👉 Tours

Russell Mini Tours
MINIBUS

(☎0800 64 64 86; www.dolphincruises.co.nz; cnr The Strand & Cass St; adult/child $29/14; ⏰10am, 11am, 1pm, 2pm, 3pm & 4pm) Minibus tour with commentary.

🛌 Sleeping

Being a tourist trap, Russell has few decent midrange options. There are several tiny budget lodges, but you'll need to book ahead at busy times. If budget is not a consideration, Russell does luxury very well.

TOP CHOICE Wainui

HOSTEL $

(☎09-403 8278; www.pelnet.org/wainui; 92d Te Wahapu Rd; dm/r $27/64; ☎) Hard to find but well worth the effort, this modern bush retreat with direct beach access has only two rooms sharing a pleasant communal space. It's 5km from Russell on the way to the car ferry. Take Te Wahapu Rd and then turn right into Waiaruhe Way.

Arcadia Lodge
B&B $$$

(☎09-403 7756; www.arcadialodge.co.nz; 10 Florance Ave; d $195-310; ☎) The characterful rooms of this 1890 hillside house are decked out with interesting antiques and fine linen, while the breakfast is probably the best you'll eat in town – organic, delicious and complemented with spectacular views from the deck.

Commodore's Lodge
MOTEL $$$

(☎09-403 7899; www.commodoreslodgemotel.co.nz; 28 The Strand; units $200-295; ☎🏊) Being the envy of every passer-by makes up for the lack of privacy in the front apartments facing the waterfront promenade. Spacious, nicely presented units are the order of the day here, along with a small pool and free kayaks, dinghies and bikes.

Orongo Bay Homestead
LODGE $$$

(☎09-403 7527; www.thehomestead.co.nz; Aucks Rd; r $650; ☎) This wooden homestead (c 1860) was NZ's first American consulate, located a discreet 4km from Russell's rabble. Accommodation is by way of three stylishly plush rooms in the converted barn facing a chocolate-box lake. When one of the charming hosts is an acclaimed food critic, you can be assured that the breakfast will be memorable (dinners by arrangement).

HONE HEKE & THE NORTHLAND WAR

Just five years after he had been the first signatory to the treaty, Ngapuhi chief Hone Heke was so disaffected that he was planning to chop down Kororareka's flagstaff, a symbol of British authority, for the fourth time. Governor FitzRoy was determined not to let that happen and garrisoned the town with soldiers and marines.

On 11 March 1845 the Ngapuhi staged a diversionary siege of the town. It was a great tactical success, with Chief Kawiti attacking from the south and another party attacking from Long Beach. While the troops rushed off to protect the township, Hone Heke felled the Union Jack on Maiki (Flagstaff Hill) for the fourth and final time. The British were forced to evacuate to ships lying at anchor. The captain of the HMS *Hazard* was wounded severely in the battle and his replacement ordered the ships' cannons to be fired on the town; most of the buildings were razed. The first of the New Zealand Wars had begun.

In the months that followed, British troops (united with Hokianga-based Ngapuhi) fought Heke and Kawiti in several battles. During this time the modern *pa* (fortified village) was born, effectively the world's first sophisticated system of trench warfare. It's worth stopping at **Ruapekapeka Pa Historic Reserve** (Ruapekapeka Rd), off SH1 south of Kawakawa, to see how impressive these fortifications were. Here you can wander the site of the last battle of the Northland War, brought to life through detailed information boards. Eventually Heke, Kawiti and George Grey (the new governor) made their peace, with no side the clear winner.

Hananui Lodge & Apartments MOTEL **$$$**
(☑09-403 7875; www.hananui.co.nz; 4 York St; units $190-320; ☜) Choose between sparkling motel-style units in the trim waterside lodge or apartments in the newer block across the road. Pick of the bunch are the upstairs waterfront units with views straight over the beach.

Ferry Landing Backpackers HOSTEL **$**
(☑09-403 7985; www.ferrylandingrussell.co.nz; 395 Aucks Rd, Okiato Pt; dm/s/d $28/50/60; @☜) More like a homestay than a hostel, with only two rooms on offer within the owners' house. It sits on the hill directly above the ferry landing in Okiato – you'll need a car to stay here.

Duke of Marlborough HISTORIC HOTEL **$$**
(☑09-403 7829; www.theduke.co.nz; 35 The Strand; r $165-360; ☜) Holding NZ's oldest pub license, the Duke boasts about 'serving rascals and reprobates since 1827', although the building has burnt down twice since then. The upstairs accommodation ranges from small, bright rooms in a 1930s extension to snazzy, spacious doubles facing the water.

🏄 **Russell Top 10** HOLIDAY PARK **$**
(☑09-403 7826; www.russelltop10.co.nz; 1 James St; sites/units from $39/80; @☜) This leafy park has a small store, good facilities, wonderful hydrangeas, tidy cabins and nice units. Showers are clean, but metered.

Russell Motel MOTEL **$$**
(☑09-403 7854; www.motelrussell.co.nz; 16 Matauwhi Bay Rd; units $125-199; ☜▣) Sitting amid well-tended gardens, this old-fashioned motel offers a good range of units and a kidney-shaped pool that the kids will love. The studios are a little dark but you really can't quibble for this price in central Russell.

Pukeko Cottage HOSTEL **$**
(☑09-403 8498; www.pukekocottagebackpackers.co.nz; 14 Brind Rd; s/d $25/50; ☜) More like staying at a mate's place than a hostel, this homely house has just two bedrooms for rent and a caravan in the back garden. It's certainly not dirty, but the cleanliness is bloke-standard. Barry, the artist owner, is always up for a chat.

🍴 **Eating & Drinking**
For a country so hooked on cafe culture and a town so touristy, it's disappointing that Russell doesn't have more on offer.

Gables MODERN NZ **$$**
(☑09-403 7670; www.thegablesrestaurant.co.nz; 19 The Strand; mains $27-42) Serving an imaginative take on Kiwi classics (lamb, beef and lots of seafood), the Gables occupies an 1847 building on the waterfront, built using whale vertebrae for foundations. Ask for a table by the windows for watery views.

Duke of Marlborough PUB **$$**
(www.theduke.co.nz; 35 The Strand; lunch $18-29, dinner $24-40) There's no better spot in Russell to while away a few hours, glass in hand, than the Duke's sunny deck. Thankfully the upmarket pub grub matches the views.

Tuk Tuk THAI
(19 York St; mains $15-24; ⊙10.30am-11pm; 🍴) Thai fabrics adorn the tables and Thai favourites fill the menu. In clement weather grab a table out front and watch Russell's little world go by.

Pizza Port PIZZERIA **$**
(Cass St; pizza $11-20; ⊙lunch & dinner) There are a couple of tables, but you're better off grabbing one of the gourmet wood-fired pizzas and battling the seagulls at the beach.

Hone's PIZZERIA, BAR **$$**
(York St; pizza $19-27) Head out to the pebbled courtyard behind the Gables restaurant for wood-fired pizza, cold beer and a good vibe.

Pub 'round the Corner PUB
(www.pubroundthecorner.co.nz; 19 York St; ⊙noon-late) A cool, cosy tavern with a beer garden and pool tables.

🛍 **Shopping**
Just Imagine... ARTS & CRAFTS
(www.justimagine.co.nz; 25 York St; ⊙10am-5pm) Full of gorgeous glassware and paintings, this gallery also offers art junkies a caffeine fix.

ℹ **Information**
Russell Booking & Information Centre (☑09-403 8020; www.russellinfo.co.nz; Russell Pier; ⊙8am-5pm, later in summer)

ℹ **Getting There & Away**
The quickest way to reach Russell by car is via the car ferry (car/motorcycle/passenger $11/5.50/1), which runs every 10 minutes from Opua (5km from Paihia) to Okiato (8km from Russell), between 6.40am and 10pm. Buy your tickets on board. If you're travelling from the south, a scenic alternative is Russell Rd.

On foot, the quickest and easiest way to reach Russell is on one of the regular passenger ferries from Paihia (adult/child one way $7/3, return $12/5). They run from 7am to 7pm (until 10pm October to May), generally every 20 minutes but hourly in the evenings. Buy your tickets on board or at the i-SITE in Paihia.

Paihia & Waitangi

POP 1800

The birthplace of NZ (as opposed to Aotearoa), Waitangi inhabits a special, somewhat complex place in the national psyche – aptly demonstrated by the mixture of celebration, commemoration, protest and apathy that accompanies the nation's birthday (Waitangi Day, 6 February).

It was here that the long-neglected and much-contested Treaty of Waitangi was first signed between Maori chiefs and the British Crown, establishing British sovereignty or something a bit like it, depending on whether you're reading the English or Maori version of the document. If you're interested in coming to grips with NZ's history and race relations, this is the place to start.

Joined to Waitangi by a bridge, Paihia would be a fairly nondescript coastal town if it wasn't the main entry point to the Bay of Islands. If you're not on a tight budget, do yourself a favour, get on a ferry and get thee to Russell, which is far nicer.

There are some good walks in the area, including an easy 5km track that follows the coast from Opua to Paihia.

⊙ Sights & Activities

Waitangi Treaty Grounds HISTORIC SITE
(☏09-402 7437; www.waitangi.net.nz; 1 Tau Henare Dr; adult/child $25/12; ⊗9am-5pm Apr-Sep, 9am-7pm Oct-Mar) Occupying a headland draped in manicured lawns and native bush, this is the most significant site in NZ's history (and as such entry is free to NZ citizens upon presentation of a passport or drivers' license). It was here on 6 February 1840 that the first 43 Maori chiefs, after much discussion, signed the Treaty of Waitangi with the British Crown (eventually over 500 would sign it).

The **Treaty House** was built in 1832 as the four-room home of British resident James Busby. It's now preserved as a memorial and museum containing displays, which include a copy of the treaty. Just across the lawn, the magnificently detailed **whare runanga** (meeting house) was completed in 1940 to mark the centenary of the treaty.

Paihia

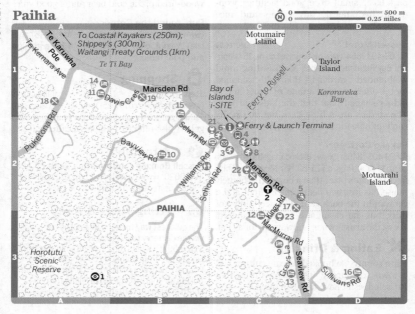

The fine carvings represent the major Maori tribes. Near the cove is the 35m **waka taua** (war canoe), which was also built for the centenary; a photographic exhibit details how it was fashioned from gigantic kauri logs.

The importance of the treaty is well understood by a NZ audience, but visitors might find it surprising that there's not more information displayed here about the role it has played in the nation's history: the long litany of breaches by the Crown, the wars and land confiscations that followed, and the protest movement that led to the current process of redress for historic injustices.

International visitors will get more out of what is already quite a pricy admission fee if they pay extra for a guided tour or cultural performance (adult/child $18/10 for each; check the website or call

for times). The 30-minute performance demonstrates traditional Maori song and dance, including that ultimate crowd-pleaser, the *haka* (war dance). The Ultimate Waitangi Experience (adult/child $30/15) is a combined ticket including a tour and a performance. In summer, a 45-minute twilight show (adult/child $25/8) is staged at 6pm.

Finally, the two-hour **Culture North Night Show** (%09-402 5990; www.culturenorth. co.nz; admission $65; h7.30pm when numbers allow) is a dramatisation of Maori history held in the *whare runanga*. It begins with a traditional Maori welcome and heads into an atmospheric theatrical performance accompanied by a sound-and-light show. Free transfers from Paihia are included in the price.

Haruru Falls   WATERFALL
(Haruru Falls Rd) A walking track (1½ hours one way, 5km) leads from the Treaty Grounds along the Waitangi River to these attractive horseshoe falls, which are lit up at night. Part of the path follows a boardwalk through the mangroves. Otherwise you can drive here, turning right off Puketona Rd onto Haruru Falls Rd.

St Paul's Church   CHURCH
(Marsden Rd) St Paul's isn't particularly old (1925), but it stands on the site of NZ's first church – a simple raupo (bulrush) hut constructed in 1823. It's an altogether charming building, built from Kawakawa stone. Look for the native birds in the stained glass above the altar – the kotare (kingfisher) represents Jesus (the king plus 'fisher of men'), while the tui (parson bird) and kereru (wood pigeon) portray the personalities of the Williams brothers (one scholarly, one forceful), who set up the mission station here.

Opua Forest   FOREST
Just behind Paihia, this regenerating forest has walking trails ranging from 10 minutes to five hours. A few large trees have escaped axe and fire, including some big kauri. If you walk up from School Rd for about 30 minutes, you'll find a couple of good lookouts. Pamphlets with details on all the Opua Forest walks are available from the i-SITE. You can drive into the forest by taking Oromahoe Rd west from Opua.

🛏 Sleeping

What makes Paihia such a desirable base for backpackers is the high standard and wide range of hostels. Kings Rd is the main 'backpackers' row'; if you can't find a bed in one of our favourite places (reviewed below), there are several other reputable places on this strip.

If your budget is more flexible, Russell has more atmosphere, but Paihia is more convenient and has a wider selection of motels, apartments and B&Bs lining the waterfront and scattered about the surrounding hills.

TOP CHOICE Seabeds   HOSTEL $

(☑09-402 5567; www.seabeds.co.nz; 46 Davis Cres; dm/s/d/apt $26/59/85/95; @🖎) Offering comfortable, friendly and quietly stylish budget digs in a converted motel, this newcomer has raised the already high bar on the Paihia scene. Of course, it helps that all the furnishings are brand new, but the little design touches suggest that it hasn't skimped on quality.

Tarlton's Lodge   B&B $$

(☑09-402 6711; www.tarltonslodge.co.nz; 11 Sullivans Rd; r $160-270; 🖎) Striking architecture combines with up-to-the-minute decor in this hilltop B&B with expansive bay views. Of the three luxurious suites in the main building, two have their own outdoor spa. The mid-priced rooms are in an older building across the lane, but they share the same aesthetic, pleasing panoramas and breakfast.

Peppertree Lodge   HOSTEL $

(☑09-402 6122; www.peppertree.co.nz; 15 Kings Rd; dm $25-28, r $69-86; @🖎) Simple, clean rooms with high ceilings and good linen. Plus there's a stash of bikes, racquets, kayaks and two barbecues for guests' use, making this a sociable choice.

Pickled Parrot   HOSTEL $

(☑09-402 6222; www.pickledparrot.co.nz; Greys Lane; sites per person $19, dm $26, s/d $60/70; @🖎) Surrounded by tropical plants, this friendly, well-maintained backpackers' stalwart has cute cabins, free bikes, free breakfast and a good vibe.

Baystay B&B   B&B $$

(☑09-402 7511; www.baystay.co.nz; 93a Yorke Rd, Haruru Falls; r $145-185; @🖎) Probably the only accommodation in NZ to have a Johnny Mnemonic pinball machine in the lounge room, this isn't your average B&B. Enjoy valley views from the spa pool of this slick, gay-friendly establishment. Yorke Rd is off Puketona Rd, just before you reach the falls.

Bay of Islands Holiday Park   HOLIDAY PARK $

(☑09-402 7646; www.bayofislandsholidaypark. co.nz; 678 Puketona Rd; site/unit from $38/70; @🖎🏊) Picturesquely placed under tall trees by a set of shallow rapids on the Waitangi River, 7km down Puketona Rd, this wonderful holiday park has excellent units and shady campsites.

Allegra House   B&B $$$

(☑09-402 7932; www.allegra.co.nz; 39 Bayview Rd; r/apt $245/275; @🖎) Offering astonishing views of the bay from an eyrie high above the township, Allegra has three handsome B&B rooms and a spacious self-contained apartment.

Cook's Lookout   MOTEL $$$

(☑09-402 7409; www.cookslookout.co.nz; Causeway Rd; apt $195-295; 🖎) Named after an All Black ex-owner rather than the good captain, Cook's is an old-fashioned motel with dated decor made creditable through a winning combination of friendly owners, breathtaking views and a solar-heated swimming pool. To get here, take Puketona Rd towards Haruru Falls, turn right into Yorke St and then take the second right into Causeway Rd.

Cap'n Bob's Beachhouse   HOSTEL $

(☑09-402 8668; www.capnbobs.co.nz; 44 Davis Cres; dm/s/tw/d $25/49/64/86; @🖎) The captain's out at sea but this small backpackers has a new first mate keeping things shipshape. Its a homely place, with sea views from the veranda and more than a touch of charm.

Te Haumi   HOMESTAY $$

(☑09-402 6818; joshlefi@xtra.co.nz; 41b Te Haumi Dr; s/d $145/165) At this proper homestay, you'll join Te Haumi's hospitable hosts for breakfast in the morning and wine and nibbles in the evening – yet once you're in your comfy downstairs room, you'll have all the privacy you'll need. The house backs on to a nature reserve and has bay views. Listen for kiwi at night. Te Haumi Dr heads inland from the main road, about halfway between Opua and Paihia.

Beachside Holiday Park   HOLIDAY PARK $
(☑09-402 7678; www.beachsideholiday.co.nz; 1290 SH11; sites/units from $18/60; @⚬) Wake up at the water's edge at this sheltered camping ground, south of the township. The angular lemon cabins have 1970s charm, and there are kayaks for hire.

Admiral's View Lodge   MOTEL $$
(☑09-402 6236; www.admiralsviewlodge.co.nz; 2 MacMurray Rd; apt $120-270; @) This hillside lodge offers natty units with balconies just begging for a relaxed sunset gin and tonic. Some have spa baths and bay views.

Swiss Chalet   MOTEL $$
(☑09-402 7615; www.swisschalet.co.nz; 3 Bayview Rd; units $175-380; ⚬) This motel has a spa, barbecue, Sky TV and a wide range of good clean rooms with balconies. There's a slight (Swiss) cheese factor but you can't accuse it of looking anonymous.

✗ Eating

TOP CHOICE **Shippey's**   FISH & CHIPS $
(www.shippeys.com; Waitangi Bridge; mains $6-12; ◷10am-late) Our favourite spot for a feed in Paihia is also one of the cheapest. Tuck into fresh fish and chips served as the good lord intended them – in newspaper with a cold beverage in hand – onboard a permanently moored 19th-century tall ship. The views over the inlet and bay are magical, particularly at sunset.

Waikokopu Cafe   CAFE $
(www.waikokopu.co.nz; Waitangi Treaty Grounds; mains $13-21; ◷9am-5pm) The setting is a cracking start – by a pond, backed by bush and overlooking the Treaty Grounds. The locale is matched by Kiwi icons on the menu: the ever popular 'fush and chups' and the Rainbow Warrior, 'French toast sunk in maple syrup, bacon and banana'.

Pure Tastes   MODERN NZ $$
(☑09-402 0003; www.puretastes.co.nz; 116 Marsden Rd; breakfast $16-19, mains $30-34; ◷breakfast, lunch & dinner) Occupying a small canvas-and-glass corner of the Paihia Beach Resort, this first-rate restaurant serves interesting, beautifully presented food using mainly Northland ingredients.

Alfresco's   PUB $$
(☑09-402 6797; 6 Marsden Rd; mains $23-32; ◷7.30am-late) It doesn't look like much but there's a reason why the locals flock to this casual restaurant/cafe/bar: great food (including plenty of local seafood), reasonable prices and a warm welcome being chief among them. Settle in for live music from 3pm to 6pm every Sunday afternoon.

Swiss Cafe & Grill   SWISS $$
(48 Marsden Rd; mains $20-32; ◷dinner) Unpretentious but excellent, this waterfront restaurant has a wide-ranging and eclectic menu, which includes pasta, nicely prepared fish dishes and Swiss comfort food such as schnitzel and homemade strudel.

Paihia Farmers' Market   MARKET
(www.bayofislandsfarmersmarket.org.nz; Village Green; ◷2-5.30pm) Stock up on local fruit, vegetables, pickles, preserves, honey, fish, smallgoods, eggs, cheese, bread, wine and oil, straight from the producer.

Countdown   SUPERMARKET
(6 Puketona Rd; ◷7am-10pm) The main place to stock up on provisions.

♟ Drinking

God bless backpackers: they certainly keep the bars buzzing. There are plenty of places along Kings Rd and in the town centre to explore, so don't feel hemmed in by our list.

Pipi Patch Bar   BAR
(18 Kings Rd; ◷5pm-late) The party hostel has the party bar: a popular spot with large video screens and a decent terrace. You'll be shuffled inside at midnight to keep the neighbours happy – although most of them are backpackers who'll be here anyway.

Mako Beach Bar   BAR
(50 Marsden Rd; ◷noon-late) If you get sick of hanging around with other travellers, head to this rough-edged locals' hang-out, where you might catch some live music on the weekends.

Bay of Islands Swordfish Club   BAR
(Swordy; www.swordfish.co.nz; upstairs, 96 Marsden Rd; ◷4pm-late) Great views, cold beer and tall tales abound at this brightly lit club bar where creatures from the deep protrude from every available surface.

❶ Information

Bay of Islands i-SITE (☑09-402 7345; www.visitnorthland.co.nz; Marsden Rd; ◷8am-5pm Mar–mid-Dec, 8am-7pm mid-Dec–Feb; @⚬) Information and internet access.

ℹ Getting There & Around

All buses serving Paihia, such as InterCity and Naked Bus, stop at the Maritime Building by the wharf.

The only buses heading to the west coast are Fullers' *Discover Hokianga* tour (p140) and the Paihia–Auckland leg of the **Magic Travellers Network** (☑09-358 5600; www.magicbus. co.nz) hop-on, hop-off service. The fare ($69, three buses weekly) includes unlimited stops and pick-ups anywhere along the route, including Opononi, Waipoua Forest, Dargaville and Matakohe. There are also tours (p125) to Cape Reinga and the Hokianga.

Ferries depart regularly for Russell.

For bikes, visit Bay Beach Hire (p123).

Urupukapuka Island

The largest of the bay's islands, Urupuka-puka is a tranquil place crisscrossed with walking trails and surrounded by aqua-marine waters. Native birds are plentiful thanks to a conservation initiative that has rendered this and all of the neighbour-ing islands predator-free; check that there aren't any rats, mice or ants stowing away on your boat or in your gear before leaving the mainland.

Most of the regular boat tours moor at Otehei Bay for a little island time; if you want to stay over, you can usually arrange to split the trip up and return at a later date. There are **DOC campsites** (www.doc.govt.nz; sites per adult/child $8.10/2) at Cable, Sunset and Urupukapuka Bays. They have water supplies, cold showers (except Sunset Bay) and composting toilets; bring food, a stove and fuel.

The **Waterfront Bar & Cafe** (www.otehei bay.co.nz; Otehei Bay; mains $15-24) serves light meals (hot chips, sandwiches, burgers, fish and chips) to passengers arriving on the boat tours, and in the height of summer also offers evening meals. Kayaks can be rented from **Bay of Islands Kayaking** (☑021 272 3353; www.bayofislandskayaking.co.nz; hire from $10, is-land transfer & guided paddle $120), based here.

Kerikeri

POP 5900

Kerikeri means 'dig dig', which is apt, as a lot of digging goes on in the fertile farm-land that surrounds the town. Famous for its oranges, Kerikeri also produces plenty of kiwifruit (don't call them kiwis unless you want to offend Kiwis), vegetables and, in-creasingly, wine. If you're looking for some back-breaking, poorly paid work that Kiwis (the people, as opposed to kiwifruit) aren't keen to do, your working holiday starts here.

A snapshot of early Maori and Pakeha (European New Zealander) interaction is offered by a cluster of historic sites centred on the picturesque river basin. In 1819 the powerful Ngapuhi chief Hongi Hika allowed Rev Samuel Marsden to start a mission un-der the shadow of his Kororipo Pa. There's an ongoing campaign to have the area recog-nised as a Unesco World Heritage Site.

⊙ Sights & Activities

Stone Store & Mission House HISTORIC BUILDINGS
(www.historic.org.nz; 246 Kerikeri Rd; ⊙10am-4pm) Sitting pretty at Kerikeri Basin, the country's most venerable architectural cou-pling represents the oldest of their kind in the country. Dating from 1836, the Stone Store is NZ's oldest stone building. It sells interesting gifts as well as the type of goods that used to be sold in the store – although these days you'll have a hard time bartering pigs for muskets. Tours ($10) of the wooden Mission House, NZ's oldest building (1822), depart from here and include entry to *The Soul Trade* exhibition on the 1st floor of the store.

Just up the hill is a marked historical walk, which leads to the site of **Kororipo Pa**. Huge war parties led by Hika once departed from here, terrorising much of the North Island and slaughtering thousands during the Musket Wars. The role of missionaries in arming Ngapuhi remains controversial. The walk emerges near the cute wooden **St James Anglican Church** (1878).

Rewa's Village MUSEUM
(Landing Rd; adult/child $5/1; ⊙9.30am-4.30pm) If you had a hard time imagining Kororipo Pa in its original state, take the footbridge across the river to this fascinating mock-up of a traditional Maori fishing village.

Aroha Island WILDLIFE RESERVE
(www.arohaisland.co.nz; 177 Rangitane Rd; admis-sion free; ⊙9.30am-5.30pm Thu-Tue) Reached via a permanent causeway through the man-groves, this 5-hectare island provides a haven for the North Island brown kiwi and other native birds, as well as a pleasant picnic spot

Kerikeri

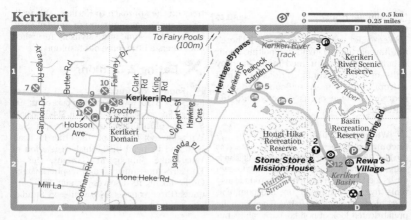

for their nonfeathered admirers. It has a visitor centre and kayaks for rent (from $18).

Kerikeri River Track WALKING
Starting from Kerikeri Basin, this 4km-long track leads past **Wharepuke Falls** and the **Fairy Pools** to the **Rainbow Falls**, where the sheet of water encloses a moss-covered cavern. Alternatively, you can reach the Rainbow Falls from Rainbow Falls Rd, in which case it's only a 10-minute walk.

🛏 Sleeping

Pagoda Lodge LODGE, CAMPSITE $
(☑09-407 8617; www.pagoda.co.nz; 81 Pa Rd; sites/safari tent from $32/100, apt $80-300; 🕸) Built in the 1930s by an oddball Scotsman with an Asian fetish, this lodge features pagoda-shaped roofs grafted onto wooden cottages. The property descends to the river and is dotted with Buddhas, gypsy caravans and safari tents with proper beds, or you can pitch your own. To get here, take Cobham Rd, turn left into Kerikeri Inlet Rd and then left into Pa Rd.

Kerikeri Farm Hostel HOSTEL $
(☑09-407 6989; www.farmhostel.co.nz; 1574 Springbank Rd (SH10); dm/s/d $24/50/56; @🕸) Less a farm, more an orange grove, this quiet rural house 4km out of town sleeps only 12. It's a homely place, with a sole chandelier adding a bit of bling to the cosy lounge.

Bed of Roses B&B $$$
(☑09-407 4666; www.bedofroses.co.nz; 165 Kerikeri Rd; r $225-350; @) It's all petals and no thorns at this stylish B&B, furnished with French antiques, luxe linens and comfy beds. The

Kerikeri

house has an art deco ambience and awesome views.

Aroha Island CAMPSITE $
(☑09-407 5243; www.arohaisland.co.nz; 177 Rangitane Rd; sites/units from $18/86) Kip among the kiwi on the eco island of love (aroha). There's a wide range of reasonably priced options, from the peaceful campsites with basic facilities by the shelly beach to a whole house. The entire island, indoors and out, is nonsmoking.

📝**Colonial House** MOTEL **$$**
(📞09-407 9106; www.colonialhousemotel.co.nz; 178 Kerikeri Rd; units $130-245; @🛜🖥) There's nothing particularly colonial-looking about it but this well-maintained motel has tidy units of various configurations set amid a tropical garden. A self-contained two-bedroom cottage opens directly onto the saltwater pool.

📝**Wharepuke Subtropical Accommodation** CABINS **$$**
(📞09-4078933;www.accommodation-bay-of-islands.co.nz; 190 Kerikeri Rd; cabins $180) Best known for its food and lush gardens, Wharepuke also rents five self-contained one-bedroom cottages hidden among the palms. They have the prefabricated look of holiday-park cabins but are a step up in terms of fixtures and space.

Kauri Park MOTEL **$$**
(📞09-407 7629; www.kauripark.co.nz; 512 Kerikeri Rd; units $130-170; @🛜🖥) Hidden behind tall trees on the approach to Kerikeri, this well-priced motel has a mixture of units of varying layouts – some quite stylishly furnished and others a little more old-fashioned.

✕ Eating & Drinking

📝**Food at Wharepuke** CAFE **$$**
(📞09-407 8936; www.foodatwharepuke.co.nz; 190 Kerikeri Rd; breakfast $14-16, lunch $14-35, dinner $26-35; ⏱10am-10pm Tue-Sat, 9am-3pm Sun) With one foot in Europe, the other in Thailand and its head in the lush vegetation of Wharepuke Subtropical Gardens, this is Kerikeri's most unusual and inspired eatery. On Friday nights it serves popular Thai banquets (three courses $45) while on Sunday afternoons it hosts live jazz.

Fishbone CAFE **$**
(88 Kerikeri Rd; mains $7-15; ⏱breakfast & lunch) Kerikeri's best brekkie spot serves excellent coffee and food. Dr Seuss fans should try the green (pesto) eggs and ham.

KERIKERI COTTAGE INDUSTRIES

You'd be forgiven for thinking that everyone in Kerikeri is involved in some small-scale artisanal enterprise or other, as the bombardment of craft shops on the way into town attests.

While Northland isn't known for its wine, a handful of vineyards near Kerikeri are doing their best to change that. The little-known red grape chambourcin has proved particularly suited to the region's subtropical humidity, along with pinotage and syrah.

Look out for the *Art & Craft Trail* and *Wine Trail* brochures for helpful maps and additional places to vist.

Kerikeri Farmers' Market (www.boifm.org.nz; Hobson Ave; ⏱8.30am-noon Sun) An excellent place to sample a range of what the region has to offer, from sausages to *limoncello*.

Get Fudged & Keriblue (www.getfudged.co.nz; 560 Kerikeri Rd; ⏱9am-5pm) An unusual pairing of ceramics and big, decadent slabs of fudge.

Makana Confections (www.makana.co.nz; 504 Kerikeri Rd; ⏱9am-5.30pm) If you're a recovering sugar junkie, you may need to drive into town with your eyes closed to avoid this boutique chocolate factory, where you can watch production through a window in the shop.

Marsden Estate (www.marsdenestate.co.nz; 56 Wiroa Rd; mains $19-22; ⏱10am-4pm) A lovely stop for tasting the area's best wine and eating lunch on the deck.

Ake Ake (www.akeakevineyard.co.nz; 165 Waimate North Rd; tastings $5, tour $5, mains $26-34; ⏱10am-6pm Tue-Sun summer, Wed-Sun winter) Offers vineyard tours (11.30am) and tastings, both of which are free if you order lunch or buy a bottle. The swanky restaurant is open for lunch and dinner on the days the cellar door is open.

Cottle Hill (www.cottlehill.co.nz; Cottle Hill Dr; tastings $5, free with purchase; ⏱10am-5pm Nov-Mar, 10am-5pm Wed-Sun Apr-Oct) Makes wine, port and grappa and has some interesting old cars kicking about.

Fat Pig Vineyard (www.fatpig.co.nz; 177 Puketotara Rd; ⏱11am-6pm) Wines and port.

PUKETI & OMAHUTA FORESTS

Inland from Kerikeri, the Puketi and Omahuta Forests form a continuous expanse of native rainforest. Logging in Puketi was stopped in 1951 to protect not only the remaining kauri but also the endangered kokako bird. Keep an eye out for this rare charmer (grey with a blue wattle) on your wanders.

The forests are reached by several entrances and contain a network of walking tracks varying in length from 15 minutes (the wheelchair-accessible Manginangina Kauri Walk) to two days (the challenging Waipapa River Track); see the DOC website for other walks.

You'll find a **DOC campsite** (☑09-407 0300; www.doc.govt.nz; Waiare Rd; sites per adult/child $7/3.50), two three-person cabins ($21) and a 18-bunk hut (exclusive use $62) at the Puketi Recreation Area on the forests' eastern fringe. The hut has hot showers, a kitchen and a flush toilet, while the cabins and campsite make do with cold showers.

Adventure Puketi (www.forestwalks.com; tours $75-155) leads guided eco-walks through the forest, including night-time tours to seek out the nocturnal wildlife.

BAY OF ISLANDS & NORTHLAND KERIKERI

Pear Tree
RESTAURANT, BAR **$$**
(☑09-407 8479; www.thepeartree.co.nz; 215 Kerikeri Rd; mains $18-33; ☺lunch & dinner) Kerikeri's best located and most upmarket restaurant occupies an old homestead right on the basin (book ahead for a table on the veranda). Mains run the gamut of bistro favourites, along with the occasional Asian dish.

Cafe Jerusalem
MIDDLE EASTERN **$$**
(Village Mall, Kerikeri Rd; mains $17-20; ☺11am-late) Northland's best falafels, served with a smile and a social vibe.

Cafe Blue
CAFE
(582 Kerikeri Rd; mains $8-20; ☺9am-3pm) It may be on the main road into town but this garden cafe is a peaceful oasis, serving sandwiches, salads, renowned Cornish pasties, pancakes and sub-$20 grills.

Cafe Zest
CAFE, BAR **$**
(73 Kerikeri Rd; mains $10-19; ☺7.30am-4pm Mon-Wed, 7.30am-8.30pm Thu-Sat, 7.30am-2pm Sun) Bathed in Kerikeri's orange glow, cute little Zest serves cafe fare during the day and tapas in the evening, but the main reason to drop by is to sample wines from all of the local producers.

Black Olive
ITALIAN **$$**
(☑09-407 9693; www.theblackolive.net; 308 Kerikeri Rd; mains $12-36; ☺dinner Tue-Sun) Call ahead for popular pasta and pizza take aways, or grab a seat in the restaurant or garden.

ⓘ Information
Procter Library (Cobham Rd; ☺8am-5pm Mon-Fri, 9am-2pm Sat, 9am-1pm Sun; @☎) Drop by for tourist brochures and free internet access.

ⓘ Getting There & Away
Air
Bay of Islands (Kerikeri) Airport (☑09-407 7147; www.bayofislandsairport.co.nz; 218 Wiroa Rd) 8km southwest of town. Air New Zealand and Salt Air Xpress both run flights (p112) to Kerikeri. **Dial-a-Ride** (☑0508 342 527; www.dial-a-ride.co.nz) Operates a shuttle service from the airport to Kerikeri, Paihia, Opua and Kawakawa.

Bus
InterCity (p112) and partner buses leave from a stop at 9 Cobham Rd, opposite the library.

THE FAR NORTH

If it sounds remote, that's because it is. Here's your chance to get off the beaten track, although that often means onto unsealed roads. The far-flung Far North is always playing second fiddle to the Bay of Islands for attention and funding, yet the subtropical tip of the North Island has more breathtaking coastline per square kilometre than anywhere but the offshore islands. Parts of the Far North are noticeably economically depressed and in places could best be described as gritty. While the 'winterless north' may be a popular misnomer, summers here are long and leisurely.

Matauri & Tauranga Bays

It's a short detour from SH10, but the exceptionally scenic loop route leading inland to these awesome beaches is a world away from the glitzy face presented for tourists in the Bay of Islands.

Matauri Bay is a long sandy surf beach, 18km off SH10, with the 17 Cavalli Islands scattered offshore. **Matauri Bay Holiday Park** (☎09-405 0525; www.matauribayholiday park.co.nz; sites from $20, units $130-180) takes up the north end of the beach and has a shop selling groceries, booze and petrol. On top of the headland above the park is a monument to the *Rainbow Warrior*; the Greenpeace ship's underwater resting place among the Cavalli Islands is a popular dive site.

DOC maintains a 12-person **hut** (☎09-407 0300; www.doc.govt.nz; sites per adult/child $13/6.10) on Motukawanui Island, but you'll need a boat or kayak to reach it and you'll need to book ahead. Only water, mattresses and a composting toilet are provided; bring everything else.

Back on the main road, the route heads west, passing through pleasant Te Ngaere village and a succession of little bays before the turn-off to Tauranga Bay, a smaller beach where the sand is a peachy pink colour. **Tauranga Bay Holiday Park** (☎09-405 0436; www.taurangabay.co.nz; sites from $18, cabins $97-170; @🔊) has campsites and log cabins on the picturesque beachfront, but it lacks trees and bears the brunt of the weather. A minimum $59 charge per night for campsites and a seven-night minimum stay apply in January.

Down a private road leading from Tauranga Bay, **Northland Sea Kayaking** (☎09-405 0381; www.northlandseakayaking.co.nz; half-/full day tours $75/95) leads kayak explorations of this magical coastline of coves, sea caves and islands. Accommodation is available in conjunction with tours for $20 extra per person.

There's no public transport to these parts or to neighbouring Whangaroa.

THE BOMBING OF THE RAINBOW WARRIOR

On the morning of 10 July 1985, New Zealanders awoke to news reporting that a terrorist attack had killed a man in Auckland Harbour. The Greenpeace flagship *Rainbow Warrior* had been sunk at its anchorage at Marsden Wharf, where it was preparing to sail to Moruroa Atoll near Tahiti to protest against French nuclear testing.

It took some time to find out exactly what had happened, but a tip-off from a Neighbourhood Watch group lead to the arrest of two French foreign intelligence service (DGSE) agents, posing as tourists. The agents had detonated two mines on the boat in staggered explosions – the first designed to cause the crew to evacuate and the second to sink her. However, after the initial evacuation, some of the crew returned to the vessel to investigate and document the attack. Greenpeace photographer Fernando Pereira was drowned below decks following the second explosion.

The arrested agents pleaded guilty to manslaughter and were sentenced to 10 years' imprisonment. In response, the French government threatened to embargo NZ goods from entering the European Economic Community – which would have crippled NZ's economy. A deal was struck whereby France paid $13 million to NZ and apologised, in return for the agents being delivered into French custody on a South Pacific atoll for three years. France eventually paid over $8 million to Greenpeace in reparation – and the bombers were quietly freed before their sentence was served.

Initially French President Mitterrand denied any government involvement in the attack, but following an inquiry he eventually sacked his Defence Minister and the head of the DGSE, Admiral Pierre Lacoste. On the 20th anniversary of the attack, *Le Monde* newspaper published a report from Lacoste dating from 1986 declaring that the president had personally authorised the operation.

The bombing left a lasting impact on NZ, and French nuclear testing at Moruroa ceased for good in 1996. The wreck of the *Rainbow Warrior* was re-sunk near Northland's Cavalli Islands, where it can be explored by divers. The masts were bought by the Dargaville Museum and overlook the town. The memory of Fernando Pereira endures in a peaceful bird hide in Thames. A memorial to the boat sits atop a Maori *pa* site at Matauri Bay, north of the Bay of Islands.

Whangaroa Harbour

Just around the headland from Tauranga Bay is the narrow entrance to Whangaroa Harbour. The small fishing village of Whangaroa is 6km from SH10 and calls itself the 'Marlin Capital of NZ'.

There are plenty of charter boats for game-fishing (December to April); prices start at around $1200 a day. If you're planning to hook a monster, insist on it being released once caught – striped marlin and swordfish are among NZ's least-sustainable fishing options.

An excellent 20-minute hike starts from the car park at the end of Old Hospital Rd and goes up **St Paul's Rock** (213m), which dominates the village. At the top you have to use a wire cable to pull yourself up, but the views make it worth the effort.

The **Wairakau Stream Track**, heading north to Pekapeka Bay, begins near the church hall on Campbell Rd in Totara North on the other side of the bay. It's an extremely beautiful, undeveloped stretch and you can cool off in swimming holes along the way. The two-hour hike passes through forest, an abandoned farm and around a steep-walled estuary before arriving at DOC's **Lane Cove Hut** (☑09-407 0300; www.doc.govt.nz; sole occupancy $164), which has 16 beds and composting toilets. Bring everything else and book well ahead; it's usually booked out by Kiwi families over summer.

Duke's Nose Track (1¼ hours return) starts behind the cottage and leads up Kairara Rocks; look for the Duke of Wellington's aquiline profile in the rock face. You'll need to haul yourself up a chain for the last 10m but the views are worth it.

If you don't fancy walking back – or if you don't fancy walking at all – **Bushmansfriend** (☑09405 1844; www.bushmansfriend.co.nz) arranges water taxis from Lane Cove ($20), one-hour boat tours ($40) and guided walks, returning by boat ($105).

On the other side of the harbour's north head is **Taupo Bay**, a surf beach that attracts a loyal Kiwi contingent in summer. On easterly swells, there are quality righthanders to surf at the southern end of the bay, by the rivermouth. It's reached by an 11km sealed road signposted from SH10.

FISH FOR THE FUTURE

While NZ's fisheries are more tightly controlled than most, conservation groups note that most fishing is still unsustainable at present levels. **Forest & Bird** (www.forestandbird.org.nz) publishes a *Best Fish Guide*, which is downloadable from its website. The following are the best and worst choices if you're hankering for a seafood chow-down.

Ten best Anchovy, pilchard, sprats, cockles, garfish, kina, skipjack tuna, kahawai, blue cod, yellow-eyed mullet

Ten worst Orange roughy, shark (porbeagle, mako, blue, lemonfish/rig), oreo (deepwater dory), southern bluefin tuna, snapper, bluenose, jack mackerel, arrow squid, skate, striped marlin

🛏 Sleeping & Eating

TOP CHOICE Kahoe Farms Hostel HOSTEL $
(☑09-405 1804; www.kahoefarms.co.nz; dm $30, r $76-96) On SH10, 10km north of the turnoff to Whangaroa, this hostel has a deservedly great reputation – for its comfortable accommodation, for its bucolic setting, for its home-cooked Italian food, but mostly for its welcoming owners. The backpackers' cottage is great, but slightly up the hill there's an even more impressive villa with excellent-value en-suite rooms.

Sunseeker Lodge HOSTEL $
(☑09-405 0496; www.sunseekerlodge.co.nz; Old Hospital Rd; dm/s/d/tr $25/50/66/90, units $120-150; @🛜) Up the hill in Whangaroa, this friendly lodge has a sublime spa with a jaw-dropping view, hires out kayaks and motor boats, and will pick you up from Kaeo on SH10.

Marlin PUB
(Whangaroa Rd; mains $15-20; ☻lunch & dinner) A friendly local pub with good honest tucker served from the attached cafe.

ℹ Information

Boyd Gallery (☑09-405 0230; Whangaroa Rd; ☻8am-7pm) The general store, but also acts as a tourist information office.

Doubtless Bay

POP 6030

The bay gets its unusual name from an entry in Cook's logbook, where he wrote that the body of water was 'doubtless a bay'. No kidding, Cap'n. It's a bloody big bay at that, with a string of pretty swimming beaches heading towards the Karikari Peninsula.

The main centre, Mangonui (meaning 'Big Shark'), retains a fishing-port feel, despite cafes and gift shops now infesting its well-labelled line of historical waterfront buildings. They were constructed in the days when Mangonui was a centre of the whaling industry (1792–1850) and exported flax, kauri wood and gum.

The popular holiday settlements of Coopers Beach, Cable Bay and Taipa are restful pockets of beachside gentrification.

◉ Sights & Activities

Grab the free *Heritage Trail* brochure from the information centre for a 3km self-guided walk taking in 22 historic sites. Other walks lead to attractive **Mill Bay**, west of Mangonui, and **Rangikapiti Pa Historic Reserve**, which has ancient Maori terracing and a spectacular view of Doubtless Bay – particularly at sunrise and sunset. A walkway runs from Mill Bay to the *pa,* but you can also drive nearly to the top.

Butler Point Whaling Museum   MUSEUM
(www.butlerpoint.co.nz; Marchant Rd; adult/child $12/2; ⊘by appointment) At Hihi, 15km northeast of Mangonui, is this small private museum and Victorian homestead (1843) set in lovely gardens. Its first owner, Captain Butler, left Dorset when he was 14 and at 24 was captain of a whaling ship. He settled here in 1839, had 13 children and became a trader, farmer, magistrate and Member of Parliament.

⌶ Sleeping

There's plenty of accommodation around the bay but most is horribly overpriced in summer. Outside the peak months things settle down considerably.

TOP
CHOICE / **Old Oak**   BOUTIQUE HOTEL $$
(✆09-406 1250; www.theoldoak.co.nz; 66 Waterfront Dr, Mangonui; s $125, d $175-225, ste $295; ⚟) A snazzy renovation has transformed this atmospheric 1861 kauri inn into an elegant boutique hotel with contemporary design and top-notch furnishings. It oozes character, not least because the building is reputedly haunted.

Mangonui Waterfront Apartments Motel   APARTMENTS $$
(✆09-406 0347; www.mangonuiwaterfront.co.nz; 88 Waterfront Dr; apt $120-225; @⚟) Sleeping two to eight people, these historic apartments on the Mangonui waterfront have loads of character, each one different but all with balconies, a sense of space and their own barbecue. Try to book 100-year-old Tahi.

Puketiti Lodge   HOSTEL $
(✆09-406 0369; www.puketitilodge.co.nz; 10 Puketiti Dr; dm/r $40/150; @⚟) If this is what they mean by flashpacking, bring it on. For $40 you get a comfy bunk in a spacious six-person dorm opening on to a large deck with awesome views, a locker big enough for the burliest backpack and, perhaps most surprisingly, breakfast. Turn inland at Midgley Rd, 6km south of Mangonui village, just after the Hihi turn-off.

◨ **By The Bay**   APARTMENTS $$$
(www.beachfrontapartments.co.nz; 16 Braemar Ave; apt $200-400; ⚟) Long, lovely Coopers Beach beckons from the bottom of the lawn at this upmarket set of apartments. The owners operate a day spa, offering in-house massage and beauty treatments.

✗ Eating

There are a few cafes, takeaways and stores scattered around the other beaches, but Mangonui has the best eating options – and they're actually pretty great.

TOP
CHOICE / **Acorn Bar & Bistro**   MODERN NZ $$
(✆09-406 0896; 66 Waterfront Dr, Mangonui; mains $26-33; ⊘dinner Wed-Mon) A fitting companion piece to its neighbour, the Old Oak, this handsome little restaurant serves a concise, seasonal menu taking advantage of the freshest seafood, straight off the wharf, and the best of the local farm produce.

Waterfront Cafe & Bar   CAFE $
(Waterfront Dr, Mangonui; brunch $11-18, dinner $14-29; ⊘8.30am-late) The best cafe in the Far North, Waterfront has water views, friendly service and old-world charm. A pizza menu kicks in at lunch and extends into dinner, where it supplements bistro dishes.

Thai Chef
THAI $$

(☎09-406 1220; www.thaichef.co.nz; 80 Waterfront Dr, Mangonui; mains $18-26; ⊘dinner Tue-Sun) The best Thai restaurant in Northland serves piquant dishes with names such as *The 3 Alcoholics*, *Spice Girls* and *Bangkok Showtime*. The *Sexy Little Duck* is irresistible.

Mangonui Fish Shop
FISH & CHIPS $

(137 Waterfront Dr; fish & chips $8.80; ⊘10am-8pm; 🔊) You can eat outdoors over the water at this famous chippie, which also sells smoked fish and seafood salads. Grab a crayfish salad and a cold beer, and all will be right with the world. If the queues are too long, the other fish and chip shop across the road is also good.

🔒 Shopping

Far North Wine Centre
WINE

(60 Waterfront Dr, Mangonui; ⊘10.30am-4.30pm Tue-Sun) Sample and purchase wine from the local Lava Rock and Manaia ranges.

Flax Bush
ART & CRAFT

(www.flaxbush.co.nz; 50 Waterfront Dr, Mangonui) Seashells, Pasifika and Maori knick-knacks.

ⓘ Information

Doubtless Bay Visitor Information Centre
(☎09-406 2046; www.doubtlessbay.co.nz; 118 Waterfront Dr, Mangonui; ⊘10am-4pm Mon-Sat; @)

ⓘ Getting There & Away

InterCity buses stop at the BP service station on Waterfront Dr in Mangonui, outside the wholesalers in Coopers Beach, opposite the shop in Cable Bay and outside the Shell station in Taipa. **Busabout Kaitaia** (☎09-408 1092; www.cbec. co.nz) has services to Kaitaia ($5, one hour).

Karikari Peninsula

The oddly shaped Karikari Peninsula bends into a near-perfect right angle. The result is beaches facing north, south, east and west in close proximity; if the wind's annoying you or you want to catch some surf, a sunrise or a sunset, just swap beaches. Despite its natural assets, the sun-baked peninsula is blissfully undeveloped, with farmers well outnumbering tourist operators. There's no public transport and you won't find a lot of shops or eateries either.

⦿ Sights & Activities

Tokerau Beach is the long, sandy stretch forming the western edge of Doubtless Bay. Neighbouring Whatuwhiwhi is smaller and more built-up, facing back across the bay. Maitai Bay, with its tiny twin coves, is the loveliest of them all, at the lonely end of the peninsula down an unsealed road. It's a great spot for swimming – the waters sheltered enough for the kids but with enough swell to body surf.

Rangiputa faces west at the elbow of the peninsula; the pure white sand and crystal-clear sheltered waters come straight from a Pacific Island daydream. A turn-off on the road to Rangiputa takes you to remote Puheke Beach, a long, windswept stretch of snow-white sand dunes forming Karikari's northern edge.

Various local watersports operators can be contacted under the umbrella of **Watersports Paradise** (☎0508 727 234; www.water sportsparadise.co.nz).

Karikari Estate
WINERY

(www.karikariestate.co.nz; Maitai Bay Rd; tastings $12; ⊘11am-4pm) An ominous sign of creeping gentrification is the luxury golf club and winery on the way to Maitai Bay. Impressive Karikari Estate produces acclaimed red wines and has a cafe attached - and while the wine tastings are shamelessly overpriced, at least the sublime views are free.

Airzone Kitesurfing School
KITESURFING

(☎021 202 7949; www.kitesurfnz.com; 1-/2-/3-day course $195/350/485) The unique set-up of Karikari Peninsula makes it one of the world's premium spots for kiteboarding, or at least that's the opinion of this experienced crew. Learners get to hone their skills on flat water before heading to the surf, while the more experienced can chase the wind around the peninsula.

A to Z Diving
DIVING

(☎09-408 3336; www.atozdiving.co.nz; 13-15 Whatu-whiwhi Rd; 2 dives incl equipment $160-230) Offers PADI courses and dive trips in Doubtless Bay and at the *Rainbow Warrior*.

Karikari Kayaks
KAYAKING

(☎09-408 7575; www.karikari-kayaking.co.nz) Hires kayaks from the northern end of Tokerau Beach.

🛌 Sleeping

📍 Whatuwhiwhi Top 10
Holiday Park   HOLIDAY PARK $
(📞09-408 7202; www.whatuwhiwhitop10.co.nz;
17 Whatuwhiwhi Rd; sites from $62, units $82-
385) Sheltered by hills and overlooking the
beach, this friendly complex has a great
location, good facilities, free barbecues and
kayaks for hire. They also offer dive fills and
PADI diving instruction.

📍 Maitai Bay DOC Campsite   CAMPSITE $
(www.doc.govt.nz; Maitai Bay Rd; sites per adult/
child $8/4) A large first-in, first-served (no
bookings) camping ground at the peninsula's most beautiful beach, with chemical
toilets, drinking water and cold showers.

📍 Carrington Resort   RESORT $$$
(📞09-408 7222; www.heritagehotels.co.nz; r $429-
476, villa $580; @🐕) There's something very
Australian-looking about this hilltop lodge,
with its wide verandas and gum trees, tem-
pered by Maori and Pacific design in the
spacious rooms and villas. The view over
the golf course to the dazzling white beach
is exquisite.

Cape Reinga & Ninety Mile Beach

Maori consider Cape Reinga (Te Rerenga-
Wairua) the jumping-off point for souls as
they depart on the journey to their spiritual
homeland. That makes the Aupouri Peninsula a giant diving board, and it even resembles one – long and thin, it reaches 108km
to form NZ's northern extremity. On its west
coast Ninety Mile Beach (Ninety Kilometre
Beach would be more accurate) is a continuous stretch lined with high sand dunes,
flanked by the Aupouri Forest.

🔘 Sights & Activities

Cape Reinga   CAPE
Standing at windswept **Cape Reinga Lighthouse** (a 1km walk from the car park) and
looking out over the ocean engenders a real
end-of-the-world feeling. This is where the
waters of the Tasman Sea and Pacific Ocean
meet, breaking together into waves up to
10m high in stormy weather. Little tufts of
cloud often cling to the ridges, giving sud-
den spooky chills even on hot days.

Visible on a promontory slightly to the
east is a spiritually significant 800-year-old
pohutukawa tree; souls are believed to slide
down its roots. Out of respect to the most
sacred site in Maoridom, don't go near the
tree and refrain from eating or drinking anywhere in the area.

Cape Reinga Coastal Walkway   TRAMPING
Contrary to expectation, Cape Reinga isn't
actually the northernmost point of the country; that honour belongs to Surville Cliffs
further to the east. A walk along Te Werahi
Beach to Cape Maria van Diemen (five hours
loop) takes you to the westernmost point.
This is one of many sections of the three- to
four-day, 53km Cape Reinga Coastal Walkway (from Kapowairua to Te Paki Stream)
that can be tackled individually. Beautiful
Tapotupotu Bay is a two-hour walk east of
Cape Reinga, via Sandy Bay and the cliffs.
From Tapotupotu Bay it's an eight-hour walk
to **Spirits Bay**, one of NZ's most beautiful
beaches. Both bays are also accessible by
road.

Te Paki Recreation Reserve   NATURE RESERVE
A large chunk of the land around Cape Reinga is part of the Te Paki Recreation Reserve
managed by DOC. It's public land with free
access; leave the gates as you found them
and don't disturb the animals. There are 7
sq km of giant sand dunes on either side of
the mouth of Te Paki Stream. Clamber up to
take flying leaps off the dunes or to tobog-
gan down them.

Great Exhibition Bay   BEACH
On the east coast, Great Exhibition Bay has
dazzling snow-white silica dunes. There's
no public road access, but some tours pay
a *koha* (donation) to cross Maori farmland
or approach the sand by kayak from Parengarenga Harbour.

Nga-Tapuwae-o-te-Mangai   TEMPLE
(6576 Far North Rd) With its two domed towers
(Arepa and Omeka, alpha and omega) and
the Ratana emblem of the star and crescent
moon, you could be forgiven for mistaking
this temple for a mosque. Ratana is a Maori
Christian sect with more than 50,000 adherents, formed in 1925 by Tahupotiki Wiremu
Ratana, who was known as 'the mouthpiece
of God'. The temple is built on land where
Ratana once stood; the name translates as
'the sacred steps of the mouthpiece'. You'll
pass it at Te Kao, 46km south of Cape Reinga.

Gumdiggers Park OUTDOOR MUSEUM
(www.gumdiggerspark.co.nz; 171 Heath Rd, Waiharara; adult/child $12/6; ⊙9am-5pm) Kauri forests covered this area for over 100,000 years, leaving ancient logs and the much-prized gum (used for making varnish and linoleum) buried beneath. Digging it out of the mud was the region's main industry from the 1870s to the 1920s. In 1900, some 7000 gumdiggers (wearing rubber gumboots – the NZ name for Wellingtons) were digging holes all over Northland, including at this site. Start with the 15-minute video telling the story of the trees, their mysterious destruction and the gum industry. Rope paths head through the bush, leading past reproductions of gumdiggers' huts, ancient kauri stumps and holes left by the diggers. It was a hard life for the workers, who used jute sacks for their tents, bedding and clothing.

Ancient Kauri Kingdom WOODTURNERS
(www.ancientkauri.co.nz; 229 Far North Rd, Awanui; ⊙8.30am-5pm; @🐾) It's tacky and overpriced, but Ancient Kauri Kingdom is still worth a stop. Here 50,000-year-old kauri stumps dragged out of swamps are fashioned into furniture, woodcraft products and a fair bit of tourist tat. The large complex includes a cafe, gift shop and workshop. A huge kauri log has an impressive spiral staircase carved into it that leads to the mezzanine level.

☞ Tours

Bus tours go to Cape Reinga from Kaitaia, Ahipara, Doubtless Bay and the Bay of Islands; there's no other public transport up here.

Cape Reinga Adventures 4WD
(☑09-409 8445; www.capereingaadventures.co.nz; half-/full-day 4WD trips $75/135) Real action men who offer 4WD tours (including sunset visits to the cape after the crowds have gone), fishing, kayaking and sandboarding as day activities or as part of overnight camping trips.

Far North Outback Adventures 4WD
(☑09-408 0927; www.farnorthtours.co.nz; price on application) Flexible, day-long tours from Kaitaia and Ahipara, including morning tea and lunch. Options include visits to remote areas such as Great Exhibition Bay.

Harrison's Cape Runner BUS
(☑0800 227 373; www.harrisonscapereingatours.co.nz; 123 North Rd, Kaitaia; adult/child $50/25)

SEED FOR THE FUTURE

The local Ngati Kuri, guardians of the sacred spaces around the Cape, have come up with a unique way of funding reforestation. For $20 you can assuage your carbon guilt by planting a native tree or bush of your choice – or, if you don't want to break a nail, letting the staff plant it for you; contact **Natives** (☑09-409 8482; www.natives.co.nz).

Day trips from Kaitaia along Ninety Mile Beach that include sandboarding and a picnic lunch.

Paradise 4x4 4WD
(☑0800 494 392; www.paradisenz.co.nz; price on application) Operates flexible 4WD tours from Doubtless Bay up Ninety Mile Beach to Cape Reinga, including a seafood lunch with local wine. Hokianga, Doubtless Bay beaches, wine and golf tours are also available.

Sand Safaris BUS
(☑0800 869 090; www.sandsafaris.co.nz; adult/child $60/35) A family-owned operation running coach trips from Ahipara and Kaitaia, including a Maori welcome, sandboarding and a picnic lunch.

Ahikaa Adventures CULTURAL
(☑09-409 8228; www.ahikaa-adventures.co.nz; tours $70-190) Maori culture permeates these tours, which can include sand-surfing, kayaking, fishing and pigging out on traditional *kai* (food).

🛏 Sleeping & Eating

Unless you're a happy camper you won't find much decent accommodation up here. Pukenui – literally 'Big Stomach' – is the best place to fill yours; there's a cafe, takeaways and grocery store. The only other options are unremarkable eateries at Ancient Kauri Kingdom and Houhora Heads.

North Wind Lodge Backpackers HOSTEL $
(☑09-409 8515; www.northwind.co.nz; 88 Otaipango Rd, Henderson Bay; dm/s/tw/d $30/60/66/80) Six kilometres down an unsealed road on the peninsula's east side, this unusual turreted house offers a homely environment and plenty of quiet spots on the lawn to sit with a beer and a book.

DOC campsites
CAMPSITES $

(www.doc.govt.nz; sites per adult/child $7.60/3.50) There are spectacularly positioned sites at Kapowairua, Tapotupotu Bay and Rarawa Beach. Only water, composting toilets and cold showers are provided. Bring a cooker, as fires are not allowed, and plenty of repellent to ward off the evil mosquitoes and sandflies. 'Freedom/Leave No Trace' camping is allowed along the Cape Reinga Coastal Walkway.

❶ Getting There & Around

Apart from numerous tours, there's no public transport past Pukenui, which is linked to Kaitaia ($5, 45 minutes) by **Busabout Kaitaia** (☑09-408 1092; www.cbec.co.nz).

As well as Far North Rd (SH1), rugged vehicles can travel along Ninety Mile Beach itself. However, cars have been known to hit soft sand and be swallowed by the tides – look out for unfortunate vehicles poking through the sands. Check tide times before setting out; avoid it 2½ hours either side of high tide. Watch out for 'quicksand' at Te Paki Stream – keep moving. Many car-rental companies prohibit driving on the sands; if you get stuck, your insurance won't cover you.

Fill up with petrol before hitting the Aupouri Peninsula.

Kaitaia

POP 5200

Nobody comes to the Far North to hang out in this provincial town, but it's a handy stop if you're after a supermarket, a post office or an ATM. It's also a jumping-off point for tours to Cape Reinga and Ninety Mile Beach.

◉ Sights

Te Ahu Centre
ARTS CENTRE

(www.teahu.org.nz; Matthews Ave) At the time of research, the cinema was the only part of this striking, multi-million-dollar new civic centrepiece that had opened. By the time you're reading this, the eclectic local-history exhibits of the Far North Regional Museum will be on display; check the website for details.

Okahu Estate Winery
WINERY

(www.okahuestate.co.nz; 520 Okahu Rd; ◎noon-4pm Mon-Fri, extended summer) Just south of town, off the road to Ahipara, Kaitaia's only winery offers free tastings and sells local produce, including the famous Kaitaia Fire chilli sauce. Enquire about tours ($5).

🛏 Sleeping & Eating

Mainstreet Lodge
HOSTEL $

(☑09-408 1275; www.mainstreetlodge.co.nz; 235 Commerce St; dm $27-34, s $55-70, d $64-78; @🛜) Maori carvings abound at this groovy old cottage, which has a modern purpose-built wing facing the rear courtyard. The friendly owners know the area inside-out.

Loredo Motel
MOTEL $$

(☑09-408 3200; www.loredomotel.co.nz; 25 North Rd; units $130-210; 🛜🎬) Opting for a breezy Spanish style (think stucco walls and terracotta tiles), this tidy motel has well-kept units set among palm trees and lawns. It's not quite Benidorm, but there is a swimming pool.

Beachcomber
RESTAURANT $$

(www.beachcomber.net.nz; 222 Commerce St; lunch $17-33, dinner $27-35; ◎lunch & dinner Mon-Sat) Easily the best place to eat in town, with a wide range of seafood and meatier fare, all deftly prepared, and a well-stocked salad bar.

❶ Information

Far North i-SITE (☑09-408 0879; www.topofnz.co.nz; South Rd; ◎8.30am-5pm; @)

❶ Getting There & Away

Kaitaia Airport (www.bayofislandsairport.co.nz; Quarry Rd) is 6km north of town. **Busabout Kaitaia** (☑09-408 1092; www.cbec.co.nz) has services to Doubtless Bay ($5, one hour), Pukenui ($5, 45 minutes) and Ahipara ($3.50, 15 minutes). Both Air New Zealand (p112) and InterCity (p112) operate services to Kaitaia.

Ahipara

POP 1130

All good things must come to an end, and Ninety Mile Beach does it at this spunky beach town. A few holiday mansions have snuck in, but mostly it's just the locals keeping it real, rubbing shoulders with visiting surfers.

The area is known for its huge sand dunes and massive gum field, where 2000 people once worked. Sandboarding and quad-bike rides are popular activities on the dunes above Ahipara and further around the Tauroa Peninsula.

NGATI TARARA

As you're travelling around the north you might notice the preponderance of road names ending in '-ich'. *Haere mai, dobro došli* and welcome (as the sign leading into Kaitaia proclaims) to one of the more peculiar ethnic conjunctions in the country.

From the end of the 19th century, men from the Dalmatian coast of what is now Croatia started arriving in NZ looking for work. Many ended up in Northland's gum fields. Pakeha society wasn't particularly welcoming to the new immigrants, particularly during WWI – they were on Austrian passports. Not so the small Maori communities of the north. Here they found an echo of Dalmatian village life, with its emphasis on extended family and hospitality, not to mention a shared history of injustice at the hands of colonial powers.

The Maori jokingly named them Tarara, as their rapid conversation in their native tongue sounded like 'ta-ra-ra-ra-ra' to Maori ears. Many Croatian men married local *wahine* (women), founding clans that have left several of today's famous Maori with Croatian surnames, like singer Margaret Urlich and former All Black Frano Botica. You'll find large Tarara communities in the Far North, Dargaville and West Auckland.

◉ Sights

Shipwreck Bay   BEACH
(Wreck Bay Rd) The best surf is to be had at this small cove at the western end of the beach, so named for the shipwrecks that are still visible at low tide.

Ahipara Viewpoint   LOOKOUT
(Gumfields Rd) Views stretch to eternity and beyond from this lookout on the bluff behind Ahipara. It's reached by an extremely rough road leading off the unsealed Gumfields Rd, which starts at the western end of Foreshore Dr.

🏃 Activities

Ahipara Adventure Centre   EQUIPMENT RENTAL
(☑09-409 2055; www.ahiparaadventure.co.nz; 15 Takahe St) Ahipara Adventure Centre hires out sandboards ($10 per half day), surfboards ($20 per hour), mountain bikes ($50 per day), kayaks ($25 per hour), blokarts for sand yachting ($65 per hour) and quad bikes ($85 per hour).

Tua Tua Tours   QUAD BIKES
(☑0800 494 288; www.ahipara.co.nz/tuatuatours/; 250 Ahipara Rd; 2hr ride per person $135, 2 people $150) This local outfit gets great word-of-mouth for its reef- and dune-rider tours and Ultimate Sand Dune Safaris (three hours including sand tobogganing, per one/two people $185/200).

Ahipara Treks   HORSE RIDING
(☑09-409 4122; ahiparahorsetreks@xtra.co.nz) Offers beach canters (from $70), including some farm and ocean riding (when the surf permits).

🛏 Sleeping

TOP CHOICE▶ Endless Summer Lodge   HOSTEL $
(☑09-409 4181; www.endlesssummer.co.nz; 245 Foreshore Rd; dm $28, d $70-85; @) Across from the beach, this superb kauri villa (1880) has been beautifully restored and converted into an exceptional hostel. There's no TV, which encourages bonding around the long table on the vine-covered back terrace. Body boards and sandboards can be borrowed and surfboards can be hired.

🏄 Beach Abode   APARTMENTS $$
(☑09-409 4070; www.beachabode.co.nz; 11 Korora St; apt $145-190; 🛜) Wander through the subtropical garden to the beach from your self-contained studio or two-bedroom apartment, or just lie in bed and lose yourself in the view.

90 Mile Beach Ahipara
Holiday Park   HOLIDAY PARK $
(☑09-409 4864; www.ahiparaholidaypark.co.nz; 168 Takahe St; sites from $20, dm/r $28/95, units $95-310; @🛜) There's a large range of accommodation on offer at this holiday park, including cabins, motel units and a worn but perfectly presentable YHA-affiliated backpackers' lodge. The communal hall has an open fire and colourful murals.

Beachfront   APARTMENTS $$
(☑09-409 4007; www.beachfront.net.nz; 14 Kotare St; apt $175-310; 🛜) Who cares if it's a bit bourgeois for Ahipara? These two upmarket, self-contained apartments have watery views and there's direct access to the beach.

✖ Eating

Gumdiggers Cafe   CAFE
(3 Ahipara Rd; mains $10-16; ⊙7am-2pm) Good coffee and huge portions are the hallmarks of this friendly little cafe, serving cooked breakfasts, nachos, burgers and platters that would polish off your average ploughman.

Bidz Takeaways   FISH & CHIPS
(Takahe St; meals $6-12; ⊙9am-8pm) You'll need a flip-top head to fit Bidz' seafood burger into your mouth – it's jam-packed with battered oysters, scallops, mussels and fish. There's a grocery store attached.

❶ Getting There & Around

Busabout Kaitaia (☑09-408 1092; www.cbec. co.nz) runs services from Kaitaia ($3.50, 15 minutes).

HOKIANGA

The Hokianga Harbour stretches out its skinny tentacles to become the fourth-biggest in the country. Its ruggedly beautiful landscape is painted in every shade of green and brown. The water itself is rendered the colour of ginger ale by the bush streams that feed it.

Of all the remote parts of Northland, this is the pocket that feels the most removed from the mainstream. Pretension has no place here. Isolated, predominantly Maori communities nestle around the harbour's many inlets, as they have done for centuries. Discovered by legendary explorer Kupe, it's been settled by Ngapuhi since the 14th century. Hippies arrived in the late 1960s and their legacy is a thriving little artistic scene.

Many of the roads remain unsealed and in poor repair after decades of neglect from government bodies. Tourism dollars are channelled eastward to the Bay of Islands, leaving this truly fascinating corner of the country remarkably undeveloped, which is the way many of the locals like it.

Mitimiti

The tiny community at Mitimiti, which consists of only 30 families and not even a shop, has the unspoilt 20km stretch of coast between the Hokianga and Whangape Harbours all to itself. The 40km drive from Kohukohu via Panguru (14km of it unsealed) is quite an experience: prepare to dodge cows, sheep, potholes and kids.

Sandtrails Hokianga (☑09-409 5035; www. sandtrailshokianga.co.nz; 32 Paparangi Dr) offers an inside perspective on Mitimiti's tight-knit Maori community, with two-hour Sandscapes dune-buggy tours, which head 12km along the beach to the giant dunes that form the harbour's north head ($155), or personally tailored tours staying overnight in the guide's house ($665 for two people).

Motuti

It's worth taking a short detour from the road to Mitimiti to visit **St Mary's Church** (Hata Maria; www.hokiangapompallier.org.nz; Motuti Rd), where NZ's first Catholic bishop is buried beneath the altar. Jean Baptiste Pompallier arrived in the Hokianga in 1838, celebrating NZ's first Mass at Totara Point. He was interred here in 2002 after an emotional 14-week pilgrimage full of Maori ceremony brought his remains back from France.

The nearby **Motuti Marae** (☑09-409 5545; www.motuti.co.nz; 318 Motuti Rd; tours 90min/day $30/60, stay $180) offers *marae* tours and stays, including a traditional Maori welcome and, on the longer tours, the opportunity to take part in flax-weaving, carving and stick games.

Kohukohu
POP 190

Quick, someone slap a preservation order on Kohukohu before it's too late. There can be few places in NZ where a Victorian village full of interesting kauri buildings has been so completely preserved with hardly a modern monstrosity to be seen. During the height of the kauri industry it was a busy town with a sawmill, shipyard, two newspapers and banks. These days it's a very quiet backwater on the north side of Hokianga Harbour, 4km from the Rawene car ferry (p148). There are no regular bus services and the only place to eat (or check your email) is the local pub. It does, however, have **Village Arts** (www.village arts.co.nz; 1376 Kohukohu Rd; ⊙10am-4pm), an excellent little commercial art gallery.

Tree House (☑09-405 5855; www.treehouse. co.nz; 168 West Coast Rd; sites/dm $18/31, s $60-68, tw & d $80, ; 🐾) is the best place to stay in the Hokianga, with helpful hosts and brightly painted little cottages set among exotic fruit and nut trees. This quiet retreat is 2km from the ferry terminus (turn sharp left as you come off the ferry).

NGAWHA SPRINGS

Near Kaikohe, these hot springs have been used by Ngapuhi for their curative powers since the 17th century. Hone Heke brought his injured warriors here during the Northland War.

Unlike many of NZ's thermal resorts, there are no hydroslides or big pools for the kids to splash about in. There aren't even any showers. Here it's all about stewing in the murky water in small pools of varying temperatures. Ngawha has two complexes, the better of which is **Ngawha Springs Pools** (☏09-405 2245; adult/child $4/2; ⊙9am-9pm).

Hidden Walks (☏021 277 7301; www.hiddenwalks.com; adult/child $28/20) offers guided walks through the thermal area taking in the remains of a historic mercury mine.

Horeke & Around

Tiny Horeke was NZ's second European settlement after Russell. A Wesleyan mission operated here from 1828 to 1855. In 1840, 3000 Ngapuhi gathered here for what was the single biggest signing of the Treaty of Waitangi.

◉ Sights & Activities

Mangungu Mission House   HISTORIC BUILDING (www.historic.org.nz; Motukiore Rd; adult/child $3/1; ⊙noon-4pm Sat & Sun) Completed in 1839, this sweet wooden cottage contains relics of the missionaries who once inhabited it and of Horeke's shipbuilding past. In the grounds there's a large stone cross and a simple wooden church. Mangungu is 1km down the unsealed road leading along the harbour from Horeke village.

Wairere Boulders

Nature Park   NATURE PARK (www.waireboulders.co.nz; McDonnell Rd; adult/child $10/5; ⊙daylight) At Wairere, massive basalt rock formations have been eroded into odd fluted shapes by the acidity of ancient kauri forests, creating a Zen-garden effect. Allow an hour for the main loop track, which follows a burbling Coca-Cola–coloured stream. It's a good path, but wear sensible shoes and expect a few ducks and climbs. An additional track leads through rainforest to a platform at the end of the boulder valley (allow 1½ hours).

The park is signposted from SH1 and Horeke; the last 3km are unsealed. If you don't have your own transport, the only way to get here is on Fullers' Discover Hokianga tour (p125), departing from Paihia.

Quad Safaris   QUAD BIKES (☏09-401 9544; www.waiwerevalley.com; 20 McDonnell Rd; 1½-hr-tour $90) Offers quad bike tours through bush to the Wairere boulder valley.

Rawene

POP 440

Founded shortly after Horeke, Rawene was NZ's third European settlement. A surprising number of historic buildings (including six churches!) remain from a time when the harbour was considerably busier than it is now. Information boards outline a heritage trail of the main sights.

There aren't any ATMs or banks, but you can get petrol here.

◉ Sights

Clendon House   HISTORIC BUILDING (www.historic.org.nz; Clendon Esplanade; adult/child $7/3.50; ⊙10am-4pm Sun May-Oct, Sat & Sun Nov-Apr) Clendon House was built in the bustling 1860s by James Clendon, a trader, shipowner and magistrate. After his death, his 34-year-old half-Maori widow Jane was left with a brood of kids and a whopping £5000 debt. She managed to clear the debt and her descendants remained in the house until 1972, when it passed to the Historic Places Trust along with many of its original chattels.

Hokianga Art Gallery   GALLERY (2 Parnell St; ⊙10am-3pm) Sells interesting contemporary art with a local focus.

🛏 Sleeping & Eating

Rawene Holiday Park   HOLIDAY PARK $ (☏09-405 7720; www.raweneholidaypark.co.nz; 1 Marmon St; dm $20, sites/units from $30/45; @🛜🐾) Tent sites shelter in the bush at this nicely managed park. The cabins are simple, with one converted into a bunkroom for backpackers (linen costs extra).

Boatshed Cafe   CAFE $ (8 Clendon Esplanade; mains $8-17; ⊙8.30am-4pm) You can eat overlooking the water at

LOCAL KNOWLEDGE

HOKIANGA *ANIKA MOA*

I love the north of the north island, the beaten, bloody and beautiful landscape and *wairua* (spirit). The small towns up north, where I grew up, reach out all along the moody west coast. As kids, my brother and I would sneak in to Ngawha Springs and have our mud baths in the morning – smelling of rotten eggs for the rest of the day. In Opononi we'd go crab hunting on the rocks with Uncle Rata, then take the car ferry from Rawene home. At Pawarenga – a dusty old Maori town – we'd go horse riding with the cuzzies, learn Maori with my Grandpa, eat *karahu* and oysters, and, as we grew up, drink with the aunties and uncles. We'd drive to Kaitaia to buy all our food for the next week, and hang at the local pubs. Then further north for the Mangonui fish 'n' chip shop, the best *kai* (food) in Aotearoa. When we were tired, we'd drive to Ahipara and sleep on the beach.

Anika Moa, singer/songwriter

this excellent cafe, a cute place with heart-warming food and a gift shop selling local art and crafts.

 ### Getting There & Away

There are no regular bus services to Rawene. From the centre of town a **car ferry** (☏09-405 2602; car & driver one way/return $16/24, passenger $2/4; ⊙7.30am-7.30pm) heads to the northern side of the Hokianga, docking 4km south of Kohukohu at least hourly. You can buy your ticket for this 15-minute ride on board. It usually leaves Rawene on the half-hour and the north side on the hour.

Opononi & Omapere

POP 480

These tranquil settlements near the south head of Hokianga Harbour more or less run into one another. The water's much clearer here and good for swimming. Views are dominated by the mountainous sand dunes across the water at North Head. If you're approaching Omapere from the south, the view of the harbour is nothing short of spectacular.

 ## Activities

Hokianga Express   SANDBOARDING
(☏09-405 8872; adult/child $25/15) A boat departs from Opononi Jetty and takes you across the harbour to the large golden sand dunes, where you can sandboard down a 30m slope and skim over the water. Boats leave on the hour, on demand; call ahead or book at the i-SITE.

Arai te Uru Heritage Walk   WALKING
Starting at the car park at the end of Signal Station Rd, this short walk (30 minutes return) follows the cliffs and passes through a tall stand of manuka before opening out to the grassy southern headland of the Hokianga and the remains of an old signal station. Built to assist ships making the treacherous passage through the harbour mouth, the station was closed in 1951 due to the decline in shipping in the harbour.

Six Foot Track   TRAMPING
The Six Foot Track at the end of Mountain Rd gives access to many Waima Forest walks.

 ## Tours

Footprints Waipoua   CULTURAL
(☏09-405 8207; www.footprintswaipoua.co.nz; adult/child $95/35) Led by Maori guides, this four-hour twilight tour into Waipoua Forest is a fantastic introduction to both the culture and the forest giants. Tribal history and stories are shared, and mesmerising *karakia* (prayer, incantation) recited before the gargantuan trees.

Sandtrails Hokianga   DUNE BUGGY
(☏09-409 5035; www.sandtrailshokianga.co.nz) Jump off the Hokianga Express boat (included in the price) and into a dune buggy for a sandy ride to Mitimiti ($185, 3¾ hours) or a 70-minute Sandsecrets tour ($95).

Sleeping & Eating

Each of these neighbouring villages has its own grocery store and takeaways.

GlobeTrekkers Lodge   HOSTEL $
(☏09-405 8183; www.globetrekkerslodge.com; SH12, Omapere; dm/s/d $26/50/65; @) Unwind in casual style at this home-style hostel with harbour views and bright dorms. Private rooms have plenty of thoughtful touches, such as writing desks, mirrors, art and fluffy

towels. There's a stereo but no TV, encouraging plenty of schmoozing in the grapevine-draped BBQ area.

Hokianga Haven B&B $$
(✆09-405 8285; www.hokiangahaven.co.nz; 226 SH12, Omapere; r $160) This modern house with original Kiwi art on the walls offers spacious accommodation on the harbour's edge and glorious views of the sand dunes. Alternative healing therapies can be arranged.

🌿Copthorne Hotel & Resort HOTEL $$
(✆09-405 8737; www.omapere.co.nz; 336 SH12, Omapere; r $145-260; 🐾🏊) Despite the original grand Victorian villa having been violated by aluminium joinery, this waterside complex remains an attractive spot for a summer's drink or bistro meal ($19 to $36). The more expensive rooms in the newer accommodation block have terraces and water views.

Opononi Hotel HOTEL $$
(✆09-405 8858; www.opononihotel.com; 19 SH12; r $129) The rooms at the old Opononi pub aren't huge but the white-paint and blond-wood makeover has left them quietly stylish. Try to grab one of the front two – they're a bit bigger and have the best views. Otherwise aim for those facing away from the pub for a quieter stay.

Opononi Lighthouse Motel MOTEL $$
(✆09-405 8824; www.lighthousemotel.co.nz; 45 SH12; units $125-210; 🐾🛜) Scrupulously clean, this refurbished motel has very comfortable harbourside units, plus a communal barbecue, a spa pool, and a cutesy lighthouse and water feature in the front garden.

ℹ️ **Information**
Hokianga i-SITE (✆09-405 8869; 29 SH12; ⏰9am-5pm; @)

ℹ️ **Getting There & Away**
There's no regular public transport to these parts but Magic Travellers Network (p134) and Crossings Hokianga are options.

Waiotemarama & Waimamaku

These neighbouring villages, nestled between the Hokianga Harbour and the Waipoua Forest, are the first of many tiny rural communities scattered along this underpopulated stretch of SH16.

🎯 **Activities**
Labyrinth Woodworks MAZE
(www.nzanity.co.nz; 647 Waiotemarama Gorge Rd; maze $4; ⏰9am-5pm) An Aladdin's cave of handmade puzzles and games. Crack the code in the outdoor maze by collecting letters to form a word.

Fern River Horse Trekking HORSE RIDING
(✆09-405 8344; www.fernriver.co.nz; 953 Waiotemarama Gorge Rd, Waimamaku; 1/2/3/4hr trek $40/75/110/120) Leads horse treks through farmland and along deserted beaches.

🍴 **Eating**
Morrell's Cafe CAFE
(7235 SH12, Waimamaku; mains $9-16; ⏰9am-4pm) Painted the colour of a block of cheddar, this cafe and craft shop occupies a former cheese factory. It's the last good eatery before Baylys Beach, so drop in for coffee or an eggy breakfast.

KAURI COAST

Apart from the odd bluff and river, this coast is basically unbroken and undeveloped for the 110km between the Hokianga and Kaipara Harbours. The main reason for coming here is to marvel at the kauri forests, one of the great natural highlights of NZ. This is one for the chubby chasers of the tree-hugging fraternity – you'd need 8m arms to get them around some of the big boys here. At the time of writing discussions were underway with a view to protecting all of the remaining forests in a new Kauri National Park; watch this space.

There are few stores or eateries and no ATMs north of Dargaville, so stock up beforehand if you're planning to spend any time here. Trampers should check DOC's website for walks in the area (www.doc.govt.nz).

Waipoua Forest

The highlight of Northland's west coast, this superb forest sanctuary – proclaimed in 1952 after much public pressure – is the largest remnant of the once-extensive kauri forests of northern NZ. The forest road (SH12) stretches for 18km and passes some huge trees – a kauri can reach 60m in height and have a trunk more than 5m in diameter.

Control of the forest has been returned to Te Roroa, the local *iwi* (tribe), as part of a settlement for Crown breaches of the Treaty of Waitangi. Te Roroa runs the **Waipoua Forest visitor centre** (☎09-439 6445; www.teroroa.iwi.nz; 1 Waipoua River Rd; ☺9am-6.30pm summer, 9am-4.30pm winter), cafe and camping ground near the south end of the park.

⊙ Sights & Activities

Tane Mahuta   TREE
Near the north end of the park, not far from the road, stands mighty Tane Mahuta, named for the Maori forest god. At 51.5m, with a 13.8m girth and wood mass of 244.5 cubic metres, he's the largest kauri alive. You don't so much look at Tane Mahuta; it's as if you're granted an audience to his hushed presence. He's been holding court here for somewhere between 1200 and 2000 years.

**Te Matua Ngahere,
Four Sisters & Yakas**   TREES
From the Kauri Walks car park, a 20-minute (each way) walk leads past the Four Sisters, a graceful stand of four tall trees that have fused together at the base, to Te Matua Ngahere (the Father of the Forest). Even the most ardent tree-hugger wouldn't consider rushing forward to throw their arms around him and call him 'Daddy', even if there wasn't a fence. At 30m he's shorter than Tane Mahuta, but he has the same noble presence, reinforced by a substantial girth – he's the fattest living kauri (16.4m). He presides over a clearing surrounded by mature trees that look like matchsticks in comparison.

A 30-minute (each way) path leads from near the Four Sisters to Yakas, the seventh-largest kauri.

Lookout   LOOKOUT
For a bird's-eye view over the canopy, head to the forest lookout, near the very south end of the park. You can either drive to it (the road is well signposted but not suitable for campervans) or take the 2.5km Lookout Track from the visitor centre.

🛏 Sleeping & Eating

Waipoua Lodge   B&B $$$
(☎09-439 0422; www.waipoualodge.co.nz; SH12; r $583) This fine old villa at the southern edge of the forest has four luxurious, spacious suites, which were originally the stables, the woolshed and the calf-rearing pen! Decadent dinners ($70) are available.

Waipoua Forest Campground   CAMPSITE $
(☎09-439 6445; www.teroroa.iwi.nz; 1 Waipoua River Rd; site/unit/house from $15/20/175) Situated next to the Waipoua River and the visitor centre, this peaceful camping ground offers hot showers, flush toilets and a kitchen. The cabins are extremely spartan, with unmade swab beds (bring your own linen or hire it). There are also whole houses for rent, sleeping 10.

Trounson Kauri Park

The 450-hectare Trounson Kauri Park has an easy half-hour loop walk leading from the picnic area by the road. It passes through beautiful forest with streams, some fine kauri stands, a couple of fallen trees and another Four Sisters – two pairs of trees with conjoined trunks. DOC operates a **campsite** (www.doc.govt.nz; sites per adult/child $11/5.10) at the edge of the park, which has a communal kitchen and hot showers.

Just 2km from SH12, **Kauri Coast Top 10 Holiday Park** (☎09-439 0621; www.kauricoasttop10.co.nz; Trounson Park Rd; dm/site/unit from $30/40/110; @) is an attractive riverside camping ground with good facilities and a small shop. It also organises night-time **nature walks** (adult/child $25/15), which explain the flora and nocturnal wildlife that thrives here. This is a rare chance to see a kiwi in the wild. Trounson has a predator-eradication program and has become a mainland refuge for threatened native bird species, so you should at least hear a morepork (a native owl) or a brown kiwi.

If you're approaching from the north, it's easier to take the second turn-off to the park, near Kaihu, which avoids a rough unsealed road.

Kai Iwi Lakes

These three trout-filled freshwater lakes nestle together near the coast, 12km off SH12. The largest, Taharoa, has blue water fringed with sandy patches. Lake Waikere is popular with water-skiers, while Lake Kai Iwi is relatively untouched. A half-hour walk leads from the lakes to the coast and it's another two hours to reach the base of volcanic **Maunganui Bluff** (460m); the hike up and down it takes five hours.

Camping (☎09-439 0986; lakes@kaipara.govt.nz; adult/child $10/5) is permitted at the side of Lake Taharoa; cold showers, drinking water and flush toilets are provided.

Baylys Beach

A village of brightly coloured baches and a few new holiday mansions, Baylys Beach is 12km from Dargaville, off SH12. It lies on 100km-long Ripiro Ocean Beach, a surf-pounded stretch of coast that has been the site of many shipwrecks. The beach is a gazetted highway: you can drive along its hard sand at low tide, although it is primarily for 4WDs. Despite being NZ's longest drivable beach, it's less well known and hence less travelled than Ninety Mile Beach. Ask locals about conditions and check your hire-car agreement before venturing onto the sand. Quad bikes (single/double $75/95) can be hired at the holiday park.

It's pretty kooky, but **Skydome Observatory** (☑09-439 1856; www.skydome.org.nz; 28 Seaview Rd; stargazing $20-40) is a massive, technologically advanced telescope and it's located on the front lawn of someone's house. Call ahead for bookings.

🛏 Sleeping

Sunset View Lodge B&B $$
(☑09-439 4342; www.sunsetviewlodge.co.nz; 7 Alcemene Lane; r $175-190; @☒) If gin-in-hand sunset-gazing is your thing, this large, modern B&B fits the bill. The upstairs rooms have terrific sea views and there's a self-service bar with an honesty box in the guest lounge.

Baylys Beach Holiday Park HOLIDAY PARK $
(☑09-439 6349; www.baylysbeach.co.nz; 24 Seaview Rd; site/unit from $16/50; @☏) Circled by pohutukawa trees, this midsized camping ground has tidy facilities and attractive cream and green units ranging from basic cabins to a cottage that sleeps six.

🍴 Eating

Funky Fish CAFE, BAR $$
(☑09-439 8883; www.thefunkyfish.co.nz; 34 Seaview Rd; lunch $14-20, dinner $22-28; ☺lunch Thu-Sun, dinner Tue-Sun) Brightly decorated with murals and mosaics, this highly popular cafe, restaurant and bar has a wonderful back garden and a wide-ranging menu, including lots of seafood. Bookings are advisable in summer.

Sharky's FISH & CHIPS
(1 Seaview Rd; mains $6-20; ☺8.30am-8pm) A handy combination of bottle shop, general store, bar and takeaway, serving all-day breakfasts.

Dargaville

POP 4500

When a town proclaims itself the 'kumara capital of NZ' (it produces two-thirds of the country's sweet potatoes), you should know not to expect too much. Founded in 1872 by timber merchant Joseph Dargaville, this once-important river port thrived on the export of kauri timber and gum. As the forests were decimated, it declined and today is a quiet backwater servicing the agricultural Northern Wairoa area.

◎ Sights & Activities

Dargaville Museum MUSEUM
(www.dargavillemuseum.co.nz; adult/child $12/2; ☺9am-4pm) Perched on top of a hill, the Dargaville Museum is more interesting than most regional museums. There's a large gumdigging display, plus maritime, Maori and musical-instrument sections and a neat model railway. Outside, the masts of the *Rainbow Warrior* are mounted at a lookout near a *pa* site and there's a recreation of a gumdiggers' camp.

Kumara Box AGRICULTURAL
(www.kumarabox.co.nz; 503 Pouto Rd; tours $20) If you want to learn about the district's knobbly purple claim-to-fame, book ahead for Kumara Ernie's show. It's surprisingly entertaining, usually involving a journey by home-built tractor-train through the fields to 'NZ's smallest church'.

🛏 Sleeping & Eating

Campervans can enjoy the views from the Dargaville Museum car park for $10 per night.

Greenhouse Backpackers HOSTEL $
(☑09-439 6342; greenhousebackpackers@ihug.co.nz; 15 Gordon St; dm/s/d $28/45/70; @☏) This converted 1921 schoolhouse has classrooms partitioned into a large dorm and a communal lounge, both painted with colourful murals. Better still are the cosy units in the back garden, decked out with heated towel rails and electric blankets.

Blah, Blah, Blah... CAFE, BAR $
(101 Victoria St; breakfast $6-20, lunch $8-28, dinner $20-28; ☺breakfast & lunch daily, dinner Tue-Sat) The number-one eatery in Dargaville (admittedly that's not saying much) has a garden area, hip music, deli-style snacks, a global menu (dukkha, confit duck, steak) and cocktails.

Riverside Produce Market   MARKET
(Kapia St; ⊘2.30-5.30pm Thu) Selling local produce and craft, it's as good a place as anywhere to stock up on kumara.

❶ Information

DOC Kauri Coast Area Office (☑09-439 3450; www.doc.govt.nz; 150 Colville Rd; ⊘8am-4.30pm Mon-Fri)
Visitor Information Centre (☑09-439 4975; www.kauriinfocentre.co.nz; 4 Murdoch St; ⊘9am-6pm; ☎) Operates out of the interesting Woodturners Kauri Gallery & Studio. Books accommodation and tours.

❶ Getting There & Away

The main bus stop is in Kapia St. Main Coachline (p112) buses and West Coaster (p112) shuttles offer services.

Pouto Point

A narrow spit descends south of Dargaville, bordered by the Tasman Sea and Wairoa River, and comes to an abrupt halt at the entrance of NZ's biggest harbour, the Kaipara. It's an incredibly remote headland, punctuated by dozens of petite dune lakes and the lonely Kaipara Lighthouse (built from kauri in 1884). Less than 10km separates Kaipara Harbour's north and south heads, but if you were to drive between the two you'd cover 267km.

A 4WD can be put to its proper use on the ocean-hugging 71km stretch of beach from Dargaville. DOC's *Pouto Hidden Treasures* is a helpful guide for motorists, with tips for protecting both your car and the fragile ecosystem. It can be downloaded at www.doc.govt.nz.

Matakohe

POP 400

Apart from the rural charms of this village, the reason for visiting is the superb **Kauri Museum** (www.kaurimuseum.com; 5 Church Rd; adult/child $25/8; ⊘9am-5pm). The giant cross-sections of trees are astounding in themselves but the entire industry is brought to life through video kiosks, artefacts, fabulous furniture and marquetry, and reproductions of a pioneer sawmill, boarding house, gum-digger's hut and Victorian home. The Gum Room holds a weird and wonderful collection of kauri gum, the amber substance that can be carved, sculpted and polished to a jewell-like quality. The museum shop stocks mementoes crafted from kauri wood and gum.

Facing the museum is the tiny kauri-built **Matakohe Pioneer Church** (1867), which served both Methodists and Anglicans, and acted as the community's hall and school. Nearby, you can wander through a historic **schoolhouse** (1878) and **post office/ telephone exchange** (1909).

🛏 Sleeping & Eating

Matakohe Holiday Park   HOLIDAY PARK $
(☑09-431 6431; www.matakoheholidaypark.co.nz; 66 Church Rd; site/unit from $19/55; @☎▣) With perhaps the cosiest lounge you'll find in a camping ground, this little park has modern amenities, plenty of space and good views of Kaipara Harbour.

Matakohe House   B&B
(☑09-431 7091; www.matakohehouse.co.nz; 24 Church Rd; s/d $135/160; @☎) A short walk from the Kauri museum, this B&B occupies a pretty villa with a cafe attached. The simply furnished rooms open out onto a veranda and offer winning touches like complimentary port and chocolates. It was for sale when we visited, so call ahead.

Petite Provence   B&B $$
(☑09-431 7552; www.petiteprovence.co.nz; 703c Tinopai Rd; s/d $110/150) This attractive, French-influenced B&B is a popular weekender for Aucklanders, so it pays to book ahead. Excellent dinners can be arranged for $45 per person.

❶ Getting There & Away

Main Coachline services operate.

Coromandel Peninsula

Best Beaches

» New Chum's Beach (p164)
» Hahei Beach (p168)
» Cathedral Cove (p167)
» Otama Beach (p164)
» Hot Water Beach (p168)

Best Places to Stay

» Black Jack Lodge (p164)
» Driving Creek Villas (p161)
» Cotswold Cottage (p159)
» Bowentown Beach Holiday Park (p172)

Why Go?

The Coromandel Peninsula juts into the Pacific east of Auckland, forming the eastern boundary of the Hauraki Gulf. Although relatively close to the metropolis, the Coromandel offers easy access to splendid isolation. Its dramatic, mountainous spine bisects it into two very distinct parts.

The east coast has some of the North Island's best white-sand beaches. When Auckland shuts up shop for Christmas/New Year, this is where it heads. The cutesy historic gold-mining towns on the west side escape the worst of the influx, their muddy wetlands and picturesque stony bays holding less appeal for the masses. This coast has long been a refuge for alternative lifestylers. Down the middle, the mountains are crisscrossed with walking tracks, allowing trampers to explore large tracts of untamed bush where kauri trees once towered and are starting to do so again.

When to Go

With the beaches playing the starring role here, summer is the best time to visit. When the pohutukawa trees put on their pre-Christmas display, the entire peninsula is edged in crimson. The population explodes during the summer school holidays (from Christmas until the end of January) and things can go a little nuts on New Year's Eve. Balmy February and March are slightly quieter. Being mountainous, the region attracts more rainfall than elsewhere on the east coast (3000mm or even 4500mm a year) – peaking from May to September.

Coromandel Peninsula Highlights

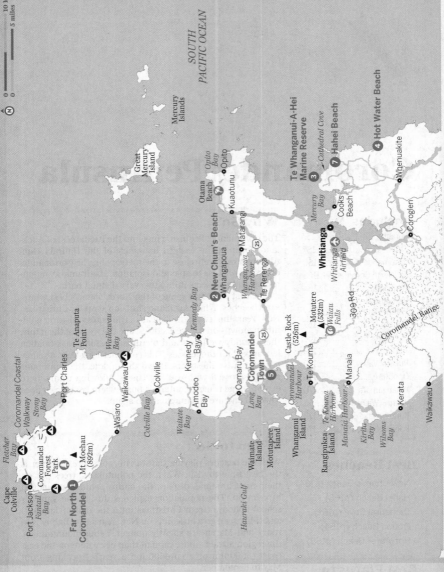

1 Travelling remote gravel roads under a crimson canopy of ancient pohutukawa trees in **Far North Coromandel** (p163)

2 Staking out your own patch of footprint-free sand at **New Chum's Beach** (p164)

3 Kayaking around the hidden islands, caves and bays of **Te Whanganui-A-Hei Marine Reserve** (p166)

4 Burning your butt in a freshly dug thermal pool in the sands of **Hot Water Beach** (p168)

5 Pigging out on smoked mussels in **Coromandel Town** (p160)

6 Penetrating the mystical depths of the dense bush of

Coromandel Forest Park (p161) and **Karangahake Gorge** (p173)

7️⃣ Watching the offshore islands glow in the dying haze of a summer sunset from **Hahei Beach** (p168)

History

This whole area, including the peninsula, the islands and both sides of the gulf, was known to the Maori as Hauraki. Various *iwi* (tribes) held claim to pockets of it, including the Pare Hauraki branch of the Tainui tribes and others descended from Te Arawa and earlier migrations. Polynesian artefacts and evidence of moa-hunting have been found, pointing to around 1000 years of continuous occupation.

The Hauraki *iwi* were some of the first to be exposed to European traders. The region's proximity to Auckland, safe anchorages and ready supply of valuable timber initially lead to a booming economy. Kauri logging was big business on the peninsula. Allied to the timber trade was shipbuilding, which took off in 1832 when a mill was established at Mercury Bay. Things got tougher once the kauri around the coast became scarce and the loggers had to penetrate deeper into the bush for timber. Kauri dams, which used water power to propel the huge logs to the coast, were built. By the 1930s virtually no kauri remained and the industry died.

Gold was first discovered in New Zealand (NZ) near Coromandel Town in 1852. Although this first rush was short-lived, more gold was discovered around Thames in 1867 and later in other places. The peninsula is also rich in semiprecious gemstones, such as quartz, agate, amethyst and jasper. A fossick on any west-coast beach can be rewarding.

Despite successful interactions with Europeans for decades, the Hauraki *iwi* were some of the hardest hit by colonisation. Unscrupulous dealings by settlers and government to gain access to valuable resources resulted in the Maori losing most of their lands by the 1880s. Even today there is a much lower Maori presence on the peninsula than in neighbouring districts.

MAORI NZ: COROMANDEL PENINSULA

Although it has a long and rich Maori history, the Coromandel Peninsula doesn't offer many opportunities to engage with the culture. Pioneer pursuits such as gold-mining and kauri logging have been given much more attention, although this is starting to change.

Historic *pa* (fortified village) sites are dotted around, with the most accessible being Paaku. There are others at Opito Beach, Hahei and Hot Water Beach.

Getting There & Around

Air

Sunair (07-575 7799; www.sunair.co.nz) Twice-daily flights to Whitianga from Auckland and Great Barrier Island, and weekday flights to Whitianga from Hamilton, Rotorua and Tauranga.

Boat

360 Discovery (0800 360 3472; www.360discovery.co.nz) Operates ferries to/from Auckland (one-way/return $55/88, two hours) via Orapiu on Waiheke Island (one-way/return $44/77, 70 minutes) five times per week (daily in summer). The boats dock at Hannafords Wharf, Te Kouma, where free buses shuttle passengers the 10km into Coromandel Town. It makes a great day trip from Auckland (same-day return $69), and there's a day-tour option that includes a hop-on, hop-off bus (adult/child $94/57).

ESSENTIAL COROMANDEL PENINSULA

» **Eat** Buckets of bivalves – mussels, oysters and scallops are local specialities
» **Drink** Boiled water from a mountain campsite
» **Read** The Penguin History of New Zealand (2003) by the late Michael King, an Opoutere resident
» **Listen to** Top Kiwi bands at the Coromandel Gold New Year's Eve festival (p166)
» **Watch** The birds in the Firth of Thames
» **Festival** The peninsula-wide Pohutukawa Festival (www.pohutukawafestival.co.nz)
» **Go green** Witness forest regeneration at the Driving Creek Railway (p161)
» **Online** www.thecoromandel.com
» **Area code** 07

Bus

Go Kiwi (☑07-866 0336; www.go-kiwi.co.nz) Has daily Auckland City–International Airport–Thames–Tairua–Whitianga shuttles year-round, with a connection to Opoutere and Whangamata. From mid-December to Easter it also runs Rotorua–Tauranga–Waihi–Whangamata–Whitianga and Coromandel Town–Whitianga shuttles.

InterCity (www.intercity.co.nz) Has two routes to/from the peninsula: Auckland–Thames–Paeroa–Waihi–Tauranga and Hamilton–Te Aroha–Paeroa–Thames–Coromandel Town. Local routes include Thames–Coromandel Town–Whitianga and Whitianga–Tairua–Thames.

Naked Bus (www.nakedbus.com) Buses on the Auckland–Tauranga–Mt Maunganui–Rotorua–Gisborne route stop at Ngatea, where local associate Tairua Bus Company continues on to Whitianga.

Tairua Bus Company (TBC; ☑07-864 7194; www.tairuabus.co.nz) As well as local buses on the Thames–Tairua–Hahei–Whitianga–Coromandel Town route, TBC has a Hamilton–Cambridge–Te Aroha–Thames–Tairua service.

Car

Car is the only option for accessing some of the more remote areas, but be careful to check hire agreements as there are plenty of gravel roads and a few streams to ford. Most of them are in good condition and even a small car can cope unless the weather's been particularly wet.

Miranda

It's a pretty name for a settlement on the swampy Firth of Thames, just an hour's drive from Auckland. The two reasons to come here are splashing around in the thermal pools and birdwatching – but doing both at the same time might be considered impolite.

This is one of the most accessible spots for studying waders or shorebirds all year round. The vast mudflat is teeming with aquatic worms and crustaceans, which attract thousands of Arctic-nesting shorebirds over the winter – 43 species of wader have been spotted here. The two main species are the bar-tailed godwit and the lesser or red knot, but it isn't unusual to see turnstones, sandpipers and the odd vagrant red-necked stint. One godwit tagged here was tracked making an 11,570km nonstop flight from Alaska. Short-haul travellers include the pied oystercatcher and the threatened wrybill from the South Island, and banded dotterels and pied stilts.

The **Miranda Shorebird Centre** (☑09-232 2781; www.miranda-shorebird.org.nz; 283 East Coast Rd; ◷9am-5pm) has bird-life displays, hires out binoculars and sells useful bird-watching pamphlets ($2). Nearby are a hide and several walks (30 minutes to two hours). The centre offers clean bunk-style accommodation (dorm beds/rooms $25/85) with a kitchen.

Miranda Hot Springs (www.mirandahotsprings.co.nz; Front Miranda Rd; adult/child $13/6; ◷9am-9.30pm), 5km south, has a large thermal swimming pool (reputedly the largest in the southern hemisphere), a toasty sauna pool and private spas ($10 extra).

Next door is **Miranda Holiday Park** (☑07-867 3205; www.mirandaholidaypark.co.nz; 595 Front Miranda Rd; sites per adult/child $21/11, dm $34, units $145-311; @🛜🏊), which has excellent sparkling-clean units and facilities, its own thermally heated pool and a floodlit tennis court.

Thames

POP 6800

Dinky wooden buildings from the 19th-century gold rush still dominate Thames, but grizzly prospectors have long been replaced by alternative lifestylers. If you're a vegetarian ecowarrior you'll feel right at home. It's a good base for tramping or canyoning in the nearby Kauaeranga Valley.

Captain Cook arrived here in 1769, naming the Waihou River the 'Thames' 'on account of its bearing some resemblance to that river in England'; you may well think otherwise. This area belonged to Ngati Maru, a tribe of Tainui descent. Their spectacular meeting house, Hotunui (1878), holds pride of place in the Auckland Museum.

After opening Thames to gold-miners in 1867, Ngati Maru were swamped by 10,000 European settlers within a year. When the initial boom turned to bust, a dubious system of government advances resulted in Maori debt and forced land sales.

◉ Sights

Goldmine Experience   MINE

(www.goldmine-experience.co.nz; cnr Moanataiari Rd & Pollen St; adult/child $15/5; ◷ 10am-4pm daily Jan-Mar, 10am-1pm Apr, May, Sep & Dec) Walk through a mine tunnel, watch a stamper battery crush rock, learn about the history of the Cornish miners and try your hand at panning for gold ($2 extra).

Thames

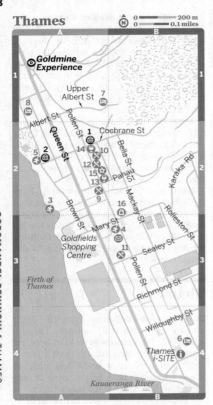

Goldmine Experience

COROMANDEL PENINSULA THAMES

School of Mines & Mineralogical Museum   MUSEUM
(www.historicplaces.org.nz; 101 Cochrane St; adult/child $5/free; ⌚11am-3pm Wed-Sun) The Historic Places Trust runs tours of these buildings, which house an extensive collection of NZ rocks, minerals and fossils. The oldest section (1868) was part of a Methodist Sunday school, situated on a Maori burial ground. The Trust also distributes a free self-tour pamphlet taking in Thames' significant buildings.

Butterfly & Orchid Garden   GARDENS
(www.butterfly.co.nz; Victoria St; adult/child $11/6; ⌚9.30am-4pm) Anyone with a fairy complex will adore the Butterfly & Orchid Garden, 3km north of town within the Dickson Holiday Park. It's an enclosed jungle full of hundreds of exotic flappers.

Historical Museum   MUSEUM
(cnr Cochrane & Pollen Sts; adult/child $5/2; ⌚1-4pm) Pioneer relics, rocks and old photographs of the town.

🏃 Activities

Hauraki Rail Trail   CYCLING
(www.haurakirailtrail.co.nz) This two-day cycle route connects Thames to Te Aroha via Paihia. Enquire at the i-SITE for more details.

Karaka Bird Hide   BIRDWATCHING
(admission free) Built with compensation funds from the *Rainbow Warrior* bombing, this hide can be reached by a boardwalk through the mangroves just off Brown St.

Thames Small Gauge Railway   NARROW-GAUGE RAILWAY
(Brown St; tickets $2; ⌚11am-3pm Sun) Young 'uns will enjoy the 900m loop ride on this cute-as-a-button train.

Canyonz
CANYONING

(☎0800 422 696; www.canyonz.co.nz; trips $290)
This outfit runs canyoning trips to the Sleeping God Canyon in the Kauaeranga Valley. Expect a vertical descent of over 300m, requiring abseiling, water-sliding and jumping.

Eyez Open
CYCLING

(☎07-868 9018; www.eyezopen.co.nz) Rents out bikes ($30 per day) and organises small-group cycling tours of the Coromandel Peninsula (one- to four-day tours from $150 to $770).

Paki Paki Bike Shop
CYCLING

(☎07-867 9026; 535 Pollen St) Rents out bikes ($25 per day) and performs repairs.

Sleeping

Cotswold Cottage
B&B $$

(☎07-868 6306; www.cotswoldcottage.co.nz; 36 Maramarahi Rd; r $165-205; ☎) Looking over the river and racecourse, 3km southeast of town, this pretty villa has had a modern makeover with luxuriant linen and an outdoor spa pool. The comfy rooms all open onto a deck.

Ocean View on Thames
B&B $$

(☎07-868 3588; www.retreat4u.co.nz; 509 Upper Albert St; ste $160, apt $180-250; ☎) Aside from the expansive views, it's the little touches that make this place so special – such as fresh flowers and, in the two-bedroom apartment downstairs, a fridge stocked with cost-price beverages offered on an honesty system.

Gateway Backpackers
HOSTEL $

(☎07-868 6339; overend@xtra.co.nz; 209 Mackay St; dm $25-27, s $50, d $62-72; @) Generations of Kiwis grew up in state houses just like this, giving this relaxed, friendly hostel a homely feel. Bathrooms are in short supply but there are pleasant rooms, a nice garden and free laundry facilities.

Coastal Motor Lodge
MOTEL $$

(☎07-868 6843; www.stayatcoastal.co.nz; 608 Tararu Rd; units $135-175; ☎) Motel and chalet-style accommodation is provided at this smart, welcoming place, 2km north of Thames. It overlooks the sea, making it a popular choice, especially in the summer months.

Grafton Cottage & Chalets
CHALET $$

(☎07-868 9971; www.graftoncottage.co.nz; 304 Grafton Rd; units $150-220; @☎☒) Perched on a hill, most of these attractive wooden chalets have decks with awesome views. The hospitable hosts provide free internet access and breakfast, as well as use of the pool, spa and barbecue areas.

Brunton House B&B
B&B $$

(☎07-868 5160; www.bruntonhouse.co.nz; 210 Parawai Rd; r $160-180, tr $195; @☎☒) Renovations of this impressive two-storey kauri villa (1875) have upgraded the kitchen and bathrooms, while staying true to the building's historic credentials (there are no en suites). Guests can relax in the grounds, by the pool, in the designated lounge or on the upstairs terrace.

Sunkist
HOSTEL $

(☎07-868 8808; www.sunkistbackpackers.com; 506 Brown St; sites from $19, dm $25-29, r $66; @☎) It's not the friendliest place, but this hostel in a character-filled 1860s heritage building has spacious dorms, a garden and free bikes. It also offers 4WD hire and shuttles to the Kauaeranga Valley ($35 return).

Eating

Rocco
MODERN NZ $$

(☎07-868 8641; 109 Sealey St; mains $23-34; ☺dinner Tue-Sun) Housed in one of Thames' gorgeous kauri villas, Rocco serves tapas and more substantial mains, making good use of local ingredients such as mussels and fish. In clement weather, take a seat among the crushed-shell and swirling brick paths outside.

Nakontong
THAI $$

(☎07-868 6821; 728 Pollen St; mains $16-20; ☺lunch Mon-Fri, dinner daily; ✍) This is the most popular restaurant in Thames by a country mile. Although the bright lighting may not induce romance, the tangy Thai dishes will provide a warm glow.

Sola Cafe
VEGETARIAN $

(720b Pollen St; mains $9-13; ☺8am-4pm; @☎✍) Bright and friendly, this meat-free cafe is first rate. Expect excellent coffee and a range of vegan, dairy-free and gluten-free options that include heavenly salads.

Coco Espresso
CAFE $

(661 Pollen St; snacks $4.50; ☺8am-2.30pm Tue-Fri, 8am-noon Sat) Occupying a corner of an old villa, this chic little cafe, decked out all in white, serves excellent coffee and enticing pastries and cakes.

COROMANDEL PENINSULA THAMES

🍃 Organic Co-op
SELF-CATERING
(736 Pollen St; ⏰9am-5pm Mon-Fri, 9am-noon Sat; 🖐) A good source of planet-friendly vegetables, nuts, bread, eggs and meat.

🍷 Drinking & Entertainment

Speak Easy
WINE BAR
(746 Pollen St; ⏰Wed-Sun) The cutest little bar on the Coromandel Peninsula, with art deco chandeliers, zany wallpaper and regular live music. It's the sort of place where a solo traveller of any gender can chill out over a glass of wine.

Junction Hotel
PUB
(www.thejunction.net.nz; 700 Pollen St) Serving thirsty gold-diggers since 1869, the Junction is the archetypal slightly rough-around-the-edges, historic, small-town pub. Live music attracts a younger crowd on the weekends, while families head to the corner-facing Grahamstown Bar & Diner for hearty pub grub.

Multiplex Cinemas
CINEMA
(www.cinemathames.co.nz; 708 Pollen St) Screening recent blockbusters in poorly sound-insulated cinemas.

🛍 Shopping
Pollen St has a good selection of gift and homeware stores selling local art and craft.

Grahamstown Market
MARKET
(Pollen St; ⏰8am-noon Sat) On Saturday mornings the Grahamstown Market fills the street with organic produce and handicrafts.

ℹ Information
Thames i-SITE (☎07-868 7284; www.thamesinfo.co.nz; 206 Pollen St; ⏰9am-5pm)

ℹ Getting There & Around
InterCity, Tairua Bus Company and Go Kiwi all run bus services (p157) to Thames.

Thames to Coromandel Town
Narrow SH25 snakes along the coast past pretty little bays and rocky beaches. Sea birds are plentiful, and you can fish, dig for shellfish and fossick for quartz, jasper and even gold-bearing rocks on the beaches. The landscape turns crimson when the pohutukawa (often referred to as the 'New Zealand Christmas tree') blooms in December.

A handful of stores, motels, B&Bs and camping grounds are scattered around the tiny settlements that front the picturesque bays. Backpackers can make themselves at home in **Wolfie's Lair** (☎07-868 2777; www.wolfieslair.co.nz; 11 Firth View Rd, Te Puru; dm/r $27/54), a tidy house in a Te Puru cul-de-sac with three rooms to rent. The wolf in question is less big and bad, more little and yappy.

At Tapu you can turn inland for a mainly sealed 6km drive to the **Rapaura Water Gardens** (☎07-868 4821; www.rapaura.com; 586 Tapu-Coroglen Rd; adult/child $15/6; ⏰9am-5pm), a marriage of water, greenery, sculpture and platitudes. There's accommodation on-site (cottage/lodge $165/275) and a well-regarded cafe (mains $14 to $29).

From Wilsons Bay the road heads away from the coast and climbs over several hills and valleys before dropping down to Coromandel Town, 55km from Thames. The view looking towards the island-studded Coromandel Harbour is exquisite.

Coromandel Town
POP 1480
Crammed with heritage buildings, Coromandel Town is a thoroughly quaint little place. Its natty cafes, interesting art stores, excellent sleeping options and delicious smoked mussels could keep you here longer than you expected.

Gold was discovered at Driving Creek in 1852. Initially the local Patukirikiri *iwi* kept control of the land and received money from digging licences. After initial financial success the same fate befell them as the Ngati Maru in Thames. By 1871, debt had forced them to sell all but 778 mountainous acres of their land. Today, fewer than 100 people remain who identify as part of this *iwi*.

◉ Sights
Heritage buffs can tour around 29 historic sites featured in the Historic Places Trust's *Coromandel Town* pamphlet (free from the i-SITE).

Coromandel Goldfield Centre & Stamper Battery
HISTORIC BUILDING
(☎07-866 8758; 360 Buffalo Rd; adult/child $10/5) The rock-crushing machine clatters into life during the informative one-hour tours of this 1899 plant; call ahead for times. You can also try panning for gold ($5). Outside of the

DON'T MISS

COROMANDEL FOREST PARK

More than 30 walks crisscross the Coromandel Forest Park, spread over several major blocks throughout the centre of the Coromandel Peninsula. The most popular hike is the challenging six- to eight-hour return journey up to the **Pinnacles** (759m) in the Kauaeranga Valley behind Thames. Other outstanding tramps include the **Coromandel Coastal Walkway** in Far North Coromandel, from Fletcher Bay to Stony Bay, and the **Puketui Valley** walk to abandoned gold mines.

The **Department of Conservation (DOC) Kauaeranga Visitor Centre** (☑07-867 9080; www.doc.govt.nz; Kauaeranga Valley Rd; ⊙8.30am-4pm) has interesting displays about the kauri forest and its history. Its staff sell maps and conservation resources and dispense advice. The centre is 14km off SH25; it's a further 9km along a gravel road to the start of the trails. Enquire at the Thames hostels about shuttles.

The DOC **Pinnacles Hut** (adult/child $15/7.50) has 80 beds, gas cookers, heating, toilets and cold showers. The 10-bunk **Crosbies Hut** (adult/child $15/7.50) is a four- to six-hour tramp from Thames or the Kauaeranga Valley. There are also four basic **back-country campsites** (adult/child $6/3) in this part of the park: one near each hut and others at Moss Creek and Billygoat Basin; expect only a toilet. A further eight **conservation campsites** (adult/child $10/5) are accessible from Kauaeranga Valley Rd. Bookings must be made online for the huts and some of the campsites.

tours it's worth stopping for a gander at NZ's largest working waterwheel.

Coromandel Mining & Historic Museum   MUSEUM
(841 Rings Rd; adult/child $3/50c; ⊙10am-1pm Sat & Sun Feb–mid-Dec, 10am-4pm daily mid-Dec–Jan) This small museum provides a glimpse of pioneer life.

Activities

Driving Creek Railway & Potteries   NARROW-GAUGE RAILWAY
(☑07-866 8703; www.drivingcreekrailway.co.nz; 380 Driving Creek Rd; adult/child $25/10; ⊙departures 10.15am & 2pm) A lifelong labour of love for its conservationist owner, this unique train runs up steep grades, across four trestle bridges, along two spirals and a double switchback, and through two tunnels, finishing at the 'Eye-full Tower'. The hour-long trip passes artworks and regenerating native forest – more than 17,000 natives have been planted, including 9000 kauri. It's worth lingering for the video about the extraordinary guy behind it all, well-known potter Barry Brickell.

Coromandel Kayak Adventures   KAYAKING
(☑07-866 7466; www.kayakadventures.co.nz) Offers paddle-powered tours ranging from half-day ecotours (from $200) to fishing trips (half/full day $200/385). Also rents kayaks (from $25/65 per hour/day).

Mussel Barge Snapper Safaris   FISHING
(☑07-866 7667; www.musselbargesafaris.co.nz; adult/child $50/25) Fishing trips with a uniquely local flavour and lots of laughs.

Tours

Tri Sail Charters   SAILING
(☑0800 024 874; www.trisailcharters.co.nz; half/full day $50/110) Cruise the Coromandel Harbour with your mates (a minimum of four) on an 11.2m trimaran (three-hulled yacht).

Argo Tours   DRIVING
(☑07-868 6633; www.argotoursnz.wordpress.com) Explore native bush and old gold workings in a mini 8WD. If you can muster a posse (up to five people), prices drop as low as $39 per person.

Coromandel Adventures   DRIVING
(☑07-866 7014; www.coromandeladventures.co.nz; adult/child $25/15) Offers various trips including a hop-on, hop-off service around Coromandel Town and a transfer to Whangapoua Beach.

Sleeping

Driving Creek Villas   COTTAGES $$$
(☑07-866 7755; www.drivingcreekvillas.com; 21a Colville Rd; villas $295-415; ⊛) This is the posh, grown-up's choice – three spacious, self-contained, modern, wooden villas with plenty of privacy. The Polynesian-influenced interior design is slick and the bush setting, complete with bubbling creek, sublime.

Anchor Lodge
MOTEL, HOSTEL $

(☑07-866 7992; www.anchorlodgecoromandel.co.nz; 448 Wharf Rd; dm $25-26, r $55-75, units $165-350; @ 🛜 ≋) Not many places can boast their own gold mine and glowworm cave, but this upmarket backpacker-motel combo has them, and a small heated swimming pool and spa to boot. The 2nd-floor units have harbour views.

Little Farm
APARTMENT $$

(☑07-866 8427; www.thelittlefarmcoromandel.co.nz; 750 Tiki Rd; r $115-130; 🛜) Overlooking a private wetland reserve at the rear of a fair-dinkum farm, these three comfortable units offer plenty of peace and quiet. The largest has a full kitchen and superb sunset views.

Green House
B&B $$

(☑07-866 7303; www.greenhousebandb.co.nz; 505 Tiki Rd; r $150-165; @🛜) Good old-fashioned hospitality and smartly furnished rooms are on offer here. The downstairs room opens onto the host's lounge, so it's worth paying $15 more for an upstairs room with a view.

Jacaranda Lodge
B&B $$

(☑07-866 8002; www.jacarandalodge.co.nz; 3195 Tiki Rd; s $80, d $135-165; 🛜) Located among 6 hectares of farmland and rose gardens, this two-storey cottage offers a bucolic retreat. Some rooms share bathrooms but expect fluffy towels and personalised soap in mini *kete* (woven flax bags).

Coromandel Motel & Holiday Park
HOLIDAY PARK $

(☑07-866 8830; www.coromandelholidaypark.co.nz; 636 Rings Rd; sites from $40, units $80-220; @🛜≋) Well kept and welcoming, with nicely painted cabins and manicured lawns, this large park includes the semi-separate Coromandel Town Backpackers. It gets busy in summer, so book ahead. Also hires bikes ($30 per day).

Tui Lodge
HOSTEL $

(☑07-866 8237; www.coromandeltuilodge.co.nz; 60 Whangapoua Rd; sites from $15, dm $25, r $60-80; @🛜) Pleasantly rural, this cheery backpackers has plenty of trees, a sauna ($5), free bikes, fruit (in season) and straight-up rooms. The pricier ones have en suites.

Lion's Den
HOSTEL $

(☑07-866 8157; www.lionsdenhostel.co.nz; 126 Te Tiki St; dm/r $26/60; 🛜) Chill out to the hippy vibe in this magical place. A tranquil garden with fish pond, fairy lights and wisteria, and a relaxed collection of comfy rooms (dotted with African bits and bobs), make for a soothing spot to rest your bones.

✖ Eating & Drinking

Umu
CAFE $

(22 Wharf Rd; breakfast $11-18, lunch $12-25, dinner $14-32; ☺breakfast, lunch & dinner; 🛜) Umu serves classy cafe fare, including excellent pizza, mouth-watering counter food (tarts and quiches around $7), superb coffee and tummy-taming breakfasts.

Pepper Tree
MODERN NZ $$

(☑07-866 8211; www.peppertreerestaurant.co.nz; 31 Kapanga Rd; lunch $22-26, dinner $26-36; ☺lunch & dinner; 🛜) Coromandel Town's most upmarket option dishes up generously proportioned meals with an emphasis on local seafood. On a summer's evening, the courtyard tables under the shady tree are the place to be.

Mussel Kitchen
SEAFOOD $$

(www.musselkitchen.co.nz; cnr SH25 & 309 Rd; mains $15-20; ☺lunch year-round, dinner Dec-Mar) Designed to look like a historic store, this cool cafe-bar sits among fields 3km south of town. Mussels are served in a multitude of ways alongside an eclectic globetrotting menu (laksa, barbecued pork ribs, pasta). In summer, the garden bar is irresistible.

🥕 Driving Creek Cafe
VEGETARIAN $

(180 Driving Creek Rd; mains $12-17; ☺9.30am-5pm; @🛜✏) A large selection of vegetarian, vegan, gluten-free, organic and fair-trade delights awaits at this funky mud-brick cafe. The food is beautifully presented, fresh and healthy. Once sated, the kids can play in the sandpit while the adults check their email.

Coromandel Smoking Co
SEAFOOD

(www.corosmoke.co.nz; 70 Tiki Rd; ☺9am-5pm) For a delicious snack or cooking supplies, Coromandel Smoking Co has a wonderful range of smoked fish and seafood. You can't leave town without trying the extremely addictive smoked mussels.

Coromandel Oyster Company
SEAFOOD

(1611 Tiki Rd; ☺9am-5pm) If you prefer your bivalves au naturel, this is the place for newly landed mussels, scallops, cooked crayfish and, of course, oysters.

Star & Garter Hotel
PUB

(www.starandgarter.co.nz; 5 Kapanga Rd; @) Making the most of the simple kauri interior of an 1873 building, this smart pub has pool tables, decent sounds and a roster of live music and DJs on the weekends. The beer garden is smartly clad in corrugated iron.

Information

Coromandel Town i-SITE (⌖07-866 8598; www.coromandeltown.co.nz; 355 Kapanga Rd; ⊙9am-5pm; @)

Getting There & Away

By far the nicest way to travel to Coromandel Town from Auckland is on a 360 Discovery (p156) ferry. The town is also serviced by InterCity, Tairua Bus Company and Go Kiwi buses (p157).

SENSIBLE CYCLISTS' LEAPFROG

There's no charge for carrying your bike on a 360 Discovery (p156) ferry. Touring cyclists can avoid Auckland's traffic fumes and treacherous roads completely by catching the ferry at Gulf Harbour to Auckland's ferry terminal, and then leapfrogging directly to Coromandel Town.

Far North Coromandel

Supremely isolated and gobsmackingly beautiful, the rugged tip of the Coromandel Peninsula is well worth the effort required to reach it. The best time to visit is summer, when the gravel roads are dry, the pohutukawa trees are in their crimson glory and camping's an option (there isn't a lot of accommodation up here).

The 1260-hectare **Colville Farm** (⌖07-866 6820; www.colvillefarmholidays.co.nz; 2140 Colville Rd; sites/units from $10/70, dm/s/d $25/38/66; @🛜) has a range of interesting accommodation, including bare-basics bush lodges and self-contained houses. Guests can try their hands at farm work (including milking) or go on horse treks ($40 to $150, one to five hours).

The nearby **Mahamudra Centre** (⌖07-866 6851; www.mahamudra.org.nz; site/dm/s/tw $15/23/45/70) is a serene Tibetan Buddhist retreat that has a stupa, a meditation hall and regular meditation courses. It offers simple accommodation in a parklike setting.

Another 1km brings you to the tiny settlement of **Colville** (25km north of Coromandel Town). It's a remote rural community by a muddy bay and a magnet for alternative lifestylers. There's not much here except for the **Green Snapper Cafe** (⌖07-866 6697; 2312 Colville Rd; mains $8-16; ⊙9am-3pm Wed, Thu, Sat & Sun, 9am-late Fri, extended in summer) and the quaint **Colville General Store** (⌖07-866 6805; Colville Rd; ⊙8.30am-5pm), selling just about everything from organic food to petrol (warning: this is your last option for either).

Three kilometres north of Colville the sealed road turns to gravel and splits to straddle each side of the peninsula. Following the west coast, ancient pohutukawa spread overhead as you pass turquoise waters and stony beaches. The small DOC-run **Fantail Bay campsite** (adult/child $9.20/2), 23km north of Colville, has running water and a couple of long-drop toilets under the shade of puriri trees. Another 7km brings you to the **Port**

Jackson campsite (adult/child $9.20/2), a larger DOC site right on the beach.

There's a spectacular lookout about 4km further on, where a metal dish identifies the various islands on the horizon. Great Barrier Island is only 20km away, looking every part the extension of the Coromandel Peninsula that it once was.

The road stops at **Fletcher Bay** – a magical land's end. Although it's only 37km from Colville, allow an hour for the drive. There's another **DOC campsite** (adult/child $10/5) here, as well as **Fletcher Bay Backpackers** (⌖07-866 6685; www.doc.govt.nz; dm $26) – a simple affair that has four rooms with four bunks in each. Bring sheets and food.

The **Coromandel Coastal Walkway** is a scenic, 3½-hour one-way hike between Fletcher Bay and **Stony Bay**. It's a relatively easy walk with great coastal views and an ambling section across farmland. If you're not keen on walking all the way back, **Coromandel Discovery** (⌖07-866 8175; www .coromandeldiscovery.co.nz; adult/child $110/65) will drive you from Coromandel Town up to Fletcher Bay and pick you up from Stony Bay four hours later.

At Stony Bay, where the east coast road terminates, there's another **DOC campsite** (adult/child $9.20/2) and a small DOC-run bach (holiday home) that sleeps five ($77). Heading south there are a couple of nice beaches peppered with baches on the way to the slightly larger settlement of Port Charles.

Tangiaro Kiwi Retreat (⌖07-866 6614; www.kiwiretreat.co.nz; 1299 Port Charles Rd; units $225-325; 🛜) offers eight brand-new one- or two-bedroom self-contained wooden cottages, each pair sharing a barbecue. There's a bush-fringed spa, an in-house masseuse ($70 per hour) and, in summer, a cafe and licensed restaurant.

Another 8km brings you to the turn-off leading back to Colville, or you can continue south to Waikawau Bay, where there's a large **DOC campsite** (07-866 1106; adult/child $9.20/2) which has a summer-only store. The road then winds its way south past Kennedy Bay before cutting back to come out near the Driving Creek Railway.

All of the DOC campsites should be booked online at www.doc.govt.nz.

Coromandel Town to Whitianga

There are two routes from Coromandel Town southeast to Whitianga. The main road is the slightly longer but quicker SH25, which enjoys sea views and has short detours to pristine sandy beaches. The other is the less-travelled but legendary 309 Rd, an unsealed, untamed route through deep bush.

STATE HIGHWAY 25

SH25 starts by climbing sharply to an incredible lookout before heading steeply down. The turn-off at Te Rerenga follows the harbour to **Whangapoua**. There's not much at this beach except for generic holiday homes, but you can walk along the rocky foreshore to the remote, beautiful and often-deserted **New Chum's Beach** (30 minutes), regarded as one of the most beautiful in the country due, in part, to its complete lack of development.

Continuing east on SH25 you soon reach **Kuaotunu**, a more interesting holiday village on a beautiful stretch of white-sand beach, with a cafe-gallery, a store and an ancient petrol pump. **Black Jack Lodge** (07-866 2988; www.black-jack.co.nz; 201 SH25; dm $33, s/tw/d from $53/76/86;) has a prime position directly across from the beach. It's a lovely little hostel with smart facilities and bikes and kayaks for hire.

For a touch more luxury, head back along the beach and up the hill to **Kuaotunu Bay Lodge** (07-866 4396; www.kuaotunubay .co.nz; SH25; s/d $270/295), an elegant B&B set among manicured gardens, offering a small set of spacious sea-gazing rooms.

Heading off the highway at Kuaotunu takes you (via an unsealed road) to one of Coromandel's best-kept secrets. First the long stretch of **Otama Beach** comes into view, deserted but for a few houses and farms. There's extremely basic camping (think long-drop toilet in a corrugated shack) in a farmer's field at **Otama Beach Camp** (07-866 2362; www.otamabeachcamp.co.nz; 400 Blackjack Rd; sites per adult/child $10/5, cottages $150-260). Down

by the beach they've recently built a couple of self-contained, ecofriendly cottages (sleeping four to six), with solar power, a composting waste-water system and ocean views.

Continue along the road and you'll be in for a shock. Just when you think you're about to fall off the end of the earth, the seal starts again and you reach **Opito** – a hidden-away enclave of 250 flash properties (too smart to be called baches), of which only 16 have permanent residents. It's more than a little weird, but it is a magical beach. You can walk to a Ngati Hei *pa* (fortified village) site at the far end.

One of the 'real' residences houses the delightful folks of **Leighton Lodge** (07-866 0756; www.leightonlodge.co.nz; 17 Stewart Pl; s $135-145, d $170-190; @). This smart B&B has a self-contained flat downstairs and an upstairs room with a view-hungry balcony.

309 ROAD

Starting 3km south of Coromandel Town, the 309 cuts through the Coromandel Range for 21km (most of which is unsealed but well maintained), rejoining SH25 7km south of Whitianga. The **Waterworks** (www.the waterworks.co.nz; 471 309 Rd; adult/child $18/12; 9am-6pm Nov-Apr, 10am-4pm May-Oct), 5km from SH25, is a wonderfully bizarre park filled with whimsical water-powered amusements made from old kitchen knives, washing machines, bikes and toilets.

Two kilometres later there's a two-minute walk through a pretty patch of bush to the 10m-high **Waiau Falls**. Stop again after another 500m for an easy 10-minute walk through peaceful native bush to an amazing kauri grove. This stand of 600-year-old giants escaped the carnage of the 19th century, giving a majestic reminder of what the peninsula once looked like. The biggest tree has a 6m circumference.

If you enjoy the remoteness and decide to linger, **Wairua Lodge** (07-866 0304; www .wairualodge.co.nz; 251 Old Coach Rd; r $145-235) is a peaceful B&B with charming hosts, nestled in the bush towards the Whitianga end of the 309. There's a riverside swimming hole on the property, a barbecue, a spa and a romantic outdoor bathtub.

Whitianga

POP 3800

Whitianga's big attractions are the sandy beaches of Mercury Bay and the diving, boating and kayaking opportunities af-

forded by the craggy coast and nearby Te Whanganui-A-Hei Marine Reserve. The pretty harbour is a renowned base for game-fishing (especially marlin and tuna, particularly between January and March). There are numerous charters on offer for would-be boaties, starting at around $500 and heading into the thousands. If you snag an overfished species, consider releasing your catch (p139).

A genuine nautical hero, the legendary Polynesian explorer and seafarer Kupe, is believed to have landed near here sometime around AD 950. The name Whitianga is a contraction of Te Whitianga a Kupe (the Crossing Place of Kupe).

◉ Sights & Activities

Beaches SWIMMING, WALKING
Buffalo Beach stretches along Mercury Bay, north of Whitianga Harbour. A five-minute passenger ferry ride will take you across the harbour to Whitianga Rock Scenic & Historical Reserve, Flaxmill Bay, **Shakespeare Cliff Lookout**, Lonely Bay, Cooks Beach and **Captain Cook's Memorial**, all within walking distance. Further afield are Hahei Beach (13km), Cathedral Cove (15km) and Hot Water Beach (18km, one hour by bike).

Lost Spring SPA
(www.thelostspring.co.nz; 121a Cook Dr; per hr/day $28/60; ⊙11am-6pm Sun-Fri, 11am-8pm Sat) This expensive but intriguing Disney-meets-Rotorua thermal complex comprises a series of hot pools in a lush junglelike setting, complete with an erupting volcano. Yet this is an adult's indulgence (children under 14 not permitted), leaving the grown-ups to marinate themselves in tropical tranquillity, cocktail in hand. There's also a day spa and cafe.

Mercury Bay Museum MUSEUM
(www.mercurybaymuseum.co.nz; 11a The Esplanade; adult/child $5/50c; ⊙10am-4pm) A small but interesting museum focusing on local history – especially Whitianga's most famous visitors, Kupe and Cook.

Dive Zone DIVING
(📞07-867 1580; www.divethecoromandel.co.nz; 7 Blacksmith Lane; trips $150-225) A PADI five-star accredited dive facility offering a range of shore, kayak and boat dives.

Seafari Windsurfing WINDSURFING
(📞07-866 0677; Brophy's Beach) Based at Brophy's Beach, 4km north of central

Whitianga

◉ Sights
1 Mercury Bay Museum B2

◉ Activities, Courses & Tours
2 Dive Zone A2
3 Lost Spring A1

◉ Sleeping
4 Beachside Resort.................................. A1
5 Cat's Pyjamas..A2
6 Mercury Bay Holiday Park A3

◉ Eating
7 Cafe Nina A2
8 Coghill House A2
9 Monk St Market......................................B2
10 Squids..B2
11 Wild Hogs B2

◉ Drinking
12 Blacksmith Bar......................................B2

◉ Entertainment
13 Mercury Twin Cinemas A2

Whitianga, Seafari hires out sailboards (from $25 per hour) and kayaks (from $15 per hour), and provides windsurfing lessons (from $40 including gear).

Twin Oaks Riding Ranch
HORSE RIDING

(☎07-866 5388; www.twinoaksridingranch.co.nz; 927 Kuaotunu-Wharekaho Rd; 2hr trek $60) Trek over farmland and through bush on horseback, 9km north of Whitianga.

Highzone
ROPES COURSE

(☎07-866 2113; www.highzone.co.nz; 49 Kaiarama Rd; activities $10-70) Hit the ropes for high adventure, including a trapeze leap, high swing and flying fox. It's located 7km south of Whitianga, just off the main road. Call for opening hours.

☞ Tours

There are a baffling number of tours to **Te Whanganui-A-Hei Marine Reserve**, where you'll see interesting rock formations and, if you're lucky, dolphins, fur seals, penguins and orcas. Some are straight-out cruises while others offer optional swimming and snorkeling.

Banana Boat
CRUISE

(☎07-866 5617; www.whitianga.co.nz/bananaboat; rides $10-30; ⊙Dec 26-Jan 31) Monkey around in Mercury Bay on the bright-yellow (naturally), motorised Banana Boat – or split to Cathedral Cove.

Cave Cruzer
CRUISE

(☎07-866 0611; www.cavecruzer.co.nz) A rigid-hull inflatable offering a one-hour (adult/child $50/30) or two-hour (adult/child $75/40) tour.

Glass Bottom Boat
CRUISE

(☎07-867 1962; www.glassbottomboatwhitianga.co.nz; adult/child $85/50) Two-hour bottom-gazing tours.

Whitianga Adventures
CRUISE

(☎0800 806 060; www.whitianga-adventures.co.nz; adult/child $65/40) Offers a two-hour Sea Cave Adventure in an inflatable.

Windborne
SAILING

(☎027 475 2411; www.windborne.co.nz; day sail $95) Day sails in a 19m 1928 schooner.

✪ Festivals & Events

Coromandel Gold Festival
MUSIC

(www.coromandelgold.co.nz; Ohuka Farm, Buffalo Beach Rd; 2-day pass $169) Top NZ and international bands \ to the stage for a two-day festival culminating in the early hours of New Year's Day.

🛏 Sleeping

Pipi Dune B&B
B&B $$

(☎07-869 5375; www.pipidune.co.nz; 5 Pipi Dune; r $160; ☜) You'll be as snug as a pipi in its shell in this attractive B&B in a quiet cul-de-sac, and you'll have a lot more room to move: pipi shells don't tend to come with guest lounges, kitchenettes, laundries and free wi-fi. To get here, head north on Cook Dr, turn left onto Surf St and then first right.

Beachside Resort
MOTEL $$

(☎07-867 1356; www.beachsideresort.co.nz; 20 Eyre St; units $175-225; ☜▨) Attached to the sprawling Oceans Resort, this modern motel has tidy units with kitchenettes and, on the upper level, balconies. Despite the name, it's set back from the beach but it does have a heated pool.

Within the Bays
B&B $$$

(☎07-866 2848; www.withinthebays.co.nz; 49 Tarapatiki Dr; r $295; @) It's the combination of charming hosts and incredible views that make this B&B set on a hill overlooking Mercury Bay worth considering. It's extremely well set up for guests with restricted mobility – there's even a wheelchair-accessible bush track on the property.

On the Beach Backpackers Lodge
HOSTEL $

(☎07-866 5380; www.coromandelbackpackers.com; 46 Buffalo Beach Rd; dm $25-27, s $38, d $70-96; @) Brightly painted and beachside, this large YHA-affiliate has a wide range of rooms, including some with sea views and en suites. It provides free kayaks, boogie boards and spades (for Hot Water Beach).

Cat's Pyjamas
HOSTEL $

(☎07-866 4663; www.cats-pyjamas.co.nz; 12 Albert St; dm $25, d $60-70; @☜) Perfectly positioned between the pubs and the beach, this converted house offers bunk-filled dorms as well as private rooms, some with their own bathroom. There's a large lounge and a sunny courtyard for mooching about in.

🏕 Mercury Bay Holiday Park
HOLIDAY PARK $

(☎07-866 5579; www.mercurybayholidaypark.co.nz; 121 Albert St; sites from $25, units $85-255; @☜▨) Strangely planted in a suburban neighbourhood, this small holiday park is comfortable and clean, with playgrounds, trampoline, swimming pool and pool table.

⚒ Eating & Drinking

Cafe Nina   CAFE $
(20 Victoria St; mains $9-19; ⊗8am-3pm) Barbecue for breakfast? Why the hell not. Too cool to be constricted to four walls, the kitchen grills bacon and eggs on an outdoor hotplate while the punters spill out onto tables in the park.

Squids   SEAFOOD $$
(☑07-867 1710; www.squids.co.nz; 15/1 Blacksmith Lane; mains $17-25; ⊗lunch & dinner Mon-Sat) On a corner facing the harbour, this informal restaurant offers that rarest of conjunctions: good-value seafood meals in a prime location. If you don't fancy the steamed mussels, smoked seafood platter, chowder or catch of the day, steak's an option.

Wild Hogs   PUB $$
(www.wildhogswhitianga.wordpress.com; 9 The Esplanade; mains $18-33; ⊗11am-late) While the name may conjure up images of hirsute, leather-clad bikers, the reality is much more genteel. The food's excellent, including juicy burgers and crispy pizzas laden with fancy toppings – best enjoyed on the shady deck.

Coghill House   CAFE $
(www.thecog.co.nz; 10 Coghill St; mains $8-17; ⊗8am-3pm) Get an early start to the day on the sunny terrace of this side-street cafe, where the counter food beckons enticingly and the toasted sandwiches have gourmet aspirations.

◢ Monk St Market   DELI
(1 Monk St; ⊗10am-6pm Mon-Sat) Self-catering foodies should head here for deli goods, imported chocolate and organic produce.

Blacksmith Bar   PUB
(www.blacksmithbar.co.nz; 1 Blacksmith Lane; ⊗10.30am-late) On the weekends, live bands keep the punters pumping until the wee hours (well, 1am). It's the kind of small-town pub that attracts all ages, styles and dancing abilities. There's a large beer garden out the back.

☆ Entertainment

Mercury Twin Cinemas   CINEMA
(☑07-867 1001; www.flicks.co.nz; Lee St) Latest-release mainstream and independent films.

❶ Information

Whitianga i-SITE (☑07-866 5555; www.whitianga.co.nz; 66 Albert St; ⊗9am-5pm Mon-Fri, 9am-4pm Sat & Sun, extended in summer) Information and internet access ($3 per 15 minutes).

❶ Getting There & Around

Sunair (p156) operates flights to Whitianga from Auckland, Great Barrier Island, Hamilton, Rotorua and Tauranga. Bus services are offered by InterCity, Tairua Bus Company and Go Kiwi.

Coroglen & Whenuakite

The blink-and-you'll-miss-them villages of Coroglen and Whenuakite are on SH25, south of Whitianga and west of Hot Water Beach. The legendary **Coroglen Tavern** (www.coroglentavern.com; 1937 SH25) is the archetypal middle-of-nowhere country pub that attracts big-name Kiwi bands in the summer.

Running from Labour Day (late October) to Queen's Birthday (early June), **Coroglen Farmers Market** (SH25; ⊗9am-1pm Sun) sells a bit of everything produced in the local area, from vegetables to compost.

Nearby, the folks at **Rangihau Ranch** (☑07-866 3875; www.rangihauranch.co.nz; Rangihau Rd; rides per hr $40) will lead you on horseback up a historic packhorse track, through beautiful bush to spectacular views.

Better than your average highway stop, **Colenso** (www.colensocafe.co.nz; SH25, Whenuakite; mains $7-14; ⊗10am-5pm) has excellent fair-trade coffee, scones, cakes and light snacks, as well as a shop selling homewares and gifts.

Hahei

POP 270 (7000 IN SUMMER)

A legendary Kiwi beach town, little Hahei balloons in summer but is nearly abandoned otherwise – apart from the busloads of tourists doing the obligatory stop-off at Cathedral Cove. It's a charming spot and a great place to unwind for a few days, especially in the quieter months. It takes its name from Hei, the eponymous ancestor of the Ngati Hei people, who arrived in the 14th century on the *Te Arawa* canoe.

◉ Sights

Cathedral Cove   BEACH
Beautiful Cathedral Cove, with its famous gigantic stone arch and natural waterfall shower, is best enjoyed early or late in the day – avoiding the worst of the hordes. At

the time of research the arch was roped off due to rock falls, but it's still worth taking the coastal walk to the cove regardless.

At the car park, 1km north of Hahei, the signs suggest that the walk will take 45 minutes, but anyone who's not on a ventilator will do it in 30. On the way there's rocky **Gemstone Bay** (which has a snorkelling trail where you're likely to see big snapper, crayfish and stingrays) and sandy **Stingray Bay**. The walk from Hahei Beach to Cathedral Cove takes about 70 minutes.

Hahei Beach
BEACH

Long, lovely Hahei Beach is made more magical by the view to the craggy islands in the distance. From the southern end of Hahei Beach, it's a 15-minute walk up to Te Pare, a *pa* site with splendid coastal views.

🏃 Activities

Cathedral Cove Sea Kayaking
KAYAKING

(☑07-866 3877; www.seakayaktours.co.nz; 88 Hahei Beach Rd; half/full day $95/150; ☺tours 9am & 2pm) This outfit runs guided kayaking trips around the rock arches, caves and islands in the Cathedral Cove area. The Remote Coast Tour heads the other way when conditions permit, visiting caves, blowholes and a long tunnel.

Cathedral Cove Dive & Snorkel
DIVING

(☑07-866 3955; www.hahei.co.nz/diving; 48 Hahei Beach Rd; dives from $80) Takes daily dive trips and rents out scuba gear, snorkelling gear ($20), bikes ($20) and boogie boards ($20). A Discover Scuba half-day beginners' course costs $190 including all the gear.

Hahei Explorer
BOAT TOUR

(☑07-866 3910; www.haheiexplorer.co.nz; adult/child $70/40) Hour-long jetboat rides touring the coast.

🛏 Sleeping & Eating

Hahei really does have a 'gone fishing' feel in the off-season. The local store remains open and the eateries take it in turns so that there's usually one option open every evening.

Tatahi Lodge
HOSTEL, MOTEL $

(☑07-866 3992; www.tatahilodge.co.nz; Grange Rd; dm $29, r $86-123, units $150-400; @☎) A wonderful place where backpackers are treated with at least as much care and respect as the lush bromeliad-filled garden. The dorm rooms and excellent communal facilities are just as attractive as the pricier motel units.

🏠 Church
COTTAGE $$

(☑07-866 3533; www.thechurchhahei.co.nz; 87 Hahei Beach Rd; cottages $135-230; @☎) Set within a subtropical garden, these beautifully kitted-out, rustic timber cottages have plenty of character. The ultracharming wooden church at the top of the drive is Hahei's swankiest eatery (mains $33 to $37), offering an ambitious (if overpriced) menu of adventurous country-style cooking.

❶ Getting There & Around

Tairua Bus Company (p157) has bus connections to Hahei. In the height of summer the council runs a bus service from the Cooks Beach side of the ferry landing to Hot Water Beach, stopping at Hahei (adult/child $3/2). Another option on the same route is the **Cathedral Cove Shuttle** (☑027 422 5899; www.cathedralcoveshuttles.co.nz; up to 5 passengers $30).

Hot Water Beach

Justifiably famous, Hot Water Beach is quite extraordinary. For two hours either side of low tide, you can access an area of sand in front of a rocky outcrop at the middle of the beach where hot water oozes up from beneath the surface. Bring a spade, dig a hole and voila, you've got a personal spa pool. Surfers stop off before the main beach to access some decent breaks. The headland between the two beaches still has traces of a Ngati Hei *pa*.

Spades ($5) can be hired from the **Hot Water Beach Store** (Pye Pl), which has a cafe attached, while surfboards ($20 per hour) and body boards ($15) can be hired from the neighbouring surf shop.

Near the beach, **Moko** (www.moko.co.nz; 24 Pye Pl; ☺10am-5pm) is full of beautiful things – art, sculpture, jewellery – with a modern Pasifika/Maori bent.

🛏 Sleeping & Eating

🏠 Hot Water Beach Top 10 Holiday Park
HOLIDAY PARK $

(☑07-866 3116; www.hotwaterbeachholidaypark.com; 790 Hot Water Beach Rd; sites from $23, units $70-250; @☎) Bordered by tall bamboo and gum trees, this is a smallish, newish, well-run camping ground with a modern shower and toilet block and good, simple cabins.

Hot Water Beach B&B
B&B $$$

(☑07-866 3991; www.hotwaterbedandbreakfast.co.nz; 48 Pye Pl; r $260) This hillside pad has priceless views (which go only part of the way towards justifying the hefty rates), a spa bath on the deck and attractive living quarters.

Hot Waves
CAFE $
(8 Pye Pl; mains $10-18; ⊗8.30am-4pm) In summer everyone wants a garden table at this excellent cafe – sometimes there are queues stretching out the door. It also hires spades for the beach ($5).

❶ Getting There & Away
The Hahei bus services stop here, but usually only on prebooked requests.

Tairua
POP 1270

Tairua and its twin town **Pauanui** sit either side of a river estuary that's perfect for windsurfing or for little kids to splash about in. Both have excellent surf beaches (Pauanui's is probably a shade better), but that's where the similarity stops. Where Tairua is a functioning residential town (with shops, ATMs and a choice of eateries), Pauanui is an upmarket refuge for over-wealthy Aucklanders – the kind who jet in and park their private planes by their grandiose beach houses before knocking out a round of golf. Friendly Tairua knows how to keep it real. Both are ridiculously popular in the summertime.

◉ Sights & Activities
Various operators offer fishing charters and sightseeing trips, including **Waipae Magic** (☑021 632 024; dewy@slingshot.co.nz), **Taranui Charters** (☑07-864 8511; www.tairua.info/taranui), **Pauanui Charters** (☑07-864 9262; www.pauanuicharters.co.nz) and **Epic Adventures** (☑07-864 8193; www.epicadventures.co.nz).

Paaku
MOUNTAIN
Around seven million years ago Paaku was a volcanic island, but now it forms the north head of Tairua's harbour. Ngati Hei had a *pa* here before being invaded by Ngati Maru in the 17th century. It's a steep 15-minute walk to the summit from the top of Paku Dr, with the pay-off being amazing views over Tairua, Pauanui and the Alderman Islands. Plaques along the way detail Tairua's colonial history, with only one rather dismissive one devoted to its long Maori occupation.

Dive Zone
DIVING
(☑07-864 8800; www.divezone.co.nz; 307 Main Rd; boat dives from $150, PADI $595; ⊗7.30am-5pm) A

SAFETY
Hot Water Beach has dangerous rips, especially directly in front of the main thermal section. It's one of the four most dangerous beaches in NZ in terms of drowning numbers, although this may be skewed by the huge number of tourists that flock here. Regardless, swimming here is *not* safe if the lifeguards aren't on patrol.

new operator making a name for itself with reliable service, including regular opening hours. Also hires snorkelling gear ($20).

Tairua Dive & Fishinn
DIVING
(☑07-864 8054; www.divetairua.co.nz; The Esplanade) Tairua Dive & Fishinn hires out kayaks (some with glass bottoms), plus scuba, snorkel and fishing gear. It also runs fishing charters, dive trips out to the Alderman Islands (including full gear $199) and PADI courses.

🛏 Sleeping

Dell Cote
B&B $$$
(☑07-864 8142; www.dellcote.com; Rewarewa Valley Rd; s/d $235/260; ⊛) Nontoxic mud bricks and macrocarpa timber give this place an organic feel, and the swooping gardens add a dose of tranquillity. The loft room is particularly lovely.

Pacific Harbour Lodge
HOTEL $$
(☑07-864 8581; www.pacificharbour.co.nz; 223 Main Rd; chalets $169-229; ⊛⊜) This 'island-style' resort in the town centre has spacious self-contained chalets, with natural wood and Gauguin decor inside and a South Seas garden outside. Discount packages are usually available.

Tairua Beach Villa Backpackers
HOSTEL $
(☑07-864 8345; www.tairuabackpackers.co.nz; 200 Main Rd; dm $25-28, s $55-72, d $65-85; ⊛⊜) Rooms are homely and casual at this estuary-edge hostel in a converted house, and the dorm scores great views. Guests can help themselves to fishing rods, kayaks, sailboards and bikes.

✗ Eating & Drinking

Manaia Cafe & Bar
CAFE $$
(☑07-864 9050; 228 Main Rd; breakfast $11-19, lunch $14-23, dinner $20-32; ⊗8.30am-4pm Mon,

8.30am-late Wed-Sun) With courtyard seating for lazy summer brunches and a burnished copper bar to prop up later in the night, Manaia is a slick addition to the Tairua strip. The dinner menu features bistro faves with some artful twists.

Old Mill Cafe CAFE **$**
(www.theoldmillcafe.co.nz; 1 The Esplanade; mains $8-19; ⊙8am-8pm Thu-Sat, 8am-4pm Sun) There's nothing run-of-the-mill about this old dear. Zooshed up with bright-pink feature walls and elegant veranda furniture, it serves interesting cafe fare, as well as tapas from 4pm.

Punters Bar & Grill PUB **$$**
(Main Rd; mains $17-19; ⊙11am-late Tue-Sun) The local pub serves decent burgers and fish and chips.

❶ Information

Tairua Information Centre (☑07-864 7575; www.tairua.info; 223 Main Rd; ⊙9am-5pm)

❶ Getting There & Around

InterCity, Tairua Bus Company and Go Kiwi all run bus services (p157) to Tairua.

Tairua and Pauanui are connected by a **passenger ferry** (☑027-497 0316; one-way/return $3/5; ⊙daily Dec & Jan), which departs every two hours from 9am to 5pm (until 11pm in January). In other months the ferry offers a water-taxi service.

Puketui Valley

Located 12km south of Tairua is the turn-off to Puketui Valley and the historic **Broken Hills gold-mine workings**, which are 8km from the main road along a mainly gravel road. There are short walks up to the sites of stamper batteries, but the best hike is through the 500m-long Collins Drive mine tunnel. After the tunnel, keep an eye out for the short 'lookout' side trail, which affords panoramic views. It takes about three hours return; remember to take a torch and a jacket with you.

There's a basic **DOC campsite** (www.doc .govt.nz; adult/child $10/5) located in a pretty spot by the river. This is a wilderness area so take care and be properly prepared. Water from the river should be boiled before drinking.

Opoutere

File this one under best-kept secrets. Maybe it's a local conspiracy to keep at bay the hordes of Aucklanders who seasonally invade Pauanui and Whangamata, as this unspoilt long sandy expanse has been kept very quiet. Apart from a cluster of houses there's nothing for miles around. Swimming can be dangerous, especially near Hikinui Islet, which is close to the beach. On the sand spit is the Wharekawa Wildlife Refuge, a breeding ground for the endangered NZ dotterel.

🛏 Sleeping

Copsefield B&B **$$**
(☑07-865 9555; www.copsefield.co.nz; 1055 SH25; r $100-180) On SH25 but closer to Opoutere than it is to Whangamata, Copsefield is a peaceful country-style villa set in attractive, lush gardens with a spa and a riverside swimming hole. The main house has three attractive B&B rooms, while cheaper accommodation is offered in a separate bach-style cottage.

Opoutere YHA HOSTEL **$**
(☑07-865 9072; www.yha.co.nz; 389 Opoutere Rd; dm $27-30, r $80-116) Housed partly in the historic Opoutere Native School, this wonderful get-away-from-it-all hostel resounds with birdsong. Kayaks, hot-water bottles, alarm clocks, stilts and hula hoops can all be borrowed.

❶ Getting There & Away

The **Go Kiwi** (☑0800 446 549; www.go-kiwi .co.nz) seasonal Auckland–Whitianga shuttle stops in Opoutere on request.

Whangamata

POP 3560

When Auckland's socially ambitious flock to Pauanui, the city's young and horny head to Whangamata to surf, get stoned and hook up. It can be a raucous spot over New Year, when the population swells to more than 40,000. It's a true summer holiday town, but in the off-season there may as well be tumbleweeds rolling down the main street.

🏃 Activities

Besides fishing (game-fishing runs from January to April), snorkelling near Hauturu

(Clarke) Island, surfing, kayaking, orienteering and mountain biking, there are excellent walks.

The **Wentworh Falls walk** takes 2½ hours (return); it starts 3km south of the town and 4km down the unsealed Wentworth Valley Rd. A further 3km south of Wentworth Valley Rd is Parakiwai Quarry Rd, at the end of which is the **Wharekirauponga walk.**, a sometimes muddy 10km return track (allow 3½ to four hours) to a mining camp, battery and waterfall that passes unusual hexagonal lava columns and loquacious bird life.

 Kiwi Dundee Adventures TRAMPING (☑07-865 8809; www.kiwidundee.co.nz) Styling himself as a local version of Crocodile Dundee, Doug Johansen offers informative one- to 16-day wilderness walks in the Coromandel Peninsula and countrywide.

🛏 Sleeping

Marine Reserved APARTMENT $$$
(☑07-865 9096; www.marinereservedapartments .co.nz; cnr Ocean Rd & Lowe St; units $330; 🕸) It's a peculiar name but the other strange thing about this excellent townhouse complex is that up to six of you can stay here in considerable comfort for $330. Units have secure ground-floor parking, full modern kitchens and barbecues on the decks.

Southpacific
Accommodation MOTEL, HOSTEL $
(☑07-865 9580; www.thesouthpacific.co.nz; 249 Port Rd; dm $27-29, s/d $70/90, units $147-168; @🕸) This hard-to-miss corner-hogging complex consists of a big barn for backpackers and self-contained motel units. Facilities are clean and modern; bikes and kayaks are available for hire.

🌿 **Wentworth Valley Campsite** CAMPSITE $
(☑07-865 7032; www.doc.govt.nz; 474 Wentworth Valley Rd; adult/child $10/5) More upmarket than most DOC camping grounds, this campsite is accessed from the Wentworth Falls walk and has toilets, showers and gas barbecues.

Breakers MOTEL $$
(☑07-865 8464; www.breakersmotel.co.nz; 324 Hetherington Rd; units $175-195; 🕸🏊) Facing the marina on the Tairua approach to Whangamata, this newish motel compensates for saggy beds with an enticing swimming pool and spa pools on the decks of the upstairs units.

🍴 Eating

Lazy Lizard CAFE $
(427 Port Rd; mains $10-17; ⊙7.30am-3.30pm Tue-Sun) Winning points for its bizarre hand-shaped stools, this funky lizard does delicious counter food, cooked breakfasts, bagels and salads. The fair-trade organic coffee is first rate.

Craig's Traditional
Fish & Chips FISH & CHIPS $
(701 Port Rd; mains $5-10; ⊙lunch & dinner Wed-Mon) All you could ask for in a chippie, Craig's scoops out pieces of grilled fresh fish and fat, salted chips. The service is friendly, and there's a TV and a stack of trashy mags to speed up the wait.

Soul Burger BURGERS $
(www.soulburger.co.nz; 441 Port Rd; burgers $10-15; ⊙5-9pm Thu, 8am-9pm Fri-Sun winter, daily summer) Serving audacious burgers with names like Soul Blues Brother and Vegan Vibe, this hip corner joint has branched out into cooked breakfasts on the weekend.

ℹ Information

Whangamata i-SITE (☑07-865 8340; www .whangamatainfo.co.nz; 616 Port Rd; ⊙9am-5pm Mon-Fri, 9.30am-3.30pm Sat & Sun)

ℹ Getting There & Away

Go Kiwi (☑0800 446 549; www.go-kiwi.co.nz) has a shuttle service to Whangamata.

Waihi & Waihi Beach

POP 4500 & 1800
Where most towns have hole-in-the-wall ATMs for people to access their riches, Waihi has a giant hole in the ground, right next to its main street. They've been dragging gold and silver out of Martha Mine, NZ's richest, since 1878. The town formed quickly thereafter and blinged itself up with grand buildings and a show-offy avenue of phoenix palms, now magnificently mature.

After closing down in 1952, open-cast-mining restarted in 1988. The mine is still productive, but only just – it takes a tonne of rock to yield 3g to 6g of gold. It's expected to run out soon, and when it does, plans are afoot to convert the town's gaping wound into a major tourist attraction. Watch this space.

While Waihi is interesting for a brief visit, it's Waihi Beach where you'll want to linger. The two places are as dissimilar as surfing is from mining, separated by 11km of farmland. The long sandy beach stretches 9km to Bowentown, on the northern limits of Tauranga Harbour, where you'll find sheltered harbour beaches such as beautiful **Anzac Bay**. There's a very popular 45-minute walk north through bush to pristine **Orokawa Bay**, which has no road access.

⊙ Sights

Seddon St   STREET
Waihi's main drag has interesting sculptures, information panels about Waihi's golden past and roundabouts that look like squashed daleks. Opposite the visitor centre, the skeleton of a derelict **Cornish Pumphouse** (1904) is the town's main landmark, atmospherically lit at night. From here the **Pit Rim Walkway** has fascinating views into the 250m-deep Martha Mine. If you want to get down into it, the mining company runs 1½-hour **Waihi Gold Mine Tours** (www.waihi goldminetours.co.nz; adult/child $28/14; ☉10am & 12.30pm Mon-Sat).

The *Historic Hauraki Gold Towns* pamphlet (free from the visitor centre) outlines walking tours of both Waihi and Paeroa.

🌿 Athenree Hot Springs   THERMAL POOLS
(www.athenreehotsprings.co.nz; 1 Athenree Rd, Athenree; adult/child $7/4.50; ☉10am-7.30pm) In those months when the waters of Waihi Beach aren't inviting, retreat to these two small but blissful outdoor hot pools, hidden within a holiday park.

Heritage Museum   MUSEUM
(www.waihimuseum.co.nz; 54 Kenny St, Waihi; adult/child $5/3; ☉10am-3pm Thu & Fri, noon-3pm Sat-Mon) The Heritage Museum has an art gallery and displays focusing on the region's gold-mining history. Prepare to squirm before the collection of miners' chopped-off thumbs preserved in glass jars.

Waihi Waterlily Gardens   GARDENS
(www.waterlily.co.nz; 441 Pukekauri Rd, Waihi; adult/ child $8.50/free; ☉11am-3pm Wed-Sun Oct-Apr) Seven hectares of ponds, peacocks and pretty things, 7km southwest of Waihi. There's a cafe on-site.

🏃 Activities

Goldfields Railway   RAILWAY
(☎07-863 8251; www.waihirail.co.nz; 30 Wrigley St, Waihi; adult/child return $15/8; ☉Fri-Mon

Apr-Aug, daily Sep-Mar) Vintage trains depart Waihi for a 7km, 25-minute scenic journey to Waikino.

Sunshine Surf Coaching   SURFING
(☎07-863 4857; www.sunshinesurfcoaching.co.nz; private lesson $120) Takes advantage of Waihi Beach's relatively gentle breaks to offer all-age surf instruction.

Over the Top Adventures   DIRT BIKING
(☎021 205 7266; www.overthetopadventures.co.nz; 1 Surrey St, Waihi; tours $90-400) Offers on/off-road dirt-bike tours, rents mountain bikes ($35 to $55 per day) and provides cycling transfers.

Dirtboard Waihi   DIRTBOARDING
(☎021 244 1646; www.dirtboard.co.nz; per hr $30) Hit the slopes on a mutant snowboard-skateboard.

Bularangi Motorbikes   MOTORBIKE TOURS
(☎07-863 6069; www.motorbikesnz.co.nz) Based in Waihi, Bularangi Motorbikes offers Harley Davidson rentals and one- to 21-day guided tours throughout the country.

🛏 Sleeping

🏆 TOP CHOICE Bowentown Beach
Holiday Park   HOLIDAY PARK $
(☎07-863 5381; www.bowentown.co.nz; 510 Seaforth Rd, Waihi Beach; sites from $25, units $95-374; @🍴🛜) Having nabbed a stunning stretch of sand this impressively maintained holiday park makes the most of it with first-rate motel units and campers' facilities. The barbecue area even has a water feature.

🌿 Athenree Hot Springs &
Holiday Park   HOLIDAY PARK $
(☎07-863 5600; www.athenreehotsprings.co.nz; 1 Athenree Rd, Athenree; sites from $24, units $70-200; @🍴🛜🏊) Harbour-hugging Athenree has smart accommodation and friendly owners. Entry to the thermal pools is free for guests, making this a top choice for the winter months.

Waihi Waterlily Gardens   COTTAGE $$$
(☎07-863 8267; www.waterlily.co.nz; 441 Pukekauri Rd, Waihi; cottages $250) After-hours you get the gardens all to yourself if you're staying in one of these two cottages. They're beautifully decked out with comfy beds, quality linen, polished concrete floors and interesting art.

🖋 Manawa Ridge
LODGE **$$$**

(☑07-863 9400; www.manawaridge.co.nz; 267 Ngatitangata Rd, Waihi; r $850) The views from this castle-like ecoretreat, perched on a 310m ridge 6km northeast of Waihi, take in the entire Bay of Plenty. Made of recycled railway timber, mud brick and lime-plastered straw walls, the rooms marry earthiness with sheer luxury.

Beachfront B&B
B&B **$$**

(☑07-863 5393; www.beachfrontbandb.co.nz; 3 Shaw Rd, Waihi Beach; r $130) True to its name with absolute beachfront and spectacular sea views, this comfortable downstairs flat has a TV, fridge and direct access to the surf.

Waihi Beach Top 10 Holiday Resort
HOLIDAY PARK **$**

(☑07-863 5504; www.waihibeach.com; 15 Beach Rd, Waihi Beach; sites from $29, units $85-265; @🛜🏊) This massive, resort-style holiday park is pretty darn flash, with a pool, gym, spa, beautiful kitchen and a smorgasbord of sleeping options.

🍴 Eating & Drinking

Porch
CAFE, BAR **$$**

(www.theporch.co.nz; 23 Wilson Rd, Waihi Beach; brunch $14-20, dinner $29-36; ⊘breakfast & lunch daily, dinner Wed-Sat) Waihi Beach's coolest chow-down spot, serving sophisticated, substantial mains.

Flatwhite
CAFE **$$**

(www.flatwhitecafe.co.nz; 21 Shaw Rd, Waihi Beach; brunch $14-20, dinner $20-27; ⊘breakfast, lunch & dinner; 🛜) Funky, licensed and right by the beach, Flatwhite has a lively brunch menu and serves decent pizzas.

Ti-Tree Cafe
CAFE **$**

(14 Haszard St, Waihi; brunch $11-18, pizza $17-24; ⊘breakfast & lunch daily, dinner Thu-Sat; 🛜) Housed in a cute little wooden building with punga-shaded outdoor seating, Ti-Tree serves fair-trade organic coffee, cooked breakfasts and wood-fired pizza.

🛍 Shopping

Artmarket
ARTS & CRAFTS

(www.artmarket.co.nz; 65 Seddon St, Waihi; ⊘10am-5pm) Stocks a first-rate selection of local arts and crafts.

ℹ Information

Waihi Visitor Centre (☑07-863 6715; www.waihi.org.nz; 126 Seddon St, Waihi; ⊘9am-5pm; @)

ℹ Getting There & Away

Waihi is serviced by InterCity buses and seasonal Go Kiwi (p171) shuttles.

Karangahake Gorge

The road between Waihi and Paeroa, through the bush-lined ramparts of the Karangahake Gorge, is one of the best short drives in the country. Walking and biking tracks take in old Maori trails, historic mining and rail detritus, and spookily dense bush. In Maori legend the area is said to be protected by a *taniwha,* a supernatural creature. The local *iwi* managed to keep this area closed to miners until 1875, aligning themselves with the militant Te Kooti.

The very worthwhile 4.5km **Karangahake Gorge Historic Walkway** takes 1½ hours (each way) and starts from the car park 14km west of Waihi. It follows the disused railway line and the Ohinemuri River to Owharoa Falls and Waikino station, where you can pick up the vintage train to Waihi, stopping in at **Waikino Station Cafe** (SH2; mains $10-18; ⊘9.30am-3pm) while you wait.

There are a range of shorter walks and loop tracks leading from the car park; bring a torch as some pass through tunnels. A two-hour tramp will bring you to Dickey's Flat, where there's a free **DOC campsite** (Dickey's Flat Rd) and a decent swimming hole. River water will need to be boiled for drinking. You'll find DOC information boards about the walks and the area's history at both the station and the main car park. A spectacular offshoot of the Hauraki Rail Trail (p158) cycling route also passes through here.

Across from the car park, **Golden Owl Lodge** (☑07-862 7994; www.goldenowl.co.nz; 3 Moresby St; dm $29, r $62-75; @🛜) is a homely, handy tramping base, sleeping only 12. Allow $5 extra for linen in the dorm rooms.

Further up the same road, **Ohinemuri Estate Winery** (☑07-862 8874; www.ohinemuri.co.nz; Moresby St; mains $19-25; ⊘10am-5pm Wed-Sun, daily summer) has Latvian-influenced architecture and serves excellent lunches. You'd be right if you thought it was an unusual site for growing grapes – the fruit is imported from other regions. Tastings are $5, refundable with purchase. If you imbibe too much, snaffle the chalet-style hut ($115 to $145 per night) and revel in the charming atmosphere of this secluded place.

Paeroa

POP 3980

If you find yourself scratching your head in Paeroa, don't worry too much about it. The whole town is an elaborate Kiwi in-joke. It's the birthplace of Lemon & Paeroa (L&P), an icon of Kiwiana that markets itself as 'world famous in NZ'. The fact that the beloved fizzy drink is now owned by global monster Coca-Cola Amatil and produced in Auckland only serves to make the ubiquitous L&P branding even more darkly ironic. Still, generations of Kiwi kids have pestered their parents to take this route just to catch a glimpse of the giant L&P bottles.

The small **museum** (37 Belmont Rd; adult/child $2/1; ⊙noon-3pm Mon-Fri) has a grand selection of Royal Albert porcelain and other pioneer and Maori artefacts – look in the drawers. If pretty crockery is your thing, Paeroa is known for its antique stores.

L&P Cafe & Bar (SH2; mains $7-20; ⊙breakfast & lunch daily, dinner Fri-Sun) has a truck-stop ambience, but is as good a place as any to find out what all the fuss is about. You can order L&P fish and chips or an L&P brekkie, washed down with the lemony lolly water itself. The cafe shares the space with the **information centre** (☑07-862 8636; www.paeroa.org.nz; ⊙9am-3pm).

Waikato & the King Country

Includes »

Best Outdoors

» Surfing at Manu Bay (p188)

» Waitomo Caves rafting (p199)

» Ngarupupu Point (p202)

» City Bridges River Tour (p181)

» Te Toto Gorge (p188)

Best Places to Stay

» Raglan Backpackers (p186)

» Solscape (p188)

» Aroha Mountain Lodge (p194)

» Abseil Inn (p200)

Why Go?

If the colour green had a homeland, this would be it. Here, verdant fields and rolling hills line New Zealand's mightiest river, the Waikato. Visitors from England might wonder why they bothered leaving home, especially in quaint towns like Cambridge where every effort has been made to replicate the 'mother country'.

But this veneer disguises another reality: this is Tainui country. In the 1850s this powerful tribal coalition elected a king to resist the loss of land and sovereignty. The fertile Waikato was forcibly taken from them, but they retained control of the limestone crags and forests of the King Country to within a whisper of the 20th century.

These days visitors can experience first-hand the region's genteel/wild dichotomy. Adrenaline junkies can hurl themsleves into Raglan's legendary surf, or into extreme underground pursuits in the extraordinary Waitomo Caves. Others will warm to the more sedate delights of Te Aroha's Edwardian thermal complex or Hamilton's gardens.

When to Go

The southern area around Taumarunui is wetter and colder than the rest of this region, which can suffer summer droughts. But either way, you're guaranteed to see a lot of green, green grass. Crowd-wise, if you avoid summer you'll avoid any accommodation shortfalls, but without the extra people around this region can seem a just a bit *too* agricultural. Raglan's surf breaks are always busy, regardless of the season (they didn't call the surf movie *The Endless Summer* for nothing).

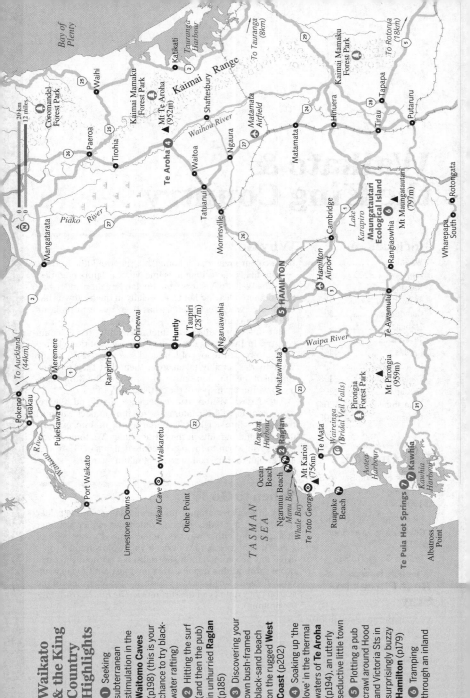

Waikato & the King Country Highlights

❶ Seeking subterranean stimulation in the **Waitomo Caves** (p198) (this is your chance to try black-water rafting)

❷ Hitting the surf (and then the pub) in unhurried **Raglan** (p185)

❸ Discovering your own bush-framed black-sand beach on the rugged **West Coast** (p202)

❹ Soaking up 'the love' in the thermal waters of **Te Aroha** (p194), an utterly seductive little town

❺ Plotting a pub crawl around Hood and Victoria Sts in surprisingly buzzy **Hamilton** (p179)

❻ Tramping through an inland

island paradise at **Maungatautari Ecological Island** (p191)

7 Indulging in Maori culture at Kawhia's **Kai Festival** (p196), and don't miss a soak at nearby **Te Puia Hot Springs** on Ocean Beach (p195)

30 Kinleith Forest

Tokoroa

Upper Atiamuri

Atiamuri

1

Taupo

Taupo Airport

Whakamaru

32

30

Lake Taupo

Titiraupenga (1042m)

Tihoi

Turangi

Rangipo

32

Pureora (1165m)

Kuratau Junction

41

Barryville

Pureora Forest Park

Rangitoto Ranges

Hauhungaroa Range

Hauhungaroa (1078m)

Pureora Forest Park

47

Kopaki

41

Otorohanga

Waitomo Caves **1**

Aratoro

Okahukura

Piriaka

Owhango

To Raurimu Spiral (4km); Tongariro National Park (11km); Ohakune (45km)

Te Kuiti

Eight Mile Junction

Mangatupoto

4

Taumarunui

Piripiri Caves Scenic Reserve

Mangapohue Natural Bridge Scenic Reserve

Marokopa Falls

Te Anga

Moeatoa

Whareorino Forest

Waikawau

WAITOMO

40

Ohura

Marokopa

Kiritehere

Tirua Point

Ngarupupu Point

3 West Coast

Herangi Range

Mokau River

Awakino River

Waitaanga

43

To Stratford (63km)

Awakino

Maniaroa Marae

Mokau

Tongaporutu

Ahiti

40

To New Plymouth (46km)

3

ESSENTIAL WAIKATO & THE KING COUNTRY

» **Eat** Rotten corn at Kawhia's Kai Festival

» **Drink** A few brews on Hamilton's Hood St

» **Read** *Potiki* (1986) by Patricia Grace

» **Listen to** Hamilton-born Kimbra's snaky/sexy debut album *Vows*, or the sacred sounds of Te Awamutu: Crowded House's 'Mean to Me'

» **Watch** *Black Sheep* (2006). Those Te Kuiti shearers should be very afraid

» **Festival** Running of the Sheep, Te Kuiti

» **Go Green** Off-the-grid tepees at Solscape (p188)

» **Online** www.hamiltonwaikato.com, www.kingcountry.co.nz

» **Area code** ☎07

ℹ Getting There & Around

Hamilton is the region's transport hub, with its airport servicing extensive domestic routes, and some international routes. Buses link the city to everywhere in the North Island. Most inland towns are also well connected on bus routes, but the remote coastal communities (apart from Mokau on SH3) are less well served.

Trains are another option but they are infrequent and surprisingly expensive on short legs. The main trunk-line between Auckland and Wellington stops at Hamilton, Otorohanga, Te Kuiti and Taumarunui.

WAIKATO

History

By the time Europeans started to arrive, this region – stretching as far north as Auckland's Manukau Harbour – had long been the homeland of the Waikato tribes, descended from the Tainui migration. In settling this land, the Waikato tribes displaced or absorbed tribes from earlier migrations.

Initially European contact was on Maori terms and to the advantage of the local people. Their fertile land, which was already cultivated with kumara and other crops, was well suited to the introduction of new fruits and vegetables. By the 1840s the Waikato economy was booming, with bulk quantities of produce exported to the settlers in Auckland and beyond.

Relations between the two cultures soured during the 1850s, largely due to the colonists' pressure to purchase Maori land. In response, a confederation of tribes united to elect a king to safeguard their interests, forming what became known as the Kingitanga (King Movement).

In July 1863 Governor Grey sent a huge force to invade the Waikato and exert colonial control. After almost a year of fighting, known as the Waikato War, the Kingites retreated south to what became branded the King Country.

The war resulted in the confiscation of 3600 sq km of land, much of which was given to colonial soldiers to farm and defend. In 1995 the Waikato tribes received a full Crown apology for the wrongful invasion and confiscation of their lands, as well as a $170 million package, including the return of land that the Crown still held.

North of Hamilton

PORT WAIKATO

The name might conjure up images of heavy industry and crusty sea dogs, but that's far from the reality of this petite village at the mouth of the mighty Waikato River. There's little here apart from a few streets of baches (holiday homes), a couple of *marae* (meeting house) complexes, a store, a holiday park and a beautiful (but treacherous) **surf beach**. Lifeguards are on duty in summer (on weekends and school holidays); strong rips render it unsafe for swimming at other times. To get here, turn off SH1 at Pokeno, 50km south of central Auckland. Go past the turn-off to Tuakau and continue until you see the Port Waikato signs.

Waikatoa Beach Lodge (☎09-232 9961; www.sunsetbeach.co.nz; 8 Centreway Rd; sites from $18, dm/s/d/f from $27/40/65/80) spoils visiting beach bums with smart rooms, decent linen, a garden scattered with seashells and a sleepy tabby cat. There's a welcoming kitchen/lounge area with gas cooking.

Continue south of Port Waikato for 28km and you'll reach **Nikau Cave** (☑09-233 3199; www.nikaucave.co.nz; 1770 Waikaretu Rd; adult/child $35/18; ☺by appointment), where a tour (minimum two people) will take you through tight, wet squeezes to glowworms, limestone formations and subterranean streams. There's a cafe here, too.

RANGIRI

Following SH1 south you're retracing the route of the colonial army in the spectacular land grab that was the Waikato War. On 20 November 1863, 1500 British troops (some say it was 850 – either way, there was a lot of 'em), backed by gunboats and artillery, attacked the substantial fortifications erected by the Maori king's warriors at Rangiriri. They were repulsed a number of times and lost 49 men, but overnight many of the 500 Maori defenders retreated; the remaining 183 were taken prisoner the next day after the British gained entry to the *pa* (fortified village) by conveniently misunderstanding a flag of truce.

The **Rangiriri Heritage Centre** (☑07-826 3663; www.nzmuseums.co.nz; 12 Rangiriri Rd; admission free, film $5; ☺7.30am-5pm) screens a short documentary about the battle, and across the road the **Maori War & Early Settlers Cemetery** (Rangiriri Rd; ☺24hr) houses the soldiers' graves and a mound covering the mass grave of 36 Maori warriors.

Next to the heritage centre is the historic, elaborately wallpapered **Rangiriri Hotel** (☑07-826 3467; 8 Talbot St; lunch mains $11-19, dinner $17-28; ☺11am-11pm), a cheery spot for lunch (try the scallops) or a beer at sunny outdoor tables.

NGARUAWAHIA & AROUND

The headquarters of the Maori King movement, Ngaruawahia (population 4940) is 19km north of Hamilton on SH1. The impressive fences of **Turangawaewae Marae** (☑07-824 5189; www.wakamaori.co.nz/maori-culture /marae/turangawaewae-marae; 29 River Rd) maintain the privacy of this important place, but twice a year visitors are welcomed. **Regatta Day** is held in mid-March, with *waka* (canoe) races and all manner of Maori cultural activities. For a week from 15 August the *marae* is open to celebrate **Koroniehana**, the anniversary of the coronation of the current king, Tuheitia.

Ask at the **post office** (3 Jesmond St) for directions

Hamilton

POP 206,400

Landlocked cities in an island nation will never have the glamorous appeal of their coastal cousins. Rotorua compensates with boiling mud and Taupo has its lake, but Hamilton and Palmerston North, despite majestic rivers, are left clutching short straws.

However, something strange has happened in Hamilton recently. The city's main street has sprouted a sophisticated and vibrant stretch of bars and eateries around Hood and Victoria Sts that – on the weekend at least – leaves Auckland's Viaduct Harbour for dead in the boozy fun stakes.

Oddly, the great grey-green greasy Waikato River rolls right through town, but the city's layout largely ignores its presence: unless you're driving across a bridge you'll hardly know it's there.

WAIKATO & THE KING COUNTRY HAMILTON

MAORI NZ: WAIKATO & THE KING COUNTRY

The Waikato/King Country region remains one of the strongest pockets of Maori influence in NZ. This is the heartland of the Tainui tribes, descended from those who disembarked from the *Tainui waka* (canoe) in Kawhia in the 14th century. Split into four main tribal divisions (Waikato, Hauraki, Ngati Maniapoto and Ngati Raukawa), Tainui are inextricably linked with the Kingitanga (King Movement), which has its base in Ngaruawahia.

The best opportunities to interact with Maori culture are the Kawhia Kai Festival, and Ngaruawahia's Regatta Day and Koroneihana celebrations. Interesting *taonga* (treasures) are displayed at museums in Hamilton and Te Awamutu. Reminders of the Waikato Land War can be found at Rangiriri, Rangiaowhia and Orakau.

Dozens of *marae* (meeting house) complexes are dotted around the countryside – including at Awakino, and at Kawhia, where the *Tainui waka* is buried. You won't be able to visit these without permission but you can get decent views from the gates. Some regional tours include an element of Maori culture, including Ruakuri Cave and Kawhia Harbour Cruises.

Hamilton

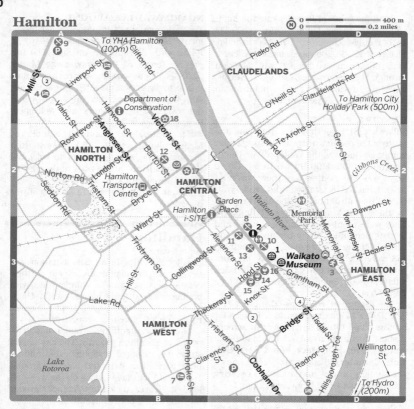

WAIKATO & THE KING COUNTRY HAMILTON

⊙ Sights

Waikato Museum   MUSEUM
(www.waikatomuseum.co.nz; 1 Grantham St; admission free-$6.50; ⊙10am-4.30pm) The excellent Waikato Museum has five main areas: an art gallery; interactive science galleries; Tainui galleries housing Maori treasures, including the magnificently carved *waka taua* (war canoe), *Te Winikawaka*; a Hamilton history exhibition entitled 'Never a Dull Moment'; and a Waikato River exhibition. The museum also runs a rigorous program of public events. Admission is charged for some exhibits.

FREE Hamilton Gardens   GARDENS
(www.hamiltongardens.co.nz; Cobham Dr; ⊙enclosed sector 7am-6pm, info centre 9am-5pm) Hamilton Gardens, spread over 50 hectares, incorporates a large park, cafe, restaurant and extravagant themed enclosed gardens. There are separate Italian Renaissance,

Chinese, Japanese, English, American and Indian gardens complete with colonnades, pagodas and a mini Taj Mahal. Equally interesting are the sustainable Productive Garden Collection, a fragrant herb garden and the precolonisation Maori Te Parapara garden. Look for the impressive *Nga Uri O Hinetuparimaunga* (Earth Blanket) sculpture at the main gates. The gardens are southeast of Hamilton city centre.

Waikato River   RIVER, PARK
The strong-flowing Waikato River is well worth investigating. Bush-covered riverside walkways run along both sides of the river and provide the city's green belt. Jogging paths continue to the boardwalk circling Lake Rotoroa, west of the centre. Memorial Park is closer to town, and has the remains of the *PS Rangiriri* – an iron-clad, steam-powered gunboat from the Waikato War – embedded in the riverbank (under restoration when we visited).

Hamilton

See Activities for some more options for exploring the river.

Riff Raff MONUMENT
(www.riffraffstatue.org; Victoria St; 🛜) One of Hamilton's more unusual public artworks is a life-size statue of *Rocky Horror Picture Show* writer Richard O'Brien aka Riff Raff, the time-warping alien from the planet Transsexual. It looks over a small park on the site of the former Embassy Theatre where O'Brien worked as a hairdresser, though it's hard to imagine 1960s Hamilton inspired the tale of bisexual alien decadence. Free wi-fi emanates from Riff Raff's three-pronged stun gun.

FREE **ArtsPost** GALLERY
(www.artspost.co.nz; 120 Victoria St; ☺10am-4.30pm) ArtsPost, near the Waikato Museum, is a contemporary gallery and gift shop housed in a grand, former post office. It focuses on the best of local art: paintings, glass, prints, textiles and photography. Check out the awesome floorboards.

Hamilton Zoo ZOO
(www.hamiltonzoo.co.nz; 183 Brymer Rd; adult/child/family $16/8/42, tours extra; ☺9am-5pm, last entry 3.30pm) Hamilton Zoo houses 500-plus species (including NZ's only tapir) and takes part in conservation breeding projects. There are various guided-tour options available, plus daily 'Meet the Keeper' talks for interesting insights from the critters' care-givers. The zoo is 8km from Hamilton city centre: take Norton Rd off Tristram St, then SH23 west towards Raglan, turn right at Newcastle Rd and then left onto Brymer Rd.

🏃 **Activities**

City Bridges River Tour KAYAKING
(📞07-847 5565; www.canoeandkayak.co.nz; ☺2hr trip adult/child $60/35) An interesting way to check out the Waikato River is on a City Bridges River Tour, a guided kayak tour through the city. No experience necessary; minimum three people.

Cruise Waikato BOAT TOUR
(📞0508 426 458; www.cruise-waikato.co.nz; Memorial Park Jetty, Memorial Dr; cruises adult/child from $25/10) Runs a range of river cruises, focused variously on sightseeing, history or your belly (coffee and muffins, *hangi* – a feast of maori food – or picnics). See the city from the river, rather than the other way around!

Extreme Edge ROCK CLIMBING
(📞07-847 5858; www.extremeedge.co.nz; 90 Greenwood St; day pass incl harness adult/child $17.50/13; ☺noon-9.30pm Mon-Fri, 10am-7pm Sat & Sun) This airy hangar near the Frankton train station contains an array of hypercoloured climbing walls, 14m of which is overhanging. There's a dedicated kids'

TAUPIRI

About 26km north of Hamilton on SH1 is Taupiri (287m), the sacred mountain of the Tainui people. You'll recognise it by the cemetery on its slopes and the honking of passing car horns – locals saying hi to their loved ones as they pass by. In August 2006 thousands gathered here as the much-loved Maori queen, Dame Te Atairangikaahu, was transported upriver by *waka* (canoe) to her final resting place, an unmarked grave on the summit.

climbing zone, and free safety lessons for vert virgins.

Wiseway Canoe Adventures   CANOEING
(☎021 988 335; www.wisewayadventures.com; 2hr trip adult/child $50/20) Wiseway Canoe Adventures offers guided trips through the city along the river, or offers freedom hire if you'd rather take things at your own pace. One- and three-hour trips also available.

Kiwi Balloon Company   BALLOONING
(☎07-843 8538, 021 912 679; www.kiwiballoon company.co.nz; flights per person $320) A hot-air ballon flight is a lovely (and surprisingly un-scary) option for gazing down on the lush Waikato countryside. The whole experience takes about four hours and includes a cham-pagne breakfast and an hour's flying time.

✹✹ Festivals & Events

Balloons Over Waikato   SPORTS
(www.balloonsoverwaikato.co.nz) In March, get a legal high with Balloons over Waikato, a colourful hot-air balloon fest.

Hamilton 400   SPORTS
(www.hamilton.v8supercars.com.au) In April rev-heads flock to town for the Hamilton 400 V8 Supercar street race, part of the Austral-ian V8 Supercars Championship. Vroom, vroom...

Hamilton River Festival   CULTURAL, SPORTS
(www.hamiltonriverfestival.co.nz) In September/ October, this month-long festival focuses on the mighty, moiling Waikato River, includ-ing a Cambridge-to-Hamilton kayak and a chilly 'Spring Dip' swim, plus food and cul-tural events around town.

🛏 Sleeping

The road into town from Auckland (Ulster St) is lined with dozens of unremarkable, traffic-noisy motels: passable for short stays.

Anglesea Motel   MOTEL $$
(☎07-834 0010, 0800 426 453; www.anglesea motel.co.nz; 36 Liverpool St; d/2-/3-br units from $138/265/310; @🗐🏊) Getting great feedback from travellers and a far preferable option to anything on Ulster St's 'motel row', the Angle-sea has plenty of space, friendly managers, free wi-fi, pool and squash and tennis courts, and not un-stylish decor. Hard to beat.

J's Backpackers   HOSTEL $
(☎07-856 8934; www.jsbackpackers.co.nz; 8 Grey St; dm/s/d/tr $28/60/66/82; @🗐) A homely

hostel occupying a characterful house near Hamilton Gardens, friendly J's offers good security, a newly renovated (but small) kitchen, free bikes and bright, tidy rooms. There's a barbecue out the back and a Mon-golian yurt lounge-space on the front lawn: sip a beer, strum a guitar and hope Ghengis Khan doesn't show up.

City Centre B&B   B&B $$
(☎07-838 1671; www.citycentrebnb.co.nz; 3 Anglesea St; r $90-150, extra person $30; @🗐🏊) At the quiet riverside end of a central city street (five minutes' walk to the Victoria/Hood St action), this sparkling self-contained apart-ment opens on to a swimming pool. There's also a bedroom available in a wing of the main house. Self-catering breakfast provided.

YWCA   HOSTEL $
(☎07-838 2219; www.ywcahamilton.org.nz; cnr Pembroke & Clarence Sts; s/d $30/60; @) You don't have to be young or female to stay at this four-storey apartment-block hostel. The rooms are cell-like but they're spotless, cheap and private. Each floor has shared bathroom facilities, good security, a kitchen and TV lounge. Weekly rates available.

Eagles Nest Backpackers   HOSTEL $
(☎07-838 2704; www.eaglesbackpackers.co.nz; 937 Victoria St; dm/d $25/60; @🗐) This laid-back 1st-floor eyrie has windowless internal rooms (with skylights) but they're clean and mercifully quiet given the hostel's busy po-sition. The roomy (and reasonably funky) communal lounge opens onto a wee balcony overlooking the Victoria St fray, with a bar-becue to sizzle a few snags.

YHA Hamilton   HOSTEL $
(☎07-957 1848; www.yha.co.nz; 140 Ulster St; dm/s $29/49, d $59-69; @🗐) Super-clean, quality linen, Sky TV, chilled-out lounge space, laundry, supermarket across the street...what's the catch? Well, the hostel oc-cupies a former 'micro hotel', so the rooms and kitchen are tiny. If you're over 6ft tall you might struggle.

Hamilton City Holiday Park   HOLIDAY PARK $
(☎07-855 8255; www.hamiltoncityholidaypark. co.nz; 14 Ruakura Rd; sites/units from $35/45; @🗐) Simple cabins and leafy sites are the rule at this shady park. The amenities block and some of the older cabins are starting to feel a bit weary, but it's reasonably close to town (2km east of the centre) and very affordable.

Eating

River Kitchen
CAFE $

(www.theriverkitchen.co.nz; 237 Victoria St; mains $7-16; ⏱7am-4pm Mon-Fri, 8am-4pm Sat & Sun; 🖉) Hip River Kitchen does things with simple style: cakes, gourmet breakfasts and fresh seasonal lunches (angle for the salmon hash), and a barista who knows his beans. It's the kind of place you visit for breakfast, come back to for lunch, then consider for breakfast the next day.

Chim-Choo-Ree
MODERN NZ $$$

(✆07-839 4329; www.chimchooree.co.nz; 244 Victoria St; mains $30-34; ⏱4.30pm-late Tue-Sat) Hip little Chim-Choo-Ree, with its clackety bentwood chairs, concrete floor and kitsch art, is a casual fine-dining option that's been wowing the critics. Launch into the five-course tasting menu ($125/85 with/without wine), or mains like manuka-smoked eel and Canadian scallops with apple-and-radish salad. Footpath tables cop some noise from the bar next door: compete with choruses of *Mary Poppins* classics.

Scott's Epicurean
INTERNATIONAL $

(✆07-839 6680; 181 Victoria St; mains $11-20; ⏱7am-4pm Mon-Fri, 8.30am-4pm Sat & Sun) This gorgeous joint features swanky leather banquettes, pressed-tin ceilings, great coffee and an interesting and affordable menu: try the *pytti panna* (Swedish bubble-and-squeak) or the ever-popular *spaghetti aglio e olio* (there'd be a riot if it ever dropped off the menu). Friendly service; fully licensed.

Rocket Coffee
CAFE $

(www.rocketcoffee.co.nz; 302 Barton St; coffees from $4; ⏱8am-4pm Mon-Fri) Duck down Barton St for what some locals say is the coolest thing about Hamilton (other than perhaps the Riff Raff statue). Rocket Coffee is a warehouse-like bean barn, roasting on-site and enticing caffeine fiends to the communal table strewn with newspapers. Staff spin old-school vinyl (and take requests) in between playing barista and packaging up sacks of beans for shipment.

Palate
MODERN NZ, FUSION $$$

(✆07-834 2921; www.palaterestaurant.co.nz; 170 Victoria St; mains $32-39; ⏱dinner Mon-Sat) Simple, sophisticated Palate has a well-deserved rep for lifting the culinary bar across regional NZ. Chef-owner Mat McLean delivers an innovative mod-NZ menu with highlights like honey-spiced duck with kumara and co-

conut puree, citrus couscous, orange salad and Cointreau jus.

Hydro
CAFE $

(www.hydrocafe.co.nz; 33 Jellicoe Dr; mains $9-21; ⏱9am-3pm Mon-Thu, 8am-3.30pm Fri-Sun; 🛜🖉) On the east side of the river (walk here along the water), Hydro is a fun cafe occupying an old block of neighbourhood shops, with tables spilling across the pavement. Great for brunch and light meals with novel taste combinations (the scallop salad with mango chilli is awesome). Wi-fi and by-the-glass NZ wines available.

Pak 'n Save
SUPERMARKET

(Mill St; ⏱8am-10pm) Just north of downtown Hamilton.

Drinking

The blocks around Victoria and Hood Sts make for a boozy bar-hop, with weekend live music and DJs.

House on Hood
BAR, CRAFT BEER

(www.houseonhood.co.nz; 27 Hood St) A crafty place for a craft beer or four, House on Hood is a 1915 barn with lots of drops to slake your thirst. Beer specials, tasting sessions and meal deals abound, plus Saturday-night bands and Sunday-afternoon DJs. Beer nirvana.

Diggers Bar
BAR

(www.diggersbar.co.nz; 17b Hood St; ⏱3pm-late Tue-Sun) This funky good-time bar has outlasted plenty of come-and-go Hood St bars, with a wealth of liquid bread on tap and nightly live music in a huge room out the back. Buy four beers on a Wednesday night and score yourself a gourmet pizza.

Limestone
BAR

(15 Hood St; ⏱8pm-late Wed, 7pm-late Thu & Sat, 4pm-late Fri) Inside Hamilton's oldest stone buliding – a former habardashery – moody Limestone offers respite from Hood St's otherwise raucous boozy nocturnal parade. An excellent range of bottled beers, a dazzling selection of spirits, and cigars to puff street-side.

⭐ Entertainment

Victoria Cinema
CINEMA

(www.victoriacinema.co.nz; 690 Victoria St; adult/child $15.50/13.50; ⏱5pm-late) Watch art-house and international films while sipping on a fine wine or cold beer at 'Hamilton's home of fine movies'. Very bohemian. Tickets are $2 cheaper on weekdays.

Lido Cinema CINEMA
(www.lidocinema.co.nz; Level 1, Centre Place, 501 Victoria St; adult/child $15/9; ⊙10am-late) Sassy Lido – all black carpet, chandeliers and gold fleurs-de-lis – offers an upmarket art-house movie experience in three 100-seat cinemas with comfy chairs and drinks to smooth the mood.

❶ Information

Anglesea Clinic (☎07-858 0800; www.angleseamedical.co.nz; cnr Anglesea & Thackeray Sts; ⊙24hr) For accidents and urgent medical assistance.

Department of Conservation (DOC; ☎07-858 1000; www.doc.govt.nz; Level 5, 73 Rostrevor St; ⊙8am-4.30pm Mon-Fri)

Hamilton i-SITE (☎07-958 5960; www.visithamilton.co.nz; 5 Garden Pl; ⊙9am-5pm Mon-Fri, 9.30am-3.30pm Sat & Sun; 🖵) Accommodation, activities and transport bookings, plus free wi-fi right across Garden Pl.

Post Office (36 Bryce St) Currency exchange available.

Waikato Hospital (☎07-839 8899; www.waikatodhb.govt.nz; Pembroke St; ⊙24hr)

❶ Getting There & Away

Air

Air New Zealand (☎0800 737 000; www.airnewzealand.co.nz) Regular direct flights from Hamilton to Auckland, Christchurch, Palmerston North and Wellington.

Pacific Blue (☎0800 670 000; www.pacificblue.com.au) International flights between Hamilton and Sydney and Brisbane.

Sunair (☎07-575 7799, 0800 786 247; www.sunair.co.nz) Direct flights to Gisborne, Napier, Great Barrier Island and Whitianga.

Bus

All buses arrive and depart from the **Hamilton Transport Centre** (☎07-834 3457; www.hamilton.co.nz; cnr Anglesea & Bryce Sts).

Waikato Regional Council's Busit! (p185) coaches serve the region, including Ngaruawahia ($3.80, 25 minutes), Cambridge ($5.40, 40 minutes), Te Awamutu ($6.40, 50 minutes) and Raglan ($7.50, one hour).

Dalroy Express (☎06-759 0197, 0508 465 622; www.dalroytours.co.nz) operates a daily both-directions service between Auckland ($23, two hours) and New Plymouth ($41, four hours) via Hamilton, stopping at most towns, including Te Kuiti ($19, 1¾ hours) and Te Awamutu ($13, 20 minutes).

InterCity (☎09-583 5780; www.intercity.co.nz) services numerous destinations:

DESTINATION	PRICE	DURATION	FREQUENCY
Auckland	$30	2hr	11 daily
Cambridge	$23	25min	9 daily
Matamata	$27	50min	3 daily
Ngaruawahia	$17	20min	9 daily
Rotorua	$35	1½hr	5 daily
Te Aroha	$10	1hr	2 daily
Te Awamutu	$22	35min	3 daily
Wellington	$55	5hr	3 daily

Naked Bus (☎0900 625 33; www.nakedbus.com) services run to the following destinations (among many others).

DESTINATION	PRICE	DURATION	FREQUENCY
Auckland	$15	2hr	5 daily
Cambridge	$20	30min	5-7 daily
Matamata	$20	1hr	1 daily
Ngaruawahia	$20	30min	5 daily
Rotorua	$15	1½hr	4-5 daily
Wellington	$40	9½hr	1-2 daily

SHUTTLE BUSES

Minibus Express (☎07-856 3191, 0800 646 428; www.minibus.co.nz) Runs a shuttle between Hamilton and Auckland Airport (one way $75).

Raglan Scenic Tours (☎07-825 0507, 021 0274 7014; www.raglanscenictours.co.nz) Runs a shuttle linking Hamilton with Raglan (one way $30). Auckland airport service also available.

Train

Hamilton is on the **Overlander** (☎0800 872 467; www.tranzscenic.co.nz; ⊙daily Oct-Apr, Fri-Sun May-Sep) route between Auckland ($68, 2½ hours) and Wellington ($129, 9½ hours) via Otorohanga ($68, 45 minutes). Trains stop at Hamilton's **Frankton train station** (Fraser St), 1km west of the city centre; there are no ticket sales here – see the website for ticketing details.

❶ Getting Around

To & From Airport

Hamilton International Airport (HIA; ☎07-848 9027; www.hamiltonairport.co.nz; Airport Rd) is 12km south of the city. International departure tax is $25 for those 12 years and over. The **Super Shuttle** (☎07-843 7778, 0800 748 885; www.supershuttle.co.nz; one way $23) offers a door-to-door service into the city. A taxi costs around $40.

Bus

Hamilton's **Busit!** (☑0800 4287 5463; www.
busit.co.nz; city routes adult/child $3.10/2.10)
network services the city-centre and suburbs
daily from around 7am to 7.30pm (later on Friday). All buses pass through Hamilton Transport
Centre. Busit! also runs a free No 51 CBD shuttle
looping around Victoria, Liverpool, Anglesea and
Bridge Sts every 10 minutes (7am to 6pm weekdays, 9am to 1pm Saturday)

Car

Rent-a-Dent (☑07-839 1049; www.rentadent.
co.nz; 383 Anglesea St; ⊙7.30am-5pm Mon-
Fri, 8am-noon Sat)

Taxi & Water taxi

Discovery River Taxis (☑0800 420 8294;
www.discoveryrivercruises.co.nz; Memorial
Park Jetty, Memorial Dr; trips from $10) Short
trips to anywhere you like, up or down the river.
Hamilton Taxis (☑07-8477 477, 0800 477 477;
www.hamiltontaxis.co.nz)

Raglan

POP 2640

Laid-back Raglan may well be NZ's perfect
surfing town. It's small enough to have escaped mass development, but it's big enough
to exhibit signs of life (good eateries, and a
bar that attracts big-name bands in summer).

The nearby surf spots – Indicators, Whale
Bay and Manu Bay – are internationally famous for their point breaks. Bruce Brown's
classic 1964 wave-chaser film *The Endless
Summer* features Manu Bay. Closer to town,
the harbour just begs to be kayaked upon.
This all serves to attract fit guys and gals
from around the planet; Raglan may also be
NZ's best-looking town!

◉ Sights & Activities

FREE Old School
Arts Centre   ARTS CENTRE, GALLERY
(www.raglanartscentre.co.nz; Stewart St; ⊙10am-
2pm Mon & Wed, exhibition hours vary) A community hub, the Old School Arts Centre
has changing exhibitions and workshops,
including weaving, carving, yoga and sto-
ry-telling. Movies screen here regularly
through summer ($11): grab a curry and a
beer to complete the experience. The hippie/
artsy **Raglan Creative Market** happens out
the front on the second Sunday of the month
(9am to 2pm).

Raglan Surf School   SURFING
(☑07-825 7873; www.raglansurfingschool.co.nz; 5b
Whaanga Rd, Whale Bay; 3hr lesson incl transport
$89) The instructors at Raglan Surf School
pride themselves on getting 95% of first-
timers standing during their first lesson. Experienced wave hounds can rent surfboards
(from $20 per hour), body boards ($5 per
hour) and wet suits ($5 per hour). It's based
at Karioi Lodge in Whale Bay.

Solscape   SURFING
(☑07-825 8268; www.solscape.co.nz; 611 Wainui
Rd, Manu Bay) Super-sustainable Solscape
offers 2½-hour surfing lessons ($85), as
well as board and wet-suit hire (per half-
day $35).

Raglan Kayak   KAYAKING
(☑07-825 8862; www.raglaneco.co.nz; Wallis St
Wharf) Raglan Harbour is great for kayaking. This outfit runs three-hour guided harbour paddles (per person $70) and rents out
kayaks (single/double per half-day $40/60).
Learn the basics on the gentle Opotoru
River, or paddle out to investigate the nooks
and crannies of the pancake rocks on the
harbour's northern edge.

Raglan Bone Carving Studio   BONE CARVING
(☑07-825 7147, 021 0223 7233; www.maoribone
carving.com; 6 Snowden Pl; workshops $69, pri-
vate lessons per hr $25) Carve your own bone
pendant (now *that's* a souvenir!) with
Rangi Wills, a reformed 'troubled teenager'
who found out he was actually really good
at carving things. Workshops run for three
to four hours, or you can book a private
lesson.

☞ Tours

Raglan Scenic Tours   GUIDED TOUR
(☑07-825 0507; www.raglanscenictours.co.nz)
These guys run an array of sightseeing tours,
including one hour around Raglan (adult/
child $30/10), 3½ to four hours around
Mount Karioi including Bridal Veil Falls and
Te Toto Gorge ($90/40), and three to four
hours to Kawhia ($70/40).

Cruise Raglan   CRUISE
(☑07-825 7873; www.raglanboatcharters.co.nz;
adult/child $40/29) Cruise Raglan offers a two-
hour sunset cruises around Raglan Harbour
on the *Wahine Moe*, with a sausage sizzle
and a few drinks.

WAIKATO & THE KING COUNTRY RAGLAN

Raglan

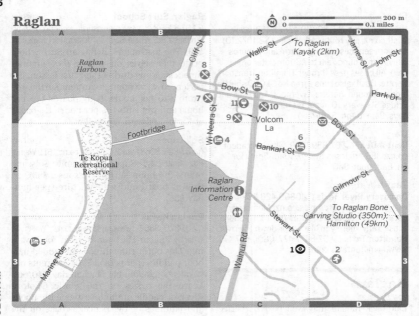

🛏 Sleeping

TOP CHOICE Raglan Backpackers　　HOSTEL $

(☏07-825 0515; www.raglanbackpackers.co.nz; 6 Wi Neera St; dm $28, s $57, tw & d $72-82; @) This chipper, purpose-built hostel has a laid-back holiday-house mood. It's right on the water, with sea views from some rooms. Other rooms are arranged around a garden courtyard. There's also a separate self-contained wing that accomodates eight people. There are free bikes and kayaks/surfboards for hire (from $30/25per half-day), or take a yoga class, snooze in a hammock, strum a guitar or drip in the sauna. No wi-fi – it 'ruins the vibe'.

Journey's End B&B　　B&B, APARTMENT $$

(☏07-825 6727; www.raglanaccommodation.co.nz; 49 Lily St; s/d $100/140, exclusive use $200; 🛜) These two attractive en-suite rooms share a central modern lounge with a kitchenette and a lovely deck overlooking the wharf and harbour. You can book out the whole place, or just one of the rooms and risk/enjoy the (potential) company of others. Fifteen minutes' walk from town.

Harbour View Hotel　　HISTORIC HOTEL $

(☏07-825 8010; harbourviewhotel@vodafone.co.nz; 14 Bow St; s from $70, tw & d from $90, f from $105) If you think that going to bed before the party's over is for the faint and feeble, then this two-storey, 106-year-old pub, with sunny verandas and kauri trimmings, is for you. Rooms are clean but you'll be sharing bathrooms (and there are no harbour views to speak of). Pub meals, live bands and big-screen rugby downstairs.

Raglan Kopua Holiday Park   HOLIDAY PARK **$**
(📞07-825 8283; www.raglanholidaypark.co.nz;
Marine Pde; sites from $34, dm/units from $56/85;
@🛜) A neatly maintained outfit with lots of
sleeping options, on the spit across the inlet from town (there's a footbridge, or drive
the long way around). No shade, but there's
beach swimming and plenty of room to run
amok.

Raglan Sunset Motel   MOTEL **$$**
(📞07-825 0050; www.raglansunsetmotel.co.nz;
7 Bankart St; d $140; 🛜) A block back from the
action, this two-storey motel with faux shut-
ters randomly adhered to the facade isn't
quite a decade old. As you'd hope, every-
thing's in good nick. The owners also have
self-contained apartments (doubles from
$150) and beach houses (four people from
$250) available around town. Bike and kay-
ak hire available (per half-day $30 and $45
respectively).

 Eating

The Shack   CAFE, INTERNATIONAL **$**
(19 Bow St; mains $9-18; ⏰8.30am-5pm Sat-Thu,
8.30am-late Fri; 🍴) Burgers, wraps, veggie fry-
ups, curries, Middle Eastern plates, tapas...
This shack ain't no hack when it comes to cafe
fare. A longboard strapped to the wall, wobbly
old floorboards, up-tempo tunes and interna-
tional staff complete a very pretty picture.

Orca   CAFE, MODERN NZ **$$**
(📞07-825 6543; www.orcarestaurant.co.nz; 2 Wal-
lis St; breakfast $11-18, mains $19-33; ⏰9am-late
Mon-Fri, 8am-late Sat & Sun) A day started at an
Orca window seat, looking over the water,
with some eggs Benedict and a superb coffee is a day well launched. Come back in the
evening for rabbit pie, wine-appreciation
nights and live music.

Raglan Roast   CAFE **$**
(www.raglanroast.co.nz; Volcom La; coffee & biscuit
$5; ⏰7.30am-5pm, reduced winter hours) This
hole-in-the-wall coffee roaster with a fold-up
front wall does the best brew in town, and
that's about all (there's not much room for
anything else). Stop by for a cup, a cookie
and a conversation.

Aloha Market Place   JAPANESE **$**
(5 Bow St; sushi $1.20-2.20, mains $10-13; ⏰11am-
5pm, reduced winter hours; 🍴) It's takeaway
without the grease, Japanese surfer-style.
Grab some delicious rolled-to-order sushi,
some udon noodles or a donburi rice bowl
and head for the harbour. 'No rice, no life'.

🍷 Drinking & Entertainment

Orca and the Harbour View Hotel both host
live music, usually on summer weekends.

Yot Club   BAR, LIVE MUSIC
(www.mukuna.co.nz/waikato/raglan/yot-club.htm;
9 Bow St; admission free-$25; ⏰9pm-late) This
raucous, nocturnal bar is where everyone
goes to dance, with visiting DJs and bands
(Harmonica Lewinsky were playing when
we visted), a pool table and imported beers.

ℹ Information

Raglan Information Centre (📞07-825 0556;
www.raglan.org.nz; 13 Wainui Rd; ⏰9.30am-
5pm Mon-Fri, 10am-5pm Sat, 10am-4pm
Sun) DOC brochures plus information about
local accommodation and activities. Reduced
winter hours.

West Coast Health Centre (📞07-825 0114;
wchc@wave.co.nz; 12 Wallis St; ⏰9am-5pm
Mon-Fri) General medical assistance.

ℹ Getting There & Around

From Hamilton, Raglan is 48km west along
SH23. Unsealed back roads connect Raglan to
Kawhia, 50km south; they're slow, winding and
prone to rockslides, but scenic and certainly off
the beaten track. Head back towards Hamilton
for 7km and take the Te Mata/Kawhia turn-off
and follow the signs; allow at least an hour.

Waikato District Council's **Busit!** (📞0800
4287 5463; www.busit.co.nz; adult/child
$7.50/3.80) heads between Hamilton and Rag-
lan (one hour) three times daily on weekdays and
twice daily on weekends.

Raglan Scenic Tours (p185) runs a Raglan–
Hamilton shuttle bus (one way $30). **Raglan
Shuttle Co** (📞0800 8873 2 7873; www.raglan
shuttle.co.nz) offers a parallel service.

Bike2Bay (📞07-825 0309; www.bike2bay.
com; 24b Stewart St; hire per hr/half/full day
$8/22/33; ⏰9.30am-5pm) has mountain bikes
for hire, does repairs and runs bike tours around
Raglan.

If you need a cab call **Raglan Taxi** (📞07-825
0506).

South of Raglan
OCEAN BEACH

Ocean Beach sits at the mouth of the harbour, 4kms southwest of Raglan down Riria
Kereopa Memorial Dr. It's popular with
windsurfers and kitesurfers, but strong
currents make it extremely treacherous for
swimmers.

WORTH A TRIP

RUAPEKE BEACH

Whale Bay marks the end of the sealed road, but a gravel road continues to the wild spans of Ruapuke Beach, 22km from Raglan, passing a couple of rusty, abandoned buses en route. It's dangerous for swimmers here, but popular with surf-casting fisherfolk. The gravel road continues to Mt Karioi and rejoins the inland road at Te Mata.

NGARUNUI BEACH

Less than 1km south of Ocean Beach, Ngarunui Beach is a great for grommets learning to surf. On the cliff-top is a clubhouse for the volunteer lifeguards who patrol part of the black-sand beach from late October until April. This is the only beach with lifeguards, and is the best ocean beach for swimming.

MANU BAY

A 2.5km journey from Ngarunui Beach will bring you to Manu Bay, a legendary surf spot said to have the longest left-hand break in the world. The elongated uniform waves are created by the angle at which the Tasman Sea swell meets the coastline (it works best in a southwesterly swell).

🛌 Sleeping

TOP CHOICE **Solscape** HOSTEL, CABINS **$**
(☎07-825 8268; www.solscape.co.nz; 611 Wainui Rd, Manu Bay; sites from $16, caboose dm/d $26/68, tepees per person $34, cottages d $115-180; @ 🛜) This hippie hilltop hostel has dorms in old train carriages. It's the ultimate greenie experience: chilling in a tepee (surprisingly comfortable, available December to April), surrounded by native bush, knowing that you're completely 'off grid' – while not sacrificing hot showers (solar) and decent toilets (composting). Self-contained sea-view cottages (try for the 'Ivy'), surf lessons and massage ($65 per hour) complete a bewildering array of services.

WHALE BAY

Whale Bay is a renowned surf spot (p185) 1km west of Manu Bay. It's usually less crowded than Manu Bay, but from the bottom of Calvert Rd you have to clamber 600m over the rocks to get to the break.

🛌 Sleeping

Karioi Lodge HOSTEL **$**
(☎07-825 7873; www.karioilodge.co.nz; 5b Whaanga Rd, Whale Bay; dm/d $30/75; @ 🛜) Deep in native bush, Karioi Lodge offers a sauna, a flying fox, mountain bikes, bush and beach walks, sustainable gardening, tree planting and the Raglan Surf School. There are no en suites but the rooms are clean and cosy. These friendly folks also run **Sleeping Lady Lodging** (☎07-825 7873; www.sleepinglady.co.nz; 5b Whaanga Rd, Whale Bay; lodges $165-570), a collection of seven luxury self-contained houses nearby, all with ocean views.

MT KARIOI

In legend, Mt Karioi (756m), the Sleeping Lady (check out that profile), is the sister to Mt Pirongia. At its base (8km south of Whale Bay) **Te Toto Gorge** is a steep cleft in the mountainside, with a vertigo-inducing lookout perched high over the chasm.

Starting from Te Toto Gorge car park, a strenuous but scenic track goes up the western slope. It takes 2½ hours to reach a lookout point, followed by an easier hour up to the summit. From the east side, the Wairake Track is a steeper 2½-hour climb to the summit, where it meets the Te Toto Track.

WAIREINGA (BRIDAL VEIL FALLS)

Just past Te Mata (a short drive south of the main Raglan–Hamilton road) is the turn-off to the 55m Waireinga (Bridal Veil Falls), 4km from the main road. From the car park, it's an easy 10-minute walk through mossy native bush to the top of the falls. It's a magical place, the effect compounded by the dancing rainbows swirling around the khaki-coloured pool far below (not suitable for swimming). A further 10-minute walk leads down to the bottom. Lock your car: theft is a problem here.

Magic Mountain Horse Treks (☎07-825 6892; www.magicmountain.co.nz; 334 Houtchen Rd, Te Mata; rides 1/2hr $50/70) runs horse treks around the hills, plus a ride to Waireinga (Bridal Veil Falls, $90).

PIRONGIA FOREST PARK

The main attraction of this 170-sq-km forest park is **Mt Pirongia** (www.mtpirongia.org.nz), its 959m summit clearly visible from much of the Waikato. The mountain is usually climbed from Corcoran Rd (three to five hours, one way) with tracks to other lookout points. Interestingly, NZ's tallest known kahikatea tree (66.5m) grows on the mountainside. There's a six-bunk DOC hut near the summit if you need to spend the night: maps and information are available from Hamilton DOC.

Te Awamutu

POP 9800

Deep into dairy-farming country, Te Awamutu (which means 'The River Cut Short'; the Waikato beyond this point was unsuitable for large canoes) is a real working town with real working people living in it – agrarian integrity by the bucketload! With a blossom-treed main street and a good museum, TA (aka Rose Town) makes a decent overnighter. (Finn fans might need longer.)

◉ Sights

Te Awamutu Museum MUSEUM
(www.tamuseum.org.nz; 135 Roche St; admission by donation; ◷10am-4pm Mon-Fri, 10am-1pm Sat, 1-4pm Sun) Te Awamutu Museum, 'where history never repeats', has a *True Colours*–painted shrine to local heroes Tim and Neil Finn. There are gold records, original lyrics, Finn memorabilia and oddities such as Neil's form-two exercise book. There's also a fine collection of Maori *taonga* (treasures), including the revered 'Uenuku', and an excellent display on the Waikato War. A great little museum.

FREE **Rose Garden** GARDEN
(cnr Gorst Ave & Arawata St; ◷24hr) The Rose Garden is next to the i-SITE and has 2500 bushes and 51 varieties with fabulously fruity names like Big Daddy, Disco Dancer, Lady Gay and Sexy Rexy. The roses usually bloom from November to May.

▣ Sleeping

Cloverdale House B&B $$
(◷07-872 1702; www.cloverdalehouse.co.nz; 141 Long Rd; d/q $140/200) Indulge your farmer fantasies at this smart new place in the dairy heartland, 8km east of Cambridge Rd. Two double rooms with en suites share a common lounge and kitchen (breakfast ingredients provided).

Rosetown Motel MOTEL $$
(◷0800 767 386, 07-871 5779; www.rosetown motel.co.nz; 844 Kihikihi Rd; d/f from $115/140; ❄▨) The older-style units at Rosetown (the new owners are weeding out the last of the teak veneer and yellow faux-marble) have kitchens, new linen and TVs, and share a spa. A solid choice if you're hankering for straight-up small-town sleeps.

✗ Eating & Drinking

Redoubt Bar & Eatery PUB $$
(www.redoubtbarandeateryta.co.nz; cnr Rewi & Alexandra Sts; mains $16-34; ◷10am-late) A relaxed little place to eat or drink, with cheap-but-potent cocktails, old photos on the walls and a decent menu stretching from pasta to curry. Watch tractors roll along the main street through fold-back windows.

Farenheight MODERN NZ, TAPAS $$
(◷07-871 5429; www.fahrenheitrestaurant.co.nz; Level 1, 13 Roche St; mains $15-36; ◷lunch & dinner Tue-Sun) Bright as a button, this new upstairs bar/restaurant on the main drag is a classy place for a drink when the sun goes down on TA. No great menu surprises (chowder, lamb rump, pork belly, steaks) but this is surely

TE AWAMUTU'S SACRED SOUND

In the opening lines of Crowded House's first single *Mean to Me*, Neil Finn single-handedly raised his sleepy hometown, Te Awamutu, to international attention. It wasn't the first time it had provided inspiration – Split Enz songs *Haul Away* and *Kia Kaha*, with big bro Tim, include similar references.

Despite NZ's brilliant songwriting brothers being far from the height of their fame, Finn devotees continue to make the pilgrimage to Te Awamutu – just ask the staff at the i-SITE. They do a brisk trade in Finn T-shirts, Finn stamps and walking-tour brochures of sites from Finn history (their childhood home at 588 Teasdale St, their school, even Neil's piano tutor's house). It's NZ's version of Graceland!

If you're hoping for a close encounter with greatness, it's unlikely: the boys skipped town decades ago.

the only place within miles that does tapas! Bee-line for the balcony.

Indian Aroma INDIAN
(☑07-871 5555; www.indianaroma.co.nz; 23 Arawata St; mains $13-17; ☺lunch Wed-Fri, dinner daily; ☝) Brightening up the town with a saffron-yellow glow, this attractive restaurant with orderly glass-topped tables serves all the fragrant favourites. The roses on the tables are fake (a sin in Rose Town?).

☆ Entertainment

Regent Theatre CINEMA
(www.regent3.itgo.com; 235 Alexandra St; adult/child $15.50/9.50; ☺10am-late) Built in 1932, this art deco cinema has five screens and fabulous movie memorabilia in the foyer. It's *deathly* serious about turning off your mobile phone.

❶ Information

Te Awamutu i-SITE (☑07-871 3259; www.teawamutuinfo.com; 1 Gorst Ave; ☺9am-5pm Mon-Fri, 10am-4pm Sat & Sun) Oodles of local information.

❶ Getting There & Away

Te Awamutu is on SH3, halfway between Hamilton and Otorohanga (29km either way). The regional bus service **Busit!** (☑0800 4287 5463; www.busit.co.nz) is the cheapest option for Hamilton (adult/child $6.40/4.30, 50 minutes, eight daily weekdays, three daily weekends).

Three daily **InterCity** (☑09-583 5780; www.intercity.co.nz) services connect Te Awamutu with Auckland ($29, 2½ hours), Hamilton ($22, 35 minutes) and Otorohanga ($22, 25 minutes).

The **Dalroy Express** (☑0508 465 622; www.dalroytours.co.nz) bus runs daily (in each direction) between Auckland ($29, 2½ hours) and New Plymouth ($40, 3½ hours), leaving from the i-SITE. Stops include Hamilton ($13, 25 minutes) and Otorohanga ($12, 20 minutes).

Around Te Awamutu

RANGIAOWHIA
Before the Waikato invasion, Rangiaowhia (located 5km east of Te Awamutu on Rangiaowhia Rd; ask at the i-SITE for directions) was a thriving Maori farming town, exporting wheat, maize, potatoes and fruit as far afield as Australia. It was home to thousands of inhabitants, two churches, a flour mill and a racecourse, and was the perfect model of what NZ under the Maori version

of the Treaty of Waitangi had desired – two sovereign peoples interacting to mutual advantage.

In February 1864 the settlement was left undefended while King Tawhiao's warriors held fortified positions further north. In a key tactical move, General Cameron outflanked them and took the town, killing women, children and the elderly. This was a turning point in the campaign, demoralising the Maori and drawing the warriors out of their near impregnable *pa* fortifications.

Sadly, all that remains of the town is the cute 1854 Anglican **St Paul's Church** (☑07-871 5568; Rangiaowhia Rd; ☺services 9am 1st & 3rd Sun of the month) and the Catholic mission's **cemetery**, standing in the midst of rich farming land – confiscated from the Maori and distributed to colonial soldiers.

The war ended further south at **Orakau**, where a roadside obelisk marks the site where 300 Maori, led by Rewi Maniapoto, repulsed three days of attacks against an unfinished *pa* by 1500 troops, before breaking out and retreating to what is now known as the King Country (losing 70 warriors).

WHAREPAPA SOUTH
A surreal landscape of craggy limestone provides some of the best **rock climbing** in the North Island. This isn't the best place for wannabe Spidermen (or women) to don their lycra bodysuits for the first time, but if you have the basic skills get ready to let your inner superhero shine.

Bryce's Rockclimbing (☑07-872 2533; www.rockclimb.co.nz; 1424 Owairaka Valley Rd; 1-day instruction for 1-2 people $440) is suited to the serious climber. On-site is NZ's largest retail climbing store, selling and hiring out a full range of gear. It also has an indoor bouldering cave, free to those staying out back in the ship-shape accommodation (dorm/double $25/66). There's a licensed cafe (open 8am to 5pm Friday to Monday, light meals $6 to $16).

Cambridge
POP 15,200
The name says it all. Despite the rambunctious Waikato River looking nothing like the Cam, the good people of Cambridge have done all they can to assume an air of English gentility: village greens, avenues of decidu-

MAUNGATAUTARI

Can a landlocked volcano become an island paradise? Inspired by the success of pest eradication and native species reintroduction in the Hauraki Gulf, a community trust has erected 47km of pest-proof fencing around the triple peaks of Maungatautari (797m) to create the impressive **Maungatautari Ecological Island** (www.maungatrust.org). This atoll of rainforest dominates the skyline between Te Awamutu and Karapiro and is now home to its first kiwi chicks in 100 years. The shortest route to the peak (1¾ hours) is from the northern side, while the entire north–south walk will take around six hours. Take Maungatautari Rd then Hicks Rd if coming from Karapiro, or Arapuni Rd then Tari Rd from Te Awamutu.

Out In The Styx (☏07-872 4505; www.styx.co.nz; 2117 Arapuni Rd, Pukeatua; dm/s/d $95/130/260), near the south end of the Maungatautari, provides a drop-off service to the northern entrance ($10 per person, minimum four), plus guided day- and night-walk options. The three stylishly furnished themed rooms (Polynesian, African or Maori) are especially nice, plus there are bunk rooms and a spa for soothing weary legs. Prices include a four-course dinner and breakfast.

ous trees, faux-Tudor houses... Even the public toilet looks like a Victorian cottage.

Famous for breeding and training thoroughbred horses, you can almost smell the wealth along the main street. Equine references are rife in public sculpture, and plaques boast of Melbourne Cup winners.

◉ Sights & Activities

FREE **Cambridge Museum**　　MUSEUM
(www.cambridgemuseum.org.nz; 24 Victoria St; ⊙10am-4pm) In a former courthouse, the quirky Cambridge Museum has plenty of pioneer relics, a military history room and a small display on the local Te Totara Pa before it was wiped out. Oh, and there's a stuffed kiwi if you haven't managed to see a real one.

Jubilee Gardens　　GARDEN, MONUMENT
(Victoria St; ⊙24hr) Apart from its Spanish Mission town clock, Jubilee Gardens is a wholehearted tribute to the 'mother country'. A British lion guards the cenotaph, with a plaque that reads, 'Tell Britain ye who mark this monument faithful to her we fell and rest content'. Outmoded sentiment or awkward grammar – either way, the soldier statue looks confused.

Lake Karapiro　　LAKE
(www.waipadc.govt.nz/district/lake+karapiro; Maungatautari Rd) Eight kilometres southeast of Cambridge, Karapiro is the furthest downstream of a chain of eight hydroelectric power stations on the Waikato River. It's an impressive sight, especially when driving across the

top of the 1947 dam. The 21km-long lake is also a world-class rowing venue. The **Boatshed Cafe** (www.theboatshed.net.nz; 21 Amber La, off Gorton Rd; ⊙10am-4pm Wed-Fri, 9am-4pm Sat & Sun) hires out basic kayaks (from $20 per half day); you can paddle to a couple of waterfalls in around an hour.

Waikato River Trails　　CYCLING, TRAMPING
(www.waikatorivertrails.com) Winding east from Cambridge, the 100km Waikato River Trails track was ascribed 'Quick Start' status as part of the Nga Haerenga, New Zealand Cycle Trail project (www.nzcycletrail.com), and opened in late 2011. You can walk or cycle the five combined trails (or parts thereof), with lots of history and local landscape en route.

Heritage & Tree Trail　　WALKING TOUR
Whether you're hip to history or tantalised by trees, this trail covers all the sights, including the Waikato River, the 1881 St Andrew's Anglican Church (look for the Gallipoli window) and leafy Lake Ko Utu. Grab a map at the Cambridge i-SITE.

Camjet　　JETBOATING
(☏0800 226 538; www.camjet.co.nz; trips adult/child $75/50) Can help adrenaline junkies shake off the cobwebs with a 35-minute spin to Karapiro dam on a jetboat. A 15-minute spin costs $45. Minimum four people.

Cambridge Thoroughbred Lodge　　GUIDED TOUR
(☏07-827 8118; www.cambridgethoroughbredlodge.co.nz; tours adult/child $12/5, show $12/5; ⊙tours

10am-2pm by arrangement) Cambridge Thoroughbred Lodge, 6km south of town on SH1, is a top-notch horse stud. Book ahead for 90-minute tours, or 'NZ Horse Magic' shows which get galloping several times a week.

🛏 Sleeping

Birches   B&B $$
(☏07-827 6556; www.birches.co.nz; 263 Maungatautari Rd; s/d $100/150; ☲) You're in luck! There's a pool, spa and tennis court at this picturesque 1930s weatherboard farmhouse, in farmland southeast of Cambridge. Sleep in the main house or self-contained cottage. Sheep and daffodils line the driveway.

Lofthouse   APARTMENT $$
(☏07-827 3693; www.lofthouse.co.nz; 17 Dunning Rd; apt from $130) If you're travelling with friends, this self-contained rural retreat is an absolute steal – sleeping four people for the price of the apartment. Jump in the spa and enjoy the awesome views. It's 3km off SH1, near the top of Karapiro, and 11km from Cambridge.

House Boat Holidays   HOUSEBOAT $$
(☏07-827 2195; www.houseboatescape.co.nz; Lake Karapiro; 2 nights $600) Humming 'Proud Mary' is acceptable as Lake Karapiro is technically still a river, but you're more likely to be relaxing than rolling. Load up this smart houseboat (sleeping eight) with kayaks and fishing gear and sail away for a splashy weekend.

Cambridge Coach House   B&B, CABIN $$
(☏07-823 7922; www.cambridgecoachhouse. co.nz; 3796 Cambridge Rd, Leamington; d from $150, cottage $195) This farmhouse accommodation is a wee bit chintzy, but if you can forgive a chandelier or two it's a beaut spot to chill out, in the thick of Waikato's bucolic splendour. There's a double in the main building, two separate doubles and a self-contained cottage. It's a couple of kilometres south of town on the way to Te Awamutu.

Cambridge Mews   MOTEL $$
(☏07-827 7166; www.cambridgemews.co.nz; 20 Hamilton Rd; apt from $155; ☎) All the spacious units in this chalet-style motel have double spa baths, decent kitchens and are immaculately maintained. The architect did a great job...the interior decorator less so. A 10-minute walk to town.

Cambridge Motor Park   HOLIDAY PARK $
(☏07-827 5649; www.cambridgemotorpark.co.nz; 32 Scott St; sites from $16, units $42-$105; ☎) A quiet, well-maintained camping ground with lots of green, green grass. The emphasis is on tents and vans here, but the cabins and units are fine. Drive over the skinny Victoria Bridge from the Cambridge town centre.

🍴 Eating

🏆 Red Cherry   CAFE $$
(☏07-823 1515; www.redcherrycoffee.co.nz; cnr SH1 & Forrest Rd; meals $7-21; ☺breakfast & lunch daily, dinner Fri & Sat; ☛) With happy staff and a cherry-red espresso machine working overtime, barn-like Red Cherry offers coffee roasted on-site, delicious counter food and impressive cooked breakfasts (oh those corn-and-pumpkin fritters). It's Cambridge's best cafe by a country mile (it's actually a country 4km out of Cambridge on the way to Hamilton).

Nash   MODERN NZ, WINE BAR $$$
(☏07-827 5596; www.thenash.net.nz; 47 Alpha St; mains $28-34; ☺lunch & dinner) All white/grey/ black paint and dapper, quick-moving staff, sexy Nash has transformed the old National Hotel, sinking the boot firmly into Ye Olde Cambridge. We hope it lasts: the braised lamb shoulder with roast-garlic mash and pea puree is sublime, and the streetside terrace is just made for people-watching while quaffing Kiwi wine.

Onyx   CAFE, RESTAURANT $$
(☏07-827 7740; 70 Alpha St; mains $20-39; ☺breakfast, lunch & dinner) All-day Onyx occupies a lofty space, with onyx-black furnishings and warm-toned timber floors. Wood-fired pizzas are the mainstay, plus salads, tortillas, sandwiches, steaks, cakes, organic coffee and 95% NZ wines. At night it's almost urbane.

ℹ Information

Cambridge i-SITE (☏07-823 3456; www. cambridge.co.nz; cnr Victoria & Queen Sts; ☺9am-5pm Mon-Fri, 10am-4pm Sat & Sun; ☻) Free Heritage & Tree Trail and town maps, and internet access.

ℹ Getting There & Away

Being on SH1, 22km southeast of Hamilton, Cambridge is well connected by bus. Environment Waikato's **Busit!** (☏0800 4287 5463; www.busit.co.nz) heads to Hamilton ($6.40, 40 minutes, seven daily weekdays, three daily weekends).

InterCity (☏09-583 5780; www.intercity.co.nz) services numerous destinations:

DESTINATION	PRICE	DURATION	FREQUENCY
Auckland	$40	2½hr	12 daily
Hamilton	$24	30min	8 daily
Matamata	$22	30min	2 daily
Rotorua	$33	1¼hr	5 daily
Wellington	$75	8½hr	3 daily

Naked Bus (☏0900 625 33; www.nakedbus.com) services to the same destinations are as follows.

DESTINATION	PRICE	DURATION	FREQUENCY
Auckland	$13	2½hr	6 daily
Hamilton	$20	30min	5 daily
Matamata	$24	2¼hr	1 daily
Rotorua	$15	1¼hr	4 daily
Wellington	$33	9½hr	1 daily

Matamata

POP 7800

Matamata was just one of those pleasant, horsey country towns you drove through until Peter Jackson's epic film trilogy *Lord of the Rings* put it on the map. During filming 300 locals got work as extras (hairy feet weren't a prerequisite). And now Jackson's *The Hobbit* is being filmed here – hobbits ahoy!

Most tourists who come to Matamata are dedicated hobbit-botherers: for everyone else there's a great cafe, avenues of mature trees and undulating green hills.

◉ Sights & Activities

Hobbiton Movie Set &
Farm Tours   MOVIE LOCATION
(☏07-888 1505; www.hobbitontours.com; 501 Buckland Rd, Hinuera; adult/child $66/5; ⊙tours 9.50am, 10.45am, noon, 1.15pm, 2.30pm, 3.45pm, 5pm) This is NZ's top attraction for *LOTR* boffins, and pretty interesting even if you haven't seen the movies. Due to copyright, all the intricately constructed movie sets around the country were dismantled after filming, but Hobbiton's owners negotiated

to keep their hobbit holes, which have been completely rebuilt for the filming of *The Hobbit*. Also on offer is a hands-on Sheep Farm Experience (adult/child $16/5), explaining all things woolly. Free transfers leave from the Matamata i-SITE. Otherwise, head towards Cambridge and turn right into Puketutu Rd and then left into Buckland Rd, stopping at the Shire's Rest Cafe. All manner of combined tour/accommodation packages also available.

Wairere Falls   WATERFALL
About 15km northeast of Matamata are the spectacular 153m-high Wairere Falls (the highest on the North Island). From the car park it's a 45-minute walk through native bush to the lookout or a steep 90-minute climb to the summit.

Firth Tower   MUSEUM, HISTORIC BUILDING
(www.firthtower.co.nz; Tower Rd; grounds free, tours adult/child $5/1; ⊙10am-4pm) Firth Tower was built by Auckland businessman Josiah Firth in 1882. The 18m concrete tower was a fashionable status symbol, and is now filled with Maori and pioneer artefacts. Around it are 10 other historic buildings (closed Tuesday and Wednesday), including a schoolroom, a church and a jail. It's located 3km east of town.

Opal Hot Springs   SWIMMING
(www.opalhotsprings.co.nz; 257 Okauia Springs Rd; adult/child $8/4, 30min private spas $10/5; ⊙9am-9pm) Opal Hot Springs isn't nearly as glamorous as it sounds but it does have three large thermal pools. Turn off just north of Firth Tower and follow the road for 2km. There's a holiday park here too.

Skydive Waikato   SKYDIVING
(☏07-888 8763; www.freefall.co.nz; tandem $245-310) Skydive Waikato offers thrilling gravity-powered plummets above Matamata Airfield, 10km north of Matamata on SH27.

⌾ Sleeping

Broadway Motel &
Miro Court Villas   MOTEL $$
(☏07-888 8482; www.broadwaymatamata.co.nz; 128 Broadway; s $86-135, d $96-159, apt $250; ❀⚞) This sprawling family-run motel complex has spread from a well-maintained older-style block to progressively newer and flasher blocks set back from the street (with

cool light fittings and funky panels of wallpaper). The nicest are the chic apartment-style Miro Court villas. There's a fun kids' play area in the centre.

Southern Belle APARTMENT **$$**
(☑07-888 5518; www.southernbelle.co.nz; 101 Firth St; r $120, extra person $40; 🐾) Taking over the top floor of a grand old house (a transported vision from Savannah or Baton Rouge), this suite has three elegant bedrooms, a comfortable lounge and a kitchenette (just a microwave for cooking, but there's a barbecue downstairs that guests can use).

✖ Eating & Drinking

TOP CHOICE **Workman's Cafe Bar** CAFE
(www.matamata-info.co.nz/workmans; 52 Broadway; lunch $15, dinner $28-32; ⊘breakfast & lunch Wed-Sun, dinner Tue-Sun) Truly eccentric (old transistor radios dangling from the ceiling; a wall-full of art deco mirrors; Johnny Cash on the stereo), this funky eatery has built itself a reputation that extends beyond Matamata. The poached salmon Benedict is a showstopper!

Redoubt Bar & Eatery PUB **$$**
(www.facebook.com/redoubtmatamata; 48 Broadway; lunch $12-20, dinner $26-34; ⊘11am-late Mon-Fri, 9.30am-late Sat & Sun) The sister establishment of Te Awamutu's Redoubt, Matamata's version is just as good: thin-crust pizzas, chowder, steaks, a winning hash stack (or 'hesh steck' in Kiwi accent), and live music every Friday. Oh, and plenty of Monteiths!

ℹ Information

Matamata i-SITE (☑07-888 7260; www.matamatanz.co.nz; 45 Broadway; ⊘9am-5pm Mon-Fri, 9am-3pm Sat & Sun) The super-helpful Matamata i-SITE has free town maps, all the guff on local attractions and extended summer hours. Hobbiton tours leave from here.

ℹ Getting There & Away

Matamata is on SH27, 20km north of Tirau.

InterCity (☑09-583 5780; www.intercity.co.nz) runs to Cambridge ($22, 40 minutes, two daily), Hamilton ($27, one hour, three daily), Rotorua ($27, one hour, one daily) and Tauranga ($23, one hour, two daily).

Naked Bus (☑0900 625 33; www.nakedbus.com) runs to Auckland ($27, 3½ hours, two daily), Cambridge ($20, two hours, one daily), Hamilton ($20, 3½ hours, two daily) and Tauranga ($14, one hour, one daily).

Te Aroha
POP 3800

Te Aroha has a great vibe. You could even say that it's got 'the love', which is the literal meaning of the name. Tucked under the elbow of the bush-clad Mt Te Aroha (952m), it's a good base for tramping or 'taking the waters' in the town's therapeutic thermal springs.

◉ Sights & Activities

Te Aroha Mineral Spas SPA
(☑07-884 8717; www.tearohapools.co.nz; Boundary St, Te Aroha Domain; 30min session adult/child $18/11; ⊘10.30am-9pm Mon-Fri, 10.30am-10pm Sat & Sun) In the quaint Edwardian Hot Springs Domain behind the Te Aroha i-SITE, this spa offers relaxing private tubs, massage, beauty therapies and aromatherapy. Also here is the temperamental Mokena Geyser – the world's only known soda geyser – which blows its top every 40 minutes or so, shooting water 3m into the air (the most ardent eruptions are between noon and 2pm).

Te Aroha Leisure Pools SWIMMING, BATHHOUSE
(www.tearohapools.co.nz; Boundary St, Te Aroha Domain; adult/child $6.50/4.50; ⊘10am-5.45pm Mon-Fri, to 6.45pm Sat & Sun) The Leisure Pools have outdoor heated freshwater pools for splashing about in. There's also a thermal bathhouse and a toddlers' pool.

Te Aroha Museum MUSEUM
(www.tearoha-museum.com; Te Aroha Domain; adult/child $4/2; ⊘11am-4pm Nov-Mar, noon-3pm Apr-Oct) Te Aroha's lovely museum is in the town's ornate former thermal sanatorium (aka the 'Treasure of Te Aroha'). Displays include quirky ceramics, old spa-water bottles, historic photos and an amazing old printing press from the *Te Aroha News*.

Mt Te Aroha TRAMPING
Trails up Mt Te Aroha start at the top of the domain. It's a 45-minute climb to Bald Spur/Whakapipi Lookout (350m), then another 2.7km (two hours) to the summit.

⌕ Sleeping

TOP CHOICE **Aroha Mountain Lodge** LODGE, B&B **$$**
(☑07-884 8134; www.arohamountainlodge.co.nz; 5 Boundary St; s/d/ste/cottage $115/135/155/250) Spread over two *aroha*-ly Edwardian villas on the hillside above town, the plush Mountain Lodge offers affordable luxury (*sooo* much nicer than a regulation motel) and op-

tional breakfast ($20 per person). The self-contained Gold Miner's Cottage sleeps six.

Te Aroha YHA
HOSTEL $

(07-884 8739, 0800 278 299; www.yha.co.nz; Miro St; dm/tr $23/56) This top-of-the-town YHA is a homely, TV-free, three-bedroom cottage with welcoming management, a well-stocked herb rack, a pile of *National Geographics* and an old nylon-string guitar leaning in the corner. A 10km mountain-bike track wheels away from the back door. Call in advance (it's closed sometimes in winter).

Te Aroha Motel
MOTEL $$

(07-884 9417; www.tearohamotel.co.nz; 108 Whitaker St; s/d/tr/q $85/100/120/150; ⚲) Welcome to the love-town motel (with a couple of palm trees out the front, this could almost be Vegas!). Inside are old-fashioned but reasonably priced and tidy units with kitchenettes, right in the centre of town. And what a lavish lawn!

Te Aroha Holiday Park
HOLIDAY PARK $

(07-884 9567; www.tearohaholidaypark.co.nz; 217 Stanley Rd; sites from $15, units $32-75; @⚲⚲) Wake up to a bird orchestra among the oaks at this site – possibly the Waikato's cheapest holiday park – equipped with grass tennis court, gym and hot pool, 2km southwest of town. The owners also speak German and Japanese.

✖ Eating

Behr Burger
BURGERS $

(176 Whitaker St; burgers $9-13; ⊘4-9pm Mon-Wed, 11am-9pm Thu-Sun) Awesome gourmet hamburgers are the go at this buzzy main-street nook. 'The Chief' (NZ rump steak, honey-smoked bacon, a free-range egg, cheddar cheese, salad and aioli) plugs the hungry hollows.

Berlusconi on Whitaker
ITALIAN, TAPAS $$

(07-884 9307; www.tearoha-info.co.nz/berlusconi; 149 Whitaker St; lunch $14-19, dinner $27-33; ⊘lunch Tue-Sun, dinner Wed-Sun) We know the defunct Italian PM has his fingers in a lot of pies, but surely they don't extend to this upmarket wine, tapas and pizza bar in Te Aroha. Mind you, it is suave enough.

ℹ Information

Te Aroha i-SITE (07-884 8052; www.tearohanz.co.nz; 102 Whitaker St; ⊘9.30am-5pm Mon-Fri, 9.30am-4pm Sat & Sun)

ℹ Getting There & Away

Te Aroha is on SH26, 21km south of Paeroa and 55km northeast of Hamilton. Waikato Regional Council's **Busit!** (0800 4287 5463; www.busit.co.nz) runs to/from Hamilton (adult/child $8/4, one hour, two daily Monday to Friday). Naked Bus (p194) runs to Hamilton ($20, one hour, one daily) and Cambridge ($20, 1½ hours, one daily).

THE KING COUNTRY

Holding good claim to the title of NZ's rural heartland, this is the kind of no-nonsense place that raises cattle and All Blacks. A bastion of independent Maoridom, it was never conquered in the war against the King Movement. The story goes that King Tawhiao placed his hat on a large map of NZ and declared that all the land it covered would remain under his *mana* (authority), and the region was effectively off limits to Europeans until 1883.

The Waitomo Caves are the area's major drawcard. An incredible natural phenomenon in themselves, they've been jazzed up even more with a smorgasbord of adrenaline-inducing activities.

Kawhia

POP 670

Along with resisting cultural annihilation, Kawhia (think mafia with a K) has avoided large-scale development, retaining its sleepy fishing-village vibe. There's not much here except for the general store, a couple of takeaways and a petrol station. Even Captain Cook blinked and missed the narrow entrance to the large harbour when he sailed past in 1770. But if low-key is what you're craving, look no further.

◉ Sights & Activities

Kayaks can be hired from Kawhia Beachside S-Cape and Kawhia Motel.

Ocean Beach
BEACH, SPRING

(Te Puia Rd) Four kilometres west of Kawhia is Ocean Beach and its high, black-sand dunes. Swimming can be dangerous, but one to two hours either side of low tide you can find the Te Puia Hot Springs in the sand – dig a hole for your own natural hot pool.

KAWHIA'S CANOE

The *Tainui waka* – a 14th-century ancestral canoe – made its final landing at Kawhia. The expedition leaders – Hoturoa, the chief/captain, and Rakataura, the *tohunga* (priest) – searched the west coast until they recognised their prophesised landing place. Pulling into shore, they tied the *waka* to a pohutukawa tree, naming it Tangi te Korowhiti. This unlabelled tree still stands on the shoreline between the wharf and Maketu Marae. The *waka* was then dragged up onto a hill and buried: sacred stones were placed at either end to mark its resting place, now part of the *marae*.

Kawhia Regional Museum & Gallery
MUSEUM, GALLERY

(www.kawhiaharbour.co.nz; Omimiti Reserve, Kawhia Wharf; admission by gold coin donation; ⊙noon-3pm Wed-Sun) Kawhia's cute waterside museum is a modest but engaging affair, with lots of local history, nautical and Maori artefacts, and regular art exhibitions. It doubles as the visitor information centre.

Kawhia Harbour Cruises
CRUISE

(☏021 966 754; www.kawhiaharbourcruises.co.nz; cruises per adult $35) There are some gorgeous beaches and kooky rock formations to check out around isolated Kawhia Harbour: bring your swimming gear! Minimum six adults.

Maketu Marae
MARAE

(www.kawhia.maori.nz; Kaora St) From the wharf, a track extends along the coast to Maketu Marae, which has an impressively carved meeting house, Auaukiterangi. Two stones here – Hani and Puna – mark the burial place of the Tainui *waka*. You can't see a lot from the road, but the *marae* is private property – don't enter without permission from the Maketu Marae Committee (info@kawhia.maori.nz).

Dove Charters
FISHING

(☏07-871 5854; www.westcoastfishing.co.nz; full day $105) Offers full-day fishing trips.

★ Festivals & Events

Kawhia Traditional Maori Kai Festival
FOOD

(www.kawhiaharbour.co.nz/maori-kai-festival.html) During the annual Kai Festival in early February, over 10,000 people descend to enjoy traditional Maori *kai* (food) and catch up with *whanau* (relations). Once you've filled up on seafood, *rewana* bread and rotten corn, settle in to watch the bands and rousing *kapa haka* (traditional Maori group singing and dancing) performances.

🛏 Sleeping & Eating

Kawhia Motel
MOTEL, RENTAL HOUSE $$

(☏07-871 0865; kawhiamotel@xtra.co.nz; cnr Jervois & Tainui Sts; s $99-155, extra person $20, house $250-300; 🖥) These six perkily painted, well-kept, old-school motel units are right next to the shops. There's also a four-bedroom house available. Kayak/bike hire costs $20/15 per hour.

Kawhia Beachside S-Cape
HOLIDAY PARK $

(☏07-871 0727; www.kawhiabeachsidescape.co.nz; 225 Pouewe St; sites from $30, cabins dm/s/d from $30/40/58, cottages $165-185) Perfectly positioned on the water's edge, this camping ground looks shabby from the road but has comfy cottages. There's a smart laundry and ablutions block, but the backpackers' area is rudimentary at best – camping is a better bet. Two-hour kayak hire is $12 per person.

Annie's Cafe & Restaurant
CAFE, RESTAURANT $

(146 Jervois St; meals $7-22; ⊙breakfast & lunch Wed-Sun winter, breakfast, lunch & dinner daily summer; 🌐) An old-fashioned licensed eatery in the main street, serving espresso, sandwiches and local specialities such as flounder and whitebait with kumara chips. There's also an internet terminal.

❶ Getting There & Away

Kawhia doesn't have a bus service. Take SH31 from Otorohanga (58km) or explore the scenic but rough unsealed road to Raglan (50km, 22km unsealed).

Otorohanga

POP 2700

One of several nondescript North Island towns to adopt a gimmick, Otorohanga's main street is festooned with images of cherished Kiwiana icons: sheep, gumboots, jandals, No 8 wire, All Blacks, pavlova, the beloved Buzzy Bee children's toy... But gimmicks aside, the Kiwi House is well worth a visit.

⊙ Sights

Otorohanga Kiwi House & Native Bird Park   ZOO

(www.kiwihouse.org.nz; 20 Alex Telfer Dr; adult/child $20/6; ⊗9am-5pm Sep-May, 9am-4.30pm Jun-Aug) This bird barn has a nocturnal enclosure where you can see active kiwi energetically digging with their long beaks, searching for food. This is the only place in NZ where you can see a Great Spotted Kiwi, the biggest of the three kiwi species. Other native birds, such as kaka, kea, morepork and weka, are also on show.

FREE Ed Hillary Walkway   MEMORIAL

(⊗24hr) As well as the Kiwiana decorating the main street, the Ed Hillary Walkway (running off Maniapoto St) has information panels on the All Blacks, Marmite, NZ competing in the America's Cup, and of course, Sir Ed.

🛏 Sleeping

Otorohanga Holiday Park   HOLIDAY PARK $

(🖉07-873 7253; www.kiwiholidaypark.co.nz; 20 Huiputea Dr; sites from $30, units $65-125; @🛜) It's not the most attractive locale, backing onto train tracks and encircled by tractor sales yards, but the owners are quick with a smile and the park's tidy facilities include a fitness centre and sauna. And if you can't find a bed in Waitomo (it happens), Otorohanga is only 16km away.

🍴 Eating & Drinking

Thirsty Weta   PUB

(www.theweta.co.nz; 57 Maniapoto St; meals $10-37; ⊗10am-1am) The top pick in town, with hearty snacks (of the pizza, pasta, surf 'n' turf and quesadilla variety) and the promise of things kicking off after dinner when the wine-bar vibe takes over and the musos plug in.

Origin Coffee Station   CAFE

(www.origincoffee.co.nz; 7 Wahanui Cres; coffee $3-5; ⊗8.30am-4.30pm Mon-Fri) It's a long way from Malawi to the old Otorohanga railway station, but the beans don't seem to mind. The folks at Origin are dead serious about coffee, sourcing, importing and roasting it themselves and then delivering it to your table, strong and perfectly formed, and possibly with a slice of cake.

Countdown   SUPERMARKET

(www.countdown.co.nz; 123 Maniapoto St; ⊗7am-10pm) As there's no supermarket at Waitomo Caves, stock up at Oto's Countdown on the Waitomo side of town.

ℹ Information

Otorohanga i-SITE (🖉07-873 8951; www.otorohanga.co.nz; 27 Turongo St; ⊗9am-5pm Mon-Fri, 10am-2pm Sat & Sun; 🛜) Free wi-fi and local information.

ℹ Getting There & Away

Bus

InterCity (🖉09-583 5780; www.intercity.co.nz) buses run from Otorohanga to Auckland ($50, 3¼ hours, four daily), Te Awamutu ($21, 30 minutes, three daily), Te Kuiti ($20, one hour, three daily) and Rotorua ($53, 2½ hours, two daily).

Naked Bus (🖉0900 625 33; www.nakedbus.com) runs one bus daily to Waitomo Caves ($20, 30 minutes), Hamilton ($25, one hour) and New Plymouth ($30, 3¼ hours).

The **Dalroy Express** (🖉0508 465 622; www.dalroytours.co.nz) bus runs daily between Auckland ($37, three hours) and New Plymouth ($35, 3¼ hours) via Otorohanga. Other stops include Hamilton ($17, 50 minutes) and Te Awamutu ($12, 25 minutes).

The **Waitomo Shuttle** (🖉07-873 8279, 0800 808 279; one-way adult/child $12/7) heads to

---

KINGITANGA

The concept of a Maori people is relatively new. Until the mid-1800s, NZ effectively comprised many independent tribal nations, operating in tandem with the British from 1840.

In 1856, faced with a flood of Brits, the Kingitanga movement formed to unite the tribes to better resist further loss of land and culture. A gathering of leaders elected Waikato chief Potatau Te Wherowhero as the first Maori king, hoping that his increased *mana* (prestige) could achieve the cohesion that the British had under their queen.

Despite the huge losses of the Waikato War and the eventual opening up of the King Country, the Kingitanga survived – although it has no formal constitutional role. A measure of the strength of the movement was the huge outpouring of grief when Te Arikinui Dame Atairangikaahu, Potatau's great-great-great-granddaughter, died in 2006 after 40 years at the helm. Although it's not a hereditary monarchy (leaders of various tribes vote on a successor), Potatau's line continues to the present day with King Tuheitia Paki.

the Waitomo Caves five times daily, coordinating with bus and train arrivals.

Train

Otorohanga is on the **Overlander** (☑0800 872 467; www.tranzscenic.co.nz; ☉daily Oct-Apr, Fri-Sun May-Sep) train route between Auckland ($98, 3¼ hours) and Wellington ($129, nine hours) via Hamilton ($68, 50 minutes) and Te Kuiti ($68, 15 minutes).

Waitomo Caves

Even if damp, dark tunnels sound like your idea of hell, take a chill pill and head to Waitomo anyway. The limestone caves and glowing bugs here are one of the North Island's premier attractions.

The name Waitomo comes from *wai* (water) and *tomo* (hole or shaft): dotted across this region are numerous shafts dropping into underground cave systems and streams. There are 300-plus mapped caves in the area: the three main caves – Glowworm, Ruakuri and Aranui – have been bewitching visitors for over 100 years.

Your Waitomo experience needn't be claustrophobic: the electrically lit, cathedral-like Glowworm Cave is far from squeezy. But if it's tight, gut-wrenching, soaking-wet, pitch-black excitement you're after, Waitomo can oblige.

◉ Sights

Caves

The big-three Waitomo Caves are all operated by the same company, based at the snazzy new **Waitomo Caves Visitor Centre** (☑0800 456 922; www.waitomo.com; Waitomo Caves Rd) behind the Glowworm Cave, which incorporates a cafe and theatre. Various combo deals are available, including a Triple Cave Combo (adult/child $80/39). Try to avoid the large tour groups, most of which arrive between 10.30am and 2.30pm.

Waitomo Caves

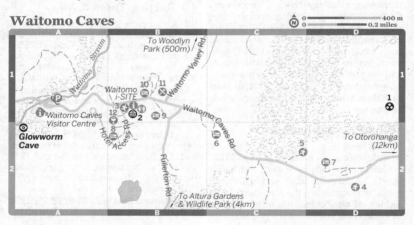

Waitomo Caves

WAITOMO CAVES DR FARAH RANGIKOEPA PALMER

The best way to experience the Waitomo glowworm caves is via black-water rafting. It's an exhilarating experience and involves getting dressed up in a wet suit (laughing at how funny everyone looks is half the fun), choosing an inflatable inner tube to sit in (another hilarious experience) and travelling through the limestone caves with two guides, your wits, and the glowworms. It is a real hands-on experience and requires some agility and the guts to jump backwards down some small waterfalls as you make your way through the tunnels. You finish off the trip quietly drifting through the caves in your tube, looking at the glowworms with your head lamp turned off.

Dr Farah Rangikoepa Palmer, former captain of the Black Ferns
(NZ's women's rugby team)

Glowworm Cave
CAVE
(adult/child $48/21; ⊘45min tours every 30min 9am-5pm) The guided tour of the Glowworm Cave, which is behind the visitor centre, leads past impressive stalactites and stalagmites into a large cavern known as the Cathedral. The acoustics are so good that Dame Kiri Te Kanawa and the Vienna Boys Choir have given concerts here. The highlight comes at the tour's end when you board a boat and swing off onto the river. As your eyes grow accustomed to the dark you'll see a Milky Way of little lights surrounding you – these are the glowworms. Conditions for their growth are just about perfect here so there are a remarkable number of them. Book your tour at the visitor centre.

Aranui Cave
CAVE
(adult/child $46/21; ⊘45min tours 10am, 11am, 1pm, 2pm, 3pm) Three kilometres west from the Glowworm Cave is Aranui Cave. This cave is dry (hence no glowworms) but compensates with an incredible array of limestone formations. Thousands of tiny 'straw' stalactites hang from the ceiling. Book tours at the visitor centre. It's an hour's walk to the caves, otherwise the visitors centre can arrange transport.

Ruakuri Cave
CAVE
(⌨07-878 6219, 0800 782 587; adult/child $67/26; ⊘2hr tours 9am, 10am, 11.30am, 12.30pm, 1.30pm, 2.30pm & 3pm) Culturally significant Ruakuri Cave has an impressive 15m-high spiral staircase, removing the need to trample through the Maori burial site at the cave entrance (as tourists did for 84 years). Tours lead through 1.6km of the 7.5km system, taking in vast caverns with glowworms, subterranean streams and waterfalls, and intricate limestone structures. For as long as this cave has been open to the public, people have described it as

spiritual – some claim it's haunted. It's customary to wash your hands when leaving to remove the *tapu* (sacred). Book your tour at the Legendary Black Water Rafting Company (p199) (tours also depart from there).

Other Sights

Waitomo Caves Discovery Centre MUSEUM
(⌨07-878 7640, 0800 474 839; www.waitomo discovery.org; 21 Waitomo Caves Rd; adult/child $5/free; ⊘8.15am-7pm Jan & Feb, 8.45am-5.30pm Nov, Dec & Mar, 8.45am-5pm Apr-Oct) Adjoining the i-SITE, the Waitomo Caves Discovery Centre has excellent exhibits explaining how caves are formed, the flora and fauna that thrive in them and the history of Waitomo's caves and cave exploration.

Altura Gardens &
Wildlife Park ZOO, HORSE RIDING
(⌨07-878 5278; www.alturapark.co.nz; 477 Fullerton Rd; adult/child $12/5; ⊘9.30am-5pm) At this 2-hectare park you can chat with a cockatoo, outstare a morepork or pat a blue-tongue lizard. There are dozens of bird and animal species here, but it's not a regular zoo – expect llamas and sheep rather than lions and giraffes. It also runs leisurely horse treks (60/90 minutes $65/80) and has B&B accommodation (a self-contained unit sleeping four; double/quad $145/185).

🏃 Activities

Underground

Legendary Black Water
Rafting Company CAVING, ADVENTURE TOUR
(⌨0800 782 5874; www.waitomo.com; 585 Waitomo Caves Rd; ⊘Black Labyrinth tour 9am, 10.30am, noon, 1.30pm & 3pm; Black Abyss tour 9am & 2pm) These guys run a Black Labyrinth tour ($119, three hours), which involves floating in a wet suit on an inner tube down a river that flows through Ruakuri Cave. The highlight

is leaping off a small waterfall and then floating through a long, glowworm-covered passage. The trip ends with showers, soup and bagels in the cafe. The Black Abyss tour ($220, five hours) is more adventurous and includes a 35m abseil into Ruakuri Cave, a flying fox and more glowworms and tubing. Minimum ages apply.

Spellbound
CAVING, GUIDED TOUR

(☑07-878 7622, 0800 773 552; www.glowworm. co.nz; 10 Waitomo Caves Rd; adult/child $70/25; ⊙3hr tours 10am, 11am, 2pm & 3pm) Spellbound is a good option if you don't want to get wet, are more interested in glowworms than an 'action' experience, and want to avoid the big groups in the main caves. Small-group tours access parts of the heavily glowworm-dappled Mangawhitiakau cave system, 12km south of Waitomo (...and you still get to ride in a raft!).

Waitomo Adventures
CAVING, ADVENTURE TOUR

(☑07-878 7788, 0800 924 866; www.waitomo. co.nz; 654 Waitomo Caves Rd) Waitomo Adventures offers five different cave adventures, with discounts for various combos and for advance bookings. The Lost World ($310/445 four/seven hours) trip starts with a 100m abseil down into the cave, then – by a combination of walking, rock climbing, wading and swimming – you journey through a 30m-high cave to get back out, passing glowworms, amazing rock formations, waterfalls and more. The price includes lunch (underground) and dinner. The shorter version skips the wet stuff and the meals.

Haggas Honking Holes ($240, four hours) includes professional abseiling instruction followed by three waterfall abseils, rock climbing and travelling along a subterranean river, traversing narrow passageways and huge caverns. Along the way you see glowworms, cave formations and cave coral.

TumuTumu Toobing ($165, four hours) is a walking, climbing, swimming and tubing trip. St Benedict's Cavern ($165, three hours) includes abseiling and a subterranean flying fox in a cave with amazing straw stalagmites.

Green Glow Eco-Adventures
CAVING, ADVENTURE TOUR

(☑0800 476 459; www.greenglow.co.nz; 1117 Oparure Rd, Te Kuiti; 6hr tours per person $180) Green Glow Eco-Adventures runs customised, small-group Waitomo tours, putting a caving, rock climbing, abseiling,

photographic or glowworm spin on your day (or all of the above!). It's based in Te Kuiti, 20 minutes from Waitomo.

CaveWorld
CAVING, ADVENTURE TOURS

(☑07-878 6577, 0800 228 338; www.caveworld. co.nz; cnr Waitomo Caves Rd & Hotel Access Rd) CaveWorld runs the Tube It ($124, two hours) black-water rafting trip through glowworm-filled Te Anaroa. Also available are a glowworm-illuminated night abseil down a 45m crevice called the Glowworm Canyon (two hours, $199), or the daytime Footwhistle Glowworm Cave Tour ($49, one hour).

Rap, Raft 'n' Rock
CAVING, ADVENTURE TOUR

(☑0800 228 372, 07-873 9149; www.caveraft.com; 95 Waitomo Caves Rd) These small-group expeditions ($160, five hours) start with abseil training, followed by a 27m descent into a natural cave, and then floating along a subterranean river on an inner tube with plenty of glowworms. After some caving, a belayed rock climb up a 20m cliff brings you to the surface.

Tramping

The Waitomo i-SITE has free pamphlets on walks in the area. The walk from **Aranui Cave** to **Ruakuri Cave** is an excellent short path. From the Waitomo Caves Visitor Centre, the 5km, three-hour-return **Waitomo Walkway** takes off through farmland, following Waitomo Stream to the **Ruakuri Scenic Reserve**, where a 30-minute return walk passes by a natural limestone tunnel. There are glowworms here at night – drive to the car park and bring a torch to find your way. Near Waitomo Adventures a steep 20-minute walk leads through bush then along farmland to the abandoned **Opapake Pa**, where terraces and kumara pits are visible.

Dundle Hill Walk
TRAMPING

(☑07-878 7788, 0800 924 866; www.waitomowalk. com; ⊙adult/child $75/35) The self-guided privately run Dundle Hill Walk is a 27km, two-day/one-night loop walk through Waitomo's bush and farmland, including overnight bunk-house accommodation high up in the bush.

🛏 Sleeping

Abseil Inn
B&B $$

(☑07-878 7815; www.abseilinn.co.nz; 709 Waitomo Caves Rd; d from $150; 🛜) A *veeery* steep driveway (abseiling in from a helicopter might be an easier approach) takes you to this

GLOWWORM MAGIC

Glowworms are the larvae of the fungus gnat. The larva glowworm has luminescent organs that produce a soft, greenish light. Living in a sort of hammock suspended from an overhang, it weaves sticky threads that trail down and catch unwary insects attracted by its light. When an insect flies towards the light it gets stuck in the threads – the glowworm just has to reel it in for a feed.

The larval stage lasts from six to nine months, depending on how much food the glowworm gets. When it has grown to about the size of a matchstick, it goes into a pupa stage, much like a cocoon. The adult fungus gnat emerges about two weeks later.

The adult insect doesn't live very long because it doesn't have a mouth. It emerges, mates, lays eggs and dies, all within about two or three days. The sticky eggs, laid in groups of 40 or 50, hatch in about three weeks to become larval glowworms.

Glowworms thrive in moist, dark caves but they can survive anywhere if they have the requisites of moisture, an overhang to suspend from and insects to eat. Waitomo is famous for its glowworms but you can see them in many other places around NZ, both in caves and outdoors.

When you come upon glowworms, don't touch their hammocks or hanging threads, try not to make loud noises and don't shine a light right on them. All of these things will cause them to dim their lights. It takes them a few hours to become bright again, during which time the grub will go hungry. The glowworms that shine most brightly are the hungriest.

delightful B&B with four themed rooms, great breakfasts and witty hosts. The biggest room has a double bath and valley views.

Waitomo Caves Guest Lodge B&B **$$**
(07-878 7641, 0800 465 762; www.waitomocaves guestlodge.co.nz; 7 Te Anga Rd; s $80, d $105-130, extra person $25, all incl breakfast; 🐾) Bag your own cosy little hillside en-suite cabin at this central operation with a sweet garden setting. The top cabins have valley views. Large continental breakfast and resident dog included. Simple and unfussy.

Waitomo Top 10 Holiday Park HOLIDAY PARK **$**
(07-878 7639, 0508 498 666; www.waitomopark. co.nz; 12 Waitomo Caves Rd; sites from $22, units $70-190; @🐾🏊) This lovely holiday park in the heart of the village has spotless facilities, some beaut new cabins (the older ones are OK too) and plenty of outdoor distractions to keep the kids busy (pool, spa, playground and neighbouring rugby pitch).

Juno Hall Backpackers HOSTEL **$**
(07-878 7649; www.junowaitomo.co.nz; 600 Waitomo Caves Rd; sites from $16, dm $28, d with/without bathroom $78/68, tr $98/88, q with bathroom $124; @🐾🏊) A slick purpose-built hostel 1km from the village with a warm welcome, a warmer wood fire in the woody lounge area, and an outdoor pool and tennis court. Comfy couches; lots of wood panelling.

Kiwi Paka HOSTEL **$**
(07-878 3395; www.waitomokiwipaka.co.nz; Hotel Access Rd; dm/s/d $30/65/70, chalets tw/d/q $95/110/150; @🐾) It's too big to be social but this classy, purpose-built, Alpine-style hostel has four-bed dorms in the main lodge, plus separate peak-roofed chalets, Morepork Cafe on-site and super-tidy facilities. Popular with big groups.

Woodlyn Park MOTEL **$$$**
(07-878 6666; www.woodlynpark.co.nz; 1177 Waitomo Valley Rd; d $170-245, extra person $15) Boasting the world's only hobbit motel (set into the ground with round windows and doors), Woodlyn Park's other sleeping options include the cockpit of a combat plane, train carriages and the *Waitanic* – a converted WWII patrol boat fitted with chandeliers, moulded ceilings and shiny brass portholes. It's extremely well done and the kids will love you for it.

✖ Eating & Drinking

The general store in Waitomo sells the basics, but a better bet is to buy provisions in Otorohanga or Te Kuiti before you visit.

TOP CHOICE **Huhu** CAFE, MODERN NZ **$$**
(07-878 6674; www.huhustore.co.nz/cafe; 10 Waitomo Caves Rd; lunch $11-19, dinner $25-30; ⏰10.30am-9pm; 🐾) Come to Huhu twice a day –

you won't be disappointed. Slick and modern with charming service, it has great views from the terrace and sublime contemporary NZ food. Sip a strong coffee, or graze through a seasonal tapas-style menu (large or small plates) of Kiwi delights like rabbit hotpot or organic braised beef, all locally sourced (right down to the specific cow). Wonderful!

Morepork Cafe   CAFE, PIZZERIA **$$**
(Kiwi Paka, Hotel Access Rd; breakfast & lunch $7-15, dinner $14-27; ☺8am-8pm) At the Kiwi Paka backpackers is this cheery joint, a jack-of-all-trades eatery serving breakfast, lunch and dinner either inside or out on the deck. The 'Caveman' pizza is a winner (the first person to ask for more pork will be shown the door).

Curly's Bar   PUB
(www.curlysbar.co.nz; Hotel Access Rd; lunch & dinner $10-25; ☺11am-2am) An easygoing tavern with lots of beers on tap, good-value pub grub (steaks, lamb shanks, nachos...), chunky wooden tables, occasional quiz nights and live music.

ⓘ Information

Note that there's no petrol in town. Curly's Bar has an ATM.
Waitomo i-SITE (☎07-878 7640, 0800 474 839; www.waitomodiscovery.org; 21 Waitomo Caves Rd; ☺8.15am-7pm Jan & Feb, 8.45am-5.30pm Nov, Dec & Mar, 8.45am-5pm Apr-Oct; @) Internet access, post office and booking agent.

ⓘ Getting There & Away

Naked Bus (☎0900 625 33; www.nakedbus. com) runs once daily to Otorohanga ($20, 20 minutes), Hamilton ($20, 1¼ hours) and New Plymouth ($30, three hours).
Waitomo Shuttle (☎07-873 8279, 0800 808 279; waikiwi@ihug.co.nz; one way adult/child $12/7) heads to the caves five times daily from Otorohanga (15 minutes away), coordinating with bus and train arrivals.
Waitomo Wanderer (☎03-477 9083, 0800 000 4321; www.travelheadfirst.com) operates a daily return services from Rotorua or Taupo, with optional caving, glowworm and tubing add-ons (packages from $133). Shuttle-only services are $99 return.

Waitomo to Awakino

This obscure route, heading west of Waitomo on Te Anga Rd, is the definition of off-the-beaten-track. It's a slow but fascinating alternative to SH3 if Taranaki's your goal.

Only 12km of the 111km route remains unsealed, but it's nearly all winding and narrow. Allow around two hours (not including stops) and fill up with petrol.

Walks in the **Tawarau Forest**, 20km west of the Waitomo Caves, are outlined in DOC's *Waitomo & King Country Tracks* booklet ($1, available from DOC in Hamilton or Te Kuitifrom), including a one-hour track to the Tawarau Falls from the end of Appletree Rd.

The Mangapohue Natural Bridge Scenic Reserve, 26km west of Waitomo, is a 5.5-hectare reserve with a giant natural limestone arch. It's a five-minute walk to the arch on a wheelchair-accessible pathway. On the far side, big rocks full of 35-million-year-old oyster fossils jut up from the grass, and at night you'll see glowworms.

About 4km further west is **Piripiri Caves Scenic Reserve**, where a five-minute walk leads to a large cave containing fossils of giant oysters. Bring a torch and be prepared to get muddy after heavy rain. Steps wind down into the gloom...

The impressively tiered, 30m **Marokopa Falls** are 32km west of Waitomo. A short track (15 minutes return) from the road leads to the bottom of the falls.

Just past Te Anga you can turn north to Kawhia, 59km away, or continue southwest to Marokopa (population 1560), a small black-sand village on the coast with some scarily big new mansions starting to appear. The whole Te Anga/Marokopa area is riddled with caves.

Marokopa Campground (☎07-876 7444; marokopacampground@xtra.co.nz; Rauparaha St; sites from $24, dm $18) ain't flash but it's in a nice spot, close to the coast. There's a small shop that will cover the catering basics (bread, milk, cheese), as well as a tennis court and tiny library.

The road heads south to Kiritehere, following a bubbling stream through idyllic farmland to Moeatoa then turning right (south) into Mangatoa Rd. Now you're in serious backcountry, heading into the dense **Whareorino Forest**. It would pay not to watch the movie *Deliverance* before tramping in this spectacularly remote tract of native bush. The 16-bunk DOC-run **Leitch's Hut** (☎07-878 1050; www.doc.govt.nz; per adult $5) has a toilet, water and a wood stove.

At Waikawau it's worth taking the 5km detour along the unsealed road to the coast near **Ngarupupu Point**, where a 100m walk through a dank tunnel opens out on an exquisitely isolated stretch of black-sand beach. Visit early and the only footprints in the sand will be yours, but think twice about swimming here; if you get caught in a rip you'll be halfway to Melbourne before your friends can reach help.

The road then continues through another twisty 28km, passing lush forest and the occasional farm before joining SH3 east of Awakino.

Te Kuiti

POP 4380

Cute Te Kuiti sits in a valley between picturesque hills. Welcome to the shearing capital of the world! You won't have any doubt as to the veracity of that statement if you're here for the very sheepish Great New Zealand Muster.

◎ Sights

Big Shearer   LANDMARK
(Rora St) The most prominent landmark in town is the 7m, 7½-tonne Big Shearer statue at the south end of the Rora St shopping strip.

Te Kuititanga-O-Nga-Whakaaro MONUMENT
(Rora St) Te Kuititanga-O-Nga-Whakaaro (the Gathering of Thoughts and Ideas) is a beautiful pavilion of etched-glass, *tukutuku* (woven flax panels) and wooden carvings that celebrates the town's history.

✾ Festivals & Events

Great New Zealand Muster CULTURAL, FOOD
(www.waitomo.govt.nz/events/the-great-nz-muster; ⊙late Mar/early Apr) The highlight of the Great New Zealand Muster is the legendary Running of the Sheep: Pamplona's got nothing on the sight of 2000 woolly demons stampeding down Te Kuiti's main street. The festival includes sheep-shearing championships, a parade, Maori cultural performances, live music, barbecues, *hangi* and market stalls.

⌖ Sleeping

TOP CHOICE Waitomo Lodge Motel   MOTEL $$
(✆07-878 0003; www.waitomo-lodge.co.nz; 62 Te Kumi Rd; d/f from $125/195; ☏) Can't find a bed in Waitomo? This snappily designed motel at the Waitomo end of Te Kuiti is a brilliant alternative. Twenty spacious, modern rooms clad in plywood feature contemporary art, moody low-voltage lighting, flat-screen TVs

and little decks overlooking Mangaokewa Stream in the units at the back. Bosco Cafe is across the street. Hipness in an un-hip town!

Simply the Best B&B   B&B $$
(✆07-878 8191; www.simplythebestbnb.co.nz; 129 Gadsby Rd; s/d incl breakfast $60/110) It's hard to argue with the immodest name when the prices are this reasonable, the breakfast this generous and the hosts this charming. Warning: the spectacular views may illicit involuntary choruses of Tina Turner anthems.

✗ Eating & Drinking

Bosco Cafe   CAFE $
(theteam@boscocafe.co.nz; 57 Te Kumi Rd; mains $10-20; ⊙breakfast & lunch; ☏) It's not damning it with faint praise to say that Bosco is the coolest place in Te Kuiti. This excellent industrial-chic cafe offers great coffee, tempting food (try the bacon-wrapped meatloaf with greens) and sweet service. It comes into its own on a sunny afternoon when the doors swing open onto Brook Park.

New World   SUPERMARKET
(www.newworld.co.nz; Te Kumi Rd; ⊙8am-8pm) Self-caterers bound for Waitomo should stock up at New World.

ⓘ Information

Department of Conservation (DOC; ✆07-878 1050; www.doc.govt.nz; 78 Taupiri St; ⊙8am-4.30pm Mon-Fri)

Te Kuiti i-SITE (✆07-878 8077; www.waitomo.govt.nz; Rora St; ⊙9am-5pm Mon-Fri, 10am-2pm Sat, noon-4pm Sun; @) Internet access and visitor information.

ⓘ Getting There & Away

Bus

InterCity (www.intercity.co.nz) uses run daily to the following destinations (among others):

DESTINATION	PRICE	DURATION	FREQUENCY
Auckland	$47	3½hr	3 daily
Mokau	$30	1hr	2 daily
New Pllymouth	$30	2½hr	2 daily
Otorohanga	$20	45min	3 daily
Taumarunui	$28	1¼	1 daily

Naked Bus (www.nakedbus.com) runs once daily to Auckland ($44, four hours), Hamilton ($20, 1½ hours), New Plymouth ($30, 2¼ hours) and Otorohanga ($20, 30 minutes).

The Dalroy Express bus runs daily between Auckland ($39, 3½ hours) and New Plymouth ($29, 2¼ hours), stopping at Te Kuiti. Other stops include Hamilton ($19, 1½ hours), Mokau ($17, one hour) and Otorohanga ($12, 15 minutes).

Train

Te Kuiti is on the Overlander train route between Auckland ($98, 3½ hours) and Wellington ($129, 8¾ hours) via Hamilton ($68, one hour) and Taumarunui ($68, 50 minutes).

Te Kuiti to Mokau

From Te Kuiti, SH3 runs southwest to the coast before following the rugged shoreline to New Plymouth. Along this scenic route the sheep stations sprout peculiar limestone formations before giving way to lush native bush as the highway winds along the course of the Awakino River.

The river spills into the Tasman at **Awakino** (population 60), a small settlement where boats shelter in the estuary while locals find refuge at the down-to-earth (or down-to-sea?) **Awakino Hotel** (☑06-752 9815; www.awakinohotel.co.nz; SH3; meals $9-20; ☉breakfast & lunch daily, dinner Mon-Sat).

A little further south the impressive **Maniaroa Marae** dominates the cliff above the highway. This important complex houses the anchor stone of the *Tainui waka* (p196) which brought this region's original people from their Polynesian homeland. You can get a good view of the intimidatingly carved meeting house, Te Kohaarua, from outside the fence – don't cross into the *marae* unless someone invites you.

Five kilometres further south, as the perfect cone of Mt Taranaki starts to take shape on the horizon, is the village of **Mokau** (population 400). It offers a fine stretch of black-sand beach and good surfing and fishing. From August to November the Mokau River (the second-longest on the North Island) spawns a whole lot of whitebait, and subsequent swarms of fiercely territorial whitebaiters.

The town's **Tainui Historical Society Museum** (☑06-752 9072; mokaumuseum@vodafone.co.nz; SH3; admission by donation; ☉10am-4pm; @) has an interesting collection of old photographs and artefacts (pianolas, whale bones, dusty photos of the Queen) from the time when this once-isolated outpost was a coal and lumber shipping port for settlements along the river.

Mokau River Cruises (☑0800 665 2874; www.mokaurivercruises.co.nz; cruises adult/child $50/15) operates a three-hour river cruise with commentary on-board the historic *MV Cygnet*. Twilight cruises are also available.

Just north of Mokau, **Seaview Holiday Park** (☑06-752 9708; seaviewhp@xtra.co.nz; SH3; sites from $10, cabins/units d from $50/85) is basic (dinky pastel-painted cabins with rickety furniture) but it's right on a broad span of big brown beach.

On the hill above the village the austere-looking but actually very friendly **Mokau Motel** (☑06-752 9725; www.mokaumotels.co.nz; SH3; s/d/ste from $90/105/120; ☎) offers fishing advice, no-nonsense self-contained units and three city-standard luxury suites (what a surprise!).

Taumarunui

POP 5140

Taumarunui on a cold day can feel a bit miserable, but this town in the heart of the King Country has potential. The main reason to stay here is to kayak on the Whanganui River or as a cheaper base for skiing in Tongariro National Park, and there are some beaut walks and cycling tracks around town.

For details on the Forgotten World Highway between Taumarunui and Stratford, see Taranaki. For details on canoeing and kayaking on the Whanganui River, see Whanganui National Park.

◎ Sights & Activities

The 3km **Riverbank Walk** along the Whanganui River runs from Cherry Grove Domain, 1km south of town, to Taumarunui Holiday Park. **Te Peka Lookout**, across the Ongarue River on the western edge of town, is a good vantage point from which to survey proceedings.

ℹ PHONE ZONE

If you've been rabidly punching the 07 area code into your phone for weeks across Waikato and the King Country, note that the code changes to 06 from around Awakino heading south into Taranaki.

Hakiaha Street
STREET

At the eastern end of Hakiaha St is **Hauaroa Whare**, a beautifully carved house. At the western end **Te Rohe Potae** memorialises King Tawhiao's assertion of his *mana* (authority) over the King Country in a sculpture of a top hat on a large rock.

Raurimu Spiral
RAILWAY

The Raurimu Spiral, 30km south of town, is a unique feat of railway engineering that was completed in 1908 after 10 years' work. Rail buffs can experience the spiral by taking the *Overlander* train to National Park township (return $136).

Taumarunui Jet Tours
JETBOATING

(☑07-896 6055, 0800 853 886; www.taumarunui jettours.co.nz; Cherry Grove Domain; 30min/1hr tour from $60/100) Taumarunui Jet Tours runs high-octane jetboat trips on the Whanganui River.

🍽 Sleeping & Eating

Taumarunui Holiday Park
HOLIDAY PARK $

(☑07-895 9345; www.taumarunuiholidaypark. co.nz; SH4; sites from $17, cabins & cottage d $50-115; @🛜) On the banks of the Whanganui River, 4km east of town, this shady camping ground offers safe river swimming and clean facilities. The new owners are fierce advocates for the town, and can give you the low-down on what to see and do.

Twin Rivers Motel
MOTEL $$

(☑07-895 8063; www.twinrivers.co.nz; 23 Marae St; units $90-215; 🛜) The 12 units at Twin Rivers are spick and span and are constantly being upgraded (new bathrooms, new fauxstone wall facing, shiny new oversized door numbers...). The bigger units sleep up to seven.

L'attitude
CAFE, TAPAS $$

(☑07-895 6611; 1 Hakiaha St; brunch $13-19, dinner tapas plates $6-12; ☺brunch Wed-Sun, dinner Fri & Sat) This black-painted box on the Te Kuiti side of town is surely the only place in Taumarunui where you can get grilled marinated sesame-seed chicken wings. There are art-hung walls, outdoor tables and plenty of NZ wines to ply yourself with.

❶ Information

Department of Conservation (DOC; ☑07-895 8201; www.doc.govt.nz; Cherry Grove Domain;

☺8am-5pm Mon-Fri) A field office not always open (call in advance).

Taumarunui i-SITE (☑07-895 7494; www.visitrua pehu.co.nz; 116 Hakiaha St; ☺9am-5pm; @) Visitor information and internet access. Pick up the *Ruapehu Chosen Pathways* brochure for regional information.

❶ Getting There & Away

Taumarunui is on SH4, 81km south of Te Kuiti and 41km north of National Park township.

InterCity (☑0508 353 947; www.intercity. co.nz) buses head to Auckland ($59, 4½ hours, one daily) via Te Kuiti ($28, one hour), and to Palmerston North ($53, 4¾ hours, one daily) via National Park ($22, 30 minutes).

Taumarunui is on the **Overlander** (☑0800 872 467; www.tranzscenic.co.nz; ☺daily Oct-Apr, Fri-Sun May-Sep) train route between Auckland ($98, 4¾ hours) and Wellington ($129, 7½ hours), via Te Kuiti ($68, 1¼ hours) and National Park ($68, 50 minutes).

Owhango
POP 210

A pint-sized village where all the street names start with 'O', Owhango makes a cosy base for walkers, mountain bikers (the 42 Traverse ends here) and skiers who can't afford to stay closer to the slopes in Tongariro National Park. Take Omaki Rd for a two-hour loop walk through virgin forest in **Ohinetonga Scenic Reserve**.

🍽 Sleeping

Forest Lodge
LODGE

(☑07-895 4854; www.forest-lodge.co.nz; 12 Omaki Rd; dm/s/d $25/45/65, units $95-120; @🛜) A snug backpackers lodge with comfortable, clean rooms, neatly folded towels with bars of soap on top, and good communal spaces. For privacy junkies there are separate self-contained motel and cottage units next door. Breakfast/dinner from $9/22; bike hire from $20 and guided fishing from $250.

Blue Duck Lodge
LODGE, HOSTEL $

(☑07-895 6276; www.blueducklodge.co.nz; RD2, Whakahoro; dm from $35, d $80-185, extra adult/child $37/20) Overlooking the Retaruke River 36km southwest of Owhango (take the Kaitieke turn-off 1km south of town), this ecosavvy place is actually three lodges, offering accommodation from dorms in an old shearers' quarters to a self-contained family cottage sleeping eight. The owners are mad-keen conservationists, restoring native bird habitats and historic buildings (you can volunteer and lend a hand).

Fernleaf B&B B&B, FARMSTAY **$$**
(☎07-895 4847; www.fernleaffarmstay.co.nz; 58 Tunanui Rd; s/d incl breakfast $85/120) This characterful villa on a third-generation cattle-and-sheep farm has two en-suite rooms with garden outlooks, plus a twin and a separate cottage double that share a bathroom. Generous breakfast and dinners ($30 per person by arrangement) are labours of love. It's just off SH4, 7km north of Owhango.

Eating & Drinking

Cafe 39 South CAFE **$**
(☎07-895 4800; www.facebook.com/cafe39south; SH4; meals $9-17; ⏲7am-3pm Wed-Sun) Transport this stylishly angular roadside cafe into any major city and it would get by just fine. The food is delicious and reasonably priced, the coffee is excellent and the electric fire will make you want to linger on cold days. The 39° South lattitude marker is just across the road.

Getting There & Away

Owhango is 14km south of Taumarunui on SH4. All the **InterCity** (☎0508 353 947; www.intercity.co.nz) buses that stop in Taumarunui also stop here.

Taranaki & Whanganui

Best Outdoors

» New Plymouth Coastal Walkway (p212)
» Surf Highway 45 (p222)
» A Mt Taranaki walk (p219)
» Whanganui River canoeing (p232)

Best Places to Stay

» Fitzroy Beach Motel (p214)
» Ahu Ahu Beach Villas (p222)
» Anndion Lodge (p227)
» Flying Fox (p235)

Why Go?

Halfway between Auckland and Wellington, Taranaki (aka 'the 'naki') is the Texas of New Zealand: oil and gas stream in from offshore rigs, plumping the region with enviable affluence. New Plymouth is the regional hub, home to an excellent art gallery and provincial museum, and enough decent espresso joints to keep you humming.

Behind the city, the moody volcanic cone of Mt Taranaki demands to be visited. Taranaki also has a glut of black-sand beaches: surfers and holidaymakers swell summer numbers.

Further east the history-rich Whanganui River curls its way through Whanganui National Park down to Whanganui city, a 19th-century river port that's aging with artistic grace.

Palmerston North, the Manawatu's main city, is a town of two peoples: tough-talkin' country fast-foodies in hotted-up cars and caffeinated Massey University literati. Beyond the city the region blends rural grace with yesterday's pace: you might even find time for a little laziness!

When to Go

Mt Taranaki is one of NZ's wettest spots, and frequently cops snowfalls, even in summer: weather on the mountain can be extremely changeable. Ironically, New Plymouth frequently tops the North Island's most-sunshine-hours list. Expect warm summers and cool winters.

Over in Whanganui the winters are milder, but they're chillier on the Palmerston North plains. Sunshine is abundant hereabouts too – around 2000 hours per year!

Taranaki & Whanganui Highlights

1 Walking up or around the massive cone of **Mt Taranaki** (p218)

2 Riding the big breaks along **Surf Highway 45** (p222)

3 Getting experimental at New Plymouth's **Govett-Brewster Art Gallery** (p211)

4 Bouncing from bean to bean in **New Plymouth's cafes** (p215)

5 Watching a glass-blowing demonstration at one of **Whanganui's glass studios** (p225)

6 Redefining serenity on a canoe or kayak trip on the **Whanganui River** (p232)

7 Traversing the rainy **Whanganui River Road** (p231) by car or bike – it's all about the journey, not how fast you get there

8 Flexing your All Blacks–spirit at Palmerston North's **New Zealand Rugby Museum** (p236)

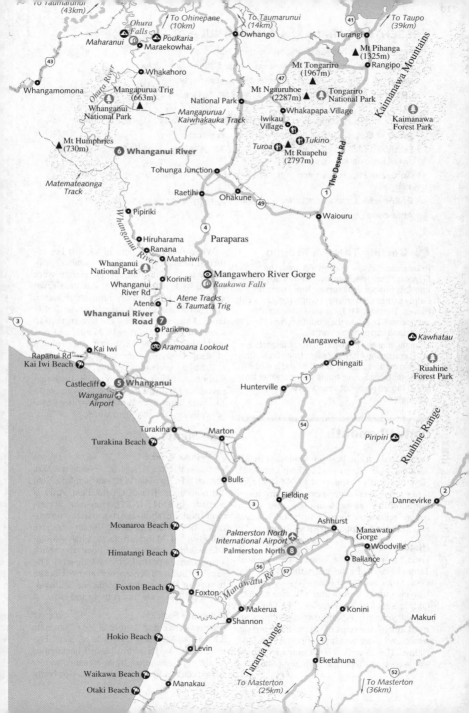

ESSENTIAL TARANAKI & WHANGANUI

» **Eat** In one of Whanganui's hip main-street eateries

» **Drink** A bottle of Mike's Mild Ale from White Cliffs Organic Brewery

» **Read** The *Wanganui Chronicle*, NZ's oldest newspaper

» **Listen to** The rockin' album *Back to the Burning Wreck* by Whanganui riff-monsters The Have

» **Watch** *The Last Samurai*, co-starring Tom Cruise (Mt Taranaki gets top billing)

» **Swim at** Oakura Beach, with its black sand and surf

» **Festival** WOMAD (World of Music Arts and Dance) every March at New Plymouth's Bowl of Brooklands

» **Go Green** Paddle a stretch of the Whanganui River, an awe-inspiring slice of NZ wilderness

» **Online** www.taranaki.co.nz, www.wanganui.com, www.ourregion.co.nz

» **Area code** ⌨06

❶ Getting There & Around

In Taranaki, Air New Zealand has domestic flights to/from New Plymouth. Naked Bus and InterCity bus services service New Plymouth; Dalroy Express is a smaller company plying local routes. Getting to Mt Taranaki is easy: shuttle services run between the mountain, New Plymouth and surrounding towns.

Whanganui and Palmerston North airports are also serviced by Air New Zealand, and both cities are also on the radar for InterCity and Naked Bus services. Tranz Scenic trains stop in Palmerston North too, en route between Auckland and Wellington.

New Plymouth

POP 52,500

Dominated (in the best possible way) by Mt Taranaki and surrounded by lush farmland, New Plymouth is this part of NZ's only international deep-water port. The city has a bubbling arts scene, some fab cafes and a rootsy, outdoorsy focus, with good beaches and Egmont National Park a short hop away.

History

Local Maori *iwi* (tribes) have long contested Taranaki lands. In the 1820s they fled to the Cook Strait region to escape Waikato tribes, who eventually took hold of the area in 1832. Only a small group remained, at Okoki Pa (New Plymouth). When European settlers arrived in 1841, the coast of Taranaki seemed deserted and there was little opposition to land claims. The New Zealand Company bought extensive tracts from the remaining Maori.

When other members of local tribes returned after years of exile, they fiercely objected to the land sale. Their claims were upheld by Governor Fitzroy, but the Crown gradually acquired more land from Maori, and European settlers sought these fertile lands. The settlers forced the government to abandon negotiations with Maori, and war erupted in 1860. By 1870 over 500 hectares of Maori land had been confiscated.

Ensuing economic growth was largely founded on dairy farming. The 1959 discoveries of natural gas and oil in the South Taranaki Bight have kept the province economically healthy in recent times.

◉ Sights

FREE **Puke Ariki**   MUSEUM
(www.pukeariki.com; 1 Ariki St; ☺9am-6pm Mon, Tue, Thu & Fri, 9am-9pm Wed, 9am-5pm Sat & Sun) Translating as 'Hill of Chiefs', Puke Ariki is home to the i-SITE (p217), a museum, library, a cafe and the fabulous Arborio (p215) restaurant. The excellent museum has an extensive collection of Maori artefacts, plus colonial and wildlife exhibits (...we hope the shark suspended above the lobby isn't life-size). The regular 'Taranaki Experience' show tells the history of the province while the audience sits in podlike seats that rumble and glow.

Pukekura Park   GARDENS
(www.pukekura.org.nz; Liardet St; ☺7.30am-6pm, 7.30am-8pm Nov-Mar) The pick of New Plymouth's parks, Pukekura has 49 hectares of gardens, playgrounds, trails, streams, waterfalls, ponds and display houses. Rowboats

(per half-hour $10, December and January only) meander across the main lake (full of arm-sized eels), next to which the **Tea House** (Liardet St; snacks $4-9; ⊙10am-5pm) serves light meals. The technicoloured Festival of Lights (p213) here draws the summer crowds, as does the classically English cricket oval.

FREE **Govett-Brewster Art Gallery** GALLERY
(www.govettbrewster.com; 42 Queen St; ⊙10am-5pm) The Govett-Brewster Art Gallery is arguably the country's best regional art gallery. Presenting contemporary – often experimental – local and international shows, it's most famous for its connection with NZ sculptor, filmmaker and artist Len Lye (1901–80). His work is well represented here, with showings of his 1930s animation as well as sculpture and super-clever kinetic works. The glass-fronted Café Govett-Brewster is also here.

Puke Ariki Landing SCULPTURE PARK
(St Aubyn St) Along the city waterfront is Puke Ariki Landing, a historic area studded with sculptures, including the wonderfully eccentric Wind Wand (www.windwand.co.nz). Designed by Len Lye – the artist who has put this town on the map in modern times – this 45m-high kooky kinetic sculpture is a beloved icon of bendy poleness.

Paritutu HILL
(Centennial Dr) Just west of town is Paritutu, a steep-sided, craggy hill (154m); its name translates appropriately as 'Rising Precipice'. From the summit you can see for miles around: out to the Sugar Loaves, down to the town and to the mountain beyond. It's a 20-minute scramble to the top.

Sugar Loaf Islands Marine Park ISLAND
(www.doc.govt.nz) A refuge for sea birds and over 400 NZ fur seals 1km offshore, these rugged islets (Nga Motu in Maori) are eroded volcanic remnants. Most seals come here from June to October but some stay all year round. Learn more about the marine park at the tiny interpretation centre on the Lee Breakwater waterfront, or take a tour.

FREE **Real Tart Gallery** GALLERY
(www.tact.org.nz; 19 Egmont St; ⊙10am-5pm Mon-Fri, 10am-4pm Sat & Sun) To see what local artists have to offer, visit the 100-year-old reconstructed warehouse Real Tart Gallery. Exhibitions change regularly and most works are for sale. Don't miss the old graffiti preserved under perspex!

Brooklands Park PARK
(www.newplymouthnz.com; Brooklands Park Dr; ⊙daylight hr) Adjoining Pukekura, Brooklands Park is home to the **Bowl of Brooklands** (www.bowl.co.nz; Brooklands Park Dr), a world-class outdoor sound-shell, hosting festivals such as WOMAD (p213) and old-school rockers like Fleetwood Mac. Park highlights include a 2000-year-old puriri tree, a 300-variety rhododendron dell and the farmy **Brooklands Zoo** (Brooklands Park Dr; ⊙9am-5pm).

Taranaki Cathedral CHURCH
(www.taranakicathedral.org.nz; 37 Vivian St; ⊙services daily) The austere Church of St Mary, built in 1846, is NZ's oldest stone church and its newest cathedral! Its graveyard has the headstones of early settlers and soldiers who died during the Taranaki Land Wars, as well as those of several Maori chiefs. Check out the fabulous vaulted timber ceiling inside.

MAORI NZ: TARANAKI & WHANGANUI

Ever since Taranaki fled here to escape romantic difficulties, the Taranaki region has had a turbulent history. Conflicts between local *iwi* and invaders from the Waikato were followed by two wars with the government – first in 1860–61, and then again in 1865–69. Following the wars there were massive land confiscations and an extraordinary passive-resistance campaign at Parihaka.

Further east, a drive up the Whanganui River Rd takes you deep into traditional Maori territory, passing the Maori villages of Atene, Koriniti, Ranana and Hiruharama along the way. In Whanganui itself, run your eyes over amazing indigenous exhibits at the Whanganui Regional Museum (p225), and check out the superb Maori carvings in Putiki Church (p226).

Over in Palmerston North, Te Manawa museum (p236) has a strong Maori focus, while the New Zealand Rugby Museum (p236) pays homage to Maori All Blacks, without whom the team would never have become a world force.

New Plymouth

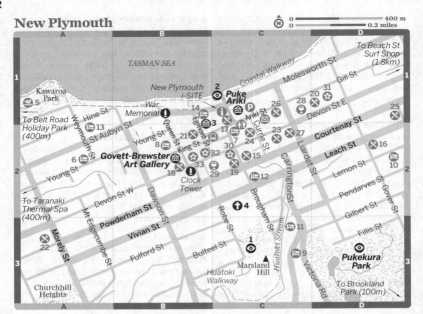

New Plymouth Observatory OBSERVATORY
(www.sites.google.com/site/astronomynp; Marsland Hill, off Robe St; adult/child/family $5/3/10; ☺7.30-9.30pm Tue Mar-Oct, 8.30-10pm Tue Nov-Feb) Atop Marsland Hill (great views!) is this wee observatory. Public nights include a planetarium program and telescope viewings if the weather is clear. Also on the hill is the cacophonous 37-bell **Kibby Carillon**, a huge automated glockenspiel-like device that tolls out across the New Plymouth rooftops.

🏃 Activities

Surfing
The black, volcanic-sand beaches of Taranaki are world renowned for surfing. Close to the eastern edge of town are **Fitzroy Beach** and **East End Beach** (allegedly the cleanest beach in Oceania). There's also decent surf at **Back Beach**, near Paritutu, at the western end of the city.

Beach Street Surf Shop SURFING
(☑06-758 0400; www.taranakisurf.com; 39 Beach St; 2hr lesson $75; ☺9am-6pm) Close to Fitzroy Beach, this surf shop offers lessons, gear hire and surf tours.

Tarawave Surf School SURFING
(☑06-752 7474, 021 119 6218; www.tarawave surfschool.com; 1½hr lesson $70) Tarawave is based 15km south of town at Oakura, on Surf Hwy 45.

Tramping
The i-SITE stocks the *Taranaki: A Walker's Guide* booklet, including coastal, local reserve and park walks. The excellent **Coastal Walkway** (13km) from Bell Block to Port Taranaki, gives you a surf-side perspective on New Plymouth and crosses the great new **Te Rewa Rewa Bridge**. The **Te Henui Walkway** (6km), from the coastal East End Reserve to the city's southern boundary, is an interesting streamside amble. **Huatoki Walkway** (5km), following Huatoki Stream, is a rambling walk into the city centre. Alternatively, the *New Plymouth Heritage Trail* brochure, taking in historic hot spots, is a real blast from the past.

Other Activities
Taranaki Thermal Spa SPA, MASSAGE
(☑06-7591666;www.windwand.co.nz/mineralpools; 8 Bonithon Ave; treatments $5-245; ☺10am-5pm Mon & Tue, 10am-9pm Wed-Fri, 3pm-9pm Sat & Sun) The warm mineral water filling the tanks at Taranaki Thermal Spa was discovered during the search for oil around 1910. The pri-

New Plymouth

vate baths are filled on arrival, and there's a suite of massage and beauty therapies available. An absolute tonic.

Todd Energy Aquatic Centre　SWIMMING
(☑06-759 6060; www.newplymouthnz.com; Tisch Ave, Kawaroa Park; adult/child $4.50/3.50, waterslide $3.50; ⊙6am-8.30pm Mon-Fri, 8.30am-7pm Sat & Sun) Just west of town in grassy Kawaroa Park is the Todd Energy Aquatic Centre, which has a waterslide, outdoor pool and indoor pool.

☞ Tours

Happy Chaddy's Charters　BOAT
(☑06-758 9133; www.windwand.co.nz/chaddies charters; Ocean View Pde; trips adult/child $35/10) Take a trip out to visit the Sugar Loaf Islands with Chaddy: expect at least four laughs a minute on a one-hour bob around on the chop. Departs daily from Lee Breakwater, tide and weather permitting. You can also hire kayaks (single/double per hour $15/30) and bikes ($10 per 30 minutes) here.

Wind Wanderers　CYCLING
(☑027 358 1182; www.windwanderers.co.nz; Nobs Line car park, East End Reserve; tours per person

$90) Wind Wanderers offers bike hire (single/tandem per hour $20/30) and three-hour guided tours along New Plymouth's excellent Coastal Walkway (cycling, not walking, obviously). Miniumum two people.

Canoe & Kayak Taranaki　KAYAKING
(☑06-769 5506; www.canoeandkayak.co.nz; half-day trips incl hire $70) Paddle out to the Sugar Loaf Islands or over the gentle Waitara River rapids.

☆ Festivals & Events

Festival of Lights　CULTURAL
(www.festivaloflights.co.nz) Complete with live music and costumed characters roaming the undergrowth, this colourful display lights up Pukekura Park from late December to mid-February.

WOMAD　MUSIC, CULTURAL
(World of Music Arts & Dance; ☑06-759 8412; www.womad.co.nz) A diverse array of local and international artists perform at the Bowl of Brooklands each March. Hugely popular, with music fans travelling from across NZ.

Taranaki International Arts Festival ARTS
(www.taft.co.nz/artsfest) The regional big-ticket arts fest happens in August ('It's warm inside' was the 2011 tagline): theatre, dance, music, visual arts, parades and plenty of food and wine.

**Taranaki Garden
Spectacuclar** HORTICULTURAL
(www.taft.co.nz/gardenfestnz) A long-running NZ flower fest, held late October/early November each year. More rhododendrons than you'll ever see in one place again.

🛏 Sleeping

TOP CHOICE **Fitzroy Beach Motel** MOTEL $$
(✆06-757 2925; www.fitzroybeachmotel.co.nz; 25 Beach St; s/d $130/150, unit $190; ☎) This quiet, old-time motel (just 160m from Fitzroy Beach) has been thoroughly redeemed with a major overhaul and extension. Highlights include quality carpets, double glazing, lovely bathrooms, LCD TVs, and an absence of poky studio-style units (all one- or two-bedroom). Free bikes too. Winner!

Seaspray House HOSTEL $
(✆06-759 8934; www.seasprayhouse.co.nz; 13 Weymouth St; dm/s/d $30/50/74; @☎) A big old house with gloriously high ceilings, Seaspray has had a recent makeover inside but remains relaxed and affordable, with well-chosen retro and antique furniture. Fresh and arty, it's a rare bunk-free backpackers with no TV (conversation encouraged). Closed June and July.

Arcadia Lodge B&B, HOSTEL $
(✆06-769 9100; www.arcadialodge.net; 52 Young St; dm/d/f incl breakfast $35/90/150; ☎) A former rest home tacked onto a big old lemon-coloured villa (built in 1904 for the local newspaper editor), Arcadia is a homey B&B with a lovely breakfast room, genteel lounge, spa, barbecue, and a superb timber-ceilinged family room upstairs with sea views.

Ariki Backpackers HOSTEL $
(✆06-769 5020; www.arikibackpackers.com; cnr Ariki & Brougham Sts; dm $25-30, d $60-90; @☎) Upstairs in the old Royal Hotel (Queen Liz stayed here once!), Ariki offers downtown hostelling with funky carpets, a roomy lounge area with retro couches, and fantastic roof terrace looking across the park to Puke Ariki. Most rooms have their own shower and toilet.

Belt Road Holiday Park HOLIDAY PARK $
(✆06-758 0228, 0800 804 204; www.beltroad.co.nz; 2 Belt Rd; sites from $18, cabins $65-125; @☎) This environmentally attuned, pohutukawa-covered holiday park sits atop a bluff overlooking the increasingly interesting Lee Breakwater area, about a 10-minute walk from town. The half-dozen best cabins have million-dollar views!

Issey Manor BOUTIQUE HOTEL $$
(✆06-758 2375; www.isseymanor.co.nz; 32 Carrington St; d $150-210) Friendly Issey is hard to miss(ey): two conjoined Victorian timber houses (1875 and 1910) painted with startling panels of white, orange and black. Inside are four stylish units (two with spa), a guest kitchen, and far more designer touches than you'd expect at these prices. Fab!

Cottage Mews Motel MOTEL $$
(✆06-758 0403; www.cottagemews.net.nz; 50 Lemon St; s/d from $115/125; ☎) A small, modest motel where you'll feel like family, rather than a guest. The well-kept rooms have interesting layouts, there's a lawn out the front instead of a car park, and you can pop next door to the co-owned Shoestring Backpackers and remember how travelling was before your career took off.

Shoestring Backpackers HOSTEL $
(✆06-758 0404; www.shoestring.co.nz; 48 Lemon St; dm/s/d/tr $30/58/78/93; @☎) Inside a labyrinthine 1920s heritage building with stripy wallpaper and fancy timberwork, this isn't the fanciest option but it's well maintained and brimming with character. The upstairs rooms are the pick: secluded, quiet and catching the morning sun. Out the back is a deck and barbecue.

Bella Vista MOTEL $$
(✆0800 235 528, 06-769 5932; www.staybellavista.co.nz; 32 Queen St; d $125-165; ☎) A dependable, vaguely Spanish-looking option right in the centre of town. Basic rooms have toast-making facilities only; fancier rooms have full kitchenettes. Bonuses such as fair-trade plunger coffee and free bicycles abound.

Egmont Eco Lodge HOSTEL $
(✆06-753 5720; www.yha.co.nz; 12 Clawton St; dm/d from $29/74; @) An immaculate YHA in a glade with chirping birds and a chuckling creek (with eels!). Mixed dorms in the main lodge; smaller pinewood cabins down below

(sleeping four). It's a hike uphill from town, but the prospect of free nightly Egmont cake will put a spring in your step. A Mt Taranaki shuttle is available.

Nice Hotel
BOUTIQUE HOTEL $$$

(06-758 6423; www.nicehotel.co.nz; 71 Brougham St; d/ste from $250/300;) This hotel is high class from top to tail; 'nice' is the understatement of the decade. The seven rooms feature luxury furnishings, designer bathrooms, imported wallpapers and select *objets d'art*. There's also a classy in-house restaurant, free bikes, and four self-contained suites next door.

New Plymouth Top 10 Holiday Park
HOLIDAY PARK $

(06-758 2566, 0800 758 256; www.nptop10.co.nz; 29 Princes St; sites/cabins from $19/75, units $85-180; @) Sequestered in Fitzroy, 3.5km east of town and a seven-minute walk to the beach, this quaint, family-run Top 10 feels a bit like a school camp, with a dinky little row of units, a life-sized chess set, trampoline, laundry and spacious kitchen.

Carrington Motel
MOTEL $$

(06-757 9431; www.carringtonmotel.co.nz; 61 Carrington St; s/d/f $95/110/165) Sixteen old but tidy units close to Pukekura Park and a 10-minute walk to town. It's very family friendly and great value (especially in winter), but noisy when the hoons careen up Carrington St. Wildly eclectic furnishings and tsunami-like showers.

BK's Egmont Motor Lodge
MOTEL $$

(0800 115 033, 06-758 5216; www.egmont motorlodge.co.nz; 115 Coronation Ave; d $125-190;) Opposite the racecourse, corporate BK's has ground-floor units and oceans of parking. Rooms are smart, comfortable and clean, and the managers (travellers too) readily share a laugh with the cleaners (a good sign). Free wi-fi and DVDs.

Waterfront
HOTEL $$$

(06-769 5301; www.waterfront.co.nz; 1 Egmont St; r $190-550; @) Sleek and snazzy, the Waterfront is *the* place to stay, particularly if the boss is paying. The minimalist studios are pretty flash, while the penthouses steal the show with big TVs and little balconies. It's got terrific views from some – but not all – rooms, but certainly from the curvy-fronted bar and restaurant.

Sunflower Lodge
HOSTEL $

(0800 422 257, 06-759 0050; www.sunflowerlodge.co.nz; 33 Timandra St; dm/s/d/tr $28/50/70/85; @) Down a steep driveway a few minutes' drive south of town, Sunflower does its best to transcend its mid-'80s rest-home origins, and (with the exception of some relentless timber panelling) succeeds. Bonuses such as quality mattresses, free local calls and a heavy-duty kitchen help the cause. Weekly rates available.

✗ Eating

TOP CHOICE Arborio
MEDITERRANEAN $$

(www.arborio.co.nz; Puke Ariki, 1 Ariki St; mains $13-34; breakfast, lunch & dinner) Despite looking like a cheese grater, Arborio, in the Puke Ariki building, is the star of New Plymouth's local food show. It's airy, arty and modern, with sea views and faultless service. The Med-influenced menu ranges from an awesome Moroccan lamb pizza to pastas, risottos and barbecued chilli squid with lychee-and-cucumber noodle salad. Cocktails and NZ wines also available.

Frederic's
TAPAS $$

(www.frederics.co.nz; 34 Egmont St; plates $10-19, mains $20-25; 2pm-late Mon-Thu, 11am-late Fri-Sun) Freddy's is a fab gastro-bar with quirky interior design (rusty medieval chandeliers, peacock-feather wallpaper, religious icon paintings), serving generous share plates. Order some meatballs with bell-pepper sauce, or some green-lipped mussels with coconut cream, chilli and coriander to go with your beer.

Elixir
CAFE $$

(www.elixircafe.co.nz; 117 Devon St E; brunch $7-18, dinner $18-31; 7am-4.30pm Mon, 7am-late Tue-Sat, 8am-4pm Sun) Behind a weird louvered wall facing onto Devon St, Elixir fosters an American-diner vibe, serving up everything from coffee, cake, bagels and eggs on toast, through to more innovative evening fare. Below a wall of rock posters, sexy staff give the coffee machine a serious work-out.

Bach on Breakwater
CAFE, RESTAURANT $$

(06-769 6967; www.bachonbreakwater.co.nz; Ocean View Pde; brunch $10-22, dinner $27-38; 9.30am-10pm Wed-Sun;) Constructed from weighty recycled timbers, this cool cafe-bistro in the emerging Lee Breakwater precinct looks like an old sea chest washed up after a storm. Expect plenty of seafood and steak, plus Asian- and Middle Eastern-influenced delights (curries, wontons, felafels) and killer coffee. The seafood chowder is a real winter warmer.

Chaos
CAFE $

(chaoscafe@xtra.co.nz; 36 Brougham St; meals $6-14; ⊙breakfast & lunch;) Not so much chaotic as endearingly boho, Chaos is a dependable spot for a coffee and a zingy breakfast. Beans with bacon, avocado and sour cream, background jazz, smiley staff and arty interior design – hard to beat! Plenty of vegetarian and gluten-free options, too.

IndiaToday
INDIAN $$

(06-758 4634; 40 Devon St E; mains $17-19; ⊙lunch & dinner;) A sumptuous gold-walled room draped with bolts of silk, IndiaToday wafts with spicy aromas and snaky tabla tunes enticing you in off the street. Dapper waiters, subcontinentally perfect in gold tunics and black pants, serve up classic and creative curries. Takeaway lunch specials from $10.

Laughing Buddha
CHINESE $$

(06-759 2065; laughingbuddha@xtra.co.nz; cnr Devon St E & Currie St; mains $16-29; ⊙dinner Tue-Sat) Red-glowing windows and a rather menacing-looking Buddha sign suggest 'nightclub'...but a wander upstairs delivers you instead to New Plymouth's best Chinese restaurant. Load up on entree plates ($4 to $8; try the steamed pork buns), or order a steaming main course (the Cantonese roast duck with plum sauce is magic). Great for groups.

Andre's Pies & Patisserie
BAKERY $

(44 Leach St; pies $4-8; ⊙6am-3.30pm Mon-Fri) Expanding waistlines since 1972, this is an easy pull-over off the main road through town. Hefty pies, buns, doughnuts and sandwiches and calorific slabs of cake.

Portofino
ITALIAN $$

(06-757 8686; www.portofino.co.nz; 14 Gill St; mains $19-60; ⊙5pm-late) This discreet little family-run eatery has been here for years, serving old-fashioned Italian pasta and pizza just like nonna used to make. The rigatoni Portofino is a knock out (spinach, fetta, garlic and sun-dried tomatoes).

Petit Paris
FRENCH $

(www.petitparis.co.nz; 34 Currie St; lunch $8-15; ⊙7.30am-4pm) Ooh-la-la: lashings of buttery treats! Flying the tricolore with pride, Petit Paris is a boulangerie and patisserie turning out crispy baguettes and *tart au citron* (lemon tart), or an omelette or croque monsieur for lunch.

Empire Tea & Coffee
CAFE $

(112 Devon St W; lunch $7-12; ⊙7.30am-4pm Mon-Fri, 9am-2pm Sat) A perfectly evolved Kiwi tearoom with china plates nailed to the walls and a sunny courtyard. Tasty sandwiches, salads, lasagne and filos, plus delectable cakes and quivering slices of lime-topped custard to finish.

André L'Escargot
FRENCH $$$

(06-758 4812; www.andres.co.nz; 37 Brougham St; mains $35-37; ⊙dinner Mon-Sat, lunch by appointment) Audaciously serving snails in the 'naki since 1976, we doff our beret to the man who has no doubt raised the bar and kept it there. All classic French fare, indulgent and largely gout-inducing, plus killer cocktails. 'Casual elegance' is the catch-cry here.

Sandwich Extreme
SANDWICHES $

(06-759 6999; 52 Devon St E; meals $8-14; ⊙8am-4pm Mon-Fri, 9am-3pm Sat) A buzzy spot for a toastie, sandwich, baked spud, coffee, salad, bagel or slice of cake, served fresh and fast by friendly staff.

Fresha
SELF-CATERING $

(www.fresha.net.nz; cnr Devon & Morley Sts; snacks $3-15; ⊙9am-6pm Mon-Fri, 9am-5pm Sat;) A drool-worthy emporium for picnic-basket essentials: meats, wines, olive oil, relish, fruit and veg, cheeses, jams and prepackaged meals (try the fish pie). There's an excellent cafe here too.

Pak 'n Save
SUPERMARKET $

(www.paknsave.co.nz; 53 Leach St; ⊙8am-11pm) Just east of downtown NP.

🍷 Drinking & Entertainment

Arthouse Cinema
CINEMA

(www.arthousecinema.co.nz; 73a Devon St W; adult/child from $12/9; ⊙11.30am-11pm) Run by a nonprofit private trust, this groovy cinema, found up a mirror-clad stairwell (this has to be an old nightclub, doesn't it?), screens the arty and the interesting. Beanbags, food platters and beer complete the picture.

Crowded House
BAR

(www.crowdedhouse.co.nz; 93 Devon St E; ⊙10am-late) A sporty hive of boozy activity with pool tables (in good nick), restaurant (fries with everything) and big-screen TVs. No sign of Neil Finn...

The Basement
LIVE MUSIC

(www.myspace.com/thebasementnp; cnr Devon St W & Egmont St; admission free-$10; ⊙varies with gigs) Underneath a regulation Irish pub, the grungy Basement is the best place in town for up-and-coming live acts, broadly sheltering under a rock, metal and punk umbrella.

Matinee
BAR

(matinee@xtra.co.nz; 69 Devon St W; ⊙9.30am-late Mon-Sat) A good option (one of the only ones, actually) for those who prefer top shelf to Tui, and electronica to '80s rock. Inside a former theatre, the design is all mirrors, silk drapes and art-nouveau wallpaper; the tables outside afford puffing and people-watching. Jazz Fridays; DJs Saturdays.

TSB Showplace
PERFORMING ARTS

(☑06-759 0021; 92 Devon St W; ⊙box office 9am-5pm Mon-Fri, 10am-1pm Sat) Housed in an old opera house, the three-venue Showplace stages a variety of big performances (Russian Ballet, Pam Ayers). For online bookings go to Ticketek (www.ticketek.co.nz) or Ticket Direct (www.ticketdirect.co.nz).

Event Cinemas
CINEMA

(www.eventcinemas.co.nz; 119 Devon St E; tickets adult/child $13.50/8.50; ⊙10am-11pm) Mainstream main street megaplex, the carpet a sea of popcorn.

ℹ Information

Department of Conservation (DOC; ☑06-759 0350; www.doc.govt.nz; 55a Rimu St; ⊙8am-4.30pm Mon-Fri)
New Plymouth i-SITE (☑06-759 6060, 0800 639 759; www.visitnewplymouthnz.co.nz; Puke Ariki, 1 Ariki St; ⊙9am-6pm Mon, Tue, Thu & Fri, 9am-9pm Wed, 9am-5pm Sat & Sun) In the Puke Ariki building, with a fantastic interactive tourist-info database.
Phoenix Urgent Doctors (☑06-759 4295; npdocs@clear.net.nz; 95 Vivian St; ⊙8.30am-8pm) Doctors available for urgent stuff (not blisters).
Post Office (21 Currie St) Foreign exchange available.
Taranaki Base Hospital (☑06-753 6139; www.tdhb.org.nz; David St; ⊙24hr) Accident and emergency.

ℹ Getting There & Away
Air

New Plymouth Airport (☑06-755 2250; www.newplymouthairport.com; Airport Dr) is 11km east of the centre off SH3. **Scott's Airport Shuttle** (☑06-769 5974, 0800 373 001; www.npairportshuttle.co.nz; adult from $25) operates a door-to-door shuttle to/from the airport.
Air New Zealand (☑0800 737 000, 06-757 3300; www.airnewzealand.co.nz; 12 Devon St E; ⊙9am-5pm Mon-Wed & Fri, 9.30am-5pm Thu) has daily direct flights to/from Auckland, Wellington and Christchurch, with onward connections.

Bus
The bus centre (p217) is on the corner of Egmont and Ariki Sts.
InterCity (☑09-583 5780; www.intercity.co.nz) services numerous destinations:

DESTINATION	PRICE	DURATION	FREQUENCY
Auckland	$70	6¼hr	4 daily
Hamilton	$58	4hr	4 daily
Palmerston North	$30	4hr	2 daily
Wellington	$41	7hr	2 daily
Whanganui	$38	3hr	2 daily

Naked Bus (☑0900 625 33; www.nakedbus.com) services run to the following destinations (among many others). Book in advance for big savings.

DESTINATION	PRICE	DURATION	FREQUENCY
Auckland	$30	6½hr	1 daily
Hamilton	$27	4hr	1 daily
Palmerston North	$20	3½hr	1 daily
Wellington	$26	6¼hr	1 daily
Whanganui	$18	2½hr	1 daily

The **Dalroy Express** (☑06-759 0197; www.dalroytours.co.nz) bus runs daily to/from Auckland ($60, six hours) via Hamilton ($41, four hours), and extending south to Hawera ($20, 45 minutes).

ℹ Getting Around

Citylink (☑0800 872 287; www.taranakibus.info; adult/child $3.50/2) services run Monday to Friday around town, as well as north to Waitara and south to Oakura. Buses depart the bus centre.
Cycle Inn Bike Hire (☑06-758 7418; www.cycleinn.co.nz; 133 Devon St E; per half-/full day $10/15; ⊙8.30am-5pm Mon-Fri, 9am-4pm Sat, 10.30am-2pm Sun) rents out bicycles, as does **Happy Chaddy's Charters** (☑06-758 9133; www.windwand.co.nz/chaddiescharters; Ocean View Pde; per 30min $10).

For cheap car hire, try **Rent-a-Dent** (☑06-757 5362, 0800 736 823; www.newplymouthcarrentals.co.nz; 592 Devon St E); for a cab call **Energy City Cabs** (☑06-757 5580).

Around New Plymouth

SOUTH OF TOWN

FREE Pukeiti Rhododendron Garden
GARDENS

(www.pukeiti.org.nz; 2290 Carrington Rd; ⊙9am-5pm) This 4-sq-km garden, 20km south of New Plymouth, is home to a masses of rhododendrons and azaleas. The flowers bloom between September and November, but it's worth a visit any time. The drive here passes between the Pouakai and Kaitake Ranges, both part of Egmont National Park. The **Gatehouse Café** (2290 Carrington Rd; meals $7-18; ⊙10am-4pm) is here too.

FREE Tupare
HISTORIC BUILDING, GARDENS

(www.tupare.info; 487 Mangorei Rd; ⊙9am-5pm, tours 11am Fri-Mon Oct-Mar) Tupare is a Tudor-style house designed by the renowned architect James Chapman-Taylor. It's as pretty as a picture, but the highlight of this 7km trip south of town will likely be the rambling 3.6 hectare garden surrounding it. Bluebells and birdsong under the boughs... picnic paradise.

Hurworth Cottage
HISTORIC BUILDING

(www.historic.org.nz; 906 Carrington Rd; adult/child/family $5/2/10; ⊙11am-3pm Sat & Sun) This 1856 cottage, 8km south of New Plymouth, was built by four-time NZ prime minister Harry Atkinson. The cottage is the sole survivor of a settlement abandoned at the start of the Taranaki Land Wars: a rare window into the lives of early settlers.

Taranaki Aviation, Transport & Technology Museum
MUSEUM

(http://tatatm.tripod.com/museum; cnr SH3 & Kent Rd; adult/child/family $7/2/16; ⊙10am-4.30pm Sat & Sun) Around 9.5km south of New Plymouth is this roadside museum, with ramshackle displays of old planes, trains, automobiles and general household miscellany. Ask to see the stuff made by the amazing bee guy (hexagons ahoy!).

NORTH VIA SH3

Heading north from New Plymouth along SH3 are various seaward turn-offs to high sand dunes and surf beaches. **Urenui**, 16km past Waitara, is a summer hot spot.

About 5km past Urenui you'll find arguably the highlight of North Taranaki – **Mike's Organic Brewery** (☎06-752 3676; www.organicbeer.co.nz; 487 Mokau Rd; tastings/tours $5/10; ⊙10am-6pm) – which offers tours (book ahead), takeaways, tastings of the legendary Mike's Pale Ale (the pilsener and lager are ace, too), and an Oktoberfest party every (you guessed it) October. A little further on is the turn-off to Pukearuhe and White Cliffs, huge precipices resembling their Dover namesakes. From Pukearuhe boat ramp you can tackle the **White Cliffs Walkway**, a seven-hour walk (one-way) with mesmerising views of the coast and mountains (Taranaki and Ruapehu).

Continuing north towards Mokau, stop at the **Three Sisters** rock formation signposted just south of the Tongaporutu Bridge – you can traverse the shore at low tide. Two sisters stand somewhat forlornly off the coast; their other sister collapsed in a heap 10 years ago, but check the progress of a new sis emerging from the eroding cliffs.

Mt Taranaki (Egmont National Park)

A classic 2518m volcanic cone dominating the landscape, Mt Taranaki is a magnet to all who catch his eye. Geologically, Taranaki is the youngest of three large volcanoes – Kaitake and Pouakai are the others – which stand along the same fault line. With the last eruption over 350 years ago, experts say that the mountain is overdue for another go. But don't let that put you off – this mountain is an absolute beauty and the highlight of any visit to the region.

History

According to Maori legend, Taranaki belonged to a tribe of volcanoes in the middle of the North Island. However, he was forced to depart rather hurriedly when he was caught with Pihanga, the beautiful volcano near Lake Taupo and the lover of Mt Tongariro. As he fled south (some say in disgrace; others say to keep the peace), Taranaki gouged out a wide scar in the earth (now the Whanganui River) and finally settled in the west in his current position. He remains here in majestic isolation, hiding his face behind a cloud of tears.

It was Captain Cook who named the mountain Egmont, after the Earl he sought to flatter at that particular moment. Egmont National Park was created in 1900, making it NZ's second oldest. Mt Taranaki eventually reclaimed its name, although the name Egmont has stuck like, well, egg. The mountain starred as Mt Fuji in *The Last Samurai* (2003), the production of which caused near-hysteria in the locals, especially when Tom Cruise came to town.

🏃 Activities

Tramping

Due to its accessibility, Mt Taranaki ranks as the 'most climbed' mountain in NZ. Nevertheless, tramping on this mountain is dangerous and should not be undertaken lightly. It's *crucial* to get advice before departing and to leave your intentions with a DOC visitor centre or i-SITE.

Most walks are accessible from North Egmont, Dawson Falls or East Egmont. Check out DOC's pamphlet *Short Walks in Egmont National Park* ($1.50), and the free *Taranaki: A Walker's Guide* booklet for more info.

From North Egmont, the main walk is the scenic **Pouakai Circuit**, a two- to three-day, 25km loop through alpine, swamp and tussock areas with awesome mountain views. Short, easy walks from here include the **Ngatoro Loop Track** (one hour), **Veronica Loop** (two hours) and **Connett Loop** (40 minutes return). The **Summit Track** also starts from North Egmont. It's a 14km poled route taking eight to 10 hours return, and should not be attempted by inexperienced people, especially in icy conditions and snow.

East Egmont has **Potaema Track** (30 minutes return) and **East Egmont Lookout** (30 minutes return); a longer walk is the steep **Enchanted Track** (two to three hours return).

At Dawson Falls you can do several short walks including **Wilkies Pools Loop** (one hour return) or the excellent but challenging **Fanthams Peak Return** (five hours return), which is snowed-in during winter. The **Kapuni Loop Track** (one-hour loop) runs to the impressive 18m **Dawson Falls** themselves. You can also see the falls on a 20-minute return walk to a viewpoint, starting 400m down the road from the visitor centre.

The difficult 55km **Around-the-Mountain Circuit** takes three to five days and is for experienced trampers only. There are a number of huts en route, tickets for which should be purchased in advance.

The **York Loop Track** (three hours), accessible from York Rd north of Stratford, is a fascinating walk following part of a disused railway line.

ℹ️ DECEPTIVE MOUNTAIN

Mt Taranaki might look like an easy peak to bag, but this cute cone has claimed more than 60 lives. The mountain microclimate changes fast: from summery to white-out conditions almost in an instant. There are also precipitous bluffs and steep icy slopes.

There are plenty of short walks here, safe for much of the year, but for adventurous trampers January to March is the best time to go. Take a detailed topographic map (the Topo50 1:50,000 *Mt Taranaki or Mt Egmont* map is good) and consult a DOC officer for current conditions. You *must* also register your tramping intentions with the DOC visitor centre or i-SITE.

You can tramp without a guide from February to March when snowfalls are low, but at other times inexperienced climbers can check with DOC for details of local clubs and guides. It costs around $300 per day to hire a guide.

Reliable operators include **Adventure Dynamics** (☎06-751 3589; www.adventuredynamics.co.nz) and **Top Guides** (☎0800 448 433, 021 838 513; www.topguides.co.nz).

Scenic Flights

Heliview SCENIC FLIGHTS (☎06-753 0123, 0800 435 426; www.heliview.co.nz; flights from $110) A 20-minute summit flight costs $200 per passenger.

New Plymouth Aero Club SCENIC FLIGHTS (☎06-755 0500; www.airnewplymouth.co.nz; flights from $69) A 50-minute, fixed-wing Mt Taranaki summit buzz costs $159 per person (minimum three people).

Precision Helicopters Limited SCENIC FLIGHTS (PHL; ☎06-752 3291, 0800 246 359; www.precisionhelicopters.com; flights from $120) A 50-minute, scenic mountain fly-around costs $300 per person (minimum four people).

Skiing

From Stratford take Pembroke Rd up to Stratford Plateau, from where it's a 1.5km walk to the small **Manganui Ski Area** (☎snow phone 06-759 1119; www.skitaranaki.co.nz). The Stratford i-SITE (p221) has daily weather and snow reports; otherwise ring the snow phone or check the webcam online.

🛏 Sleeping

Several DOC huts are scattered about the mountain, accessible by tramping tracks. Most cost $15 per night (Syme and Kahui cost $5); purchase hut tickets in advance from DOC. BYO cooking, eating and sleeping gear, and bookings are not accepted – it's first come, first served. Remember to carry out *all* your rubbish.

Alpine Lodge   B&B $$
(✆06-765 6620; www.andersonsalpinelodge.co.nz; 922 Pembroke Rd; s/tw/d incl breakfast from $50/100/140; P🛜) With picture-postcard mountain views, this lovely Swiss-style lodge is on the Stratford side of the mountain. Inside are four rooms (three with en suite) and lots of nifty timberwork; outside are billions of birds, a hot tub and some wandering black-faced sheep.

Camphouse   HOSTEL $
(✆06-756 9093; www.mttaranaki.co.nz; Egmont Rd; dm/d/f $30/70/160) Bunkhouse-style accommodation behind the North Egmont visitor centre in a historic 1850 corrugated-iron building, complete with bullet holes in the walls (from shots fired at settlers by local Maori during the Taranaki Land Wars). Endless horizon views from the porch.

Mountain House   LODGE $$
(✆06-765 6100; www.stratfordmountainhouse. co.nz; Pembroke Rd; r $155) This upbeat lodge, on the Stratford side of the mountain (15km from the SH3 turn-off and 3km to the Manganui ski area), has recently renovated, motel-style rooms and a European-style **restaurant/cafe** (Pembroke Rd; mains $30-35; ⏰breakfast, lunch & dinner). Dinner, bed and breakfast packages available.

🍃 Eco Inn   HOSTEL $
(✆06-752 2765; www.ecoinn.co.nz; 671 Kent Rd; s/d $30/60; @🛜) About 6.5km up the road from the turn-off at the Aviation, Transport & Technology Museum, this ecofriendly place is made from recycled timber and runs on solar, wind and hydropower. There's a spa and pool table, too. Good for groups.

Rahiri Cottage   B&B $$
(✆06-756-9093; www.mttaranaki.co.nz; Egmont Rd; d with/without breakfast $195/145, whole cottage $225, extra person $45) Right on the edge of Egmont National Park on the way to North Egmont, this 1929 clinker-brick cottage was once the park tollgate (it once cost two shillings and six pence to drive past), and today offers rustic B&B rooms in a bush setting. Sleeps five.

Konini Lodge   HOSTEL $
(✆06-756 0990; www.doc.govt.nz; Upper Manaia Rd; dm adult/child $25/10) Basic bunkhouse accommodation 100m downhill from the Dawson Falls visitor centre. The six dorm rooms feed off a huge communal space and kitchen.

Missing Leg Lodge   HOSTEL $
(✆06-752 2570; www.missinglegbackpackers.co.nz; 1082 Junction Rd; sites/dm/s/d from $15/27/35/64; @🛜) This eccentric, bicycle-strewn backpackers has a strange lack of natural light – OK for sleeping! Dorm accommodation is up in the loft, plus there's a handful of shabby-chic baches outside.

ℹ Information

Dawson Falls Visitor Centre (✆027 443 0248; www.doc.govt.nz; Manaia Rd; ⏰daily Dec-Feb, 9am-4pm Thu-Sun Mar-Nov) On the southeastern side of the mountain, fronted by an awesome totem pole.

MetPhone (✆0900 999 06) Mountain weather updates.

North Egmont Visitor Centre (✆06-756 0990; www.doc.govt.nz; Upper Manaia Rd; ⏰8am-4.30pm) Current and comprehensive national park info, plus a greasy-spoon cafe (meals $10 to $18).

ℹ Getting There & Away

There are three main entrance roads to Egmont National Park, all of which are well signposted and either pass by or end at a DOC visitor centre. Closest to New Plymouth is North Egmont: turn off SH3 at Egmont Village, 12km south of New Plymouth, and follow the road for 14km. From Stratford, turn off at Pembroke Rd and continue for 15km to East Egmont and the Manganui Ski Area. From the southeast, Upper Manaia Rd leads up to Dawson Falls, 23km from Stratford.

There are no public buses to the national park but numerous shuttle-bus/tour operators will gladly take you there for around $40/55 one-way/return:

Cruise NZ Tours (✆0800 688 687, 027 497 3908; kirkstall@xtra.co.nz) Mountain shuttle bus departing New Plymouth 7.30am for North Egmont; returns 4.30pm. Other pick-ups/drop-offs by arrangement. Tours also available.

FORGOTTEN WORLD HIGHWAY

The 150km road between Stratford and Taumarunui (SH43) has become known as the Forgotten World Hwy. The drive winds through hilly bush country with 11km of unsealed road, passing Maori *pa* (fortified villages), abandoned coal mines and memorials to those long gone en route. Allow four hours and plenty of stops, and fill up with petrol at either end (there's no petrol along the route itself). Pick up a pamphlet from i-SITEs or DOC visitor centres in the area.

The town of **Whangamomona** (population 170) is a highlight. This quirky village declared itself an independent republic in 1988 after disagreements with local councils. The town celebrates Republic Day in January every two years, with a military-themed extravaganza. In the middle of town is the unmissable grand old **Whangamomona Hotel** (✆06-762 5823; www.whangamomonahotel.co.nz; 6018 Forgotten World Hwy; accommodation per person incl breakfast $65, meals $10-20; ⊗11am-late), a pub offering simple accommodation and big country meals.

If you're not driving, **Eastern Taranaki Experience** (✆06-765 7482, 027 471 7136; www.eastern-taranaki.co.nz; day trips per person from $45) runs tours through the area.

Eastern Taranaki Experience (✆06-765 7482, 027 471 7136; www.eastern-taranaki.co.nz) Departs from Stratford; extra charge from New Plymouth. Tours also available.

Outdoor Gurus (✆06-758 4152, 027 270 2932; www.outdoorgurus.co.nz) Pick-up points (New Plymouth) and times to suit; gear hire available.

Taranaki Tours (✆06-757 9888, 0800 886 877; www.taranakitours.com) New Plymouth to North Egmont return. Tours also available.

Around Mt Taranaki

INGLEWOOD
POP 3090

Handy to the mountain on SH3, the little main-street town of Inglewood (www.inglewood.co.nz) is an adequate stop for supermarket supplies and a noteworthy stop for a steak-and-egg pie at **Nelsons Bakery** (✆06-756 7123; 45 Rata St; pies $3-4; ⊗ 6am-4.30pm Mon-Fri, 7am-4pm Sat). Inglewood's other shining light is the cute **Fun Ho! National Toy Museum** (✆06-756 7030; www.funhotoys.co.nz; 25 Rata St; adult/child $6/3; ⊗10am-4pm), exhibiting (and selling) old-fashioned sand-cast toys. It doubles as the local visitor information centre.

On the road into town from New Plymouth, **White Eagle Motel** (✆06-756 8252; www.whiteeaglemotel.co.nz; 87b Rata St; s/d from $90/98, extra person $20) is basic but tidy and quiet. The two-bedroom units feel bigger than they are.

Inside a fire-engine-red heritage building, jazzy **Macfarlane's Caffe** (✆06-756 6665; 1 Kelly St; brunch $9-18, dinner $23-30; ⊗9am-5pm Sun-Wed, 9am-late Thu-Sat) sells super-sized custard squares and coffee during the day and wild-boar sausages at night (among other things). The venison Taranaki Burger rules. Nearby, **Funkfish Grill** (✆06-756 7287; www.funkfishgrill.co.nz; 32 Matai St; takeaways $8-10, mains $22-38; ⊗4pm-late Tue-Thu, Sat & Sun, 3pm-late Fri) is a hip pizzeria and fish-and-chippery doing eat-in and takeaway meals, and doubles as a bar at night. Try the tempura scallops.

STRATFORD
POP 5330

Forty kilometres southeast of New Plymouth on SH3, Stratford plays up its namesake of Stratford-upon-Avon, Shakespeare's birthplace, by naming its streets after bardic characters. Stratford also claims NZ's first **glockenspiel**. Four times daily (10am, 1pm, 3pm and 7pm) this clock doth chime out Shakespeare's greatest hits with some fairly wooden performances.

Stratford i-SITE (✆06-765 6708, 0800 765 6708; www.stratfordnz.co.nz; Prospero Pl; ⊗8.30am-5pm Mon-Fri, 10am-3pm Sat & Sun) also houses the **Percy Thomson Gallery** (✆06-765 0917; www.percythomsongallery.org.nz; ⊗10.30am-4pm Mon-Fri, 10.30am-3pm Sat & Sun), a community gallery (named after the former mayor) displaying eclectic local and touring art shows.

One kilometre south of Stratford on SH3, the **Taranaki Pioneer Village** (✆06-765 5399; www.pioneervillage.co.nz; SH3; adult/child/family $10/5/20; ⊗10am-4pm) is a 4-hectare outdoor museum that houses 40 historic buildings. It's very bygone-era and more than a little spooky.

Seemingly embalmed in calamine lotion, the pretty-in-pink **Stratford Top Town Holiday Park** (☎06-765 6440; www.stratford toptownholidaypark.co.nz; 10 Page St; sites/dm/cabins/units from $14/22/40/90; @⚲) is a trim caravan park offering one-room cabins, motel-style units and backpackers' bunks.

All stone-clad columns, jaunty roof angles, timber louvres and muted cave colours, flashy **Amity Court Motel** (☎06-765 4496; www.amitycourtmotel.co.nz; 35 Broadway N; d $120, apt $140-160; @⚲) is the new kid on the Stratford block, upping the town's accommodation standings 100%.

Across the street from Stratford i-SITE is the disarmingly retro, trapped-in-a-time-warp tearoom, **Casa Pequena** (☎06-765 6680; casa@xtra.co.nz; 280 Broadway; snacks $3-5, meals $12-28; ⚫6am-4pm Mon-Fri, 7am-1.30pm Sat), serving classics such as bangers-and-mash and hot beef-and-gravy sandwiches.

Surf Highway 45

Sweeping south from New Plymouth to Hawera, the 105km-long SH45 is known as Surf Hwy 45. There are plenty of black-sand beaches dotted along the route, but don't expect to see waves crashing ashore the whole way. The drive generally just undulates through farmland – be ready to swerve for random tractors and cows. Pick up the *Surf Highway 45* brochure at visitor centres.

OAKURA
POP 1220

From New Plymouth, the first cab off the rank is laid-back Oakura, 15km southwest on SH45. Its broad sweep of beach is hailed by waxheads for its right-hander breaks, but it's also great for families (take sandals – that black sand scorches feet). A surf shop on the main road, **Vertigo** (☎06-752 7363; www.vertigosurf.com; 2hr lessons $75; ⚫9am-5pm Mon-Fri, 10am-4pm Sat), runs surf lessons. See also Tarawave Surf School (p212).

⚐ Sleeping & Eating

TOP CHOICE **Ahu Ahu Beach Villas**
BOUTIQUE HOTEL **$$$**
(☎06-752 7370; www.ahu.co.nz; 341 Lower Ahu Ahu Rd; d from $210; ⚲) Pricey, but pretty amazing. Set on a knoll overlooking the wide ocean, these luxury, architect-designed villas are superbly eccentric, with huge recycled timbers, bottles cast into walls, lichen-covered French tile roofs and polished-concrete floors with inlaid paua. A new lodge addition sleeps four. Even rock stars stay here!

PARIHAKA

From the mid-1860s Parihaka, a small Maori settlement east of SH45 near Pungarehu, became the centre of a peaceful resistance movement, one that involved not only other Taranaki tribes, but Maori from around the country. Its leaders, Te Whiti-o-Rongomai and Tohu Kakahi, were of both Taranaki and Te Ati Awa descent.

After the Land Wars, confiscation of tribal lands was the central problem faced by Taranaki Maori, and under Te Whiti's leadership a new approach to this issue was developed: resisting European settlement through nonviolent methods.

When the government started surveying confiscated land on the Waimate plain in 1879, unarmed followers of Te Whiti, wearing the movement's iconic white feather in their hair and in good humour, obstructed development by ploughing troughs across roads, erecting random fences and pulling survey pegs. Many were arrested and held without trial on the South Island, but the protests continued and intensified. Finally, in November 1881 the government sent a force of over 1500 troops to Parihaka. Its inhabitants were arrested or driven away, and the village was later demolished. Te Whiti and Tohu were arrested and imprisoned until 1883. In their absence Parihaka was rebuilt and the ploughing campaigns continued into the 1890s.

In 2006 the NZ government issued a formal apology and financial compensation to the tribes affected by the invasion and confiscation of Parihaka lands.

Te Whiti's spirit lives on at Parihaka, with annual meetings of his descendants and a public music-and-arts Parihaka International Peace Festival held early each year. Parihaka is open to the public on the 18th and 19th of each month. For more info see www.parihaka.com.

Wave Haven
HOSTEL **$**

(☑06-752 7800; www.thewavehaven.co.nz; cnr Lower Ahu Ahu Rd & SH45; dm/s/d $25/50/60; @) A surfy backpackers close to the big breaks, this colonial charmer has a coffee machine, a large deck to chill out on, and surfboards and empty wine bottles strewn about the place.

Oakura Beach Holiday Park
HOLIDAY PARK **$**

(☑06-752 7861; www.oakurabeach.com; 2 Jans Tce; sites from $18, cabins $70-140; @☎) Squeezed between the cliffs and the sea, this classic beachside park caters best to caravans but has simple cabins and well-placed spots to pitch a tent (absolute beachfront!).

Oakura Beach Motel
MOTEL **$$**

(☑06-752 7680; www.oakurabeachmotel.co.nz; 53 Wairau Rd; d from $115; ☎) A very quiet, seven-unit motel set back from the main road, just three minutes' walk to the beach. It's a '70s number, but the Scottish owners keep things shipshape, and there are 300 DVDs to choose from!

Carriage Café
CAFE **$**

(1145 SH45; meals $4-14; ☺8am-4pm) Housed in a very slow-moving 1914 railway carriage set back from the main street, this is an unusual stop for good-value breakfast stacks, bacon-and-egg pies and cheese scones. Good coffee, too.

Snickerdoodle
BAKERY **$**

(1151 SH45; snacks $4-7; ☺7am-4pm Mon-Fri, 8.30am-4pm Sat & Sun) On the main road this tiny bakery bakes daily. Swing in for a chunky cheese scone, a chicken-and-apricot quiche, some delectable pumpkin bread or a coffee.

OAKURA TO OPUNAKE

From Oakura, SH45 veers inland, with detours to sundry beaches along the way. On the highway near Okato the buttermilk-coloured, 130-year-old **Stony River Hotel** (☑06-752 4253; www.stonyriverhotel.co.nz; 2502 SH45; s/d/tr incl breakfast $80/120/180, mains $10-28.; ☺dinner Wed-Sat) has simple country-style en suite rooms and a straight-up public bar.

Just after Warea is **Stent Rd**, a legendary shallow reef break suitable for experienced surfers (look for the painted-boulder sign: the street sign kept being stolen). Another famous spot is **Kumara Patch**, down Komene Rd west of Okato, which is a fast 150m left-hander.

Another coastward turn-off at **Pungarehu** leads 4km to **Cape Egmont Lighthouse**, a photogenic cast-iron lighthouse moved here from Mana Island near Wellington in 1881. Abel Tasman sighted this cape in 1642 and called it 'Nieuw Zeeland'. The road to Parihaka leads inland from this stretch of SH45.

OPUNAKE
POP 1500

A summer town and the surfie epicentre of the 'naki, Opunake has a sheltered family beach and plenty of challenging waves further out.

☆ Activities

Dreamtime Surf Shop
SURFING

(☑06-761 7570; cnr Tasman & Havelock Sts; surfboards/bodyboards/wetsuits per half-day $30/20/10; ☺9am-5pm; @) Dreamtime Surf Shop has internet access and surf-gear hire; hours can be patchy – call in advance.

⛏ Sleeping & Eating

Headlands
HOTEL **$$**

(☑06-761 8358; www.headlands.co.nz; 4 Havelock St; d $120-250) Just 100m back from the beach, Headlands is a new(ish) operation encompassing a mod, airy **bistro** (mains $10-35; ☺breakfast, lunch & dinner) and an upmarket, three-storey accommodation tower. The best rooms snare brilliant sunsets. B&B and DB&B packages available.

Opunake Motel & Backpackers
MOTEL, HOSTEL **$**

(☑06-761 8330; www.opunakemotel.co.nz; 36 Heaphy Rd; dm $30, d $100-120) Opunake Motel & Backpackers is much more low-key, with old-style motels and a funky dorm lodge (a triumph in genuine retro) on the edge of some sleepy fields.

Opunake Beach Holiday Park
HOLIDAY PARK **$**

(☑0800 758 009, 06-761 7525; www.opunakebeachnz.co.nz; Beach Rd; sites/cabins/cottages $18/68/98; @☎) Opunake Beach Holiday Park is a mellow spot right on the surf beach. The laugh-a-minute host will direct you to your grassy site, the big camp kitchen and the cavernous amenities block.

TOP CHOICE Sugar Juice Café
CAFE **$$**

(42 Tasman St; snacks $4-10, mains $25-29; ☺8.30am-4pm Tue, 8.30am-late Wed-Sun) Sugar Juice Café has the best food on SH45. It's buzzy and brimming with delicious, filling things

SNELLY!

Opunake isn't just about the surf – it's also the birthplace of iconic middle-distance runner Peter Snell (b 1938), who showed his rivals a clean set of heels at the 1960 Rome and 1964 Tokyo Olympics. Old Snelly won the 800m gold in Italy, then followed up with 800m and 1500m golds in Japan. Legend! Check out his funky running statue outside the library.

(try the basil-crusted snapper or cranberry lamb shanks). Terrific coffee, salads, wraps, tarts, cakes and big brekkies too – don't pass it by. Open Mondays too in summer.

ℹ Information

Opunake Library (☑0800 111 323, 06-761 8663; opunakel@stdc.govt.nz; Tasman St; ☺8.30am-5pm Mon-Fri, 9.30am-1pm Sat; @) The Opunake Library doubles as the local visitor information centre and has internet access.

HAWERA
POP 11,000

Don't expect much urban virtue from agricultural Hawera, the largest town in South Taranaki. Still, it's a good pit stop for supplies, to stretch your legs, or to bed down for a night. And don't miss Elvis!

◉ Sights & Activities

TOP CHOICE **KD's Elvis Presley Museum**　MUSEUM
(www.elvismuseum.co.nz; 51 Argyle St; admission by donation; ☺by appointment only) Elvis lives! At least he does at Kevin D Wasley's astonishing museum, which houses over 10,000 of the King's records and a mind-blowing collection of Elvis memorabilia collected over 50 years. 'Passion is an understatement', says KD. Just don't ask him about the chubby Vegas-era Elvis: his focus is squarely on the rock 'n' roll King from the '50s and '60s.

Hawera Water Tower　TOWER, LOOKOUT
(vistorinfo@stdc.govt.nz; 55 High St; adult/child/family $2.50/1/6; ☺10am-2pm) The austere Hawera Water Tower beside the i-SITE is one of the coolest things in Hawera. Grab the key from the i-SITE, ascend the 215 steps, then scan the horizon for signs of life (you can see the coast and Mt Taranaki on a clear day).

Tawhiti Museum　MUSEUM
(www.tawhitimuseum.co.nz; 401 Ohangai Rd; adult/child $10/3; ☺10am-4pm Fri-Mon Feb-Apr & Sep-Dec, Sun only Jun-Aug, daily Jan) The excellent Tawhiti Museum houses a collection of exhibits, dioramas and creepily lifelike human figures modelled on people from the region. A large collection of tractors pays homage to rural heritage; there's also a bush railway and 'Traders & Whalers' boat ride here (extra charges for both). It's near the corner of Tawhiti Rd, 4km north of town.

🛏 Sleeping & Eating

Hawera Central Motor Lodge　MOTEL $$
(☑06-278 8831; www.haweracentralmotorlodge.co.nz; 53 Princes St; d $135-170; ☏) The pick of the town's motels (better than any of those along South Rd), the shiny Hawera Central does things with style: grey-and-eucalypt colour scheme, frameless-glass showers, big flat-screen TVs, good security, DVD players, free movie library... Nice one!

Wheatly Downs Farmstay　FARMSTAY $
(☑06-278 6523; www.mttaranaki.co.nz; 484 Ararata Rd; sites from $20, dm/s & tw $30/70, d with/without bathroom $115/70; @) Set in a rural idyll, this heritage building is a classic, with its clunky wooden floors and no-nonsense fittings. Host Gary is an affable bloke, and might show you his special pigs. To get there, head past the turn-off to Tawhiti Museum and continue on Ararata Rd for 5.5km. Pick-ups by arrangement.

Indian Zaika　INDIAN $$
(☑06-278 3198; 91 Princes St; mains $16-20; ☺lunch Tue-Sat, dinner daily; ☑) For a fine lunch or dinner, try this spicy-smelling, black-and-white diner, serving decent curries in upbeat surrounds. The $10 takeaway lunches are a steal.

ℹ Information

South Taranaki i-SITE (☑06-278 8599; www.southtaranaki.com; 55 High St; ☺9.30am-4pm Mon-Fri, 10am-3pm Sat & Sun) The South Taranaki low-down. Reduced winter hours.

Whanganui
POP 39,700

With rafts of casual Huck Finn sensibility, Whanganui is a raggedy historic town on the banks of the wide Whanganui River. The local arts community is thriving: old port buildings are being turned into glass-art studios, and the town centre has been rejuvenated – there are few more appealing

WHANGANUI OR WANGANUI?

Yeah, we know, it's confusing. Is there an 'h' or isn't there? Either way, the pronunciation is identical: 'wan-ga', not (as in the rest of the country) 'fan-ga'.

Everything was originally spelled Wanganui, because in the local dialect *whanga* (harbour) is pronounced 'wan-ga'. However, in 1991 the New Zealand Geographic Board officially adopted the correct Maori spelling (with an 'h') for the Whanganui River and Whanganui National Park. This was a culturally deferential decision: the Pakeha-dominated town and region retained the old spelling, while the river area – Maori territory – adopted the new.

In 2009 the Board assented that the town and region should also adopt the 'h'. This caused much community consternation, opinions on the decision split almost evenly (outspoken Mayor Michael Laws was particularly anti-'h'). Ultimately, NZ Minister for Land Information Maurice Williamson decreed that either spelling was acceptable, and that adopting the querulous 'h' is up to individual businesses or entities. A good old Kiwi compromise! Whanderful...

places to while away a sunny afternoon than beneath Victoria Ave's leafy canopy.

History

Maori settlement at Whanganui dates from around 1100. The first European on the river was Andrew Powers in 1831, but Whanganui's European settlement didn't take off until 1840 when the New Zealand Co could no longer satisfy Wellington's land demands – settlers moved here instead.

When the Maori understood that the gifts the Pakeha settlers had given them were in permanent exchange for their land, they were understandably irate, and seven years of conflict ensued. Thousands of government troops occupied the Rutland Stockade in Queens Park. Ultimately, the struggle was settled by arbitration; during the Taranaki Land Wars the Whanganui Maoris assisted the Pakeha.

◉ Sights & Activities

Whanganui Regional Museum MUSEUM
(www.wrm.org.nz; Watt St, Queens Park; adult/child $8.50/free; ⊙10am-4.30pm) The Whanganui Regional Museum is one of NZ's better natural-history museums. Maori exhibits include the carved Te Mata o Houroa war canoe and some vicious-looking *mere* (greenstone clubs). The colonial and wildlife installations are first rate, and there's plenty of button-pushing and drawer-opening to keep the kids engaged.

FREE **Sarjeant Gallery** GALLERY
(www.sarjeant.org.nz; Queens Park; ⊙10.30am-4.30pm) The elegant neoclassical Sarjeant Gallery covers the bases from historic to contemporary with its extensive permanent art exhibition and frequent special exhibits (including glass from the annual Wanganui Festival of Glass). What a lovely place!

FREE **Whanganui Riverboat Centre** MUSEUM
(www.riverboats.co.nz; 1a Taupo Quay; ⊙10am-4pm) The historical displays are interesting, but everyone's here for the *Waimarie,* the last of the Whanganui River paddle steamers. In 1900 she was shipped from England and paddled the Whanganui until she sank ingloriously at her mooring in 1952. Submerged for 41 years, she was finally raised, restored, then relaunched on the first day of the 21st century. She now offers two-hour tours along the Whanganui.

FREE **Chronicle Glass Studio** GALLERY
(☎06-347 1921; www.chronicleglass.co.nz; 2 Rutland St; ⊙9am-5pm Mon-Fri, 10am-3pm Sat & Sun) The pick of Whanganui's many glass studios is the Chronicle Glass Studio where you can watch glass-blowers working, check out the gallery, take a weekend glass-blowing course ($375) or a one-hour 'Make a Paperweight' lesson ($100), or just hang out and warm up on a chilly afternoon.

Durie Hill Elevator TOWER
(Anzac Pde; adult/child one-way $2/1; ⊙8am-6pm Mon-Fri, 10am-5pm Sat & Sun) Across City Bridge from downtown Whanganui, this elevator was built with grand visions for Durie Hill's residential future. A tunnel burrows 213m into the hillside, from where the

Whanganui

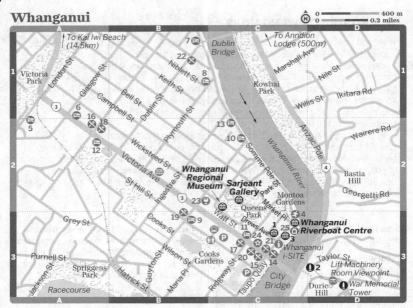

elevator rattles 65.8m to the top. At the summit you can climb the 176 steps of the **War Memorial Tower** and scan the horizon for Mt Taranaki and Mt Ruapehu.

FREE **Wanganui Community Arts Centre**   GALLERY
(www.communityartscentre.org.nz; 19 Taupo Quay; ☺10am-4pm Mon-Fri, 9am-4pm Sat, 1-4pm Sun) By the river's edge is the Wanganui Community Arts Centre, which exhibits mostly local artists and musters up a decidedly South Pacific vibe with glass, ceramics, jewellery, photography and painting.

Putiki Church   CHURCH
(20 Anaua St; per person $2 plus deposit $20; ☺service 9am Sun) Across the City Bridge from town and 1km towards the sea is the Putiki Church, aka St Paul's Memorial Church. It's unremarkable externally but, just like the faithful pew-fillers, it's what's inside that counts: the interior is magnificent, completely covered in Maori carvings and *tukutuku* (wall panels). Show up for Sunday service, or borrow a key from the i-SITE.

Kai Iwi Beach   BEACH
Kai Iwi Beach is a wild ocean frontier, strewn with black sand and masses of bro-

ken driftwood. To get here follow Great North Rd 4km north of town, then turn left onto Rapanui Rd and head seawards for 10km.

Splash Centre   SWIMMING
(www.splashcentre.co.nz; Springvale Park, London St; adult/child $4.50/3, waterslide $3; ☺6am-8pm Mon-Fri, 8am-6pm Sat & Sun) If the sea is angry, try the Splash Centre for a safe swim.

☞ Tours

See also Whanghanui National Park for Whanganui River canoe, kayak and jetboat tours.

Waimarie Paddle-Steamer Tours   BOAT
(☎06-347 1863, 0800 783 2637; www.river boats.co.nz; 1a Taupo Quay; adult/child/family $39/15/89; ☺tours 11.30pm daily) Take a two-hour trip up ol' man Whanganui on the historic *Waimarie,* the last of the river paddle steamers.

Scenic Flights   SCENIC FLIGHTS
(☎06-345 0914; www.wanganuiaeroclub.co.nz; Whanganui Airport, Airport Rd; flights from $50) Mile-high fixed-wing panoramas above Whanganui, Mt Ruapehu and Whanganui National Park.

Whanganui

🎉 Festivals & Events

NZ Masters Games   SPORTS
(www.nzmg.com) The country's biggest multi-sport event (67 sports!), held in early February every odd-numbered year.

Wanganui Festival of Glass   ARTS
(www.wanganuiglass.co.nz) Classy glass fest in September. Plenty of open studios, demonstrations and workshops.

Wanganui Literary Festival   CULTURAL
(www.writersfest.co.nz) Thoughts, words, and thoughts about words every September.

Cemetery Circuit Motorcycle Race   SPORTS
(www.cemeterycircuit.co.nz) Pandemonic Boxing Day motorcycle race around Whanganui's city streets. The southern hemisphere's version of the Isle of Man TT?

🛏 Sleeping

TOP CHOICE Anndion Lodge   HOSTEL $
(☑06-343 3593, 0800 343 056; www.anndion lodge.co.nz; 143 Anzac Pde; s/d/f/ste from $75/88/105/130; @🛜⛵) Hell-bent on constantly improving and expanding their fabulous hyper-hostel, hosts Ann and Dion (Anndion, get it?) go to enormous lengths to

make things homey: stereo systems, big TVs, spa, swimming pool, barbecue area, restaurant, bar, courtesy van etc. 'No is not in our vocabulary', says super-helpful Ann.

Aotea Motor Lodge   MOTEL $$
(☑06-345 0303; www.aoteamotorlodge.co.nz; 390 Victoria Ave; d/apt from $150/190; 🛜) It gladdens the heart to see a job done well, and the owners of one of Whanganui's newest motels have done just that. On the upper reaches of Victoria Ave, this flashy, two-storey contemporary motel features roomy suites, lavish linen, dark-timber furniture and plenty of marble and stone – classy stuff.

Tamara Backpackers Lodge   HOSTEL $
(☑06-347 6300; www.tamaralodge.com; 24 Somme Pde; dm $31, s from $54, d & tw with/without bathroom $86/72; @) Tamara is a photogenic, mazelike two-storey heritage house with a wide balcony, lofty ceilings (people weren't taller in 1904 were they?), kitchen, TV lounge, free bikes and a leafy, hammock-hung back garden. Ask for one of the beaut doubles overlooking the river.

Grand Hotel   HOTEL $$
(☑0800 843 472, 06-345 0955; www.thegrand hotel.co.nz; cnr St Hill & Guyton Sts; s/d/ste from

$79/99/120; 🖥) If you can't face another soulless motel room, rooms at this stately old-school Whanganui survivor (built 1927) have a bit more personality. Singles and doubles are basic but good value; suites are spacious. The Grand Irish Pub and a restaurant are downstairs.

Braemar House YHA
HOSTEL $

(✆06-348 2301; www.braemarhouse.co.nz; 2 Plymouth St; dm/d & tw $29/70, guesthouse incl breakfast s/d $100/130; @🖥) Riverside Braemar brings together an 1895 Victorian B&B guesthouse and a reliable YHA backpackers. Centrally heated guesthouse rooms are floral and fancy; airy dorms conjure up a bit more fun out the back.

Kembali B&B
B&B $$

(✆06-347 1727; www.bnb.co.nz/kembali.html; 26 Taranaki St, St Johns Hill; s/d incl breakfast from $80/110) Up on leafy St Johns Hill on the way to Taranaki, this home-spun B&B has two private upstairs guest rooms sleeping four, available on an exclusive-use basis. It's a sedate place overlooking some wetlands, all achirp with tuis, pukekos and native whistling frogs.

151 on London Motel
MOTEL $$

(✆06-345 8668; www.151onlondon.co.nz; 151 London St; d & ste $110-280; 🖥) Since opening in 2009, this snappy-looking spaceship of a motel has won plenty of fans with its architectural angles, quality carpets and linen, natty lime, silver and black colour scheme and big TVs. At the top of the price tree are some excellent upstairs/downstairs apartment-style units: about as ritzy as Whanganui accommodation gets.

Siena Motor Lodge
MOTEL $$

(✆06-345 9009, 0800 888 802; www.siena.co.nz; 335 Victoria Ave; d $130-150; 🖥) Aiming for Tuscany but hitting Taranaki, the compact rooms here are five star and spotless. Business travellers enjoy double glazing, a DVD library, heated towel rails, coffee plungers and real coffee.

Whanganui River Top 10
Holiday Park
HOLIDAY PARK $

(✆06-343 8402, 0800 272 664; www.wrivertop10.co.nz; 460 Somme Pde; sites/cabins/units from $21/72/135; @🖥🏊) This tidy Top 10 park sits on the Whanganui's west bank 6km north of Dublin Bridge. Facilities (including pool and jumping pillow) are prodigious. Kayak hire also available: the owners shuttle you up river

then you paddle back to camp. Self-catering or dining in town is your best bet food-wise.

Avro Motel & Caravan Park
HOLIDAY PARK $

(✆0800 367 287, 06-345 5279; www.wanganui accommodation.co.nz; 36 Alma Rd; sites/units from $20/85; 🖥🏊) Avro's yellow biplane heralds the closest camping to the city centre, 1.5km west. Both powered and unpowered sites have their own freestanding bathrooms, and the camp kitchen is a wee winner. Standard motel units also available.

Riverview Motel
MOTEL $$

(✆06-345 2888, 0800 102 001; www.wanganui motels.co.nz; 14 Somme Pde; d $98-150; 🖥) Take your pick from one of 15 '80s-style kitchenette units in the main block or the five spiffy spa suites out the back. Nothing too flash (and the river views are mostly glimpses), but a decent central option with a charming Irish host.

Astral Motel
MOTEL $$

(✆06-347 9063, 0800 509 063; www.astralmotel. co.nz; 46 Somme Pde; s/d/f from $85/95/110; 🏊) Astrally aligned with the very terrestrial Dublin Bridge nearby, rooms here are a bit dated and a tad noisy but are well serviced, roomy and good bang for your buck. There's also 24-hour check-in if you're rolling in off the midnight highway.

Rutland Arms Inn
HOTEL $$

(✆06-347 7677, 0800 788 5263; www.rutlandarms. co.nz; 48 Ridgway St; ste $140-165; 🖥) Carving off a slice of the 'upmarket heritage' pie, this restored 1849 building has an old-fashioned pub downstairs with colonial-style accommodation above. Rooms have TV, phone, flowery wall friezes, double glazing and spine-straightening beds. English hunting scenes adorn the bar's beer taps.

✖ Eating

Cracked Pepper
CAFE $

(21 Victoria Ave; mains $5-18; ⊘7am-4.30pm; 🅿) Hungry? Hungover? Hedonistic? Head straight for Cracked Pepper, the best cafe in Whanganui serving (arguably) the best eggs Benedict in NZ. Staff are spot-on, and the 1890s building is a beauty (formerly a Japanese tearoom, a menswear store and a confectioner). Great coffee and plenty of vegetarian and gluten-free options.

Stellar
CAFE, BAR $$

(www.stellarwanganui.co.nz; 2 Victoria Ave; mains $15-35; ⊘3pm-late Mon, 9am-late Tue-Sun; 🖥)

Stellar lives up to its name – a cavernous bar-cum-restaurant with a convivial family atmosphere, it's the town's pride and joy. Reclining contentedly on leather couches, locals and tourists alike sip premium lagers and feast on bar morsels, gourmet pizzas and surf 'n' turf fare. Frequent bands, DJs and quiz nights to boot.

Rapido Espresso House   CAFE $
(rapidoltd@hotmail.com; 71 Liverpool St; snacks $3-6; ⊙7.30am-6pm Mon-Fri, 9am-3pm Sat) If you're hungry, don't expect more than a wedge of cake, a scone or some sushi at this raffish, royal blue cafe – what you're here for is the coffee. Organic and fair-trade all the way, the brew here is the best in town.

Red Eye Café   CAFE $
(96 Guyton St; meals $6-18; ⊙6.30am-3.30pm Mon-Fri, 7am-10.30pm Sat; ✍) With inexplicable familiarity (maybe it's the friendly staff), this bohemian urban cafe has colourful local art, tasty light snacks (bagels, nachos, salads) as well as more substantial meals (curries, organic chicken sandwiches). Good coffee, too.

Orange   CAFE $
(51 Victoria Ave; meals $9-22; ⊙7.30am-5pm Mon-Fri, 9am-5pm Sat & Sun; ☎) Inside a gorgeous old Whanganui red-brick building, Orange is a babbling espresso bar serving gourmet burgers, big breakfasts, muffins, cakes and sandwiches (try the BLT). The outdoor tables go berserk during summer.

Ceramic   CAFE, LOUNGE $$
(51 Victoria Ave; mains $9-22; ⊙3pm-late Tue-Sat; ☎) In a split-business arrangement with adjacent Orange, Ceramic takes over for the dinner shift, serving upmarket cafe food (killer quesadillas) in a low-lit, rust-coloured interior. Occasional DJs ooze tunes across the tables to cocktail-sipping seducers.

Yellow House Café   CAFE $
(cnr Pitt & Dublin Sts; meals $6-20; ⊙8am-4pm Tue-Sun; ✍) Take a walk away from the main drag for funky tunes, buttermilk pancakes, local art, great omelettes and courtyard tables beneath a chunky-trunk cherry blossom tree. Actually, it's more of a taupe colour...

Spice Guru   INDIAN $$
(✆06-348 4851; 23 Victoria Ave; mains $17-23; ⊙lunch Mon-Sat, dinner daily; ✍) There are a few Indian joints in the River City (an af-finity with the Ganges, perhaps?), but the Guri takes the cake for its charismatic black-and-chocolate coloured interior, attentive service and flavoursome dishes (the chicken tikka masala is great). Plenty of vego options.

Al Ponte   ITALIAN $$
(✆06-345 9955; 49 Taupo Quay; mains $18-32; ⊙dinner Tue-Sun; ☎) Al Ponte's moody riverside building has been a merchant store and a brothel, but today it's a time-and-space vortex delivering you straight to Roma. There's plenty of seafood for the *poisson*-impassioned, plus zingy pizzas (the Salciccia is a vego delight: tomato, mozzarella, zucchini, artichoke hearts and black olives); or dive into a classic *penne alla putanesca*.

New World   SUPERMARKET
(www.newworld.co.nz; 374 Victoria Ave; ⊙7am-9pm) Your best self-catering option.

🍷 Drinking
See also Rutland Arms Inn (p228), Stellar (p228) and Ceramic (p229).

Grand Irish Pub   IRISH PUB
(www.thegrandhotel.co.nz; cnr St Hill & Guyton Sts; ⊙11am-late) Siphoning into NZ's insatiable (and, it has to be said, annoying) passion for Irish pubs, the Grand Hotel's version is as good a spot as any to elbow down a few pints of Guinness on a misty river afternoon. Good pub meals too.

Spirit'd   BAR
(75 Guyton St; ⊙10am-late) Pool tables, Jack Daniels, Metallica on the jukebox and local young bucks trying to out-strut each other – just like 1989 minus the cigarettes.

☆ Entertainment
Embassy 3 Cinemas   CINEMA
(www.embassy3.co.nz; 34 Victoria Ave; tickets adult/child $12.50/8.50, Tue tickets $8; ⊙11am-midnight) Nightly new-release blockbusters selling out faster than you can say 'bored Whanganui teenagers'.

🛍 Shopping
River Traders Market   FARMERS MARKET
(www.therivertraders.co.nz; Taupo Quay; ⊙9am-1pm Sat) The Saturday-morning River Traders Market, next to the Riverboat Centre, is crammed with local crafts and organic produce.

ⓘ Information

Post Office (119 Victoria Ave)
Whanganui Hospital (☎06-348 1234; www.
wdhb.org.nz; 100 Heads Rd; ⏰24hr) Accident
and emergency.
Whanganui i-SITE (☎0800 926 426, 06-349
0508; www.wanganui.com; 31 Taupo Quay;
⏰8.30am-5pm Mon-Fri, 9am-3pm Sat & Sun;
@🤍) Tourist and DOC information in an impressive renovated riverside building (check out
the old floorboards!). Internet access available.

ⓘ Getting There & Away

Air

Whanganui Airport (WAG; ☎06-348 0536;
www.wanganuiairport.co.nz) is 4km south of
town, across the river towards the sea.
  Air New Zealand (☎06-348 3500, 0800 737
000; www.airnewzealand.co.nz; 133 Victoria
Ave; ⏰9am-5pm Mon-Fri) has daily direct flights
to/from Auckland and Wellington, with onward
connections.

Bus

InterCity (☎09-583 5780; www.intercity.co.nz)
buses operate from the **Whanganui Travel
Centre** (☎06-345 7100; www.tranzit.co.nz; 160
Ridgway St; ⏰8.15am-5.15pm Mon-Fri). Some
destinations:

DESTINATION	PRICE	DURATION	FREQUENCY
Auckland	$83	8hr	5 daily
New Plymouth	$32	2½hr	2 daily
Palmerston North	$22	1½hr	3 daily
Taumarunui	$48	2¾hr	1 daily
Wellington	$42	4hr	3 daily

Naked Bus (☎0900 625 33; www.nakedbus.
co.nz) departs from Whanganui i-SITE to most
North Island centres, including the following:

DESTINATION	PRICE	DURATION	FREQUENCY
Auckland	$40	9¼hr	1 daily
Hamilton	$32	7hr	1 daily
New Plymouth	$18	2½hr	1 daily
Palmerston North	$12	1hr	1 daily
Wellington	$23	4hr	1 daily

ⓘ Getting Around

Bicycle

Bike Shed (☎06-345 5500; www.bikeshed.
co.nz; cnr Ridgway & St Hill Sts; ⏰8am-5.30pm
Mon-Fri, 9am-2pm Sat) Hires out bikes from
$35 per day, including helmet and lock.

Bus

Tranzit City Link (☎0508 800 800;
www.horizons.govt.nz; tickets adult/child
$2.50/1.50; ⏰7am-6pm Mon-Fri, 10.30am-
5.30pm Sat) Operates four looped local bus
routes departing from the Maria Pl bus stop,
including routes 5 and 6 past the Whanganui
River Top 10 Holiday Park in Aramoho.

Taxi

Rivercity Cabs
(☎06-345 3333, 0800 345 3333)
Wanganui Taxis
(☎06-343 5555, 0800 343 5555)

Whanganui National Park

The Whanganui River – the lifeblood of
Whanganui National Park – curls 329km
from its source on Mt Tongariro to the Tasman Sea. It's the longest navigable river in
NZ, a fact that's been shaping its destiny for
centuries. The river today conveys canoes,
kayaks and jetboats, its waters shifting from
deep mirror greens in summer to turbulent
winter browns.

The native bush here is thick podocarp
broad-leaved forest interspersed with ferns.
Occasionally you'll see poplar and other introduced trees along the river, remnants of
long-vanished settlements. Traces of Maori
settlements also crop up here, with old *pa*
(fortified village) and *kainga* (village) sites,
and Hauhau *niu* (war and peace) poles at
the convergence of the Whanganui and
Ohura Rivers at Maraekowhai.

The impossibly scenic Whanganui River
Rd, a partially unsealed river-hugging road
from Whanganui to Pipiriki, makes a fabulous alternative to the faster but less magical SH4.

History

In Maori legend the Whanganui River was
formed when Mt Taranaki, after brawl-
ing with Mt Tongariro over the lovely Mt
Pihanga, fled the central North Island for
the sea, leaving a long gouge behind him.
He turned west at the coast, finally stopping at his current address. Mt Tongariro
sent cool water to heal the gouge – thus the
Whanganui River was born.

Kupe, the great Polynesian explorer, is
believed to have travelled 20km up the
Whanganui around AD 800; Maori lived
here by 1100. By the time Europeans put
down roots in the late 1830s, Maori settle-

ments lined the river valley. Missionaries sailed upstream and their settlements – at Hiruharama, Ranana, Koriniti and Atene – have survived to this day.

Steamers first tackled the river in the mid-1860s, a dangerous time for Pakeha. Aligned with Taranaki Maoris, some river tribes joined the Hauhau Rebellion – a Maori movement seeking to expel settlers.

In 1886 a Whanganui company established the first commercial steamer transport service. Others soon followed, utilising the river between Whanganui and Taumarunui. Supplying river communities and linking the sea with the interior, the steamers' importance grew, particularly after 1903 when the Auckland railway reached Taumarunui from the north.

New Zealand's contemporary tourism leviathan was seeded here. Internationally advertised trips on the 'Rhine of Maoriland' became so popular that by 1905, 12,000 tourists a year were making the trip upriver from Whanganui to Pipiriki or downriver from Taumarunui. The engineering feats and skippering ability required on the river became legendary.

From 1918 land upstream of Pipiriki was granted to returning WWI soldiers. Farming here was a major challenge, with many families struggling for years to make the rugged land productive. Only a few endured into the early 1940s.

The completion of the railway from Auckland to Wellington and the improving roads ultimately signed river transport's death warrant; 1959 saw the last commercial riverboat voyage. Today, just one old-fleet vessel cruises the river – the *Waimarie*.

Sights

Whanganui River Road

The scenery along the Whanganui River Rd en route to Pipiriki is camera conducive – stark, wet mountain slopes plunge into lazy jade stretches of the Whanganui River. A French Catholic mission led by Suzanne Aubert established the Daughters of Our Lady of Compassion in Jerusalem in 1892. Around a corner in the road, the picture-perfect, red-and-mustard spire of **St Joseph's Church** stands tall on a spur of land above a deep river bend.

Whanganui National Park Area

Whanganui National Park Area

Sights
1	Aramoana Hill	B4
2	Bridge to Nowhere	A1
3	Kawana Flour Mill	B3
4	Operiki Pa	B3
5	St Joseph's Church	B3

Sleeping
6	Bridge to Nowhere Lodge	A2
7	Downes Hut	B3
8	Flying Fox	B3
9	Kohu Cottage	B3
10	Koriniti Marae	B3
11	Ngapurua Hut	A2
12	Omaru Hut	A2
13	Operiki Farmstay	B3
14	Pouri Hut	A2
15	Puketotara Hut	A2
16	Rivertime Lodge	B4
	St Joseph's Church	(see 5)
17	Tieke Kainga	B2
18	Whakahoro Hut	B1

WHANGANUI RIVER *PETER GORDON*

Whanganui has a good black-sand surfing beach out at Castlecliff where I'm from, and a famous 'upside-down' river (as Dad calls it) where all the silt floats on the top – muddy coloured, but still gorgeous. The river is truly breathtaking and also happens to be the longest navigable river in the country. Join a guided canoe or boat trip down the river, over rapids that are challenging but not deathly, through spectacular broody lush bush and visit historical places like Jerusalem – where one of our more famous poets James K Baxter lived for a while.

Peter Gordon, chef, food writer & restaurateur

Other sights along the road include the restored 1854 **Kawana Flour Mill** near Matahiwi, **Operiki Pa** and other *pa* sites, and **Aramoana Hill**, near the southern end of the road, from where there's a panoramic view. The Maori villages of **Atene**, **Koriniti**, **Ranana** and **Hiruharama** crop up along the way – ask a local before you go sniffing around. You can wander around Koriniti Marae (p235; between the road and the river: look for the signs) unless there's a *marae* function happening. The *marae* also offers accommodation for groups. Note that the River Rd is unsealed between Ranana and 4km south of Pipiriki, although road crews are making steady progress in sealing the entire route.

Pipiriki is beside the river at the north end of Whanganui River Rd. It's a rainy river town without much going on (no shops or petrol), but was once a humming holiday hot spot serviced by river steamers and paddleboats. Seemingly cursed, the old Pipiriki Hotel, formerly a glamorous resort full of international tourists, burned to the ground twice. Recent attempts to rebuild it have stalled due to funding issues; it's been vandalised and stripped of anything of value, leaving a hollow brick husk riddled with potential. Pipiriki is the end point for canoe trips coming down the river and the launching pad for jetboat rides.

Standing in mute testimony to the optimism of the early settlers is the **Bridge to Nowhere**, built in 1936. The walking track from Mangapurua Landing (upstream from Pipiriki, accessible by jetboat) to the lonesome bridge was part of a long-lost 4.5m-wide roadway from Raetihi to the river.

🏃 Activities
Canoeing & Kayaking
The most popular stretch of river for canoeing and kayaking is downstream from Taumarunui to Pipiriki. This has been added to the NZ Great Walks system and is called the 'Whanganui Journey' (despite the fact that there's more sitting down than walking involved). It's a Grade II river – easy enough for the inexperienced, with enough moiling rapids to keep things interesting.

Great Walk charges apply from 1 October to 30 April for the use of huts and campsites for overnight stays between Taumarunui and Pipiriki (adults $10 to $31, kids free). Outside the main season you'll only need a **Backcountry Hut Pass** (1yr per adult/child $122/61, 6 months $92/46), or you can pay on a night-by-night basis (adults $5 to $15, kids free). If you're just paddling and not sleeping anywhere, there's no charge. Note that during summer, hut wardens and conservation officers patrol the river.

All passes and tickets can be purchased directly on the DOC website (www.doc.govt.nz), or through the DOC Whakapapa visitor centre, the Taumarunui, Ohakune or Whanganui i-SITEs, and some local canoe-hire/trip operators (a booking fee may be charged for this service).

Taumarunui to Pipiriki is a five-day/four-night trip, Ohinepane to Pipiriki is a four-day/three-night trip, and Whakahoro to Pipiriki is a three-day/two-night trip. Taumarunui to Whakahoro is a popular overnight trip, especially for weekenders, or you can do a one-day trip from Taumarunui to Ohinepane or Ohinepane to Whakahoro. From Whakahoro to Pipiriki, 88km downstream, there's no road access so you're wed to the river for a few days; this is the trip everyone clamours to do. Most canoeists stop at Pipiriki.

The season for canoe trips is usually from September to Easter. Up to 5000 people make the river trip each year, mostly between Christmas and the end of January. During winter the river is almost deserted – the winter currents run swift and deep, as cold weather and short days deter potential paddlers.

To hire a two-person Canadian canoe for one/three/five days costs around $80/220/300 per person not including transport (around $50 per person). A single-person kayak costs about $60 per day. Operators provide you with everything you need, including life jackets, waterproof drums (essential if you go bottom-up), and sometimes cover the mandatory DOC camping/hut fees.

GUIDED TRIPS

You can also take guided canoe or kayak trips – prices start at around $300/800 per person for a two-/five-day guided trip.

Operators from include the following; see also Jetboating for operators who also run canoe trips:

Blazing Paddles CANOEING
(☑07-895 5261, 0800 252 946; www.blazing paddles.co.nz)

Whanganui River Canoes CANOEING
(☑06-385 4176, 0800 408 888; www.whanganui rivercanoes.co.nz)

Wades Landing Outdoors CANOEING
(☑07-895 5995, 0800 226 631; www.whanganui. co.nz)

Canoe Safaris CANOEING
(☑0800 272 335, 06-385.9237; www.canoesafaris. co.nz)

Taumarunui Canoe Hire CANOEING
(☑07-895 7483, 0800 226 6348; www.taumarunui canoehire.co.nz)

Awa Tours CANOEING
(☑06-385 8012; www.awatours.co.nz)

Whanganui Kayak Hire KAYAKING
(☑021 133 6938; www.kayakhire.co.nz)

Yeti Tours CANOEING
(☑06-385 8197, 0800 322 388; www.canoe.co.nz)

Jetboating

Hold onto your hats – jetboat trips give you the chance to see parts of the river that would otherwise take you days to paddle through. Jetboats depart from Pipiriki and Whanganui; four-hour tours start at around $110 per person. The following operators can also provide transport to the river ends of the Matemateaonga and Mangapurua Tracks:

Spirit of the River Jet JETBOATING
(☑06-342 5572, 0800 538 8687; www.spiritof theriverjet.co.nz)

Bridge to Nowhere Tours JETBOATING, CANOEING
(☑0800 480 308; www.bridgetonowhere.co.nz) Canoe trips also available.

Whanganui River Adventures JETBOATING, CANOEING
(☑0800 862 743; www.whanganuiriveradventures. co.nz) Canoe trips also available.

Whanganui Scenic Experience Jet JETBOATING, CANOEING
(☑06-342 5599, 0800 945 335; www.whanganui scenicjet.com) Canoe trips also available.

Tramping
BRIDGE TO NOWHERE TRACK

The most popular track in Whanganui National Park is the 40-minute walk from Mangapurua Landing to the Bridge to Nowhere, 30km upstream from Pipiriki by jetboat. Contact jetboat operators for transport (around $100 per person one way).

TRACKS FROM ATENE

At Atene, on the Whanganui River Rd about 22km north of the SH4 junction, you can tackle the short **Atene Viewpoint Walk**, about a one-hour ascent (quicker on the way down). The track travels through native bush and farmland along a 1959 roadway built by the former Ministry of Works and Development during investigations for a Whanganui River hydro-electric scheme (a dam was proposed at Atene that would have flooded the river valley almost as far as Taumarunui). From the ridge-top there are great views across the national park.

From the Viewpoint Walk you can continue along the circular 18km **Atene Skyline Track**. The track takes six to eight hours, showcasing native forest, sandstone bluffs and the **Taumata Trig** (523m), with its broad views as far as Mt Ruapehu, Mt Taranaki and the Tasman Sea. The track

---

ℹ️ REMOTE TRACK ACCESS

The Matemateaonga and Mangapurua/Kaiwhakauka Tracks are brilliant longer tramps (DOC booklets \$1, or see www.doc.govt.nz for up-to-date track info). Both are one-way tracks beginning (or ending) at remote spots on the river, so you have to organise jetboat transport to or from the river trailheads – ask any jetboat operator. Between Pipiriki and the Matemateaonga Track is around \$50 per person; for the Mangapurua Track it's around \$100.

---

ends back on the Whanganui River Rd, 2km downstream from the starting point.

MATEMATEAONGA TRACK

Three to four days from end to end, the 42km Matemateaonga Track gets kudos as one of NZ's best walks. Probably due to its remoteness, it doesn't attract the hordes of trampers that amass on NZ's more famous tracks. Penetrating deep into wild bush and hill country, it traces an old Maori track and a disused settlers' dray road between the Whanganui and Taranaki regions. It follows the crest of the Matemateaonga Range along the route of the Whakaihuwaka Rd, started in 1911 to create a more direct link from Stratford to the railway at Raetihi. WWI interrupted planning and the road was never finished.

On a clear day, a 1½-hour side trip to the top of Mt Humphries (730m) rewards you with sigh-inducing views all the way to Mt Taranaki and the volcanoes of Tongariro. There's a steep section between the Whanganui River (75m above sea level) and the Puketotara Hut (427m above sea level) but mostly it's easy walking. There are four DOC backcountry huts along the way: Omaru, Pouri, Ngapurua and Puketotara; hut tickets cost \$15 per person per night. There's road access at the track's western end.

MANGAPURUA/KAIWHAKAUKA TRACK

The Mangapurua/Kaiwhakauka Track is a 40km trail between Whakahoro and the Mangapurua Landing, both on the Whanganui River. The track runs along the Mangapurua and Kaiwhakauka Streams (both Whanganui River tributaries). Be-

tween these valleys a side track leads to the 663m Mangapurua Trig, the area's highest point, from which cloudless views extend to the Tongariro and Egmont National Park volcanoes. The route also passes the Bridge to Nowhere (p232) and abandoned farming land cleared by settlers in the 20th century. Unless you're an insane tramping dynamo, walking the track takes 20 hours (three to four days). The Whakahoro Hut (p235) at the Whakahoro end of the track is the only hut, but there's plenty of good camping. There's road access to the track both at the Whakahoro end and from a side track from the end of the Ruatiti Valley–Ohura Rd (from Raetihi).

Mountain Biking

Aside from cycling down the Whanganui River Rd, the Mangapurua/Kaiwhakauka Track has recently been upgraded to form part of the Mountains to Sea Ohakune-to-Whanganui bike track, part of the Nga Haerenga, New Zealand Cycle Trail (www.nzcycletrail.com) project. It takes about six hours to ride along the Mangapurua Track from the Ruatiti Rd end through to the Whanganui River (where you'll need to pre-arrange a jetboat to take you downriver to Pipiriki). After rain, some sections get slippery and muddy: dismount and walk your bike across. For bike hire/track info try Bike Shed (p230) in Whanganui; for info on the track from the Ohakune end see p285.

👉 Tours

See also Activities for info on canoe and jetboat tours on the Whanganui River.

Whanganui Tours   VAN
(☎ 06-345 3475; www.whanganuitours.co.nz) Join the mailman on the Whanganui River Rd to Pipiriki (\$63, departs 7am) with lots of social and historical commentary. Returns mid-afternoon. Ask about the option of taking the mail van to Pipiriki then cycling back down the road to Whanganui.

Whanganui River Road Tours   BUS
(☎ 0800 201 234; www.whanganuiriverroad.com; tours per person \$80) Take a five-hour minibus ride up the River Rd with lots of stops and commentary. Or, you can take an abbreviated tour up to Pipiriki then cycle back to Whanganui (\$100 per person). Minimum four people on both tours.

🛏 Sleeping

WHANGANUI NATIONAL PARK

The park has a sprinkling of huts, a lodge and numerous camping grounds. Along the Taumarunui–Pipiriki section are three huts classified as Great Walks Huts during summer and Backcountry Huts in the off-season ($10 to $31 per person per night in summer; $10 to $15 off-season): **Whakahoro Hut** (free), John Coull Hut and Tieke Kainga, which has been revived as a marae (you can stay here, but full marae protocol must be observed). On the lower part of the river, Downes Hut is on the west bank, opposite Atene.

Bridge to Nowhere Lodge   LODGE, HOSTEL

(☑06-385 4622, 0800 480 308; www.bridgeto nowhere.co.nz; sites from $20, per adult/child self-catering $45/20, incl meals $245/75) Across the river from the Tieke Kainga *marae*, this remote lodge lies deep in the national park, 21km upriver from Pipiriki near the Matemateaonga Track. The only way to get here is by jetboat from Pipiriki or on foot. It has a licensed bar, and meals are quality home-cooked affairs. The lodge also runs jetboat, canoe and mountain-bike trips.

WHANGANUI RIVER RD

There's an informal campsite with toilets and cold water at Pipiriki, and another one (even less formal) just north of Atene.

Book the following places in advance – no one's going to turn you away, but they appreciate a bit of warning! From south to north, accommodation includes the following:

Rivertime Lodge   LODGE $$

(☑06-342 5595; www.rivertimelodge.co.nz; 1569 Whanganui River Rd; d $130, extra adult/child $45/35) A rural idyll: grassy hills folding down towards the river and the intermittent bleating of sheep. Rivertime is a moss green farmhouse with three bedrooms, a barbecue, a lovely deck overlooking the river and no TV! Sleeps six.

📷 Flying Fox   LODGE, HOSTEL $$

(☑06-342 8160; www.theflyingfox.co.nz; Whanganui River Rd; sites $20, d $100-200) This eco-attuned getaway is on the riverbank across from Koriniti. You can self-cater in the Brewhouse, James K or Glory Cart (self-contained cottages), opt for B&B ($120 per person), or pitch a tent in a bush clearing. Access is by jetboat; otherwise you can park across the river from the accommodation then soar over the river on the flying fox.

Kohu Cottage   RENTAL HOUSE $

(☑06-342 8178; kohu.cottage@xtra.co.nz; Whanganui River Rd; d $70) A snug little cream-coloured weatherboard cottage (100 years old!) above the road in Koriniti, sleeping three bods. There's a basic kitchen and a wood fire for chilly riverside nights.

Koriniti Marae   LODGE $

(☑06-342 8198; www.koriniti.com; Koriniti Pa Rd; dm $30) This *marae* on the east bank offers dorm-style beds for pre-booked groups; offer *koha* (a donation) plus the fee. It also runs a 24-hour 'cultural experience' for groups, including a *haka* (war dance), weaving, storytelling and three meals ($190 per person).

Operiki Farmstay   FARMSTAY $

(☑06-342 8159; operiki@farmside.co.nz; Whanganui River Rd; incl breakfast & dinner s/d $55/110) On a steep hillside 1.5km north of Koriniti, this is a cheery in-with-the-family farmhouse. There are scenic walks around the property, and macadamia-nut muffins come hot from the oven. The friendliest place this side of Disneyland.

St Joseph's Church   HOSTEL $

(☑06-342 8190; www.compassion.org.nz; Whanganui River Rd; dm adult/child $25/15, linen $10) Taking in bedraggled travellers and offering 20 dorm-style beds and a simple kitchen, the sisters at St Joe's await to issue your deliverance – book ahead for the privilege. Moutoa Island, site of a historic 1864 battle, is just downriver.

ℹ Information

For national park information, try the affable Whanganui (p230) or Taumarunui i-SITEs, or check out www.doc.govt.nz or www.whanganui river.co.nz online. Otherwise, a more tangible resource is the NZ Recreational Canoeing Association's *Guide to the Whanganui River* ($10). The **Wanganui Tramping Club** (☑06-346 5597; www.wanganuitrampingclub.org.nz) puts out the quarterly *Wanganui Tramper* magazine.

There's no mobile-phone coverage along the River Rd, and no petrol or shops. There are a couple of takeaway food vans in Pipiriki open during summer, plus the casual **Matahiwi Gallery cafe** (☑06-342 8112; www.matahiwi gallery.com; 3926 Whanganui River Rd; snacks $3-5; ☺9am-3.30pm Thu-Sun) in Matahiwi (call ahead to ensure they're open).

Getting There & Away

From the north, there's road access to the Whanganui River at Taumarunui, Ohinepane and Whakahoro, though the latter is a long, remote drive on mostly unsealed roads. Roads to Whakahoro lead off from Owhango and Raurimu, both on SH4. There isn't any further road access to the river until Pipiriki.

From the south, the Whanganui River Rd veers off SH4, 14km north of Whanganui, rejoining it at Raetihi, 91km north of Whanganui. It takes about two hours to drive the 79km between Whanganui and Pipiriki. The full circle from Whanganui through Pipiriki and Raetihi and back along SH4 takes about four hours. Alternatively, take a River Rd tour from Whanganui.

Palmerston North

POP 82,400

The rich sheep- and dairy-farming Manawatu region embraces the districts of Rangitikei to the north and Horowhenua to the south. The hub of it all, on the banks of the Manawatu River, is Palmerston North, with its moderate high-rise attempts reaching up from the plains. Massey University, NZ's largest, informs the town's cultural and social structures. As a result 'Palmy' has an open-minded, rurally bookish vibe.

None of this impressed a visiting John Cleese who scoffed, 'If you ever do want to kill yourself, but lack the courage, I think a visit to Palmerston North will do the trick.' The city exacted revenge by naming a rubbish dump after him.

⊙ Sights & Activities

TOP CHOICE **New Zealand Rugby Museum** MUSEUM

(www.rugbymuseum.co.nz; 326 Main St; adult/child/family \$12.50/5/30; ⊙10am-5pm) Fans of the oval ball holler about the New Zealand Rugby Museum, an amazing new space overflowing with rugby paraphernalia, from a 1905 All Blacks jumper to a scrum machine and the actual whistle used to start the first game of every Rugby World Cup. Of course, NZ hosted the 2011 Rugby World Cup and beat France 7-8 in the final: don't expect anyone here to stop talking about it until 2015...

FREE **Te Manawa** MUSEUM

(www.temanawa.co.nz; 326 Main St; ⊙10am-5pm) Te Manawa merges a museum, art gallery and science centre into one experience. Vast collections join the dots between 'life, art and mind'. The museum has a strong Maori focus, while the gallery's exhibits change frequently. Kids will get a kick out of the hands-on exhibits at the science centre. The New Zealand Rugby Museum is in the same complex.

The Square LANDMARK

(The Square) Taking the English village-green concept to a whole new level, The Square is Palmy's heart and soul. Seventeen spacey acres, with a clock tower, duck pond, Maori carvings, statues and trees of all seasonal dispositions. Locals eat lunch on the manicured lawns in the sunshine.

Lido Aquatic Centre SWIMMING

(www.lidoaquaticcentre.co.nz; 50 Park Rd; adult/child \$4/3, hydroslide \$5; ⊙6am-8pm Mon-Thu, 6am-9pm Fri, 8am-8pm Sat & Sun) When the summer plains bake, dive into the Lido Aquatic Centre. It's a long way from Lido Beach in Venice, but it has a 50m pool, waterslides, cafe and gym.

☞ Tours

Feilding Saleyard Tours CULTURAL

(☎06-323 3318; www.feilding.co.nz; 10 Manchester Sq; tours \$5; ⊙tours 11am Fri) Local farmers instruct you in the gentle art of selling livestock at this small town north of the city centre. Farmers market from 9am to 2pm every Friday.

Manawatu Gorge Experience Jet JETBOATING

(☎06-342 5599, 0800 945 335; www.manawatugorgejet.com; 25min tours per person \$65) Jetboat tours through gorgeous Manawatu Gorge, departing Woodville Ferry Domain on SH3, 25 minutes from Palmy.

Tui Brewery Tours BREWERY

(☎06-370 6600, 0800 471 227; www.tuibrewery.co.nz; 5hr tour per person \$50; ⊙noon-5pm Fri) Even if you're more of a craft-beer fan than a drinker of ubiquitous Tui, this boozy tour is a worthwhile outing. Check out the interesting brewery and museum and taste a Tui or two. Minimum numbers apply.

Festivals & Events

Festival of Cultures CULTURAL, FOOD & WINE

(www.foc.co.nz) Massive arts/culture/lifestyle festival in late March, with a food-and-craft market in the Square.

Palmerston North

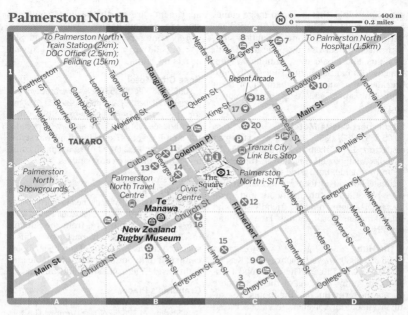

Palmerston North

◎ Top Sights
New Zealand Rugby Museum B3
Te Manawa... B3

◎ Sights
1 The Square C2

🛏 Sleeping
2 @ the Hub B2
3 Bentleys Motor Inn C3
4 Café de Paris B3
5 Empire Hotel... C2
6 Fitzherbert Castle Motel C3
7 Grandma's Place................................... C1
8 Pepper Tree Hostel............................... C1
9 Rose City Motel C3

🍴 Eating
10 Aqaba D1
11 Café Cuba B2
12 Halikarnas Café C2
13 Indian2nite B2
14 Moxies B2
15 Pak 'n Save C3

🍷 Drinking
16 Brewer's Apprentice B3
17 Celtic Inn.. C1
18 Fish C1

⭐ Entertainment
19 Centrepoint Theatre B3
    CinemaGold ....(see 20)
20 Downtown Cinemas C2

**Reel Earth Environmental
Film Festival**   FILM
(www.reelearth.org.nz) Nature and environment films from across Oceania flicker onto
Palmy's screens in May.

International Jazz & Blues Festival   MUSIC
(www.jazzandblues.co.nz) All things jazzy, blue-
sy and swingin' in late May/early June, including plenty of workshops.

Manawatu Wine & Food Festival   FOOD & WINE
(www.mwff.co.nz) Mid-June weekend fiesta of
culinary creations and the best local drops.

🛏 Sleeping

TOP CHOICE Plum Trees Lodge   LODGE, B&B $$
(☎06-358 7813; www.plumtreeslodge.co.nz; 97
Russell St; s/d incl breakfast from $135/150; 🛜)
In a flat-grid town with more motels than

seems plausible, this secluded lodge comes as sweet relief. It's brilliantly designed using recycled timbers from demolition sites, with raked timber ceilings punctuated with skylights, and a balcony set among swaying boughs. Romantic nights slide lazily into breakfast – a sumptuous hamper of fresh fruit, croissants, jams, eggs, cheese, coffee and juice.

Fitzherbert Castle Motel MOTEL $$
(06-358 3888, 0800 115 262; www.fitzherbert castle.co.nz; 124 Fitzherbert Ave; d $110-195;) It looks unapologetically like a Tudor castle from outside, but inside it's more like an intimate hotel. Fourteen immaculate rooms with cork-tiled bathroom floors and quality carpets, plenty of trees, friendly staff and small kitchens in some units. Free wi-fi and laundry.

@ the Hub HOTEL, HOSTEL $
(06-356 8880; www.atthehub.co.nz; 10 King St; s/d $40/55, units $80;) There are lots of students in Palmy, and lots of them stay here during the term. But half the rooms are usually available for travellers: book a serviced en-suite double unit with kitchenette, or a simple student shoebox (also with en suite). Great location, great value!

Pepper Tree Hostel HOSTEL $
(06-355 4054; www.peppertreehostel.co.nz; 121 Grey St; dm/s/d $28/53/70;) Inexplicably strewn with green-painted boots, this endearing 100-year-old house is the best budget option in town. Mattresses are thick, the kitchen will never run out of spatulas, and the piano and wood fire make things feel downright homey. Doubles off the kitchen are a bit noisy – angle for one at the back.

Empire Hotel HOTEL $
(06-357 8002; www.empirehotel.co.nz; cnr Princess & Main Sts; s/d/f $80/80/140;) With slicker-than-average, colonial-style pub rooms upstairs, the Empire is a solid central option. Beyond a tandem bike poised bizarrely in the stairwell, rooms have TV, bathroom and fridge. The pub downstairs gets raucous – steer for a room far from the beer cheer.

Bentleys Motor Inn MOTEL, APARTMENT $$
(06-358 7074, 0800 2368 5397; www.bentleys motorinn.co.nz; cnr Linton & Chaytor Sts; ste $155-320) The highest peak on Palmerston North's motel range, Bentleys' five-star

apartments are worth the investment. Inside are new appliances, DVD player, spa, stereo, contemporary furnishings and Sky TV; outside are a full-blown gym, squash court and sauna.

Rose City Motel MOTEL $$
(0508 356 538, 06-356 5388; www.rosecitymotel. co.nz; 120 Fitzherbert Ave; units $125-145;) One for the postmodern aesthetes, Rose City's townhouse-style units are spacey (especially the split-level ones) and shipshape but stylistically rather '90s. Free DVDs, a squash court and a kids' play area are bonuses.

Palmerston North Holiday Park HOLIDAY PARK $
(06-358 0349; www.palmerstonnorthholiday park.co.nz; 133 Dittmer Dr; sites/cabin/unit d from $16/45/80;) About 2km from the Square, off Ruha St, this shady park with daisy-speckled lawns has a bit of a wheezy boot-camp feel to it, but it's quiet, affordable and right beside Victoria Esplanade gardens.

Grandma's Place HOSTEL $
(06-358 6928; www.grandmas-place.com; 146 Grey St; dm/s/d $28/52/70;) Ignore the terrifying spectre of Grandma on the sign out the front – inside are tidy, old-fashioned rooms with floral wallpaper and macramé rugs. There are plenty of beds and a functional kitchen.

Café de Paris HOTEL $
(06-355 2130; www.cafedeparisinn.co.nz; 267 Main St; s/d $60/80) It ain't Montmartre, but this friendly, 1893 boozer three minutes' walk from the Square has a warren of surprisingly decent pub accommodation upstairs, all rooms with TV, en suite and eclectic furnishings. Off-street parking out the back is limited.

Eating

Moxies CAFE $$
(moxies@hotmail.com; 67 George St; meals $6-20; 7am-5pm Mon-Sat, 7.30am-5pm Sun;) This chipper corner cafe is a real George St fixture, decked out in primary colours with big windows. Staff members are equally upbeat, the all-day menu is top value (stellar omelettes) and if you've got gluten issues, this is the place for you.

Halikarnas Café TURKISH $$
(15 Fitzherbert Ave; mains $16-20; lunch Tue-Fri, dinner daily) Angling for an Ali-Baba-and-the-Forty-Thieves vibe, with magic carpets, brass hookahs and funky trans-Bosphorus

beats, Halikarnas plates up generous Turkish delights, from lamb shish kebabs to felafels and kick-arse Turkish coffee. Takeaway kebabs next door.

Café Cuba
CAFE $$

(cnr George & Cuba Sts; meals $10-30; ⊗7am-midnight; 🖋) Need a sugar shot? Proceed to day-turns-to-night Café Cuba – the cakes here are for professional chocoholics only. Supreme coffees and traditional cafe fare (risottos, salads, corn fritters) also draw the crowds. Live music Friday nights.

Izakaya Yatai
JAPANESE $$

(🖋06-356 1316; www.yatai.co.nz; 316 Featherstone St; dishes $9-24; ⊗dinner Tue-Sat) Simple, fresh, authentic Japanese food cooked by Atsushi Taniyama in an unpretentious suburban house with empty sake bottles lining the window sills. Front-of-house host Barbara comes with a big personality. Set menus available.

Indian2nite
INDIAN $$

(🖋06-353 7400; www.indian2nite.com; 22 George St; mains $10-20; ⊗lunch Wed-Sat, dinner daily; 🖋) A million miles from Bollywood schmaltz, this upmarket place won't break the bank. Behind George St picture windows and tucked under a curved wall-cum-ceiling, northern Indian curries are served by super-polite waiting staff. Try the *dahl makhani*.

Aqaba
INTERNATIONAL $$

(186 Broadway Ave; meals $12-32; ⊗7.30am-late Mon-Fri, 9am-late Sat & Sun) Family-friendly cafe classics (pasta, fish and chips, soups, nachos, steaks, salads and curries) served inside a cavernous, colourful former Masonic Hall (no secret handshake required). R&B beats; Egyptian interiors.

Pak 'n Save
SUPERMARKET

(www.paknsave.co.nz; 335 Ferguson St; ⊗7am-11pm) Cheap and cheerful.

🍷 Drinking

Fish
COCKTAIL BAR

(Regent Arcade; ⊗4-11pm Wed, 4pm-1am Thu, 4pm-3am Fri & Sat) A progressive, stylish, Pacifically-hewn cocktail bar, the Fish has got its finger firmly on the Palmy pulse. DJs smooth over the week's problems on Friday and Saturday nights as a sexy, urbane crew sips Manhattans and Tamarillo Mules (yes, they kick).

Brewer's Apprentice
PUB

(www.brewersapprentice.co.nz; 334 Church St; ⊗11am-late Mon-Fri, 10am-late Sat & Sun) What was once a grungy student pub is now a slick Monteiths-sponsored bar. Business crowds flock for lunch ($10 to $17, dinner $27 to $29), and 20-somethings fill the beer terrace after dark. Live music Friday nights.

Celtic Inn
IRISH PUB

(www.celticinn.co.nz; Regent Arcade; ⊗11am-3am Mon-Sat, 4pm-11am Sun) The Celtic expertly offsets the Fish nearby with its good old-fashioned pub stuff, labourers, travellers and students bending elbows with a few tasty pints of the black stuff. Friendly staff, live music, red velvet chairs, kids darting around parents' legs – it's all here.

☆ Entertainment

CinemaGold
CINEMA

(www.cinemagold.co.nz; Downtown Shopping Arcade, Broadway Ave; adult/child $16/11; ⊗10am-midnight) In the same complex as the Downtown Cinemas, CinemaGold ups the ante with plush seats and a booze licence to enhance art-house classics and limited-release screenings.

Centrepoint Theatre
THEATRE

(www.centrepoint.co.nz; 280 Church St) A mainstay of the simmering Palmerston North theatre scene, Centrepoint serves up big-name professional shows, theatre sports and seasonal plays.

Downtown Cinemas
CINEMA

(www.dtcinemas.co.nz; Downtown Shopping Arcade, Broadway Ave; adult/child $15.40/9.40; ⊗10am-midnight) The capacious Downtown Cinemas megaplex shows mainstream new-release flicks. All Tuesday tickets $9.40.

ℹ Information

Palmerston North i-SITE (🖋0800 626 292, 06-350 1922; www.manawatunz.co.nz; The Square; ⊗9am-5pm Mon-Fri, 10am-2pm Sat & Sun; 🛜) A super-helpful source of tourist information; free wi-fi throughout the Square.

Department of Conservation (DOC; 🖋06-350 9700; www.doc.govt.nz; 717 Tremaine Ave; ⊗8am-4.30pm Mon-Fri) DOC information 3km north of the Square.

Palmerston North Hospital (🖋06-356 9169; www.midcentraldhb.govt.nz; 50 Ruahine St; ⊗24hr) Accident and emergency assistance.

Post Office (cnr Main St & the Square)

TARANAKI & WHANGANUI PALMERSTON NORTH

Radius Medical, The Palms (☑06-354 7737; www.radiusmedical.co.nz; 445 Ferguson St; ⊘8am-7pm Mon-Fri, 9am-6pm Sat & Sun) Accident and emergency, plus doctors by appointment and a pharmacy.

❶ Getting There & Away

Air

Palmerston North International Airport (PMR; ☑06-351 4415; www.pnairport.co.nz; Airport Dr) is 4km north of the town centre. Air New Zealand runs daily direct flights to Auckland, Christchurch and Wellington.

Bus

InterCity (☑09-583 5780; www.intercity. co.nz) buses operate from the **Palmerston North Travel Centre** (☑06-355 4955; cnr Main & Pitt Sts; ⊘8.45am-5pm Mon-Thu, 8.45am-7.45pm Fri, 9am-2.45pm Sat, 9am-2.45pm & 4-7.15pm Sun). Destinations include the following:

DESTINATION	PRICE	DURATION	FREQUENCY
Auckland	$70	9hr	2 daily
Napier	$34	3hr	2 daily
Taupo	$35	4hr	2 daily
Wellington	$30	2¼hr	7 daily
Whanganui	$24	1½hr	3 daily

Naked Bus (p230) services also depart the Travel Centre, servicing North Island centres including these:

DESTINATION	PRICE	DURATION	FREQUENCY
Auckland	$25	9¼hr	1 daily
Napier	$16	2½hr	2 daily
Taupo	$20	4¼hr	2 daily
Wellington	$14	2¼hr	4 daily
Whanganui	$12	1¼hr	1 daily

Train

Tranz Scenic (☑04-495 0775, 0800 872 467; www.tranzscenic.co.nz) runs long-distance trains between Wellington and Auckland, stopping at the retro-derelict **Palmerston North Train Station** (Mathews Ave), off Tremaine Ave about 2.5km north of the Square. From Palmy to Wellington, take the *Overlander* ($68, 2½ hours, one daily) departing at 5pm (Friday to Sunday, May to November); or the *Capital Connection* ($24, two hours, one daily Monday to Friday) departing Palmy at 6.15am. To Auckland, the *Overlander* ($129, 9½ hours, one daily) departs at 9.45am. Buy tickets from Tranz Scenic di-

rectly, or on the train for the *Capital Connection* (no ticket sales at the station).

❶ Getting Around

To & From the Airport

There's no public transport between the city and airport, but taxis abound or **Super Shuttle** (☑09-522 5100, 0800 748 885; www.super shuttle.co.nz; $18) can whiz you into town in a minivan (pre-booking required).

Bicycle

Crank It Cycles (☑06-358 9810; www.crank itcycles.co.nz; 203 Cuba St; ⊘8am-5.30pm Mon-Fri, 9am-3pm Sat) Hires out mountain bikes from $20/40 per half-/full day, including helmet and lock.

Bus

Tranzit City Link (☑06-952 2800, 0508 800 800; www.horizons.govt.nz; adult/child $2.50/1.50) Runs daytime buses departing from the Main St bus stop on the east side of the Square. Bus 12 goes to Massey University; none go to the airport.

Taxi

A city-to-airport taxi costs around $15. **Gold & Black Taxis** (☑06-351 2345) is a family-run local outfit.

Around Palmerston North

Just south of 'Student City' in the underrated Horowhenua district, **Shannon** (population 1510) and **Foxton** (population 2000) are sedentary country towns en route to Wellington.

Our fine feathered friends at **Owlcatraz** (☑06-362 7872; www.owlcatraz.co.nz; SH57; adult/child incl tour $17.50/8; ⊘9am-5pm) have obligingly adopted oh-so-droll names like Owlvis Presley and Owl Capone. It's a 30-minute drive south from Palmerston North.

Foxton Beach is one of a string of broad, shallow Tasman Sea beaches along this stretch of coast – brown sand, driftwood and holiday houses proliferate. Other worthy beaches include **Himatangi**, **Hokio** and **Waikawa**.

The town of **Levin** (population 19,550) is more sizeable, but suffers from being too close to both Wellington and Palmerston North to warrant the through-traffic making a stop.

Manawatu Gorge & Around

About 15km northeast of Palmerston North, SH2 dips into **Manawatu Gorge**. Maori named the gorge Te Apiti (the Narrow Passage), believing the big reddish rock near the centre of the gorge was its guardian spirit. The rock's colour is said to change intensity when a prominent Rangitane tribe member dies or sheds blood. It takes around four hours to walk through the gorge from either end, or you can see it via jetboat.

On the southwestern edge of the gorge, about 40 minutes drive from Palmerston North, is the **Tararua Wind Farm** (☑07-574 4754, 0800 878 787; www.trustpower.co.nz; Hall Block Rd), allegedly the largest wind farm in the southern hemisphere. From Hall Block Rd there are awesome views of the turbines. Spinning similarly, north of the gorge is **Te Apiti Wind Farm** (☑03-357 9700, 0800 496 496; www.meridianenergy.co.nz; Saddle Rd, Ashhurst). There are great views from Saddle Rd – ask the i-SITE for directions.

Alternatively, flee the city with a visit to **Timeless Horse Treks** (☑06-376 6157; www.timelesshorsetreks.co.nz; Gorge Rd, Ballance; 1/2hr rides from $40/60). Gentle trail rides take in the Manawatu River and surrounding hills, or you can saddle up for an overnight all-inclusive trek ($175). Palmerston North pick-up/drop-off available.

Taupo & the Central Plateau

Includes »

Best Places to Eat

» Bistro Lago (p254)

» Vine Eatery (p254)

» Cyprus Tree (p269)

» Brantry (p254)

» Tongariro Lodge (p259)

Best Places to Stay

» Riverstone Backpackers (p258)

» Creel Lodge (p258)

» Lake (p253)

» Powderhorn Chateau (p269)

» Station Lodge (p269)

Why Go?

From river deep to mountain high, New Zealand's geology takes centre stage in this diverse region – and my-oh-my does it get its shimmy on. Much of the pizzazz comes from the Taupo Volcanic Zone – a line of geothermal activity that stretches, via Rotorua, to Whakaari/White Island in the Bay of Plenty. It's the commotion below the surface that has gifted the region with some of the North Island's star attractions, including the country's largest lake and the three hot-headed peaks of Tongariro National Park.

And the thrills don't stop there, for this area now rivals Rotorua for daredevil escapades. Perhaps you fancy fly-fishing in the trout-filled Tongariro River, hooning up to Huka Falls in a jetboat, or bouncing on a bungy over the Waikato River? Or skydiving, skiing or just soaking in a thermal pool? If so, mark Taupo as a must-do on your North Island itinerary.

When to Go

Equally popular in winter as in summer, there's not really a bad time to visit. The ski season runs roughly from July to October, but storms and freezing temperatures can occur at any time on the mountains, and above 2500m there is a small permanent cap of snow. Due to its altitude, the Central Plateau has a generally cool climate, with average high temperatures ranging from around 3°C in winter up to around 24°C in summer. In summer, the lake becomes the epicentre of a whirl of outdoor activity.

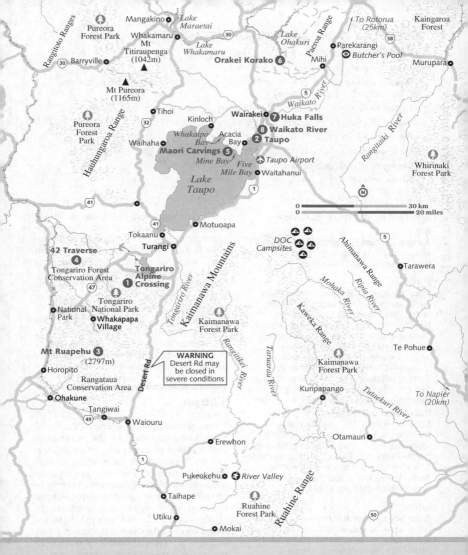

Taupo & Central Plateau Highlights

1. Exploring fascinating volcanic terrain while tramping the **Tongariro Alpine Crossing** (p262)

2. Hurtling to earth strapped to a complete stranger in the world's skydiving capital, **Taupo** (p250)

3. Carving fresh powder on **Mt Ruapehu** (p260)

4. Biking till your bum burns on the **42 Traverse** (p262)

5. Paddling Lake Taupo to check out the modern **Maori carvings** (p245)

6. Rediscovering the 'lost valley' of **Orakei Korako** (p256)

7. Rocketing up the Waikato River to the base of **Huka Falls** (p245) in a jetboat

8. Plunging 47m over the **Waikato River** (p251) on the end of a rubber band

ESSENTIAL TAUPO & CENTRAL PLATEAU

» **Eat** Trout – but you'll have to catch it first!

» **Drink** A mouthful of water from the Waikato River as you bungy over it

» **Read** *Awesome Forces* by Hamish Campbell and Geoff Hicks – the geological story of New Zealand in explosive detail

» **Listen to** *Ka mate* – the famous haka, written on the shores of Lake Rotoaira

» **Watch** *The Return of the King*, starring Ngauruhoe as Mt Doom

» **Festival** Lake Taupo Cycle Challenge

» **Go green** Explore Tongariro National Park's alpine flora and geological oddities

» **Online** www.greatlaketaupo.com; www.visitruapehu.com

» **Area Code** 07

Getting There & Away

Air

Air New Zealand (0800 737 000; www.airnz.co.nz) Direct flights to Taupo from Auckland, Whanganui and Wellington.

Bus

InterCity (07-348 0366; www.intercity.co.nz) Runs coaches through the region on the following routes: Auckland–Hamilton–Rotorua–Taupo–Turangi–Waiouru–Taihape–Palmerston North–Wellington; Auckland–Hamilton–Taupo–Napier–Hastings; Auckland–Hamilton–National Park–Ohakune–Whanganui–Palmerston North Tauranga–Rotorua–Taupo–Turangi–Waiouru–Taihape–Palmerston North–Wellington; Tauranga–Rotorua–Taupo–Napier–Hastings.

Naked Bus (0900 62533, per minute $1.99; www.nakedbus.com) Operates on the following routes: Auckland–Hamilton–Taupo–Turangi–Waiouru–Taihape–Palmerston North–Wellington; Tauranga–Rotorua–Taupo–Turangi–Waiouru–Taihape–Palmerston North–Wellington; Taupo–Napier–Hastings; Turangi–National Park–Ohakune.

Train

Tranz Scenic (www.tranzscenic.co.nz) Overlander services stop at National Park, Ohakune and Taihape on the Auckland–Hamilton–Palmerston North–Wellington route.

LAKE TAUPO REGION

NZ's largest lake, Lake Taupo, sits in the caldera of a volcano that began erupting about 300,000 years ago. The caldera was formed by a collapse during the Oruanui eruption about 26,500 years ago, which threw out 750 cu km of ash and pumice, making Krakatoa (8 cu km) look like a pimple.

The last major cataclysm was in 180AD, shooting up enough ash into the atmosphere for the red skys to be noted by the ancient Romans and Chinese. The area is still volcanically active and, like Rotorua, has fascinating thermal hot spots.

Today the 606-sq-km lake and its surrounding waterways are serene enough to attract fishing enthusiasts from all around the world. Well positioned by the lake, both Taupo and Turangi are popular tourist centres. Taupo, in particular, has plenty of activities and facilities to cater for families and independent travellers alike.

Taupo

POP 22,600

With a postcard-perfect setting on the northeastern shores of the lake, the increasingly exciting town of Taupo now rivals Rotorua as the North Island's adrenaline capital. There's an abundance of blood-pumping activities on offer but for those with no appetite for white knuckles and churned stomachs, there's plenty of enjoyment to be had simply strolling by the lake and enjoying the views, which on clear days reveal the snowy peaks of Tongariro National Park. Stop at the lookout on the way into town and you'll see exactly what we mean.

NZ's longest river, the Waikato, originates from Lake Taupo at the township, before crashing its way through the Huka Falls and Aratiatia Rapids and then settling down for a sedate ramble to the west coast, just south of Auckland.

History

When Maori chief Tamatea-arikinui first visited this area, his footsteps reverberated, making him think the ground was hollow; he therefore dubbed the area Tapuaeharuru (Resounding Footsteps). The modern name, however, originates from the story of Tia. After Tia discovered the lake and slept beside it draped in his cloak, the area became known as Taupo Nui a Tia (The Great Cloak of Tia).

Europeans settled here in force during the East Coast Land War (1868–72), when it was a strategic military base. A redoubt was built in 1869 and a garrison of mounted police remained until the defeat of Te Kooti later that year.

In the 20th century the mass ownership of the motorcar saw Taupo grow from a lakeside village of about 750 people to a large resort town, easily accessible from most points of the North Island. Today the population still grows considerably at peak holiday times, when New Zealanders and international visitors alike flock to the lakeshore.

◉ Sights

LAKESIDE

Taupo's main attraction is the lake and all the things you can do in, on and around it. The water is famously chilly, but in several places (such as **Hot Water Beach** (Map p248), immediately south of the centre) there are thermal springs just below the surface. You can swim in front of the township, but **Acacia Bay**, 5km west, is a particularly pleasant spot. Even better and quieter is **Whakaipo Bay**, another 7km further on.

Maori Carvings   CARVINGS
Accessible only by boat, these 10m-high carvings were etched into the cliffs near Mine Bay by master carver Matahi Whakataka-Brightwell in the late 1970s. They depict Ngatoro-i-rangi, the visionary Maori navigator who guided the Tuwharetoa and Te Arawa tribes to the Taupo area a thousand years ago. There are also two smaller Matahi figures here, both of Celtic design, which depict the south wind and a mermaid.

Taupo Museum   MUSEUM
(Map p246; www.taupomuseum.co.nz; Story Pl; adult/child $5/free; ◷10am-4.30pm) With an excellent Maori gallery and quirky displays, which include a 1960s caravan set up as if the occupants have just popped down to the lake, this little museum makes an interesting rainy-day diversion. The centrepiece is an elaborately carved Maori meeting house, *Te Aroha o Rongoheikume*. Set up in a courtyard, the *Ora Garden of Wellbeing* is a re-creation of NZ's gold-medal-winning entry into the 2004 Chelsea Flower Show. Historical displays cover local industries, a mock-up of a 19th-century shop and a moa skeleton, and there's also a gallery devoted to visiting exhibitions.

WAIRAKEI PARK

Huka Falls   WATERFALL
(Map p248; Huka Falls Rd) Clearly signposted and with a car park and kiosk alongside, these falls mark the spot where NZ's longest river, the Waikato, is slammed into a narrow chasm, making a dramatic 10m drop into a surging pool. As you cross the footbridge, you can see the full force of this torrent that the Maori called Hukanui (Great Body of Spray). On sunny days the water is crystal clear and you'll be able to

---

MAORI NZ: CENTRAL PLATEAU

The North Island's central region is home to a group of mountains that feature in several Maori legends of lust and betrayal, which end with a few mountains fleeing to other parts of the island (see Mt Taranaki's sad tale).

Long after all that action was over, the *tohunga* (priest) Ngatoro-i-rangi, fresh off the boat from Hawaiki, explored this region and named the mountains that remained. The most sacred was Tongariro, consisting of at least 12 volcanic cones, seen as the leader of all the other mountains.

The major *iwi* (tribe) of the region is **Ngati Tuwharetoa** (www.tuwharetoa.co.nz), one of the few *iwi* in NZ that has retained an undisputed *ariki* (high chief). The current *ariki* is Sir Tumu Te Heuheu Tukino VIII, whose great-great-grandfather, Te Heuheu Tukino IV (a descendent of Ngatoro-i-rangi), gifted the mountains of Tongariro to NZ in 1887.

To discover the stories of local Maori and their ancestors, visit Taupo Museum, the carved cliff faces at Mine Bay, Wairakei Terraces, or take a tour with pureORAwalks, Rafting NZ, Wai Maori, Awhina Wilderness Experience or Kai Waho.

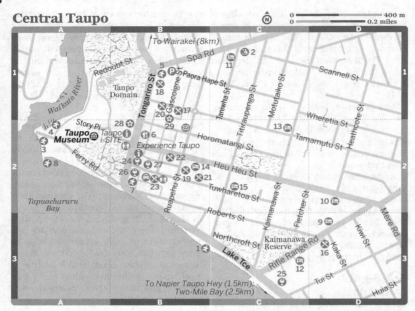

Central Taupo

take great photographs from the lookout on the other side of the footbridge. You can also take a few short walks around the area or pick up the Huka Falls Walkway back to town, or the Aratiatia Rapids Walking Track to the rapids.

Wairakei Terraces & Thermal Health Spa   THERMAL AREA

(Map p248; ☎07-378 0913; www.wairakeiterraces. co.nz; Wairakei Rd; thermal walk adult/child $18/9, pools $25; ⊙8.30am-5pm) Known to Maori as Waiora and latterly as Geyser Valley, this was one of the most active thermal areas in the world (with 22 geysers and 240 mud pools and springs) until 1958, when it was significantly affected by the opening of the geothermal power station. Today it's the site of a re-created Maori village, a small meeting house, a carving centre, massage rooms and a set of healing thermal pools. These sit alongside artificially made geysers and silica terraces, re-creating, on a smaller scale, the famous Pink and White Terraces, which were destroyed by the Tarawera eruption in 1886.

The nighttime Maori Cultural Experience – which includes a traditional challenge, welcome and concert, as well as a *hangi* meal – gives an insight into Maori life in the geothermal areas of the county (adult/child $95/48).

Craters of the Moon   THERMAL AREA

(Map p248; www.cratersofthemoon.co.nz; Karapiti Rd; adult/child $6/2.50; ⊙8.30am-5.30pm) This lesser-known geothermal area sprang to life as a result of the hydroelectric tinkering that created the power station. When underground water levels fell and pressure shifted, new steam vents and bubbling mud pools sprang up. The perimeter loop walk takes about 45 minutes and affords great views down to the lake and mountains beyond. There's a kiosk at the entrance, staffed by volunteers who kindly keep an eye on the car park. It's signposted from SH1, about 5km north of Taupo.

Aratiatia Rapids   WATERFALL

(Map p248) Two kilometres off SH5, this was a spectacular part of the Waikato River until the government plonked a hydroelectric dam across the waterway, shutting off the flow. But the spectacle hasn't disappeared completely, with the floodgates opened from October to March at 10am, noon, 2pm and 4pm and from April to September at 10am, noon and 2pm. You can see the water crash through the dam from two good vantage points.

Central Taupo

◎ Top Sights
Taupo Museum A2

⊕ Activities, Courses & Tours
1 Big Sky Parasail B3
2 Canoe & Kayak C1
3 Chris Jolly Outdoors A2
4 Fish Cruise Taupo A2
5 Greenstone Fishing B1
6 Pointons Ski Shop B2
7 Taupo Rod & Tackle B2
8 Taupo's Floatplane A2

⊟ Sleeping
9 Beechtree D3
10 Bella Vista D2
11 Blackcurrant Backpackers C1
12 Catelli's of Taupo C3
13 Silver Fern Lodge C2
14 Taupo Urban Retreat B2
15 Tiki Lodge......................................C2

✕ Eating
16 Brantry D3
17 Eruption..B1
18 Lotus B1
19 Piccolo...B2
20 Pimentos B1
21 Plateau B2
22 Replete B2
23 Vine Eatery B2

◉ Drinking
24 Finn MacCuhal's B2
25 Jolly Good Fellows C3
26 Mulligans B2
27 Shed...B2

◎ Entertainment
28 Great Lake Centre B2
29 Starlight Cinema Centre B1

Volcanic Activity Centre MUSEUM
(Map p248; www.volcanoes.co.nz; Karetoto Rd; adult/child $10/6; ☺9am-5pm Mon-Fri, 10am-4pm Sat & Sun) What's with all the geothermal activity around Taupo? This centre has the answers, with excellent, if text-heavy, displays on the region's geothermal and volcanic activity, including a live seismograph keeping a watch on what's currently going on. A favourite exhibit with kids is the Earthquake Simulator, which is a little booth you can sit in to experience an earthquake, complete with teeth-chattering shudders and sudden shakes. You can also configure your own tornado and then watch it wreak havoc, or see a simulated geyser above and below ground. There is a small theatre that screens footage of the 1995 Ruapehu eruption and the 2007 breach of the crater lake.

Huka Prawn Park FARM
(Map p248; www.hukaprawnpark.co.nz; Karetoto Rd; adult/child $24/14; ☺9.30am-4pm) One of the world's only geothermally heated freshwater prawn farms, this place offers a surprising array of activities, including prawn 'fishing' and Killer Prawn Golf, shooting for rings floating in the prawn ponds. And, of course, there's a restaurant.

FREE **Honey Hive** STORE
(Map p248; www.honeyhivetaupo.com; 65 Karetoto Rd; ☺10am-5pm) Has a glass-enclosed viewing hive, honey tastings, a cafe and sells all manner of bee products – edible, medicinal and cosmetic – as well as mead.

✦ Activities
Adrenaline addicts should look out for special deals that combine several activities for a reduced price. Some operators offer backpacker discounts.

Water-based

FREE **Spa Park Hot Spring** SWIMMING
(Map p248; Spa Park) The hot thermal waters of the Otumuheke Stream meet the bracing Waikato River at this pleasant and well-worn spot under a bridge, creating a free natural spa bath. Take care: people have been known to drown while trying to cool off in the fast moving river. It's near the beginning of the Huka Falls Walkway, about 20 minutes from the centre of town.

Hukafalls Jet JETBOATING
(Map p248; ☎07-374 8572; www.hukafallsjet.com; 200 Karetoto Rd; trips adult/child $105/59) This 30-minute thrill ride takes you up the river to the spray-filled foot of the Huka Falls and down to the Aratiatia Dam, all the while doing acrobatic 360-degree turns. Trips run all day (prices include transport from Taupo) and you can bundle it in with a helicopter ride.

Rapids Jet JETBOATING
(Map p248; ☎07-374 8066; www.rapidsjet.com; Nga Awa Purua Rd; adult/child $105/60) This sensational 35-minute ride shoots along the

Taupo & Wairakei

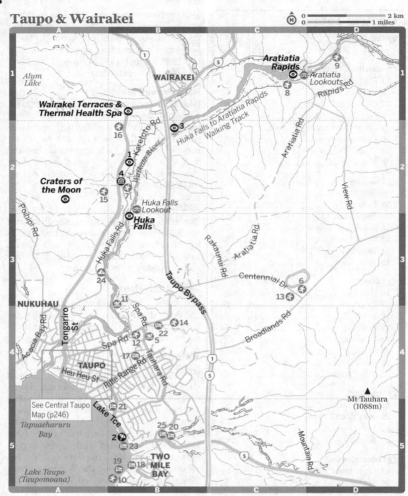

lower part of the Aratiatia Rapids – rivalling the Huka Falls trip for thrills. The boat departs from the end of the access road to the Aratiatia lookouts. Go down Rapids Rd and look for the signpost to the National Equestrian Centre.

Huka Falls River Cruise CRUISE
(Map p248; ☎0800 278 336; www.hukafallscruise. co.nz; Aratiatia Dam; adult/child $35/15; ⊙10.30am, 12.30pm & 2.30pm) For a photo-friendly ride, this boat offers a relaxed jaunt (80 minutes) from Aratiatia Dam to Huka Falls.

Taupo DeBretts Spa Resort SWIMMING
(Map p248; ☎07-377 6502; www.taupodebretts. co.nz; 76 Napier Taupo Hwy; adult/child $20/12; ⊙7.30am-9.30pm) A variety of mineral-rich indoor and outdoor thermal pools are on offer. The kids will love the giant dragon waterslide, while the adults can enjoy a wide choice of treatments, such as massage and body scrubs.

AC Baths SWIMMING, CLIMBING
(Map p248; ☎07-376 0350; www.taupovenues. co.nz; AC Baths Ave; adult/child $7/3, slides $5, climbing wall adult/child $10/6; ⊙6am-9pm,

Taupo & Wairakei

climbing wall hours vary) At the Taupo Events Centre, about 2km east of town, this large complex has a big, heated pool with a waterslide, as well as an indoor kids' pool, private mineral pools and a sauna. There are also a climbing wall and gym.

Wilderness Escapes   KAYAKING
(☑07-376 8981; www.wildernessescapes.co.nz; half-day $90) Well-regarded, long-standing operator offering half- or full-day kayaking trips to the Maori carvings, as well as sunset paddles on the lake.

Chris Jolly Outdoors   CRUISE, KAYAKING
(Map p246; ☑07-378 0623; www.chrisjolly.co.nz; Marina; ⊙9am-5.30pm) Operates the Cruise Cat, a large, modern launch that offers fishing trips and daily cruises to the Maori carvings (adult/child $44/16, 10.30am and 1.30pm). Sunday brunch trips (adult/child $62/34) are especially worthwhile. It also hires kayaks (single/double per hour $20/30) and self-drive boats ($70 to $85 per hour), and offers guided mountain-biking trips.

🚣 **Barbary**   SAILING
(☑07-378 3444; www.sailbarbary.com; adult/child $40/10; ⊙10.30am & 2pm year-long plus 5pm

summer) A classic 1926 yacht offering 2½-hour cruises to the Maori rock carvings every day, as well as a three-hour movie and barbecue cruise in summer ($65, 8pm, December to April).

**Rapid Sensations &
Kayaking Kiwi**   KAYAKING, RAFTING
(Map p248; ☑0800 35 34 35; www.rapids.co.nz; 413 Huka Falls Rd) This operator offers kayak trips to the Maori carvings (four hours, $98), a gentle paddle along the Waikato (two hours, $48), white-water rafting on the Tongariro River ($88 to $145) and guided mountain-bike rides ($75).

Canoe & Kayak   CANOEING, KAYAKING
(Map p246; ☑07-378 1003; www.canoeandkayak.co.nz; 77 Spa Rd; ⊙9am-5pm Mon-Sat) Instruction and boat hire, as well as guided tours, including a two-hour trip on the Waikato River ($45) or a half-day to the Maori carvings ($90).

**Sailing & Watersports
Centre Two Mile Bay**   SAILING, KAYAKING
(Map p248; ☑0274 967 350; www.sailingcentre.co.nz; Lake Tce; ⊙9am-10pm) Has a lakeside cafe/bar and hires out kayaks (from $25), canoes (from $25), windsurfers (from $30),

ABOUT TROUT

Ever since trout were introduced into Lake Taupo in 1898 there have been yarns of fish weighing more than a sack of spuds and measuring the length of a surfboard. The truth is that more than 28,000 brown and rainbow trout of legal size are bagged annually and fishing enthusiasts head here from all over the world to try their luck.

February and March are the best months for brown trout but rainbow fishing is good year-round on the Tongariro River (near Turangi). Fly-fishing is the only fishing permitted on all rivers flowing into the lake and within a 300m radius of the river mouths. Spin fishing is allowed only on the Waikato River (flowing *out* of the lake) and on the Tokaanu tailrace, flowing into the lake from the Tokaanu Power Station.

This unique fishery is protected by special conditions, including a bag limit of three fish, no use of bait (except flies) and a minimum size of 40cm, depending on where you fish – this is detailed on your licence, which you must carry at all times while fishing. Licences are available from DOC, i-SITEs and fishing stores (per day/week/season $17/38/90).

There are numerous fishing guides operating out of Taupo and Turangi, offering transport, gear, licences and, most importantly, local knowledge. Many are happy to negotiate a price depending on the trip; $250 for a half-day is a rough ballpark. Likewise there are shops in each town that hire and sell gear, and handle bookings for guides and charters. Refer to the activities section of each town for recommended operators.

sailboats ($65) and catamarans (from $70); rates are per hour.

Fish Cruise Taupo
BOATING

(Launch Office; Map p246; ☑07-378 3444; www.fishcruisetaupo.co.nz; Marina; ⊙9am-5pm Dec-Mar, 9.30am-3pm Apr-Nov) Representing 18 different boats belonging to the Taupo Launchmen's Association, this is the best place to book a private charter – whether for fishing or for a cruise.

Greenstone Fishing
FISHING

(Map p246; ☑07-378 3714; 147 Tongariro St; gear hire from $15; ⊙8am-5pm Mon-Sat, 9am-3pm Sun) Central fishing shop that sells licences, hires gear and arranges guided trips.

Taupo Rod & Tackle
FISHING

(Map p246; ☑07-378 5337; www.tauporodandtackle.co.nz; 7 Tongariro St; gear hire $20-35; ⊙8am-6pm Sat & Sun, 8am-8pm Fri) Rental gear, fishing guides and boat charters.

Skydiving

More than 30,000 jumps a year are made from Taupo, which makes it the skydiving capital of the world. It's certainly a terrific spot to do it: all those beautiful places you see from ground level are patchworked together in a brilliant blanket of natural colour, the highlights of which are the deep blue lake and the brilliant white of the snow-capped peaks.

Skydive Taupo
SKYDIVING

(☑0800 586 766; www.skydivetaupo.co.nz; 12,000ft/15,000ft $250/340) Packages are available (from $439) that include town pick-ups in a white limousine, DVDs, photos and T-shirts.

🌿 Taupo Tandem Skydiving
SKYDIVING

(☑0800 826 336; www.taupotandemskydiving.com; 12,000ft/15,000ft $249/339) Various packages that include DVDs, photos, T-shirts etc ($388 to $679) are available.

Freefall!
SKYDIVING

(☑0800 373 335; www.freefall.net.nz; 12,000/15,000ft $249/339) DVDs and photos are extra.

Other Activities

There are good mountain-bike tracks just out of town in the Wairakei and Pureora Forests, and along the Waikato River. You can download maps for these from www.biketaupo.org.nz or pick them up at the i-SITE. While you're there, check on the status of the **Great Lake Trail**, a purpose-built 97km track from Whakaipo Bay to Waihaha in the remote western reaches of the lake. At the time of research only the **W2K** section had been completed, from Whakaipo to Kinloch.

There are some great walks in and around Taupo, ranging from sedate ambles to more gnarly all-dayers; collect a booklet from the i-SITE.

Great Lake Walkway
WALKING

This pleasant path follows the Taupo lakefront south to Five Mile Bay (8km). It's a flat, easy walk along public-access beaches.

Huka Falls Walkway
WALKING

Starting from the Spa Park car park at the end of County Ave (off Spa Rd), this scenic, easy walk takes just over an hour to reach the falls, following the east bank of the Waikato River. Continuing on from the falls is the 7km Huka Falls to Aratiatia Rapids walking track (another two-plus hours).

Taupo Bungy
BUNGY

(Map p248; 07-377 1135; www.taupobungy.co.nz; 202 Spa Rd; solo/tandem $149/298; 8.30am-5pm, extended in summer) Sitting on a cliff edge over the mighty Waikato River, this picturesque bungy site is the most popular on the North Island, with plenty of vantage points if you're too chicken to jump. Nonchickens will be led onto a platform jutting 20m out over the cliff (the world's first cantilever jump, for engineering boffins) and convinced, with masterly skill, to throw themselves off the edge. A heart-stopping 47m hurtle and a few bounces back and it's safely into the boat. You can opt for a slight dunk in the river, or strap yourself to a friend and leap off together. Alternatively, try the giant swing (solo/tandem $99/180).

If you want all of the glory and none of the terror, the wonders of Photoshop and a blue screen now allow you to 'Fake It' ($25).

Taupo Horse Treks
HORSE RIDING

(Map p248; 07-378 0356; www.taupohorsetreks.co.nz; Karapiti Rd; per hr $70, pony ride $30) Conducts treks through some fine forest with good views over the Craters of the Moon.

Big Sky Parasail
PARASAILING

(Map p246; 0800 724 4759; www.bigskyparasail.co.nz; Lake Tce; 400ft/800ft $79/89; 9am-5pm Dec-Apr) Parasailing flights from the lakefront, taking off hourly; bookings essential.

Rock'n Ropes
ROPES COURSE

(Map p248; 07-374 8111; www.rocknropes.co.nz; 65 Karetoto Rd; giant swing $20, adrenaline combo $40, half-day $65) A vertiginous and challenging high-ropes course that includes balancing in teetering 'tree-tops', negotiating a tricky two-wire bridge and scaling ropes. The combo includes the swing, high beam and trapeze.

Kaimanawa Heli-Biking
MOUNTAIN BIKING

(07-384 2816; www.kaimanawahelibiking.co.nz; 4hr ride $395) For luxury rough riding, Heli-Biking will pick you up in a helicopter and drop you on top of the highest point in the Kaimanawa range, allowing you to ride all the way down.

Formula Challenge
MOTOR RACING

(Map p248; 07-377 0338; www.fcr.co.nz; Broadlands Rd; driving experience $340-740) Thrill seekers with petrol-head tendencies should head to the Taupo Motorsport Park, a state-of-the-art 3.5km racetrack and drag circuit that has staged the A1 Grand Prix. There's often something to watch here, from sidecar races to 'drifters' and, on occasion, the police testing their skills. Best of all, this outfit allows you to get behind the wheel in a V8 or Formula Challenge racer.

Taupo Gliding Club
GLIDING

(Map p248; 07-378 5627; www.taupoglidingclub.co.nz; Centennial Dr; flights $120-195) Flights daily by appointment (weather permitting).

Pointons Ski Shop
SKIING

(Map p246; 07-377 0087; www.pointons.co.nz; 57 Tongariro St; ski/snowboard hire $30/40) Taupo is tantalisingly close to the ski fields, being 1¼ hours drive from Whakapapa and two hours from Turoa. This shop hires gear and stays open from 7am to 7pm throughout the season.

Wairakei Golf & Sanctuary
GOLF

(Map p248; 07-374 8152; www.wairakeigolfcourse.co.nz; SH1; 18 holes $155-225) In late 2009 a 2m-high, 5km-long pest-proof fence was erected, turning the whole course into a native bird sanctuary. It's a challenging 18 holes set in 150 hectares of beautiful countryside.

Taupo Golf Club
GOLF

(Map p248; 07-378 6933; www.taupogolf.co.nz; 32 Centennial Dr; 18 holes $52-60, club hire $25-50) Has two good 18-hole courses; one is a park course and the other an inland links.

Tours

pureORAwalks
CULTURAL TOUR

(021-042 2722; www.pureorawalks.com; adult/child $105/97) Nature-Culture walks in Pureora Forest Park, Lake Rotopounamu and Whirinaki Forest Park, offering insight into *Maoritanga* (things Maori) – including local history, legends and traditional uses for flora and fauna.

Kai Waho Experience

CULTURAL TOUR

(www.kaiwaho.co.nz; price on application) Whisks you to a remote *pa* in wilderness east of the lake for a day of Maori culture and a *hangi*-cooked feast.

Taupo Quad Adventures

QUAD BIKES

(07-377 6404; www.taupoquads.co.nz; SH1, Maroa; 1hr to full day $85-299) Offers fully guided off-road quad-bike trips, 24km north of town opposite the turn-off to Orakei Korako.

Helipro

SCENIC FLIGHTS

(07-377 8805; www.helipro.co.nz; flights $99-1150) Specialises in heli-tours, which include alpine and White Island landings, as well as shorter scenic flights over the town, lake and volcanoes.

Helistar Helicopters

SCENIC FLIGHTS

(Map p248; 07-374 8405; www.helistar.co.nz; 415 Huka Falls Rd; flights $99-995) Offers a variety of scenic helicopter flights, from 10 minutes to two hours. Combine a Helistar trip with the Huka Falls Jet in the Huka Star combo (from $193).

Izardair

SCENIC FLIGHTS

(07-378 7835; www.izardair.com; flights $100-310) Luxury light aircraft flights over Taupo, Orakei Korako or the volcanoes.

Taupo Air Services

SCENIC FLIGHTS

(07-378 5325; www.taupoair.com; flights $100-550) Runs light aircraft flights, from the 15-minute Local Look to a two-hour trip to White Island.

Taupo's Floatplane

SCENIC FLIGHTS

(Map p246; 07-378 7500; www.tauposfloatplane.co.nz; flights $85-625) Located at the entrance to the marina, the floatplane offers a variety of trips, including quick flights over the lake and longer ones over Mt Ruapehu or White Island. Packages include the Taupo Trifecta (floatplane trip, followed by a jet-boat trip and a walk through Orakei Korako; $440).

Paradise Tours

BUS TOUR

(07-378 9955; www.paradisetours.co.nz; adult/child $99/45) Three-hour tours to the Aratiatia Rapids, Craters of the Moon and Huka Falls. Also offers day tours to Tongariro National Park, Orakei Korako, Rotorua, Hawke's Bay and Waitomo Caves.

Festivals & Events

Heralding itself as the events capital of NZ, Taupo plays host to numerous big shindigs throughout the year, many of them of a sporting nature – and many of which you can enter and participate in. See www.great laketaupo.com for more details.

Epic Swim

SPORTS

(www.epicswim.co.nz) Brave the lake waters in mid-January alongside some of the best swimmers in NZ. Courses range from 1km to 10km.

NZ Body Painting Festival

ARTS

(www.bodyartawards.co.nz) Three days of decorated flesh brightens up the lakeside in late January.

Great Lake Relay

SPORTS

(www.relay.co.nz) Hustle together 10 to 18 mates (or badger some backpackers) for a tag-team circumnavigation of the lake. It takes place mid-February and it doesn't matter whether you walk or run, as long as you finish your allotted leg.

Ironman New Zealand

SPORTS

(www.ironman.co.nz) Bring a magnet, as buns of steel are plentiful during this pimped-up triathlon. Held in early March, it's the country's biggest annual one-day event. A half-ironman (half fluffy bunny?) is held in December.

100K Flyer

SPORTS

(www.100kflyer.co.nz) A 100km road-cycling race from Rotorua to Taupo; late March.

Erupt Festival

ARTS

(www.erupt.co.nz/Erupt-Festival) Biennial arts festival, held over 11 days in May on even numbered years.

Winterfest

FAMILY

Billed as a festival of old-fashioned family fun, this July celebration includes a trolley derby and temporary snowpark.

Day-Night Thriller

SPORTS

(www.daynightthriller.co.nz; Spa Park) Held in September, this 12-hour event attracts more than 3000 mountain bikers, competing in teams or as individuals.

BikeFest & Lake Taupo Cycle Challenge

SPORTS

(www.bikefest.co.nz) One of NZ's biggest annual cycling events, the 160km Lake Taupo Cycle Challenge, sees around 10,000 people pedalling around the lake on the last Saturday in November. It's preceded by a week-long festival.

🛏 Sleeping

Taupo is motel central, with many spread out along the lake, especially southeast of the town centre at Waipahihi and Two Mile Bay. Acacia Bay, 5km to the west, has some good B&Bs. Areas have been designated for Freedom Campers between the hours of 5pm and 10am at the Ferry Rd parking bay and at the marina. Best of all is the **Reid's Farm Recreation Reserve** (Map p248; Huka Falls Rd), a beautiful spot beside the Waikato River.

Lake
MOTEL $$

(Map p248; ☑07-378 4222; www.thelakeonline. co.nz; 63 Mere Rd; apt $155-220) A reminder that 1960s and '70s design wasn't all Austin Powers–style groovaliciousness, this unusual boutique motel is crammed with furniture from the era's signature designers. The studio is a tight fit, but the four one-bedroom units all have kitchenettes and dining/living areas.

Beechtree
MOTEL $$

(Map p246; ☑07-377 0181; www.beechtreemotel. co.nz; 56 Rifle Range Rd; apt $140-390; @🛜) The Beechtree, and its sister motel Miro next door, offer classy rooms at reasonable rates. The design is fresh and modern, with neutral-toned decor, large windows, ground-floor patios and upstairs balconies.

Cottage Mews
MOTEL $$

(Map p248; ☑07-378 3004; www.cottagemews. co.nz; 311 Lake Tce, Two Mile Bay; apt $115-210; 🛜) Few motels muster much charm, but this cute gable-roofed block, festooned with hanging flowers, manages to seem almost rustic. Some units have lake views, most have spa baths and all have a small private garden.

Blackcurrant Backpackers
HOSTEL $

(Map p246; ☑07-378 9292; www.blackcurrentbp. co.nz; 20 Taniwha St; dm $27-28, s/d $60/78; @🛜) Fashioned from an ageing motel, our favourite Taupo hostel has private rooms with en suites and supercomfy beds. The staff rival the cartoon blackcurrants in the Ribena ads for chirpiness.

Sacred Waters
APARTMENTS $$$

(Map p246; ☑07-376 1400; www.sacredwaters. co.nz; 221-225 Lake Tce, Waipahihi; apt $360-670; 🛜🛁) Apart from some awful mass-produced 'art', these large apartments are stylish and well-designed. Each has a contemporary kitchen and its own private thermal plunge pool, and most have wonderful lake views.

Acacia Cliffs Lodge
B&B $$$

(☑07-378 1551; www.acaciacliffslodge.co.nz; 133 Mapara Rd, Acacia Bay; r $700; @🛜) Pushing the romance switch way past 'rekindle', this luxurious B&B, high in the hills above Acacia Bay, offers four modern suites – three with sumptuous lake views and one that compensates for the lack of them with a curvy bath and a private garden.

Taupo Urban Retreat
HOSTEL $

(Map p246; ☑07-378 6124; www.tur.co.nz; 65 Heu Heu St; dm $25-29, r $70; @) A younger crowd gravitates to this purpose-built hostel, attracted by its publike hub and carefree style. It's refreshingly modern in design with a beach-house feel, despite being on a busy road.

🏆 Catelli's of Taupo
MOTEL $$

(Map p246; ☑07-378 4477; www.catellis.co.nz; 23-27 Rifle Range Rd; apt $135-230; 🛜) The exterior is all hobbitish '80s curves, sloping roofs and nipple-pink trim, but these orderly motel units have a fresh feel inside. In summer it's worth paying the extra $5 for a garden studio.

🏆 Hilton Lake Taupo
HOTEL $$$

(Map p248; ☑07-378 7080; www.hilton.com/lake taupo; 80-100 Napier Taupo Hwy; from $230; @🛜🛁) Occupying the historic Terraces Hotel (1889) and a recent extension, this large complex offers the expected Hilton standard of luxury in non-threatening shades of grey. It's a little out of town but is handy for the DeBretts thermal complex.

🏆 Taupo DeBretts Spa Resort
HOLIDAY PARK $

(Map p248; ☑07-378 8559; www.taupodebretts. com; 76 Napier Taupo Hwy; sites from $20, units $90-275; @🛜) More of a holiday park than a flashy resort, DeBretts offers everything from tent sites to motel-style units. It's a five-minute drive from downtown, but it's well worth the hop for the indulgent thermal pools that share its home.

Reef Resort
APARTMENTS $$

(Map p248; ☑07-378 5115; www.accommodation taupo.com; 219 Lake Tce; apt $145-480; 🛜🛁) Like the ducks that congregate here in winter, warming their butts in the hot springs, so too do Taupo's apartment complexes jostle for the free thermal waters on this stretch of the lake. Reef offers attractive, well-priced units of varying sizes, including a luxurious three-bedroom apartment that is right by the shore.

Bella Vista
MOTEL $$
(Map p246; 07-378 9043; www.bellavistamotels.co.nz; 145 Heu Heu St; apt $120-190;) The canine-adverse may find the owners' big docile dog a little offputting, but the units here are clean and comfortable, if a little bland. There's a communal barbecue at the rear of the complex.

Silver Fern Lodge
HOSTEL $
(Map p246; 07-377 4929; www.silverfernlodge.co.nz; cnr Tamamutu & Kaimanawa Sts; dm $25, r $60-110;) Rooms range from 10-bed dorms to studio en suite units in this large, custom-built complex, trimmed in shiny corrugated aluminium yet still strangely lifeless, decorwise. There's a large communal kitchen and lounge.

Tiki Lodge
HOSTEL $
(Map p246; 07-377 4545; www.tikilodge.co.nz; 104 Tuwharetoa St; dm $27, r $80-90;) This hostel has lake and mountain views from the balcony, a spacious kitchen, comfy lounges, lots of Maori artwork and a spa pool out the back.

All Seasons
HOLIDAY PARK $
(Map p248; 07-378 4272; www.taupoallseasons.co.nz; 16 Rangatira St; sites from $20, dm $47, units $75-240;) A pleasant holiday park, located five minutes' walk from town, with well-established trees and hedgerows between sites, a playground, games room, thermal pool, bike hire and good kitchen facilities.

Lake Taupo Top 10 Holiday Resort
HOLIDAY PARK $
(Map p248; 07-378 6860; www.taupotop10.co.nz; 41 Centennial Dr; sites from $50, units $123-365;) The slickest of the local camping grounds, this 20-acre park has all the mod cons, including heated swimming pool, tennis courts and an on-site shop. It's about 2.5km from the i-SITE.

Chelmswood
MOTEL $$
(Map p248; 07-378 2715; www.chelmswood.co.nz; 250 Lake Tce, Waipahihi; r $115-295;) It's starting to look a little tired, but this Tudor-style motel has simple studios and larger family rooms, most with their own mineral pool. There's a heated outdoor pool, a sauna, and a sandpit for the littlies.

Eating

Bistro Lago
ITALIAN $$$
(Map p248; 07-377 1400; www.bistrolago.co.nz; 80-100 Napier Taupo Hwy; breakfast $25-35, pizza $22-23, mains $37-42; breakfast, lunch & dinner) Under the long-distance tutelage of Auckland-based celebrity chef Simon Gault, the Hilton's inhouse restaurant delivers inventive Italian-influenced dishes using quality regional ingredients. The view, stretching over the lake to the distant mountains, only adds to the magic.

Vine Eatery
TAPAS $$
(Map p246; www.sceniccellars.co.nz; 37 Tuwharetoa St; tapas $9-20; 9am-late) Sharing the Scenic Cellars wine store, this chic eatery continues the communal ethos with a 'shared plates' menu – offering traditional tapas alongside heftier divisible dishes. Of course, the wine list is excellent.

Brantry
MODERN NZ $$$
(Map p246; 07-378 0484; www.thebrantry.co.nz; 45 Rifle Range Rd; mains $38-42, 2-/3-course set menu $45/60; dinner) It's an unusual set-up, operating out of an unobtrusive 1950s house, but the Campbell sisters have turned Brantry into one of the most well-regarded restaurants in the region. The menu makes use of top-quality cuts of beef and lamb.

Pimentos
INTERNATIONAL $$
(Map p246; 07-377 4549; 17 Tamamutu St; mains $28-30; dinner Wed-Mon) Pimentos is such a local favourite that you'd be wise to book ahead. The lamb shanks and mash are legendary, but the relatively short menu offers plenty of well-considered experimentation.

Plateau
PUB $$
(Map p246; www.plateautaupo.co.nz; 64 Tuwharetoa St; mains $20-35; lunch & dinner) Plateau is a great place for a drink (Monteith's beer being the main poison), but it's as a gastro-pub that it shines. The menu offers rustic pub classics with fancy fusion tweaks.

L'Arté
CAFE $
(www.larte.co.nz; 255 Mapara Rd, Acacia Bay; mains $10-19; 9am-4pm Wed-Sun, daily Jan) Lots of mouth-watering treats are made from scratch at this fantastically artful cafe on the hill that backs Acacia Bay. After your arty latte, check out the sculpture garden and gallery.

Eruption
CAFE $

(Map p246; www.eruptioncoffee.co.nz; Suncourt Centre, Tamamutu St; mains $7-17; ⊙7.30am-3.30pm) Shelter behind one of the free newspapers while Eruption's espresso machine steams and spurts out black rivers topped with creamy foam. The food selection is limited but good.

Replete
CAFE $

(Map p246; www.replete.co.nz; 45 Heu Heu St; mains $7-18; ⊙8.30am-4pm) The counter at Replete is packed full of delicatessen delights – running the gamut from sandwiches and salads to sweets. Its pastry selection is particularly commendable. A blackboard menu offers inexpensive and interesting light meals.

Lotus
THAI $$

(Map p246; www.lotusthai.co.nz; 137 Tongariro St; mains $16-21; ⊙lunch Wed-Fri, dinner Wed-Mon; ☑) A warm and inviting restaurant with Siamese trimmings throughout, offering standard Thai fare in plentiful portions.

Piccolo
CAFE $

(Map p246; 41 Ruapehu St; mains $11-19; ⊙7am-4pm; ☜) Good coffee, tasty food and free wifi – that's something to toot your flute about.

Drinking

Things get lively in the height of summer when the town fills up with travellers. The rest of the year it might pay to take a newspaper to read over your pint.

Shed
PUB

(Map p246; www.theshedbar.co.nz; 18 Tuwharetoa St; ⊙3pm-late Mon & Tue, noon-late Wed-Sun) A lively place to sup a beer and catch the big game, sit outside and watch the world go by, or strut your stuff to DJs on the weekends. Food is punter-pleasing pub fare in man-sized portions.

Finn MacCuhal's
IRISH PUB

(Map p246; www.finns.co.nz; cnr Tongariro & Tuwharetoa Sts; ⊙11am-late) With Irish ephemera nailed to the walls and a backpackers' next door, you can be sure that there will be plenty of craic here. DJs and bands play on the weekends.

Jolly Good Fellows
PUB

(Map p246; 76 Lake Tce; ⊙11am-late) Corr, Guvnor! You ain't seen a pub like this since old Blighty, with lashings of cultural cliches and Old Speckled Hen, Tetleys and Bulmers cider on tap.

Mulligans
IRISH PUB

(Map p246; 15 Tongariro St; ⊙11am-late) A good spot for a quiet Guinness among the locals.

☆ Entertainment

Great Lake Centre
CONCERT VENUE

(Map p246; www.taupovenues.co.nz; Tongariro St) Hosts performances, exhibitions and conventions. Ask at the i-SITE for the current program.

Starlight Cinema Centre
CINEMA

(Map p246; www.starlightcinema.co.nz; Starlight Arcade, off Horomatangi St; adult/child $13/8.50) Screens the latest Hollywood blockbusters.

❶ Information

Experience Taupo (☎07-377 0704; www.experiencetaupo.co.nz; 29 Tongariro St; ⊙9am-6pm; @) A private agency booking activities, tours and transport. It also offers internet access.

Taupo i-SITE (☎07-376 0027; www.greatlaketaupo.com; Tongariro St; ⊙8.30am-5pm) Handles bookings for accommodation, transport and activities; dispenses cheerful advice; and stocks Department of Conservation (DOC) maps and town maps.

❶ Getting There & Away

Taupo Airport (☎07-378 7771; www.taupoairport.co.nz; 33 Anzac Memorial Dr) is 8km south of town. InterCity buses stop at the **Taupo Travel Centre** (☎07-378 9005; 16 Gascoigne St), which operates as a booking office. Naked Bus services (p244) stop outside the i-SITE.

Shuttle services (p265) operate year-round between Taupo, Turangi and Tongariro National Park. In winter, services run to Whakapapa Ski Area (1½ hours) and can include package deals for lift tickets and ski hire.

❶ Getting Around

Shuttle 2U (☎07-376 7638; www.shuttle2u.co.nz; per stop $4-10, day pass $15) operates an on-demand shuttle service, picking up from local accommodation and stopping at all major attractions in and around Taupo.

Hotbus (☎0508 468 287; www.alpinehotbus.co.nz; 1st stop $15, then per stop $5) is a hop-on, hop-off minibus that covers similar sights, departing from the i-SITE.

Taxi companies include **Taupo Taxi** (☎07-378 5100; www.taupotaxi.co.nz) and **Top Cabs** (☎07-378 9250; 23 Tuwharetoa St). Expect to pay about $25 for a cab from the airport to the centre of town.

Around Taupo

ORAKEI KORAKO

A bit off the beaten track, **Orakei Korako** (☏07-378 3131; www.orakeikorako.co.nz; adult/ child $34/14; ⊙8am-5pm) gets fewer visitors than other thermal areas. Yet, since the destruction of the Pink and White Terraces, it is arguably the best thermal area left in NZ, even though three-quarters of the original site now lies beneath the dam waters of Lake Ohakuri.

A walking track that's steep in parts largely follows a boardwalk around the colourful silica terraces for which the park is famous, and passes geysers and **Ruatapu Cave** (allow 1½ hours). This impressive natural cave has a jade-green pool, thought to have been used as a mirror by Maori women preparing for rituals (Orakei Korako means 'the place of adorning'). Entry includes a boat ride across Lake Ohakuri.

It's about 35 minutes to Orakei Korako from Taupo. Take SH1 towards Hamilton for 23km, and then travel for 14km from the signposted turn-off. From Rotorua the turn-off is on SH5, via Mihi.

Alternatively, **NZ River Jet** (☏07-333 7111; www.riverjet.co.nz; SH5, Mihi; 2½hr entry incl entry to Orakei Korako adult/child $159/79) will zip you there in thrilling fashion from Mihi, 20km upstream on the Waikato River. The operator also offers The Squeeze – a highly recommended jetboat ride through Tutukau Gorge to a spot where you can disembark in warm water and edge your way through a crevice to a concealed natural thermal waterfall surrounded by native bush ($139).

If it was difficult to resist all that enticing but scalding water at Orakei Korako, but you don't fancy a squeeze, a 30km detour will take you to **Butcher's Pool** (admission free), a bedecked but otherwise purely natural thermal spring in the middle of a farmer's paddock. Alongside is a small parking area and changing sheds. To get there, turn left onto SH5 at Mihi (follow the signs to Rotorua). After 4km look out for Homestead Rd on your right. Follow it to the end, turn left and look for a row of trees lining a gravel driveway off to your right about 300m away (the signpost can be difficult to spot as it's pointing from the other side of the road).

MANGAKINO & WHAKAMARU

These neighbouring towns, like their respective lakes (Maraetai and Whakamaru), are by-products of hydroelectric schemes on the Waikato River. The power stations are still in operation, but the main drawcards today are activities on or around the lakes.

🏄 Activities

Paddleboat Company   CRUISE
(☏07-882 8826; www.paddleboat.co.nz; 1/2hr cruise $25/35) Splash along the lake in a paddleboat, which over the course of a century has transported everything from cattle to the Queen.

M-I-A Wakeboarding   WAKEBOARDING
(☏021 864 254; www.m-i-a.co.nz; wakeboard/wakeskate/wakesurf $100/100/75) M-I-A tears up the water on Mangakino's Lake Maraetai, offering wakeboarding, wakeskating and wakesurfing as well as basic backpacker accommodation (dorm/double $23/54).

Waikato River Trails   TRAMPING, CYCLING
(www.waikatorivertrails.com) Mangakino and Whakamaru are stops on this 100km walking and cycling route, which follows the river from near the southern end of Lake Karapiro to Atiamuri, 38km north of Taupo.

🛏 Sleeping & Eating

Freedom camping is permitted near the **Bus Stop Café** (mains $6-9; ⊙Tue-Sun), which dishes out burgers and toasties from the back of an old Bedford bus on the Maraetai lakefront.

PUREORA FOREST PARK

Fringing the western edge of Lake Taupo, the 78,000-hectare Pureora Forest is home to NZ's tallest totara tree. Logging was stopped in this forest in the 1980s after a long campaign by conservationists, and the subsequent regeneration is impressive. There are mountain-bike tracks and hiking routes through the park, including tracks to the summits of **Mt Pureora** (1165m) and the rock pinnacle of **Mt Titiraupenga** (1042m). A 12m-high tower, a short walk from the Bismarck Rd car park, provides a canopy-level view of the forest for birdwatchers.

To stay overnight in one of three standard DOC huts (adult/child $5.10/2.50) you'll need to buy hut tickets in advance, unless you have a backcountry hut pass. The three campsites (adult/child $8/2) have self-registration boxes. Hut tickets, maps and information on the park are available from DOC.

Awhina Wilderness Experience (www.awhinatours.co.nz; per person $175) offers five-hour walking tours with local Maori guides through virgin bush to the summit of Titiraupenga, their sacred mountain. Farmstay accommodation is also available.

Turangi & Around

POP 3500

Once a service town for the nearby hydro-electric power station, sleepy Turangi's claim to fame nowadays is as the 'Trout Fishing Capital of the World' and as one of the country's premier white water–rafting destinations. Set on the Tongariro River, the town is a shortish hop for snow-bunnies from the ski fields and walking tracks of Tongariro National Park.

◉ Sights & Activities

There are several short walks around town. A favourite is the **Tongariro River Lookout Track** (one-hour loop), a riverside amble affording views of Mt Pihanga. This track joins the **Tongariro River Walkway** (three hours return), which follows the river to the Red Hut suspension bridge, and will eventually hook up with the **Tongariro River Trail** (www.tongariirorivertrail.co.nz), a multiday walking and mountain-biking route, which was being finalised at the time of research.

Other good leg-stretchers include **Hine-mihi's Track**, near the top of Te Ponanga Saddle, 8km west of Turangi on SH47 (15 minutes return); **Maunganamu Track**, 4km west of Turangi on SH41 (40 minutes return); and **Tauranga-Taupo River Walk** (30 minutes), which starts at Te Rangiita, 12km north of Turangi on SH1.

The Tongariro River has some superb Grade III rapids for river rafting, as well as Grade I stretches suitable for beginners in the lower reaches during summer.

It's also a likely spot for trout fishing (p250).

Tongariro National Trout Centre AQUARIUM
(Map p261; www.troutcentre.com; SH1; adult/child $10/free; ☺10am-3pm) The DOC-managed trout hatchery has polished educational displays, a collection of rods and reels dating back to the 1880s and freshwater aquariums displaying river life, both nasty and nice. A gentle stroll along the landscaped walkway leads to the hatchery, keeping ponds, an underwater viewing chamber and a picnic area.

Tokaanu Thermal Pools SWIMMING
(Map p261; Mangaroa St, Tokaanu; adult/child $6/4, private pools per 20min $10/6; ☺10am-9pm) Soak in thermally heated water at this unpretentious, family-orientated facility, 5km north-west of Turangi. A 20-minute stroll along the boardwalk (wheelchair accessible) showcases

Turangi

Turangi

◉ Activities, Courses & Tours
1 Barry Greig's Sporting World	A1
Creel Tackle House	(see 6)
2 Rafting NZ	B1
3 Sporting Life	A2
4 Tongariro River Rafting	A3
Vertical Assault	(see 7)

◉ Sleeping
5 Anglers Paradise Motel	A2
6 Creel Lodge	B2
7 Extreme Backpackers	B1
8 Judges Pool Motel	B2
9 Parklands Motor Lodge	B2
10 Riverstone Backpackers	B1
11 Sportmans Lodge	B1

◉ Eating
12 Grand Central Fry	B1

boiling mud pools, thermal springs and a trout-filled stream.

Rafting NZ RAFTING
(Map p257; ☎0800 865 226; www.raftingnew zealand.com; 41 Ngawaka Pl) Offering a warm welcome, hot showers and a taste of Maori culture, this operator is a popular choice.

The main trips offered are Tongariro White-water with an optional waterfall jump (Grade III, four hours, adult/child $119/109) and the Family Fun raft over more relaxed rapids (Grade II, three hours, adult/child $75/65). Groups of four or more can tackle an overnighter (Grade III+, per person $350), rafting to a riverside campsite and then hitting more rapids the following day.

Tongariro River Rafting RAFTING
(Map p257; ☑07-386 6409; www.trr.co.nz; Atirau Rd; adult/child $109/99) Test the white waters with a Gentle Family Float (adult/child $75/65), splash straight into the Grade III rapids (adult/child $115/105), or try a full day's raft fishing (summer only, price on enquiry). The operator also hires out mountain bikes and runs guided trips and shuttles on the 42 Traverse, Tongariro River Track, Moerangi Station, Tree Trunk Gorge and Fishers Track. Kayaking and multi-activity combos are also available.

Wai Maori KAYAKING
(☑07-386 0315; www.waimaori.com; Tokaanu) Offers guided white-water kayaking (November to April, per person $159) or trips accompanied only by trout down the gentle Tokaanu Stream to Lake Taupo, passing boiling mud, hot pools and wetlands on the way (90 minutes/half-day/full day $30/40/65).

Flyfishtaupo.com FISHING
(☑07-377 8054; www.flyfishtaupo.com; prices on application) Guide Brett Pirie offers a range of fishing excursions, including seniors-focussed 'Old Farts & Tarts' trips.

Central Plateau Fishing FISHING
(☑027 285 6593; www.cpf.net.nz; half-/full day from $300/550) Guided fly-fishing, boat charters (per hour $100) and quad-bike adventure fishing in Tongariro National Park (from $750). Licences extra.

Ian & Andrew Jenkins FISHING
(☑07-386 0840; www.tui-lodge.co.nz; half-/full day $350/600) Father and son fly-fishing guides.

John Somervell FISHING
(☑07-386 5931; www.nymphfish.com; half-/full day from $225/450) Well-priced guided fly-fishing.

AJ Charters FISHING, CRUISE
(☑07-386 7992; www.ajtaupocharters.com; per hr from $120) Fishing trips and scenic lake cruises on a two-storey catamaran.

Barry Greig's Sporting World FISHING
(Map p257; ☑07-386 6911; www.greigsports.co.nz; 59 Town Centre) Hires and sells gear and handles bookings for guides and charters.

Creel Tackle House FISHING
(Map p257; ☑07-386 7929; 183 Taupahi Rd) Fishing equipment and tips.

Sporting Life FISHING
(Map p257; www.sportinglife-turangi.co.nz; Town Centre) This sports store is laden with fishing paraphenalia. Its website details the latest fishing conditions.

Motuoapa Hire Boats BOATING
(☑07-386 7000; Motuoapa Esplanade; per hr $39) Hires aluminium dinghies for lake fishing, 10km northeast of Turangi.

Vertical Assault CLIMBING
(Map p257; www.extremebackpackers.co.nz; 22 Ngawaka Pl; adult/child $20/15; ⊗9am-5pm Thu-Tue, 9am-8pm Wed) For wet-weather thrills, head here to scale walls built to challenge all skill levels.

🛏 Sleeping

Riverstone Backpackers HOSTEL $
(Map p257; ☑07-386 7004; www.riverstoneback packers.com; 222 Tautahanga Rd; dm $25-30, r $62-84; @) Reborn as a bijou backpackers, this cleverly refitted old house has an enviable kitchen, comfortable lounge and a stylish landscaped yard (with pizza oven). It's a true home away from home.

Creel Lodge LODGE $$
(Map p257; ☑07-386 8081; www.creel.co.nz; 183 Taupahi Rd; s $110-130, d $125-145; ☎) Set in green and peaceful grounds, this heavenly hideaway backs onto a fine stretch of the Tongariro River. It's worth upgrading to an executive garden suite for a smarter unit in an attractive punga-fenced garden.

Oreti Village APARTMENTS $$$
(Map p261; ☑07-386 7070; www.oretivillage.com; Mission House Dr, Pukawa; apt $220-280; ☎) This enclave of luxury self-contained apartments might give you a hankering for 'village' life – which in Oreti's case entails gazing at blissful lake views from the comfort of a rolled-arm leather couch. Take SH41 for 15km, heading northwest of Turangi, and turn right into Pukawa Rd.

Sportmans Lodge GUESTHOUSE $$
(Map p257; ☎07-386 8150; www.sportsmanslodge.
co.nz; 15 Taupahi Rd; r $72, cottage $105-130; ☎)
Backing on to the river, this lodge is a hidden bargain for trout-fishing folk unbothered by punctuation. All the rooms share the lounge and well-equipped kitchen. The self-contained cottage sleeps four.

Extreme Backpackers HOSTEL $
(Map p257; ☎07-386 8949; www.extremeback
packers.co.nz; 22 Ngawaka Pl; dm $25-27, s $46-56,
d $62-72; @☎) Crafted from pine and corrugated iron, this modern backpackers has the bonus of a climbing wall, a cafe, a lounge with an open fire and a sunny courtyard with hammocks. Dorms range from four to eight beds and the pricier private rooms have en suites. The operators also run shuttles to Tongariro National Park.

Parklands Motor Lodge MOTEL $
(Map p257; ☎07-386 7515; www.parklandsmotor
lodge.co.nz; 25 Arahori St; sites from $17, units $110-
140; ☎☎) On SH1 but set back beyond an epic front lawn, Parklands offers a small but functional area for campervans and splay of well-presented units. There's a swimming pool and play area for the kids.

Anglers Paradise Motel MOTEL $$
(Map p257; ☎07-386 8980; www.anglersparadise.
co.nz; cnr Ohuanga Rd & Raukura St; units $119-160;
@☎) Looking like something out of Twin Peaks, this very old-fashioned motel sits in a 1-hectare leafy pocket where privacy prevails. It's geared up for anglers, with guides happily arranged and a smokehouse on-site.

Judges Pool Motel MOTEL $$
(Map p257; ☎07-386 7892; www.judgespoolmotel.
co.nz; 92 Taupahi Rd; units $105-145; ☎) This older motel has tidy, spacious rooms with kitchenettes. All one-bedroom units have outdoor decks for relaxing beers, although the barbecue area is the best place to talk about the one that got away.

✗ Eating

Tongariro Lodge MODERN NZ $$
(Map p261; ☎07-386 7946; www.tongarirolodge.
co.nz; 83 Grace Rd; mains $30-42; ☉dinner) Some of the world's most famous blokes (Robert Mitchum, Liam Neeson, Larry Hagman, Jimmy Carter, Timothy Dalton) have come to this luxury riverside fishing lodge, set in 9 hectares of parkland north of the town, to relax in wood-panelled anonymity. Not surprisingly, the menu is orientated around man-sized slabs of meat but the real squeals of delight come when lucky lodgers are presented with their day's catch, smoked and served to perfection.

Oreti Village FRENCH $$
(Map p261; ☎07-386 7070; Mission House Dr, Pukawa; mains $30-38; ☉lunch Sat & Sun, dinner Tue-Sun) It's hard to imagine a more romantic spot to while away a balmy summer's evening than looking over the lake from Oreti's terrace. It's an added bonus that the French-influenced food matches up.

Grand Central Fry FAST FOOD $
(Map p257; 8 Ohuanga Rd; meals $3-8; ☉11am-
8.30pm) This local legend serves top fish and chips, plus burgers and anything else fryable.

Licorice CAFE $
(57 SH1, Motuoapa; mains $9-17; ☉7am-4pm Wed-
Sat, 9am-4pm Sun) Look for the giant licorice allsort on the roof of this roadside cafe, 8km north of Turangi. It's better than any of the cafes in the town itself.

❶ Information
Turangi i-SITE (☎07-386 8999; www.great
laketauponz.com; Ngawaka Pl; ☉8.30am-5pm;
@☎) A good stop for information on Tongariro National Park, Kaimanawa Forest Park, trout fishing, and snow and road conditions. It issues DOC hut tickets, ski passes and fishing licences, and makes bookings for transport, accommodation and activities.

❶ Getting There & Away
Both InterCity (p244) and Naked Bus (p244) coaches stop outside the i-SITE.

THE CENTRAL PLATEAU

Tongariro National Park
Established in 1887, Tongariro was NZ's first, and the world's fourth, national park, and is one of NZ's three World Heritage Sites. Its three towering, active volcanoes – Ruapehu, Ngauruhoe and Tongariro – rise from a vast, scrub-covered alpine plateau, making this one of the nation's most spectacular locations. In summer it offers excellent short walks and longer tramps, most notably the Tongariro Northern Circuit and the Tongariro Alpine Crossing. In winter it's a busy ski area.

The three peaks were a gift to NZ from Ngati Tuwharetoa, the local *iwi* (tribe), who saw the act as the only way to preserve an area of spiritual significance.

◉ Sights

Mt Ruapehu   VOLCANO
(www.mtruapehu.com) The multipeaked summit of Ruapehu (2797m) is the highest and most active of the park's volcanoes, and the centre-piece of the national park, with Whakapapa Village (pronounced 'fa-ka-pa-pa'), numerous walking tracks and three ski fields on its slopes.

The name means 'pit of sound', a reference to its regular eruptions. It began erupting over 250,000 years ago and remains active today, with major eruptions roughly every 50 years. During the spectacular 1995 eruptions, Ruapehu spurted volcanic rock and cloaked the area in clouds of ash and steam. From June to September the following year the mountain rumbled, groaned and thrust ash clouds high into the sky, writing off the 1996 ski season. The latest eruption, accompanied by a small earthquake, came out of the blue in September 2007, seriously injuring a climber sleeping in a hut on the mountain.

The mountain was the cause of one of NZ's deadliest natural disasters. Eruptions in 1945 blocked the overflow of the crater lake, causing the water levels to rise dramatically. On Christmas Eve 1953 the dam burst and the flood of volcanic mud (known as a lahar) swept down the mountain and took out a railway bridge at Tangiwai (between Ohakune and Waiouru), just moments before a crowded express train arrived. The train was derailed and 153 people lost their lives.

The crater lake was blocked again by the 1995–96 eruption. As the levels rose, it was foreseen that a major lahar could lead to another catastrophe. Alarm systems were set up at the crater lake's edge and in March 2007 they were triggered when a moderate lahar swept down the Whangaehu Valley. No one was injured and there was little damage to infrastructure.

Mt Ngauruhoe   VOLCANO
Much younger than the other two volcanoes, it is estimated that Ngauruhoe (2287m) formed in the last 2500 years. In contrast to the others, which have multiple vents, Ngauruhoe is a conical, single-vent volcano with perfectly symmetrical slopes – which is the reason that it was chosen to star as Mt Doom in Peter Jackson's *Lord of the Rings*. It can be climbed in summer, but in winter (under snow) this steep climb is only for experienced mountaineers.

Mt Tongariro   VOLCANO
The Red Crater of Mt Tongariro (1968m) last erupted in 1926. This ancient, but still active, volcano has coloured lakes dotting its uneven summit. The Tongariro Alpine Crossing, a magnificent walk, passes beside the lakes, right through several craters, and down through lush native forest.

🏃 Activities

The DOC and i-SITE visitor centres at Whakapapa, Ohakune and Turangi have maps and information on walks in the park, as well as track and weather conditions. Each January, DOC offers an excellent guided-walks program in and around the park; ask at DOC centres for information or book online. The national park is a popular skiing destination (p34).

Whakapapa &
Turoa Ski Areas   SKIING, SNOWBOARDING
(☑Turoa 06-385 8456, Whakapapa 07-892 4000; www.mtruapehu.com; daily lift pass adult/child $95/57, valid at both resorts) These linked resorts straddle either side of Mt Ruapehu and are NZ's two largest ski areas. Each offers similar skiing at an analogous altitude (around 2300m), with areas to suit each level of experience – from beginners' slopes to

---

Tongariro National Park & Around

black diamond runs for the pros. The same lift passes cover both ski areas. At the time of research a new lift was being planned for Turoa, providing access to a glacial area further up the mountain.

The only accommodation at the ski fields is in private lodges (mainly owned by ski clubs), so most Whakapaka visitors stay at Whakapaka or National Park Village. Turoa is only 16km from Ohakune, which has the best après-ski scene.

Tongariro National Park & Around

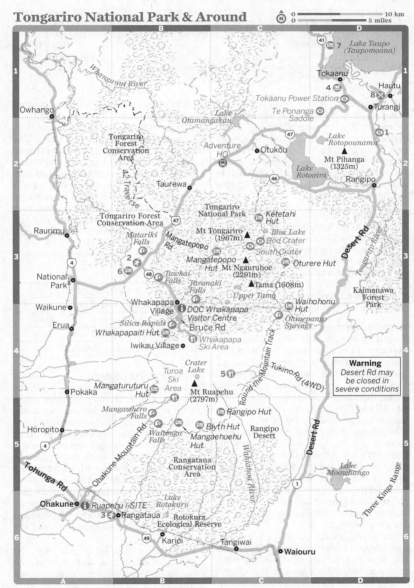

HOTHEADS TO THE RESCUE

Maori legend tells of the great *tohunga* (priest) and explorer Ngatoro-i-rangi, who first climbed Mt Tongariro. At the summit, realising he was close to freezing to death, he called out for assistance: *'ka riro au i te tonga'* ('I am carried away by the cold south wind') – and from these words the name Tongariro is derived.

The fire spirits, Te Pupu and Te Hoata, roared underground from the sacred island homeland of Hawaiki to find Ngatoro-i-rangi, but stuck their heads up first at Whakaari (White Island), then exploded out at Rotorua before finally bursting forth in the volcanoes of Tongariro to warm the explorer.

Because of this divine intervention, Maori revere these sites and once used the pools around them for rituals as well as cooking, dyes and medicine.

Tukino Ski Area
SKIING, SNOWBOARDING

(Map p261; ☎06-387 6294, 0800 885 466; www. tukino.co.nz; daily lift pass adult/child $50/30) Club-operated Tukino is on Mt Ruapehu's east, 46km from Turangi. It's quite remote, 14km down a gravel road from the sealed Desert Rd (SH1), and you need a 4WD vehicle to get in. Uncrowded, with mostly beginner and intermediate runs.

42 Traverse
MOUNTAIN BIKING

This four- to six-hour, 46km mountain-bike trail through the Tongariro Forest is one of the most popular one-dayers on the North Island. The Traverse follows old logging tracks, making for relatively dependable going, although there are plenty of ups and downs – more downs as long as you start from Kapoors Rd (off SH47) and head down to Owhango.

Tongariro Northern Circuit
TRAMPING

Classed as one of NZ's Great Walks, the Northern Circuit circumnavigates Ngauruhoe and affords spectacular views all around, particularly of Mt Tongariro. As a circuit, there are several start and finish points, including Whakapapa Village, Ketetahi Rd and Desert Rd. The walk covers the famous Tongariro Alpine Crossing.

Highlights of the circuit include tramping through or past several volcanic craters, including the South Crater, Central Crater and Red Crater; brilliantly colourful volcanic lakes, including the Emerald Lakes, Blue Lake and the Upper and Lower Tama Lakes; the cold Soda Springs; and various other volcanic formations, including cones, lava flows and glacial valleys.

There are several possibilities for side trips that take from a few hours to overnight. The most popular side trip from the main track is to Ngauruhoe's summit (three hours return), but it is also possible to climb Tongariro from Red Crater (two hours return) or walk to the cold-water Ohinepango Springs from Waihohonu Hut (one hour return).

The safest and most popular time to walk the track is from December to March. The track is served by four well-maintained huts: Mangatepopo, Ketetahi, Oturere and Waihohonu. The huts have mattresses, gas cookers in summer, toilets and water. This track is quite difficult in winter, when it is covered in snow, and becomes a tough alpine trek requiring ice axes and crampons. You may need to factor in significant extra walking time, or not attempt it at all.

Estimated walking times in summer:

ROUTE	TIME
Whakapapa Village to Mangatepopo Hut	3-5hr
Mangatepopo Hut to Emerald Lakes	3½hr
Emerald Lakes to Oturere Hut	1½hr
Oturere Hut to Waihohonu Hut	3hr
Waihohonu Hut to Whakapapa Village	5½hr

Tongariro Alpine Crossing
TRAMPING

Reputedly the best one-day walk in NZ, the Tongariro Alpine Crossing traverses spectacular volcanic geography, from an active crater to steaming vents and beautiful coloured lakes. And the views aren't bad either. The track passes through vegetation zones ranging from alpine scrub and tussock to places at higher altitudes where there is no vegetation at all, to the lush podocarp forest as you descend from Ketetahi Hut towards the end of the track. It covers the most spectacular features of the Tongariro Northern Circuit between the Mangatepopo and Ketetahi Huts.

Although achievable in one day, the Crossing is exhausting and shouldn't be taken lightly. Weather can change without warning, so make sure you are adequately equipped. If you're not in top walking condition you may prefer to take two days, spending a night at Ketatahi Hut

Worthwhile side trips from the main track include ascents to the summits of Mts Ngauruhoe and Tongariro. Ngauruhoe can be ascended most easily from the Mangatepopo Saddle, reached near the beginning of the track after the first steep climb. It's a challenging unmarked ascent on a scree surface where rocks are easily dislodged – look out for those falling from above and take care if people are walking below you. The summit of Tongariro is reached by a poled route from Red Crater.

The Tongariro Alpine Crossing can be reached from Mangatepopo Rd, off SH47, and from Ketetahi Rd, off SH46. The Mangatepopo Hut, reached via Mangatepopo Rd, is near the start of the track, and the Ketetahi Hut is a couple of hours before the end. Theft from parked vehicles is a problem at both ends: don't leave valuables in the car and keep everything out of sight.

Because of its popularity, there are plenty of shuttle services to both ends of the track. The shuttles need to be booked and you'll be expected to complete the track in a reasonable time.

Note: this may be one of the world's great walks, but it's not an experience you'll enjoy if you're badly prepared or the weather is awful. In winter, the colourful lakes are hidden under a blanket of snow and the effect is quite different. If it's blowing a gale, pelting with rain or if you're wearing unsuitable clothing (jeans and flip-flops aren't alpine-appropriate), you're all but guaranteed to have a miserable, not to mention potentially dangerous, time.

Estimated summer walking times:

ROUTE	TIME
Mangatepopo Rd end to Mangatepopo Hut	15min
Mangatepopo Hut to South Crater	1½-2hr
South Crater to Mt Ngauruhoe summit (side trip)	2-3hr (return)
Red Crater to Tongariro summit (side trip)	1½hr (return)
South Crater to Emerald Lakes	1-1½hr
Emerald Lakes to Ketetahi Hut	1½hr
Ketetahi Hut to road end	1½hr

Round the Mountain Track   TRAMPING

This off-the-beaten-track hike is a quieter alternative to the busy Northern Circuit, but it's particularly tough, has some potentially tricky river crossings, and is not recommended for beginners or the unprepared. Looping around Mt Ruapehu, the trail takes in a diversity of country, from glacial rivers to tussocky moors to majestic mountain views. You should allow at least four days to complete the hike, with six days a realistic estimate if you're including side trips to the Blyth Hut or Tama Lakes.

You can get to the Round the Mountain trail from Whakapapa Village, the junction near Waihohonu Hut, Ohakune Mountain Rd, or Whakapapaiti Hut. Most trampers start at Whakapapa Village and return there to finish the loop.

The track is safest from December to March when there is little or no snow, and less chance of avalanche. At other times of year, navigation and walking is made difficult by snow, and full alpine gear (ice axe, crampons and specialised clothing) is a requirement. To attempt the track you should prepare thoroughly. Take sufficiently detailed maps, check on the latest conditions, and carry clothing for all climes and more-than-adequate food supplies. Be sure to leave your plans and intended return date with a responsible person and check in when you get back.

This track is served by Waihohonu, Rangipo, Mangaehuehu, Mangaturuturu and Whakapapaiti Huts, and a side trip can be made to Blyth Hut. Estimated summer walking times:

ROUTE	TIME
Whakapapa Village to Waihohonu Hut	5-6hr
Waihohonu Hut to Rangipo Hut	5hr
Rangipo Hut to Mangaehuehu Hut	5-6hr
Mangaehuehu Hut to Mangaturuturu Hut	5hr
Mangaturuturu Hut to Whakapapaiti Hut	6hr
Whakapapaiti Hut to Whakapapa Village	2-3hr
Tama Lakes (side trip)	1½hr
Blyth Hut (side trip)	1hr

ⓘ MOUNTAIN SAFETY

Many visitors to NZ come unstuck in the mountains. The weather can change quicker than you expect, and rescues (and fatalities) are not uncommon. When heading out on remote tracks, you must be properly equipped and take safety precautions, including leaving your itinerary with a responsible person.

Crater Lake
TRAMPING

The unmarked rugged route up to Ruapehu's Crater Lake (seven hours return) is a good one, allowing you to see the acidic lake up close, but this walk is strictly off limits when there's volcanic activity. This moderate-to-difficult walk begins at Iwikau Village at the top of the Bruce Rd. You can cut three hours off it by catching the **chairlift** (adult/child $26/16; ⊙9am-3.30pm mid-Dec–April) from Whakapapa Ski Area. **Guided walks** (⊠0508 782 734; www.mtruapehu.com; adult/child incl lift pass $145/95) to Crater Lake run from mid-December to mid-April, weather dependent. Like most of the walks in Tongariro, you'll need to check conditions before heading out and don't attempt it in winter unless you're a mountaineer.

Tama Lakes Track
TRAMPING

Starting at Whakapapa Village, this 17km track leads to the Tama Lakes, on the Tama Saddle between Ruapehu and Ngauruhoe (five to six hours return). The upper lake affords fine views of Ngauruhoe and Tongariro (beware of winds on the saddle).

Ridge Track
TRAMPING

A 30-minute return walk from Whakapapa that climbs through beech forest to alpine-shrub areas for views of all three peaks.

Silica Rapids Track
TRAMPING

From Whakapapa Village this 2½-hour, 7km loop track leads to the Silica Rapids, named for the silica mineral deposits formed there by rapids on the Waikare Stream.

Taranaki Falls Track
TRAMPING

A two-hour, 6km loop track heads from Whakapapa to the 20m Taranaki Falls on the Wairere Stream.

Whakapapa Nature Walk
WALKING

Suitable for wheelchairs, this 15-minute loop track begins about 200m above the visitor centre, passing through beech forest and gardens typical of the park's vegetation zones.

Tongariro Quads
QUAD BIKES

(⊠07-378 2662; www.tongariroquads.com; half-/full day $199/299) Takes guided trips through the Tongariro Forest Park along the 42 Traverse.

🛩 Mountain Air
SCENIC FLIGHTS

(Map p261; ⊠0800 922 812; www.mountainair. co.nz; junction SH47 & SH48; flights $115-220) Offers scenic flights ranging from 15 to 35 minutes covering the volcanoes and lakes. They also depart from Turangi ($275, 45 minutes) and Taupo ($299, 65 minutes).

🛩 Edge to Edge
SNOW SPORTS

(⊠0800 800 754; www.edgetoedge.co.nz; Skotel Alpine Resort; 1-day full ski gear $35-65, 1-day snowboard gear $43-71) Stocks a full range of skiing, climbing and alpine gear for hire.

🛏 Sleeping & Eating

Whakapapa Village has limited accommodation and prices quoted here are for summer; rates are generally much higher during the ski season. National Park village and Ohakune offer a greater range of options. National Park has the best selection of budget accommodation while Ohakune is a proper town, with a better array of eateries and shops.

🛩 Whakapapa Holiday Park
HOLIDAY PARK $

(⊠07-892 3897; www.whakapapa.net.nz; Whakapapa Village; sites from $19, dm $25, units $69-149) This popular DOC-associated park has a wide range of accommodation options, including campsites perched on the edge of beautiful bushland, a 32-bed backpackers lodge (linen required), cabins (linen required) and a self-contained unit. The camp store stocks basic groceries.

Skotel Alpine Resort
HOSTEL $

(⊠07-892 3719; www.skotel.co.nz; Whakapapa Village; s/tw/tr without bathroom $40/55/75, r with bathroom $110-185, cabin $185) If you think of it more as a hostel than a hotel, you'll excuse the odd bit of stained carpet or cheap lino, and enjoy the timber-lined alpine ambience and decidedly non-hostel-like facilties: sauna, spa pool, gym, ski hire, restaurant and bar.

Bayview Chateau Tongariro HOTEL **$$**
(07-892 3809; www.chateau.co.nz; Whakapapa Village; r from $155; @) NZ's great missed tourism opportunity promises much, with its sublime setting and manor house grandeur, but the old-world charm is fading fast. Which is a shame, as a cashed-up interior designer could swiftly transform the Chateau back into the iconic hotel it was when it first opened its doors in 1929. Still, you may just run into one-armed big-game hunters in the bar here, or cane-wielding silver-medal skiers from the seventies, or ex-colonels twisting their fine little moustaches as they eye you through their greasy monocles – it has that kind of vibe. Within the hulking complex are a cinema, the elegant **Ruapehu Room** (mains $36-38; dinner), **Pihanga Cafe** (mains $20-27; lunch & dinner) and the T-bar, a cosy spot for a warming winter tipple. The operators also manage the neighbouring nine-hole public golf course, **Fergusson's Cafe** (mains $5-10; breakfast & lunch; @) and Fergusson Motel, which has self-contained family chalets (from $155).

DOC campsites CAMPSITES **$**
(www.doc.govt.nz; sites per adult/child $6/3) Apart from the huts and associated campsites, there are two basic DOC camping grounds in this area: Mangahuia, between National Park village and the SH48 turn-off heading to Whakapapa; and Mangawhero, near Ohakune. Both have cold water and pit toilets.

ⓘ Information

Further national park information is available from the i-SITEs in Ohakune (p270) as well as Turangi (p259).

DOC Whakapapa Visitor Centre (07-892 3729; www.doc.govt.nz; Whakapapa Village; 8am-5pm) Has maps and info on all corners of the park, including walks, huts and current skiing, track and weather conditions. It also has interesting exhibits on the geological and human history of the area, including an audio-visual display and a small shop – making it the perfect place for rainy days. The detailed *Tongariro National Park* map ($19) is worth buying before tramping.

ⓘ Getting There & Around
Bus

There are numerous shuttle services to Whakapapa Village, the Tongariro Alpine Crossing and other key destinations from Taupo, Turangi,

HUT PASSES

Scattered around the park's tramping tracks are 10 huts that can be used for accommodation. Prices vary according to hut and season, but range from $15 to $31 per person. You can camp beside the huts for $5 to $21 per person. The DOC centres and i-SITEs in Turangi, Whakapaka and Ohakune sell hut tickets and Backcountry Hut Passes.

In the Great Walk season – from late October to April – advance reservations are required for the four Tongariro Northern Circuit huts (Mangatepopo, Ketetahi, Oturere and Waihohonu). You're best to book online at www. doc.govt.nz, but bookings may also be made at DOC visitor centres and some i-SITES, where a booking fee may apply.

National Park and Ohakune. In summer tramping trips are their focus, but in winter most offer ski-field shuttles. Book your bus in advance to avoid unexpected strandings. As well as those listed below, most of the Turangi and National Park hostels offer their own shuttles at similar rates.

Adventure HQ (07-386 0969; www.adventure hq.co.nz) Runs scheduled Tongariro Alpine Crossing services ($35) from its base on SH47. They also sell and hire gear.

Alpine Hotbus (0508 468 287; www.alpine hotbus.co.nz) Provides shuttles to the Crossing from Rotorua ($99), Taupo ($55) and Turangi ($40), and from Taupo to Whakapapa and National Park village ($60).

Matai Shuttles (06-385 8724; www. mataishuttles.co.nz) Runs ski shuttles from Ohakune to Turoa (return $25) and Whakapapa (return $30), a winter-only nighttime loop around Ohakune ($4), and shuttles to various walking and cycling trails.

Snow Express (06-385 4022; www.dempsey buses.co.nz; return $25) Offers transport from Ohakune to the Turoa ski field.

Tongariro Expeditions (0800 828 763; www.tongariroexpeditions.com) Runs shuttles from Taupo ($59, 1½ hours), Turangi ($40, 45 minutes) and Whakapapa ($35, 15 minutes) to the Crossing and the Northern Circuit.

Turangi Alpine Shuttles (07-386 8226; www.turangirentals.co.nz) Plys the Turangi–Whakapapa route (one-way/return $35/45) and has Crossing shuttles ($40).

Car & Motorcycle

Tongariro National Park is bounded by roads: SH1 (called the Desert Rd) to the east, SH4 to the west, SH46 and SH47 to the north and SH49 to the south. The main road up into the park is SH48, which leads to Whakapapa Village and continues further up the mountain as Bruce Rd leading to the Whakapapa Ski Area. Ohakune Mountain Rd leads up to the Turoa Ski Area from Ohakune. The Desert Rd is regularly closed when the weather is bad – large signs will direct you to other routes. Likewise, Ohakune Mountain Rd and Bruce Rd are subject to closures, and access beyond certain points may be restricted to 4WDs or cars with snow chains.

National Park Village

POP 460

Named for nearby Tongariro National Park, this tiny outpost lies at the junction of SH4 and SH47, 15km from the hub of Whakapapa Village. In ski season the township is packed, but in summer it's sleepy – despite being a handy base for activities in and around the park.

There's little to do in the village itself, its major enticement being its proximity to the ski fields, national-park tramps, the 42 Traverse mountain-bike trail and canoe trips on the Whanganui River. Daily shuttles leave from here to the Tongariro Alpine Crossing and Whakapapa Village in summer, and the ski area in winter.

As you'll discover, it's railway country around here. About 20km south on SH4 at Horopito is a monument to the Last Spike, the spike that marked the completion of the Main Trunk Railway Line between Auckland and Wellington in 1908. Five kilometres north from National Park, at Raurimu, is evidence of the engineering masterpiece that is the 'spiral'. Trainspotters will marvel, while non-trainspotters will probably wonder what the hell they're looking at (there's not much to see).

Activities

Most accommodation in town offers packages for lift passes and ski hire, sparing you the steeper prices further up the mountain. Ski gear can be hired from **Eivins** (07-892 2843; www.nationalpark.co.nz/eivins; Carroll St), **Snow Zone** (07-892 2757; www.snowzone.co.nz; 25-27 Buddo St) and **Ski Biz** (07-892 2717; www.skibiz.co.nz; 10 Carroll St).

Fishers Track   MOUNTAIN BIKING
Starting from National Park village, this track is a 17km downhill blast, and now forms part of the Ruapehu Whanganui Trails (p269).

Adrift Guided Outdoor Adventures   CANOEING, TRAMPING
(07-892 2751; www.adriftnz.co.nz) Runs guided canoe trips on the Whanganui River (one to six days, $245 to $999), as well as freedom canoe hire and all necessary transfers. It also offers guided tramps in Tongariro National Park (two hours to three days, $95 to $850).

Wade's Landing Outdoors   CANOEING, KAYAKING
(07-895 5995; www.whanganui.co.nz; 29 Kaitieke Rd, Raurimu) Offers freedom kayak and canoe hire for Whanganui River expeditions, including jetboat/road transfers to trail heads (one to five days, $80 to $180). There are also mountain-biking shuttles, *Lord of the Rings* tours and a 'prehistoric driftwood sculpture park'.

Climbing Wall   CLIMBING
(07-892 2870; www.npbp.co.nz; 4 Findlay St; adult/child $15/10; 9am-8pm) For rainy days there's an 8m-high indoor climbing wall at National Park Backpackers. Outdoor climbers with their own gear can find spots near Manataupo Valley and Whakapapa Gorge.

Sleeping

National Park is a town of budget and mid-range accommodation. This makes sense, as you'll probably spend most of your time in the great outdoors. We list summer prices here; be warned that they increase in the ski season, when accommodation is tight and bookings are essential.

Tongariro Crossing Lodge   LODGE $$
(07-892 2688; www.tongarirocrossinglodge.com; 27 Carroll St; s $115-125, d $140-185;) As pretty as a picture, this white weatherboard cottage is decorated with a baby-blue trim and rambling blooms in summer. Accommodation ranges from standard doubles to larger self-contained apartments.

Discovery Lodge   LODGE $
(Map p261; 07-892 2744; www.discovery.net.nz; SH47; sites from $16, units $60-300;) Handy for skiers, this lodge is midway between the village and the Whakapapa turn-off. The restaurant has excellent views of Ruapehu, plus there's a bar and comfy lounge. Cabins are basic, but large chalets provide upmarket getaways for up to four people.

Plateau
HOSTEL **$**

(☎07-892 2993; www.plateaulodge.co.nz; 17 Carroll St; dm $28, d $65-85, apt $155-195; @🔊) Plateau has cosy rooms, some with en suite and TV, and an attractive communal lounge, a kitchen and a hot tub. The dorms don't get bigger than two sets of bunks and there are nice two-bedroom apartments (sleeping up to six) available as well. This place also offers Crossing, Northern Circuit and 42 Traverse shuttles.

Park
HOSTEL **$**

(☎07-892 2748; www.the-park.co.nz; 2/6 Millar St; dm $35-40, r $120-140, apt $160-200; @🔊) There's no way you can miss this big flashpackers on the highway. Inside it's smart and comfortable, with a garden courtyard surrounded by 200 beds' worth of dorms, doubles and self-contained micro-apartments, as well as an in-house cafe and a railway-inspired bar. Bikes are available for hire (per hour/day $15/60).

Adventure Lodge & Motel
HOSTEL, MOTEL

(☎07-892 2991; www.adventurenationalpark.co.nz; 21 Carroll St; lodge dm/r $30/70, units $120-210; @🔊) This place caters particularly to Tongariro Alpine crossers, offering accommodation and transfers, with all-inclusive packages available (two nights' accommodation, breakfasts, lunch, dinner, T-shirt and transport for $170 to $240). Chill out post-walk in the relaxing lounge or one of the spa pools. The motel units are clean but unspectacular.

✖️ Eating & Drinking

Station
CAFE **$$**

(www.stationcafe.co.nz; Findlay St; lunch $9-16, dinner $29-36; ⏱lunch daily, dinner Wed-Mon) Count your blessings ye who find this little railway station along the line, a lovely old dear, carefully restored and now serving eggy brunch, pies, coffee and cakes, plus an impressive à la carte evening menu.

Schnapps
PUB

(www.schnappsbarruapehu.com; Findlay St; mains $19-28; ⏱noon-late) This popular pub serves better-than-average grub and has a handy ATM. Bands pack the place out on wintry Saturday nights.

Mill Bar & Grill
PUB

(www.nationalpshoteltongariro.co.nz; 61 Carroll St; mains $19-25; ⏱10am-11pm) A good old-fashioned Kiwi boozer with real live locals

having a few quiet ones, a selection of local microbrewed beers and a menu of stomach-warming favourites.

ℹ️ Information
There's no i-SITE in the village, so visit www.nationalpark.co.nz for info.

ℹ️ Getting There & Away
InterCity (☎09-583 5780; www.intercity.co.nz), Naked Bus and **Tranz Scenic** (☎04-495 0775; www.tranzscenic.co.nz; tickets $49-81) all offer services.

Ohakune
POP 1100

Expect to see carrots crop up all over Ohakune, for this is undisputedly the country's carrot capital. They not only creep into burgers and sneak onto pizzas, but also litter the roadside in season. To learn more (and you know you want to), visit during October's annual **Carrot Carnival** (www.carrotcarnival.org.nz).

But locals needn't mention liver cleansing and eyesight improvement to win us over to the charms of this little town. A pretty retreat in the summer offering outdoor adventure galore, Ohakune springs to life in winter when the snow drifts down on Turoa Ski Area and the snow bunnies invade (they no doubt love carrots themselves).

There are two distinct parts to the town: the commercial hub strings along the highway, but in winter the northern end around the train station, known as the Junction, is the epicentre of action.

🏃 Activities
There are several scenic walks near the town, many starting from the Ohakune Mountain Rd, which stretches 17km from Ohakune to the Turoa Ski Area on Mt Ruapehu. The handy DOC brochure *Walks in and around Tongariro National Park* ($3) is a good starting point, available from the i-SITE.

Tramps in Tongariro National Park, including the Tongariro Alpine Crossing, are easily accessible from Ohakune, and shuttle services are provided by Matai Shuttles (p265). The Round the Mountain (p263) track can be accessed by continuing on the Waitonga Falls track.

Old Coach Road WALKING, MOUNTAIN BIKING
(www.ohakunecoachroad.co.nz) The original 16km coach track from Ohakune to Horopito dates from 1886, when it was built largely by hand by workers living in canvas tents and operating in harsh winter conditions. It was gradually upgraded to carry passengers and goods, and used until 1909, when SH49 opened. A recent restoration has rescued it from obscurity, creating this excellent walking and cycling route.

The gently graded route contains a number of unique engineering features, including the historic Hapuawhenua and Toanui viaducts – these are the only two remaining curved viaducts in the southern hemisphere. It passes through ancient forest of giant rimu and totara that survived the Taupo blast, being in the lea of Ruapehu.

If you're cycling, you're best to start at Horopito for a slightly downhill ride finishing at Ohakune Railway Station (allow four hours). Mountain Bike Station offers transfers to Horopito or you can undertake a full-day's return ride.

Mangawhero Forest Walk WALKING
An easy stroll starting near the beginning of Ohakune Mountain Rd (one hour return, 3km), taking in native forest and the Mangawhero River. It is well graded and suitable for wheelchairs and pushchairs.

Waitonga Falls &
Lake Surprise Tracks TRAMPING
The path to Waitonga Falls (1½ hours return, 4km), Tongariro's highest waterfall (39m), offers magnificent views of Mt Ruapehu. A more challenging walk climbs to shallow Lake Surprise (five hours return,

9km). Both tracks start from Ohakune Mountain Rd.

Ruapehu Homestead HORSE RIDING
(Map p261; ☎027-267 7057; cnr Piwara St & SH49, Rangataua; 30min-3hr adult $30-120, child $15-90) Located four kilometres east of Ohakune (near Rangataua), Ruapehu Homestead offers guided treks around its paddocks, as well as longer rides along the river and on backcountry trails that have views of the mountain.

Canoe Safaris CANOEING, RAFTING
(☎0800 272 3353; www.canoesafaris.co.nz; 6 Tay St) Offers guided canoeing trips on the Whanganui River (one to five days, $165 to $950) and Rangitikei River (one to four days, $145 to $825), canoe and kayak hire (two to five days, $150 to $195), and guided rafting trips on the Mohaka (two to four days, $425 to $950).

Yeti Tours CANOEING, KAYAKING
(☎06-385 8197; www.yetitours.co.nz; 61 Clyde St; guided tours 2-10 days $420-1500, 2-6 day hire $160-210) Leads guided canoeing safaris on the Whanganui and Mokau Rivers, and hires canoes and kayaks.

Heliview SCENIC FLIGHTS
(☎06-753 0123; www.heliview.co.nz; flights $110-420) Offers scenic helicopter flights ranging from 12 minutes over Ohakune to 45-minute flights over the peaks or Whanganui National Park.

Mountain Bike
Station & SLR MOUNTAIN BIKING
(☎06-385 8797; www.mountainbikestation.co.nz; 60 Thames St) Rents mountain bikes (half-/full-day from $35/50) and provides transfers to local mountain-biking routes, including the Old Coach Road ($20); bike and transport packages are available. SLR, the winter sports part of the business, rents ski and snowboard gear (from $25).

TCB EQUIPMENT HIRE
(☎06-385 8433; www.tcbskiandboard.co.nz; 29 Ayr St) A good source of information about local mountain-biking routes, TCB publishes a free bike trail map and rents mountain bikes (from $40) and skiing and snowboarding gear (from $20).

Ski Shed EQUIPMENT HIRE
(☎06-385 9173; www.skished.com; 71 Clyde St) Hires skiing (from $35) and snowboard-

---

DON'T MISS

THE BIG CARROT

Maybe not so much 'Don't Miss' as 'Impossible to Miss', this roadside tribute to Ohakune's biggest crop, the **Big Carrot** (Rangataua Rd) was erected in 1984 and quickly became one of NZ's most hugged 'Big Things'. Carrots were first grown in the area during the 1920s by Chinese settlers, who cleared the land by hand and explosives. Ohakune now grows two-thirds of the North Island's total crop.

MOUNTAIN BIKING FROM MOUNTAIN TO SEA

Traversing two national parks, the Ruapehu Whanganui Trails (Nga Ara Tuhono) is a 317km route linking up various established tracks and stretches of rural road to provide a mountain-biking route from Mt Ruapehu to the sea at Whanganui.

Starting at Turoa with a descent down the sealed Ohakune Mountain Rd (check those brakes first!), it follows the Old Coach Road (p268) to Horopito. Here it takes rural roads to the Fishers Track (p266), connects to the Mangapurua Track across the Bridge to Nowhere and continues on the Kaiwhakauka Track (p234).

ing (from $43) gear, and snow-appropriate clothing.

Powderhorn Snow Centre   EQUIPMENT HIRE
(☑06-385 9100; www.snowcentre.co.nz; 194 Mangawhero Tce) Sells and hires snow gear and mountain bikes (half-/full-day $35/50).

🛏 Sleeping

The prices listed here are for summer; expect to pay up to 50% more in winter and book ahead. Savings can be made on winter rates by booking midweek.

TOP CHOICE Station Lodge   HOSTEL $
(☑06-385 8797; www.stationlodge.co.nz; 60 Thames St; dm $27, r $54, unit $100-200; @☎) Housed in a lovely old villa with wooden floors and high ceilings, this excellent backpackers has a well-equipped kitchen, comfortable lounge and a spa pool. In winter the demand is so high that it only rent beds, not whole rooms; if you're after privacy, separate chalets and apartments are available. The clued-up young owners also run Mountain Bike Station and SLR.

Powderhorn Chateau   HOTEL $$$
(☑06-385 8888; www.powderhorn.co.nz; cnr Thames St & Mangawhero Tce; r from $199; @☎❋) Enjoying a long-standing reputation as the hub of activity during the ski season, the Powderhorn has a Swiss-chalet feel with woody interiors, slate floors and exposed rafters. The grotto-like indoor pool is a relaxing way to recover from the slopes before enjoying revelry in the popular in-house establishments.

Snowhaven   APARTMENTS, B&B $$
(☑06-385 9498; www.snowhaven.co.nz; 92 Clyde St; apt $95-110, r $195, townhouse $245; ☎) A tasty trio is on offer at Snowhaven: modern studio apartments in a slate-fronted block on the main drag; three self-contained, three-bedroom townhouses by the Junction;

or luxury B&B rooms somewhere between the other two. All are top options.

Peaks   MOTEL $$
(☑06-385 9144; www.thepeaks.co.nz; cnr Mangawhero Tce & Shannon St; units $110-124; @☎) This well-kept motel offers spacious rooms with good bathrooms but dubious decor. Communal facilities include a basic gym, a large outdoor spa and a sauna.

Tussock Grove   HOTEL $$
(☑06-385 8771; www.tussockgrove.co.nz; 3 Karo St; r $145-165; ☎) Cooking on holiday? No way, mister. In a town full of motels this small hotel fills a gap for those who just want a decent midrange room, perhaps with a mountain view.

🌿Ohakune Top 10   HOLIDAY PARK $
(☑0800 825 825; www.ohakune.net.nz; 5 Moore St; sites from $20, units $32-203; @☎) A bubbling stream borders this holiday park, and while it's not as flash as some of the Top 10 chain, neither is it as expensive. Extras include a playground, barbecue area and spa pool.

Mountain View   MOTEL $
(☑06-385 8675; www.mountain-viewmotel.co.nz; 2 Moore St; units $70-100; ☎) In this old, vaguely Tudor-styled motel, the no-nonsense rooms are clean, quiet and good value, with all necessary facilities, including a spa pool.

🍴 Eating & Drinking

The Junction is the après-ski place to be, but in summer the action (such that it is) drifts to the other end of town. Many hotels sprout restaurants during the ski season.

Cyprus Tree   ITALIAN $$
(☑06-385 8857; www.thecyprustree.co.nz; 19a Goldfinch St; mains $22-31; ⊙4pm-late Mon-Fri, 9am-late Sat & Sun) Open all year round, this restaurant and bar serves up a tasty menu of Italian-influenced dishes – pizza, pasta and

WORTH A TRIP

LAKE ROTOKURA

Rotokura Ecological Reserve is 14km southeast of Ohakune, at Karioi, just off SH49 (*karioi* means 'places to linger'). There are two lakes here: the first is Dry Lake, actually quite wet and perfect for picnicking; the furthest is Rotokura, *tapu* (sacred) to Maori, so eating, fishing and swimming are prohibited. The round-trip walk will take you 45 minutes; longer if you linger to admire the ancient beech trees and waterfowl such as dabchicks and paradise ducks.

antipasto – in a large yet relaxed space. Or you can just drop in for a cocktail.

Bearing Point   INTERNATIONAL **$$**
(06-385 9006; Clyde St; mains $25-35; ⊘dinner Tue-Sat) Hearty après-ski fare is offered at this upmarket establishment run by local identities. Warm your cockles with aged eye fillet, maple-glazed salmon, lamb rump or a seafood curry.

Mountain Kebabs   KEBABS **$**
(29 Clyde St; kebabs $10-13) Any old kebabery can come up with the basic lamb, chicken or felafel varieties – but here camembert, hummus, sprouts and olives are rolled into the mix, too.

Powderkeg & Matterhorn   PUB
(www.powderhorn.co.nz; cnr Thames St & Mangawhero Tce; bar menu $12-18, à la carte $31-35; ⊘lunch & dinner) The Powderkeg is the party bar of the Powderhorn Chateau, with bands in winter and regular dancing on the tables – once the detritus of the burgers and nachos have been cleared. Upstairs is the swankier Matterhorn, serving cocktails and relaxed but chic à la carte dining. In summer the Matterhorn closes and its menu moves to the Powderkeg.

Utopia   CAFE **$**
(47 Clyde St; mains $10-17; ⊘8am-2.30pm; 🛜) A funky, upbeat and perennially popular destination for cooked breakfasts and fresh homemade counter food. If it's pumping downstairs, there are usually quieter tables upstairs.

❶ Information
Ohakune Public Library (06-385 8364; 15 Miro St; ⊘9am-5pm Mon-Fri; @) Offers free internet access.
Ruapehu i-SITE (06-385 8427; www.visit ruapehu.com; 54 Clyde St; ⊘9am-5pm) Can

make bookings for activities, transport and accommodation; DOC officer on hand from 9am to 3.30pm, Wednesday to Sunday.

❶ Getting There & Around
InterCity (p244) buses and Tranz Scenic (p244) trains service Ohakune, and Matai Shuttles (p265) and Snow Express (p265) run up to Turoa. Matai runs a handy night shuttle around Ohakune's pubs during the ski season.

Waiouru
POP 1400
At the junction of SH1 and SH49, 27km east of Ohakune, Waiouru is primarily an army base and a refuelling stop for the 56km-long Desert Rd leading to Turangi. **Rangipo Desert** isn't a true desert, as it receives plenty of rainfall; its stunted scrubby vegetation is due to its high altitude, windswept nature and the Taupo eruption that obliterated the ancient forests, affected the soil quality and caused a mass sterilisation of seeds. The road often closes in winter due to snow.

Housed in a large, concrete castle at the south end of the township, the **National Army Museum** (www.armymuseum.co.nz; adult/child $15/5; ⊘9am-4.30pm) preserves the history of the NZ army and its various campaigns, from colonial times to the present. Moving stories are told through displays of arms, uniforms, medals and memorabilia.

Once you're done with playing soldier, head 11km south to **Lazy H Horseback Riding & Adventures** (06-388 1144; www.lazyh. co.nz; 159 Maukuku Rd; 1hr-overnight $50-295), where you can channel your inner cowboy. Sadly, this is where the Village People–themed pursuits end.

Taihape & Around

POP 1800

If you have an ill-defined interest in rubber boots, a visit to Taihape, 20km south of Waiouru, is a must. The town has the dubious distinction of being the Gumboot Capital of the World, celebrated with – you guessed it – a giant corrugated gumboot on the main street. It is also the access point for **Gravity Canyon** (⏱06-388 9109; www.gravitycanyon.co.nz; Mokai; ⊙9am-5pm), 20km southeast, where adrenaline-junkies can take a 1km, 170m-high flying-fox ride at speeds of up to 160km/h ($155); dive from the North Island's highest bridge bungy (80m, $179); or freefall for 50m on a tandem swing ($159). Multi-thrill packages are available.

If you didn't give horseback riding a go in Ohakune or Waiouru, giddy-up to **River Valley** (⏱06-388 1444; www.rivervalley.co.nz), 28km northeast of Taihape (follow the signs from Taihape's Gretna Hotel). Enjoy views of Mt Ruapehu, the Ruahine Range and the Rangitikei River on two-hour ($109), half-day ($175) or day-long ($235) excursions. On summer evenings the three-hour Sundowner ride ends with a glass of bubbles ($139). White-water rafting trips are also offered.

Rotorua & the Bay of Plenty

Best Outdoors

» Surfing at Mt Maunganui (p299)

» Waimangu Volcanic Valley (p291)

» KG Kayaks (p311)

» Agroventures (p278)

» Redwoods Whakarewarewa Forest (p289)

Best Places to Stay

» Regent of Rotorua (p283)

» Warm Earth Cottage (p304)

» Captain's Cabin (p308)

» Opotiki Beach House Backpackers (p313)

Why Go?

Captain Cook christened the Bay of Plenty when he cruised past in 1769, and plentiful it remains. Blessed with sunshine and sand, the bay stretches from Waihi Beach in the west to Opotiki in the east, with the holiday hubs of Tauranga, Mt Maunganui and Whakatane in between.

Offshore from Whakatane is New Zealand's most active volcano, Whakaari (White Island). Volcanic activity defines this region, and nowhere is this subterranean sexiness more obvious than in Rotorua. Here the daily business of life goes on among steaming hot springs, explosive geysers, bubbling mud pools and the billows of sulphurous gas responsible for the town's 'unique' eggy smell.

Rotorua and the Bay of Plenty are also strongholds of Maori tradition. There are plenty of opportunities to engage with NZ's rich indigenous culture: check out a power-packed concert performance, chow down at a *hangi* (Maori feast) or learn the techniques behind Maori arts and crafts.

When to Go

The Bay of Plenty is a beachy haven: it's one of NZ's sunniest regions, with Whakatane recording a brilliant 2350 average hours of sunshine per year. Summers here are gorgeous, with maximum temperatures hovering between 20°C and 27°C. Of course, everyone else is here too, but the holiday vibe is heady. Winter can see the mercury fall as low as 5°C overnight, although it's usually warmer on the coast. Visit Rotorua any time: geothermal activity is a year-round wonder, and there are enough beds in any season.

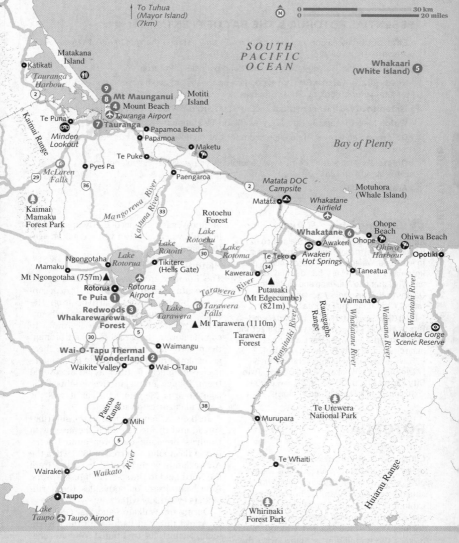

Rotorua & the Bay of Plenty Highlights

1 Watching Rotorua's famous geyser Pohutu blow its top at **Te Puia** (p275), then tucking into a steaming-hot Maori *hangi*

2 Ogling kaleidoscopic colours and bubbling mud pools at **Wai-O-Tapu Thermal Wonderland** (p291)

3 Mountain biking on tracks (both humble and hardcore) in the **Redwoods Whakarewarewa Forest** (p289)

4 Carving up the surf over NZ's first artificial reef at **Mt Maunganui** (p299)

5 Flying or boating to NZ's only active marine volcano, **Whakaari (White Island)** (p310)

6 Kicking back in **Whakatane** (p306) – NZ's most underrated seaside town?

7 Swimming with dolphins at **Tauranga** (p292)

8 Drinking in **Mt Maunganui** (p299) after a day at the beach

ESSENTIAL ROTORUA & THE BAY OF PLENTY

» **Eat** A buttery corn cob, cooked in Rotorua's only genuine thermal *hangi* at Whakare-warewa Thermal Village

» **Drink** Croucher Brewing Co's microbrewed pale ale in Rotorua

» **Read** *How to Watch a Bird,* an exposition on the joys of avian observation, written by Mt Maunganui schoolboy Steve Braunias

» **Listen to** *Kora,* the eponymous rootsy album from Whakatane's soulful sons

» **Watch** Maori TV and Te Reo, NZ's two Maori TV stations

» **Go green** See www.sustainablenz.com for tips on how to make your Rotorua visit more ecofriendly

» **Online** www.rotoruanz.com, www.bayofplenty.co.nz; www.lonelyplanet.com/new-zealand/rotorua

» **Area code** ☑07

ⓘ Getting There & Away

Air New Zealand (www.airnewzealand.co.nz) has direct flights from Tauranga and Rotorua to Auckland, Wellington and Christchurch, plus Rotorua to Sydney (every Tuesday and Saturday) and Whakatane to Auckland and Wellington. Qantas (p287) also links Auckland with Tauranga, Whakatane and Rotorua.

InterCity (www.intercity.co.nz) and **Naked Bus** (www.nakedbus.com) services connect Tauranga, Rotorua and Whakatane with most other main cities in NZ. **Bay Hopper** (☑0800 422 928; www.baybus.co.nz) bus services run between Tauranga, Whakatane and Opotiki. **Twin City Express** (☑0800 422 928; www.baybus.co.nz) buses link Tauranga and Rotorua.

ROTORUA

POP 70,400

Catch a whiff of Rotorua's sulphur-rich, asthmatic airs and you've already got a taste of NZ's most dynamic thermal area, home to spurting geysers, steaming hot springs and exploding mud pools. The Maori revered this place, naming one of the most spectacular springs Wai-O-Tapu (Sacred Waters). Today 35% of the population is Maori, with their cultural performances and traditional *hangi* as big an attraction as the landscape itself.

Despite the pervasive eggy odour, 'Sulphur City' is one of the most touristed spots on the North Island, with nearly three million visitors annually. Some locals say this steady trade has seduced the town into resting on its laurels, and that socially Rotorua lags behind more progressive towns like Tauranga and Taupo. And with more motels than nights in November, the urban fabric of 'RotoVegas' isn't particularly appealing... but still, where else can you see a 30m geothermal geyser!

History

The Rotorua area was first settled in the 14th century when the canoe *Te Arawa,* captained by Tamatekapua, arrived from Hawaiki at Maketu in the central Bay of Plenty. Settlers took the tribal name Te Arawa to commemorate the vessel that had brought them here. Tamatekapua's grandson, Ihenga, explored much of the inland forest, naming geographical features as he discovered them. Ihenga unimaginatively dubbed the lake Rotorua (Second Lake) as it was the second lake he came across.

In the next few hundred years, subtribes spread and divided through the area, with conflicts breaking out over limited territory. A flashpoint occurred in 1823 when the Arawa lands were invaded by tribes from the Northland in the so-called Musket Wars. After heavy losses on both sides, the Northlanders eventually withdrew.

During the Waikato Land War (1863–64) Te Arawa threw in its lot with the government against its traditional Waikato enemies, gaining troop support and preventing East Coast reinforcements getting through to support the Kingitanga movement.

With peace in the early 1870s, word spread of scenic wonders, miraculous landscapes and watery cures for all manner of diseases. Rotorua boomed. Its main attraction was the fabulous Pink and White Terraces, formed by volcanic silica deposits. Touted at the time as the eighth natural wonder of the world, they were destroyed in the 1886 Mt Tarawera eruption.

⊙ Sights

Te Whakarewarewa
THERMAL RESERVE

Rotorua's main drawcard is Te Whakare-warewa (pronounced fa-ka-re-wa-re-wa), a thermal reserve 3km south of the city centre. This area's full name is Te Whakareware-watanga o te Ope Taua a Wahiao, meaning 'The Gathering Together of the War Party of Wahiao', although many people just call it 'Whaka'. Either way, the reserve is as famous for its Maori cultural significance as its steam and bubbling mud. There are more than 500 springs here, including a couple of famed geysers. The two main tourist operations are Te Puia and Whakarewarewa Thermal Village.

Te Puia
GEYSER, CULTURAL TOUR

(Map p290; ☑0800 837 842, 07-348 9047; www.tepuia.com; Hemo Rd; adult/child tour & daytime cultural performance $57.50/29, tour, evening concert & hangi $110/55, combination $145/72.50; ☺8am-6pm Nov-Apr, to 5pm May-Oct) The most famous Te Whakarewarewa spring is **Pohutu** ('Big Splash' or 'Explosion'), a geyser which erupts up to 20 times a day, spurting hot water up to 30m skyward. You'll know when it's about to blow because the **Prince of Wales' Feathers** geyser will start up shortly before. Both these geysers form part of Te Puia, the most polished of NZ's Maori cultural attractions. Also here is the National Carving School and the National Weaving School, where you can discover the work and methods of traditional Maori woodcarvers and weavers, plus a carved meeting house, a cafe, galleries, a kiwi reserve and a gift shop.

Tours take 1½ hours and depart hourly from 9am (the last tour an hour before closing). Daytime 45-minute cultural performances start at 10.15am, 12.15pm and 3.15pm; nightly three-hour Te Po indigenous concerts and *hangi* feasts start at 6pm.

Whakarewarewa Thermal Village
SPRING, CULTURAL TOUR

(Map p290; ☑07-349 3463; www.whakarewarewa.com; 17 Tryon St; tour & cultural performance adult/child $30/13; ☺8.30am-5pm) Whakarewarewa Thermal Village, on the eastern side of Te Whakarewarewa, is a living village, where *tangata whenua* (the locals) still reside, as they and their ancestors have for centuries. It's these local villagers who show you around and tell you the stories of their way of life and the significance of the steamy bubbling pools, silica terraces and the geysers that, although inaccessible from the village, are easily viewed from vantage points (the view of Pohutu is just as good from here as it is from Te Puia, and considerably cheaper).

The village shops sell authentic arts and crafts, and you can learn more about Maori traditions such as flax weaving, carving, and *ta moko* (tattooing). Nearby you can eat tasty, buttery sweetcorn ($2) pulled straight out of the hot mineral pool – the only genuine geothermal *hangi* in town. There are cultural performances at 11.15am and 2pm, and guided tours at 9am, 10am, 11am, noon, 1pm, 3pm and 4pm.

ROTORUA IN...

Two Days

Order breakfast at **Third Place Cafe**, after which stroll the lakeside at **Ohinemutu**, continuing back into town via steamy **Kuirau Park**. Next stop is the fabulous **Rotorua Museum**, followed by a soak at the **Blue Baths**. In the evening, catch a *hangi* and concert at **Tamaki Maori Village** or **Mitai Maori Village**.

Start the second day with a tour of **Whakarewarewa Thermal Village** and watch **Pohutu** geyser blow its top. From here, it's a quick hop to the **Redwoods Whakarewarewa Forest** for a couple of hours' mountain biking. Head across town to dangle in a gondola at **Skyline Rotorua** or see the swooping falcons at **Wingspan Birds of Prey Trust**.

Four Days

Too much geothermal excitement is barely enough! Explore the hot spots to the south: **Waimangu Volcanic Valley** and **Wai-O-Tapu Thermal Wonderland**. The nearby **Waikite Valley Thermal Pools** are perfect for an end-of-day plunge.

On your last day, head southeast and visit the **Buried Village**, swim in **Lake Tarawera**, or take a long walk on one of the tracks at nearby **Lake Okataina**. Back in town, cruise the restaurants and bars on **Tutanekai St** and toast your efforts with a few cold beers.

Rotorua

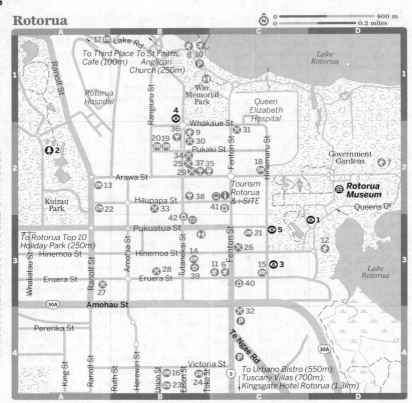

TOP CHOICE Rotorua Museum MUSEUM, GALLERY
(Map p276; www.rotoruamuseum.co.nz; Queens
Dr, Government Gardens; adult/child \$18/7;
⊙9am-5pm Apr-Sep, to 8pm Oct-Mar, tours hourly
10am-4pm plus 5pm Dec-Feb) This outstanding museum occupies a grand Tudor-style edifice. It was originally an elegant spa retreat
called the Bath House (1908); displays in
the former shower rooms give a fascinating
insight into some of the eccentric therapies
once practised here, including 'electric
baths' and the Bergonie Chair.

A gripping 20-minute film on the history
of Rotorua, including the Tarawera eruption, runs every 20 minutes from 9am (not
for small kids – the seats vibrate and the
eruption noises are authentic). The fabulous new **Don Stafford Wing** houses eight
object-rich galleries dedicated to Rotorua's
Te Arawa people, featuring woodcarving,
flax weaving, jade, interactive audiovisual
displays and the stories of the revered WWII

28 Maori Battalion (a movie on the battalion
runs every 30 minutes from 9.30am). Also
here are two **art galleries** (with air swabbed
clean of hydrogen sulphide), and a cool cafe
with garden views (although the best view in
town can be had from the viewing platform
on the roof).

Lake Rotorua LAKE
Lake Rotorua is the largest of the district's
16 lakes and is – underneath all that water –
a spent volcano. Sitting in the lake is Mokoia
Island, which has for centuries been occupied by various subtribes of the area. The
lake can be explored by boat, with several
operators situated at the lakefront.

Government Gardens GARDENS
The manicured English-style Government
Gardens surrounding the Rotorua Museum
are pretty as a picture, with roses aplenty,
steaming thermal pools dotted about and
civilised amenities such as croquet lawns

Rotorua

ROTORUA & THE BAY OF PLENTY ROTORUA

and bowling greens. Also here is the upmarket Polynesian Spa and Government Gardens Golf.

Blue Baths   BATHHOUSE
(Map p276; 🖉07-350 2119; www.bluebaths. co.nz; Government Gardens; adult/child/family $11/6/30; ⏰noon-6pm Apr-Nov, 10am-6pm Dec-Mar) The gorgeous Spanish Mission–style Blue Baths opened in 1933 (and, amazingly, were closed from 1982 to 1999). Today you can visit a small museum recalling the building's heyday, with recorded anecdotes and displays in the old changing rooms. If it all makes you feel like taking a dip yourself, the heated pool (adult/child/family $11/6/30) awaits. Ask about occasional dinner-and-cabaret shows (from $125 per person).

Kuirau Park   PARK
(Map p276; cnr Ranolf & Pukuatua Sts) Want some affordable geothermal thrills? Just west of central Rotorua is Kuirau Park, a volcanic area you can explore for free. In 2003 an eruption covered much of the park (including the trees) in mud, drawing crowds of spectators. It has a crater lake, pools of boiling mud and plenty of huffing steam. Take care – the pools here really are boiling, and accidents have happened.

Ohinemutu   MAORI VILLAGE
Ohinemutu is a charmingly ramshackle lakeside Maori village (access via Kiharoa, Haukotuku or Korokai Sts off Lake St, north of Rotorua Hospital) that traces the fusing of European and Maori cultures. A highlight is the 1905 Tama-te-kapua Meeting House (corner of Kiharoa St and Mataiawhea St),

DON'T MISS

MAORI CONCERTS & HANGI

Maori culture is a big-ticket item in Rotorua and, although it is commercialised, it's a great opportunity to learn about the indigenous culture of New Zealand. The two big activities are concerts and *hangi* feasts, often packaged together in an evening's entertainment featuring the famous *hongi* (Maori greeting; the pressing of foreheads and noses, and sharing of life breath) and *haka* and *poi* dances.

An established favourite, **Tamaki Maori Village** (☑07-349 2999; www.maoriculture .co.nz; booking office 1220 H inemaru St; adult/child/family $105/60/250; ⊘tours depart 5pm, 6pm & 7.30pm Nov-Apr, 6.30pm May-Oct) does an excellent twilight tour to a *marae* (meeting house) and Maori village 15km south of Rotorua. Buses collect from the Hinemaru St booking office and local accommodation. The experience is very hands-on, taking you on an interactive journey through Maori history, arts, traditions and customs from pre-European times to the present day. The concert is followed by an impressive *hangi*.

The family-run **Mitai Maori Village** (Map p290; ☑07-343 9132; www.mitai.co.nz; 196 Fairy Springs Rd; adult/child 5-9yr/child 10-15yr/family $107/21/53/279; ⊘6.30pm) offers a popular three-hour evening event with a concert, *hangi* and glowworm bushwalk. The experience can be combined with a tour of Rainbow Springs Kiwi Wildlife Park (p288) next door, with coloured nightlights and a walk through the kiwi enclosure (four hours total, adult/child 5-9yr/child 10-15yr $125/35/65). Pick-ups available.

Te Puia (p275) and Whakarewarewa Thermal Village (p275) also put on shows, and many of the big hotels offer Maori concerts and *hangi*, making up for what they lack in ambience with convenience. Some of the main venues:

» **Kingsgate Hotel Rotorua** (Map p290; ☑07-348 0199; www.millenniumhotels.co.nz; 328 Fenton St; concert adult/child $30/15, incl hangi $45/22.50)

» **Millennium Hotel Rotorua** (Map p276; ☑07-347 1234; www.millenniumrotorua.co.nz; cnr Eruera & Hinemaru Sts; concert adult/child $30/15, incl hangi $70/35)

» **Novotel Rotorua** (Map p276; ☑07-346 3888; www.novotelrotorua.co.nz; 11 Tutanekai St; concerts adult/child $39/18, incl hangi $59/28)

» **Pohutu Cultural Theatre** (Map p290; ☑07-348 1189, 0800 476 488; www.pohutu theatre.co.nz; cnr Froude & Tryon Sts; concerts & hangi adult/child $69/34.50)

named for the captain of Te Arawa canoe. This sacred meeting house for Te Arawa people isn't open to visitors, but you can check out the exterior.

St Faith's Anglican Church　CHURCH
(☑07-348 2393; cnr Mataiawhea & Korokai Sts; admission by donation; ⊘8am-6pm, services 9am Sun & 10am Wed) Ohinemutu's historic timber St Faith's Anglican Church is intricately decorated with Maori carvings, *tukutuku* (woven panels), painted scrollwork and stained-glass windows. One window features an etched image of Christ wearing a Maori cloak as he appears to walk on the waters of Lake Rotorua.

🏃 Activities

Note that several of the following operators have teamed up under the banners of **Rotorua Adventure Combos** (☑0800 338 786, 07-357 2236; www.rotoruacombos.com), **Rotorua Hot Deals** (☑0800 768 678; www.rotoruahotdeals.com) and **Rotorua CitySights** (☑0800 744 487; www.

citysights.co.nz), delivering a slew of good-value skydiving, white-water rafting, river sledging, jetboating and helicopter experiences (plus zorbing, gondola rides, mountain biking...).

Extreme Sports

Agroventures　EXTREME SPORTS
(Map p290; ☑07-357 4747, 0800 949 888; www. agroventures.co.nz; Western Rd; ⊘9am-5pm) Agroventures is a hive of action, 9km north of Rotorua on SH5 (shuttles available). Prices following are for single activities but combo deals abound.

Start off with the 43m bungy (adult/child $95/80) and the Swoop (adult/child $49/35), a 130km/h swing that can be enjoyed alone or with friends. If that's not enough for you, try Freefall Xtreme (3min per adult/child $49/35), which simulates skydiving by blasting you 5m into the air on a column of wind.

Also here is the Shweeb (adult/child $39/29), a monorail velodrome from which you hang in a clear capsule and pedal yourself along recumbently at speeds of up to 60km/h. Alongside is the Agrojet (adult/child \$49/35), allegedly NZ's fastest jetboat, splashing around a 1km course.

Zorb   EXTREME SPORTS
(Map p290; 07-357 5100, 0800 227 474; www.zorb.com; cnr Western Rd & SH5; rides from \$30; 9am-5pm, to 7pm Dec-Mar) The Zorb is 9km north of Rotorua on SH5 – look for the grassy hillside with large, clear, people-filled spheres rolling down it. Your eyes do not deceive you! There are three courses: 150m straight, 180m zigzag or 250m 'Drop'. Do your zorb strapped in and dry, or freestyle with water thrown in.

Ogo   EXTREME SPORTS
(Map p290; 0800 646 768; www.ogo.co.nz; 525 Ngongotaha Rd; rides from \$35; 9am-5pm, to 6.30pm Dec-Feb) The Ogo (about 5km north of town) involves careening down a grassy hillside in a big bubble, with water or without. Silly? Fun? Terrifying? All of the above...

Skyline Rotorua   EXTREME SPORTS
(Map p290; 07-347 0027; www.skyline.co.nz; Fairy Springs Rd; adult/child gondola \$25/12.50, luge 3 rides \$41/31, sky swing \$52/41; 9am-11pm) This gondola cruises up Mt Ngongotaha, about 3km northwest of town, from where you can take in panoramic lake views or ride a speedy luge back down on three different tracks. For even speedier antics, try the Sky Swing, a screaming swoosh through the air at speeds of up to 160km/h.

Also at the top are a restaurant, cafe and walking tracks.

The Wall   ROCK CLIMBING
(Map p276; 07-350 1400; www.thewall.co.nz; 1140 Hinemoa St; adult/child incl harness \$16/12, shoe hire \$5; noon-10pm Mon-Fri, 10am-10pm Sat & Sun) Get limbered up at the Wall, which has a three-storey indoor climbing wall with overhangs aplenty.

NZONE   SKYDIVING
(Map p290; 07-345 7520, 0800 376 796; www.nzone.biz; Rotorua Airport; dives from \$269) NZONE offers tandem skydives from 9000ft, 12,000ft or 15,000ft, giving you a bird's-eye view of the lakes and volcanoes. Town pickups available.

Kawarau Jet   JETBOATING
(Map p276; 07-343 7600, 0800 538 7746; www.kjetrotorua.co.nz; Lakefront; 30min adult/child \$74/54) Speed things up by jetboating with Kawarau Jet, which tears around the lake. Parasailing also available.

Mountain Biking
On the edge of town is the Redwoods Whakarewarewa Forest (p289), home to some of the best mountain-bike trails in the country. There are close to 100km of tracks to keep bikers of all skill levels happy for days on end. Note that not all tracks in the forest are designated for bikers, so adhere to the signposts. Pick up a trail map at the forest visitor centre.

For more information, the Rotorua i-SITE stocks the *Get on Your Bike* Rotorua cycle

---

MAORI NZ: ROTORUA & THE BAY OF PLENTY

The Bay of Plenty's traditional name, Te Rohe o Mataatua, recalls the ancestral *Mataatua* canoe, which arrived here from Hawaiki to make an eventful landfall at Whakatane. The region's history stretches back further than that, though, with the Polynesian settler Toi setting up what's claimed to be Aotearoa's first settlement in about AD 800.

Major tribal groups in the region are the Ngati Awa (www.ngatiawa.iwi.nz) of the Whakatane area, Whakatohea (www.whakatohea.co.nz) of Opotiki, Ngai Te Rangi (www.ngaiterangi.org.nz) of Tauranga, and Te Arawa (www.tearawa.iwi.nz) of Rotorua. Tribes in this region were involved on both sides of the Land Wars of the late 19th century, with those fighting against the government suffering considerable land confiscations that have caused legal problems right up to the present day.

There's a significant Maori population in the bay, and there are many ways for travellers to learn about the Maori culture. Opotiki has Hiona St Stephen's Church (p312) – the death here of government spy Reverend Carl Volkner in 1865 inspired the charming eyeball-eating scene in *Utu*. Whakatane has a new main-street marae (p306) (meeting house complex) and Toi's Pa (p281), perhaps NZ's oldest *pa* (fortified village) site. Rotorua has traditional villages at Te Whakarewarewa (p275) and Ohinemutu (p277), cultural performances and *hangi* (p278), and much, much more.

HINEMOA & TUTANEKI

Hinemoa was a young woman of a *hapu* (subtribe) that lived on the western shore of Lake Rotorua, while Tutanekai was a young man of a Mokoia Island *hapu*. The pair met and fell in love during a regular tribal meeting. While both were of high birth, Tutanekai was illegitimate, and so while Hinemoa's family thought he was a fine young man, marriage between the two was forbidden.

Home on Mokoia, the lovesick Tutanekai played his flute for his love, the wind carrying the melody across the water. Hinemoa heard his declaration, but her people took to tying up the canoes at night to ensure she wouldn't go to him.

Finally, Tutanekai's music won her over. Hinemoa undressed and swam the long distance from the shore to the island. When she arrived on Mokoia, Hinemoa found herself in a quandary. Shedding her clothing in order to swim, she could hardly walk into the island's settlement naked. She hopped into a hot pool to think about her next move.

Eventually a man came to fetch water from a cold spring beside the hot pool. In a deep man's voice, Hinemoa called out, 'Who is it?' The man replied that he was Tutanekai's slave on a water run. Hinemoa grabbed the slave's calabash and smashed it to pieces. More slaves came, but she smashed their calabashes too, until finally Tutanekai came to the pool and demanded that the interloper identify himself – imagine his surprise when it turned out to be Hinemoa. He secreted her into his hut.

Next morning, after a suspiciously long lie-in, a slave reported that someone was in Tutanekai's bed. The two lovers were rumbled, and when Hinemoa's superhuman efforts to reach Tutanekai had been revealed, their union was celebrated.

Descendants of Hinemoa and Tutanekai still live around Rotorua today.

map (downloadable from www.rdc.govt.nz) and the *Rotorua Mountain Biking* brochure (www.rotoruanz.com).

Mountain Bike Rotorua   BICYCLE RENTAL
(Map p290; ☎0800 682 768; www.mtbrotorua.co.nz; Waipa State Mill Rd; mountain bikes per 2hr/day from $30/45, guided half-/full-day rides $120/185; ☉9am-5pm) This outfit hires out bikes at the Waipa Mill car park entrance to the Redwoods Whakarewarewa Forest, the starting point for the bike trails. There's also a satellite bike depot across the forest at the visitor centre, so you can ride through the trees one-way then catch a shuttle back.

Bike Barn   BICYCLE RENTAL
(Map p276; ☎07-347 1151; www.bikebarn.co.nz; 1275 Fenton St; mountain bikes per half/full day from $45/60; ☉8.30am-5.30pm Mon-Fri, 9am-5pm Sat, 10am-5pm Sun) Bike hire and repairs in downtown Rotorua.

Lady Jane's Ice Cream Parlour   BICYCLE RENTAL
(Map p276; ☎07-347 9340; ladyjanes@xtra.co.nz; 1092 Tutanekai St; bikes per 3hr/day $25/35; ☉10am-late) Bike hire down near Lake Rotorua.

White-Water Rafting & Sledging

There's plenty of white-water action around Rotorua with the chance to take on the Grade V **Kaituna River**, complete with a startling 7m drop at Okere Falls. Most of these trips take a day. Some companies head further out to the **Rangitaiki River** (Grade III–VI) and **Wairoa River** (Grade V), raftable only when the dam is opened every second Sunday. Sledging (in case you didn't know) is zooming downriver on a body board. Most operators can arrange transport.

River Rats   RAFTING
(☎07-345 6543, 0800 333 900; www.riverrats.co.nz) Takes on the Wairoa ($119), Kaituna ($99) and Rangitaiki ($129), and runs a scenic trip on the lower Rangitaiki (Grade II) that is good for youngsters (adult/child $129/100).

Kaituna Cascades   RAFTING
(☎07-345 4199, 0800 524 8862; www.kaituna cascades.co.nz) Does rafting on the Kaituna ($82), Rangitaiki ($118) and Wairoa ($98), plus kayaking options.

Wet 'n' Wild   RAFTING
(☎07-348 3191, 0800 462 7238; www.wetnwild rafting.co.nz) Runs trips on the Kaituna ($99), Wairoa ($110) and Mokau ($160), as well as easy-going Rangitaiki trips (adult/child $125/90) and longer trips to remote parts of the Motu and Mohaka (two to five days, $595 to $975).

Raftabout RAFTING, RIVER SLEDGING

(☑07-343 9500, 0800 723 822; www.raftabout. co.nz) Does rafting on the Kaituna ($99), Rangitaiki ($129) and Wairoa ($129), plus sledging on the Kaituna ($115).

Kaitiaki Adventures RAFTING, RIVER SLEDGING

(☑07-357 2236, 0800 338 736; www.kaitiaki.co.nz) Offers white-water rafting trips on the Kaituna ($95), Wairoa ($99) and Rangitaki ($125), plus sledging on the Wairoa ($299) and a Grade III section of the Kaituna ($109).

Kayaking

River Rats KAYAKING

(☑07-345 6543, 0800 333 900; www.riverrats. co.nz) Kayaking options include freedom hire (from $30/40 per half/full day) and guided four-hour Lake Rotoiti trips ($95).

Go Wild Adventures KAYAKING

(☑07-533 2926; www.adventurekayaking.co.nz) Takes trips on Lakes Rotorua, Rotoiti, Tarawera and Okataina (from $80/95/140 for two hours/half-day/full day); also offers freedom hire (from $50 per day).

Kaituna Kayaks KAYAKING

(☑07-362 4486; www.kaitunakayaks.com; half-day trip $199, lessons half/full day $199/299) Guided tandem trips and kayaking lessons (cheaper for groups) on the Kaituna River.

Thermal Pools & Massage

Geothermal complexes in the area include Hell's Gate & Wai Ora Spa (p288), 16km northeast of Rotorua, and Waikite Valley Thermal Pools (p291), 30km south.

Polynesian Spa SPA, MASSAGE

(Map p276; ☑07-348 1328; www.polynesianspa. co.nz; Government Gardens, off Hinemoa St; adults-only pools $21.50, private pools per half-hour adult/child from $18.50/6.50, family pool adult/child/family $14.50/6.50/36, spa therapies from $85; ☺8am-11pm, spa therapies 9am-8pm) A bath-house opened at these Government Gardens springs in 1882, and people have been swearing by the waters ever since. There is mineral bathing (36°C to 42°C) in several picturesque pools at the lake's edge, marble-lined terraced pools and a larger, main pool. Also here are luxury therapies (massage, mud and beauty treatments) and a cafe.

Tramping

There are plenty of opportunities to stretch your legs around Rotorua, with day walks a speciality. The booklet *Walks in the Ro-*

torua Lakes Area ($2.50), available from the i-SITE, showcases town walks, including the popular lakefront stroll (20 minutes). See also www.doc.govt.nz.

The **Eastern Okataina Walkway** (three hours one way) goes along the eastern shoreline of Lake Okataina to Lake Tarawera and passes the Soundshell, a natural amphitheatre that has *pa* (fortified village) remains and several swimming spots. The Western Okataina Walkway (five hours one way) mimics this route on the western side of the lake.

The **Northern Tarawera Track** (three hours one way) connects to the Eastern Okataina Walkway, creating a two-day walk from either Ruato or Lake Okataina to Lake Tarawera with an overnight camp at either Humphries Bay (sites free) or Tarawera Outlet (sites per adult/child $6/3). From Tarawera Outlet you can walk on to the 65m **Tarawera Falls** (four hours return). There's a forestry road into Tarawera Outlet from Kawerau, a grim timber town in the shadow of Putauaki (Mt Edgecumbe), off the road to Whakatane; access costs $5, with permits available from the **Kawerau visitor centre** (☑07-323 6300; www.kawerauonline.com; Plunkett St bus terminal; ☺8am-6pm Nov-Apr, 9am-4pm May-Oct).

The **Okere Falls** are about 21km northeast of Rotorua on SH33, with an easy track (30 minutes return) past the 7m falls (popular for rafting), through native podocarp (conifer) forest and along the Kaituna River. Along the way is a lookout over the river at Hinemoa's Steps.

Just north of Wai-O-Tapu on SH5, the **Rainbow Mountain Track** (1½ hours one way) is a strenuous walk up the peak known to Maori as Maungakakaramea (Mountain of coloured earth). There are spectacular views from the top towards Lake Taupo and Tongariro National Park.

There are also a couple of good walks at Mt Ngongotaha, 10km northwest of Rotorua: the easy 3.2km **Nature Walk** loop through native forest, and the steep 5km return **Jubilee Track** to the (viewless) summit. See www.ngongotaha.org.

Horse Riding

Paradise Valley Ventures HORSE RIDING

(☑07-348 3300; www.paradisetreks.co.nz; 679 Paradise Valley Rd; 60/90min $65/90) The very safe and professional Paradise Valley Ventures takes treks for novices and experienced riders through a 280-hectare farm northwest of Rotorua. Pony rides for the kids, too.

Farmhouse   HORSE RIDING
(Map p290; ☑07-332 3771; www.thefarmhouse.
co.nz; 55 Sunnex Rd, off Central Rd; 30/60/120min
$26/42/74) North of Lake Rotorua at the
Farmhouse you can saddle-up for a short
horse-riding trip for beginners, or a longer
trek for experienced riders.

Fishing
There's always good trout fishing to be had
somewhere around Rotorua. Hire a guide
or go solo: either way a licence (per day/
season $23/116) is essential, available from
O'Keefe's Fishing Specialists (Map p276;
☑07-346 0178; www.okeefesfishing.co.nz; 1113
Eruera St; ☺8.30am-5pm Mon-Fri, 9am-2pm Sat,
9am-1pm Sun). You can fish Rotorua's lakefront with a licence, though not all lakes can
be fished year-round; check with O'Keefe's
or the i-SITE.

Recommended guides include Mana Adventures (p283) and the following operators.

Trout Man   FISHING
(☑0800 876 881, 07-357 5255; www.waiteti.com;
2hr/day trip from $35/120) Learn to fish with
experienced angler Harvey Clark, from a
couple of hours to multiday trips.

Clark Gregor   FISHING
(☑07-347 1123; www.troutnz.co.nz; per hr $105)
Fly- and boat fishing.

Gordon Randle   FISHING
(☑07-349 2555; www.rotoruatrout.co.nz; half-/
full-day charters $370/750) Reasonable hourly
rates also available.

Golf

Government Gardens Golf   GOLF
(Map p276; ☑07-348 9126; www.government
gardensgolf.co.nz; Queens Dr, Government Gardens; ☺7.30am-8pm) Government Gardens
Golf has a nine-hole course (adult/child
$20/14), minigolf ($11/8) and driving range
(80 balls $11). A $40 golf package incudes
clubs, green fees, balls and tees. There's also
a baseball batting cage (bucket of balls $9).

☞ Tours

Geyser Link Shuttle   TOUR
(☑07-343 6764; www.geyserlink.co.nz) Tours of
some of the major sights, including Wai-O-
Tapu (adult/child $65/32.50, half-day) and
Waimangu Volcanic Valley ($60/30, half-
day), or both ($115/57.50, full day). Transport-
only options available too.

Affordable Adventures   TOUR
(☑0508 278 946; www.affordableadventures.co.nz)
Runs a shuttle to Wai-O-Tapu ($25 return),
plus a full-day geothermal tour (adult/child
$120/60).

Indigenous Trails   TOUR
(☑07-542 1074; www.itrails.co.nz; tours adult/child
$338/250) Full-day Maori-guided tours around
Rotorua, with a bungy jump, river cruise,
kiwi-meeting, cultural show and *hangi*.

Elite Adventures   TOUR
(☑07-347 8282; www.eliteadventures.co.nz; tours
adult/child half-day from $85/55, full-day from
$220/130) Small-group tours covering a se-
lection of Rotorua's major cultural and natural highlights.

Rotorua Duck Tours   TOUR
(☑07-345 6522; www.rotoruaducktours.co.nz;
adult/child/family $68/38/155; ☺tours 11am,
1pm & 3.30pm Oct-Apr, 11am & 2.15pm May-Sep)
Ninety-minute trips in an amphibious bio-
fuelled vehicle taking in the major sites
around town and heading out onto three
lakes (Rotorua, Okareka and Tikitapu/
Blue). Longer Lake Tarawera trips also
available.

Tim's Wai-O-Tapu
Thermal Cultural Shuttle   TOUR
(☑027 494 5508) Goes to Wai-O-Tapu (return
including entry $50) and the Buried Village
and Waimangu Volcanic Valley on request.

Volcanic Air Safaris   SCENIC FLIGHTS
(Map p276; ☑07-348 9984, 0800 800 848; www.
volcanicair.co.nz; Lakefront; trips $70-862) A va-
riety of floatplane and helicopter flights
taking in Mt Tarawera and surrounding
geothermal sites including Hell's Gate, the
Buried Village and Waimangu Volcanic Valley. A 3¼-hour Whakaari (White Island)/Mt
Tarawera trip is also available.

Helipro   SCENIC FLIGHTS
(Map p290; ☑07-357 2515, 0800 435 477; www.
helipro.co.nz; Hemo Rd; flights $95-895) Helipro
plies the skies over Rotorua in nippy little
red choppers (eight-minute city sightseeing
flights $95), also extending to Mt Tarawe-
ra and as far as Whakaari (White Island).
Landings in various places cost extra.

Pure Cruise New Zealand   SAILING
(☑0800 272 456, 027 272 4561; www.purecruise.
co.nz; cruises adult/child morning or sunset
$110/70, half-day $135/75) Slow-boat catamaran

cruises on Lake Rotoiti; take a morning sail with a hot-spring soak, a sunset cruise or half-day exploration.

Mokoia Island Wai
Ora Experiences   CRUISE, CULTURAL TOUR
(Map p276; ☑07-349 0976; www.mokoiaisland. co.nz; Lakefront; tours adult/child $75/38; ⊙9.30am & 2pm) This operator takes visitors out to Mokoia Island on a 2½-hour Ultimate Island Experience tour. The tour includes wildlife-spotting, hearing tales of the island, and letting you dip your toes in the legendary hot pool of Hinemoa.

Lakeland Queen   CRUISE
(Map p276; ☑07-348 0265, 0800 572 784; www.lake landqueen.com; Lakefront) The *Lakeland Queen* paddlesteamer offers one-hour breakfast cruises (adult/child $45/22.50) and longer cruises (lunch $54/27.50; Saturday-night summer dinner $70/35) on Lake Rotorua.

Mana Adventures   CRUISE, KAYAKING
(Map p276; ☑07-348 4186, 0800 333 660; www. manaadventures.co.nz; Lakefront) To explore the lake under your own steam, head for Mana Adventures, which offers (weather permitting) rental pedal boats ($9/6 per adult/child per 20 minutes) and kayaks ($25/50 per hour/half-day). It also runs one-hour lake cruises ($55/39 per adult/child), trout-fishing charters and three-hour tours to Mokoia Island ($75/30 per adult/child).

🛏 Sleeping

Rotorua has plenty of holiday parks and an ever-changing backpacker scene. Generic motels crowd Fenton St: better and more interesting rooms are away from the main drag.

TOP CHOICE Regent of Rotorua   BOUTIQUE HOTEL $$$
(Map p276; ☑07-348 4079, 0508 734 368; www. regentrotorua.co.nz; 1191 Pukaki St; d/ste from $169/239; 🕸🏊) Wow! It's about time Rotorua showed some slumbering style, and the Regent (a renovated 1960s motel) delivers. 'The '60s was a glamorous time to travel,' say the owners: the decor follows suit, with hip black-and-white tones, funky mirrors, retro wallpaper and colourful splashes. There's a pool and restaurant too, and the Tutanekai St eateries are an amble away.

🖋 Funky Green Voyager   HOSTEL $
(Map p276; ☑07-346 1754; www.funkygreenvoyager. co.nz; 4 Union St; dm from $25, d with/without bath-

room $68/59; @🕸) Green on the outside and the inside – due to several cans of paint and a dedicated environmental policy – the shoe-free Funky GV features laid-back tunes and plenty of sociable chat among a spunky bunch of guests and worldly-wise owners, who know what you want when you travel. The best doubles have bathroom; dorms are roomy with quality mattresses.

Waiteti Trout Stream
Holiday Park   HOLIDAY PARK $
(Map p290; ☑07-357 5255, 0800 876 881; www. waiteti.com; 14 Okona Cres; sites $36, dm from $22, d cabin/motel from $55/105; @🕸) This well-maintained park is a great option if you don't mind the 8km drive into town. Set in 2 acres of garden on the banks of a trout-filled stream, it's a cute classic with character-filled motel units, compact cabins, a tidy backpackers lodge and beaut campsites by the stream. Free kayaks and dinghies; fly-fishing lessons $30.

Tuscany Villas   MOTEL $$
(Map p290; ☑07-348 3500, 0800 802 050; www. tuscanyvillasrotorua.co.nz; 280 Fenton St; d from $145; 🕸) With its Italian-inspired architecture and pointy conifers, this family-owned eye-catcher is the pick of the Fenton St motels. It pitches itself perfectly at both the corporate and leisure traveller, who will appreciate the lavish furnishings, multiple TVs, DVD players and huge, deep spa baths.

Crank Backpackers   HOSTEL $
(Map p276; ☑0508 224 466, 07-348 0852; www. crankbackpackers.co.nz; 1140 Hinemoa St; dm $22-25, d & tw with/without bathroom $62/56; @🕸) A cavernous hostel determined to compete with the old stagers, Crank occupies a former shopping mall (you might be sleeping in a florist or delicatessen). Dorms over the street are sunny, and there are sexy co-ed bathrooms, a free gym and the Wall rock-climbing facility, as well as the art-house Basement Cinema downstairs.

Regent Flashpackers   HOSTEL $
(Map p276; ☑07-348 5111; www.regentflashpackers. co.nz; 1181 Pukaki St; dm/d from $25/79; @🕸) Angling for a mature, upscale backpacker market (is there such a thing?), the very decent Regent does it with style: sturdy bunks, cosy kitchen, quality linen, underfloor heating and fill-your-own mineral pools out the back. There's also a bar, which helps lower the tone a little.

Jack & Di's Troutbeck Lodge LODGE, MOTEL $$

(Map p290; ☑07-357 4294, 0800 522 526; www.
jackanddis.co.nz; 5 Arnold St; d/lodge from
$99/399; ☎) A lakeside position in quiet, se-
cluded Ngongotaha makes this large lodge a
good retreat from central Rotorua (no sulphur smell!). The lodge (with full kitchen)
caters for families or groups of up to 11, or
there are motel-style doubles. Good winter
rates; free kayaks.

Rotorua YHA HOSTEL $

(Map p276; ☑07-349 4088, 0800 278 299; www.
yha.co.nz; 1278 Haupapa St; dm $28-35 d with/with-
out bathroom $87/77; @☎) Bright and spar-
kling-clean, this classy, purpose-built hostel
is great for those wanting to get outdoors,
with staff eager to assist with trip bookings,
and storage for bikes and kayaks. Pricier
rooms come with bathroom, and there's
a barbecue area and deck for hanging out
on (though this ain't a party pad). Off-street
parking a bonus.

Rotorua Top 10 Holiday Park HOLIDAY PARK $

(☑07-348 1886, 0800 223 267; www.rotoruatop10.
co.nz; 1495 Pukuatua St; sites from $20, d cabin/
motel from $65/95; @☎🏊) A small but per-
fectly formed holiday park with a continual
improvement policy that has seen a new
playground, shower/toilet blocks and mineral hot pools installed. Cabins are in good
nick and have small fridges and microwaves.
Plenty of shrubberies and picnic tables.

Sandi's Bed & Breakfast B&B $$

(Map p290; ☑0800 726 3422, 07-348 0884; www.
sandisbedandbreakfast.co.nz; 103 Fairy Springs Rd;
d/f incl breakfast $130/160; ☎🏊) A friendly,
family B&B run by the well-humoured Sandi
who offers tourist advice with a ready smile.
The best bets are the two bohemian chalets
with TV and plenty of room to move. It's on
a busy road a couple of kilometres north of
town, but thoughtful extras include fresh
fruit with breakfast and a sun deck.

Rotorua Central Backpackers HOSTEL $

(Map p276; ☑07-349 3285; www.rotoruacentral
backpackers.co.nz; 1076 Pukuatua St; dm $25, d
$60; @☎) This heritage hostel was built in
1936 and retains historic features including
dark-wood skirting boards and door frames,
deep bathtubs and radiators that are geo-
thermally powered. Dorms have no more
than six beds (and no bunks), plus there's a
spa pool and barbecue, all within strolling
distance of the museum.

Jack & Di's Lake View Lodge LODGE $$

(Map p276; ☑07-357 4294, 0800 522 526; www.
jackanddis.co.nz; 21 Lake Rd; r/apt from $99/199 ;
☎) Lake views and a central but secluded location make this unique lodge a persuasive
option. The upstairs penthouse is ideal for
couples, while downstairs is better for families or groups (three bedrooms, three bathrooms). A spa pool, lazy lounge areas and
full kitchens add to the appeal.

Crash Palace HOSTEL $

(Map p276; ☑07-348 8842, 0800 892 727; www.
crashpalace.co.nz; 1271 Hinemaru St; dm/s/d from
$22/35/60; @☎) This newcomer occupies a
big, mustard-coloured 1930s hotel near Government Gardens. The atmosphere strikes a
balance between party and pristine, without
too much of either. The nicest rooms have
floorboards, and there's lots of art on the
walls. Crash (aka Chris) and Nero the black
cat man the reception desk. Limited off-steet
parking.

Rotorua Thermal
Holiday Park HOLIDAY PARK $

(Map p290; ☑07-346 3140; www.rotoruathermal.
co.nz; 463 Old Taupo Rd; sites from $16, d cabins/
units from $51/98; @☎🏊) This super-friendly
holiday park on the edge of town is deep in
the leisure groove, with barbecues, a playground, rows of cabins and tourist flats,
campsites galore and a shop and seasonal
cafe. There's plenty of room to move, with
lots of open grassy areas, plus hot mineral
pools to soak the day away.

Millennium Hotel Rotorua HOTEL $$$

(Map p276; ☑07-347 1234; www.millenniumrotorua.
co.nz; cnr Eruera & Hinemaru Sts; d from $250;
@☎🏊) The slick Maori-inspired lobby sets
the scene for this elegant five-storey motel.
Lakefront rooms afford excellent views as
does the club lounge, popular with the suits
and internationalists swanning about. The
poolside *hangi* (p278) is fab, as is the in-
house restaurant Nikau.

Six on Union MOTEL $$

(Map p276; ☑07-347 8062, 0800 100 062; www.six
ononion.co.nz; 6 Union St; d/f from $105/145; ☎🏊)
Hanging baskets ahoy! This modest place is
an affordable bonanza with pool, spa and
small kitchenettes in all units. Rooms are
functional, and the new owners (from Yorkshire) keep the swimming-pool area in good
nick. It's away from traffic noise, but still an
easy walk into town.

Victoria Lodge
MOTEL **$$**

(Map p276; 0800 100 039, 07-348 4039; www.victorialodge.co.nz; 10 Victoria St; d/apt from $115/160;) The friendly Vic has seen a lot of competitors come and go, maintaining its foothold in the market with individual-feeling rooms: the studios are particularly attractive with their thermally heated plunge pools. Fully equipped, freshly painted apartments can squeeze in seven, though four would be very comfortable.

Ann's Volcanic Rotorua Motel
MOTEL **$$**

(Map p290; 07-347 1007, 0800 768 683; www.rotoruamotel.co.nz; 107 Malfroy Rd; d/ste from $99/115;) Ann's is an affordable motel that has family charm and an ever-friendly host with loads of advice on things to see and do around Rotorua. Larger rooms feature courtyard spas and facilities for travellers with disabilities, with a house next door available for big groups. Rooms close to the street can be a tad noisy.

Princes Gate Hotel
LUXURY HOTEL **$$$**

(Map p276; 07-348 1179, 0800 500 705; www.princesgate.co.nz; 1057 Arawa St; d/ste from $165/220; @) The Princes Gate is a well-loved and warmly welcoming 19th-century dame with 54 different rooms, such as the opulent Marvelly suite – perhaps too pink for all but Barbara Cartland. Sink into the bottomless bath, however, and all is forgiven. Other amenities include cascading mineral baths, sauna and restaurant. Cabaret nights, too.

Base Rotorua
HOSTEL **$**

(Map p276; 07-348 8636, 0800 227 369; www.stayatbase.co.nz; 1286 Arawa St; dm/s/d $28/70/70; @) A link in the Base chain, this huge hostel is ever-popular with partying backpackers who love the Lava Bar (cheap meals, toga parties, disco nights etc). Dorms can be tight (up to 12 beds), but extras such as girls-only rooms, en suites in all doubles, a large outdoor heated pool and off-street parking compensate.

Kiwi Paka
HOSTEL **$**

(07-347 0931; www.kiwipaka.co.nz; 60 Tarewa Rd; sites from $15, dm/s/d $29/55/64, chalets with bathroom d/tr/q $87/107/147; @) This rambling complex is a short walk through Kuirau Park to town. The vibe is a bit like a school camp, with acceptable amenities and a range of accommodation from campsites to plain dorms, lodge rooms and two-storey pine-clad chalets. There's a cafe and bar on-site.

Eating

The lake end of Tutanekai St has a strip of good eating places, but there are plenty of other options all over town.

TOP CHOICE Third Place Cafe
CAFE **$$**

(07-349 4852; www.thirdplacecafe.co.nz; 36 Lake Rd; mains $15-18; 8am-4pm Mon-Fri, 8am-3pm Sat) A really interesting cafe away from the hubbub, Third Place has leapfrogged into first by our reckoning. All-day breakfast/brunch sidesteps neatly between chicken jambalaya, fish and chips, and an awesome 'mumble jumble' of crushed kumara (sweet potato), green tomatoes and spicy chorizo topped with bacon, poached egg and hollandaise sauce. Hangover? What hangover? Slide into a red-leather couch or score a window seat overlooking Ohinemutu.

Lime Caffeteria
CAFE **$$**

(Map p276; 07-350 2033; cnr Fenton & Whakaue Sts; mains $13-24; 7.30am-4.30pm;) Occupying a quiet corner near the lake, this refreshing cafe is especially good for alfresco breakfasts and dishes with a welcome twist: try the chicken-and-chorizo salad or prawn-and-salmon risotto in lime sauce. It also offers classy counter snacks, excellent coffee and outdoor tables. 'This is the best lunch I've had in ages,' says one happy punter.

Indian Star
INDIAN **$$**

(Map p276; 07-343 6222; www.indianstar.co.nz; 1118 Tutanekai St; mains $14-22; lunch & dinner;) This is one of several Indian eateries around town, elevating itself above the competition with immaculate service and marvellous renditions of subcontinental classics. It has sizeable portions and good vegetarian selections (try the chickpea masala). Book for dinner.

Fat Dog Cafe & Bar
CAFE **$$**

(Map p276; 07-347 7586; 1161 Arawa St; mains breakfast & lunch $12-20, dinner $27-32; breakfast, lunch & dinner;) With paw prints and silly poems painted on the walls, this is the town's friskiest and most child-friendly cafe. During the day it dishes up burgers (try the Dogs Bollox version), nachos, salads and sandwiches; in the evening it's candlelit lamb and venison. The only cafe in NZ brave enough to play *Unskinny Bop* by Poison.

Capers Epicurean
CAFE, DELICATESSEN

(Map p276; 07-348 8818; www.capers.co.nz; 1181 Eruera St; mains breakfast & lunch $6-20, dinner

ROTORUA & THE BAY OF PLENTY ROTORUA

ROTORUA & THE BAY OF PLENTY ROTORUA

$13-28; ⊘7.30am-9pm; 🍴) This slick, barnlike deli is always busy with diners showing up for cabinets crammed full of delicious gourmet sandwiches, pastries, salads and cakes, and an excellent blackboard menu of breakfasts and other tasty hot foods (try the carrot, leek and feta lasagne). There's also a deli section stocked with olive oils, marinades, relishes, jams and chocolates.

Weilin's Noodle House NOODLES, CHINESE $
(Map p276; ☎07-343 9998; 1148 Tutanekai St; mains $8-17; ⊘lunch & dinner Wed-Mon) A neat and tidy shop serving trad (and refreshingly un-fatty/salty/stodgy) Chinese dumplings and oodles of noodles in soups and stir-fries. Eat in or take away.

Urbano Bistro MODERN NZ, CAFE $$
(Map p290; ☎07-349 3770; www.urbanobistro.co.nz; cnr Fenton & Grey Sts; mains breakfast & lunch $14-21, dinner $24-43; ⊘9am-11pm Mon-Sat, to 3pm Sun) This suburban cafe, with its mega-checkerboard floor and striking wallpaper, is a bold move by reputable local restaurateurs. It serves some of the most delicious fare in town (try the beef, pineapple and kumara curry), rich in flavour and well executed. Fine wines and five-star service.

Sabroso LATIN AMERICAN $$
(Map p276; ☎07-349 0591; www.sabroso.co.nz; 1184 Haupapa St; mains $18-45; ⊘5-10pm Thu-Tue) What a surprise! This modest Latin American cantina – adorned with sombreros, guitars, hessian tablecloths and salt-and-pepper shakers made from Corona bottles – serves adventurous south-of-the-border fare to spice up bland Kiwi palates. The black-bean chilli is a knock-out (as are the margaritas).

Bistro 1284 MODERN NZ $$$
(Map p276; ☎07-346 1284; www.bistro1284.co.nz; 1284 Eruera St; mains $34-39; ⊘6pm-late) Definitely one of RotoVegas' fine-dining hot spots, this intimate place (all chocolate and mushroom colours) serves stylish NZ cuisine with an Asian influence. It's an excellent place to sample local ingredients (the lamb is always good); be sure to leave room for some delectable desserts.

Amazing Thai THAI $$
(Map p276; ☎07-343 9494; 1246 Fenton St; mains $19-28; ⊘lunch & dinner) This large, glass-fronted restaurant dishes up better-than-average, spicy-as-you-like Thai food in generous servings. There are obligatory portraits of Thai royals and sundry elephants, and takeaways available.

Ali Baba's Tunisian Takeaway MIDDLE EASTERN, TUNISIAN $
(Map p276; ☎07-348 2983; 1146 Tutanekai St; meals $9-15; ⊘11.30am-late; 🍴) Follow the belly-dancing music (and your nose) into this neat little eatery serving kebabs and Tunisian-inspired pizzas, salads, pastas and rice meals. Eat in or take away.

Pak 'n Save SUPERMARKET
(Map p276; www.paknsave.co.nz; cnr Fenton & Amohau Sts; ⊘8am-10pm) Centrally located.

Drinking & Entertainment

Brew BAR, CRAFT BEER
(Map p276; www.brewpub.co.nz; 1103 Tutanekai St) Run by the lads from Croucher Brewing Co, Rotorua's best microbrewers, Brew sits in a sunny spot on Rotorua's main eat-street. Sip down a pint of fruity pale ale, aromatic drunken hop bitter or malty pilsener and wonder how you'll manage a sleep-in tomorrow morning. Good coffee, too.

Pig & Whistle PUB, BREWERY
(Map p276; www.pigandwhistle.co.nz; cnr Haupapa & Tutanekai Sts) Inside a former police station, this busy microbrewery-pub serves up Swine lager, big-screen TVs, a beer garden and live music Thursday to Saturday, plus simple grub (mains $15 to $30). The menu runs the gamut from crispy pork-belly salad to burgers and vegetarian nachos.

Belgian Bar BAR, LIVE MUSIC
(Map p276; www.facebook.com/pages/belgian-bar/137762819598058; 1151 Arawa St; ⊘Tue-Sun) The best bar in town for lovers of gigs and good beer. Half a dozen Euro-beers on tap and 42 in the bottle accompany regular blues and acoustic acts ('Clapton is God' is spraypainted behind the stage).

Pheasant Plucker PUB, LIVE MUSIC
(Map p276; www.thepheasantplucker.co.nz; 1153 Arawa St) A place for a proper pint, the pleasant Pheasant proffers locally brewed and Brit beers, along with pub food and open-mic, blues, rock, roots and singer-songwriter acts.

Basement Cinema CINEMA
(Map p276; www.basementcinema.co.nz; 1140 Hinemoa St) Part of the same complex as the Wall rock-climbing gym, the Basement offers up offbeat, foreign-language and art-house flicks.

🛍 Shopping

Rotorua and souvenirs go hand-in-hand: look for genuine Maori and NZ-made arts and crafts. South of town, Te Puia and Whakarewarewa Thermal Village have excellent selections of genuine Maori-made arts.

Rotorua Night Market   MARKET
(Map p276; www.rotoruanightmarket.co.nz; Tutanekai St; ⊘4.30pm-late Thu) Tutanekai St is closed off on Thursday nights between Haupapa and Pukuatua Sts to allow the Rotorua Night Market to spread its wings. Expect local arts and crafts, souvenirs, cheesy buskers, coffee, wine and plenty of deli-style food stalls for dinner.

Mountain Jade   ARTS & CRAFTS, JEWELLERY
(Map p276; www.mountainjade.com; 1288 Fenton St; ⊘9am-6pm) High-end hand-crafted greenstone jewellery and carvings. You can watch the carvers at work through the streetside window.

Out of New Zealand   ARTS & CRAFTS, JEWELLERY
(Map p276; 1189 Fenton St; ⊘10am-6pm, to 9pm Dec-Mar) Stocks NZ-made craft and gifts including carvings, ceramics and jewellery: affordable, packable souvenirs.

ℹ Information

There are plenty of ATMs around town, and a Travelex at the i-SITE. Most banks offer currency exchange.

Lakes Prime Care (☑07-348 1000; 1165 Tutanekai St; ⊘8am-10pm) Urgent medical care.

Police (☑111, non-emergency 07-348 0099; www.police.govt.nz; 1190-1214 Fenton St)

Post office (cnr Tutanekai & Pukuatua Sts)

Rotorua Hospital (☑07-348 1199; www.lakesdhb.govt.nz; Arawa St; ⊘24hr) Round-the-clock medical care.

Rotorua Sustainable Tourism (www.sustainablenz.com) Make your Rotorua visit more ecofriendly.

Tourism Rotorua & i-SITE (☑07-348 5179, 0800 768 678; www.rotoruanz.com; 1167 Fenton St; ⊘8am-6pm Sep-May, to 5.30pm Jun-Aug) The hub for travel information and bookings, including Department of Conservation (DOC) walks. Also has an exchange bureau, a cafe, showers and lockers.

ℹ Getting There & Away

Air

Air New Zealand (☑07-343 1100; www.airnewzealand.co.nz; 1267 Tutanekai St; ⊘9am-5pm Mon-Fri) Has direct flights between Rotorua and Auckland, Wellington and Christchurch, plus Sydney (every Tuesday and Saturday).

Qantas (www.qantas.com.au) Links Rotorua with Auckland.

Bus

All the major bus companies stop outside the Rotorua i-SITE, from where you can arrange bookings.

InterCity (www.intercity.co.nz) destinations include the following:

DESTINATION	PRICE	DURATION	FREQUENCY
Auckland	$50	3½hr	7 daily
Gisborne	$82	9hr	1 daily
Hamilton	$32	1½hr	5 daily
Napier	$53	3hr	3 daily
Taupo	$32	1hr	4 daily
Tauranga	$30	1½hr	3 daily
Wellington	$65	8hr	5 daily
Whakatane	$34	1½hr	1 daily

Naked Bus (www.nakedbus.com) services the following destinations. Substantial fare savings can be made by booking in advance.

DESTINATION	PRICE	DURATION	FREQUENCY
Auckland	$19	4hr	6 daily
Gisborne	$27	4¾hr	1 daily
Hamilton	$16	1½hr	5 daily
Napier	$29	3hr	3 daily
Taupo	$15	1hr	2 daily
Tauranga	$12	1½hr	5 daily
Wellington	$36	8hr	2 daily
Whakatane	$18	1½hr	1 daily

Twin City Express (☑0800 422 928; www.baybus.co.nz) buses run twice daily Monday to Friday between Rotorua and Tauranga/Mt Maunganui via Te Puke ($11.60, 1½ hours).

White Island Shuttle (☑07-308 9588, 0800 733 529; www.whiteisland.co.nz; one-way/return $35/60), run by White Island Tours in Whakatane, operates return shuttles to Whakatane from Rotorua. It's ostensibly for tour customers, but you can use the service without taking the tour.

ℹ Getting Around

To/From the Airport

Rotorua Airport (☑07-345 8800; www.rotorua-airport.co.nz; SH30) is 10km northeast of town.

Super Shuttle (☑09-522 5100, 0800 748 885; www.supershuttle.co.nz) offers a door-to-door airport service for $22 for the first person then

$6 per additional passenger. Cityride (p288) runs a daily airport bus service ($2.30). A taxi to/from the city centre costs about $25.

Bus

Many local attractions offer free pick-up/drop-off shuttle services. Shuttle services (p282) are also available to/from outlying attractions.

Cityride (☑0800 422 928; www.baybus. co.nz) operates local bus services around town, and also to Ngongotaha (route 1, $2.30) and the airport (route 10, $2.30).

Car

The big-name car-hire companies vie for your attention at Rotorua Airport. The following smaller companies share a premises located on Fenton St.

A2B Car Rentals (☑0800 666 703; www.a2b-carrentals.co.nz; 1234 Fenton St)
Ezi-Rent Car Hire (☑07-349 1629, 0800 652 565; www.ezirentcarhire.co.nz; 1234 Fenton St)
Nationwide Rental Cars (☑0800 803 003; www.nationwiderentalcars.co.nz; 1234 Fenton St)

Taxi

Fast Taxis (☑07-348 2444)
Rotorua Taxis (☑07-348 1111)

AROUND ROTORUA

North of Rotorua

◉ Sights & Activities

Rainbow Springs Kiwi Wildlife Park
WILDLIFE RESERVE
(Map p290; ☑0800 724 626; www.rainbowsprings. co.nz; Fairy Springs Rd; 24hr pass adult/child/family $35/22.50/103; ⊗8am-late) About 3km north of central Rotorua, Rainbow Springs is a family-friendly winner. The natural springs here are home to wild trout and eels, which you can peer at through an underwater viewer. There are interpretive walkways, a new 'Big Splash' water ride, and plenty of animals, including tuatara (a native reptile), introduced species (wallabies, rainbow lorikeets) and native birds (kea, kaka and pukeko).

A highlight is the Kiwi Encounter, offering a rare peek into the lives of these endangered birds: excellent 30-minute tours have you tiptoeing through incubator and hatchery areas. Also available are joint four-hour evening tours (adult/child $125/65) with neighbouring Mitai Maori Village (p278).

Wingspan Birds of Prey Trust
WILDLIFE CENTRE
(☑07-357 4469; www.wingspan.co.nz; 1164 Paradise Valley Rd; adult/child $25/8; ⊗9am-3pm) Wingspan Birds of Prey Trust is dedicated to conserving three threatened NZ birds: the falcon, hawk and owl. Learn about the birds in the museum display, then take a sneaky peek into the incubation area before walking through the all-weather aviary. Don't miss the 2pm flying display.

aMAZEme
MAZE
(Map p290; ☑07-357 5759; www.amazeme.co.nz; 1335 Paradise Valley Rd; adult/child/family $16/9/45; ⊗9am-5pm Dec-Feb, 10am-4pm Mar-Nov) This amazing 1.4km maze is constructed from immaculately pruned, head-high escallonia hedge. Lose yourself (or the kids) in the endless spirals.

Paradise Valley Springs
WILDLIFE RESERVE
(☑07-348 9667; www.paradisevalleysprings.co.nz; 467 Paradise Valley Rd; adult/child $29/14.50; ⊗8am-dusk) In Paradise Valley at the foot of Mt Ngongotaha, 8km from Rotorua, is Paradise Valley Springs, a 6-hectare park with trout springs, big slippery eels and various land-dwelling animals such as deer, alpacas, possums and a pride of lions (fed at 2.30pm; see the two new cubs before they grow up). There's also a coffee shop and an elevated treetop walkway.

Agrodome
AGRICULTURAL
(Map p290; ☑07-357 1050; www.agrodome. co.nz; Western Rd; 1hr tour adult/child/family $38.50/19.50/82, 1hr show $29/14.50/77, tour & show $56/28/115; ⊗8.30am-5pm, shows 9.30am, 11am & 2.30pm, tours 10.40am, 12.10pm, 1.30pm & 3.40pm) Learn everything you need to know about sheep at the educational Agrodome. Shows include a parade of champion rams, a livestock auction, and shearing and doggy displays. The tour lets you check out farm animals including, among others, sheep. Other agro-attractions include a shearing-shed museum and cafe.

Northeast of Rotorua

◉ Sights & Activities

Hells Gate & Wai Ora Spa
VOLCANIC AREA, SPA
(Map p290; ☑07-345 3151; www.hellsgate. co.nz; SH30, Tikitere; admission adult/child/family $30/15/75, mud bath & spa $105, massage per 30/60min $85/135; ⊗8.30am-8.30pm) Known

as Tikitere to the Maori, Hells Gate is an impressive geothermal reserve 16km northeast of Rotorua on the Whakatane road (SH30). Tikitere is an abbreviation of *Taku tiki i tere nei* (My youngest daughter has floated away), remembering the tragedy of a young girl jumping into a thermal pool. The English name originates from a 1934 visit by George Bernard Shaw. The reserve covers 10 hectares, with a 2.5km walking track to the various attractions, including a hot thermal waterfall. You can also see a master woodcarver at work, and learn about flax weaving and other Maori traditions.

Long regarded by Maori as a place of healing, Tikitere also houses the Wai Ora Spa, where you can get muddy with a variety of treatments. A courtesy shuttle to/from Rotorua is available.

3D Maze
MAZE
(Map p290; ☑07-345 5275; www.3dmaze.co.nz; 1135 Te Ngae Rd; adult/child $9/6; ☺9am-5pm) Three kilometres beyond Rotorua Airport is this 1.7km-long wooden maze that will entertain kids for an hour or so.

Southeast of Rotorua
◉ Sights & Activities

Redwoods Whakarewarewa Forest FOREST
(www.redwoods.co.nz; ☺5.30am-8.30pm) This magical forest park is 3km southeast of town on Tarawera Rd. It was originally home to over 170 tree species (a few less now), planted from 1899 to see which could be grown successfully for timber. Radiata pine proved a hit (as evident throughout New Zealand), but it's the mighty Californian redwoods that give the park its grandeur today.

Clearly signposted walking tracks range from a half-hour wander through the Redwood Grove to an enjoyable whole-day route to the Blue and Green Lakes. Most walks start from the **Redwoods Gift Shop & Visitor Centre** (Map p290; ☑07-350 0110; Long Mile Rd; ☺8.30am-5.30pm Mon-Fri, 10am-5pm Sat & Sun Oct-Mar, 8.30am-4.30pm Mon-Fri, 10am-4pm Sat & Sun Apr-Sep), where you can get maps and view displays about the forest. Aside from walking, the park is great for picnics, and is acclaimed for its accessible mountain biking. Mountain Bike Rotorua (p280) offers bike hire, across the park off Waipa State Mill Rd.

Buried Village ARCHAEOLOGICAL SITE, MUSEUM
(Map p290; ☑07-362 8287; www.buriedvillage.co.nz; 1180 Tarawera Rd; adult/child/family $31/8/62; ☺9am-5pm Nov-Mar, to 4.30pm Apr-Oct) Fifteen kilometres from Rotorua on Tarawera Rd, beyond the pretty Blue and Green Lakes, is the buried village of Te Wairoa, interred by the eruption of Mt Tarawera in 1886. Te Wairoa was the staging post for travellers coming to see the Pink and White Terraces. Today a museum houses objects dug from the ruins, and guides in period costume escort groups through the excavated sites. There's also a walk to the 30m **Te Wairoa Falls** (not suitable for kids or oldies), and a teahouse if you're feeling more sedate.

Lake Tarawera LAKE
(www.doc.govt.nz) Tarawera means 'Burnt Spear', named by a visiting hunter who left his bird spears in a hut and, on returning the following season, found both the spears and hut had been burnt. The lake is picturesque and good for swimming, fishing, cruises and walks.

A good place to access the lake is at the Landing, about 2km past the buried village. Here you'll find **Clearwater Cruises** (Map p290; ☑07-345 6688, 0508 253 279; www.clearwater.co.nz; per hr cruise vessel/self-drive runabout $550/140), which runs scenic cruises for groups and trout-fishing trips aboard a variety of vessels. Also here is the **Landing Café** (www.thelandinglaketarawera.co.nz; mains $26-30; ☺breakfast & lunch daily, closed Mon & Tue Jun-Aug), serving hearty mains like spiced lamb rump, salmon pasta and seafood chowder. Around 2km beyond the Landing is **Lake Tarawera Water Taxi** (☑07-362 8080; www.laketaraweraescape.co.nz; 93 Spencer Rd; from $60), which can take you anywhere on the lake, at any time.

There are campsites managed by **DOC** (www.doc.govt.nz) at **Hot Water Beach** (Map p290; adult/child $10/5) (boat access only), **Tarawera Outlet** (Map p290; adult/child $6/3) and **Humphries Bay** (Map p290) (free, but rudimentary). The **Blue Lake Top 10 Holiday Park** (Map p290; ☑07-362 8120, 0800 808 292; www.bluelaketop10.co.nz; 723 Tarawera Rd; sites from $18.50, cabins $56-139, units $99-229; @🖢) offers camping next to the Blue Lake (good for swimming and kayaking), 6km before you get to Lake Tarawera; well run, it has spotless facilities and a handy range of cabins.

ROTORUA & THE BAY OF PLENTY SOUTHEAST OF ROTORUA

Around Rotorua

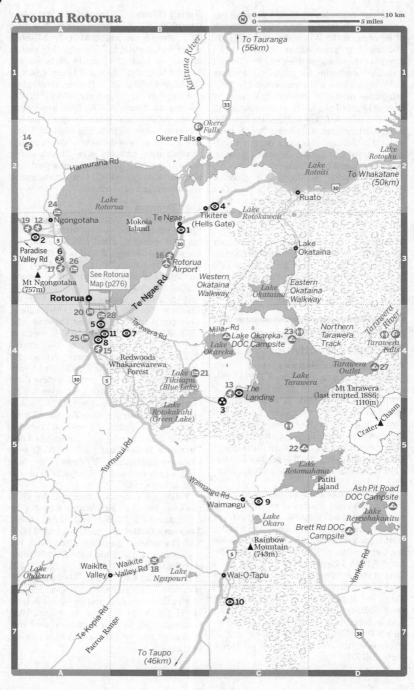

N

0 ————————— 10 km
0 ————————— 5 miles

To Tauranga (56km)

Kaituna River

33

Okere Falls

Okere Falls

Lake Rotoiti

Lake Rotoehu

Hamurana Rd

14

Lake Rotorua

Mokoia Island

Te Ngae

Tikitere (Hells Gate)

4

1

Ngongotaha

24

19 12

2

Paradise Valley Rd

6

17 26

Mt Ngongotaha (757m)

See Rotorua Map (p276)

Rotorua

Lake Rotokawau

Ruato

To Whakatane (50km)

30

Lake Okataina

16

Rotorua Airport

Te Ngae Rd

Western Okataina Walkway

Lake Okataina

Eastern Okataina Walkway

Tarawera River

Tarawera Falls

20

28

5

11 7

8

15

25

Tarawera Rd

Millar Rd

Lake Okareka DOC Campsite

23

Northern Tarawera Track

Tarawera Outlet

27

Redwoods Whakarewarewa Forest

Lake Okareka

Lake Tikitapu (Blue Lake)

21

Lake Tarawera

Mt Tarawera (last erupted 1886; 1110m)

Crater Chasm

Lake Rotokakahi (Green Lake)

13

The Landing

3

22

Lake Rotomahana

Patiti Island

Ash Pit Road DOC Campsite

Waimangu Rd

Waimangu

Lake Okaro

9

Lake Rerewhakaaitu

Brett Rd DOC Campsite

Rainbow Mountain (743m)

Waikite Valley

Waikite Valley Rd

18

Lake Ngapouri

Wai-O-Tapu

Yankee Rd

Lake Ohakuri

Te Kopia Rd

Paeroa Range

10

38

To Taupo (46km)

Around Rotorua

South of Rotorua
◎ Sights & Activities

Waimangu Volcanic Valley
VOLCANIC AREA, SPRING

(Map p290; ☑07-366 6137; www.waimangu.com; 587 Waimangu Rd; adult/child walking tour $34.50/11, boat cruise $42.50/11; ☺8.30am-5pm daily, to 6pm Jan, last admission 3.45pm, 4.45pm Jan) This interesting thermal area was created during the eruption of Mt Tarawera in 1886, making it young in geological terms. Waimangu (Black Water) refers to the dark, muddy colour of much of the water here.

Taking the easy downhill stroll through the valley you'll pass many spectacular thermal and volcanic features, including Inferno Crater Lake, where overflowing water can reach 80°C, and Frying Pan Lake, the largest hot spring in the world. The walk continues down to Lake Rotomahana (meaning 'Warm Lake'), from where you can either get a lift back up to where you started or take a 45-minute boat trip on the lake, past steaming cliffs and the former site of the Pink and White Terraces.

Waimangu is 20 minutes south of Rotorua, 14km along SH5 (towards Taupo) and then 6km from the marked turn-off.

Wai-O-Tapu Thermal Wonderland
VOLCANIC AREA, GEYSER

(Map p290; ☑07-366 6333; www.waiotapu.co.nz; 201 Waiotapu Loop Rd, off SH5; adult/child/family $32.50/11/80; ☺8.30am-5pm, last admission 3.45pm) Wai-O-Tapu (Sacred Waters) is a fairly commercial operation with a lot of interesting geothermal features packed into a small area, including the boiling, multi-hued Champagne Pool, bubbling mud pool, stunning mineral terraces and Lady Knox Geyser, which spouts off (with a little prompting from an organic soap) punctually at 10.15am and gushes up to 20m for about an hour (be here by 9.45am to see it).

Wai-O-Tapu is 27km south of Rotorua along SH5 (towards Taupo), and a further 2km from the marked turn-off.

Waikite Valley Thermal Pools
SWIMMING

(Map p290; ☑07-333 1861; www.hotpools.co.nz; 648 Waikite Valley Rd; public pools adult/child/family $14/7/35, private pools 40min $18; ☺10am-9pm) Approximately 30km south of Rotorua are these excellent open-air pools, formalised in the 1970s but utilised for centuries before then. There are four main pools, two more relaxing, smaller pools, and four private spas, all ranging from 35°C to 40°C. There's also a cafe and camping (sites from $18; pools free for campers).

To get here, turn right off SH5 opposite the Wai-O-Tapu turn-off, and continue 6km (worth the drive if only for the gorgeous valley view as you come over the hill).

BAY OF PLENTY

The Bay of Plenty stretches along the pohutukawa-studded coast from Waihi Beach to Opotiki and inland as far as the Kaimai Range. This is where New Zealanders have come on holiday for generations, lapping up salt-licked activities and lashings of sunshine.

Tauranga

POP 121,500

Tauranga (pronounced Tao-wronger) has been booming since the 1990s and remains one of NZ's fastest-growing cities. It's also NZ's busiest port – with petrol refineries and mountains of coal and lumber – but it's beach-seeking holidaymakers who have seen the old workhorse reborn as a show pony. Restaurants and bars line the revamped waterfront, fancy hotels rise high, and the once-sleepy burbs of Mt Maunganui and Papamoa have woken up to new prosperity. This is about as Riviera as NZ gets. Online, www.downtowntauranga.co.nz is a commercial but useful resource.

◎ Sights

FREE Tauranga Art Gallery   GALLERY
(www.artgallery.org.nz; cnr Wharf & Willow Sts; ◷10am-4.30pm) The Tauranga Art Gallery presents historic and contemporary art, and houses a permanent collection along with frequently changing local and visiting exhibitions. The building itself is a former bank, although you'd hardly know it – it's an altogether excellent space with no obvious compromise (cue: applause). Touring the ground and mezzanine galleries, with a stop to poke your nose into the video cube, will take an hour or so.

Elms Mission House   HISTORIC BUILDING
(www.theelms.org.nz; 15 Mission St; house adult/child $5/50c, gardens free; ◷house 2-4pm Wed, Sat & Sun, gardens 9am-5pm daily) Built in 1847, Elms Mission House is the oldest building in the Bay of Plenty. Furnished in period style, it sits among other well-preserved mission buildings in leafy gardens. The spooky Mission Cemetery (cnr Marsh St & Dive Cres; ◷24hr) lies not far away – a shady tangle of trees and headstones, it's good for a little epitaph-reading.

Classic Flyers NZ   MUSEUM
(www.classicflyersnz.com; 8 Jean Batten Dr; adult/child/family $10/5/25; ◷10am-4pm) Out near the airport, Classic Flyers NZ is an interesting aviation museum (biplanes, retired US Airforce jets, helicopters etc) with a buzzy on-site cafe.

FREE Monmouth
Redoubt   ARCHAEOLOGICAL SITE, PARK
(Monmouth St; ◷24hr) Shaded by huge pohutukawa trees, spooky Monmouth Redoubt was a fortified site during the Maori Wars. Next door is Robbins Park (Cliff Rd), a verdant pocket of roses with sweeping views across to Mt Maunganui. At the foot of the

---

WORTH A TRIP

WHIRINAKI FOREST PARK

This lush podocarp (conifer) forest park is 90km southeast of Rotorua off SH38, en route to Te Urewera National Park (take the turn-off at Te Whaiti to Minginui). Also here are canyons, waterfalls, lookouts and streams, plus the **Oriuwaka Ecological Area** and **Arahaki Lagoon**.

Walking tracks here vary in length and difficulty: the Department of Conservation (DOC) booklet *Walks in Whirinaki Forest* ($2.50) details walking and camping options. Pick one up at DOC's **Murupara visitor centre** (☏07-366 1080; www.doc.govt.nz; SH38, Murupara).

A good short walk is the **Whirinaki Waterfalls Track** (four hours return), which follows the Whirinaki River. Longer walks include the **Whirinaki Track** (two days), which can be combined with **Te Hoe Track** (four days). There's also a rampaging 16km **mountain-bike track** here.

There are several accessible camping areas and 10 backcountry huts (free to $15) in the park; pay at the DOC office.

Tauranga

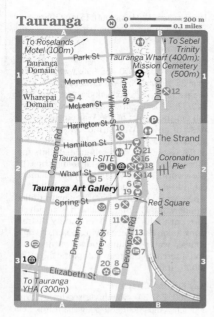

ROTORUA & THE BAY OF PLENTY TAURANGA

Redoubt on the end of the Strand is Te Awa nui Waka, a replica Maori canoe, on display in an open-sided building.

Brain Watkins House   HISTORIC BUILDING
(www.nzhistoricalsocieties.org.nz; cnr Elizabeth St & Cameron Rd; adult/child/family $4/2/10; ⊙2-4pm Sun) A demure Victorian villa and one of Tauranga's best-preserved colonial homes, Brain Watkins House was built in 1881 from kauri (wood). It was bequeathed to the Historical Society in 1979 following the death of Elva Brain Watkins.

Minden Lookout   LOOKOUT
(Minden Rd) From Minden Lookout, about 10km west of Tauranga towards Katikati, there's a superb view back over the Bay of Plenty. To get there, take SH2 to Te Puna and turn off south on Minden Rd; the lookout is about 4km up the road.

Mills Reef Winery   WINERY
(☑07-576 8800; www.millsreef.co.nz; 143 Moffat Rd; ⊙10am-5pm) Stately Mills Reef, 7km from the town centre at Bethlehem, has tastings of its award-winning wines (dig the cab sav) and a refined restaurant (read: great food but not much fun) that's open for lunch daily and dinner by reservation (mains $23 to $39).

FREE **Huria Marae**   MARAE
(☑07-578 7838; www.ngaitamarawaho.maori.nz; Te Kaponga St) Huria Marae is on a nondescript suburban street, but has sensational carvings both inside and out. Call to organise permission to visit.

🏃 Activities

White-water rafting on the Wairoa River (accessible from Tauranga) is definitely for thrill-seekers. The Wairoa's levels are controlled by a dam, so it can only be rafted 26 days of the year: advance bookings are essential. Contact local operators (p280) for more information.

The free *Tauranga City Walkways* pamphlet details walks around Tauranga and Mt Maunganui, including the **Waikareao Estuary Walkway** and the popular **Mauao**

Base Track in Mt Maunganui. History buffs should pick up the free *Historic Tauranga* brochure and stroll around the town's cache of historic sites. Pick up pamphlets at the Tauranga and Mt Maunganui i-SITEs.

FREE **Kaimai Mamaku Forest Park** TRAMPING (www.doc.govt.nz; SH29) The backdrop to the Western Bay of Plenty is the rugged 70km-long Kaimai Mamaku Forest Park, 35km southwest of Tauranga, with tramps for the intrepid and huts (per person per night $5 to $15) and campsites ($6). For more info see DOC's pamphlet *Kaimai to Coast* ($2.50), or contact **Kaimai New Zealand Tours** (☑07-552 6338; www.kaimai-new-zealand-tours.com) to arrange a guided tramp.

FREE **McLaren Falls Park** TRAMPING (☑07-577 7000; www.tauranga.govt.nz; McLaren Falls Rd; sites adult/child $6/free; ☺8am-5.30pm May-Oct, to 7.30pm Nov-Apr) In the Wairoa River valley, 15km southwest of Tauranga just off SH29, McLaren Falls Park is a 190-hectare lakeland park with wonderful trees, short walks and picnic areas. There's a basic modern hostel here ($110 per night for exclusive use, or $20 per person) and campsites. Also accessible from McLaren Falls is **Marshalls Animal Park** (☑07-543 1099; www.marshalls animalpark.co.nz; McLaren Falls Rd; adult/child/family $12/6/32; ☺10am-2pm Wed & Thu, to 4.30pm Sat & Sun), which has animal petting, a flying fox, a playground and pony rides.

Butler's Swim with Dolphins WILDLIFE TOUR (☑07-578 3197, 0508 288 537; www.swimwith dolphins.co.nz; full-day trips adult/child $135/110; ☺departs Tauranga 9am, Mt Maunganui 9.30am) Even without dolphins (and you're guaranteed of seeing them), these trips are always entertaining, particularly with Cap'n Butler, a real old salt who protested against nuclear testing at Mururoa Atoll.

Dolphin Blue WILDLIFE TOUR (☑07-576 4303; www.dolphinblue.co.nz; day trips from $135; ☺departs 8.30am) Small-group, unhurried day trips (15 people maximum) across Tauranga harbour and out onto the Bay of Plenty in pursuit of pods of dolphins.

Dolphin Seafaris WILDLIFE TOUR (☑07-577 0105, 0800 326 8747; www.nzdolphin. com; half-day trip adult/child $110/95; ☺departs Tauranga 8am, Mt Maunganui 8.15am) Offers eco-attuned dolphin-spotting trips.

Waimarino Adventure Park KAYAKING, WATER SPORTS (☑07-576 4233, 0800 456 996; www.waimarino. com; 36 Taniwha Pl; kayak tours from $65, kayak hire per hr/day $26/55, park day-pass adult/child $40/32; ☺10am-6pm Aug-Apr, reduced hours May-Jul) On the banks of the Wairoa River 8km west of town, Waimarino offers freedom kayak hire for leisurely paddles along 12km of flat water, and runs self-guided tours further up the river and sea kayaking trips. Its Glowworm Tour ($120 per person) is a magical after-dark journey at McLaren Falls Park where you slip into a secret glowworm-filled wonderland. Waimarino also has an adventure park with all kinds of watery distractions: a kayak slide, a diving board, a ropes course, water-walking zorbs, warm pools, and a terrifying human catapult called 'The Blob' – intense!

Bay Fishing Charters FISHING (☑0800 229 347; www.bayfishingcharters.co.nz; adult/child trips from $80/50, game fishing from $1800) Small-group fishing charters (half- and full-day) and longer game-fishing epics.

Blue Ocean Charters FISHING (☑07-544 3072, 0800 224 278; www.blueocean. co.nz; day trips from $100) Fishing, diving and sightseeing trips (including one to Tuhua Island) on the TS *Ohorere*, MV *Te Kuia* and MV *Ratahi*.

Dive Zone DIVING (☑07-578 4050; www.divezone.co.nz; 213 Cameron Rd; trips/courses from $95/600) PADI-qualifying courses or trips to local wrecks and reefs, plus gear rental.

Earth2Ocean DIVING (☑07-571 5286; www.earth2ocean.co.nz; trips/courses from $100/500) Runs an extensive range of diving courses and trips.

Elements Watersports WATER SPORTS (☑0800 486 729; www.elementsonline.co.nz; lessons from $80) If you're new to the sea and want to splash safely into the big blue, Elements Watersports runs sailing, windsurfing and jetskiing lessons, and has gear for hire.

Tauranga Tandem Skydiving SKYDIVING (☑07-576 7990, 0274 968 408; www.tandemskydive. co.nz; 2 Kittyhawk Way; jumps 8000/10,000/12,000ft $269/299/349) Landlubbers might consider jumping out of a plane...or maybe not.

Tauranga Tandem Skydiving offers jumps from three different heights, with views of Whakaari (White Island), Mt Ruapehu and the East Cape on the way down.

☞ Tours

Adventure Bay of Plenty
KAYAKING, MOUNTAIN BIKING
(☑0800 238 267; www.adventurebop.co.nz; 2hr/half-day/full-day tours from $85/125/175) Offers an enticing array of adventure tours by kayak, mountain bike and horse. Half-day paddles around Mt Maunganui with a stop on Matakana Island cost $125/70 per adult/child. A two-to-three hour cycle around Tauranga costs $85.

No.8 Farm Tours
GUIDED TOUR
(☑07-579 3981; www.no8farmtours.co.nz; tours adult/child from $95/69) Half-day Tauranga tours, plus 4WD tours of a working NZ farm, featuring shearing, milking, sheep dogs, deer and morning tea.

Touring Company
GUIDED TOUR
(☑07-577 0057; www.newzealandadventure.co.nz; tours from $79) Half- and full-day local scenic tours and trips further afield to Waitomo, Rotorua and Whakaari (White Island).

Tauranga Tasting Tours
GUIDED TOUR
(☑07-544 1383; www.tastingtours.co.nz; tours $130) Whips around a local brewery, Mills Reef and Morton Estate wineries, and back to town for cocktails.

Aerius Helicopters
SCENIC FLIGHTS
(☑0800 864 354; www.aerius.co.nz; flights from $59) Local flights and aerial excursions as far away as Waitomo, Rotorua and Whakaari (White Island), departing Mt Maunganui or Te Puke.

Gyrate
SCENIC FLIGHTS
(☑07-575 6583; www.gyrate.co.nz; flights from $95) Flights in a gyroplane (the jetski of the sky), from local, scenic flights to learn-to-fly packages.

Vulcan Helicopters
SCENIC FLIGHTS
(☑07-308 4188, 0800 804 354; www.vulcanheli.co.nz; flights from $870) If you feel like (and can afford) a rotor-propelled spin out to explore Whakaari (White Island), Vulcan Helicopters is for you.

Mount Classics Tours
BUS TOUR
(☑07-574 1779; www.shoretrips.co.nz; half-day tours from $65) Short-hop trips around Tauranga and to Te Puke, aimed at cruise-boat passen-

gers finding their land legs. Longer tours to Rotorua from Tauranga also available.

⚘ Festivals & Events

National Jazz Festival
MUSIC, FOOD & WINE
(www.jazz.org.nz) An Easter extravaganza of big blowers and scoobee-doobee-doobop, with concerts and food and wine galore.

Tauranga Arts Festival
ARTS
(www.taurangafestival.co.nz) Kicking off on Labour weekend in October (in odd-numbered years), showcasing dance, comedy, plays and other things arty.

🛏 Sleeping

Ambassador Motor Inn
MOTEL $$
(☑07-578 5665, 0800 735 294; www.ambassador-motorinn.co.nz; 9 Fifteenth Ave; d/f from $110/175; 🐾🖾) This tidy motel has noise-reducing glass for peaceful sleeps, a swimming pool, and a long list of 'new' things: TVs, kitchens, bedspreads, towels, sheets... Some rooms have spa baths; all have kitchen facilities. It's not overtly ambassadorial, but spotlessly clean, and the owner calls you 'Honey' and might pick you up from the pub if it's not too late.

Roselands Motel
MOTEL $$
(☑0800 363 093, 07-578 2294; www.roselands.co.nz; 21 Brown St; d/ste from $110/135; 🖾) Tarted up with splashes of orange paint and new linen, this sweet, old-style motel is in a quiet but central location. Expect roomy units (all with kitchens), friendly first-name-basis hosts and new TVs. Nice one.

Harbourside City Backpackers
HOSTEL $
(☑07-579 4066; www.backpacktauranga.co.nz; 105 The Strand; dm/d from $28/72; @🖾) Enjoy sea views from this sociable hostel (a renovated former hotel), which is all too handy to the Strand's bars. Rooms are smallish but clean, and you'll spend more time on the awesome roof terrace anyway. There's no car park, but down the road is a public car park that's empty at the right time.

Harbour City Motor Inn
MOTEL $$
(☑0800 253 525, 07-571 1435; www.taurangaharbourcity.co.nz; 50 Wharf St; d from $150; 🖾) With a winning location right in the middle of town (and with plenty of parking), this newish, lemon-yellow motor inn has all the mod cons. There are spa baths in each room, and friendly staff who can offer sound advice on your itinerary.

Tauranga YHA
HOSTEL $

(☎0800 278 299, 07-578 5064; www.yha.co.nz; 171 Elizabeth St; dm from $29, d with/without bathroom $106/89; @🖥🛜) A well-kept, deceptively big YHA with a large grassy backyard and a nearby mangrove swamp boardwalk to explore. Inviting dorms have individual lockers, and there's also info available on local walking trails and a noticeboard for all things green.

Loft 109 Backpackers
HOSTEL $

(☎07-579 5638; www.loft109.co.nz; 109 Devonport Rd, upstairs; dm/d/tr from $28/62/82; @) This central spot feels like somebody's flat, with an intimate kitchen and lounge, rooftop balconies in upper rooms, and (oddly) two halves of a boat built into the ceiling. It's bright, with plenty of skylights and a gas fire for colder days. Super-relaxed without being lax about things like security or boozy bad behaviour.

Just the Ducks Nuts Backpackers
HOSTEL $

(☎07-576 1366; www.justtheducksnuts.co.nz; 6 Vale St; dm from $29, d with/without bathroom $78/66; @🛜) Just out of the town centre, this is a friendly place with colourful rooms, a fulsome library, TVs strewn about and quirky touches like flowers planted in a bathtub and duck-themed toilets – like a university share-house minus the parties. Free shuttles to/from the bus stop; self-contained flats also available.

Hotel on Devonport
HOTEL $$$

(☎07-578 2668; www.hotelondevonport.net.nz; 72 Devonport Rd; d/ste $165/195; @) City-centre Devonport is top of the town, with bay-view rooms, noise-reducing glass, slick interiors and sassy staff, all of which appeal to business travellers and upmarket weekenders. No in-room wi-fi is a surprising downer.

City Suites
HOTEL $$

(☎07-577 1480, 0800 4787 474; www.puriri.co.nz; 32 Cameron Rd; ste $130-225; @🛜🏊) A 2011 refurb of this hotel has sent the mood upmarket, the large rooms (all with either terrace or balcony) taking on a decidedly regal feel, with Louis XIV bedspreads, king-sized beds and full kitchens. A swimming pool and secure parking complete the list of essentials for wandering business bods.

Sebel Trinity Wharf Tauranga
HOTEL $$$

(☎0800 937 373, 07-577 8700; www.mirvachotels. com; 51 Dive Cres; d from $180; @🛜🏊) This blocky high-rise near the harbour bridge has a slick, contemporary lobby – all retro white vinyl and trendy plush greys – leading to the upmarket in-house restaurant **Halo** (mains lunch $14 to $32, dinner $30 to $39). Rooms are supersized and luxurious in tones au naturel. Amenities include an underutilised gym, an infinity-edge swimming pool and a baby grand piano in the lobby. Very flashy.

Tauranga Tourist Park
HOLIDAY PARK $

(☎07-578 3323; www.taurangatouristpark.co.nz; 9 Mayfair St; sites/cabins from $20/50; @🛜) On the harbour's edge, this is a good option for tenters and campervans with decent grassed sites and a new TV lounge. The layout feels a bit tight (don't expect rolling acres), but it's well maintained, clean and tidy.

🍴 Eating

Devonport Rd is the place to grab lunch, but places on the Strand excel at dinner with drinks to follow. Tauranga's pubs also do solid meals.

Grindz Café
CAFE $

(☎07-579 0017; grindzcafe@xtra.co.nz; 50 First Ave; meals $5-15; ⏰7am-4pm Mon-Fri, 8am-3pm Sat & Sun; 🛜🚲) The undisputed highlight of wide-open First Ave is Grindz, a hip cafe with scattered footpath tables. Inside it's a roomy, split-level affair, with funky wallpaper, antiques and retro relics. Bagels, veggie stacks, muffins, cakes and salads are the order of the day, plus creative coffee (try 'The Trough' if you're sleepy: a four-shot soup bowl of caffeine heaven). Free wi-fi too.

Naked Grape
MODERN NZ, WINE BAR $$

(☎07-579 5555; www.nakedgrape.co.nz; 97 The Strand; breakfast & lunch $9-19, dinner mains $21-32; ⏰breakfast & lunch daily, dinner Mon-Sat) With cheery staff, wine-coloured rugs and lilting jazz, this hip Strand wine bar draws the daytime crowds with pastas, pizzas, salads, good coffee and beaut breakfasts. At night it's moodier, with mains like spice-rubbed salmon with citrus salsa and eggplant parmesan with toasted pine nuts.

Mediterraneo Café
CAFE, MEDITERRANEAN $$

(The Med; ☎07-577 0487; www.mediterraneocafe. co.nz; 62 Devonport Rd; mains $12-19; ⏰7am-4pm Mon-Fri, 7.30am-4pm Sat, 8am-4pm Sun; 🚲) A hot spot reeling with regulars enjoying terrific coffee and scrumptious all-day breakfasts. Order from the blackboard or from the cabinet that is crammed with sandwiches, salads, flans and cakes. Lunchtime crowds can be frantic (but the chicken salad is worth it). Plenty of gluten-free and vegetarian options.

Zeytin on the Strand   TURKISH $$
(07-579 0099; 83 The Strand; mains $16-29; ⊙lunch & dinner Tue-Sun) Ask the locals to name their favourite restaurant, and odds-on they'll name Zeytin – a Turkish delight indeed. Real food, real cheap, with something for everyone along the lines of kebabs, delicious homemade breads, dips and healthy salads, wood-fired pizza and a few exotic surprises.

Fresh Fish Market   FISH & CHIPS $
(07-578 1789; 1 Dive Cres; meals from $5; ⊙lunch & dinner) A local legend serving up fresh fish and chips, with hexagonal outdoor tables right on the water's edge and plenty of seagulls to keep you company.

Collar & Thai   THAI $$
(07-577 6655; www.collarandthai.co.nz; Goddards Centre, 21 Devonport Rd; mains lunch $15-17, dinner $21-31; ⊙lunch Mon-Sat, dinner daily) No tie required at this upstairs eatery that artfully elaborates on Thai standards and uses plenty of fresh seafood. Perfect for a pre-movie meal (the Rialto Cinemas are right next door). Good-value lunch specials, too.

Cafe Bravo   CAFE, MEDITERRANEAN $$
(07-578 4700; www.cafebravo.co.nz; Red Sq; mains $22-32; ⊙breakfast & lunch daily, dinner Tue-Sat; 🖉) Set back from the Strand fray, this refined restaurant-bar is a quiet spot for breakfast or a substantial lunch (try the cider-braised pork belly), or lighter stuff like sandwiches, salads, wood-fired pizzas and freshly squeezed juices. There's outside seating on the pedestrianised street, and a couple of good vegetarian options.

Shima   JAPANESE $$
(07-571 1382; 15 Wharf St; mains $12-30; ⊙lunch & dinner Mon-Sat) Shima is a simple, unpretentious sushi and sashimi bar, hung with Japanese fans, umbrellas and lanterns. Bento boxes and set-price menus are great bang for your buck.

Somerset Cottage   MODERN NZ $$$
(07-576 6889; www.somersetcottage.co.nz; 30 Bethlehem Rd; mains $38-40; ⊙lunch Wed-Fri, dinner Tue-Sun) The most awarded restaurant in the bay, Somerset Cottage is a simple-but-elegant venue for that special treat. The food is highly seasonal, made from the best NZ ingredients, impressively executed without being too fussy. Standout dishes include blue cheese soufflé, duck with coconut kumara and the famous liquorice ice cream.

City Markets   MARKET
(cnr Willow & Hamilton Sts; ⊙9am-5pm Mon-Fri, to noon Sat) Self caterers should swing by the fruit-and-veg City Markets, in a warehouse a block back from the Srand. Freshly baked bread, too.

Pak 'n Save   SUPERMARKET
(www.paknsave.co.nz; 476 Cameron Rd; ⊙8am-10pm) This place is a short drive south of central Tauranga.

🍷 Drinking

De Bier Haus   BAR
(www.debierhaus.com; 109 The Strand) With a pavement packed with happy punters, this hot *haus* features Belgian beers, big-screen TVs and manly hunting-lodge interiors with an antler or two in the midst. Kitchen-work is swift and savvy, turning out cajun chicken sandwiches, roast-duck spring rolls and seafood chowder (mains $15 to $36).

Crown & Badger   PUB
(www.crownandbadger.co.nz; cnr The Strand & Wharf St) A particularly convincing black-painted Brit boozer that does pukka pints of Tennent's and Guinness, and food along the lines of bangers and mash and BLTs (mains $15 to $23). Things get happening at the weekends with live bands.

CornerStone   PUB
(www.cornerstonepub.net.nz; 55 The Strand) This cheerful watering hole features on-the-ball staff and a mature crowd (let's say over-25s... folks who wouldn't mind Gordon Lightfoot on the sound system). A no-surprises menu offers whopping meals (mains $15 to $31), while sports fans can watch the game on the big TV and groovers can swing a hip (live music Thursday to Sunday).

☆ Entertainment

Rialto Cinemas   CINEMA
(www.rialtotauranga.co.nz; Goddards Centre, 21 Devonport Rd) Home to the Tauranga Film Society, the Rialto is the best spot in town to

catch a flick: classic, offbeat, art-house and international. And you can sip a coffee or a glass of wine in the darkness.

Buddha Lounge CLUB, COCKTAIL BAR
(www.thebuddhalounge.co.nz; 61b The Strand; ☺Thu-Sat) Up a staircase beyond a big set of varnished plywood doors (and some heavy-duty bouncers), this clubby cocktail lounge hosts local and visiting DJs. There's a beaut outdoor terrace up above the street. Don't dress down.

Bay City Cinemas CINEMA
(www.baycitycinemas.co.nz; 45 Elizabeth St) A mainstream Megaplex a few blocks back from the action.

ⓘ Information

Paper Plus (17 Grey St; ☺8.30am-5.30pm Mon-Fri, 9am-4pm Sat, 10am-3pm Sun) The local NZ Post branch.

Tauranga Hospital (☏07-579 8000; www. bopdhb.govt.nz; 375 Cameron Rd; ☺24hr) A couple of kilometres south of town.

Tauranga i-SITE (☏07-578 8103; www.bay ofplentynz.com; 95 Willow St; ☺8.30am-5.30pm Mon-Fri, 9am-5pm Sat & Sun, reduced winter hours; ☏) Local tourist information, bookings, InterCity bus tickets and DOC maps.

ⓘ Getting There & Away

Air
Air New Zealand (☏07-577 7300; www. airnewzealand.co.nz; cnr Devonport Rd & Elizabeth St; ☺9am-5pm Mon-Fri) Has daily direct flights to Auckland, Wellington and Christchurch, with connections to other centres.

Bus
Twin City Express (☏0800 422 928; www. baybus.co.nz) buses run twice daily Monday to Friday between Tauranga/Mt Maunganui and Rotorua via Te Puke ($11.60, 1½ hours).

InterCity (www.intercity.co.nz) tickets and timetables are available at the i-SITE. Destinations including the following:

DESTINATION	PRICE	DURATION	FREQUENCY
Auckland	$46	4hr	7 daily
Hamilton	$33	2hr	2 daily
Rotorua	$30	1½hr	2 daily
Taupo	$50	3hr	3 daily
Wellington	$59	9hr	4 daily

Naked Bus (www.nakedbus.com) offers substantial fare savings when you book in advance. Destinations include the following:

DESTINATION	PRICE	DURATION	FREQUENCY
Auckland	$15	4¼hr	3 daily
Hamilton	$20	2hr	3 daily
Napier	$50	4½hr	2 daily
Rotorua	$9	1½hr	3-5 daily
Taupo	$25	2½hr	2 daily
Wellington	$27	9hr	1 daily
Whakatane	$19	6¼hr	1 daily

SHUTTLE BUS

White Island Shuttle (☏07-308 9588, 0800 733 529; www.whiteisland.co.nz; shuttle-only one way/return $35/60), run by White Island Tours in Whakatane, runs return shuttles to Whakatane from Tauranga. It's ostensibly for tour customers, but you can use the service without taking the tour.

A couple of companies can pick you up at Auckland or Rotorua airports and bus you to Tauranga (though you'll pay upwards of $100 for the privilege):

Luxury Airport Shuttles (☏07-547 4444, 0800 454 678; www.luxuryairportshuttles.co.nz)

Apollo Connect Shuttles (☏07-218 0791; www.taurangashuttles.co.nz)

Car
If you're heading to Hamilton on route K, don't forget the toll road costs $1.

ⓘ Getting Around

Bicycle
Cycle Tauranga (☏07-571 1435, 0800 253 525; www.cycletauranga.co.nz; 50 Wharf St; per half-/full-day $29/49) Cycle Tauranga, at Harbour City Motor Inn, has road-trail hybrid bikes for hire, including helmets, locks, saddle bags and maps. Tours also available.

Bus
Tauranga's bright yellow **Bay Hopper** (☏0800 422 928; www.baybus.co.nz) buses run to most locations around the area, including Mt Maunganui ($2.60, 15 minutes) and Papamoa ($3.20, 30 minutes). There's a central stop on Wharf St; timetables available from the i-SITE.

Car
Numerous car-rental agencies have offices in Tauranga, including **Rent-a-Dent** (☏07-578 1772, 0800 736 823; www.rentadent.co.nz; 19 Fifteenth Ave).

Taxi

A taxi from the centre of Tauranga to the airport costs around $20.

Citicabs (☑07-577 0999)

Tauranga Mount Taxis (☑07-578 6086; www.taurangataxis.co.nz)

Mt Maunganui

POP 18,600

Named after the hulking 232m hill that punctuates the sandy peninsula occupied by the township, up-tempo Mt Maunganui is often just called 'the Mount', or Mauao, which translates as 'caught by the light of day'. It's considered part of greater Tauranga, but really it's an enclave unto itself, with great cafes and restaurants, hip bars and fab beaches. Sun-seekers flock to the Mount in summer, supplied by an increasing number of 10-storey apartment towers studding the spit. Online, see www.mountmaunganui.org.nz for information.

👁 Sights & Activities

The Mount lays claim to being NZ's premier surfing city (they teach surfing at high school!). You can carve up the waves at **Mount Beach**, which has lovely beach breaks and a 100m artificial surf reef not far offshore. Learn-to-surf operators include the following:

Hibiscus (☑07-575 3792, 027 279 9687; www.surfschool.co.nz; 2hr/2-day lesson $80/150)

Discovery Surf School (☑027 632 7873; www.discoverysurf.co.nz; lessons 1hr $60, 2hr group/private $90/150)

Mount Surf Shop (☑07-575 9133; www.mountsurfshop.co.nz; 96 Maunganui Rd; rental per day wetsuit/bodyboard/surfboard $15/20/30, 2hr lesson $80)

East Coast Paddler (☑07-574 2674, 021 0230 0746; www.eastcoastpaddler.co.nz; lessons 1hr group/private $50/75)

TOP
CHOICE **Mauao**   MOUNTAIN, LOOKOUT

Mauao (Mt Maunganui) itself can be explored via walking trails, winding around it and leading up to the summit. The summit walk takes about 40 minutes and gets steep near the top. You can also climb around the rocks on Moturiki Island, which adjoins the peninsula. The island and the base of Mauao also make up the Mauao base track (3½km, 45 minutes), wandering through magical groves of pohutukawa trees that bloom between November and January. Pick up a map at the i-SITE.

THE WRECK OF THE RENA

On 5 October 2011, the 47,000 tonne cargo ship MV *Rena*, loaded with 1368 containers and 1900 tonnes of fuel oil, ran aground on Astrolabe Reef 22km off the coast of Mt Maunganui. The ship had been attempting to enter Tauranga Harbour, NZ's busiest port, but inexplicably hit one of the most consistently charted obstacles in the way. Pitched acutely on the reef with a rupturing hull, the *Rena* started spilling oil into the sea and shedding containers from its deck. Over subsequent days, disbelieving locals watched as oil slicks, containers and dead fish and seabirds washed up on their glorious beaches.

The blame game began: the captain? The owners? The company that chartered the vessel? Thousands of volunteers pitched in to help with the clean-up as bad weather delayed attempts to pump oil from the vessel and remove the containers still on deck. Salvors eventually managed to remove most of the oil, but on 8 January 2012 the *Rena* finally broke in two, spilling remnant oil and dozens more containers into the sea.

By 10 January, the stern section was almost completely submerged. With the initial focus on preventing an oil spill, the elephant in the corner of the room – the *Rena* herself – seemed a problem too large. With refloating the ship no longer an option, will the bow section of the boat be dragged off the rocks and scuttled, and the stern section sunk in entirety? A future dive site for the Bay of Plenty? Whatever happens, the grounding has been an environmental and economic disaster, with beaches soiled, fisheries ravaged and countless local businesses suffering. Time will tell how far reparations – both environmental and fiscal – will go towards improving the situation.

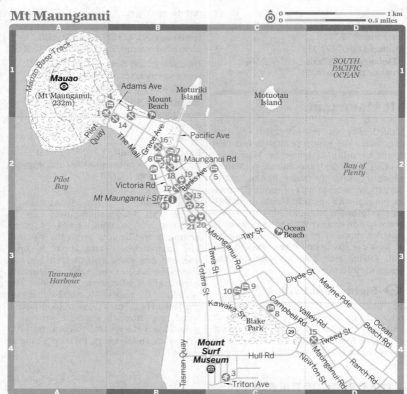

FREE Mount Surf Museum   MUSEUM
(www.mountsurfshop.co.nz; 139 Totara St; ⊙9am-
5pm Mon-Sat, 9.30am-5pm Sun) To learn about
surfing in the area (and beyond) visit the
amazing Mount Surf Museum, inside the
Totara St branch of the Mount Surf Shop.

Mount Maunganui Hot
Saltwater Pools   SWIMMING
(www.tcal.co.nz; 9 Adams Ave; adult/child/family
$11/8/30; ⊙6am-10pm Mon-Sat, 8am-10pm Sun)
If you've worked up a sweat walking up and
down Mauao, take a long relaxing soak at
these hotwater pools at the foot of the hill.

Canoe & Kayak   KAYAKING
(☎07-574 7415; www.canoeandkayak.co.nz; tours
adult/child from $89/69) Canoe & Kayak run
2½-hour kayaking trips around Mauao
checking out seals, rock formations and
hearing local legends, plus 1½-hour nocturnal glowworm paddles in nearby McLarens
Falls Park.

Rock House   ROCK CLIMBING
(www.therockhouse.co.nz; 9 Triton Ave; adult/child
$16.50/12.50, gear hire extra; ⊙noon-9pm Tue-Fri,
10am-6pm Sat & Sun) Try rock climbing at the
Rock House, a huge blue steel shed with
huge blue climbing walls inside it.

Baywave   SWIMMING
(☎07-575 0276; www.tcal.co.nz; cnr Girven &
Gloucester Rds; adult/child $7.50/5, hydroslide
$4.50; ⊙6am-9pm Mon-Fri, 7am-7pm Sat & Sun)
Don't like salt in your hair? For traditional
swimming-pool action plus NZ's biggest
wave pool, a hydroslide and aqua aerobics,
visit Baywave.

🛏 Sleeping

Seagulls Guesthouse B&B   B&B, HOSTEL $
(☎07-574 2099; www.seagullsguesthouse.co.nz; 12
Hinau St; dm/s/d/f from $30/60/70/100; @🖲)
Can't face another crowded, alcohol-soaked
hostel? On a quiet street not far from town,

Mt Maunganui

Seagulls is a gem: an immaculate, upmarket backpackers where the emphasis is on peaceful enjoyment of one's surrounds rather than wallowing in the excesses of youth (...not that there's anything wrong with that). The best rooms have bathrooms and TVs. Breakfast costs $8; bike hire is $25.

**Pacific Coast Lodge
& Backpackers**   HOSTEL $
(☎07-574 9601, 0800 666 622; www.pacificcoast lodge.co.nz; 432 Maunganui Rd; dm/d from $26/72; @☞) Not far from the action, this efficiently run, clean hostel is sociable but not party-focused, with drinkers gently encouraged to migrate into town after 10pm. Purpose-built bunkrooms are roomy and adorned with jungle murals.

Beachside Holiday Park   HOLIDAY PARK $
(☎07-575 4471; www.mountbeachside.co.nz; 1 Adams Ave; sites from $35, on-site vans $60-80, cabins $80-130; ☞) With three different camping areas nooked into the foot of Mt Maunganui itself, this community-run park has spectacular camping with all the requisite facilities, plus it's handy to the Mount Maunganui Hot Saltwater Pools (who offer a discount for campers) and a strip of good eateries.

Mission Belle Motel   MOTEL $$
(☎07-575 2578, 0800 202 434; www.missionbelle motel.co.nz; cnr Victoria Rd & Pacific Ave; d/f from $125/185; ☞) With a distinctly Tex-Mex exterior (like something out of an old Clint Eastwood movie), this family-run motel goes all modern inside, with especially good two-storey family rooms with large bathtubs, plus sheltered barbecue and courtyard areas.

Westhaven Motel   MOTEL $$
(☎07-575 4753; www.westhavenmotel.co.nz; 27a The Mall; units $100-250; ☞) The 1970s architecture here is soooo *Brady Bunch,* with wooden shelving between kitchen and lounge, and funky mirrors to retune your afro. Full kitchens are perfect for self-caterers, plus there are new TVs and DVDs, and free fishing rods and kayaks. The cheapest motel in miles.

Mount Backpackers   HOSTEL $
(☎07-575 0860; www.mountbackpackers.co.nz; 87 Maunganui Rd; dm/tw/tr from $28/72/84; @☞) A tight but tidy hostel, bolstered by location – close to the beach and a mere stagger from the Mount's best restaurants and bars – plus extras like a travel desk, cheap weekly rates and deals on activities including surf lessons.

Belle Mer   HOTEL, APARTMENTS $$$
(☎0800 100 235, 07-575 0011; www.bellemer.co.nz; 53 Marine Pde; apt $190-450; ☞▣) A classy beachside complex of one-, two- and three-bedroom apartments, some with sea-view balconies and others opening onto private courtyards (though you'll more likely head for the resort-style pool terrace). Rooms are tastefully decorated in warm tones with soft edges, and have everything you need for

longer stays, with proper working kitchens and laundries.

Cosy Corner Holiday Park HOLIDAY PARK $
(☑0800 684 654, 07-575 5899; www.cosycorner. co.nz; 40 Ocean Beach Rd; sites from $40, cabins & flats $70-120; @🛜🛏) This spartan camping ground has a sociable feel, with barbecues, trampolines and a games room. And it's possibly the only accommodation in NZ where prices have actually come down since the last edition of this book. Handy for the beach, too.

Mount Maunganui B&B B&B $$
(☑07-575 4013; www.mountbednbreakfast.co.nz; 463 Maunganui Rd; s/d incl cooked breakfast from $65/100; @🛜) This good-value five-room B&B on the main road into town offers a cosy guest lounge, basic shared kitchen, pool table, BBQ and cable TV. The two rooms at the front cop a bit of traffic noise, but the rest are fine. Good for groups.

✘ Eating

TOP CHOICE Slowfish CAFE $
(☑07-574 2949; www.slowfish.co.nz; Shop 5, Twin Towers, Marine Pde; meals $7-20; ⏱6.30am-4.30pm; 🍴) There's no slacking-off in the kitchen of this award-winning, eco-aware cafe, which promotes the art of savouring fine, locally sourced food. It's a hit with the crowds: you'll have to crowbar yourself in the door or pounce on any available alfresco seat, but it's worth it for its free-range eggs and ham, Greek salads and divine counter selection, all made on-site.

Providores Urban Food Store CAFE, DELICATESSEN $
(☑07-572 1300; 19a Pacific Ave; meals $5-18; ⏱7.30am-5pm; 🍴) Surf videos set the mood as your eyes peruse fresh-baked breads, buttery croissants, home-smoked meats and cheeses, organic jams and free-range eggs – perfect ingredients for a bang-up breakfast or a hamper-filling picnic on the beach. Superb.

Mount Bistro MODERN NZ $$$
(☑07-575 3872; www.mountbistro.co.nz; 6 Adams Ave; ⏱dinner Tue-Sun) The buttermilk-coloured Mount Bistro, an unpretentious fine-dining experience at the foot of Mauao, is onto a good thing: quality local meats (fish, lamb, beef, crayfish, chicken, duck) creatively worked into classic dishes (lamb

shanks, seafood chowder) and served with élan. Makes for a classy night out.

Gusto CAFE $$
(☑07-575 5675; 200 Maunganui Rd; breakfast $7-16, lunch $15-17; ⏱7am-3.30pm, from 8am Sat & Sun; 🍴) This friendly spot keeps its menu affordable but interesting, with pancakes, fritters, bagels, omelettes, BLATs and Kiwi standards like lamb and kumara, given a fresh spin. Cool tunes, sassy staff, no weird culinary surprises... As reliable as a cafe can get.

Zeytin at the Mount TURKISH, MEDITERRANEAN $$
(☑07-574 3040; 118 Maunganui Rd; mains $19-21; ⏱lunch & dinner Tue-Sun; 🍴) Sister establishment to Tauranga's Zeytin on the Strand, this version has earned a following for its slow-cooked tagines, spanakopita and moussaka, plus live jazz every second Wednesday. Stripy cushions and Arabic lanterns adorn the cavelike interior. Magic felafels (you can buy the mixture and whip up some more back at the hotel).

Kwang Chow CHINESE $$
(☑07-575 5063; 241 Maunganui Rd; lunch/dinner $13/20; ⏱lunch & dinner Tue-Sun) This all-you-can-eat Chinese place is a local favourite for a bargain bite that maintains tasty flavours rather than resorting to a bland melange. And great puddings. Cavernous interior with floorboards and refreshingly little gold/crimson/mirror festoonery.

New World SUPERMARKET
(www.newworld.co.nz; cnr Tweed St & Maunganui Rd; ⏱7am-9pm) A haven for self-caterers.

🍷 Drinking & Entertainment

TOP CHOICE Major Tom's BAR, LIVE MUSIC
(www.majortomsbar.com; 297 Maunganui Rd; ⏱Tue-Sat) A funky little bar set back from the main drag in what looks like Major Tom's spaceship. Inside it's all kooky antiques, vintage couches, dangling inverted desk lamps and prints of Elvis, the *Mona Lisa* and (of course) David Bowie. Fabulous streetside terrace, cool tunes, free wi-fi and occasional live acts. Everybody sing: 'Planet Earth is blue, and there's nothing I can do...'

Latitude 37 BAR
(www.37.co.nz; 181 Maunganui Rd; 🛜) A slick, up-market bar with stone-faced walls, fold-back windows and flaming torches out the front. A lot of folk come here to eat (lunch $15 to $22, dinner $22 to $34...oh, the pork-belly

sandwich!), but it's also a beaut spot for a cold Heineken after a day in the surf.

Rosie O'Grady's   IRISH PUB

(www.rosiesnz.com; 2 Rata St) Rosie's is usually not too blokey, with NZ boutique beers, jam nights, pool tables, big screens and good-value pub grub (mains $11 to $28). The beer garden has *actual grass* – ideal for a pint or two of the black stuff.

Bay City Cinemas   CINEMA

(www.baycitycinemas.co.nz; 249 Maunganui Rd) Mainstream cinematic offerings, run in parallel with Bay City Cinemas in Tauranga.

ℹ Information

Mt Maunganui i-SITE (☏07-575 5099; www. bayofplentynz.com; Salisbury Ave; ☻9am-5pm) The friendly Mt Maunganui i-SITE can assist with information and bookings (transport, accommodation and activities).

ℹ Getting There & Away

Bus

InterCity (www.intercity.co.nz) and **Naked Bus** (www.nakedbus.com) services visiting Tauranga also stop at Mt Maunganui, with fares similar to those to/from Tauranga (p298). All buses depart from the i-SITE.

Car

Mt Maunganui is across the harbour bridge from Tauranga, or accessible from the south via Te Maunga on SH2. For car hire, try **Rite Price Rentals** (☏0800 250 251; www.ritepricerentals. co.nz; 25 Totara St).

Papamoa

POP 20,100

Papamoa is a burgeoning 'burb next to Mt Maunganui, separated now by just an empty paddock or two, destined for subdivision. With big new houses on pristine streets, parts of Papamoa have the air of a gated community, but the beach beyond the sheltering dunes is awesome – you can't blame folks for moving in.

Back a few kilometres from the beach, **Blo-kart Heaven** (☏07-572 4256; www .blokartheaven.co.nz; 176 Parton Rd; blokarting 30min $30; ☻10am-4.30pm) is the place to attempt land-sailing around a custom-built speedway (blokarts are like seated windsurfers on wheels).

The sprawling **Papamoa Beach Top 10 Holiday Resort** (☏0800 232 243, 07-572 0816; www.papamoabeach.co.nz; 535 Papamoa Beach Rd; sites from $40, villas & units $88-250; @☏) is a spotless, modern park, primed and priced beyond its caravan-park origins, with an array of accommodation including self-contained villas. If you're quiet you'll hear the surf breaking just over the dunes.

With its angular corrugated-iron exterior and tasteful caneware furnishings, **Beach House Motel** (☏0800 429 999, 07-572 1424; www.beachhousemotel.co.nz; 224 Papamoa Beach Rd; d from $120; ☏☒) offers an immaculate, upmarket version of the Kiwi bach holiday, relaxed and close to the beach. There's a pool if the beach is too windy, and orange daisies poking up through rock gardens.

Bluebiyou (☏07-572 2099; www.bluebiyou .co.nz; 559 Papamoa Beach Rd; mains $15-38; ☻breakfast Sat & Sun, lunch & dinner Wed-Sun) is a casual, breezy restaurant riding high on the dunes, serving big brunches and seafood specialities. The orange-scented French toast with maple syprup and bacon is a sure-fire Saturday start-me-up.

Tuhua (Mayor Island)

Commonly known as Mayor Island, this dormant volcano is 35km north of Tauranga. It's a privately owned island noted for its black, glasslike obsidian rock and birdlife, including a clutch of kiwi, introduced to the predator-free isle in 2006. Walking tracks cut through the overgrown crater valley, and the northwest corner is a marine reserve.

You need permission to visit from the island's *kaitiaki* (guardians), via the **Tuhua Trust Board** (☏07-577 0942). There's a $5 landing fee, and visitors must observe strict quarantine regulations. Accommodation is limited to basic camping/cabins ($10/30); bring your own food and water (no fridges). The landing fee is included in accommodation costs. Several boat-charter companies will take you to Tuhua, including Blue Ocean Charters (p294). Contact **DOC** (☏07-578 7677; taurangainfo@doc.govt.nz) in Tauranga for more info.

Matakana Island

About 24km long and forming the seaward side of Tauranga Harbour, Matakana is laced with secluded white-sand surf beaches on its eastern shore (for the experienced only) and enjoys a laid-back island lifestyle. The only way to visit it is on a kayak tour with Adventure Bay of Plenty (p295).

ROTORUA & THE BAY OF PLENTY PAPAMOA

HOT FUZZ: KIWIFRUIT

The humble kiwifruit earns New Zealand more than a billion dollars every year, and with the Bay of Plenty in the thick of the action, it's no wonder the locals are fond of them.

The fruit's origins are in China, where it was called the monkey peach (they were considered ripe when the monkeys munched them). As they migrated to NZ, they were renamed the Chinese gooseberry – they were a lot smaller then, but canny Kiwis engineered them to more generous sizes and began exporting them in the 1950s. The fruit was then sexily rebranded as the Zespri. Today the Zesprians grow two types of kiwifruit: the common fuzzy-covered green fruit, and the gold fruit with its smooth complexion. To learn more about the kiwifruit, visit **Kiwi360** (☑07-573 6340, 0800 549 4360; www.kiwi360. com; 35 Young Rd, off SH2; admission free, tour adult/child $20/6; ☺9am-5pm).

For visitors after a dollar or two, there's always kiwifruit-picking work around the area – most of it during harvest (May and June), and odd jobs at other times. Enquire at Mural Town Backpackers (p305) in Katikati and regional i-SITEs, or check online at www.picknz.co.nz.

Katikati

POP 3580

'Katikat' to the locals, this small town was the only planned Ulster settlement in the world, and celebrates this history with colourful murals adorning the town's buildings. The **Mural Town Information Centre** (☑07-549 1658; www.katikati.co.nz; 36 Main Rd; ☺8am-5pm Mon-Fri, 9am-2pm Sat, 10am-2pm Sun; @) sells a guide to the various murals for $2.50, but you can also take a small-group guided tour (☑07-549 2977; per person $5).

◉ Sights & Activities

Katikati Heritage Museum   MUSEUM
(katikati.heritage.museum@xtra.co.nz; 3 Wharawhara Rd; adult/child $7.50/5; ☺8.30am-4.30pm) This rusty old museum traces local history with an engaging mix of Maori artefacts and Ulster history, some moa bones and reputedly the largest bottle collection in the southern hemisphere.

FREE Haiku Pathway   WALKWAY
(www.katikati.co.nz/kk_text/haiku.html; ☺24hrs) From the information centre you can also explore the Haiku Pathway, rambling along the Uretara River past boulders inscribed with haiku verses.

Katikati Bird Gardens   WILDLIFE RESERVE
(☑07-549 0912; www.birdgardens.co.nz; 263 Walker Rd E; adult/child/family $9/5/24; ☺10am-4.30pm) Located about 7km south of town, the 4-hectare Katikati Bird Gardens is all aflap with native birdlife (ever seen a kawaupaka?). There's a cafe and gallery here

too, plus boutique cottage accommodation (double rooms $160).

Morton Estate   WINERY
(www.mortonestatewines.co.nz; 2389 SH2; ☺9.30am-5pm) The monastic-looking Morton Estate, one of NZ's bigger wineries, is located on SH2, 8km south of Katikati, and open for tastings and stock-ups. Try the smooth-as-cream chardonnay.

🛏 Sleeping

TOP CHOICE Warm Earth Cottage   CABIN, B&B $$$
(☑07-549 0962; www.warmearthcottage.co.nz; 202 Thompsons Track; d $220) Re-ignite your romance or simmer in simple pleasures at this rural idyll, 5km south of town then 2km west of SH2. Two pretty, electricity-less cottages sit by the swimmable Waitekohe River. Fire up the barbecue (generous BBQ packs $85), or melt into a wood-fired outdoor bath. Big DIY breakfasts are included in the price, and there's a lovely new guest lounge/ library.

Panorama Country Lodge   B&B $$$
(☑07-549 1882; www.panoramalodge.co.nz; 901 Katikati North Rd; d from $185; ☞☒) Run by jocular Brits, this neat little B&B is set in diverse orchards 9km north of town, and lives up to its name with sweeping views of the bay. It's a real farm experience, with quail and alpacas wandering around. Plush rooms have extras beyond brass beds and DVDs, including slippers and fresh coffee.

Kaimai View Motel   MOTEL $$
(☑07-549 0398; www.kaimaiview.co.nz; 78 Main Rd; d from $120; ☞☒) Beyond a funky mural on

the streetside wall, this jaunty, mod motel offers neat rooms (all named after NZ native trees) with CD player, kitchenette and, in larger rooms, spa. Breakfast available on request.

Mural Town Backpackers   HOSTEL **$**
(☏07-549 5150, 021 184 1403; 5 Main Rd; dm $25; @) Inside a converted 1935 barbershop, this basic two-storey hostel is *really* casual, and is usually full of backpackers here to work in the local orchards (kiwifruit, citrus, flowers, avocados etc). The owners can help find you farm work and offer good weekly rates.

✖ Eating

Talisman   PUB **$$**
(7 Main Rd; mains $18-36; ☻lunch & dinner) The Talisman is the local boozer, with occasional live music, and the Landing restaurant serving all-day grub including pizza, steak and chips, lamb Wellington, pan-fried salmon and surf 'n' turf.

Katz Pyjamas   CAFE **$**
(cnr SH2 & Beach Rd; meals $5-15; ☻8am-4pm Mon-Fri) Royal blue outside, rude orange inside, this informal main-street cafe serves homemade soups, salads, pies and cakes and a reasonable jolt of java.

Twickenham
Restaurant & Cafe   CAFE, RESTAURANT **$$**
(www.twickenham.co.nz; cnr SH2 & Mulgan St; mains lunch $17-23, dinner $24-30; ☻brunch Tue-Sun, dinner Thu-Sun) In a century-old villa surrounded by manicured gardens, this place is a bit twee but makes amends with admirable Devonshire teas. During the day it's Thai beef salad, omelettes and ploughman's platters; at night it's roast duck, pork fillets and steaks.

Te Puke
POP 7150

Welcome to the 'Kiwifruit Capital of the World', a busy town during the picking season when there's plenty of work around. The **Te Puke visitor information centre** (☏07-573 9172; www.tepuke.co.nz; 130 Jellicoe St; ☻8am-5pm Mon-Fri, 9am-noon Sat) is in the same building as the public library (staff will confirm that 'Puke' rhymes with cookie, not fluke).

For the low-down on all things kiwifruit, swing into Kiwi360 (p304) at the turn-off for Maketu. Sitting among orchards of nashi pears, citrus, avocados and (you guessed it) kiwifruit, this visitor centre peels off a range of attractions, including a 35-minute kiwicart orchard tour, kiwifruit viewing tower and a cafe serving up a variety of kiwifruit delights.

After something sweeter? About 10km south of Te Puke in Paengaroa, **Comvita** (☏07-533 1987, 0800 493 782; www.comvita.com; 23 Wilson Rd S; ☻8.30am-5pm Mon-Fri, 9.30am-4pm Sat & Sun) is home to NZ's most famous honey- and bee-derived health-care products. There's a gallery, shop, cafe and educational talks available. Grab a pot of vitamin E cream with bee pollen and manuka honey on your way out.

Not far from Comvita, **Spring Loaded** (☏07-533 1515, 0800 867 386; www.springloaded adventures.co.nz; 316 SH33; adult/child jetboat $95/45, 4WD $60/35, helicopter 12min $105; ☻8.30am-4.30pm Nov-Apr, 9am-4pm May-Oct) offers various adventures from jetboat rides on a lovely stretch of the Kaituna River and Tauranga Harbour, to 'mud bug' 4WD trips, helicopter flights and rafting and sledging trips. There's a cafe on-site.

Homestays and farmstays dapple the Te Puke area: ask the visitor centre for a list. A cute, private self-contained cottage, **Lazy Daze B&B** (☏07-573 8188; www.lazydaze cottage.co.nz; 144 Boucher Ave; d cottage/house incl breakfast $130/110) sits out the back of Mel and Sharron's property and has a deck overlooking its own garden. Breakfast

---

WORTH A TRIP

PADDLES & PIES: MAKETU

Take SH2 through Te Puke then turn left onto Maketu Rd, and you'll find yourself deposited at this historic seaside town that has seen better days.

Maketu (population 1240) played a significant role in New Zealand's history as the landing site of *Te Arawa* canoe in 1340, commemorated with a somewhat underwhelming 1940 monument on the foreshore. Arguably, though, the town is more famous for **Maketu Pies** (☏07-533 2358; www.maketupies.co.nz; 6 Little Waihi Rd), baked fresh daily here and employing a good proportion of the population. The factory shopfront was being renovated when we visited, but you can buy a pie at the store next door (go for a lamb-and-mint or smoked fish).

provisions are included and there's also a tidy two-bedroom, self-contained house available next door, sleeping six. Call for directions. For fruit-pickers and doyens of dorm-life there's rudimentary hostel accommodation at **Hairy Berry** (☎07-573 8015; www.hairyberrynz.com; 2 No 1 Rd; sites $15, dm/tw/d from $22/56/60), a barn-like affair on the Whakatane side of town with a roomy communal space and small, tidy bedrooms.

Whakatane

POP 18,750

A true pohutukawa paradise, Whakatane (pronounced Fokka-*tar*-nay) sits on a natural harbour at the mouth of the river of the same name. It's the hub of the Rangitaiki agricultural district, but there's much more to Whakatane than farming – blissful beaches, a sunny main-street vibe and volcanic Whakaari (White Island) for starters. And (despite Nelson's protestations) it's officially NZ's sunniest city.

◉ Sights

FREE **Te Manuka Tutahi Marae**   MARAE
(www.mataatua.com; Muriwai Dr) The centrepiece of this brand-new Ngati Awa *marae* isn't new: Mataatua Wharenui (The House That Came Home) is a fantastically carved 1875 meeting house. In 1879 it was dismantled and shipped to Sydney, before spending 71 years in the Otago Museum from 1925. It was returned to the Ngati Awa in 1996. Still a work in progress when we visited, a cultural experience for visitors is planned: until its completion you can enter the *marae* and check out Mataatua Wharenui from the outside (behave respectfully).

Wairere Falls   WATERFALL
(Toroa St) Tumbling down the cliffs behind the town, picture-perfect Te Wairere (Wairere Falls) occupies a deliciously damp nook, and once powered flax and flour mills and supplied Whakatane's drinking water. It's a gorgeous spot, and goes almost completely unheralded: in any other county there'd be a ticket booth, interpretive audiovisual displays and a hotdog van!

FREE **Whakatane**
Museum & Gallery   MUSEUM, GALLERY
(☎07-306 0505; www.whakatanemuseum.org.nz; 51-55 Boon St; ☺10am-4.30pm Mon-Fri, 11am-

3pm Sat & Sun) This impressive regional museum has artfully presented displays on early Maori and European settlerment in the area: *taonga* (treasures) of local Maori trace their lineage back to the *Mataatua* canoe. The art gallery presents a varied program of NZ and international exhibitions. It's rumoured to be relocating: call the number if it's not where it's supposed to be.

Pohaturoa   LANDMARK, MONUMENT
(cnr The Strand & Commerce St) Beside a roundabout on the Strand is Pohaturoa, a large *tapu* (sacred) rock outcrop, where baptism, death, war and *moko* (tattoo) rites were performed. The Treaty of Waitangi was signed here by Ngati Awa chiefs in 1840; there's a monument to the Ngati Awa chief Te Hurinui Apanui here too.

Muriwai's Cave   CAVE
(Muriwai Dr) The partially collapsed Te Ana o Muriwa (Muriwai's Cave) once extended 122m into the hillside and sheltered 60 people, including Muriwai, a famous seer and aunt of Wairaka (p308). Along with Wairere Falls and a rock in the harbour-mouth, the cave was one of three landmarks Toroa was told to look for by his father Irakewa, when he arrived in the *Mataatua waka*.

Te Papaka &
Puketapu   ARCHAEOLOGICAL SITES, LOOKOUTS
On the clifftops behind the town are two ancient Ngati Awa *pa* sites – Te Papaka and Puketapu – both of which offer sensational (and very defendable) outlooks over Whakatane.

Whakatane Observatory   ASTRONOMY
(www.skyofplenty.com; Hurinui Ave; adult/child/family $15/5/35; ☺dusk Tue & Fri) Up on a hilltop behind the town, Whakatane Observatory offers a great chance to star-spot when the sky is clear.

☀ Activities

The i-SITE sells Discover the Walks Around Whakatane ($2), a booklet detailing walks ranging from 30 minutes to half a day. Most walks are part of the Nga Tapuewae o Toi Track (Footsteps of Toi; 13 hours, 18km), large loop which actually comprises three separate walks: the Kohi Point Walkway, the walk along Ohope Beach up into Ohope Reserve at the base of Ohope Hill, and the walk back down into Whakatane through Mokoroa Reserve.

Whakatane

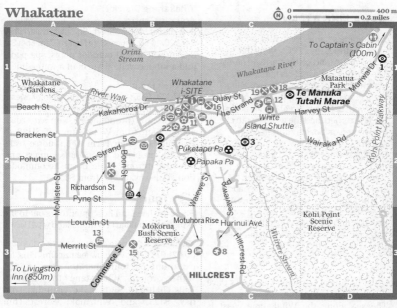

ROTORUA & THE BAY OF PLENTY WHAKATANE

Whakatane

The Kohi Point Walkway is highly recommended: a bushy four-hour, 5.5km track with panoramic clifftop views and a genuine 'gasp' moment when you set eyes on Otarawairere Bay. A short detour rewards you with amazing views from Toi's Pa (Kapua te rangi), reputedly the oldest's pa site in NZ. You can also get to Toi's Pa by a party unsealed access road off the Whakatane–Ohope road. From Ohope, you can catch the bus back to Whakatane if there aren't any more kilometres left in your legs.

A flatter option is the River Walk (two to three hours), following the Whakatane River

WAKA LIKE A MAN

Whakatane's name originated some eight centuries ago, 200 years after the original Maori settlers arrived here. The warrior Toroa and his family sailed into the estuary in a huge ocean-going *waka* (canoe), the *Mataatua*. As the men went ashore to greet local leaders, the tide turned, and the *waka* – with all the women on board – drifted out to sea. Toroa's daughter, Wairaka, cried out *'E! Kia whakatane au i ahau!'* (Let me act as a man!) and, breaking the traditional *tapu* (taboo) on women steering a *waka*, she took up the paddle and brought the boat safely ashore. A whimsical **statue of Wairaka** stands proudly atop a rock in Whakatane's harbour in commemoration of her brave deed.

past the Botanical Gardens, Muruwai's Cave and on to Wairaka's statue.

The sea along the Whakatane coast is alive with marine mammals including dolphins (25,000 of them!), fur seals, orca, pilot and minke whales; plus birdlife including gannets and little blue penguins. The area is also renowned for diving and big-game fishing.

See also Dive White Island (p311).

Dolphin & Whale Nature Rush
ECOTOUR, WILDLIFE TOUR

(☑07-308 9588, 0800 733 529; www.dolphin andwhale.co.nz; 15 The Strand; trips adult/child $80/50; ⏱10am daily Jan-Mar) Run by White Island Tours, Dolphin & Whale Nature Rush offers a two-hour trip out to Motuhora (Whale Island), with plenty of critter-spotting in the sea and sky.

Diveworks Dolphin & Seal Encounters
DIVING, WILDLIFE TOUR

(☑07-308 2001, 0800 354 7737; www.whaleisland tours.com; 96 The Strand; dolphin & seal swimming adult/child $160/130, diving incl gear from $215) This dive/ecotour company runs dolphin- and seal-swimming trips from Whakatane (cheaper if you're just watching from the boat), plus dive trips to Motuhora (Whale Island) and Whakaari (White Island). Fishing tours and dive lessons also available (two Whale Island dives with instructor and gear $475).

Whakatane District Aquatic Centre
SWIMMING

(www.tlc.net.nz; 28 Short St; adult/child/family $4/2.20/10.50; ⏱6am-8pm Mon-Fri, 7am-6pm Sat & Sun) Indoor and outdoor pools, spa pools and a tubular yellow worm of a waterslide.

Tui Glen Farm
HORSE RIDING

(☑07-323 6457; www.tuiglenfarm.com; Kawerau Loop Rd; rides adult/child from $40/30) Close to Kawerau (pronounced 'Kuh-*way*-roo'), about 35km from Whakatane off SH30 to Rotorua, Tui Glen Farm offers horse treks through bush and farm for beginners and the adventurous. Basic dorm accommodation, is also available (from $35).

☞ Tours

There are boat and helicopter tours out to the explosive Whakaari (White Island) (p311).

Kiwi Feet Adventures
TRAMPING, OUTDOORS

(☑021 077 7789; www.kiwifeetnz.com) This local tramping tour operator runs guided walks around Whakatane to Tarawera Falls (half-day, $60), Lake Okataina (full day, $125) and Whirinaki Forest (full day, $150). All tours include lunch. Horse riding, kayaking and fishing options also available.

🛏 Sleeping

Captain's Cabin
APARTMENT $$

(☑07-308 5719; www.captainscabin.co.nz; 23 Muriwai Dr; r $125) In a serene part of town with sparkling harbour views, this homely self-contained unit is the perfect spot if you're hanging round for a few days (rates drop for stays of two nights or more). A cosy living area cleverly combines bedroom, lounge, kitchen and dining, with a second smaller room and bijou bathroom – all sweetly decorated along nautical lines. Sleeps three (extra person $25).

Whakatane Hotel
HOTEL $

(☑07-307 1670; www.whakatanehotel.co.nz; 79 The Strand; dm/s $25/40, d with/without bathroom from $75/50; 🛜) This lovely old art deco classic has 27 basic (but very decent) rooms upstairs in two wings. Clean shared bathrooms, high ceilings, communal kitchen… Great value for money. Some rooms do cop a bit of noise from the pub downstairs, but the owners try to shuffle people around to dodge the din.

White Island Rendezvous HOTEL, B&B $$
(☑07-308 9588, 0800 242 299; www.whiteisland.
co.nz; The Strand; d from $140, apt $260, B&B $190;
☎) An immaculate 26-room complex run by
the on-the-ball White Island Tour people.
Lots of balcony and deck space for inhaling
the sea air, while interiors are decked out
with timber floors for a nautical vibe. Deluxe
rooms come with spas; disabled-access facil-
ities available. The B&B next door includes
cooked breakfast.

Windsor Backpackers HOSTEL $
(☑07-308 8040; www.windsorlodge-backpackers.
co.nz; 10 Merritt St; dm/s/d from $25/48/66; @☎)
Whakatane's best backpackers occupies a
converted funeral parlour, so expect a rest-
ful sleep. Excellent rooms range from serv-
iceable dorms to a couple of motel-standard
doubles out the front. The communal kitch-
en, lounge and barbecue courtyard are spa-
cious and tidy.

Tuscany Villas MOTEL $$
(☑07-308 2244, 0800 801 040; www.tuscanyvillas.
co.nz; 57 The Strand; d $155-200; @☎) This mod
motel may be a long way from Florence, but
still offers a few rays of Italian sunshine with
interesting architecture, wrap-around balconies and floral plantings wherever there's
room. Rooms are luxurious and comfy, with
super-king beds and spa pools.

Motuhora Rise B&B B&B $$$
(☑07-307 0224; www.motuhorarise.com; 2 Mo-
tuhora Rise; s/d incl breakfast $205/220; @☎) At
the top of the town in both senses (the drive-
way is steep!), this jaunty hilltop spot feels
vaguely Rocky Mountains, and affords a dis-
tant glimpse of Motuhora (Whale Island).
You can expect a gourmet cheeseboard on
arrival, along with other extras such as a
DVD home-theatre suite, outdoor spa-pool
deck, and fishing rods and golf clubs. Kid-
free zone.

Livingston Inn MOTEL $$
(☑07-308 6400, 0800 770 777; www.livingston.
co.nz; 42 Landing Rd; d/f $130/220; ☎) This
spotless, ranch-style motel is the pick of the
half-dozen dotted along the Landing, with
spacious, well-kept units and comfy beds.
Large spas in executive suites are a great
fringe benefit.

Awakeri Hot Springs HOLIDAY PARK $
(☑07-304 9117; www.awakerisprings.co.nz; SH30;
sites $32, d cabins/flats/units $70/85/95) Sixteen
kilometres from Whakatane on the road to

Rotorua (SH30) you'll come to the immaculate Awakeri Hot Springs, an old-fashioned
holiday park complete with (as the name
suggests) hot springs (adult/child $6/4),
picnic areas and a bed for every budget.

🍴 Eating

Wally's on the Wharf FISH & CHIPS $
(☑07-307 1100; www.whakatane.info; The Wharf,
The Strand; meals $6-19; ☺11am-7pm) Wally
knows a thing or two about fish and chips:
hoki, snapper, flounder, john dory and
tarakihi – done in the deep fry, on the grill
or in a burger. Whitebait fritters in season,
and chips that score well on the crispom-
eter. The reconstituted squid rings are a tad
disappointing (but the seagulls don't seem
to mind).

Cafe Coco CAFE $
(☑07-308 8337; 10 Richardson St; mains $5-17;
☺7.30am-6.30pm, to 4.30pm winter) Just 10
months old when we visited, Coco is a hip,
L-shaped corner spot serving bright, fresh
cafe fare: bagels, paninis, corn fritters, juices,
French toast, cakes, organic fair-trade coffee, eggs any-which-way...and the 'Crepe of
the Week'. Very kid-friendly, too.

Wharf Shed INTERNATIONAL $$
(☑07-308 5698, 0800 863 463; www.wharfshed.
com; The Wharf, The Strand; mains $18-32; ☺lunch
& dinner) An award winner for beef and lamb
but famous for fish (this is Whakatane, after
all), which includes locally bagged crayfish,
corpulent mussels and fresh Pacific oysters.
Right on the waterside with alfresco dining
on balmy evenings.

Roquette MODERN NZ, MEDITERRANEAN $$$
(☑07-307 0722; www.roquette-restaurant.co.nz; 23
Quay St; mains $20-35; ☺10am-late Mon-Sat) A
modern waterside restaurant on the ground
floor of one of the town's big new apartment
building, sunny Roquette serves up refreshing Mediterranean-influenced fare with lots
of summery salads, risotto and fish dishes.
Laid-back tunes, lots of glass and mosaics,
good coffee and sexy staff to boot. Try the
haloumi salad nicoise.

The Bean CAFE $
(☑07-307 0494; www.thebeancafe.co.nz; 72 The
Strand; snacks $5-12; ☺8am-4pm Mon-Sat , 9am-
3pm Sun) The loungiest spot in town to get
good coffee (roasted on the premises). Pull
up a chair, and get yourself going with a
quick fix and a freshly baked biscuit, roll or

bagel. Local art on the walls; retro furniture on the floor.

Countdown
SUPERMARKET

(www.countdown.co.nz; 105 Commerce St; ⊙7am-10pm) Stock up on supplies.

🍷 Drinking & Entertainment

Craic
IRISH PUB

(www.whakatanehotel.co.nz; Whakatane Hotel, 79 The Strand) The Craic is a busy locals' boozer of the Irish ilk, good for a pint or two, or a mug of hot chocolate if you're feeling sub-par. Fantastic streetside terrace for sunny afternoons, and solid pub-grub (mains $13 to $22).

Office
BAR

(82 The Strand) The upmarket Office does what it does well: beer, big meals with chips and salad all over (mains $17 to $27), and live bands and/or DJs on Friday and Saturday nights.

Boiler Room
CLUB, LIVE MUSIC

(www.whakatanehotel.co.nz; Whakatane Hotel, 79 The Strand) Next door to the Craic at the Whakatane Hotel, the Boiler Room is a cavernous, hedonistic space dotted with pool tables. In fact, it's Whakatane's only club. DJs and live bands engage your ears for Friday and Saturday nights respectively.

Cinema 5
CINEMA

(www.cinema5.co.nz; 101 The Strand) Right in the middle of the Strand, Cinema 5 screens new-release movies. Cheap tickets before 4.30pm.

ℹ Information

Post office (4 Commerce St) Also has foreign exchange.

Whakatane Hospital (☎07-306 0999; www.bopdhb.govt.nz; cnr Stewart & Garaway Sts; ⊙24hr) For emergency medical treatment.

Whakatane i-SITE (☎07-306 2030, 0800 924 528; www.whakatane.com; cnr Quay St & Kakahoroa Dr; ⊙8am-5pm Mon-Fri, 10am-4pm Sat & Sun; @🛜) Free internet access (including 24-hour wi-fi on the terrace outside the building), tour bookings, accommodation and general enquiries for DOC.

ℹ Getting There & Around

Air

Air New Zealand (☎07-308 8397, 0800 737 000; www.airnewzealand.com) has daily flights linking Whakatane to Auckland, with connections to other centres.

Bus

InterCity (www.intercity.co.nz) buses stop outside the i-SITE and connect Whakatane with Rotorua ($34, 1½ hours, one daily), Tauranga ($27, three hours, one daily; via Rotorua) and Gisborne ($45, three hours, one daily; via Opotiki), with onward connections.

Naked Bus (www.nakedbus.com) services run to the following destinations. Book in advance for big savings.

DESTINATION	PRICE	DURATION	FREQUENCY
Auckland	$33	5½hr	1 daily
Gisborne	$20	3¼hr	1 daily
Hamilton	$20	1½hr	1 daily
Rotorua	$15	1½hr	1 daily
Tauranga	$18	5½hr	1 daily
Wellington	$70	10½hr	1 daily

Local **Bay Hopper and Beach Runner** (☎0800 422 928; www.baybus.co.nz) buses run to Ohope ($2.60, 45 minutes, seven daily), Opotiki ($8, 1¼ hour, two daily Monday and Wednesday) and Tauranga ($12.60, five hours, one daily Monday to Saturday).

SHUTTLE BUS

White Island Shuttle (☎0800 733 529; www.whiteisland.co.nz) runs Rotorua–Whakatane and Tauranga–Whakatane return shuttles that can be used by nontour travellers (adult/child return $60/35 from either town).

GKM Shuttles (☎0800 007 005, 07-308 9906; www.whakatane.info) to/from the airport cost $20 per adult for the first adult, with discounted prices per additional passenger.

Taxi
Dial a Cab (☎07-308 0222, 0800 342 522)

Whakaari (White Island)

NZ's most active volcano (it last erupted in 2000) lies 49km off the Whakatane coast. The small island was originally formed by three separate volcanic cones of different ages. The two oldest have been eroded, while the younger cone has risen up between them. Mt Gisborne is the highest point on the island at 321m. Geologically, Whakaari is related to Motuhora (Whale Island) and Putauaki (Mt Edgecumbe), as all lie along Taupo Volcanic Zone.

The island is dramatic, with hot water hissing and steaming from vents over most of the crater floor. Temperatures of 600°C to 800°C have been recorded.

MOTUHORA (WHALE ISLAND)

Nine kilometres off Whakatane is Motuhora (Whale Island) – so-called because of its leviathan shape. This island is yet another volcano along the Taupo Volcanic Zone but is much less active, although there are hot springs along its shore. The summit is 353m high and the island has several historic sites, including an ancient *pa* (fortified village) site, a quarry and a camp.

Whale Island was originally home to a Maori settlement. In 1829, Maori massacred sailors from the trading vessel *Haweis* while it was anchored at Sulphur Bay. In 1867 the island passed into European ownership and remains privately owned, although since 1965 it has been a Department of Conservation–protected wildlife refuge for seabirds and shorebirds.

The island's protected status means landing is restricted, with tours running only from January to March. Operators include Dolphin & Whale Nature Rush (p308), Diveworks Dolphin & Seal Encounters (p308) and KG Kayaks (p311).

The island is privately owned so you can only visit it with a licensed tour operator. Fixed-wing air operators run flyover tours only, while boat and helicopter tours will usually include a walking tour around the island including a visit to the ruins of the sulphur-mining factory – an interesting story in itself.

Numerous helicopter and fixed-wing operators run trips out of Rotorua and Tauranga; there are also a number of local operators.

Tours

White Island Tours BOAT TOUR
(07-308 9588, 0800 733 529; www.whiteisland. co.nz; 15 The Strand, Whakatane; 6hr tours adult/ child $185/120; ⊙departures btwn 7am-12.30pm) The only official boat trip to Whakaari (on board the good ship *Pee Jay*), with dolphin-spotting en route and a two-hour tour of the island.

Dive White Island DIVING
(07-307 0714, 0800 348 394; www.divewhite. co.nz; 186 The Strand, Whakatane; snorkelling/diving trips per person $190/345) Full-day snorkelling and diving trips with lunch and gear provided; underwater volcanic terrain and lots of fish to look at.

Vulcan Helicopters SCENIC FLIGHTS
(07-308 4188, 0800 804 354; www.vulcanheli. co.nz; flights per person from $550) A two-hour trip to Whakaari (departing from Whakatane) that includes a one-hour guided walk on the volcano.

White Island Flights SCENIC FLIGHTS
(0800 944 834; www.whiteislandflights.co.nz; flights per person $220) Fixed-wing scenic flights over Whakaari, with lots of photo opportunities. A Whakaari/Mt Tarawera combo flight costs $299.

Ohope
POP 2760
Just 7km over the hill from Whakatane, Ohope has great beaches, perfect for lazing or surfing, and is backed by sleepy Ohiwa Harbour. Just beyond the harbour is the small Sandspit Wildlife Refuge.

Activities

KG Kayaks KAYAKING
(027 272 4073; www.kgkayaks.co.nz; tours $75-145, 2hr hire s/d $50/70) Explore the harbour with KG Kayaks, which offers freedom hire and 2½-hour guided tours, plus four-hour kayak trips around Motuhora (Whale Island), which involves a boat trip initially.

By Salt Surf School SURFING
(07-312 4909, 0211 491 972; beaver@e3.net.nz; 2hr lesson $90) If you want to splash around in the Ohope Beach surf, get some lessons from Beaver at By Salt Surf School, which provides all gear and offers discounts for groups.

Sleeping

Ohope Beach Top 10 Holiday Park HOLIDAY PARK $
(0800 264 673, 07-312 4460; www.ohopebeach. co.nz; 367 Harbour Rd; sites/cabins/units/apts from $23/90/136/190; @🐶🕸) The Ohope Beach Top 10 Holiday Park is the very model of a modern holiday park, with a raft of family-friendly facilities: sports courts, minigolf,

pool... Plus some great apartments peeking over the dunes at the Bay of Plenty. Busy as a woodpecker in summer.

Aquarius Motor Lodge MOTEL $
(☎07-312 4550; www.aquariusmotorlodge.co.nz; 103 Harbour Rd; d $85-150; ☀) For a quiet, affordable motel-style option, roll into Aquarius Motor Lodge, a basic complex with various room configurations, all with kitchens and just 100m from the beach (you don't need a swimming pool).

✖ Eating

Ohiwa Oyster Farm SEAFOOD, FAST FOOD $
(Wainui Rd; meals $6-17; ☺9am-8pm, to 7pm winter) Poised over a swampy back-reach of Ohiwa Harbour (serious oyster territory), this classic roadside fish shack is perfect for a fish-and-chip (and oyster) picnic.

Toi Toi Bar & Brasserie MODERN NZ $$
(☎07-312 5623; www.toitoi-ohope.co.nz; 19 Pohutukawa Ave; mains lunch $13-18, dinner $25-35; ☺breakfast & lunch Sat & Sun, dinner Tue-Sun) With polished wooden floorboards, white vinyl chairs and a fold-back window wall, Toi Toi is a ritzy new bistro making a splash in little Ohope's shopping strip. Try some sautéed paua (shellfish) with chilli, lime and mussel fritters, or some peppered duck breast with orange, ginger and honey glaze. There are occasional jazz-and-dinner nights, too. Classy stuff indeed.

Opotiki
POP 4180

The Opotiki area was settled from at least 1150, some 200 years before the larger 14th-century Maori migration. Maori traditions are well preserved here, with the work of master carvers lining the main street and the occasional facial *moko* passing by. The town acts as a gateway to the East Coast, and has excellent beaches – Ohiwa and Waiotahi – and an engaging museum.

◉ Sights & Activities

Pick up the *Historic Opotiki* brochure from the i-SITE (or download from www.opotikinz.com) for the low-down on the town's heritage buildings.

Opotiki Heritage & Agriculture Museum MUSEUM
(ohas@xtra.co.nz; 123 Church St; adult/child $10/5; ☺10am-4pm Mon-Fri, to 2pm Sat) Opotiki's excellent museum offers a chance to learn much about the rich history of the area. Run by volunteers, the museum has interesting heritage displays including Maori *taonga*, militaria, recreated shopfronts (a barber, carpenter, printer...), and agricultural items including tractors and a horse-drawn wagon. Admission to the Shalfoon & Francis Museum is included in the ticket price.

Shalfoon & Francis Museum MUSEUM
(ohas@xtra.co.nz; 129 Church St; adult/child $10/5) Opotiki's original general store has been born again, with shelves piled high with old grocery and hardware products. Handbags, sticky-tape dispensers, sets of scales, books – you name it, they had it. An amazing collection. Admission is included in your ticket to the Opotiki Heritage & Agriculture Museum.

Hiona St Stephen's Church CHURCH
(hiona-st.stephens@xtra.co.nz; 128 Church St; ☺services 8am & 9.30am Sun, 10am Thu) White-weatherboard St Stephen's (1862) is an Anglican church with a perfectly proportioned timber-lined interior. Reverend Carl Volkner, known by the local Whakatohea tribe to have acted as a government spy, was murdered here in 1865. In 1992 the Governor-General granted Mokomoko, the man who hanged for the crime, a full pardon, which hangs in the lobby.

FREE **Hukutaia Domain** FOREST, ARCHAEOLOGICAL SITE
(☎07-315 6167; Woodlands Rd; ☺daily) Around 8km south of the town centre is Hukutaia Domain, home to one of the finest collections of native plants in NZ. In the centre is Taketakerau, a 23m puriri tree estimated to be more than 2000 years old and a burial place for the distinguished dead of the Upokorehe *hapu* (subtribe) of Whakatohea. The remains have since been reinterred elsewhere.

Waioeka River Kayaks KAYAKING, WATER SPORTS
(☎07-315 5553; www.newzealandsbestspot.co.nz; 3666 Waioeka Rd; adult/child $20/10; ☺Dec-Apr) Have a paddle on the scenic and easy Waioeka River, or try a rope swing, an 8m cliff jump or just bobbing around in an innertube. About 16km south of Opotiki on SH2 on the way to Gisborne.

Motu River Jet Boat Tours JETBOATING
(www.motujet.co.nz; trips from $90) Runs as many as three 1½-hour trips on the Motu River (which runs through the Raukumara Ranges near Opotiki) every day through summer. Winter trips by arrangement.

Wet 'n' Wild RAFTING
(0800 462 7238, 07-348 3191; www.wetnwild rafting.co.nz; trips from $875) Offers two- to five-day rafting and camping adventures on the Motu (Grade III–IV rapids).

★ Festivals & Events

Opotiki Rodeo RODEO
(www.opotikirodeo.co.nz) Dust off your spurs and cowboy hat for the annual Opotiki Rodeo in December. Giddyup.

🛌 Sleeping

Opotiki Beach House Backpackers HOSTEL $
(07-315 5117; www.opotikibeachhouse.co.nz; 7 Appleton Rd; sites/dm/d $20/28/66; 🌐) A cruisy, shoe-free beachside pad with a sunny, hammock-hung deck, sea views and plenty of opportunities to get in the water (kayaks/body boards cost $5/3 per hour). Beyond the dorms and breezy lounge are decent doubles and a quirky caravan for those who want a real taste of the Kiwi summer holiday. About 5km west of town; sleeps 12.

Capeview Cottage COTTAGE
(07-315 7877, 0800 227 384; www.capeview.co.nz; 167 Tablelands Rd; d $145; 🌐) Set amid chirruping birds and kiwifruit orchards, this serene, self-contained cottage has two bedrooms, a barbecue and a brilliant outdoor spa from which you can soak up some rather astonishing coastal views. Weekly rates available.

Central Oasis Backpackers HOSTEL $
(07-315 5165; www.centraloasisbackpackers.co.nz; 30 King St; dm/d $24/54; ✳🌐) Inside a late-1800s kauri (timber) house, this central backpackers is run by a super-laid-back German a long way from home. It's a snug spot with spacious rooms, a crackling fire and a big front yard to hang out in. The pet rabbit keeps the grass down.

Kukumoa Lodge LODGE, GUESTHOUSE
(07-315 8545; www.kukumoalodge.co.nz; 19a Bairds Rd; d $90-110, f $300; 🌐✲) This imposing farmhouse is five minutes from town on the way to Ohope, and sports a spacious double and a family area sleeping up to six. There's a games room for the kids, a pool and spa, and a large balcony and patio for swanning around in the sunshine.

Eastland Pacific Motor Lodge MOTEL $$
(0800 103 003, 07-315 5524; www.eastland pacific.co.nz; cnr Bridge & St John Sts; d/units from $105/145; 🌐) Bright, clean Eastland is a well-kept motel with new carpets, spa baths as standard, and a tidy rose garden in the car park. The two-bedroom units are top value.

🍴 Eating

Two Fish CAFE $
TOP CHOICE
(mudslide@xtra.co.nz; 102 Church St; snacks $4-8, mains $9-19; ⊗8am-4pm Mon-Fri, 8.30am-2pm Sat) Decent eating options are thin on the ground in Opotiki, so what a surprise to discover the best cafe this side of Tauranga! Serving up hefty burgers, chowder, toasties, fab muffins and salads plus a jumbo selection in the cabinet, Two Fish has happy staff, Cuban tunes and a retro-groovy interior and courtyard. Nice one.

Nikau CAFE, RESTAURANT $$
(07-315 5760; 95 Church St; mains lunch $9-16, dinner $16-28; ⊗breakfast & lunch daily, dinner Tue-Sun) Seemingly the only real restaurant within miles, Nikau does a steady cafe trade during the day (good coffee, toasted sandwiches, BLATs, eggs florentine), and more sophisticated dinners at night ('The warm beef salad is di-VINE!' says one happy customer). Hip, minimal, informal.

New World SUPERMARKET
(www.newworld.co.nz; 19 Bridge St; ⊗8am-8pm) Self-catering supplies.

☆ Entertainment

De Luxe Cinema CINEMA
(127 Church St) The beguiling old De Luxe Cinema shows the occasional movie and brass-band concert. Check the window for upcoming events, including the annual Silent Film Festival in September.

ℹ Information

DOC (07-315 1001; www.doc.govt.nz; 70 Bridge St; ⊗8am-2.30pm Mon-Fri) In the same building as the i-SITE.

Opotiki i-SITE (07-315 3031; www.opotikinz .com; 70 Bridge St; ⊗9am-4.30pm Mon-Fri, 9am-1pm Sat & Sun) The i-SITE takes bookings for activities and transport and stocks the indispensable free East Coast booklet *Pacific Coast Highway*.

❶ Getting There & Away

Travelling east from Opotiki there are two routes: SH2, crossing the spectacular Waioeka Gorge, or SH35 around East Cape. The SH2 route offers some day walks in the Waioeka Gorge Scenic Reserve, with the gorge getting steeper and narrower as you travel inland, before the route crosses typically green, rolling hills, dotted with sheep, on the descent to Gisborne.

Bus

Buses pick up/drop off at the Hot Bread Shop on the corner of Bridge and St John Sts, though tickets and bookings are made through the i-SITE or **Travel Shop** (☑07-315 8881; travelshop@xtra.co.nz; 104 Church St; ⏲8am-5pm Mon-Fri, to noon Sat). The Travel Shop also rents out bikes (per half-/full day $30/45).

InterCity (www.intercity.co.nz) has daily buses connecting Opotiki with Whakatane ($22, 45 minutes), Rotorua ($34, 2½ hours) and Auckland ($69, seven hours). Heading south, daily buses connect Opotiki with Gisborne ($34, two hours).

Naked Bus (www.nakedbus.com) runs daily services to destinations including the following. Book in advance for big savings.

DESTINATION	PRICE	DURATION
Auckland	$35	6¼hr
Gisborne	$18	2¼hr
Rotorua	$23	2¼hr
Tauranga	$36	6¼hr
Wellington	$50	11¼hr

The local **Bay Hopper** (☑0800 422 928; www.baybus.co.nz) bus runs to Whakatane ($8, 1¼ hour, two daily Monday and Wednesday).

The East Coast

Best Outdoors

» Cape Kidnappers (p345)

» Cooks Cove Walkway (p322)

» Hawke's Bay Cycle Trails (p336)

» Surf Gisborne (p324)

» Lake Waikaremoana Track (p329)

Best Places to Stay

» Kennedy Park Top 10 Resort (p337)

» Waikawa B&B (p320)

» Clive Colonial Cottages (p342)

» Knapdale Eco Lodge (p325)

Why Go?

New Zealand is known for its mix of wildly divergent landscapes, but in this region it's the sociological contours that are most pronounced. From the earthy settlements of the East Cape to Havelock North's wine-soaked streets, there's a full spectrum of NZ life.

Maori culture is never more visible than on the East Coast. Exquisitely carved *marae* (meeting house complexes) dot the landscape, and while the locals may not be wearing flax skirts and swinging *poi* (flax balls on strings) like they do for the tourists in Rotorua, you can be assured that *te reo* and *tikanga* (the language and customs) are alive and well.

Intrepid types will have no trouble losing the tourist hordes – along the Pacific Coast Hwy, through rural back roads, on remote beaches, or in the mystical wilderness of Te Urewera National Park.

When the call of the wild gives way to caffeine withdrawal, a fix will quickly be found in the urban centres of Gisborne and Napier. You'll also find plenty of wine, as the region strains under the weight of grapes. From *kaimoana* (seafood) to berry fruit and beyond, there are riches here for everyone.

When to Go

The East Coast basks in a warm, mainly dry climate. Summer temperatures around Napier and Gisborne nudge 25°C, rarely dipping below 8°C in winter. The Hawke's Bay region also suns itself in mild, dry, grape-growing conditions, with an average annual rainfall of 800mm. Heavy downpours sometimes wash out sections of the Pacific Coast Hwy (State Hwy 35, SH35).

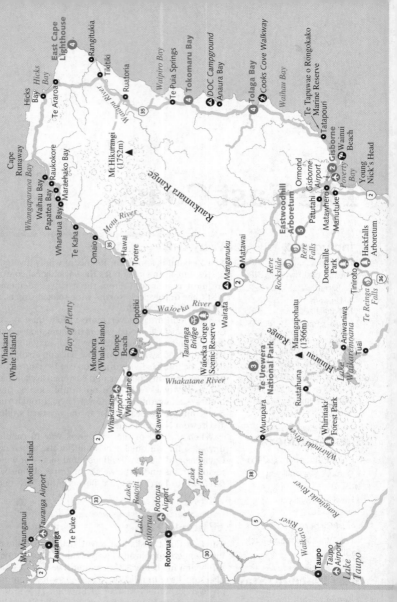

The East Coast Highlights

1 Time-warping to the 1930s amid the art deco delights of **Napier** (p332)

2 Sniffing and sipping around the wineries of **Hawke's Bay** (p344) or **Gisborne** (p323)

3 Losing yourself in the mighty forests and Maori culture of **Te Urewera National Park** (p328)

4 Cruising the coast, taking in landmarks such as **Cape Kidnappers** (p345), **Tolaga Bay** (p321), **Tokomaru Bay** (p321) and the **East Cape Lighthouse** (p320)

5 Searching for wood nymphs among the magical forest paths of **Eastwoodhill Arboretum** (p323)

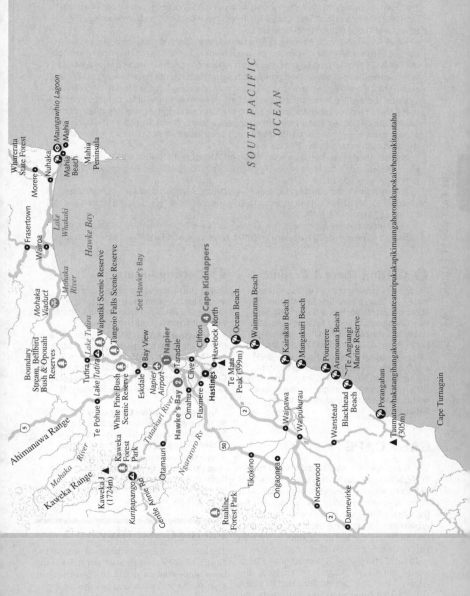

SOUTH PACIFIC

OCEAN

Whararata State Forest

Morere

Nuhaka

Maungawhio Lagoon

Mahia

Mahia Beach

Mahia Peninsula

Frasertown

Wairoa

Lake Whakaki

Hawke Bay

Mohaka River

Mohaka Viaduct

Boundary Stream, Bellbird Bush & Opouahi Reserves

Te Pohue

Tutira

Lake Tutira

Waipatiki Scenic Reserve

Tangoio Falls Scenic Reserve

See Hawke's Bay

Ahimanawa Range

Mohaka River

White Pine Bush Scenic Reserve

Eskdale

Bay View

Napier Airport

Napier

Taradale

Cape Kidnappers

Clifton

Havelock North

Ocean Beach

Waimarama Beach

Kaweka Range

Kaweka J (1724m)

Kaweka Forest Park

Kuripapango

Otamauri

Gentle Annie Rd

Tutaekuri River

Hawke's Bay

Omahu

Flaxmere

Clive

Hastings

Te Mata Peak (399m)

Kairakau Beach

Mangakuri Beach

Pourerere

Aramoana Beach

Te Angiangi Marine Reserve

Waipawa

Waipukurau

Wanstead

Blackhead Beach

Porangahau

Taumatawhakatangihangakoauauotamateaturipukakapikimaungahoronukupokaiwhenuakitanatahu (305m)

Cape Turnagain

Ngaruroro Ry.

Tikokino

Ongaonga

Ruahine Forest Park

Norsewood

Dannevirke

MAORI NZ: THE EAST COAST

The main *iwi* (tribes) in the region are Te Whanau-a-Apanui (west side of East Cape), Ngati Porou (east side of East Cape), Ngati Kahungunu (the coast from Hawke's Bay down) and Tuhoe (inland in Te Urewera).

Ngati Porou and Ngati Kahungunu are the country's second- and third-biggest *iwi*. In the late 19th century they produced the great leaders James Carroll (the first Maori cabinet minister) and Apirana Ngata (who was briefly acting prime minister). Ngata, whose face adorns the $50 bill, worked tirelessly in parliament to orchestrate a cultural revival within Maoridom. The region's magnificent carved meeting houses are part of his legacy.

Maori life is at the forefront around the East Cape, in sleepy villages centred upon the many *marae* that dot the landscape. Living in close communities, drawing much of their livelihoods off the sea and the land, the *tangata whenua* (local people) of the Cape offer a fascinating insight into what life might have been, had they not been so vigorously divested of their land in the 19th century.

You will meet Maori people wherever you go. For accommodation with a distinctly Maori flavour, consider Maraehako Bay Retreat (p320), Eastender Backpackers (p321) or Hikihiki's Inn (p330).

For an intimate introduction to *Maoritanga* (things Maori), consider a guided tour. Look out for Motu River Jet Boat Tours (p319), Tipuna Tours (p325), Long Island Guides (p341) or Te Hakakino (p341).

For a more passive brush with the culture, visit Dive Tatapouri (p322), Gisborne's Tairawhiti Museum (p322), Otatara Pa (p335) in Napier, and Tikitiki's St Mary's Church.

ⓘ Getting There & Around

The region's only airports are in Gisborne and Napier. Air New Zealand flies to both from Auckland and Wellington, and also to Napier from Christchurch. Sunair Aviation connects Gisborne and Napier to Hamilton, Palmerston North, Rotorua, Tauranga and Whakatane.

Regular bus services ply State Hwy 2 (SH2) and State Hwy 5 (SH5), connecting Gisborne, Wairoa, Napier, Hastings and Waipukurau with all the main centres. Transport is much more limited around East Cape and Te Urewera National Park.

EAST CAPE

The East Cape is a unique and special corner of NZ. It's a quiet place, where everyone seems to know everyone, their community ties built on rural enterprise and a shared passion for the ocean. The pace is slow and the people are wound down. Horse-back riding, tractors on the beach, fresh fish for dinner – it's all part of daily life around these parts.

Inland, the wild Raukumara Range forms the Cape's jagged spine. Near the edge of the sea, the 323km Pacific Coast Hwy (SH35) runs from Opotiki to Gisborne. Lonely shores lie strewn with driftwood, while picture-postcard sandy bays lure in a handful of visitors.

ⓘ Getting Around

Unless you're behind the wheel, transport around East Cape can be tricky, especially on weekends, but couriers regularly link Opotiki with Gisborne via Hicks Bay.

Bay Hopper (☑021 0260 4885) runs between Opotiki and Potaka/Cape Runaway Tuesdays and Thursdays only ($15, two hours); they will drive on to Te Araroa for an additional fee. **Cook's Couriers** (☑021 371 364) runs between Te Araroa and Gisborne ($40, 3½ hours) Monday to Saturday.

An alternative is **Kiwi Experience** (☑09-366 9830; www.kiwiexperience.com; per person $395), which runs the four-day 'East As' backpacker bus leaving from Taupo or Rotorua.

For a shortcut through this region, you can shun the coastal highway and zip through the Waioeka Gorge from Opotiki to Gisborne on **InterCity** (☑06-868 6139; www.intercity.co.nz) (from $15, two hours).

Pacific Coast Hwy

The long and often winding road around the North Island's easternmost point has long been somewhat of a rite of road-trip passage for New Zealanders, but overseas visitors could be forgiven for wondering what all the fuss is about. It has its highlights, for sure, but for much of the journey between Opotiki and Gisborne, the Pacific Coast is far away beyond the hills, and the road snakes through farmland that missed its makeover by the quaintillator.

That said, if you like cruisy drives or are skilled in cadging lifts, and don't mind attractions that are few, far between and largely centred upon people, horses, and piles of driftwood, you will likely find this journey surprisingly intrepid and captivating.

If you're short on time or not up for hit-and-miss, you can head for Gisborne via the **Waioeka Gorge**. This 144km alternative route takes 2½ hours to drive, although you could easily make a day of it by the time you stop at various picnic spots including the historic **Tauranga Bridge**. The loop walk here (three hours) is well worth the effort if you like bushy valleys or haven't yet had a glimpse into the pioneer past that was 'farm fails: terrain too tough'.

For a taste of the Pacific Coast Hwy, drive from Opotiki to the macadamia farm (p320). It's a picturesque section that captures the essence of this scenic route: shimmering turquoise ocean seen betwixt the crimson blooms of gnarled pohutukawa trees.

Both routes, along with several more in the region, are covered in the excellent *Pacific Coast Highway Guide*, available at Gisborne and Opotiki i-SITEs and outlets along the way.

Set off with a full petrol tank, and stock up on snacks and groceries – shops and petrol stations are in short supply. Sleeping and eating options are pretty spread out, so we've listed them in the order you'll find them.

OPOTIKI TO TE KAHA

The first leg offers hazy views across to Whakaari (White Island), a chain-smoking active volcano. The desolate beaches at **Torere**, **Hawai** and **Omaio** are steeply shelved and littered with flotsam. Check out the magnificent *whakairo* (carving) on the Torere school gateway. Hawai marks the boundary of the Whanau-a-Apanui tribe whose *rohe* (traditional land) extends to Cape Runaway.

About 42km east of Opotiki the road crosses the broad pebbly expanse of the **Motu River**, the first river in NZ to be designated as a protected wilderness area. Departing from the Motu bridge on the highway, **Motu River Jet Boat Tours** (☑07-325 2735; www.motujet.co.nz; 45min ride $85, min 2 people) blats up the river all year round,

ESSENTIAL EAST COAST

» **Eat** Delicious fresh produce from the Hastings Farmers Market (p343)

» **Read** Witi Ihimaera's novel *Whale Rider*, then watch the powerful movie adaptation

» **Listen to** Uawa FM (88.5, 88.8, 99.3 FM) in Tolaga Bay

» **Watch** *Boy* (2010), Taika Waititi's record-breaking and hilarious film, shot at Waihau Bay

» **Festival** Art deco weekend (p337) in Napier and Hastings

» **Go Green** Millton vineyard (p323) – organic, biodynamic, and delicious to boot

» **Online** www.hawkesbaynz.com; www.gisbornenz.com

» **Area code** Opotiki east to Hicks Bay ☑07; rest of the region ☑06.

weather permitting. **Wet 'n' Wild Rafting** (☑0800 462 7238; www.wetnwildrafting.co.nz; 2-5 days $825-975) offers multiday excursions, with the longest taking you 100km down the river. The two-day tour requires you to be helicoptered in, therefore costing almost as much as the five-day trip.

Twenty-five kilometres further along, the fishing town of **Te Kaha** once sounded the death knell for passing whales. There's a shop here, a modern waterside hotel with a bar and restaurant, and several accommodation options including **Tui Lodge** (☑07-325 2922; www.tuilodge.co.nz; Copenhagen Rd, Te Kaha; s/d incl breakfast $125/150; @). This capacious guesthouse sits on groomed three-acre gardens, irresistible to tui and many other birds. Meals are available by arrangement, as are horse-trekking, fishing and diving trips.

TE KAHA TO CAPE RUNAWAY

A succession of sleepy bays extends from Te Kaha. At **Papatea Bay** stop to admire the gateway of **Hinemahuru marae**, intricately carved with images of WWI Maori Battalion soldiers. Nearby **Christ Church Raukokore** (1894) is a sweet beacon of belief on a lonely promontory (look out for the mouse on high). **Waihau Bay** has an all-in-one petrol station–post office–store–takeaway at its western end, alongside the pub. **Cape Runaway**, where

THE EAST COAST PACIFIC COAST HWY

FREEDOM TO CAMP

Gisborne District Council (GDC) is one of the few authorities to permit freedom camping (extremely cheap informal camping), but only at a handful of designated sites from the end of September to April. You can apply for a permit online (www.gdc.govt.nz/freedom-camping/) for two, 10 or 28 consecutive nights at a cost of $10, $25 and $60 respectively. Freedom camping is a privilege, so please follow the requirements in the GDC *Freedom Camping* leaflet, available online or at visitor centres. Your own gas cooker, chemical toilet and water supply are obligatory.

kumara was first introduced to NZ, can only be reached on foot.

There are few accommodation options in these parts, and what you will find will be small and personal. Nestled among ancient pohutukawa trees, the waterfront **Maraehako Bay Retreat** (☏07-325 2648; www.maraehako.co.nz; SH35; dm/s/d $28/43/66; @) is a hostel that looks like it was cobbled together from flotsam and jetsam washed up in the craggy cove. It's rustic, but unique, for what it lacks in crossed t's and dotted i's it more than makes up for in *manaakitanga* (hospitality). Enjoy a spa under the stars ($5), free kayaks, as well as fishing charters, *marae* tours, guided walks, horse treks and more, at reasonable prices. Run by the same *hapu* (subtribe) as the retreat next door is **Maraehako Camping Ground** (☏07-325 2901; SH35; sites per adult/child $12/8). Little more is offered than clean toilets, showers and beachfront nirvana.

Towards **Whanarua Bay**, the magical **Waikawa B&B** (☏07-325 2070; www.waikawa.net; 7541 SH35; d $120-135; @) sits in a private rocky cove with views of the sunset and White Island. The artful buildings blend weathered timber, corrugated iron and paua inlay to great effect. There are two double B&B rooms, and a two-bedroom self-contained bach ($150 to $220), perfect for two to four people.

There are plenty of beds at **Oceanside Apartments** (☏07-325 3699; www.waihaubay.co.nz; 10932 SH35; d $110-130; @), between two nicely-kept apartments and a next-door bach. Meals and picnic lunches are available by arrangement. Bookings can be made for kayak hire and local activities.

Heaven is a tub of homemade macadamia and honey ice cream at **Pacific Coast Macadamias** (☏07-325 2960; www.macanuts.co.nz; SH35, Whanarua Bay; snacks $2-9; ⊙9am-4pm), accompanied by views along one of the most spectacular parts of the coast. Toasted sandwiches and nutty sweet treats make this a great lunch stop.

CAPE RUNAWAY TO EAST CAPE

The road heads inland from Whangaparaoa, crossing into Ngati Porou territory before hitting the coast at **Hicks Bay**, a real middle-of-nowhere settlement with a grand beach. Brilliant views distract from the barrack ambience at the sprawling **Hicks Bay Motel Lodge** (☏06-864 4880; www.hicksbaymotel.co.nz; 5198 SH35; dm $23, d $75-145; ☏⊠), perched high above the bay. The old-fashioned rooms are nothing flash, although the restaurant, shop, pool and glowworm grotto offer some compensation.

Nearly 10km further is **Te Araroa**, a lone-dog village with two shops, petrol station, takeaway and beautifully carved *marae*. The geology changes here from igneous outcrops to sandstone cliffs, but it is the dense regenerating bush backdrop that gives this place its flavour. More than 350 years old, 20m high and 40m wide, Te-Waha-O-Rerekohu, allegedly NZ's largest pohutukawa tree, stands in Te Araroa schoolyard. The progressive **East Cape Manuka Company** (www.eastcapemanuka.co.nz; 4464 Te Araroa Rd; ⊙9am-4pm daily Nov-Mar, Mon-Fri Apr-Oct) is also here, selling soaps, oils, creams and honey made from potent East Cape manuka. It's a good stop for coffee.

From Te Araroa, drive out to see the **East Cape Lighthouse**, the easterly tip of mainland NZ. It's 21km (30 minutes) east of town along a mainly unsealed road, with a 25-minute climb to the lighthouse. Set your alarm and get up there for sunrise.

EAST CAPE TO TOKOMARU BAY

Heading through farmland south of Te Araroa, the first town you come to is **Tikitiki**. If you haven't yet made it onto a *marae,* you'll get a fair idea of what you're missing out on by visiting the extraordinary **St Mary's Church** (1924). It's nothing special from the outside, but step inside for a sensory overload. There are woven *tukutuku* (flax panels) on the walls, geometrically patterned stained-glass windows, painted beams and amazing carvings – check out the little guys holding up the pulpit. A stained-glass crucifixion scene behind the pulpit depicts WWI Maori Battalion soldiers in attendance.

The farming sprawl of **Rangitukia**, 8km down towards the coast from Tikitiki, would be unremarkable were it not for a couple of welcoming visitor experiences. **Eastender Backpackers** (☎06-864 3820; eastenderbackpackers@xtra.co.nz; 836 Rangitukia Rd; campsites per person $10, dm $25, d $50) is a down-to-earth farmstay with a choice of dorms or cabins. Conveniently, **Eastender Horse Treks** (☎06-864 3033; www.eastenderhorsetreks.co.nz; 836 Rangitukia Rd; 2hr treks $85) can be found next door, and either operator can hook you up with bone-carving lessons (from $55), and you might even get to try a *hangi* (Maori feast; $14). The nearby beach is dicey for swimming but there's a safe waterhole if you're keen.

Mt Hikurangi (1752m), jutting out of the Raukumara Range, is the highest nonvolcanic peak on the North Island and the first spot on Earth to see the sun each day. According to local tradition it was the first piece of land dragged up when Maui snagged the North Island. The Ngati Porou version of the Maui story has his canoe and earthly remains resting here on their sacred mountain.

Continuing south, the road passes **Ruatoria** and **Te Puia Springs**. Along this stretch a 14km loop road offers a rewarding detour to **Waipiro Bay**.

Eleven kilometres south of Te Puia is **Tokomaru Bay**, perhaps the most interesting spot on the entire route, with its broad beach framed by sweeping cliffs. The town has weathered hard times since the freezing works closed in the 1950s, but it still sports several attractions including good beginner surfing, swimming, and **Te Puka Tavern** (☎06-864 5465; www.tepukatavern.co.nz; Beach Rd; meals $10-25; ⊙11am-10pm; @🖙). The well-run pub with cracker ocean views is a cornerstone of the community, keeping everyone fed and watered, and now offering visitors a place to stay. Four units sleep up to five and there's room for a couple of campervans. You'll also find a small supermarket, takeaway and post office, and some crumbling surprises at the far end of the bay. Up on the hill, **Brian's Place** (☎06-864 5870; www.briansplace.co.nz; 21 Potae St; campsites per person $15, dm/s/d $28/45/66) scores the awards for views and eco-loos. There are two tricky loft rooms for sharing, a double downstairs and three sweet

THE BALLAD OF FOOTROOT FLATS *MURRAY BALL*

Where the black Raukumara Ranges
Lie out east of everywhere,
The land's been stripped by sun and rain,
Until its bones are bare.
In this land of snarl-lipped razor backs
Of possums, deer and rats,
They talk a lot of working dogs
And the man from Footrot Flats.

cabins. Tenters have a panoramic knoll on which to pitch.

TOKOMARU BAY TO GISBORNE

After a bucolic 22km of highway is the turnoff to **Anaura Bay**, 7km away. It's a definite 'wow' moment when it springs into view far below. Captain Cook arrived here in 1769 and commented on the 'profound peace' in which the people were living and their 'truly astonishing' cultivations. **Anaura Bay Walkway** is a two-hour ramble through steep bush and grassland, starting at the northern end of the bay. There's a standard Department of Conservation (DOC) campsite here (adult/child $6/3; fully self-contained campers only).

Campers are catered for best around these parts, although a few B&Bs come and go in the midst. **Anaura Bay Motor Camp** (☎06-862 6380; anaurabay@farmside.co.nz; Anaura Bay Rd; sites per adult/child from $16/6) is all about the location – right on the beachfront by the little stream where James Cook once stocked up with water. There's a decent kitchen, showers and toilets.

Back on the highway it's 14km south to **Tolaga Bay**, East Cape's largest community. There's an **information centre** (☎06-862 6862; 55 Cook St; ⊙6am-6pm Mon-Fri) in the foyer of the local radio station (Uawa FM; 88.5, 88.8, 99.3FM). Just off the main street, **Tolaga Bay Cashmere Company** (www.cashmere.co.nz; 31 Solander St; ⊙10am-4pm Mon-Fri) inhabits the art deco former council building. Watch the knitters at work, then perhaps purchase one of their delicate handiworks; the seconds are sold at a discount.

Tolaga is defined by the remarkable **historic wharf** (1929) – the longest in the southern hemisphere at 660m – which is slowly surrendering to the sea (although work is under way to preserve it). Take the time to walk its length. Nearby is **Cooks Cove Walkway** (5.8km, 2½ hours; closed August to October), an easy loop through farmland and native bush to another cove where the captain landed. At the northern end of the beach is the **Tatarahake Cliffs Lookout**, a sharp 10-minute walk to an excellent vantage point.

Tolaga Bay Holiday Park (☑06-862 6716; www.tolagabayholidaypark.co.nz; 167 Wharf Rd; sites from $14, units $55-90) is right next to the wharf. The stiff ocean breeze tousles Norfolk Island pines as open lawns bask in the sunshine. It's a pretty special spot. Back in town, the 1930s faux-Tudor **Tolaga Inn** (☑06-862 6856; 12 Cook St; dm/s/d $25/50/75) is an up-and-comer with basic but clean rooms. Downstairs is a pub and cafe (meals $9 to $30) with home-baking.

Around 16km north of Gisborne, **Te Tapuwae o Rongokako Marine Reserve** is a 2450-hectare haven for many species of marine life including fur seals, dolphins and whales. Get out amongst it with **Dive Tatapouri** (☑06-868 5153; www.divetatapouri.com; SH35, Tatapouri Beach, Tatapouri Beach), which offers an array of watery activities including dive trips, snorkel hire, a reef ecology tour, shark-cage diving and even stingray feeding.

Gisborne

POP 34,300

Gizzy to her friends, Gisborne's a pretty thing, squeezed between surf beaches and a sea of chardonnay. It proudly claims to be the first city on Earth to see the sun, and once it does it hogs it and heads to the seaside. Poverty Bay starts here, hooking south to Young Nick's Head.

Perhaps it's the isolated location that's helped Gisborne maintain its small-town charm and interesting main street. Grand Edwardian buildings sit alongside modernist 1950s, five-storey 'skyscrapers' and the odd slice of audacious art deco.

It's a good place to put your feet up for a few days, hit the beaches and sip heavenly wine.

History

The Gisborne region has been settled for over 700 years. A pact between two migratory *waka* (canoe) skippers, Paoa of the *Horouta* and Kiwa of the *Takitimu,* led to the founding of Turanganui a Kiwa (now Gisborne). Kumara flourished in the fertile soil and the settlement blossomed.

In 1769 this was the first part of NZ sighted by Cook's expedition. Eager to replenish supplies and explore, they set ashore, much to the amazement of the locals. Setting an unfortunate benchmark for intercultural relations, the crew opened fire when the Maori men performed their traditional blood-curdling challenge, killing six of them.

The *Endeavour* set sail without provisions. Cook, perhaps in a fit of petulance, named the area Poverty Bay as 'it did not afford a single item we wanted'.

European settlement began in 1831 with whaling and farming, with missionaries following. In the 1860s battles between settlers and Maori erupted. Beginning in Taranaki, the Hauhau insurrection spread to the East Coast, culminating in the battle of Waerenga a Hika in 1865.

To discover Gisborne's historical spots, pick up the *Historic Walk* pamphlet from the i-SITE.

◎ Sights

Tairawhiti Museum   MUSEUM
(www.tairawhitimuseum.org.nz; 18 Stout St; adult/child $5/free, Mon free; ⊙10am-4pm Mon-Sat, 1.30-4pm Sun) The Tairawhiti Museum focuses on East Coast Maori and colonial history. Its gallery is Gisborne's arts hub, with rotating exhibits, and excellent historic photographic displays. There's also a maritime wing, with displays on *waka*, whaling and Cook's Poverty Bay, although these pale in comparison to the vintage surfboard collection.

There's a shop and tearoom-style cafe overlooking Kelvin Park, while outside is the reconstructed **Wyllie Cottage** (1872), Gisborne's oldest house.

Titirangi Park   PARK
High on Kaiti Hill overlooking the city, Titirangi was once a *pa* (fortified village). You can reach it by driving or walking up Queens Dr, or pick up the walking track at the Cook Monument. Near the summit is **Titirangi Lookout** and yet another Cook edifice, **Cook's Plaza**. Due to a cock-up of historic proportions, the Cook statue here looks nothing like Cap'n Jim. A plaque proclaims, 'Who was he? We have no idea!' Further on is the **Cook Observatory** (public viewing $5; ⊙viewing 8.30pm Tue Oct-Mar, 7.30pm Tue Apr-Sep), the world's easternmost stargazing facility.

Cook Monument   MONUMENT
At the foot of Titirangi Park is the spot
where Cook first got NZ dirt on his boots.
This important site is little more than a
patch of lawn with a grim obelisk facing
the end of the wharves. The scrappy site
is made even more significant by being
the landing point of the *Horouta waka*.
Look out for the remnants of terracing and
kumara pits on the steep track to the top
of Kaiti Hill, which starts near the monument.

Statue of Young Nick   MONUMENT
There's no let-up in the *Endeavour* en-
deavours, because in the riverside park is
a statue of Nicholas Young, Cook's cabin
boy, whose eagle eyes were the first to spot
NZ (the white cliffs at Young Nick's Head).
There's a **Captain Cook statue** nearby,
erected on a globe etched with his roaming
routes.

Te Tauihu Turanga Whakamana   MONUMENT
(The Canoe Prow; cnr Gladstone Rd & Customhouse
St) Te Tauihu Turanga Whakamana is a large
modern sculpture in the shape of a *tauihu*
(canoe prow) that celebrates early Maori
explorers.

Gisborne Botanic Gardens   GARDENS
(Aberdeen Rd) The town gardens sit prettily
beside the Taruheru River and are a pleasant place for a picnic.

TOP
CHOICE **Eastwoodhill Arboretum**   GARDENS
(06-863 9003; www.eastwoodhill.org.nz; 2392
Wharekopae Rd, Ngatapa; adult/child $15/free;
9am-5pm) Arboreal nirvana, Eastwoodhill
Arboretum is the country's largest collection
of imported trees and shrubs. It's staggeringly beautiful, and you could easily lose a
day wandering around the 25km of themed
tracks in this pine-scented paradise. It's well
signposted, 35km northwest of Gisborne.

**East Coast Museum of
Technology & Transport**   MUSEUM
(www.ecmot.org.nz; SH2, Makaraka; adult/child
$5/2; 10am-4.30pm) Think analogue, rather
than digital; old-age rather than space-age.
Located 5km west of the town centre, this
improbable medley of farm equipment, fire
engines, domestic appliances and an elec-
tron microscope has found an appropriate
home in a motley old milking barn and surrounding outhouses. Oh, the irony of the
welcome sign...

THE EAST COAST GISBORNE

GISBORNE WINERIES

With hot summers and fertile loam soils, the land to the northwest of Gisborne is of New
Zealand's foremost grape-growing areas. Centred upon the Waipaoa River valley, geographically and climatically diverse terroir – river plains, gently sloping hills, sheltered
valleys and plateau – produce a wide variety of distinct wines. It is traditionally famous
for its chardonnay but increasingly being noticed for other white varietals, particularly
gewürztraminer and pinot gris.

Some vineyards charge a nominal fee, deducted from subsequent purchases. Pick up
the winery guide from the i-SITE, or visit www.gisbornewine.co.nz for a map of all cellar
doors. The following are open daily from around 11am to 4pm, but scale back opening
hours out of peak season.

» **Bushmere Estate** (www.bushmere.com; 166 Main Rd, Matawhero) Great chardonnay,
gewürztraminer, cafe lunches, and live music on summer Sundays.

» **Kirkpatrick Estate** (www.kew.co.nz; 569 Wharekopae Rd, Patutahi) Sustainable winery
with lovely wines across the board, including a delicious malbec. Enjoy a guided tour
and antipasto platter in the sun.

» **Matawhero** (www.matawhero.co.nz; Riverpoint Rd, Matawhero) Home of a particularly
buttery chardy. Enjoy your picnic in a bucolic setting, accompanied by a flight of fine
wines.

» **Millton** (www.millton.co.nz; 119 Papatu Rd, Manutuke) Sustainable, organic and biodynamic to boot. Bring a picnic and linger in the beautiful gardens.

» **Gisborne Wine Centre** (www.gisbornewine.co.nz; Shed 3, 50 The Esplanade; 10am-
5pm Sun-Wed, 10am-7pm Thu-Sat) Harbourside spot with a wide selection of the region's
vino to sample, plus local winery information.

Gisborne

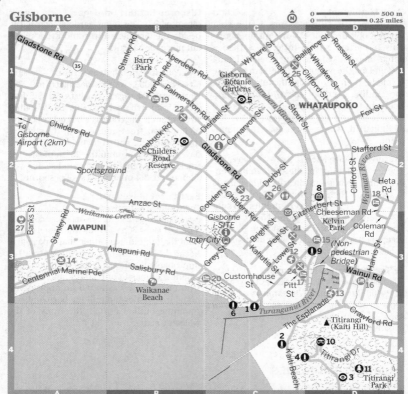

Presbyterian Church CHURCH
(Church Ln, Matawhero) Some 7km west of the centre in the suburb of Matawhero, this historic Presbyterian church is the only building in the village to have survived Te Kooti's 1868 raid. It's a sweetly simple affair with lovingly tended gardens.

FREE **Sunshine Brewing
Company** BREWERY
(✆06-867 7777; www.gisbornegold.co.nz; 109 Disraeli St; ⊕9am-6pm Mon-Sat) Sunshine Brewing Company, Gisborne's own natural brewery, offers four quality beers including the famous Gisborne Gold and its big brother Green. Free tours and tastings by arrangement.

🏃 Activities
Water Sports
Surfing is mainstream in Gisborne, with the teenage population looking appropriately shaggy. **Waikanae Beach** and **Roberts Road** are good for learners and young ones; experienced surfers get tubed south of town at the **Pipe**, or east at **Sponge Bay** and **Tuamotu Island**. Further east along SH35, **Wainui** and **Makorori** also have quality breaks.

Wainui is home to **Surfing with Frank** (✆021 119 0971; www.surfingwithfrank.com; 58 Murphy Rd, Wainui Beach, Wainui Beach; lessons $50-75), which offers lessons as well as tours of the best East Coast and Taranaki breaks. Don't miss the Wainui Store if you're in the vicinity and are looking for something to fill your belly.

There's plenty of good swimming in the area. In town, swim safely between the flags at **Waikanae** and **Midway** beaches, or if you prefer the parameters of a swimming pool, the **Olympic Pool** (Centennial Marine Pde, Midway Beach; adult/child $3.60/2.60; ⊕6am-8pm) has 50m lane-swimming, and a wormlike waterslide.

Gisborne

Awaken your sense of mortality with a shark-cage dive from **Surfit Charters** (✆06-867 2970; www.surfit.co.nz; per person $310). Tamer fishing and snorkelling trips can also be arranged.

The extreme in local watery sports has to be **Rere Rockslide** (Wharekopae Rd). This natural phenomenon occurs in a section of the Rere River 50km northwest of Gisborne along Wharekopae Rd. Grab a tyre tube or boogie board to cushion the worst of the bumps and slide down the 60m-long rocky run into the pool at the bottom. Three kilometres downriver, the **Rere Falls** send a 30m-wide curtain of water over a 10m drop; you can walk behind it if you don't mind getting wet.

Walking

There are stacks of walks to tackle in the area, starting with a gentle stroll along the river. The i-SITE can provide you with brochures for the **Historic Walk** and the **Arts & Crafts Trail**. The *Walking Trails of Gisborne City* brochure details a further five walks around the city cenre.

Winding its way through farmland and forest with commanding views, the **Te Kuri Walkway** (two hours, 5.6km, closed August to October) starts 4km north of town at the end of Shelley Rd.

☞ Tours

Tipuna Tours CULTURAL TOUR
(✆027 240 4493, 06-862 6118; www.tipunatours.com; half-day tour $60-120) Anne offers meaningful insights into Maori culture on her small-group tours, including the half-day trip to Tolaga Bay. Visit the sites and hear the stories, including the *Whale Rider* legend.

Gisborne Cycle Tours CYCLING
(✆06-927 7021; www.gisbornecycletours.co.nz; Poverty Bay Club, 38 Childers Rd; half-day tour $100, freedom hire from $50 per day) Half-day to multiday guided cycle tours around local sights and further afield including wineries and Eastwoodhill Aboretum. Take the half-day cultural tour and you can keep the bike all day. Cheaper rates for multiday freedom bike hire (maps and advice on tap).

✸✸ Festivals & Events

Gisborne Food & Wine Festival FOOD & WINE
(www.gisbornewine.co.nz; tickets $75) On October's Labour Day weekend, local wine makers and foodies pool talents for the Gisborne Food & Wine Festival held at a local vineyard. Top NZ musical talent usually makes an appearance.

🛏 Sleeping

Gisborne's speciality is midrange motor lodges and the ubiquitous beachside motel. Budget travellers will find their options limited.

Knapdale Eco Lodge LODGE $$$
(✆06-862 5444; www.knapdale.co.nz; 114 Snowsill Rd, Waihirere; d incl breakfast $398-472; @⊛)

Indulge and relax at this tranquil idyll complete with lake, farm animals and home-grown produce. The stunning modern lodge is filled with international artwork, its glassy frontage flowing out to an expansive patio area, with brazier, barbecue and pizza oven. Five-course dinner by arrangement ($85). The lodge is 10km northwest of Gisborne, via Back Ormond Rd.

Te Kura B&B B&B $$
(☑06-863 3497; www.tekura.co.nz; 14 Cheeseman Rd; d $120-140; ☻🖥🌊) Play lord of the manor at this lovely 1920s Arts and Crafts–style riverside home. Two guest rooms (one with clawfoot-bath en suite) share a stately lounge and a bright breakfast room opening on to the swimming pool and Waimata River.

Teal Motor Lodge MOTEL $$
(☑0800 838 325, 06-868 4019; www.teal.co.nz; 479 Gladstone Rd; d $125-135, tr/q $175/215; @🖥🌊) With super street appeal on the high street (500m to town), the mildly aeronautical Teal boasts a solid offering of tidy, family-friendly units with the bonus of a pleasant swimming-pool area and lots of lawn to run around on.

Gisborne YHA HOSTEL $
(☑06-867 3269; www.yha.co.nz; 32 Harris St; dm/s/d $26/48/64; @🖥) A short stroll across the river from town, this rambling mansion houses a well-kept hostel. The rooms are large and comfortable, while outside there's a pleasant deck and lawns for communing. Family ensuite unit available.

Eastwoodhill Arboretum LODGE $
(☑06-863 9003; www.eastwoodhill.org.nz; 2392 Wharekopae Rd, Ngatapa; dm/tw $40/70) The bunks and private rooms are basic and you'll still need to pay the garden admission on the first day (adult/child $15/free), but once you're here, endless woody delights can fill your days and nights. Meals can be provided by arrangement, or you can use the fully-equipped kitchen. Remember to bring food though as there's nothing for miles around.

**Waikanae Beach
Top 10 Holiday Park** HOLIDAY PARK $
(☑0800 867 563, 06-867 5634; www.waikanae beachtop10.co.nz; Grey St; sites from $18, units $60-145; @🖥) Right by the beach and a pleasant 10-minute walk to town, this grassy holiday park offers good-value built accommodation and grassy lanes for pitching tents and parking vans.

Emerald Hotel HOTEL $$
(☑06-868 8055; www.emeraldhotel.co.nz; cnr Reads Quay & Gladstone Rd; r $140-280; @🖥🌊) The modern Emerald is all about the swimming pool and patio area, which makes a reasonable fist of looking like a foxy international. Surrounding it are 48 luxury suites running along epic corridors connecting the various wings. There's a gym, day spa, and the Grill Room restaurant (mains $28 to $35).

Pacific Harbour Motor Inn MOTEL $$
(☑06-867 8847; www.pacific-harbour.co.nz; 24 Reads Quay; r $130-190, ste $130-195; @🖥) Overlooking the harbour, this apartment-style inn offers well-kept units with no-frills decor and the bonus of good balconies.

✖ Eating

TOP CHOICE **USSCO Bar & Bistro** MODERN NZ $$
(☑06-868 3246; 16 Childers Rd; mains $30; ⊗dinner) Housed in the restored Union Steam Ship Company building (hence the name), this place is all class. Silky kitchen skills shine in a highly seasonal menu featuring the likes of pan-fried fish with ratatouille and creamed mussel sauce. Devilishly good desserts, plus plenty of local wines and NZ craft beers. Generous portions, multi-course deals and live piano on some nights.

Villaggio CAFE $$
(☑06-863 3895; 57 Ballance St; lunch mains $18-28, dinner mains $28-32; ⊗8am-4pm Sun-Wed, til late Thu-Sat) On the north side of the river, not far from the Botanic Gardens, this dear old art deco home has been respectfully stripped back, its new scheme of red, white and wood making this cafe super-smart and edgy. The food's on the modern side too, offering fresh takes on the classics (seafood chowder, fish and chips), as well as a colourful array of Med-style dishes such as spaghetti with tomato, goat cheese and herbs, and Moroccan vegetable tagine. Pleasant garden invites loitering over lunchtime wines.

Café 1874 CAFE $
(38 Childers Rd; meals $10-22; ✐) The creaky old grandeur of the Poverty Bay gentleman's club (1874) is reason enough to visit. This cafe within it certainly adds impetus: appealing counter food, all-day brunch, pizza, blackboard specials, reasonable prices and

a pleasant garden. Bike hire and boutique shopping share the building.

Bookshop Café
CAFE $

(62 Gladstone Rd; meals $7-12; 🖉) Situated above Muirs Bookshop, a beloved, age-old independent in a lovely heritage building, this simple cafe offers a small but sweet selection of counter food and excellent salads. Fans of fine espresso coffee and literature may need to be forcibly removed. Atmospheric balcony for those balmy days.

Morrell's
BAKERY $

(437 Gladstone Rd; ⊗7am-2pm Tue-Sat; 🖉) Artisan bakers with killer pies, wholesome bread and delicious patisserie.

Yoko Sushi
SUSHI $

(87 Grey St; sushi $5-12) Looks like the Gisbonites have well and truly taken to sushi, if the lunchtime trade at this sparky sushi bar is anything to go by. Commendable sushi, along with the usual miso-lany of extras including the bento box and octopus dumplings. Ample seating for eating in, plus pavement tables.

Pak N Save
SUPERMARKET

(274 Gladstone Rd; ⊗7am-9pm) Fill up the trolley, and don't forget your Gisborne oranges.

🍷 Drinking & Entertainment

The Rivers
PUB

(cnr Gladstone Rd & Reads Quay) This well-run, British-style pub does the business, offering steak-and-ale pie, proper pudding, big-screen telly and pool. It's also family-friendly and cosy, with some stonework and choice artefacts adding a veneer of history in what could otherwise be a plain, corner pub in the bottom of a big new hotel.

Smash Palace
PUB

(24 Banks St) Get juiced at the junkyard. Iconic drinking den full to the gunwales with ephemera and its very own DC3 crash-landed in the garden bar. Occasional live music.

Poverty Bay Club
LIVE MUSIC, CINEMA

(www.thepovertybayclub.co.nz; 38 Childers Rd) Sharing this lovely old historic building with a cafe and art shop is Winston's Bar where occasional music events are held, as well as the bean-bagged **Dome Cinema** (🖉08-324 3005; www.domecinema.co.nz), which shows arthouse films on Wednesday, Thursday and Sunday evenings.

ℹ️ Information

The major banks are located along Gladstone Rd.
DOC (🖉06-869 0460; www.doc.govt.nz; 63 Carnarvon St; ⊗8am-4.30pm Mon-Fri) Tourist information.
Gisborne Hospital (🖉06-869 0500; Ormond Rd)
Gisborne i-SITE (🖉06-868 6139; www.gisborne nz.com; 209 Grey St; ⊗8.30am-5.30pm Mon-Fri, 9am-5pm Sat, 10am-4pm Sun; @) Beside a doozy of a Canadian totem pole, this information centre has all and sundry, as well as a travel booking office, internet access, toilets and a minigolf course ($4).
Police Station (🖉06-869 0200; cnr Gladstone Rd & Customhouse St)
Post Office (cnr Gladstone Rd & Bright St)

ℹ️ Getting There & Around

The **Travel Centre** (🖉06-868 6139; 209 Grey St) at the i-SITE handles bookings for many local and national transport services.

Air

Gisborne Airport (www.eastland.co.nz/airport; Aerodrome Rd) is 3km west of the city. **Air New Zealand** (🖉0800 737 000; www.airnewzealand. co.nz) flies to/from Auckland and Wellington, with onward connections. Check the website for fares and special offers.

Sunair Aviation (🖉0800 786 247; www. sunair.co.nz) offers flights on weekdays to Hamilton, Napier, Paparaumu, Rotorua and Tauranga (from $280).

Bus

InterCity (p318) buses depart daily from the i-SITE for Napier (from $30) via Wairoa (from $15), and Auckland (from $38) via Opotiki (from $18) and Rotorua (from $23).

Organised penny-pinchers can take advantage of limited $1 advance fares on **Naked Bus** (www. nakedbus.com) to Auckland via Opotiki and Rotorua.

For courier services from Gisborne to Opotiki travelling via East Cape's scenic SH35, see East Cape (p318).

Car

Conveniently, **Gisborne Airport Car Rental** (🖉0800 556 606; www.gisborneairportcarhire. co.nz) is an agent for 10 car-hire companies including the big brands and local outfits.

Taxi

A city-to-airport taxi fare costs about $20.
Eastland Taxis (🖉0800 282 947, 06-867 6667)
Gisborne Taxis (🖉0800 505 55523, 06-867 2222)

Gisborne to Hawke's Bay

From Gisborne, heading south towards Napier you're confronted with a choice: follow SH2, which runs closer to the coast, or take SH36 inland via Tiniroto. Either way you'll end up in Wairoa.

The coastal route is a marginally better choice, being quicker and offering occasional views out to sea. However, SH36 (Tiniroto Road) is also a pleasant drive with several good stopping points en route. **Doneraille Park**, 49km from Gisborne, is a peaceful bush reserve with a frigid river to jump into and freedom camping for self-contained vehicles. Avid tree-lovers might like to check out **Hackfalls Arboretum** (entry $10), a 4km detour from the turn-off at the tidy Tiniroto Tavern. The snow-white cascades of **Te Reinga Falls**, 12km further south, are well worth a stop.

The busier SH2 route heads inland and soon enters the **Wharerata State Forest** (so beware of logging trucks around these parts). Just out of the woods, 55km from Gisborne, **Morere Hot Springs** (www.morerehotsprings. co.nz; SH2; adult/child $6/3; ⊙10am-5pm, to 9pm summer) burble up from a fault line in the **Morere Springs Scenic Reserve**. You might want to tackle the bushwalks (20 minutes to two hours) before taking the plunge. The main swimming pool is near the entrance, but a five-minute walk through virgin rainforest leads to the Nikau Baths. The reserve is quite lovely, much favoured by locals who visit for a family day out. Long may it continue, although with the spring outlet threatened by landslips upriver, the day may soon come when the hot tap is turned off.

There's accommodation at Morere. You won't miss the **Morere Tearooms & Camping Ground** (☑06-837 8792; SH2; campsites from $30, d $60-90) where you can get a respectable toasted sandwich and avail yourself of campsites and basic cabins alongside the babbling Tunanui Stream. Just over the stream is **Morere Hot Springs Lodge** (☑06-837 8824; www.morerehotsprings.co.nz; SH2; s/d/tr/q $80/95/115/135), a farmy enclave where the lambs gambol and the dog wags her tail at you nonstop. Sleeping options are a classic 1917 farmhouse with sweet sleepout, or two adorable cabins.

From Gisborne on SH2, keep an eye out for the unusually brightly painted **Taane-nui-a-Rangi Marae**. You can get a decent view from the road; don't enter unless invited.

SH2 continues south to Nuhaka at the northern end of Hawke Bay. From here it's west to Wairoa or east to the salty **Mahia Peninsula**. Not far from the Nuhaka roundabout is **Kahungunu Marae**. From the street you can see the carving at the house's apex of a standing warrior holding a *taiaha* (spear). It's less stylised than most traditional carving, opting for simple realism.

Te Urewera National Park

Shrouded in mist and mysticism, Te Urewera National Park is the North Island's largest, encompassing 212,673 hectares of virgin forest cut with lakes and rivers. The highlight is **Lake Waikaremoana** (Sea of Rippling Waters), a deep crucible of water encircled by the Lake Waikaremoana Track, one of NZ's Great Walks. Rugged bluffs drop away to reedy inlets, the lake's mirror surface disturbed only by mountain zephyrs and the occasional waterbird taking to the skies.

The name Te Urewera still has the capacity to make Pakeha New Zealanders feel slightly uneasy – and not just because

---

WORTH A TRIP

MAHIA PENINSULA

The Mahia Peninsula's eroded hills, sandy beaches and vivid blue sea make it a mini-ringer of the Coromandel, without the tourist hordes and fancy subdivisions, and with the bonus of dramatic Dover-ish cliffs. It's an enduring holiday spot for East Coasters, who come largely for boaty, beachy stuff, and you can easily get in on the action if you have your own transport. A day or two could easily be spent visiting the scenic reserve and the bird-filled Maungawhio Lagoon, hanging out at the beach (Mahia Beach at sunset can be spectacular), or even playing a round of golf at the friendly golf course.

Mahia has several small settlements offering between them a couple of guesthouses, a grotty campsite, a decent pub and a dairy. See www.voyagemahia.co.nz for more information.

Lake Waikaremoana Track

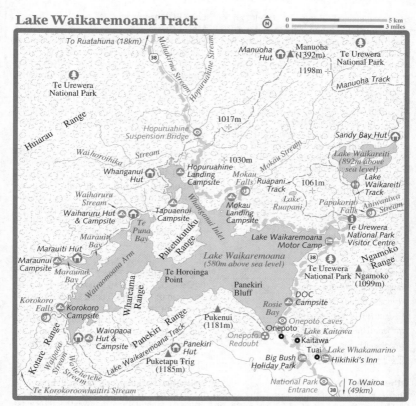

THE EAST COAST TE UREWERA NATIONAL PARK

it translates as 'The Burnt Penis'. There's something primal and untamed about this wild woodland, with its rich history of Maori resistance.

The local Tuhoe people – prosaically known as the 'Children of the Mist' – never signed the Treaty of Waitangi and fought with Rewi Maniapoto at Orakau during the Waikato Wars. The army of Te Kooti (p331) took refuge here during running battles with government troops. The claimant of Te Kooti's spiritual mantle, Rua Kenana, led a thriving community beneath the sacred mountain Maungapohatu (1366m) from 1905 until his politically motivated 1916 arrest. This effectively erased the last bastion of Maori independence in the country. Maungapohatu never recovered, and only a small settlement remains. Nearby, Ruatahuna's extraordinary Mataatua Marae celebrates Te Kooti's exploits.

Tuhoe remain proud of their identity and traditions, with around 40% still speaking *te reo* (the language) on a regular basis.

🏃 Activities

Lake Waikaremoana Track

The 46km, three- to four-day tramp scales the spectacular Panekiri Bluff, with open panoramas interspersed with fern groves and forest. The walk is rated as moderate with the only difficult section being the Panekiri ascent, and during summer it can get busy.

Although it's a year-round track, winter rain deters many people and makes conditions much more challenging. At this altitude (580m above sea level), temperatures can drop quickly, even in summer. Walkers should take portable stoves and fuel as there are no cooking facilities en route.

There are five huts (adult/child $32/ free) and campsites (per night adult/child

$14/free) spaced along the track, all of which must be prebooked through DOC, regardless of the season. Book at the Aniwaniwa, Gisborne, Wairoa, Whakatane or Napier DOC offices, i-SITEs or online at www.doc.govt.nz.

If you have a car, it is safest to leave it at the Lake Waikaremoana Motor Camp or Big Bush Holiday Park then take a water taxi to the trailheads. Alternatively, you can take the fully catered, four-night guided tour offered by the enthusiastic and experienced people at **Walking Legends** (☑0800 925 569; www.walkinglegends.com; adult/child $1290/1000).

Propel yourself onto the trail either clockwise from just outside **Onepoto** in the south or anticlockwise from **Hopuruahine Suspension Bridge** in the north.

Estimated walking times:

ROUTE	TIME
Onepoto to Panekiri Hut	5hr
Panekiri Hut to Waiopaoa Hut	3-4hr
Waiopaoa Hut to Marauiti Hut	5hr
Marauiti Hut to Waiharuru Hut	2hr
Waiharuru Hut to Whanganui Hut	2½hr
Whanganui Hut to Hopuruahine Suspension Bridge	2hr

Other Walks

There are dozens of walks within the park's vast boundaries, most of which are outlined in DOC's *Lake Waikaremoana Walks* and *Recreation in Northern Te Urewera* pamphlets ($2.50).

With its untouched islands, **Lake Waikareiti** (892m) is an enchanting place. Starting nearby the DOC visitor centre, it's an hour's walk to its shore. Once you're there, a fitting way to explore it is in a rowboat (unlock one with a key collected from the visitor centre for $20 for four hours). You may also be lured in for a skinny dip.

The **Ruapani Track** (six hours), starting at the same place, is a circuit that passes seven wetlands as it wends through dense, virgin forest.

Numerous shorter walks (less than an hour) are easily accessible from the visitor centre and Waikaremoana Motor Camp.

🛏 Sleeping & Eating

DOC has more than 30 huts and campsites within the park, most of which are very basic.

Lake Waikaremoana Motor Camp
HOLIDAY PARK $
(☑06-837 3826; www.lake.co.nz; campsites per adult/child $15/5, cabins $55, units $90-160) Right on the shore, this place has Swiss-looking chalets, fisherman's cabins and campsites, most with watery views. The on-site shop is full of essentials such as hot pies, chocolate and a swarm of fishing flies. The camp can also hook you up with water taxis, shuttles and petrol.

Hikihiki's Inn
B&B $$
(☑06-837 3701; www.hikihiki.co.nz; 9 Rotten Row, Tuai; s/d $80/160) In the sweet little settlement of Tuai, 6km from Onepoto, this beautifully kept home now serves as a B&B run by '100% Kiwi' hosts. The little weatherboard gem is quintessential NZ, with hospitality to match, including continental breakfast and other meals at extra cost (24 hours notice required).

Big Bush Holiday Park
HOLIDAY PARK $
(☑0800 525 392; www.lakewaikaremoana.co.nz; SH38; campsites from $15, dm/d $30/95) Located 4km from the Onepoto trailhead, Big Bush offers tent sites, trim cabins and acceptable backpacker rooms. Pick-ups, water taxis/scenic charters and storage are available.

❶ Information

Te Urewera National Park Visitor Centre (☑06-837 3803; www.doc.govt.nz; SH38, Aniwaniwa; ◷8am-4.45pm) has weather forecasts, accommodation information and hut or campsite passes for the Lake Waikaremoana Track.

See also www.teurewera.co.nz.

❶ Getting There & Around

Approximately 95km of SH 38 between Wairoa and Rotorua remains unsealed and it'll take around four bone-rattling hours to do the entire journey (Wairoa to Aniwaniwa 61km, Aniwaniwa to Rotorua 139km).

Big Bush Water Taxi (☑0800 525 392; www.lakewaikaremoana.co.nz) will ship you to either Onepoto or Hopuruahine trailhead ($35 return), with hut-to-hut pack transfers for the less gung-ho. It also runs shuttles to and from Wairoa ($40 one way). More shuttle action is offered by **Route 38 Shuttles** (☑021 042 9972).

Home Bay Water Taxi & Shuttles (☑06-837 3826; www.waikaremoana.com) does boat runs from Lake Waikaremoana Motor Camp to stops all around the lake (trailhead $40 return), offers lake cruises ($40) and runs a shuttle to Wairoa ($80 for four people).

TE KOOTI

Maori history is littered with mystics, prophets and warriors, one of whom is the legendary Te Kooti (rhymes with naughty, not booty).

In 1865 he fought with the government against the Hauhau (adherents of the Pai Marire faith, founded by another warrior-prophet) but was accused of being a spy and imprisoned on the Chatham Islands without trial.

While there, Te Kooti studied the Bible and claimed to receive visions from the archangel Michael. His charismatic preaching and 'miracles' – including producing flames from his hands (his captors claimed he used phosphorus from the head of matches) – helped win over the Pai Marire to his distinctly Maori take on Christianity.

In 1867 Te Kooti led an astounding escape from the Chathams, hijacking a supply ship and sailing to Poverty Bay with 200 followers. En route he threw a doubter overboard as a sacrifice. Upon their safe arrival, Te Kooti's disciples raised their right hands in homage to God rather than bowing submissively; *ringa tu* (upraised hand) became the name of his church.

Te Kooti requested a dialogue with the colonial government but was once again rebuffed, with magistrate Reginald Biggs demanding his immediate surrender. Unimpressed by Pakeha justice, Te Kooti commenced a particularly effective guerrilla campaign – starting by killing Biggs and around 50 others (including women and children, Maori and Pakeha) at Matawhero near Gisborne.

A four-year chase ensued. Eventually Te Kooti took refuge in the King Country, the Maori king's vast dominion where government troops feared to tread.

Proving the pointlessness of the government's approach to the whole affair, Te Kooti was officially pardoned in 1883. By this time his reputation as a prophet and healer had spread and his Ringatu Church was firmly established – at the most recent census it boasted over 16,000 adherents.

HAWKE'S BAY

Hawke Bay, the name given to the body of water that stretches from the Mahia Peninsula to Cape Kidnappers, looks like it's been bitten out of the North Island's eastern flank. Add an apostrophe and an 's' and you've got a region that stretches south and inland to include fertile farmland, surf beaches, mountainous ranges and forests.

The southern edge of the bay is a travel-channel come to life – food, wine and architecture are the shared obsessions. It's smugly comfortable but thoroughly appealing, and is best viewed through a rosé-tinted wineglass. If the weather's putting a dampener on your beach-holiday plans, it's a great place to head.

Wairoa to Napier

The small town of **Wairoa** is trying hard to shirk its rough-edged reputation, and a walk along its riverside promenade on a sunny day will leave you wondering whether those edges are smoothing off. Not scintillating enough to warrant an extended stay, the town has a couple of points of interest, including an exceptional pie shop called **Oslers**. Non-consumable attractions include the **Wairoa Museum** and the nearby **Whakaki Lake** wetland. The town has a couple of motels and a cracker little campsite.

The stretch of highway between Wairoa and Napier traipses through unphotogenic farmland and forestry blocks for much of its 117km. Most of it follows a railway line that is currently only used for freight – you'll see what a travesty that is when you pass under the **Mohaka viaduct** (1937), the highest rail viaduct in Australasia (97m). The litter-strewn roadside rest area here does little to honour this grand construction.

Occupied by early Maori, **Lake Tutira** has walkways and a bird sanctuary. At Tutira village, just north of the lake, Pohokura Rd leads to the wonderful **Boundary Stream Reserve**, a major conservation area. Three loop tracks start from the road, ranging in length from 40 minutes to three hours. Also along this road you'll find the **Opouahi** and **Bellbird Bush Scenic Reserves**, which both offer rewarding walks.

Hawke's Bay

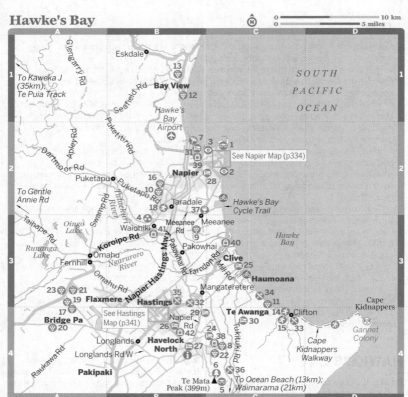

Eskdale

13

Bay View

12

Hawke's Bay Airport

SOUTH PACIFIC OCEAN

7   3   1
31
See Napier Map (p334)
39
Napier
28   2

16
10   Taradale   *Hawke's Bay Cycle Trail*
Puketapu   4   37
18
Waiohiki   41   Meeanee   Meeanee
Rd   9
Pakowhai   *Hawke Bay*
40
Clive
Omahu   25
Fernhill   **Haumoana**

23   21   Mangateretere   34
19   **Flaxmere**   11   Cape Kidnappers
17   **Hastings**   35   32   **Te Awanga** 14   Clifton
Bridge Pa 20   29   30   *Gannet Colony*
Longlands   Napier Rd   15   33
26   42   24   **Havelock North**   *Cape Kidnappers Walkway*
Longlands Rd W   27   38   8
6   22
20   36
Pakipaki
Te Mata Peak (399m)   5   To Ocean Beach (13km); Waimarama (21km)

To Kaweka J (35km); Te Puia Track

Glengarry Rd
Seafield Rd
Puketitiri Rd
Apley Rd
Dartmoor Rd
Puketapu
To Gentle Annie Rd
Taihape Rd
Oingo Lake
Ruanga Lake
Titiokura River
Tutaekuri River
Swamp Rd
Koroipo Rd
Ngaruroro River
Omahu Rd
Napier Hastings Mwy
Pakowhai Rd
Farndon Rd
Mill Rd
Tukituki Rd
Raukawa Rd
See Hastings Map (p341)

Cape Kidnappers

See Napier Map (p334)
See Hastings Map (p341)

Off Waipatiki Rd, 34km outside Napier, Waipatiki Beach is a beaut spot boasting a low-key campsite and the 64-hectare **Waipatiki Scenic Reserve**. Further down the line, **White Pine Bush Scenic Reserve**, 29km from Napier on SH2, bristles with kahikatea and nikau palms. **Tangoio Falls Scenic Reserve**, 27km north of Napier, has Te Ana Falls, stands of wheki-ponga (tree ferns) and native orchids. Between White Pine and Tangoio reserves the **Tangoio Walkway** (three hours return) follows Kareaara Stream.

The highway surfs the coast for the last 25km, with impressive views towards Napier. Hawke's Bay wine country starts in earnest at the mouth of the Esk River. Even the driver should safely be able to stop for a restrained tasting at one of the excellent vineyards just off SH2 (or both if you're spitting).

Esk Valley Estate is a lovely spot to bring your picnic and enjoy some great reds. With its relaxed, rustic feel, **Crab Farm Winery** (Map p332; www.crabfarmwinery.co.nz; 511 Main Rd, Bay View; tastings free; ☺10am-5pm Fri-Sun, cafe 12-3pm Fri-Sun, dinner Fri) is a good stop for lunch and a glass of rosé (among others).

Napier

POP 58,800

The Napier of today is the silver lining of the dark cloud that was one of NZ's worst natural disasters. Rebuilt after the deadly 1931 earthquake in the popular styles of the time, the city retains a unique concentration of art deco buildings to which architecture obsessives flock from all over the world. Don't expect the Chrysler Building – Napier's art deco is resolutely low-rise – but you will find intact 1930s streetscapes, which can

Hawke's Bay

THE EAST COAST NAPIER

provoke a *Great Gatsby* swagger in the least romantic soul.

For the layperson it's a charismatic, sunny, composed city with the air of an affluent English seaside resort about it.

History

The area has been settled since around the 12th century and was known to Maori as Ahuriri. By the time James Cook eyeballed it in October 1769, Ngati Kahungunu was the dominant tribe, controlling the coast to Wellington.

In the 1830s whalers malingered around Ahuriri, establishing a trading base in 1839. By the 1850s the Crown had purchased – by often dubious means – 1.4 million acres of Hawke's Bay land, leaving Ngati Kahungunu with less than 4000 acres. The town of Napier was planned in 1854 and obsequiously named after the British general and colonial administrator Charles Napier.

At 10.46am on 3 February 1931, the city was levelled by a catastrophic earthquake (7.9 on the Richter scale). Fatalities in Napier and nearby Hastings numbered 258. Napier suddenly found itself 40 sq km larger, as the earthquake heaved sections of what was once a lagoon 2m above sea level (Napier airport was once more 'port', less 'air'). A fevered rebuilding program ensued, constructing one of the world's most uniformly art deco cities.

Napier

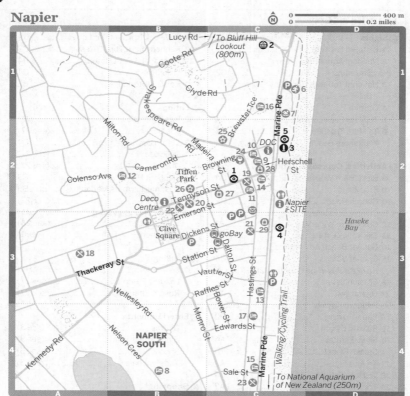

☉ Sights

Napier's claim to fame is undoubtedly its architecture, and a close study of these treasures could take several days (especially if you stop often to shop and eat). There are, however, many other interesting diversions, not least of all the area's many wineries (p344).

Architecture

The 1931 quake demolished most of Napier's brick buildings. Frantic reconstruction between 1931 and 1933 caught architects in the throes of global art deco mania. Art deco, along with Spanish Mission and Stripped Classical, was cheap (debts were high), safe (falling stone columns and balconies had killed many during the earthquake) and contemporary (residents wanted to make a fresh start).

The place to start your art deco exploration is the home of the Art Deco Trust, the **Deco Centre** (www.artdeconapier.com; 163 Ten-

nyson St; ☉9am-5pm) opposite colourful Clive Sq. Its one-hour guided deco walk ($16) departs the i-SITE daily at 10am; the two-hour version ($21) leaves the Centre at 2pm daily and includes an introductory spiel. These excellent walks include an introductory spiel, DVD screening and refreshments. The Deco Centre has a lovely little shop, and stocks brochures for the excellent self-guided *Art Deco Walk* ($5), *Art Deco Scenic Drive* ($5) and *Marewa Meander* ($3). You can also hire art deco–style bikes from here, and set off on a self-guided tour of up to four hours ($50).

If you haven't got time for guided or self-guided art deco walking tours of Napier, just take to the streets – particularly Tennyson and Emerson. Remember to look up! The **Daily Telegraph Building** (Map p334; 49 Tennyson St) is one of the stars of the show, with superb zigzags, fountain shapes and ziggurat aesthetic. If the building is open, nip inside and ogle at the painstakingly restored foyer.

Napier

Around the shore at Ahuriri, the **National Tobacco Company Building** (Map p332; cnr Bridge & Ossian Sts) is arguably the region's deco masterpiece. Built in 1933, it combines art deco forms with the natural motifs of art nouveau. Roses, *raupo* (bulrushes) and grapevines frame the elegantly curved entrance. During business hours it's possible to pull on the leaf-shaped brass door handles and enter the first two rooms.

Other Sights

Marine Parade   STREET

Napier's elegant avenue is lined with huge Norfolk Island pines, and dotted with motels and charming timber villas. Along its length are parks, **sunken gardens** (Map p334), a minigolf course, a swimming complex and aquarium. Near the north end of the parade is the **Tom Parker Fountain** (Map p334), which is best viewed at night when it is lavishly lit. Next to it is **Pania of the Reef** (Map p334) (1954), with her dubious boobs.

**National Aquarium of
New Zealand**   AQUARIUM

(Map p332; www.nationalaquarium.co.nz; 546 Marine Pde; adult/child/family $17.40/8.70/41.90; ⊙9am-5pm, feedings 10am & 2pm) Inside this modern complex with its stingray-inspired roof are piranhas, terrapins, eels, kiwi, tuatara and a whole lotta fish. 'Behind the Scenes' tours (adult/child $34.80/17.40) leave at 9am and 1pm and snorkellers can swim with sharks ($60).

Napier Prison   HISTORIC BUILDING

(Map p334; www.napierprison.com; 55 Coote Rd; tours $20) If you fancy going to jail, Napier Prison Tours offers fascinating self-guided audio tours in 16 languages (9am to 9pm) and hosted tours (9.30am and 3pm).

Bluff Hill Lookout   LOOKOUT

(Map p332) The circuitous route to the top (102m) makes a pleasant wander and rewards with expansive views. The well-loved lookout itself is a nice spot for a picnic, which might just give you the excuse you need to drive up in your car.

Otatara Pa   ARCHAEOLOGICAL SITE

(Map p332) Wooden palisades, carved *pou* (memorial posts) and a carved gate help bring this *pa* site to life. An hour-long loop walk across grassy hills passes barely-discernible archaeological remains but affords terrific views of the surrounding countryside. From the city head southwest on Taradale Rd and Gloucester St. Turn right into Springfield Rd just before the river.

⚡ Activities

Most of the city's activities require energy to burn and moderate risk of personal injury. Speaking of which, Napier's pebbly beach isn't safe for swimming; locals head north

CYCLE THE BAY

The expanding network of **Hawke's Bay Cycle Trails** offers cycling opportunities from short, city scoots to hilly, single-track shenanagins.

Napier is cycle-friendly, particularly along Marine Parade where you'll find **Fishbike** (Map p334; www.fishbike.co.nz; 26 Marine Pde; bike hire from $15; ☺9am-5pm) renting comfortable bikes – including tandems for those willing to risk divorce.

Dedicated cycle trails stretch from Napier, north to Westshore and Bay View, inland to Taradale and the wineries around Flaxmere, and south along the coast all the way to Clifton. The *Hawke's Bay Cycle Map* can be picked up from the i-SITE or www.hawkesbaynz.com/visit/cyclinghawkesbay. Fit mountain bikers should head to **Eskdale Mountain Bike Park** (www.hawkesbaymtb.co.nz; 3-week permit $7) for a whole lot of fun in the forest. Hire mountain bikes from **Pedal Power** (Map p332; ☎06-844 9771; www.pedalpower.co.nz; 340 Gloucester St; half-/full day from $30/60), just out of the city centre in Taradale.

Given the condusive climate, terrain and multitudinous tracks, it's no surprise that numerous cycle companies pedal their fully geared-up tours around the Bay. These include:

» **Bike About Tours** (☎06-845 4836; www.bikeabouttours.co.nz; half- to full day $35-60)

» **Bike D'Vine** (☎06-833 6697; www.bikedevine.com; adult/child from $45/25)

» **On Yer Bike** (☎06-879 8735; www.onyerbikehb.co.nz; full day without/with lunch $50/60)

» **Takaro Trails** (☎06-836 5385; www.takarotrails.co.nz; half- to full day $55-85)

» **Village Cycle Tours & Hire** (☎06-650 7722; www.villagecycletours.co.nz; half-/full day $40/60)

of the city to **Westshore** (Map p332) or to the surf beaches south of Cape Kidnappers.

Ocean Spa SWIMMING
(Map p334; www.oceanspa.co.nz; 42 Marine Pde; adult/child $9/7, private pools 30min adult/child $12/9; ☺6am-10pm Mon-Sat, 8am-10pm Sun) A spiffy waterfront pool complex that features a lane pool, hot pools, a beauty spa and gym.

Pandora Kayaks KAYAKING
(Map p332; www.pandorakayaks.co.nz; 53 Pandora Rd; kayaks per hr from $14, bikes per day from $30) Situated on the shore of Pandora Pond, these folks hire out kayaks, surfboards, windsurfers, stand-up paddle boards, small yachts and bikes. Windsurfing and sailing lessons available.

Mountain Valley ADVENTURE SPORTS
(☎06-834 9756; www.mountainvalley.co.nz; 408 McVicar Rd, Te Pohue; horse treks from $30, rafting from $60) Sixty kilometres north of Napier on SH5, Mountain Valley is a hub of outdoorsy activities including horse trekking, whitewater rafting, kayaking and fly fishing. There's also accommodation on-site.

☞ Tours

Numerous operators offer tours of the art-deco delights and excursions around the local area.

Absolute de Tours GUIDED TOUR
(☎06-844 8699; www.absolutedetours.co.nz) Runs the 'Deco Tour' of the city, Marewa and Bluff Hill ($38, 75 minutes) in conjunction with the Deco Centre, as well as half-day tours of Napier and Hastings ($60).

Ferg's Fantastic Tours GUIDED TOUR
(☎0800 428 687; www.fergstours.co.nz; tours $40-120) Tours from two to seven hours, exploring Napier and surrounding areas.

Hawke's Bay Scenic Tours GUIDED TOUR
(☎06-844 5693; www.hbscenictours.co.nz; tours $50-90) Five tour options including the 'Napier Whirlwind' and wineries.

Hawke's Bay Wine Country Cat BOAT TOUR
(Map p332; ☎0800 946 322; www.experiencehawkesbay.co.nz; West Quay; cruises $30-70) Schmooze out on a lunch or dinner cruise, or shorter trips morning and afternoon. Also operates the fun, family-friendly Duck tours (one hour adult/child/family $45/30/130), jet boat rides (adult/child $55/30), and winery tours (from $55).

Packard Promenade GUIDED TOUR
(☎06-835 0022; www.packardpromenades.co.nz; tours up to 4 people $140-600) Offers deco and wine tours, in a 1939 Packard Six vintage car.

★★ Festivals & Events

Art Deco Weekend CULTURAL
(www.artdeconapier.com) In the third week of February, Napier and Hastings co-host the sensational Art Deco Weekend. Dinners, picnics, dances, balls, bands and Gatsby-esque fancy dress fill the week with shenanigans, many of which are free. Bertie, Napier's art-deco ambassador, is omnipresent. (See if he'll flex his biceps for you.)

🛏 Sleeping

TOP CHOICE Kennedy Park Top
10 Resort HOLIDAY PARK $
(Map p332; ☎0800 457 275, 06-843 9126; www.kennedypark.co.nz; Storkey St; sites $48, units $89-227; @🌐🏊) Less a campsite and more an entire suburb of holidaymakers, this complex is top dog on the Napier camping scene and winner of many awards. It's the closest campsite to town (2.5km out, southwest of the centre) and has every facility imaginable, although a larger kitchen would be nice.

Criterion Art Deco Backpackers HOSTEL $
(Map p334; ☎06-835 2059; www.criterionartdeco.co.nz; 48 Emerson St; dm $26, s $49-85, d $65-85, tr/q $90/120 all incl continental breakfast; @🌐) If it's interesting architecture and a central location you're after, here you have it. The vast communal area showcases the impressive internal features of what is Napier's best Spanish Mission specimen. Deals for guests in the bar-restaurant downstairs.

Masonic Hotel HOTEL $$
(Map p334; ☎06-835 8689; www.masonic.co.nz; cnr Herschell & Tennyson Sts; s $85-95, d $95-130, tr $120-140; 🌐) The art deco Masonic is arguably the heart of town, its accommodation, restaurants and bars taking up most of a city block. It's undergoing a gradual but much-needed refurb, and is shaping up nicely around its charming old bones. Lovers of heritage hotels will likely fall in love with it, especially once they've experienced the 1st-floor balcony.

Archie's Bunker HOSTEL $
(Map p334; ☎06-833 7990; www.archiesbunker.co.nz; 14 Herschell St; dm/s $24/35, d $60-64; @🌐) One street back from the foreshore, Archie's is a shipshape modern hostel in an old office building. A few of the rooms are windowless, but on the whole this is a well-ventilated, quiet and secure arrangement with friendly owners and bike hire.

Napier YHA HOSTEL $
(Map p334; ☎06-835 7039; www.yha.co.nz; 277 Marine Pde; dm $29-32, s/d $40/70; @🌐) Napier's friendly YHA is housed in a beachfront earthquake survivor with a seemingly endless rabble of rooms. There's a fabulous overhanging reading nook and a sunny rear courtyard. Bob will help with bookings and local info.

Stables Lodge Backpackers HOSTEL $
(Map p334; ☎06-835 6242; www.stableslodge.co.nz; 370 Hastings St; dm $22-28, d $64; @🌐) Formerly an actual stables, this is a friendly place to get off your horse with pot-luck dinners, a barbecue courtyard, murals, resident cats and free internet.

Aqua Lodge HOSTEL $
(Map p334; ☎06-835 4523; aquaback@inhb.co.nz; 53 Nelson Cres; campsites per person $18, dm $26, d $62-76; @🌐🏊) Aqua Lodge sprawls between neighbouring houses on a quiet suburban street, with campsites on the back lawn. It's a fun place, with a wee pool and gardens.

Seaview Lodge B&B B&B $$
(Map p334; ☎06-835 0202; www.aseaviewlodge.co.nz; 5 Seaview Tce; s $130-140, d $170-180; 🌐) This grand Victorian villa (1890) is queen of all she surveys – which is most of the town and a fair bit of ocean. The elegant rooms have tasteful period elements and either bathroom or en suite. It's hard to resist a sunset tipple on the veranda, which opens off the relaxing guest lounge.

Rocks Motorlodge MOTEL $$
(Map p332; ☎06-835 9626; www.therocksmotel.co.nz; 27 Meeanee Quay, Westshore; units $110-180; @🌐) Located just 80m from the beach, the Rocks has corrugated stylings and wood-carving that have raised the bar on Westshore's motel row. Interiors are plush with a colour-splash, and some have a spa bath, others a clawfoot. Free internet, free gym, and laundry.

Sea Breeze B&B $$
(Map p334; ☎06-835 8067; seabreeze.napier@xtra.co.nz; 281 Marine Pde; s $95, d $110-130; 🌐) Inside this Victorian seafront villa are three richly coloured themed rooms (Chinese, Indian and Turkish), decorated with a cornucopia of artefacts and exotic flair.

Manor on Parade B&B $$
(Map p334; ☎06-834 3885; www.manoronparadenapier.co.nz; 283 Marine Pde; d $155-195; 🌐) Comfortable and friendly, this two-storey wooden villa on the waterfront has proved itself a

solid option, having survived the earthquake and in its latter-day incarnation as a B&B. The back room has a sunny deck while at the front are views out to sea.

Green House on the Hill   B&B $$

(Map p334; ✆06-835 4475; www.the-green-house.co.nz; 18b Milton Rd; s/d $110/135; ☞) This meat-free B&B is up a steep hill and rewards with leafy surrounds and city 'n' sea views. The guest floor has one en suite room and one with its own bathroom. Home-baked goodies and fine herbal teas are likely to make an appearance. Free wi-fi most definitely on.

County Hotel   HOTEL $$$

(Map p334; ✆06-835 7800; www.countyhotel.co.nz; 12 Browning St; r/ste $350/488; ☞) There's luxury infused between the masonry at this elegantly restored Edwardian building (a rare brick earthquake survivor). Chambers restaurant breathes refined formality at dinner (mains $30 to $40) while Winston's portrait gazes victoriously over Churchill's Champagne and Snug Bar.

Nautilus   MOTEL $$$

(Map p334; ✆0508 628 845, 06-974 6550; www.nautilusnapier.co.nz; 387 Marine Pde; d $175-225; ☞) A newish hotel and a relatively good bit of architecture, too. Views from every room, kitchenettes, decor with spunk, spa baths, private balconies and an in-house restaurant. Apartments can sleep up to six ($300).

Crown Hotel   HOTEL $$$

(Map p332; ✆06-833 8300; www.thecrownnapier.co.nz; cnr Bridge St & Hardinge Rd, Ahuriri; apt from $200; ☞) The conversion of this 1932 pub into a ritzy apartment-style hotel must have broken a few fishermen's hearts. The new wing may be generically modern but it offers superb ocean views. There's also a gym.

Eating

Napier is strong on cafes, but sketchy when it comes to evening dining. Some of the best food can be found at the Bay's wineries (p344).

Groove Kitchen Espresso   CAFE $

(Map p334; www.groovekitchen.co.nz; 112 Tennyson St; meals $9-19; ☺breakfast & lunch ; ☞) A sophisticated cafe squeezed into small, groovy space where the turntable spins and the kitchen cranks out A1 brunch along with trendsetting wraps, baps and salads, plus ginger gems your granny would be proud of. Killer coffee. With luck you'll be around for one of the intermittent Thursday night gigs.

Kitchen Table   CAFE $

(Map p334; 138 Tennyson St; brunch $8-19; ☺breakfast & lunch; ☞) Sharing an airy gallery space with a local photography studio, this colourful and crafty cafe produces classic modern fare from scones to goat cheese salad. Plenty to inspire, both on the walls and on the menu.

Restaurant Indonesia   INDONESIAN $$

(Map p334; ✆06-835 8303; 409 Marine Pde; mains $20-27; ☺dinner Tue-Sun; ☞) Crammed with Indonesian curios, this intimate space oozes authenticity. Lip-smacking Indo-Dutch *rijst-tafel* smorgasbords are the house speciality (14 dishes, $30 to $36). A romantic option for those inclined. Bookings advisable.

Café Ujazi   CAFE $

(Map p334; 28 Tennyson St; snacks $4-10, meals $9-19; ☞) The most bohemian of the city's cafes, Ujazi folds back its windows and lets the alternative vibe spill out onto the pavement where coffee and conversation carry on all day long. This is a long-established, consistent performer offering blackboard meals and hearty counter food. Try the classic *rewana* special – a big breakfast on traditional Maori bread.

Burger Fuel   BURGERS $

(Map p334; 70 Carlyle St; burgers $9-15; ☞) Big, beautiful burgers that feel like a good square meal, especially if you add a side of fries with aioli and a malted milkshake. Pleasant dine-in experience – a little bit Fonzie, a little bit Prince in *Purple Rain*.

Westshore Fish Café   FISH & CHIPS $

(Map p332; 112a Charles St, Westshore; takeaway $5-8, meals $14-28; ☺lunch Thu-Sun, dinner Tue-Sun) If you're the type who needs cutlery, sit-down meals are served in the dining room. Otherwise grab some of the acclaimed fish and chips and contend with the gulls on the beach.

Kilim Café   TURKISH $

(Map p334; ✆06-835 9100; 193 Hastings St; meals $9-17; ☺11am-late; ☞) Authentic Turkish cuisine in a smart cafe environment, adorned with suitably Ottoman cushions and wall hangings. The kebabby, felafelly, saladly meals are fresh and tasty, which is just as well as the service can be a bit on the sluggish side.

Farmers Market   FARMERS MARKET

(Map p334; Lower Emerson St; ☺8.30am-12.30pm Sat) This is your chance to score super-fresh local produce including fruit, veggies, bread and dairy products.

Drinking & Entertainment

When it comes to nightlife, Napier hedges its bets between the more traditional options downtown, and the strip of brassy restaurant-cum-bars around the shore at Ahuriri. Here you'll find a numer of fairly average establishments tailored to the weekend fun-lovers who flock here, particularly in high summer. Expect barnlike interiors, big screens, nautical themes, open fires, outdoor seating (a highlight) and limited beer options. A definite upside is the possibility of live music, as is the spectacle of excitable people breaking out their best dance moves – there's nothing like a bit of '70s twang-rock to bring folk out of their shell. Ahuriri's best is arguably **Shed 2** (Map p332), followed closely the **Thirsty Whale** (Map p332) and the **Gintrap** (Map p332). Oh, hang on a minute: that's just about all of them.

Napier town's options for an evening out have a bit more character, and are pretty much centred around Hastings St.

Med Bar
BAR
(Map p334; Masonic Hotel, cnr Herschell & Tennyson Sts) Napier's s most civilised bar by a long shot, the Med's warm terracotta tones, tiling and mosaic make for atmosphere plus. Brisk staff, cocktails, good coffee, bistro fare ($24 to $30) and location in the waterfront Masonic Hotel complete the package.

Brazen Head
BAR
(Map p334; 21 Hastings St) Poker machines compromise the vibe at this Irish bar, but the beer's cold and the outdoor deck is a brazen spot to get through a few.

Cabana Bar
LIVE MUSIC
(Map p334; www.cabana.net.nz; 11 Shakespeare Rd) This legendary music venue of the '70s, '80s and '90s died in 1997, but thanks to some forward-thinking, toe-tapping folk, it's risen from the grave to save the day for Napier's gig lovers.

Napier Municipal Theatre
THEATRE
(Map p334; www.napiermunicipaltheatre.co.nz; 119 Tennyson St) Not only the city's largest venue for the likes of concerts, dance and drama, but also one of the world's few working art-deco theatres. Worth going for the foyer lighting alone. Box office on-site.

Globe Theatrette
CINEMA
(Map p332; www.globenapier.co.nz; 15 Hardinge Rd, Ahuriri) A vision in purple, this boutique cinema screens art-house flicks in a sumptuous cinema lounge with ready access to upmarket snacks.

 # Shopping

Although a relatively small town centre, Napier has plenty of interesting, independent retailers stocking a surprisingly diverse range of goods. Antiques, unsurprisingly, are in reasonable supply, although for a thorough trawl pick up the free *Hawke's Bay Antique Trail* brochure from the i-SITE. Instant gratification can be found at **Decorum** (Map p334; www.decorum-napier.com; cnr Tennyson & Herschell Sts), especially if you like crazy clothing from a bygone era.

Art and craft galleries are listed in another free brochure, the *Hawke's Bay Art Guide*, published annually.

For all-natural snugly gear, head straight to **Opossum World** (Map p334; 157 Marine Pde), or to **Classic Sheepskins** (Map p332; 22 Thames St) on the edge of the city centre.

Bookworms should wriggle into **Beattie & Forbes** (Map p334; www.beattieandforbes.co.nz; 70 Tennyson St), a long-standing independent, strong on NZ titles.

 # Information

Banks cluster around the corner of Hastings and Emerson Sts, with ATMs scattered throughout the centre. Internet access is available at the i-SITE and several cafes in the city.

DOC (06-834 3111; www.doc.govt.co.nz; 59 Marine Pde; 9am-4.15pm Mon-Fri) Maps, advice and passes.

Napier Health Centre (06-878 8109; 76 Wellesley Rd; 24hr)

Napier i-SITE (06-834 1911; www.napiercity.co.nz; 100 Marine Pde; 9am-5pm; @) Handy and helpful.

Napier Police Station (06-831 0700; Station St; 24hr)

Napier Post Office (151 Hastings St)

Getting There & Away

Air

Hawke's Bay Airport (06-835 3427; www.hawkesbay-airport.co.nz) is 8km north of the city.

Air New Zealand (06-833 5400; www.airnewzealand.co.nz; cnr Hastings & Station Sts) Daily direct flights to Auckland (from $89), Wellington (from $79) and Christchurch (from $129).

Sunair Aviation (0800 786 247; www.sunair.co.nz) Offers direct flights on weekdays between Napier and Gisborne ($280) with connections to other select North Island towns.

Bus

InterCity (www.intercity.co.nz) buses can be booked online or at the i-SITE, and depart from the **Dalton St Bus Stop**. Services run daily to Auckland (from $51, seven hours) via Taupo (from $18, two hours), Gisborne ($30, four hours) via Wairoa (from $13, 2½ hours), and Wellington (from $22, 5½ hours) via Waipukurau (from $13, one hour), plus four daily services to Hastings (from $18, 30 minutes).

If you're super-organised you can take advantage of $1 advance fares on **Naked Bus** (www.nakedbus.com) on the Auckland–Wellington route via Hastings and Taupo.

❶ Getting Around

Most key sights in the city are reachable on foot, or you can speed things up by hiring a bicycle from Fishbike (p336).

Bus

goBay (☑06-878 9250; www.hbrc.govt.nz) runs the local bus service, covering Napier, Hastings, Havelock North and thereabouts. There are ample services between the main centres Monday to Friday, including three different routes between Napier and Hastings (adult/child $4.50/2.50) taking between 30 minutes (express) and 55 minutes (all stops). Buses depart from the Dalton St Bus Stop.

Car

Conveniently, **Napier Airport Car Rental** (☑0800 556 606; www.napierairportcarehire.co.nz) acts as agent for 10 car-hire companies including the big brands and local outfits. **Rent-a-Dent** (☑06-834 0688; www.napiercarrentals.co.nz) is locally owned and based at the airport.

Taxi

A city-to-airport taxi ride will cost you around $22. **Napier Taxis** (☑06-835 7777) **Super Shuttle** (☑0800 748 885; www.supershuttle.co.nz)

Hastings & Around

POP 66,100

Positioned at the centre of the Hawke's Bay fruit bowl, bustling Hastings is the commercial hub of the region, 20km south of Napier. A few kilometres of orchards still separate it from Havelock North, with its prosperous village atmosphere and the towering backdrop of Te Mata Peak.

◉ Sights & Activities

As with Napier, Hastings was similarly devastated by the 1931 earthquake and also boasts some fine art deco and Spanish Mission buildings, built in the aftermath. Main street highlights include the **Westerman's Building** (Map p341; cnr Russell & Heretaunga St E, Hastings), arguably the Bay's best example of the Spanish Mission style, although there are many other architectural gems if you cast your eye around. The i-SITE stocks the *Art Deco Hastings* brochure ($2), detailing two self-guided walks of the CBD.

FREE **Hastings City Art Gallery**   GALLERY
(Map p341; www.hastingscityartgallery.co.nz; 201 Eastbourne St E, Hastings; ☉10am-4.30pm) The city's gallery presents contemporary NZ and international art in a pleasant, purpose-built space.

Te Mata Peak   PARK
Rising melodramatically from the Heretaunga Plains, Te Mata Peak, 16km south of Havelock North, is part of the 98-hectare **Te Mata Trust Park** (Map p332). The road to the 399m summit passes sheep trails, rickety fences and vertigo-inducing stone escarpments cowled in a bleak, lunar-meets-Scottish-Highland atmosphere. The **lookout** (Map p332) still awaits its makeover, but it's really all about the views which – on a clear day – fall away to Hawke Bay, Mahia Peninsula and distant Mt Ruapehu.

The view of Te Mata is also extraordinary. To local Maori this is the sleeping giant Te Mata O Rongokako. From the fields around Havelock North, a little imagination will conjure up the giant, lying on his back with his head to the right. The park's network of trails offers walks from 30 minutes to two hours. Our pick is the Peak Trail for views, but all are detailed in the *Te Mata Trust Park* brochure available from local visitor centres.

Splash Planet   SWIMMING
(Map p332; www.splashplanet.co.nz; Grove Rd, Hastings; adult/child $26/18; ☉10am-5.30pm Nov-Feb) This massive complex has plenty of pools, slides and aquatic excitement.

Airplay Paragliding   PARAGLIDING
(☑06-845 1977; www.airplay.co.nz) Te Mata Peak is a paragliding hotspot, with voluminous updraughts offering exhilarating whooshes through the air. Airplay Paragliding has tandem paragliding ($140) and full-day beginners' courses (from $180).

Hastings

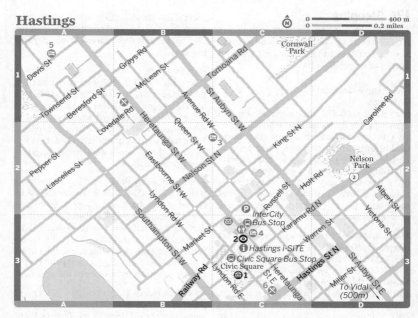

👉 Tours

Long Island Guides
GUIDED TOURS

(✆06-874 7877; www.longislandtoursnz.com; half-day from $180) Customised and personalised tours across a wide range of interests including Maori culture, bushwalks, kayaking, horse riding and, inevitably, food and wine.

Te Hakakino
CULTURAL TOUR

(✆021 057 0935; www.waimaramaori.com; 2-3hr tours $60-120) Guided tours of a historic hill fortress revealing archaeological remains and cultural insights en route.

Early Morning Balloons
BALLOONING

(✆06-879 4229; www.hotair.co.nz; per person $345) Provides inflated views over grapey Hawke's Bay.

Wine Tours

The majority of tours in this part of the world are focused on wine. Plenty of operators offer self-guided cycle tours (p336) of the vines, but there are also plenty of motorised options, usually by minibus, lasting three to seven hours and starting at $60 per person.

» **Bay Tours & Charters**
(✆06-845 2736; www.baytours.co.nz)

» **Grape Escape**
(✆0800 100 489; www.grapeescape.net.nz)

Hastings

◎ Sights
1 Hastings City Art Gallery C3
2 Westerman's Building C3

🛏 Sleeping
3 Gloucester House Motel C2
4 Rotten Apple C3
5 Sleeping Giant A1

🍴 Eating
6 Opera Kitchen C3
7 Rush Munro's B1

» **Odyssey NZ**
(✆0508 639 773; www.odysseynz.com)
» **Prinsy's**
(✆06-845 3703; www.prinsyexperience.co.nz)
» **Vince's World of Wine**
(✆06-836 6705; www.vincestours.co.nz)

✨ Festivals & Events

Hastings Blossom Festival
CULTURAL

(✆06-878 9447; www.blossomfestival.co.nz) The Hastings Blossom Festival, a petalled spring fling, happens in the second half of September, with parades, arts, crafts and visiting artists.

🛏 Sleeping

Much of the superior accommodation lies outside the city's confines. As for Hastings' hostels, you'll have to fight for your bed with hordes of seasonal workers.

TOP CHOICE Clive Colonial Cottages
RENTAL HOUSES $$

(Map p332; 📞06-870 1018; www.clivecolonialcot tages.co.nz; 198 School Rd, Clive; d from $135; 🛜) Two minutes walk to the beach and almost equidistant from Hastings, Napier and Havelock, these three purpose-built character cottages sit around a courtyard garden on a two-acre garden property. Pleasant communal areas include barbecue, games room and pétanque court. Bikes on-site; trail on doorstep.

Mangapapa Petit Hotel
BOUTIQUE HOTEL $$$

(Map p332; 📞06-878 3234; www.mangapapa.co.nz; 466 Napier Rd, Havelock North; d incl breakfast $450-1500; @🛜) Five minutes' drive from Hastings, this large heritage home (1885), surrounded by leafy gardens, a tennis court, swimming pool and short golf course, has been sympathetically adapted into a boutique hotel. Twelve suites offer period-style luxury; a restaurant and day spa up the indulgence factor.

Hastings Top 10 Holiday Park
HOLIDAY PARK $

(Map p332; 📞06-878 6692; www.hastingstop10. co.nz; 610 Windsor Ave, Hastings; sites $42, units $78-145; @🛜🏊) Putting the 'park' back into holiday park, within its leafy confines are sycamore hedges, a topiary 'welcome' sign, stream, ducks and plenty of serenity. New pool and spa complex will satisfy young and old.

Gloucester House Motel
MOTEL $$

(Map p341; 📞06-876 3741; www.gloucesterhouse motel.co.nz; 404 Avenue Rd W, Hastings; units $99-125; 🛜🏊) Picket fences and colourful roses welcome you to this spick-and-span motel, five minutes' walk from the centre of town. The 11 units are spotlessly clean and spacious, with kitchen facilities and separate lounge-dining areas. Cool off with a dip in the pool.

Sleeping Giant
HOSTEL $

(Map p341; 📞06-878 5393; sleepinggiant@ xtra.co.nz; 109 Davis St, Hastings; dm/tw/d $20/50/60; 🛜) A comfy backpackers in a suburban street, 10 minutes walk to town. A posse of tanned, wiry agricultural workers ensures an atmosphere of laid-back sociability, in the fairly close communal confines of lounge and courtyard where the odd barbecue takes place. Off-street parking is available.

Rotten Apple
HOSTEL $

(Map p341; 📞06-878 4363; www.rottenapple.co.nz; 114 Heretaunga St E, Hastings; dm $26, s/d $50/70; 🛜) The central city option and a fairly fruity affair with a few orchard workers settled in paying keen weekly rates. Flat-screen telly, a bit of balcony, decent kitchen, sociable vibe – all good things for Rotten Apple turnover. Free evening parking.

Arataki Holiday Park
HOLIDAY PARK $

(Map p332; 📞06-877 7479; www.aratakiholiday park.co.nz; 139 Arataki Rd, Havelock North; sites from $20, caravan from $60, cabins $70, units from $130; 🛜🏊) This place has seen better days, probably way back before the suburbs arrived. That said, if you like colourful, cheap, old-fashioned campsites, Arataki will do the trick if you want to be close to the action.

Havelock North Motor Lodge
MOTEL $$

(Map p332; 📞06-877 8627; www.havelocknorth motorlodge.co.nz; 7 Havelock Rd, Havelock North; units $135-195; @🛜) Smack-bang in the middle of Havelock North, this modern motel is a cut above the rest. Tidy one- and two-bedroom units feature spa baths, Sky TV and kitchenettes.

Millar Road
RENTAL HOUSES $$$

(Map p332; 📞06-875 1977; www.millarroad.co.nz; 83 Millar Rd; villa $600, house $950; 🛜🏊) Set in the Tuki Tuki Hills with vineyard and bay views, Millar Road is architecturally heaven-sent. Two plush villas (each sleep four) and a super-stylish house (sleeps up to eight) are filled with NZ-made furniture and local artworks. Explore the 20-hectare grounds or look cool by the communal pool.

🍴 Eating

It is the wineries and artisan food producers we have to thank for this area's culinary highlights, which include some particularly fine vineyard lunches (p344), ice cream, and a perplexing amount of pickle.

Opera Kitchen
CAFE $$

(Map p341; 312 Eastbourne St E, Hastings; snacks $5-7, meals $9-22; ⏱breakfast & lunch; 🍴) This modern and stylish cafe has an interesting menu including healthy brekkie options, such as granola and fruit compote. For the less calorie-conscious, the farmer's breakfast is a real winner, too. Heavenly baked goods, great coffee and snappy staff round things out nicely. Eat in or outside in the suntrap courtyard.

Deliciosa
TAPAS $$

(Map p332; ✆06-877 6031; 21 Napier Rd, Havelock North; tapas $8-17; ⊘4pm-late Mon-Wed, 11am-late Thu-Sat) Great things come in small packages at this intimate tapas bar with a rosy glow. The menu has almost as many influences as the United Nations, as duck rillette battles Lebanese seven-spice beef and Waldorf salad. Luckily for diners, flare in the kitchen and great local ingredients keep the peace.

BJs Bakery
BAKERY $

(Map p332; 12 Havelock Road, Havelock North; pies $3-5; ✐) This outpost of one of the Bay's biggest bakeries is stacked with handsome cakes and sandwiches as well as arguably the region's best pies. It also offers hot meals, good espresso, wine if you fancy it, a pleasant environment, and whip-cracking service.

Diva
MODERN NZ $$

(Map p332; ✆06-877 5149; 1/10 Napier Rd, Havelock North; meals $12-32; ⊘lunch Tue-Fri, dinner Tue-Sat) The most happening place in Havelock, Diva offers good-value lunch (from fish and chips to Caesar salad) and a bistro-style menu featuring fresh seafood and seasonal specialities. Eating is divided between flash dining room and groovy bar (snacks from $6), plus lively pavement tables.

Pipi
PIZZERIA $$

(Map p332; ✆06-877 8993; 16 Joll Rd, Havelock North; mains $16-24; ⊘4-10pm Tue-Sun; ✐) Shockingly pink with candy stripes and mismatched furniture, Pipi cheekily thumbs its nose at small-town conventionality. The food focus is on simple pasta dishes and Roman-style thin-crusted pizza.

Bay Espresso
CAFE $

(Map p332; 141 Karamu Rd, Hastings; snacks & lunches $6-19; ⊘7am-4pm; ✐) An easy pit stop on the main road, this enduringly popular cafe serves up house-roasted organic coffee as well as handsome counter food and reasonable brunch, best enjoyed in the sunny courtyard out back.

Rush Munro's
ICE CREAM $

(Map p341; 704 Heretaunga St W, Hastings; ice cream $3-8) Rush Munro's is a Hastings icon, serving up locally made ice cream since 1926.

Hastings Farmers Market
FARMERS MARKET

(Map p332; Showgrounds, Kenilworth Rd; ⊘8.30am-12.30pm Sun) If you're around on Sunday, the Hastings market is not to be missed. Bring an empty stomach, cash and a roomy shopping bag.

Drinking

Few standout options exist beyond the winery gates.

Rose & Shamrock
PUB

(Map p332; cnr Napier Rd & Porter Dr, Havelock North) A carpeted, dark-wood, British-style boozer complete with a few British brews on tap and hearty pub grub (mains $14 to $26). Occasional live music on Saturday nights.

Loading Ramp
PUB

(Map p332; 6 Treachers Lane, Havelock North; ⊘3pm-late) This lofty timber space pulls a mixed crowd of young 'uns up to high jinks, especially on the weekends when the queue can stretch well down the road. Also offers pub-style meals.

Filter Room
BREWERY

(Map p332; www.hbib.co.nz; Awatoto Rd, Meeanee; ⊘10am-5pm Sun-Thu, 10am-7pm Fri & Sat) Surrounded by orchards, these folk offer a large range of craft beers and ciders, all brewed on-site, plus a great-value $15 tasting tray and tummy-filling food.

Shopping

The Hastings area appears to exist largely for the satisfaction of our appetites. Beyond a great big bunch of wineries (p344), there is a plethora of boutique food producers, of which the following are just a few:

Arataki Honey
FOOD

(Map p332; www.aratakihoney.co.nz; 66 Arataki Rd, Havelock North; ⊘9am-5pm) Stock up on buzzy by-products for your toast or your skin. There are family-fun, hands-on displays outlining the whole sticky cycle from flower to jar.

Hohepa Organic Cheeses
FOOD

(Map p332; www.hohepa.com; 363 Main Rd, Clive; ⊘9am-5pm Mon-Fri, 9.30am-2.30pm Sat) Part of a Steiner-based community of people with intellectual disabilities, this shop sells local produce, including cheese (made on-site), biodynamic fruit and vegetables, candles and clothing.

HAWKE'S BAY WINERIES

Once upon a time, this district was most famous for its orchards. Today it's vines that have top billing, with Hawke's Bay now NZ's second-largest wine-producing region. A bunch of grapes are grown around Havelock North and the Tuki Tuki River, by the coast at Te Awanga, and in the stony Gimblett Gravels west of Flaxmere. Between them they produce some excellent Bordeaux-style reds, syrah and chardonnay.

Best Wining & Dining

» **Vidal** (Map p332; ☑06-872 7440; www.vidal.co.nz; 913 St Aubyn St, Hastings; lunch mains $20-30, dinner mains $28-39; ☺11.30am-late) There's nothing pedestrian about this winery restaurant despite being tucked into the backstreets of suburban Hastings. The warm, wood-lined dining room is a worthy setting for the elegant food. The pancetta and tarragon roasted baby chicken was a summer highlight.

» **Elephant Hill** (Map p332; ☑06-872 6060; www.elephanthill.co.nz; 86 Clifton Rd, Te Awanga; mains $32-38; ☺11am-10pm) Ubermodern winery with edgy architecture, and food, wine and service to rival the stunning sea views; we went quackers over the duck tasting plate. At night, enjoy an aperitif or dessert in the slinky sunken bar.

» **Terrôir at Craggy Range** (Map p332; ☑06-873 0143; www.craggyrange.com; 253 Waimarama Rd, Havelock North; mains $37-40; ☺lunch Mon-Sun, dinner Mon-Sat) Housed in a cathedral-like 'wine barrel', Terrôir is one of the region's most consistent fine-dining experiences. Impressive views of Te Mata peak from the terrace.

A Taste of the Tastings

Cellar doors are open for tastings throughout the summer, with shorter hours in winter. Tastings are generally free, but there's a small charge at some (refundable on purchase). Pick up the *Hawke's Bay Winery Guide*, or download it from www.winehawkesbay.co.nz.

» **Black Barn Vineyards** (Map p332; ☑06-877 7985; www.blackbarn.com; Black Barn Rd, Havelock North) Bistro, gallery, popular Saturday growers market and an amphitheatre.

» **Brookfields** (Map p332; www.brookfieldsvineyards.co.nz; 376 Brookfields Rd, Meeanee) Excellent reds. The 'sun-dried' malbec is a delicious rendition of Italy's amarone.

» **Church Road** (Map p332; www.churchroad.co.nz; 150 Church Rd, Taradale) Winery and museum tours (11am and 2pm).

» **Clearview Estate Winery** (Map p332; ☑06-875 0150; www.clearviewestate.co.nz; 194 Clifton Rd, Te Awanga) Award-winning wines, quality restaurant, relaxed and family-friendly.

» **Crab Farm Winery** (☑06-836 6678; www.crabfarmwinery.co.nz; 511 Main North Rd, Bay View; ☺10am-5pm Fri-Sun, 6pm-late Fri) Decent, reasonably priced wines and a great cafe.

» **Esk Valley Estate** (Map p332; www.eskvalley.co.nz; 745 Main North Rd, Bay View) Excellent Bordeaux-style reds, chardonnay and riesling.

» **Mission Estate** (Map p332; ☑06-845 9354; www.missionestate.co.nz; 198 Church Rd, Napier) NZ's oldest winery; beautiful grounds and restaurant housed within a restored seminary.

» **Ngatarawa** (Map p332; www.ngatarawa.co.nz; 305 Ngatarawa Rd, Bridge Pa) Historic stables with rustic cellar door and picnicking opportunities.

» **Salvare** (Map p332; www.salvare.co.nz; 403 Ngatarawa Rd, Bridge Pa) Small winery punching well above its weight in terms of wine and cellar-door experience.

» **Sileni Estates** (Map p332; www.sileni.co.nz; 2016 Maraekakaho Rd, Bridge Pa) Wine, cheese, chocolate and charming cellar-door experience.

» **Te Awa** (Map p332; ☑06-879 7602; www.teawa.com; 2375 SH50) Casually stylish winery and a good lunch option, where the kids can come too.

» **Te Mata Estate** (Map p332; www.temata.co.nz; 349 Te Mata Rd, Havelock North) Legendary Coleraine red and Elston chardonnay.

» **Trinity Hill** (Map p332; www.trinityhill.com; 2396 SH50) Sip serious reds and top-ranking chardonnay at this baroque-industrial cellar door.

Silky Oak Chocolate Company　FOOD
(Map p332; www.silkyoakchocs.co.nz; 1131 Links Rd, Waiohiki; ⊙9am-5pm Mon-Thu, to 4pm Fri, 10am-4pm Sat & Sun) Watch the chocolatiers at work while deliberating over mouth-watering truffles and chocolate rugby balls. The museum (adult/child $8/5) offers a chocolate-drenched history and the odd ancient Mayan artefact. There's a cafe next door.

Strawberry Patch　FOOD
(Map p332; www.strawberrypatch.co.nz; 76 Havelock Rd, Havelock North; ⊙9am-5.30pm) Pick your own berries in season, and call in all year round for fresh produce, picnic supplies and real fruit ice cream.

Telegraph Hill　FOOD
(Map p332; www.telegraphhill.co.nz; 1279 Howard St, Hastings; ⊙9am-5pm Mon-Fri, 10am-3pm Sat) A small producer of olives, oils and all sorts of Mediterranean-influenced gourmet treats. Four-person picnic baskets ($30) available for on-site indulgence.

❶ Information

Hastings i-SITE (☑06-873 0080; www.hastings.co.nz; cnr Russell St & Heretaunga St E; ⊙8.30am-5pm Mon-Fri, 9am-4pm Sat, to 3pm Sun; ◉) Internet access, free maps, trail brochures and bookings.

Havelock North Information Centre (☑06-877 9600; www.havelocknorthnz.com; cnr Te Aute & Middle Rds, Havelock North; ⊙10am-4pm Mon-Fri, to 2pm Sat & Sun) Information, bike hire and more.

Hawke's Bay Hospital (☑06-878 8109; Omahu Rd)

Police Station (☑06-873 0500; Railway Rd)

Post Office (cnr Market St & Heretaunga St W)

❶ Getting There & Away

Napier's Hawke's Bay Airport (p339) is a 20-minute drive away. **Air New Zealand** (☑06-873 2200; www.airnewzealand.co.nz; 117 Heretaunga St W) has an office in central Hastings.

The **InterCity Bus Stop** is on Russell St. Book **InterCity** (☑06-835 4326; www.intercity.co.nz) and **Naked Bus** (www.nakedbus.com) buses online or at the i-SITE.

❶ Getting Around

goBay (p340) runs the local bus service, covering Napier, Hastings, Havelock North and thereabouts. There are ample daily services between the main centres including three different routes between Napier and Hastings taking between 30 minutes (express) and 55 minutes (all stops). Buses depart from the **Civic Square Bus Stop**.

Fares are up to adult/child $4.50/2.50. Services between Hastings and Havelock North run from Monday to Saturday (adult/child $3/2, 35 minutes). Signal the driver and pay on the bus.

Hastings Taxis (☑06-878 5055) is the local cab service.

Cape Kidnappers

From mid-September to late April, Cape Kidnappers (named when local Maori tried to kidnap Cook's Tahitian servant boy) erupts with squawking gannets. These big birds usually nest on remote islands but here they settle for the mainland, completely unfazed by human spectators.

The birds nest as soon as they arrive, and eggs take about six weeks to hatch, with chicks arriving in early November. In March the gannets start their migration; by May they're gone.

Early November to late February is the best time to visit. Take a tour or the walkway to the colony: it's about five hours return from the Clifton Reserve car park (parking $3), located at the Clifton Motor Camp. You'll find interesting cliff formations, rock pools, a sheltered picnic spot, and the birds themselves. The walk is tide dependent. Leave no earlier than three hours after high tide; start back no later than 1½ hours after low tide.

No regular buses go to Clifton, but the tour operators below will transport you for an additional fee, or you could bike (p336).

Refreshments out this way can be had at the pleasant **Clifton Bay Café** (Map p332; 468 Clifton Rd; meals $12-25; ⊙10am-4pm), a breezy place for a meal before or after you run the gannet gauntlet.

☞ Tours

All trips depart according to tide times; the region's i-SITEs and individual operators have schedules.

TOP CHOICE **Gannet Beach Adventures**　ECOTOUR
(Map p332; ☑0800 426 638; www.gannets.com; adult/child/family $39/24/95) Ride along the beach on a tractor-pulled trailer before wandering out on the Cape for 90 minutes. A great, guided return trip of four hours, departing from Clifton Reserve.

Gannet Safaris　ECOTOUR
(Map p332; ☑0800 427 232; www.gannetsafaris.co.nz; Summerlee Station; adult/child $60/30)

Overland 4WD trips across farmland into the gannet colony. Three-hour tours depart at 9.30am and 1.30pm. Also operate small-group Wilderness Safaris (www.kidnapperssafaris.co.nz) heading behind the vermin-proof fence into the conservation zone.

Central Hawke's Bay

Grassy farmland stretches south from Hastings, dotted with the grand homesteads of Victorian pastoralists. It's an untouristed area, rich in history and deserted beaches. Waipukurau (aka 'Wai-puk'), the main town, isn't exactly thrilling but it's worth calling in to the extremely helpful **Central Hawke's Bay Information Centre** (☑06-858 6488; www.centralhawkesbay.co.nz; Railway Esp; ⊙9am-5pm Mon-Fri, to 1pm Sat) in the old railway station. It can sort you out with the comprehensive *Experience Central Hawke's Bay* brochure and pamphlets outlining heritage trails and DOC reserves and walkways.

◉ Sights

There are no fewer than six windswept and interesting beaches along the coast here: **Kairakau**, **Mangakuri**, **Pourerere**, **Aramoana**, **Blackhead** and **Porangahau**. The first five are good for swimming, and between the lot they offer a range of sandy, salty activities including surfing, fishing, and driftwoody, rock-pooly adventures. Between Aramoana and Blackhead Beach lies the **Te Angiangi Marine Reserve** – bring your snorkel.

It's a nondescript hill in the middle of nowhere, but the place with the world's second-longest name is good for a photo op. **Taumatawhakatangihangakoauauotamateaturipukakapikimaungahoronukupokaiwhenuakitanatahu** is actually the abbreviated form of 'The Brow of a Hill Where Tamatea, the Man with the Big Knees, Who Slid, Climbed, and Swallowed Mountains, Known as Land Eater, Played his Flute to his Brother'. To get there, fuel-up in Waipukurau and drive 40km to the Mangaorapa junction on route 52. Turn left and go 4km towards Porangahau. At the intersection with the signposts, turn right and continue 4.3km to the sign.

Ongaonga, an historic village 16km west of Waipawa, has interesting Victorian and Edwardian buildings. Pick up a pamphlet for a self-guided walking tour from the information centre in Waipukurau.

The **Central Hawke's Bay Settlers Museum** (www.chbsettlersmuseum.co.nz; 23 High St; $2; ⊙10am-4pm) in **Waipawa** has pioneer artefacts, informative 'homestead' displays and a good specimen of a river *waka* (canoe).

🛏 Sleeping & Eating

Lochlea Backpacker Farmstay   FARMSTAY $
(☑06-855 4816; 344 Lake Rd, Wanstead; campsites from $23, dm/d/q $26/60/106; ☒) As far removed from urban stress as possible, this idyllic farm has breezy stands of trees on grazing slopes. Rooms are simple but the communal lounge is cosy. There's a pool, tennis court and endless paddocks to wander.

Gwavas Garden Homestead   B&B $$$
(☑06-856 5810; www.gwavasgarden.co.nz; 5740 SH50, Tikokino; d incl breakfast $245-285; ☎) Six kilometres from Tikokino, this grand old 1890 homestead has enjoyed a faithful room-by-room renovation with pretty floral wallpaper, period furnishings and divine linens. Enjoy breakfast on the veranda before a spot of lawn tennis or a wander through the internationally renowned 9-hectare 'Cornish' garden.

Misty River Café   CAFE $$
(12 High Street, Waipawa; mains $14-20; ⊙9am-4pm Wed-Sun) A little bit of continental chic on the functional high street, this darling cafe makes lip-smacking salads as well as fresh ham, pasta, nachos and other global favourites. Drop-dead-gorgeous baking.

Paper Mulberry Café   CAFE $
(SH2, Pukehou; meals $8-17; ⊙7am-4pm Thu-Mon) Halfway between Waipukurau and Hastings, this rustic cafe and art gallery serves excellent coffee and home-style food (and yummy fudge). Well worth a stop for a chomp and a shop.

Oruawharo   CAFE $$
(☑06-855 8274; www.oruawharo.com; 379 Oruawharo Rd, Takapau; morning and afternoon tea $15, lunch $20-25) One of the area's rural mansions, Oruawharo (1879) is a grand setting for high tea or lunch served on fine bone china. Call ahead for sittings.

❶ Getting There & Away

InterCity (www.intercity.co.nz) and **Naked Bus** (www.nakedbus.com) pass through Waipawa and Waipukurau on their Wellington–Napier routes.

Kaweka & Ruahine Ranges

The remote Kaweka and Ruahine ranges separate Hawke's Bay from the Central Plateau. These forested wildernesses offer some of the North Island's best tramping. See the DOC pamphlets *Kaweka Forest Park & Puketitiri Reserves* and *Eastern Ruahine Forest Park* for details of tracks and huts.

An ancient Maori track, now know as the **Gentle Annie Road**, runs inland from Omahu near Hastings to Taihape, via Otamauri and Kuripapango (where there is a basic but charming DOC campsite, $5). The route is scenic and will take around three hours.

Kaweka J, the highest point of the range (1724m), can be reached by a three-to-five-hour tramp from the end of Kaweka Rd; from Napier take Puketitiri Rd then Whittle Rd. The drive is worthwhile in itself; it's partly unsealed and takes three hours return.

Enjoy a soak in natural hot pools before or after the three-hour walk on **Te Puia Track**, which follows the picturesque **Mohaka River**. From Napier, take Puketitiri Rd, then Pakaututu Rd, then Makahu Rd to the road-end **Mangatutu Hot Pools**.

The Mokaha can be rafted with **Mohaka Rafting** (☑027 825 8539, 06-839 1808; www.mohakarafting.com; from $75).

Wellington Region

Best Places to Eat

» Ortega Fish Shack (p364)

» Trio Café at Coney Winery (p377)

» Moore Wilson Fresh (p367)

» Logan Brown (p365)

» Scopa (p365)

» Schoc Chocolates (p379)

Best Places to Stay

» YHA Wellington City (p360)

» Ohtel (p360)

» Martinborough Top 10 Holiday Park (p377)

» Moana Lodge (p360)

Why Go?

If your New Zealand travels thus far have been all about the great outdoors and sleepy rural towns, Wellington will blow the cobwebs away. Art-house cinemas, funky boutiques, hip bars, live-music venues and lashings of restaurants – all can be found in the 'cultural capital'.

As the crossing point between the North and South Islands, travellers have long been passing through these parts. Te Papa and Zealandia now stop visitors in their tracks, and even a couple of days' pause will reveal myriad other attractions, including a beautiful harbour and walkable waterfront, hillsides clad in pretty weatherboard houses, ample inner-city surprises, and some of the freshest city air on the planet.

Less than an hour away to the north, the Kapiti Coast offers more settled weather and a beachy vibe, with Kapiti Island nature reserve a highlight. An hour away over the Rimutaka Range, the Wairarapa farm plains are dotted with sweet towns and famed wineries, hemmed in by a wind-swept coastline.

When to Go

'You can't beat Wellington on a good day', they say, and such days are a lot more frequent than you might think. For while the nickname 'Windy Welly' is justly deserved, Wellington's climate is largely pleasant, and the Kapiti Coast and Wairarapa are even better.

November to April are the warmer months, with average maximums hovering around 20°C. From May to August it's colder and wetter – daily temperatures lurk around 12°C. No matter: there's plenty to do indoors.

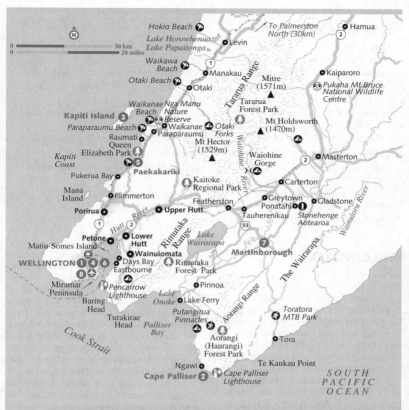

WELLINGTON REGION

Wellington Region Highlights

1 Getting interactive at NZ's finest museum, Wellington's **Te Papa** (p358)

2 Scaling the lighthouse steps on wild and remote **Cape Palliser** (p378)

3 Meeting real live kiwi on a **Kapiti Island** night-time walk (p375)

4 Exploring the capital's creative side on **Cuba Street**

5 Rambling the dunes of **Queen Elizabeth Park** (p373) near beachy Paekakariki

6 Riding the ratchety **cable car** (p355) from Lambton Quay to the leafy **Wellington Botanic Gardens** (p355)

7 Maintaining a straight line on your bicycle as you tour the picturesque **Martinborough wineries** (p**378**)

8 Discovering the joys of NZ single-track on the trails of **Makara Peak Mountain Bike Park** (p357)

ⓘ Getting There & Around

Wellington is the North Island port for the inter-island ferries. Long-distance **Tranz Scenic** (☏ 0800 872 467, 04-495 0775; www.tranz scenic.co.nz) trains run from Wellington to Auckland via Palmerston North. Wellington Airport is serviced by international and domestic airlines.

InterCity (☏ 04-385 0520; www.intercity. co.nz) is the main North Island bus company, trav-

elling just about everywhere. Approaching Wellington city from the north, you'll pass through either the Kapiti Coast to the west via State Hwy1 (SH1), or the Wairarapa and heavily populated Hutt Valley to the east via State Hwy2 (SH2).

Getting into and out of Wellington on regional trains and buses is a breeze. Metlink (p372) is the one-stop-shop for regional transport services, from Wellington to the Kapiti Coast and the Wairarapa.

ESSENTIAL WELLINGTON

» **Eat** yourself silly: Wellington has a gut-busting number of great cafes and restaurants; bring trousers with an elasticated waistband

» **Drink** in pursuit of hoppiness at one of Wellington's numerous craft beer bars

» **Read** the moving, sometimes rousing literary sculptures along the waterfront's Writers Walk

» **Listen** to Radio Active (88.6FM, www.radioactive.co.nz), for loads of Kiwi music and local banter

» **Watch** 'Golden Days' – the frenetic short film screened non-stop at Te Papa (p358)

» **Festival** Summer City (p359) – free fun in the sun, *in theory*

» **Go green** Check out rare NZ wildlife at Zealandia (p357), Wellington's mainland 'conservation island'

» **Online** www.wellingtonnz.com, www.naturecoast.co.nz, www.wairarapanz.com; www.lonelyplanet.com/new-zealand/wellington

» **Area code** ✆04

WELLINGTON

POP 199,200 (CITY), 393,400 (REGION)

A small city with a big reputation, Wellington is most famous for being NZ's capital. It is *infamous* for its weather, particularly the gale-force winds wont to barrel through, wrecking umbrellas and obliterating hairdos. It also lies on a major fault line. And negotiating the inner-city one-way system is like the Krypton Factor on acid.

But don't be deterred. 'Welly' is a wonderful city, voted 'the coolest little capital in the world' in Lonely Planet's *Best in Travel* (2011). For a starter it's lovely to look at, draped around bushy hillsides encircling a magnificent harbour. There are super lookouts on hilltops, golden sand on the prom, and spectacular craggy shores along the south coast. Downtown, the city is compact and vibrant, buoyed by a surprising number of museums, theatres, galleries and boutiques. A cocktail- and caffeine-fuelled hospitality scene fizzes and pops among the throng.

History

Maori legend has it that the explorer Kupe was first to discover Wellington harbour. Wellington's original Maori name was Te Whanganui-a-Tara (great harbour of Tara), named after the son of a chief named Whatonga who had settled on the Hawke's Bay coast. Whatonga sent Tara and his halfbrother to explore the southern part of the North Island. When they returned over a year later, their reports were so favourable that Whatonga's followers moved there, founding the Ngati Tara tribe.

The first European settlers arrived in the New Zealand Company's ship *Aurora* on 22 January 1840, not long after Colonel William Wakefield arrived to buy land from the Maori. However, Maori denied they had sold the land at Port Nicholson, or Poneke as they called it, as it was founded on hasty and illegal buying by the New Zealand Company. As in many parts of NZ, land rights struggles ensued, and would plague the country for years to come.

By 1850 Wellington was a thriving settlement of around 5500 people, despite a lack of flat land. Originally the waterfront was along Lambton Quay, but reclamation of parts of the harbour began in 1852. In 1855 a significant earthquake razed many parts of Wellington, including the lower Hutt Valley and the land on which the modern Hutt Rd now runs.

In 1865 the seat of government was moved from Auckland to Wellington, due to its central location in the country.

One blustery day back in 1968 the wind blew so hard it pushed the almost-new Wellington–Christchurch ferry *Wahine* onto Barrett Reef at the harbour entrance. The disabled ship dragged its anchors, drifted into the harbour and slowly sank – 51 people perished. The Museum of Wellington City & Sea has a moving exhibit commemorating this tragedy.

⊙ Sights

Museums & Galleries

FREE Museum of
Wellington City & Sea   MUSEUM
(Map p352; www.museumofwellington.co.nz; Queens
Wharf; ⊙10am-5pm) For an imaginative, interactive experience of Wellington's social and
salty maritime history, swing into the Museum of Wellington. Highlights include a
moving documentary about the tragedy
of the *Wahine*, and ancient Maori legends
dramatically told using tiny hologram actors
and special effects. The building itself is an
old Bond Store dating from 1892.

FREE City Gallery   GALLERY
(Map p362; www.citygallery.org.nz; Civic Sq, Wakefield St; charges may apply for major exhibits;
⊙10am-5pm) Housed in the monumental
old library in Civic Sq, Wellington's much-
loved City Gallery does a cracking job of
securing acclaimed contemporary international exhibitions, as well as unearth-
ing and supporting those at the forefront
of the NZ scene. A jam-packed events calendar and excellent Nikau Gallery Cafe
enhance endearment.

FREE New Zealand Film Archive   CINEMA
(Map p362; ☏film info line 04-499 3456; www.
filmarchive.org.nz; cnr Taranaki & Ghuznee Sts;
movies $8; ⊙9am-5pm Mon-Fri, evening cinema
screenings Wed-Sat) The Film Archive is a
veritable vortex of NZ moving images, into

which you could well get sucked for days on
end. Its library holds more than 150,000 titles spanning feature films, documentaries,
short films, home movies, newsreels, TV
programs and advertisements. There are
regular screenings in the cinema ($8), as
well as a viewing library (free) where you
can ferret out and watch films until you're
square-eyed. Groovy on-site cafe.

Carter Observatory   ASTRONOMY
(Map p352; ☏04-910 3140; www.carterobserva
tory.org; 40 Salamanca Rd; adult/child $18.50/8;
⊙10am-5pm, to 9.30pm Tue & Sat) At the top of
the Botanic Gardens (p355), the Carter Observatory features a full-dome planetarium
offering regular shows with virtual tours
of the local skies; a multimedia display of
Polynesian navigation, Maori cosmology and
European explorers; and some of NZ's finest
telescopes and astronomical artefacts. Check
the website for evening star-gazing times.

FREE Academy Galleries   GALLERY
(Map p352; www.nzafa.com; 1 Queens Wharf;
⊙10am-5pm) The showcase of the New Zealand Academy of Fine Arts, Academy Galleries presents frequently changing exhibitions
by NZ artists.

FREE New Zealand
Portrait Gallery   GALLERY
(Map p352; www.portraitgallery.nzl.org; Shed 11,
Queens Wharf; ⊙10.30am-4.30pm) Housed in his-
toric waterfront Shed 11, this gallery presents

WELLINGTON IN ...

Two Days

To get a feel for the lie of the land, walk (or drive) up to the **Mt Victoria Lookout**, or ride
the **cable car** up to the **Wellington Botanic Gardens**. After lunch on cool **Cuba Street,**
immerse yourself in all things Kiwi at **Te Papa** or the **Museum of Wellington City & Sea**.
Drink beer by the jug and meet fun-loving locals at **Mighty Mighty**.

The next day, fuel-up with coffee and eggs at **Nikau** in the City Gallery, then head to
Zealandia to meet the birds and learn about NZ conservation, or encounter some other
bird-brains in a tour of **Parliament House**. For dinner, try **Chow** or **Phoenician Falafel**,
then spend your evening **bar-hopping** along Courtenay Pl. Nocturnal entertainment
could involve live music, a movie at the gloriously restored **Embassy Theatre**, or a midnight snack at a late-closing cafe – or all three.

Four Days

Shake and bake the two-day itinerary, then decorate with the following: hightail it out of
Wellington for some wine tasting around **Martinborough**, followed by a seal-spotting
safari along the wild **Cape Palliser**. The next day, have a picnic in **Paekakariki**, plunge in
for a swim, and take a wander around **Queen Elizabeth Park** next door.

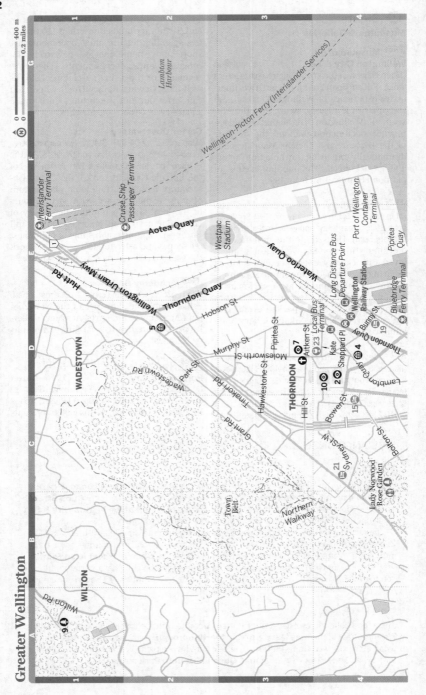

Greater Wellington

400 m
0.2 miles

Lambton
Harbour

Wellington-Picton Ferry (Interislander Services)

Interislander
Ferry Terminal

Cruise Ship
Passenger Terminal

Aotea Quay

Westpac
Stadium

Waterloo Quay

Hutt Rd

Wellington Urban Mwy

Thorndon Quay

Port of Wellington
Container
Terminal

Pipitea
Quay

Hobson St

Long Distance Bus
Departure Point

Bluebridge
Ferry Terminal

Wellington
Railway Station

Murphy St

Pipitea St

Aitken St

7

23 Local Bus
Terminal

Bunny St

19

WADESTOWN

Park St

Tinakori Rd

Molesworth St

Hawkestone St

THORNDON

Kate

Sheppard Pl

Thorndon Quay

4

Wadestown Rd

Grant Rd

10

2

Lambton Quay

Hill St

Bowen St

15

Town
Belt

Northern
Walkway

Sydney St W

21

Bolton St

Lady Norwood
Rose Garden

WILTON

Wilton Rd

6

353

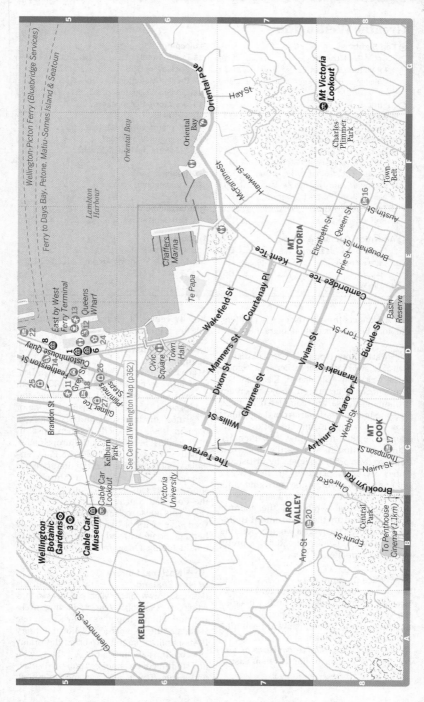

WELLINGTON REGION WELLINGTON

Greater Wellington

New Zealanders through the eyes of painters, sculptors, illustrators and photographers.

FREE Parliament House   CULTURAL BUILDING
(Map p352; www.parliament.nz; Bowen St; ⊙tours on the hour 10am-4pm Mon-Fri, 10am-3pm Sat, 11am-3pm Sun) The austere grey-and-cream Parliament House was completed in 1922. Free one-hour tours depart from the ground-floor foyer (arrive 15 minutes prior). Next door is the 1899 neo-Gothic Parliamentary Library building, as well as the modernist **Beehive** (Map p352) designed by British architect Sir Basil Spence and built between 1969 and 1980. Controversy surrounded its construction and – love it or loathe it – it's the architectural symbol of the country. Across the road are the **Government Buildings** (Map p352), the largest wooden building in the southern hemisphere, doing a pretty good impersonation of stone.

FREE Weta Cave   MUSEUM
(www.wetanz.com; cnr Camperdown Rd & Weka St, Miramar; ⊙9am-5.30pm) Film buffs will enjoy the Weta Cave, a fun, mind-boggling mini-museum of the Academy Award–winning company that brought *The Lord of the Rings*, *King Kong*, *The Adventures of Tintin* and *The Hobbit* to life. It's 9km east of the city centre, a pleasant waterside bike ride or 20 minutes on the No 2 bus.

Katherine Mansfield's Birthplace   HISTORIC BUILDING
(Map p352; www.katherinemansfield.com; 25 Tinakori Rd, Thorndon; adult/child $8/2; ⊙10am-4pm Tue-Sun) Often compared to Chekhov and Maupassant, Katherine Mansfield is one of NZ's most distinguished authors. She was born in 1888, and died of tuberculosis in 1923 aged 34. She mixed with Europe's most famous writers (DH Lawrence, TS Eliot, Virginia Woolf), and married the literary critic and author John Middleton Murry. Her short stories can be found in one volume, the *Collected Stories of Katherine Mansfield*. This house in Tinakori Rd is where she spent five years of her childhood, a lovely heritage home with exhibitions in her honour, including a biographical film.

FREE National Library of New Zealand   CULTURAL BUILDING
(Map p352; www.natlib.govt.nz; cnr Molesworth & Aitken Sts; ⊙9am-5pm Mon-Sat) Putting 'exciting' and 'library' happily side by side in one sentence, the re-emerged National Library hosts public programs exploring the brainy side of the nation. There's a gallery, wi-fi and multimedia technology, pop-up displays and a cafe. This is also a chance to eyeball

nationally significant documents such as the Treaty of Waitangi and the women's suffrage petition.

FREE **The Dowse** GALLERY
(www.dowse.org.nz; 45 Laings Rd, Lower Hutt; ⊙10am-4.30pm Mon-Fri, 10am-5pm Sat & Sun) Fifteen minutes' drive or via regular buses from downtown Wellington, the Dowse is worth visiting for its architecture alone (the pink is positively audacious). It's also a friendly, accessible art museum showcasing NZ art, craft and design. Nice cafe.

FREE **Petone Settlers Museum** MUSEUM
(www.newdowse.org.nz; The Esplanade, Petone; ⊙10am-4pm Wed-Sun) On the shell-strewn Petone foreshore, 10 to 15 minutes' drive from downtown Wellington or reachable by regular bus services, the art deco Petone Settlers Museum recalls local migration and settlement, in its charming *Tatou Tatou* exhibition.

Gardens & Lookouts

FREE **Wellington Botanic Gardens** GARDENS
(Map p352) The hilly, 25-hectare botanic gardens can be *almost* effortlessly visited via a cable-car ride (nice bit of planning, eh?). They boast a tract of original native forest along with varied collections including a beaut rose garden and international plant collections. Add in fountains, a cheerful playground, sculptures, duck pond, cafe, magical city views and much more, and you've got a grand day out. The gardens are also accessible from the Centennial Entrance on Glenmore St (Karori bus 3).

Cable Car & Museum CABLE CAR
(Map p352; www.wellingtoncablecar.co.nz; one-way adult/child $3.50/1, return $6/2; ⊙departs every 10min, 7am-10pm Mon-Fri, 8.30am-10pm Sat, 9am-9pm Sun) One of Wellington's most famous attractions is the little red cable car that clanks up the steep slope from Lambton Quay to Kelburn. At the top are the Wellington Botanic Gardens, the Carter Observatory (p351) and the small-but-nifty **Cable Car Museum** (Map p352; www.cablecarmuseum.co.nz; admission free), which tells the cable car's story since it was built in 1902 to open up hilly Kelburn for settlement. Take the cable car back down the hill, or ramble down through the gardens (a 30- to 60-minute walk, depending on your wend).

Mt Victoria Lookout LOOKOUT
(Map p352) For a readily accessible viewpoint of the city, harbour and surrounds, venture up to the lookout atop the 196m Mt Victoria, east of the city centre. You can take bus 2 some of the way up, but the rite of passage is to sweat it out on the walk (ask a local for directions or just follow your nose). If you've got your own wheels, take Oriental Pde along the waterfront and then scoot up Carlton Gore Rd. If this whets your appetite, ask a local how to get to the wind turbine or Mt Kaukau – these are even higher viewpoints that'll blow your socks off.

FREE **Otari-Wilton's Bush** PARK
(Map p352; 160 Wilton Rd; ⊙dawn-dusk) About 3km west of the city is Otari-Wilton's Bush, the only botanic gardens in NZ specialising in native flora. There are more than 1200 plant species here, including some of the

MAORI NZ: WELLINGTON

In legend the mouth of Maui's Fish, and traditionally known as Te Whanganui-a-Tara, the Wellington area became known to Maori in the mid-19th century as 'Poneke' (a transliteration of Port Nicholas, its European name at the time).

The major *iwi* (tribes) of the region were Te Ati Awa and Ngati Toa. Ngati Toa was the *iwi* of Te Rauparaha, who composed the now famous *Ka Mate haka*. Like most urban areas the city is now home to Maori from many *iwi*, sometimes collectively known as Ngati Poneke.

New Zealand's national museum, Te Papa (p358), presents excellent displays on Maori culture, traditional and modern, as well as a colourful *marae* (meeting house). In its gift store you can see excellent carving and other crafts, as you can in both Kura (p370) and Ora (p370) galleries nearby.

Kapiti Island Nature Tours (p375) offers an intimate insight into the Maori culture of Wellington.

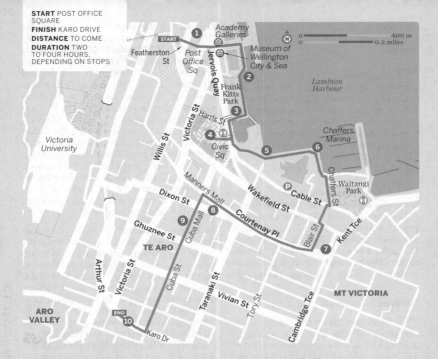

START POST OFFICE SQUARE
FINISH KARO DRIVE
DISTANCE TO COME
DURATION TWO TO FOUR HOURS, DEPENDING ON STOPS

Academy Galleries

START

Featherston St

Post Office Sq

Jervois Quay

Museum of Wellington City & Sea

Lambton Harbour

0   400 m
0   0.2 miles

Frank Kitts Park

Victoria St

Harris St

Chaffers Marina

Willis St

Civic Sq

Wakefield St

Cable St

Waitangi Park

Victoria University

Manners Mall

Dixon St

Courtenay Pl

Chaffers St

Kent Tce

Ghuznee St

Cuba Mall

Blair St

TE ARO

Arthur St

Victoria St

Cuba St

Taranaki St

Vivian St

Tory St

Cambridge Tce

MT VICTORIA

ARO VALLEY

END

Karo Dr

Walking Tour
City Sculpture

❯ To begin, send yourself to Post Office Sq, where Bill Culbert's ❶ **SkyBlues** spaghetti's into the air, then cross Jervois Quay to pass between the New Zealand Academy of Fine Arts and Museum of Wellington City & Sea. At the Queens Wharf waterfront, turn south, past the big shed to the ❷ **Water Whirler**, the largely lifeless needle of experimental kineticist Len Lye that whirrs crazily into life on the hour several times a day.

Continue along the promenade or deviate through Frank Kitts Park, under which lies Kaffe Eis on the edge of the lagoon and next to the ❸ **Albatross Fountain**. A short detour over the flotsam City to Sea Bridge, Civic Sq is surrounded by the i-SITE, library, and City Gallery. Neil Dawson's ❹ **Ferns** hangs in the air, attendant by a stand of nikau palms.

Back on the waterfront, continue past Te Raukura *whare waka* (canoe house), and ❺ **Hikitia**, the world's oldest working crane ship. Keep to the wharf, past the bronze form of ❻ **Solace in the Wind** leaning over the edge, alongside Katherine Mansfield's breezy contribution to the Wellington Writers Walk.

Cross the footbridge to Waitangi Park to eyeball the graffiti wall and some roller action, before heading south to Courtenay Pl via Chaffers St, and Blair St with its century-old warehouses.

On Courtenay Pl, check out the leggy form of the industrial ❼ **Tripod**, before heading west. Cross Taranaki St to ❽ **Te Aro Park** with its canoe prow and other ceramic elements.

Both Dixon and Manners St will see you intersect with Cuba St, where you should turn south and head up the pedestrian mall, home of the ridiculous, malicious ❾ **Bucket Fountain**. It's out to get you. See the sly, schadenfreude smile on the face of the tuatara slide?

Change down to granny gear and wander through doorways, all the way to the top of Cuba, into the remnant heritage precinct cut through by the controversial inner-city bypass. The Lady McLeods at Arthur's & Martha's cafes could well tell the tale, poignantly illustrated by Regan Gentry's brilliant but ghostly ❿ **Subject to Change**, and the Tonk's Well alongside.

WORTH A TRIP

DAYS BAY & MATIU-SOMES ISLAND

The small **East By West Ferry** (📞04-499 1282; www.eastbywest.co.nz; Queens Wharf) plies Wellington harbour between Queens Wharf and Days Bay in Eastbourne, via Matiu-Somes Island, and on fine weekends Petone and Seatoun as well.

Locals have been jumping on a boat to **Days Bay** for decades, where there's a beach, park and cafe, and a boatshed with kayaks, rowboats and bikes for hire. A 10-minute walk from Days Bay leads to Eastbourne, a beachy township with more cafes, a cute pub, and numerous other diversions.

The ferry also stops at at **Matiu-Somes Island** in the middle of the harbour, a DOC-managed reserve where you might see weta, tuatara, kakariki and little blue penguins, among other critters. The island is rich in history, having once been a prisoner-of-war camp and quarantine station. Take a picnic lunch, or even stay overnight in the campsite (adult/child $10/5) or in the DOC house – book online at www.doc.govt.nz or at Wellington's DOC visitor centre (p371).

It's a 20- to 30-minute chug across the harbour. There are 16 sailings on weekdays, eight on Saturday and Sunday (return fare adult/child $22/11.50).

city's oldest trees, as well as 11km of walking trails and delightful picnic areas. Bus 14 from the city passes the gates.

Wildlife

Zealandia WILDLIFE RESERVE
(📞04-920 9200; www.visitzealandia.com; Waiapu Rd; adult/child/family exhibition only $18.50/9/46, exhibition & valley $28.80/14.50/71.50; ⊙10am-5pm, last entry 4pm) This groundbreaking eco-sanctuary is tucked in the hills about 2km west of town (bus 3 passes nearby, or see the Zealandia website for the free shuttle). Living wild within the fenced valley are more than 30 native bird species, including rare takahe, saddleback, hihi and kaka, as well as NZ's most accessible wild population of tuatara and little spotted kiwi. An excellent exhibition relays NZ's natural history and world-renowned conservation story. More than 30km of tracks can be explored and there's a daily tour (11.15am). The night tour provides an opportunity to spot nocturnal creatures including kiwi, frogs and glow-worms (adult/child $76.50/36). Cafe and shop on-site.

Wellington Zoo ZOO
(www.wellingtonzoo.com; 200 Daniell St; adult/child $20/10; ⊙9.30am-5pm, last entry 4.15pm) Committed to conservation, research and rescuing wayward Antarctic penguins, Wellington Zoo is also home to a plethora of native and non-native wildlife, including lions and chimpanzees. The nocturnal house has kiwi and tuatara. Check the website for info on 'close encounters', which allow you to meet the big cats, red pandas and giraffes (for a fee). The zoo is 4km south of the city; catch bus 10 or 23.

Staglands Wildlife Reserve WILDLIFE RESERVE
(www.staglands.co.nz; Akatarawa Rd, Upper Hutt; adult/child $19/8; ⊙10am-5pm) The drive from Upper Hutt to Waikanae (on the Kapiti Coast) along the windy, scenic Akatarawa Rd passes the 10-hectare Staglands Wildlife Reserve, which helps to conserve native NZ birds and animals, such as the blue duck (whio). It's 16km from SH2, 20km from SH1.

🏃 Activities

Ferg's Kayaks KAYAKING
(Map p352; www.fergskayaks.co.nz; Shed 6, Queens Wharf; ⊙10am-8pm Mon-Fri, 10am-6pm Sat & Sun) Punish your tendons with indoor rock climbing (adult/child $15/10), cruise the waterfront on a pair of in-line skates ($15 for two hours) or paddle around the harbour in a kayak or on a stand-up paddleboard (from $15 for one hour). There's also bike hire (one hour from $15) and guided kayaking trips.

Makara Peak Mountain Bike Park MOUNTAIN BIKING
(www.makarapeak.org; South Karori Rd, Karori; admission by donation) In the hills of Karori, 4km west of the city centre (bus 3, 17 or 18), this excellent 200-hectare park is laced with 24km of single-track ranging from beginner to expert. The nearby **Mud Cycles** (📞04-476 4961; www.mudcycles.co.nz; 421 Karori Rd; half-/full-day/weekend bike hire from $30/45/75; ⊙8.30am-6.30pm Mon-Fri, 9am-5pm Sat, 10am-5pm Sun) has mountain bikes for hire, and

runs guided tours for riders of all abilities. Wellington is fast becoming a MTB mecca – visit tracks.org.nz for details of the dozens of other rides around the capital.

Wild Winds   WINDSURFING

(Map p352; ☎04-384 1010; www.wildwinds.co.nz; 36 Customhouse Quay) With all this wind and water, Wellington was made for windsurfing, kiteboarding, and stand-up paddleboarding. Take on one or all three with Wild Winds, with lessons starting from $110 for two hours.

👉 Tours

Walk Wellington   GUIDED TOUR

(☎04-802 4860; www.walkwellington.org.nz; adult/child $20/10; ⊗tours 10am daily, plus 5.30pm Mon, Wed & Fri Nov-Mar) Informative and great-value two-hour walking tours focusing on the city and waterfront, departing the i-SITE. Book online, phone or just turn up.

Flat Earth   GUIDED TOUR

(☎0800 775 805, 04-472 9635; www.flatearth.co.nz; half- & full-day tours $159-385) An array of themed small-group tours (city highlights, Maori treasures, arts and Middle-earth filming locations).

Hammonds Scenic Tours   GUIDED TOUR

(☎04-472 0869; www.wellingtonsightseeingtours.com; city tour adult/child $55/27.50, Kapiti Coast $100/50, Wairarapa $195/97.50) Runs a 2½-hour city highlights tour, four-hour tour of the Kapiti Coast, and a full-day Wairarapa experience including Cape Palliser.

Zest Food Tours   GUIDED TOUR

(☎04-801 9198; www.zestfoodtours.co.nz; tours from $128) Runs 2½- to 5½-hour small-group city sightseeing tours; longer tours include lunch with matched wines at Logan Brown (p365).

Wild About Wellington   GUIDED TOUR

(☎027 441 9010; www.wildaboutwellington.co.nz; tours from $95) Small-group walking and public-transport tours including City of Style, Sights & Bites, Wild About Chocolate or Boutique Beer Tasting. From a few hours to a full day.

Movie Tours   GUIDED TOUR

(☎027 419 3077; www.adventuresafari.co.nz; tours from adult/child $45/30) Half- and full-day tours for real movie fiends – more props, clips, film locations and Middle-earth than you can shake a staff at.

Wellington Rover   GUIDED TOUR

(☎0800 426 211, 04-471 0044; www.wellingtonrover.co.nz; tours from adult/child $50/25) Half- to full-day tours of the city and plenty of Hobbit action.

Helipro   SCENIC FLIGHTS

(Map p352; ☎04-472 1550; www.helipro.co.nz; Shed 1, Queens Wharf; 10/15/25/35min flights per person $95/190/240/375) Buzz around Welly in a chopper. Heli-lunch trips to the Wairarapa and Marlborough Sounds also available.

Festivals & Events

Check at the Wellington i-SITE or visit www.wellingtonnz.com/event for comprehensive festival listings; most tickets can be booked through Ticketek (p369).

DON'T MISS

TREASURES OF TE PAPA

Te Papa (Map p362; www.tepapa.govt.nz; 55 Cable St; admission free; ⊗10am-6pm Fri-Wed, to 9pm Thu) is the city's 'must-see' attraction, and for reasons well beyond the fact that it's NZ's national museum. It's highly interactive, fun and full of surprises.

Aptly, 'Te Papa Tongarewa' loosely translates as 'treasure box'. The riches inside include an amazing collection of Maori artefacts and the museum's own colourful *marae*; natural history and environment exhibitions; Pacific and NZ history galleries; national art collection, and themed hands-on 'discovery centres' for children. Exhibitions occupy impressive gallery spaces with a high-tech twist (eg motion-simulator rides and a house shaking through an earthquake). Big-name, temporary exhibitions incur an admission fee.

You could spend a day exploring Te Papa's six floors but still not see it all. To cut to the chase, head to the information desk on level two. For exhibition highlights and to get your bearings, the one-hour 'Introducing Te Papa' tour ($14) is a good idea; tours leave from the info desk at 10.15am, noon and 2pm daily in winter, more frequently in summer. Two cafes and two gift shops complete the Te Papa experience, one which could well take a couple of visits.

TANA UMAGA, FORMER ALL BLACKS CAPTAIN

Wellington is a beautiful city, with a striking waterfront surrounded by bush-clad hills, and sightseeing and photo opportunities are plentiful. Downtown, it's easy to get around on foot and there are plenty of cafes and restaurants to stop at for a break. It's also a very family-friendly city: Wellington Zoo (p357) is a special place to take the family to check out the brave one-legged kiwi, while just a short bus ride away, Te Papa (p358), the national museum, mixes history and modern technology under the one roof. Wellingtonians are always really friendly and welcoming and ready to help visitors to their city.

Summer City CULTURAL
(www.wellingtonnz.com) A two-month celebration commencing mid-January that includes countless free outdoor events.

New Zealand International Sevens SPORTS
(www.sevens.co.nz) The world's top seven-a-side rugby teams compete, but it's the crowd that plays up. Held in February.

Fringe NZ CULTURAL
(www.fringe.org.nz) Three weeks across February and March of way-out-there experimental visual arts, music, dance and theatre.

New Zealand International Arts Festival CULTURAL
(www.festival.co.nz) A month-long biennial (even years) spectacular of theatre, dance, music, visual arts and literature. International acts aplenty. Usually held late February to March.

ASB Gardens Magic CULTURAL
(www.wellingtonnz.com) Free evening concerts in the Botanic Gardens. Get there early with blanket and picnic. In March.

New Zealand Comedy Festival COMEDY
(www.comedyfestival.co.nz) Three weeks of hysterics across April/May. World-famous-in-NZ comedians, and some truly world-famous ones, too.

Matariki CULTURAL
(www.tepapa.govt.nz) Celebrating the Maori New Year (in June) with a free festival of dance, music and other events at Te Papa.

International Film Festival FILM
(www.nzff.co.nz) Two-week indie film fest screening the best of NZ and international cinema. Held over July/August.

Beervana BEER
(www.beervana.co.nz) A barrel-load of craft-beer aficionados roll into town for a weekend of supping and beard-stroking. In August.

Wellington on a Plate FOOD
(www.wellingtononaplate.com) Lip-smacking program of gastronomic events, and bargains aplenty at restaurants around the city. Held in August.

World of WearableArt FASHION
(www.worldofwearableart.com) A two-week run in September of the spectacular nightly extravaganza of amazing garments. Tickets are hot property.

Toast Martinborough FOOD & DRINK
(www.toastmartinborough.co.nz) A day of hedonism around the Martinborough vineyards. Tickets = hot cakes. Held in November.

🛏 Sleeping

Wellington accommodation is generally more expensive than in regional areas. Standards are reasonably high, and there are plenty of options right in or within easy walking distance of the city centre. One hassle is the lack of parking; if you have your own wheels, ask about car parking when you book (and be aware you'll probably have to pay for it).

Wellington's budget accommodation largely takes the form of multistorey hostel megaliths. There's no 'motel alley' in Wellington, but motels are scattered around the city fringe. Being the hub of government and business, self-contained apartments are popular, and bargains can often be found at weekends.

During the peak season (December to February), or during major festivals, book your bed well in advance.

Campsites are as rare as bad coffee in Wellington. Tenters should head to the Harcourt Holiday Park (p363) in the Hutt Valley, the Wellington Top 10 Holiday Park (p363) in Seaview, or Paekakariki Holiday Park (p374). Motorhomers, however, can en-

WELLINGTON FOR CHILDREN

With ankle-biters in tow, your best bet is a visit to colourful **Capital E** (Map p362; ☑04-913 3740; www.capitale.org.nz; Civic Sq; events free-$15; ☉9am-5pm Mon-Fri, 10am-4pm Sat), an educational entertainment complex designed especially for kids. Expect interactive rotating exhibitions, children's theatre and TV, readings, workshops and courses. Call or check the website for the events calendar and prices.

Te Papa (p358) is fantastic for children. The Discovery Centres are loaded with inter-active activities, and StoryPlace is designed for children aged five and under. See the dedicated Kids page on the website for more details. Along the waterfront on either side of Te Papa are **Frank Kitts Park** and **Waitangi Park**, both with playgrounds perfect for expending pent-up energy.

A ride up the cable car (p355) and a lap around the Wellington Botanic Gardens (p355) will pump plenty of fresh air into young lungs, and when darkness descends head to the Carter Observatory (p351) where kids can gaze at galaxies far, far away. On a more terrestrial bent, check out some living dinosaurs (aka tuatara) at the Wellington Zoo (p357) or Zealandia (p357).

For online ideas, search the Sights & Activities section of www.wellingtonnz.cm.

---

joy the unbelievably convenient Wellington Waterfront Motorhome Park (p363).

⭐ YHA Wellington City
HOSTEL **$**

(Map p362; ☑04-801 7280; www.yha.co.nz; cnr Cambridge Tce & Wakefield St; dm $29-36, d with/without bathroom $120/88; @ 🖛) Wellington's best hostel wins points for fantastic com-munal areas including two big kitchens and dining areas, games room, reading room and dedicated movie room with high-tech projector. Sustainable initiatives (recycling, composting and energy-efficient hot water) impress, and there's a compre-hensive booking service at reception, along with espresso.

Ohtel
BOUTIQUE HOTEL **$$$**

(Map p362; ☑04-803 0600; www.ohtel.com; 66 Ori-ental Parade; d $265-395; 🖛) Aesthetes check in and don't want to check out at this bijou hotel on Oriental Parade. Individually decorated rooms are beautified with stylish furniture and contemporary artwork and ceramics, avidly collected by the architect-owner. The bathrooms in the deluxe rooms and suites, with their vista walls and deep tubs, are a designer's wet dream.

Nomads Capital
HOSTEL **$**

(Map p362; ☑0508 666 237, 04-978 7800; www.nomadscapital.com; 118 Wakefield St; dm $28-36, d with bathroom $95-105; @ 🖛) Smack-bang in the middle of town, Nomads has good security, spick-and-span rooms, an on-site cafe-bar (free modest nightly meals) and dis-counts for longer stays. Kitchen and lounge

spaces are short on elbow room, but herit-age features (such as the amazing stairwell) stop you dwelling on the negatives.

Moana Lodge
HOSTEL **$**

(☑04-233 2010; www.moanalodge.co.nz; 49 Moana Rd, Plimmerton; dm $33, d with shared bathroom $76-94; @ 🖛) Just off SH1 and only a short train ride or drive from Wellington (25km), this exceptional backpackers right on the beach is immaculate and inviting, with friendly owners super-keen to infuse you with their local knowledge. Kayaks and bikes available. From Wellington catch the Tranz Metro Kapiti train to Plimmerton.

Cambridge Hotel
HOSTEL **$**

(Map p362; ☑04-385 8829; www.cambridgehotel.co.nz; 28 Cambridge Tce; dm $23-25, s with/without bathroom $95/65, d $105/85; @ 🖛) Comforta-ble, affordable accommodation in a heritage hotel. En suite rooms have Sky TV, phone and fridge (try for a room at the back if you're a light sleeper). The backpacker wing has a snug kitchen/lounge, flash bathrooms and dorms with little natural light but sky-high ceilings. The $2 breakfast is a plus.

Capital View Motor Inn
MOTEL **$$**

(Map p362; ☑0800 438 505, 04-385 0515; www.capitalview.co.nz; 12 Thompson St; d $125-160; 🖛) Many of the rooms in this well-maintained, multistorey buiilding close to Cuba St do indeed enjoy capital views – especially the large, good-value penthouse (sleeps five, $220). All are self-contained, and recent renovations have freshened things up.

Booklovers B&B
B&B **$$**

(Map p352; ✆04-384 2714; www.booklovers.co.nz; 123 Pirie St; s/d from $150/180; @🖥🛜) This gracious, book-filled B&B run by award-winning author Jane Tolerton has four guest rooms with TV, CDs and CD/DVD player. Three have en suites, one has a private bathroom. Bus 2 runs from the front gate to Courtenay Pl and the train station, and the city's 'green belt' begins right next door. Free wi-fi and parking.

Comfort & Quality Hotels
HOTEL **$$**

(Map p362; ✆04-385 2156, 0800 873 553; www.hotelwellington.co.nz; 223 Cuba St; d $104-200; @🖥🏊) Two hotels in one: the sympathetically renovated historic Trekkers building with its smaller, cheaper rooms (Comfort); and the snazzier high-rise Quality with modern styling and a swimming pool. Both share the in-house bar and dining room (mains $22 to $30). Two solid options in the heart of Cuba.

City Cottages
RENTAL HOUSES **$$**

(Map p362; ✆021 073 9232; www.citybedandbreakfast.co.nz; Tonks Grove; d/q $170/200; 🖥) Saved only after protracted public protest when the new bypass went through, these two tiny 1880 cottages sit amongst a precious precinct of historic Cuba St buildings. Clever conversion has transformed them into all-mod-con, self-contained one-bedroom pads, comfortable for two but sleeping up to four thanks to a sofa bed. Stylish, convenient, and veerrrry Cuba. Ask about road noise.

Museum Hotel
HOTEL **$$$**

(Map p362; ✆0800 994 335, 04-802 8900; www.museumhotel.co.nz; 90 Cable St; r & apt Mon-Thu $205-399, Fri-Sun $199-349; @🖥🏊) Formerly known as 'Museum Hotel de Wheels' (to make way for Te Papa, it was rolled here from its original location 120m away), this art-filled hotel keeps the quirk-factor high. Bright-eyed staff, a very good restaurant with outrageous decor, and groovy tunes piped into the lobby make a refreshing change from homogenised business hotels. Tasty weekend/weekly rates.

Mermaid
GUESTHOUSE **$$**

(Map p352; ✆04-384 4511; www.mermaid.co.nz; 1 Epuni St; s $95-130, d $105-145; 🖥) In the uber-cool Aro Valley 'hood, Mermaid is a small women-only guesthouse in a colourfully restored villa. Each room is individually themed with artistic flair (one with private

bathroom, three with shared facilities). The lounge, kitchen and deck are homely and laid-back. Great cafe, bakery and deli on the doorstep.

Victoria Court
MOTEL **$$**

(Map p362; ✆04-385 7102; www.victoriacourt.co.nz; 201 Victoria St; r $149-205; 🖥) Our top motel choice in the city centre, with plenty of parking. The affable owners offer modern, spacious studios and apartments with spa baths, kitchenettes, slick blond-wood joinery and TVs. Two disabled-access units; larger units sleep six.

Trek Global
HOSTEL **$**

(Map p362; ✆04-471 3480, 0800 868 735; www.trekglobal.net; 9 O'Reilly Ave; s $59, tw with/without bathroom $89/69, d with/without bathroom $99/79; 🖥) Wellington's groovy new hostel is slightly squeezed into its back-lane location, hence some tight but funky communal areas (the lounge is a highlight). Multistorey, colour-coded accommodation wings are a little bit rabbit-warren, but what counts is that it's relatively quiet, the rooms are fresh, the service is good, and there are laudable extras such as bike hire, bookings, and a fab women-only dorm with a suntrap terrace.

Downtown Backpackers
HOSTEL **$**

(Map p352; ✆0800 225 725, 04-473 8482; www.downtownbackpackers.co.nz; 1 Bunny St; dm $25-29, s $65, d $82-95; @🖥) An old charmer at the railway end of town, housed in a grand art-deco building. Downtown has clean, bright rooms and plenty of character-filled communal areas (be sure to check out the carved fireplace in the bar). Budget meals available in the cafe morning and night.

🏆 Bolton Hotel
HOTEL **$$$**

(Map p352; ✆0800 996 622, 04-472 9966; www.boltonhotel.co.nz; cnr Bolton & Mowbray Sts; d $174-334; @🖥🏊) Slick and well serviced, the lofty Bolton deserves its five stars. Room options are varied but share a common theme of muted tones, fine linens and colourful artwork. Most are spacious with full kitchen facilities and some enjoy park or city views. Warm your cockles in the heated pool, spa and sauna.

CityLife Wellington
APARTMENTS **$$$**

(Map p352; ✆04-922 2800, 0800 368 888; www.heritagehotels.co.nz; 300 Lambton Quay; d Mon-Thu $229-249, Fri-Sun $179-199; @🖥) Luxurious serviced apartments in the city centre,

Central Wellington

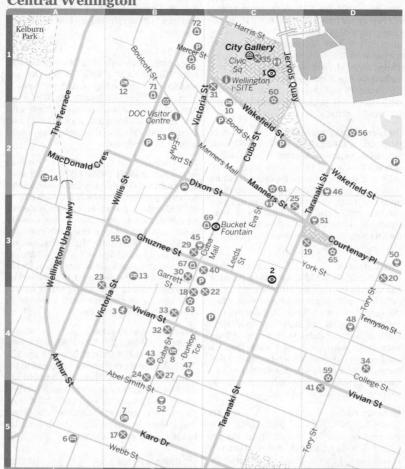

ranging from studios to three-bedroom arrangements, some with a harbour glimpse. Features include full kitchen, CD/DVD player, and in-room laundry facilities. Weekend rates are great bang for your buck. The vehicle entrance is from Gilmer Tce, off Boulcott St (parking $15.50 per day).

Shepherds Arms Hotel HISTORIC HOTEL **$$**
(Map p352; ☑0800 393 782, 04-472 1320; www.shepherds.co.nz; 285 Tinakori Rd; s without bathroom $65-75, d with bathroom $100-140; ☎) With wall-to-wall heritage buildings and proximity to the Botanic Gardens, Thorndon makes an

atmospheric home base. This well-preserved hotel serves its patrons in fitting style, with a restaurant and bar, and good-value rooms upstairs. The ovine artwork isn't baaaad.

Apollo Lodge MOTELS **$$**
(Map p362; ☑0800 361 645, 04-385 1849; www.apollolodge.co.nz; 49 Majoribanks St; d $135-160, q $190-260; ☎) Within staggering distance of Courtenay Pl, Apollo Lodge is a loose collation of 35 varied units (one and two bedrooms), ranging from studios to family-friendly units with full kitchen. Nearby apartments available for longer-term stays.

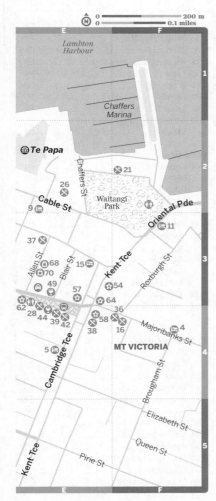

Carillon Motor Inn GUESTHOUSE $

(Map p352; ☑04-384 8795; www.carillon.co.nz; 33 Thompson St; s/d $85/95; ☎; ☐7) Wow, what a relic! Carillon is a rickety old Victorian mansion that's somehow evaded the wrecking ball, developers' ambitions and renovators' brushstrokes. With its air of *Fawlty Towers* and cheap price, its en suite rooms are a character-filled alternative to the city hostels.

Worldwide Backpackers HOSTEL $

(Map p362; ☑04-802 5590, 0508 888 555; www. worldwidenz.co.nz; 291 The Terrace; dm/d with shared bathroom incl breakfast $29/75; @☎) In

a 110-year-old house, Worldwide is a small hostel that's reasonably tidy, with winning features such as free wi-fi, breakfast, and regular barbecues. It's youthful, down-to-earth and chilled out.

Wellington Waterfront Motorhome Park MOTORHOME PARK $

(Map p352; ☑04-472 3838; www.wwmp.co.nz; 12 Waterloo Quay; powered sites $50; ☎) In reality it's simply a waterfront car park, but it's nonetheless unbelievably convenient, offering overnight stays, and modest hourly rates for day-parking. Facilities comprise a sharp ablution block and power supply. Book online.

Wellington Top 10 Holiday Park HOLIDAY PARK $

(☑04-568 5913, 0800 948 686; www.wellington top10.co.nz; 95 Hutt Park Rd, Seaview; sites $45, cabins $58-105, motels $111-168; @☎) Holiday park, 13km northeast of Wellington, that's convenient for the ferry. Family-friendly facilities include communal kitchens, games room, jumping pillow and a playground, but its industrial location detracts. Follow the signs off SH2 for Petone and Seaview, or take regular public transport.

Harcourt Holiday Park HOLIDAY PARK $

(☑04-526 7400; www.harcourtholidaypark.co.nz; 45 Akatarawa Rd, Upper Hutt; unpowered/powered sites $32/44, cabins & tourist flats $45-100, motels $120; @☎) Veritably verdant park 35km northeast of Wellington (a 35-minute drive), just off SH2, set in parkland by the trout-filled Hutt River.

✖ Eating

Wellington is an exciting place in which to eat. There's a bewildering array of options in a very small area, and keen competition keeps standards high and prices reasonable. Varied, contemporary NZ dining is nicely complemented by legions of budget fare including oodles of noodles. The recent opening of Le Cordon Bleu cookery school puts some icing on Wellington's culinary cake, bolstering its status as a bona fide gastronomic destination.

Three excellent food markets run from dawn till around 2pm on Sundays – the seriously fruit-and-veggie **Farmers Market** (Map p362; cnr Victoria & Vivian Sts), and the more varied **Harbourside Market** (Wakefield St) next to Te Papa where you'll also find artisan producers seducing foodies with their wares in the **City Market** (Map p362; Chaffers Dock Bldg, 1 Herd St; ⊙8.30am-12.30pm Sun).

Central Wellington

TOP
CHOICE **Ortega Fish Shack**   SEAFOOD $$$
(Map p362; ☎04-382 9559; www.ortega.co.nz; 16 Marjoribanks St; mains $32-34; ☺dinner Tue-Sat) Fishing floats, salty portraits and Egyptian floor tiles set a colourful Mediterranean scene, a good hook on which to hang a sea-food dinner. Fish comes many ways (with ratatouille and crayfish butter; on pork-and-prawn kedgeree with *nam prik* spicy relish) while the afters head straight for France

courtesy of orange crêpes and one of Welly's best cheeseboards. Excellent food in a relaxed yet upbeat environment.

Scopa   ITALIAN $$
(Map p362; cnr Cuba & Ghuznee Sts; mains $15-26; ⊙9am-late Mon-Sun; 🍴) Perfect pizza, proper pasta and other authentic Italian treats make dining at this modern *cucina* a pleasure. The *bianche* (white) pizzas make a refreshing change as do the *pizzaiolo* – pizzas of the week. Watch the groovy 'Cubans' from a seat in the window. Lunchtime specials; sexy evenings complete with cocktails.

Fidel's   CAFE $
(Map p362; 234 Cuba St; meals $9-20; ⊙7.30am-late; 🍴) A Cuba St institution for caffeine-craving, alternative types. Eggs any-which-way, pizza and splendid salads are cranked out of the itsy kitchen, along with Welly's best milkshakes. Revolutionary memorabilia adorns the walls of the funky interior; decent outdoor areas too. A superbusy crew copes with the chaos admirably.

Capitol   MODERN NZ $$
(Map p362; www.capitolrestaurant.co.nz; cnr Kent Tce & Majoribanks St; mains $23-33; ⊙lunch & dinner daily, brunch from 9.30am Sat & Sun) Simple, seasonal food using premium local ingredients, lovingly prepared with a nod to the classic Italian style. The rabbit pappardelle is to die for (for the rabbit, at least). The dining room is a bit cramped and noisy, but elegant nonetheless. And who's going to gripe when presented with food of this quality for the price? No dinner bookings are taken, but it's well worth waiting with an aperitif at the tiny bar.

Phoenician Falafel   LEBANESE $
(Map p362; 10 Kent Tce; meals $8-16; ⊙11.30am-9.30pm; 🍴) Authentic falafel, shish and *shawarma* (kebab) served up by cheery Lebanese owners. The best kebabs in town, although its sistership, Phoenician Cuisine at 245 Cuba St, comes a very close second.

Nikau Gallery Cafe   CAFE $$
(Map p362; City Gallery, Civic Sq; lunch $14-25; ⊙7am-4pm Mon-Fri, 8am-4pm Sat; 🍴) An airy affair at the sophisticated end of the cafe scene, Nikau consistently dishes up some of the simplest but most delightful fare in town. Refreshing aperitifs, legendary kedgeree and sage eggs, divine sweets, and sunny courtyard.

Logan Brown   MODERN NZ $$$
(Map p362; ☎04-801 5114; www.loganbrown.co.nz; 192 Cuba St; mains $39-48; ⊙noon-2pm Mon-Sat, 5.30pm-late Mon-Sun) Located in a 1920s banking chamber, Logan-Brown oozes class without being pretentious or overly formal. Believe the hype, sample the lamb two ways, snapper and paua, and peruse the epic wine list. The pre-theatre menu ($39.50) is a fine way of indulging without cleaning out your account. Bookings recommended.

KK Malaysian Cafe   MALAYSIAN $
(Map p362; 54 Ghuznee St; mains $9-14; ⊙lunch Mon-Sat, dinner Mon-Sun; 🍴) Decked out like a dirty protest, tiny KK is one of Wellington's most popular cheap Malaysian joints in a city obsessed with Southeast Asian cuisine. Scrumptious satay and rendang to put a smile on your face, accompanied by the ubiquitous roti, of course.

Chow   FUSION $$
(Map p362; 45 Tory St; small plates $7-17, mains $15-24; ⊙noon-midnight; 🛜🍴) Home of the legendary blue-cheese-and-peanut wonton, Chow is a stylish pan-Asian restaurant-cum-bar: a must-visit for people who love exciting food in sociable surroundings, accompanied by the odd cocktail. Daily deals, free wi-fi, and the fun Library bar through the back door.

Midnight Espresso   CAFE $
(Map p362; 178 Cuba St; meals $8-17; ⊙7.30am-late Mon-Fri, 8am-late Sat & Sun; 🍴) The city's original hip cafe, with food that's hearty, tasty and inexpensive – heavy on the wholesome and vegetarian. Sitting in the window with Havana coffee and cake is the quintessential Wellington cafe experience.

Aunty Mena's   VEGETARIAN $
(Map p362; 167 Cuba St; meals $10-18; ⊙11.30am-9.30pm; 🍴) One of many Cuba St noodle houses, cheap-and-cheerful Aunty Mena's cranks out yummy veggie/vegan Malaysian and Chinese dishes to a diverse clientele. Easy-clean, over-lit interior.

Sweet Mother's Kitchen   AMERICAN $
(Map p362; 5 Courtenay Pl; mains $10-27; ⊙8am-late; 🍴) Perpetually full, predominantly with young cool cats, Sweet Mother's serves dubious takes on the Deep South, such as burritos, nachos, po' boys and jambalaya. Key lime pie is about as authentic as it gets. It's cheap, cute, has craft beer and good sun.

WELLINGTON REGION WELLINGTON

Ambeli
MODERN NZ **$$$**

(Map p362; ☎04-385 7577; www.theambeli.co.nz; 18 Marjoribanks St; ☺lunch Tue-Fri, dinner daily) Seriously good, super-fine fare served in the refined surroundings of an inner-city colonial cottage. Exciting dishes flavoured with seasonal, top-end ingredients (confit pork cheek with hand-pounded broad beans; citrus-cured salmon) are complemented by a wine list much-lauded maître d' Shae Moleta claims to know better than he knows his mother. Exquisite desserts. Bookings recommended.

Le Métropolitain
FRENCH **$$**

(Map p362; www.lemetropolitain.co.nz; cnr Garrett & Cuba Sts; mains $19-34; ☺lunch & dinner Tue-Sat) Prepare to be transported to the heart of France via unpretentious bistro fare in a suitably Gallic environment. Classics are well covered and include *moules* (mussels), onion soup, *steak frites,* coq au vin and escargot. Scrumptious cheese for afters, although you'll probably want the tart that you saw in the window.

Great India
INDIAN **$$**

(Map p362; 141 Manners St; mains $15-29; ☺lunch & dinner; ☒) This is not your average curry house. While a tad more expensive than its competitors, this place consistently earns its moniker. With any luck you'll be served by Rakesh, one of the capital's smoothest maître d's.

Regal
CHINESE **$$**

(Map p362; ☎04-384 6656; 7 Courtenay Pl; yum cha around $20) Yum cha is popular in Wellington, with Regal just one of many Chinese restaurants clustered around Courtenay Pl that pack in the punters for their weekend ritual. Despite having arguably the least charm of the lot, Regal nevertheless pleases with excellent delivery speed, volume and quality, and excellence in the departments of prawn steamed dumplings, barbecue pork buns, Peking duck and coconut buns. Booking advised.

Shinobi Sushi Lounge
SUSHI **$$**

(Map p362; 43 Vivian St; sushi plates $19-35, California rolls $7-19; ☺noon-2pm Tue-Fri, 5.30pm-10pm Tue-Sun) Super-fresh fish, Japanese training and Kiwi flair combine to create the most exciting sushi joint in town, while seriously good cocktails and a quality drinks list keeps things lubricated. Non-fishy dishes include killer *karaage* (fried)

chicken, *kounomono* (pickled vegetables) and seaweed salad.

Burger Fuel
BURGERS **$**

(Map p362; 101 Courtenay Pl; burgers $5-15; ☺11am-late; ☒) Fast food how it should be. Tasty burgers of all description made with fresh, natural ingredients, beating the pants off Ronald and the Colonel.

Deluxe
CAFE **$**

(Map p362; 10 Kent Tce; snacks $4-10; ☺7am-late Mon-Fri, 8am-late Sat & Sun; ☒) A stalwart of the late-night cafe scene, with off-beat, oft-changing local art adorning the walls. Cranking, teeny wee space next to the Embassy Cinema that serves hundreds of coffees a day and mainly vegetarian/vegan counter food and pizza slices to loyal customers.

Duke Carvell's
TAPAS **$$**

(Map p362; 6 Swan Ln; lunch $12-20, small plates $15-19, large plates $30-42; ☺noon-late Mon-Fri, 9am-late Sat & Sun) Join the Duke for a culinary tour of the Mediterranean, and choose from small plates and large plates, or get piggy with a charcuterie platter. A mishmash of classic artwork adorns the walls while thrift-shop chandeliers cast a low, sexy light on proceedings. Snappy staff brighten the atmosphere as do dishes of flaming ouzo cheese.

Lido
CAFE **$$**

(Map p362; cnr Victoria & Wakefield Sts; brunch & lunch $9-21, dinner $19-26; ☺7.30am-3pm Mon, to late Tue-Sat, 9am-9pm Sun) Swing into Lido, at the bottom of a racy old office block, for a wide selection of consistent and reasonably priced Med-inspired food. Pancakes and pasta sit happily alongside fish, burgers, antipasto and salad. Great coffee and sweet treats, too. Live jazz Saturday and Sunday evenings.

Wellington Trawling Sea Market
FISH & CHIPS **$**

(Map p362; 220 Cuba St; meals $7-15; ☺11.30am-9.30pm) Locals' favourite fresh-off-the-boat fish and chips, plus other salty delicacies in season. Burgers, too.

Arthur's & Martha's
CAFE **$**

(Map p362; 272 & 276 Cuba St; snacks $3-8, meals $12-22) Run by the McLeods, whose roots in this neighbourhood descend several generations, this pair of Ladies & Gentlemen tearooms commemorate their heritage in delicious style. Martha proffers finger sandwiches, delicate tarts, and tea in fine bone china, while Arthur wears plaid and dishes up a manly fry-up and pork crackling snacks.

Heaven
PIZZERIA **$**

(Map p362; 247 Cuba St; pizzas $8-22; ☺noon-late; ☑) Divine pizzas emerge from the flames of a woodfired oven, straddled by a monolithic sculpture of St George and the Dragon. Eat inside this groovy space with its rustic and recycled decor, or take away. Pizzas also available by the slice.

Kaffe Eis
ICE CREAM **$**

(Map p362; 29 Courtenay Pl; ice cream $3-7) Ice cream made the Italian way, but with NZ ingredients (think extraordinarily good cream, luscious fruit including the inimitable feijoa) – Kaffe Eis brings you heaven by way of waffle or spoon. Go for the double scoop: vanilla on the bottom, gingernut on top. Look out for satellite branches along the waterfront.

Pandoro Panetteria
BAKERY **$**

(Map p362; 2 Allen St; items $3-6; ☺7am-5pm Mon-Fri, to 4pm Sat & Sun; ☑) An excellent Italian bakery with smooth coffee, cakes, pastries and a range of yummy savoury, bready, scrolly, rolly things.

Moore Wilson Fresh
SUPERMARKET

(Map p362; cnr College & Tory Sts; ☺7.30am-7pm Mon-Fri, to 6pm Sat, 9am-5pm Sun) An unsurpassed array of (predominantly NZ) produce, baked treats, smallgoods, mountains of cheese...just endless goodies. Positively swoon-inducing.

🍸 Drinking

Wellingtonians love a late night, and it's common to see the masses heading into town at a time when normal folk would be boiling the kettle for cocoa. A lively music scene keeps things cranking, along with some famously good bar food, competitive cocktail concocting, fine wines and microbrews.

In fact it's the craft-beer scene that has most recently gone through the roof, with updraught encouraged by a burgeoning local brewing scene and more bars than you can lob a hop at. See www.craftbeer capital.com for more propaganda.

Most of the action in Wellington's clusters around two hubs: Courtenay Pl – bustling, brassy and positively let-your-hair-down; and Cuba St – edgy, groovy and sometimes too cool for school.

TOP CHOICE Mighty Mighty
BAR

(Map p362; 104 Cuba St; ☺4pm-late Wed-Sat) This is the hippest of the capital's drinking and music venues. Inside-a-pinball-machine decor, pink velvet curtains, kitsch gewgaws and Wellington's best barmaid make this an essential port of call for those wanting to tilt or bang a bumper. A colourful slice of NZ bar life.

Hashigo Zake
CRAFT BEER

(Map p362; www.hashigozake.co.nz; 25 Taranaki St) The headquarters of the capital's underground beer movement, this brick-walled basement bar pours only quality craft brews to a wide range of hopheads. An oft-changing selection of a dozen beers on tap is reinforced by a United Nations of around 140 beers by the bottle.

Havana
BAR

(Map p362; www.havanabar.co.nz; 32 Wigan St; ☺11am-late Mon-Fri, 3pm-late Sat) Much like the proverbial light under a bushel, one of Welly's most seductive bars is hidden away down a side-street you'll never stumble across. (This is your cue to turn to our map.) You'll find it in two adjacent heritage cottages, where you can eat tapas, drink your way along the top shelf, then chinwag, smoke, flirt and dance until very near dawn.

Malthouse
CRAFT BEER

(Map p362; www.themalthouse.co.nz; 48 Courtenay Pl; ☺3pm-late Sun-Thu, noon-3am Fri & Sat) At last count there were 150 reasons to drink at this, the capital's original craft-beer bar. Savvy staff will recommend brews from an epic list that showcases beers from NZ and around the globe. Enquire about new arrivals, and the aged selection of brews if you're a well-heeled beer geek.

Southern Cross
PUB

(Map p362; www.thecross.co.nz; 35 Abel Smith St; ☺9am-late) Welly's most stylish crowd-pleasing pub combines a laid-back restaurant, lively bar, regular music, dance floor, pool table, the best garden bar in town and a welcoming attitude to children. Independent beer on tap and a good bowl of chips. Choice!

Ancestral
BAR

(Map p362; www.ancestral.co.nz; 31 Courtenay Pl; ☺11am-late Tue-Fri, 3pm-late Mon & Sat) Asian-infused Ancestral has broken new ground in the Wellington bar scene. It's designed by the architects responsible for the legendary Matterhorn, and no effort has been spared to get every line and level right – lighting, music, shirt collars and cocktails. Whisky and cigars in the stripped and pimped garden bar are a highlight, but there's heaps to please here, including sake and the smoke, spark and crackle of the yakitori grill ($4 to $17).

Matterhorn
BAR

(Map p362; www.matterhorn.co.nz; 106 Cuba St; ⊙3pm-late Mon-Fri, 10am-late Sat & Sun) We're still gettin' the Horn, despite a change of ownership and some stiff competition. A perennially popular joint with three distinct but equally pleasing areas (long bar, dining room and garden bar), the Matterhorn still honours its patrons with reputable food (tapas from mid-arvo, dinner daily, brunch weekends), solid service and regular live music.

Vivo
WINE BAR

(Map p362; www.vivowinebar.co.nz; 19 Edward St; ⊙3pm-late Mon-Fri, 5pm-late Sat) A tomelike list of approximately 600 wines from around the world, with more than 60 available by the glass. Exposed bricks and timber beams give Vivo an earthy cellarlike feel, while the fairy lights look like stars set against the dark ceiling. Excellent, inexpensive tapa-esque food (small plates $6 to $14).

Good Luck
BAR

(Map p362; basement, 126 Cuba St; ⊙5pm-late Tue-Sun) Cuba St's Chinese opium den, without the opium. This is a slickly run, sultry basement bar playing multiflavoured upbeat tunes. It also mixes the best mint juleps in town, and sports a middle-of-the-mall al fresco lounge – great for watching the Cubacade.

Hawthorn Lounge
BAR

(Map p362; 82 Tory St; ⊙6pm-late Tue-Sat) Akin to a 1920s speakeasy, complete with waistcoats and wide-brimmed fedoras. Sip cocktails and play poker, or simply enjoy the behind-the-bar theatrics.

Library
BAR

(Map p362; 53 Courtenay Pl; ⊙5pm-late Mon-Thu, 4pm-late Fri-Sun) Velveteen booths, books, booze and board games. A real page-turner, with cocktails you won't want to put down.

Betty's
BAR

(Map p362; 32 Blair St; ⊙5pm-3am Wed-Sat) Brassy joint with on-to-it staff, apothecary theme and wraparound digital screen covering three walls. DJs and VJs drop quality beats.

Hummingbird
WINE BAR

(Map p362; www.hummingbird.net.nz; 22 Courtenay Pl; ⊙3pm-late Mon-Fri, 10am-late Sat & Sun) Popular with the sophisticated set, Hummingbird is usually packed – both inside in the intimate, stylish dining room and bar, and outside on street-side tables. Croony music (with regular live jazz), exciting brunch-to-supper menus, and impressive drinks including fine wines and cocktails.

Molly Malone's
PUB

(Map p362; cnr Courtenay Pl & Taranaki St) A highly polished Irish bar, complete with daily live music, well-priced pub grub (bar menu $6 to $19, meals $23 to $30) and a suntrap balcony. If the craic downstairs is too much for you, head up to the piano bar for a calming dram.

Backbencher
PUB

(Map p352; 34 Molesworth St; ⊙11am-late) You might spot the odd parliamentarian on the turps at this pub opposite the Beehive, where rubbery puppets of NZ pollies are mounted trophy-style on the walls (Aunty Helen is much more beautiful in real life). Quiz nights and other events keep things lively.

☆ Entertainment

Wellington's entertainment scene is a bit like the Tardis: it looks small from the outside, but inside it holds big surprises. Not only does it boast an inordinate number of local performers, plenty of high-quality acts visit from around NZ and abroad, too. Hungry, appreciative crowds help things along.

Listings can be found in the *Capital Times* – the free weekly rag found all over town. Look out, also, for the *Groove Guide* (www.grooveguide.co.nz), which has a gig guide and pertinent articles.

Entry to most gigs and club nights can be gained via a door sale. Popular gigs, however, may well sell out, so it pays to buy advance tickets from advertised outlets – often Ticketek (p369), www.underthera-dar.co.nz or **Cosmic** (www.cosmiccorner.co.nz; 97-99 Cuba Mall).

Live Music & Clubs

Listed below are Wellington's main players, although live music is also a staple of many of the capital's bars, including

Mighty Mighty (p367), Havana (p367), Molly Malone's (p368), the Matterhorn (p368) and the Southern Cross (p367).

San Francisco Bath House
LIVE MUSIC

(Map p362; www.sfbh.co.nz; 171 Cuba St; ⊗4pm-late Tue-Sat) Wellington's best midsized live-music venue, playing host to the cream of NZ artists, as well as quality acts from abroad. Somewhat debauched balcony action, five deep at the bar, but otherwise well run and lots of fun when the floor starts bouncing.

Bodega
LIVE MUSIC

(Map p362; www.bodega.co.nz; 101 Ghuznee St; ⊗4pm-late) A trailblazer of the city's modern live-music scene, and still considered an institution despite its move from a derelict heritage building to a concrete cavern. 'The Bodge' offers a full and varied program of gigs in a pleasant space with a respectable dance floor.

Happy
LIVE MUSIC

(Map p362; www.happybar.co.nz; cnr Tory & Vivian Sts; ⊗Wed-Sun 5pm-late) A loungey basement bar championing performance-focused acts from virtually all genres – expect indie folk right through to hardcore. Craft beers, sushi from Shinobi (p366) across the road and free jazz on Sundays.

Sandwiches
CLUB

(Map p362; www.sandwiches.co.nz; 8 Kent Tce; ⊗4pm-late Wed-Sat) Get yourself a slice of NZ's electronic artists and DJs, regular multiflavoured international acts and a great sound system. Gritty club run by a dedicated team that isn't just in it for the bread.

Theatres

Wellington's accessible performing-arts scene sustains a laudable number of professional and amateur companies. Tickets for many events can be purchased from the **Ticketek box offices** (www.ticketek.co.nz) at two of the major venues: **St James Theatre** (Map p362; ✆04-802 4060; www.stjames.co.nz; 77 Courtenay Pl) and the **Michael Fowler Centre** (Map p362; ✆04-801 4231; www.wellingtonconvention-centre.com; 111 Wakefield St). Discount same-day tickets for some productions are often available at the i-SITE. The two other key show venues are the **Opera House** (Map p362; www.stjames.co.nz; 111 Manners St) and **TSB Bank Arena** (Map p352; 4 Queens Wharf).

The capital has three noteworthy theatre companies presenting regular performances:

BATS
THEATRE

(Map p362; ✆04-802 4175; www.bats.co.nz; 1 Kent Tce) Wildly alternative BATS presents cutting-edge and experimental NZ theatre – varied, cheap and intimate.

Circa
THEATRE

(Map p362; ✆04-801 7992; www.circa.co.nz; 1 Taranaki St) Circa's main auditorium seats 240 people, its studio 100. Cheap tickets are available for preview shows, and there are standby tickets available an hour before the show (anything from pantomime to international comedy).

Downstage
THEATRE

(Map p362; ✆04-801 6946; www.downstage.co.nz; 12 Cambridge Tce) Original NZ plays, dance, comedy and musicals in a 250-seat auditorium.

Cinemas

Movie times are listed in the local newspapers and at www.film.wellington.net.nz, and most cinemas have discounts early in the week or during the day. We can't list all the many excellent indy cinemas in Wellywood – we just ain't got the room! Here are our inner-city picks.

Embassy Theatre
CINEMA

(Map p362; ✆04-384 7657; www.deluxe.co.nz; 10 Kent Tce; from adult/child $15.50/12.50) Wellywood's cinema mothership, built in the 1920s. Screens mainstream films; bars and cafe on-site.

WELCOME TO WELLYWOOD

In recent years Wellington has stamped its place firmly on the world map as the home of NZ's dynamic film industry, earning itself the nickname 'Wellywood'. Acclaimed director Peter Jackson still calls Wellington home; the success of his *The Lord of the Rings (LOTR)* films and subsequent productions such as *King Kong*, *The Adventures of Tintin* and *The Hobbit* have made him a powerful Hollywood player, and have bolstered Wellington's reputation.

LOTR fans and movie buffs can experience some local movie magic by visiting minimuseum, the Weta Cave (p354), or one of many film locations around the region – a speciality of local guided-tour companies (p358).

Paramount CINEMA
(Map p362; 04-384 4080; www.paramount.co.nz; 25 Courtenay Pl; from adult/child $13/9; noon-midnight) A lovely old complex screening largely art-house, documentary and foreign flicks.

Penthouse Cinema CINEMA
(04-384 3157; www.penthousecinema. co.nz; 205 Ohiro Rd, Brooklyn; from adult/child $11.50/9.50) Art deco charmer screening a smart range of films. Nice cafe too. Well worth the bus ride – take number 7 or 8 south from town.

Shopping

Wellington supports a high number of independent shops including scores of designer boutiques. To 'Buy Kiwi Made', head straight to Cuba St to score a good hit rate, or try the gift shop at Te Papa.

A short drive or train ride away, Petone's Jackson Street is well worth a wander for lunching and shopping.

Starfish CLOTHING
(Map p362; 128 Willis St) Wellingtonian fashionista favourite treat. Beautiful clothing, sustainably made.

Hunters & Collectors VINTAGE
(Map p362; 134 Cuba St) Off-the-rack and vintage clothing (punk, skate and mod), plus shoes and accessories. Best-dressed window in NZ.

Mandatory CLOTHING
(Map p362; 108 Cuba Mall) Great service and sharp men's tailoring for the capital's cool cats.

Kura ARTS & CRAFTS
(Map p362; 19 Allen St) Contemporary indigenous art: painting, ceramics, jewellery and sculpture.

Ora Design Gallery ARTS & CRAFTS
(Map p362; 23 Allen St) The latest in Pacific and Maori art: beautiful sculpture, weaving and jewellery.

Vault ARTS & CRAFTS
(Map p352; 2 Plimmer Steps) Jewellery, clothing, bags, ceramics, cosmetics – a bonny store with beautiful things.

Unity Books BOOKS
(Map p362; 57 Willis St) Setting the standard for every bookshop in the land.

Bivouac Outdoor OUTDOOR EQUIPMENT
(Map p362; 39 Mercer St) The best of several outdoor shops clustered around Mercer St.

Old Bank Shopping Arcade SHOPPING CENTRE
(Map p352; www.oldbank.co.nz; cnr Lambton Quay & Willis St) This is a dear old building home to some satisfying and self-indulgent boutiques.

Kirkcaldie & Stains DEPARTMENT STORE
(Map p352; 165-177 Lambton Quay) NZ's answer to Bloomingdale's or Harrods, established in 1863. Bring your travels documents with you for tax-free bargains.

Information

Emergency
Ambulance, fire service & police (111)
Wellington Police Station (04-381 2000; www.police.govt.nz; cnr Victoria & Harris Sts)

Internet Access
Free wi-fi is available in most of the CBD (www.cbdfree.co.nz); the i-SITE (p371) also has internet access.

Media
Best of Wellington (www.bestofwellington. co.nz) 'Insiders', independent guidebook aimed at longer-staying visitors.
Capital Times (www.capitaltimes.co.nz) Free weekly newspaper with local news, gossip and gig listings.
Stuff (www.stuff.co.nz) Online news service incorporating Wellington's newspaper, the *Dominion Post*.

Medical Services
Wellington Accident & Urgent Medical Centre (04-384 4944; 17 Adelaide Rd, Newtown; 8am-11pm) No appointment necessary; also home to the after-hours pharmacy. It's close to the Basin Reserve around the northern end of Adelaide Rd.
Wellington Hospital (04-385 5999; www.ccdhb.org.nz; Riddiford St, Newtown; 24hr) One kilometre south of the city centre.

Money
Major banks have branches on Courtenay Pl, Willis St and Lambton Quay. Moneychangers include the following:
City Stop (107 Manners St; 24hr) Convenience store that exchanges travellers cheques.
Travelex (www.travelex.co.nz; 120 Lambton Quay; 8.30am-5.30pm Mon-Fri) Foreign-exchange office. Also has branches at the airport.

Post
Post Office (2 Manners St)

Tourist Information

DOC Visitor Centre (Department of Conservation; ☑04-384 7770; www.doc.govt.nz; 18 Manners St; ⊙9am-5pm Mon-Fri, 10am-3.30pm Sat) Bookings, passes and information for national and local walks, parks, huts and camping, plus permits for Kapiti Island.

Hutt City i-SITE (☑04-560 4715; www.hutt valleynz.com; 25 Laings Rd; ⊙9am-5pm Mon-Fri, to 4pm Sat & Sun) Information centre covering Upper Hutt, Lower Hutt and Petone.

Wellington i-SITE (☑04-802 4860; www. wellingtonnz.com; Civic Sq, cnr Wakefield & Victoria Sts; ⊙8.30am-5pm) Staff book almost everything, and cheerfully distribute Wellington's *Official Visitor Guide*, other maps and walking guides. Internet access and cafe.

Websites

Positively Wellington Tourism (www. wellingtonnz.com) Official tourism website for the city.

Word on the Street (www.wordonthestreet. co.nz) Magazine-style site dedicated to news, previews and reviews.

Wotzon.com (www.wotzon.com) Arts and events listings for Wellington and surrounds.

❶ Getting There & Away

Air

Wellington is an international gateway to NZ.
Wellington Airport (WLG; ☑04-385 5100; www.wellington-airport.co.nz; Stewart Duff Dr, Rongotai; ⊙4am-1.30am) has touch-screen information kiosks in the luggage hall. There's also currency exchange, ATMs, car-rental desks, cafes, shops etc. If you're in transit or have an early flight, you can't linger overnight inside the terminal. Departure tax on international flights is adult/child $25/10.

Air New Zealand (☑0800 737 000, 04-474 8950; www.airnewzealand.co.nz; cnr Lambton Quay & Grey St; ⊙9am-5pm Mon-Fri, 10am-1pm Sat) offers flights between Wellington and most domestic centres, including Auckland (from $69), Christchurch (from $59), Queenstown (from $89) and Nelson (from $79).

Jetstar (☑0800 800 995; www.jetstar.com) flies between Wellington and Auckland (from $49), Christchurch (from $49) and Queenstown (from $59).

Soundsair (☑0800 505 005, 03-520 3080; www.soundsair.com) flies between Wellington and Picton up to eight times daily (from $90), Nelson (from $107) and Blenheim (from $90).

Air2there (☑0800 777 000, 04-904 5130; www.air2there.com) flies between Wellington and Blenheim ($99), and from Kapiti Coast Airport (p373) to Blenheim ($125) and Nelson ($135).

Travel agents include Air New Zealand and **Flight Centre** (www.flightcentre.co.nz; cnr Cuba & Manners Sts; ⊙9am-5.30pm Mon-Wed & Fri, 9am-7pm Thu, 10am-4pm Sat).

Boat

On a clear day, sailing into Wellington Harbour or through the Marlborough Sounds is magical. Cook Strait is notoriously rough, but the big ferries handle it well, and sport lounges, cafes, bars, information desks and cinemas but no pool tables. There are two options for crossing the strait between Wellington and Picton: Bluebridge and the Interislander.

Book ferries at hotels, by phone, online, at travel agents and with operators directly (online is the cheapest option). Bluebridge is based at Waterloo Quay, opposite the Wellington train station. The Interislander terminal is about 2km northeast of the city centre; a shuttle bus ($2) runs to the Interislander from platform 9 at Wellington train station (where long-distance buses also depart). It also meets arriving ferries, returning passengers to platform 9. There's also a taxi stand at the terminal.

Car-hire companies allow you to pick-up/ drop-off vehicles at ferry terminals. If you arrive outside business hours, arrangements can be made to collect your vehicle from the terminal car park.

Bluebridge Ferries (☑04-471 6188, 0800 844 844; www.bluebridge.co.nz; 50 Waterloo Quay; adult/child from $51/26) Crossing takes three hours 20 minutes; up to four sailings in each direction daily. Cars and campervans up to 5.5m from $118; motorbikes $51; bicycles $10.

Interislander (☑04-498 3302, 0800 802 802; www.interislander.co.nz; Aotea Quay; adult/ child from $55/28) Crossing takes three hours 10 minutes; up to five sailings in each direction daily. Cars are priced from $118; campervans (up to 5.5m) from $133; motorbikes from $56; bicycles $15.

Bus

Wellington is a bus-travel hub, with connections north to Auckland and all major towns in between. **InterCity** (☑04-385 0520; www. intercity.co.nz) and **Newmans** (☑04-385 0521; www.newmanscoach.co.nz) buses depart from platform 9 at the train station. Tickets are sold at the Intercity/Newmans ticket window in the train station. Typical fares include Auckland (from $29, 11 hours), Palmerston North (from $14, 2¼ hours) and Rotorua (from $26, 7½ hours). There are good savings when booked online.

Naked Bus (☑0900 625 33; www.nakedbus. com) runs north from Wellington to all major North Island destinations, including Palmerston North (from $11, 2½ hours), Napier (from $19, five hours), Taupo (from $25, 6½ hours) and

Auckland (from $28, 11½ hours), with myriad stops en route. Buses depart from opposite the Amora Hotel in Wakefield St, and collect more passengers at Bunny St opposite the railway station. Book online or at Wellington i-SITE; get in early for the cheapest fares.

Train

Wellington train station has six **ticket windows** (☎0800 801 700; ☉6.30am-8pm Mon-Thu, to 1pm Fri & Sat, to 3pm Sun), two selling tickets for Tranz Scenic trains, Interislander ferries and InterCity and Newmans coaches; the other four ticketing local/regional **Tranz Metro** (☎0800 801 700; www.tranzmetro.co.nz) trains (Johnsonville, Melling, Hutt Valley, Kapiti and Wairarapa lines).

Long-haul **Tranz Scenic** (☎0800 872 467; www.tranzscenic.co.nz) routes include the daily *Overlander* between Wellington and Auckland (from $79, 12 hours, Thursday to Sunday May to September); and the *Capital Connection* between Wellington and Palmerston North (from $26, two hours, one daily Monday to Friday).

⒈ Getting Around

Metlink (☎0800 801 700; www.metlink.org.nz) is the one-stop shop for Wellington's regional bus, train and harbour ferry networks all detailed below.

To & From Airport

Super Shuttle (☎0800 748 885; www.super shuttle.co.nz; 1/2 passengers $16/21; ☉24hr) provides a door-to-door minibus service between the city and airport, 8km southeast of the city. It's cheaper if two or more passengers are travelling to the same destination. Shuttles meet all arriving flights.

The **Airport Flyer** (☎0800 801 700; www. metlink.co.nz; airport–city per adult/child $8.50/5) bus runs between the airport, Wellington and the Hutt Valley. Buses run from around 6am to 9.30pm.

A taxi between the city centre and airport costs around $30.

Bicycle

If you're fit or keep to the flat, bicycle hire is a viable option. City hirers include **On Yer Bike** (Map p362; ☎04-384 8480; www.onyerbikeavanti plus.co.nz; 181 Vivian St; half-day $20-30, full day $30-40, week $150) and **Penny Farthing** (☎04-385 2279; www.pennyfarthing.co.nz; 65 Dixon St; half-/full day from $40/60).

Bus

Frequent and efficient bus services cover the whole Wellington region and run between approximately 6am and 11.30pm. Major bus terminals are at the Wellington train station, and on

Courtenay Pl near the Cambridge Tce intersection. Pick up route maps and timetables from the i-SITE and convenience stores, or online from Metlink (p372). Fares are determined by zones: a trip across the city centre (Zone 1) costs $2, and all the way up the coast to Otaki (Zone 13) costs $16.50.

Metlink also runs the **After Midnight** bus service, departing from two convenient city stops (Courtenay Pl and Cuba St) between midnight and 4.30am Saturday and Sunday. on a number of routes to the outer suburbs. Fares range from $6 to $12, depending on how far away your bed is.

Car

There are a lot of one-way streets in Wellington, the traffic is surprisingly snarly and parking can be a royal (and expensive) pain in the rump. If you've got a car or a caravan, park on the outskirts and walk or take public transport into the city centre. Campervans can also park during the day at the Wellington Waterfront Motorhome Park (p363) and the car park outside Te Papa (p358).

Aside from the major international rental companies, Wellington has several operators that will negotiate cheap deals, especially for longer-term rental of two weeks or more, but rates generally aren't as competitive as in Auckland. Rack rates range from around $40 to $80 per day; cars are usually a few years old and in pretty good condition. Operators include the following:

Ace Rental Cars (☎0800 535 500, 04-471 1176; www.acerentalcars.co.nz; 126 Hutt Rd, Kaiwharawhara)

Apex Car Rental (☎04-385 2163, 0800 300 110; www.apexrentals.co.nz; 186 Victoria St)

Omega Rental Cars (☎04-472 8465, 0800 667 722; www.omegarentalcars.com; 96 Hutt Rd)

If you plan on exploring both North and South Islands, most companies suggest you leave your car in Wellington and pick up another one in Picton after crossing Cook Strait. This is a common (and more affordable) practice, and car-hire companies make it a painless exercise.

There are often cheap deals on car relocation from Wellington to Auckland (most renters travel in the opposite direction). A few companies offer heavy discounts on this route, with the catch being that you may only have 24 or 48 hours to make the journey.

Taxi

Packed ranks can be found on Courtenay Pl, at the corner of Dixon and Victoria Sts, on Featherston St, and outside the railway station. Two of many operators:

Green Cabs (☎0508 447 336)
Wellington Combined Taxis (☎04-384 444)

Train

Tranz Metro (p372) operates four train routes running through Wellington's suburbs to regional destinations. Trains run frequently from around 6am to 11pm, departing Wellington train station. The routes: Johnsonville, via Ngaio and Khandallah; Kapiti, via Porirua, Plimmerton, Paekakariki and Paraparaumu; Melling, via Petone; the Hutt Valley via Waterloo to Upper Hutt. A train service also connects with the Wairarapa, calling at Featherston, Carterton and Masterton. Time-tables are available from convenience stores, the train station, Wellington i-SITE and online. Standard fares from Wellington to the ends of the five lines range from $4.50 to $17.50. A Day Rover ticket ($13) allows unlimited off-peak and weekend travel on all lines except Wairarapa.

KAPITI COAST

With wide, crowd-free beaches, the Kapiti Coast acts as a summer playground and suburban extension for Wellingtonians. The region takes its moniker from Kapiti Island, a bird and marine sanctuary 5km offshore from Paraparaumu.

In the Tararua Range, Tararua Forest Park forms a dramatic backdrop along the length of the coastline and has some accessible day walks and longer tramps.

The Kapiti Coast makes an easy day trip from Wellington, but if you're after a few restful days there's enough of interest to keep you happy.

ℹ Information

Comprehensive visitor information can be found at **Paraparaumu visitor information centre** (☑04-298 8195; www.naturecoast.co.nz; Coastlands, Rimu Rd; ⊙9am-5pm Mon-Fri, 10am-3pm Sat & Sun). Pick up the *Nature Coast* brochure while you're there.

ℹ Getting There & Around

Getting here from Wellington is a breeze: just track north on SH1. By car, it's about a 30-minute drive to Paekakariki, and around 45 minutes to Paraparaumui, much of it by motorway.

Air

Kapiti Coast Airport (PPQ; www.kapitiairport. co.nz; Toru Rd, Paraparaumu Beach) in Paraparumu was expanded in 2011, and is a regular destination for **Air2there** (☑0800 777 000; www.air2there.com) , with daily flights to Blenheim and Nelson, and Air New Zealand (p371) , which flies direct to Auckland.

Bus

InterCity (p371) stops at major Kapiti Coast towns on its services between Wellington and the north. At the outside, you're looking at $34 from Wellington, and $68 from Taupo; cheaper if you book in advance and online.

The daily services into/out of Wellington run by **White Star Express** (☑04-478 4734, 0800 465 622; www.whitestarbus.co.nz) and Naked Bus (p371) also stop at major Kapiti Coast towns.

Metlink (p372) runs good local bus services around Paraparaumu, and up to Waikanae and Otaki, calling at highway and beach settlements.

Train

Tranz Metro (p372) commuter trains between Wellington and the coast are easier and more frequent than buses. Services run from Wellington to Paraparaumu ($12, generally half-hourly off-peak between 6am and 11pm, with more services at peak times), stopping en route in Paekakariki ($9.50). Weekday off-peak fares (9am to 3pm) are up to $3 cheaper.

Tranz Scenic (p372) has long-distance *Overlander* trains connecting Wellington and Auckland stopping at Paraparaumu, while the weekday-only, peak-hour *Capital Connection*, travelling to Wellington in the morning and back to Palmerston North in the evening, stops at Paraparaumu, Waikanae and Otaki.

Paekakariki

POP 1730

Paekakariki is a little seaside village stretched along a black-sand beach, serviced by a train station and passed by the highway to Wellington, 41km to the south.

◉ Sights & Activities

FREE **Queen Elizabeth Park**   PARK
(SH1; ⊙gates open 8am-8pm) This rambling but rather beautiful 650-hectare beachside park offers plenty of opportunities for swimming, walking, cycling and picnicking, as well as being the location of the Stables on the Park and Tramway Museum. There are three entrances: off Wellington Rd in Paekakariki, at MacKay's Crossing on SH1, and off the Esplanade in Raumati to the north.

Tramway Museum   MUSEUM
(www.wellingtontrams.org.nz; MacKay's Crossing entrance, Queen Elizabeth Park; admission by donation, all-day tram rides adult/child/family $8/4/20; ⊙museum 10am-4.30pm daily, trams 11am-4.30pm Sat & Sun, daily 26 Dec–late Jan) A glimpse into historic Wellington by way of restored wooden trams and museum displays inside their

big garage. A 2km track curls through Queen Elizabeth Park down to the beach. On-site ice-cream kiosk.

Stables on the Park   HORSE RIDING
(☎027 448 6764, 06-364 3336; www.stablesonthe park.co.nz; MacKay's Crossing entrance, Queen Elizabeth Park; 30-90min ride $35-90; ⊙open most days in summer) Mandy and friends run guided rides on well-mannered horses. The 1½-hour ride will see you trot along the beach with views of Kapiti Island before heading inland on park tracks. Beginners are welcome.

🛏 Sleeping & Eating

Paekakariki Holiday Park   HOLIDAY PARK $
(☎04-292 8292; www.paekakarikiholidaypark. co.nz; 180 Wellington Rd; sites per adult $15, cabins & flats from $65; @🛜) A pleasant, large, leafy park approximately 1.5km north of the township at the southern entrance to Queen Elizabeth Park. Just a hop, skip and a jump from the beach.

Hilltop Hideaway   GUESTHOUSE $
(☎04-902 5967; www.wellingtonbeachbackpack ers.co.nz; 11 Wellington Rd; d $80; @🛜) Formerly Paekakariki Backpackers, Peter and Denise now offer two double en suite rooms in their hilltop home, one with sea and sunset views. The great-value rooms are homely but elegant, much like the hosts themselves.

Finn's   HOTEL $$
(☎04-292 8081; www.finnshotel.co.nz; 2 Beach Rd; d $125-135; 🛜) Finn's is the flashy beige suit of the cutesy railway village, but redeems itself with spacious rooms, good-value meals (mains $17 to $27), and independent beer on tap. The hush glass keeps the highway at bay.

Beach Road Deli   CAFE $
(5 Beach Rd; snacks $3-8, pizza $13-22; ⊙7am-8pm Wed-Sun) Bijou deli and pizzeria, packed with home-baked bread and patisserie, cheese, charcuterie and assorted imported goodies. Heaven-sent for the highway traveller, picnic provisioner, or those looking for a sausage to fry and a bun to put it in. Ace coffee.

Paraparaumu
POP 6840
Low-key Paraparaumu is the principal town on the Kapiti Coast, and a suburban satellite of Wellington. The rough-and-tumble beach is the coast's most developed, sustaining cafes, motels and takeaway joints. Boat trips to Kapiti Island set sail from here.

The correct pronunciation is 'Pah-ra-pah-ra-oo-moo', meaning 'scraps from an oven', which is said to have originated when a Maori war party attacked the settlement and found only scraps of food remaining. It's a bit of a mouthful to pronounce; locals usually just corrupt it into 'Para-par-am'.

👁 Sights & Activities
There are two hubs to Paraparaumu: the main town on the highway, with shopping galore, and Paraparaumu Beach with its waterside park and walkway, decent swimming and other beachy attractions, including the stunning view out to Kapiti Island.

Southward Car Museum   MUSEUM
(www.southwardcarmuseum.co.nz; Otaihanga Rd; adult/child $12/3; ⊙9am-4.30pm) This museum has one of Australasia's largest collections of antique and unusual cars. Check out the DeLorean and the 1950 gangster Cadillac.

Paraparaumu Beach Golf Club   GOLF
(☎04-902 8200; www.paraparaumubeachgolfclub. co.nz; 376 Kapiti Rd; green fees $150; ⊙7.30am-dusk) This challenging and beautiful links course is ranked among NZ's best. It has hosted the New Zealand Open 12 times and tamed Tiger in 2002. Visitors are welcome: call for tee times, or book online. Clubs, carts and shoes can be hired.

🛏 Sleeping

Barnacles Seaside Inn   HOSTEL $
(☎04-902 5856; www.seasideyha.co.nz; 3 Marine Pde; dm/s/f $29/50/93, d $72-82; @🛜) Opposite Paraparaumu Beach, this homely YHA hostel resides in a 1920s heritage building. Snug rooms are individually decorated with antique dressers and have sinks and heaters; some have electric blankets and sea views. Note that all rooms share a bathroom.

Wrights by the Sea   MOTEL $$
(☎0508 902 760, 04-902 7600; www.wrightsmotel. co.nz; 387 Kapiti Rd; units $120-160; @🛜) In fact about a minute's walk to the sea, this modern motel complex in the conservative style has light, airy rooms, Sky TV and off-road parking. Some rooms have full kitchen.

🍴 Eating
If you're around on a Saturday, head for the **farmers market** (9am to 1pm) held in a carpark on Marine Parade at Paraparaumu Beach. Picnic heaven!

Fed Up Fast Foods
FISH & CHIPS **$**

(40 Marine Pde; meals $6-15; ⊙10am-9pm Mon-Thu, 9.30am-9.30pm Fri-Sun) A beachside chippy with the usual battery of fries as well as good-value dinner deals, eggy brekkies, espresso and Kapiti ice cream. Alfresco tables with views to the blue yonder.

Ambience Café
CAFE **$**

(10 Seaview Rd; lunch $12-20; ⊙8am-4pm Sun-Thu; ☑) A very 'Wellington' cafe, with both light and substantial meals made with relish, such as fish cakes, the BLT, and colourful veggie options. Cake cabinet at full capacity, and great coffee (of course).

Soprano Ristorante
ITALIAN **$$**

(☑04-298 8892; 7 Seaview Rd; mains $25-30; ⊙6pm-late Mon-Sat) A welcoming family-run joint with the liveliest evening atmosphere at the beach township. Pasta and other Italian-influenced fare, *carne e pesce*. Sweet treats include the ubiquitous tiramisu and delicious homemade *limoncello* (lemon liqueur). No-nonsense, affordable food and wine in a homely environment – *bella*!

Mediterranean Food Warehouse
PIZZA **$**

(Coastlands car park, SH1; meals $11-20; ⊙9am-9pm) A handy highway pit stop in Paraparaumu town, with excellent wood-fired pizza, luscious cakes and gelato – food so good you'll forget you're in the middle of a car park.

❶ Information

Coastlands shopping centre has all the services you'll need: banks, ATMs, post office, supermarkets and cinema, as well as the Paraparaumu visitor information centre (p373).

Kapiti Island

Kapiti Island is the coatline's dominant feature, a 10km by 2km slice that since 1897 has been a protected reserve. It's largely predator-free, allowing a remarkable range and number of birds – including many species that are now rare or extinct on the mainland – to thrive on the island.

The island is open to visitors, limited to 86 people per day (or you can stay overnight with Kapiti Island Nature Tours), and it's essential that you book and obtain a permit (adult/child $11/5) online (www.doc.govt.nz), in person at Wellington's DOC visitor centre (p371), or via email (wellingtonvc@doc.govt.nz).

Transport is booked separately from the permit (arrange your permit before your boat trip). Two commercial operators are licensed to take visitors to the island, both running to/from Paraparaumu Beach (which can be reached by train). Departures are between 9am and 9.30am daily, returning between 3pm and 4pm; call in the morning to confirm departure (sailings are weather dependent). And don't forget to bring your lunch.

Make all your bookings in advance; more information can be found in DOC's *Kapiti Island Nature Reserve* brochure.

☞ Tours

TOP CHOICE Kapiti Island

Nature Tours & Lodge
LODGE

(☑06-362 6606; www.kapitiislandnaturetours.co.nz; per person incl 3 meals $250-330) The Barrett and Clark *whanau* (family), which have a long-standing connection to the island, run very special nature tours that touch on the birds (in incredible range and number), seal colony, history and Maori traditions. Lodge accommodation is in four-bunk cabins or two-bedroom house and, importantly, offers the after-dark chance to spot the cutest-ever bird, the rare little spotted kiwi.

❶ Getting There & Away

The following operators provide boat transport to and from Kapiti Island, a couple of times a day:

Kapiti Marine Charter (☑04-297 2585, 0800 433 779; www.kapitimarinecharter.co.nz; adult/child $60/35)

Kapiti Tours (☑04-237 7965, 0800 527 484; www.kapititours.co.nz; adult/child $60/35)

THE WAIRARAPA

The Wairarapa is the large slab of land east and northeast of Wellington, beyond the craggy Tararua and Rimutaka Ranges. Named after Lake Wairarapa (Shimmering Waters), a shallow. 8000-hectare lake, the region has traditionally been a frenzied hotbed of sheep farming. More recently, wineries have sprung up, accompanied by a vigorous foodie culture – around Martinborough, most famously – which has turned the region into a decadent weekend retreat.

See www.wairarapanz.com for regional info, but also check out the **Classic New Zealand Wine Trail** (www.classicwinetrail.co.nz) – a useful tool for joining the dots

WORTH A TRIP

WAIKANAE

With a particularly nice stretch of beach, NZ's 2008 'Top Town' (and retirees' favourite) is a viable option as your Kapiti Coast rest stop.

As well as the beach and a couple of good cafes right next to it, the main attraction here is **Nga Manu Nature Reserve** (www.ngamanu.co.nz; 281 Ngarara Rd; adult/child/family $15/6/35; ⏲10am-5pm), a 15-hectare bird sanctuary dotted with picnic areas, bushwalks, aviaries and a nocturnal house with kiwi, owls and tuatara. The eels are fed at 2pm daily, and guided tours run at weekends at 2pm (Sunday only in winter). To get here, turn seawards from SH1 onto Te Moana Rd and then right down Ngarara Rd and follow the signs.

The Waikanae Estuary is a hotspot for birds, with around 60 species visiting during the year. **Waikanae Estuary Bird Tours** (☎04-905 1001; www.kapitibirdtours.co.nz; 2hr tours $35) offer highly personalised, passionate tours, so if you're looking to make feathered friends (and like a cup of tea and a freshly baked scone), this is a great opportunity.

A couple of breezy cafes sit side by side on the road that runs behind the dunes. The crowd-pleasing **Long Beach** (40 Tutere St; meals $16-22) offers an extensive menu from Cloudy Bay clams and beef cheek, though to pizza and fish and chips. With a large conservatory, it's bright, airy and suitably beachy.

Next door, the **Front Room** (42 Tutere St; meals $10-31) has a stylish, pared-back interior and is home to some simple and seasonal yet rather sophisticated fare such as watermelon and feta salad, and Waikanae crab, a regional speciality. The pleasant garden out back sports a fireplace, welcome on cool evenings.

throughout the Wairarapa and its neighbouring wine regions of Hawke's Bay and Marlborough.

Note that the telephone area code over here is 06, not 04 like most of the rest of the Wellington region.

Getting There & Around

From Wellington, **Tranz Metro** (☎0800 801 700; www.tranzmetro.co.nz) commuter trains run to Masterton ($17.50, five or six daily on weekdays, two daily on weekends), calling at seven Wairarapa stations including Featherston and Carterton. For towns off the railway line, catch a local bus.

Tranzit Coachlines (☎0800 471 227, 06-370 6600; www.tranzit.co.nz) runs services between all major Wairarapa towns (maximum fare $7.50) as well as north to Palmerston North ($21).

Martinborough

POP 1360

The sweetest visitor spot in the Wairarapa, Martinborough is a pretty town with a leafy town square and some charming old buildings, surrounded by a patchwork of pasture and a pinstripe of grapevines. It is famed for its wineries, which draw in visitors to nose the pinot, avail themselves of excellent eateries, and snooze it off at boutique accommodation.

Sights & Activities

With so many wineries scattered around town (p378), there are no points for guessing what is the town's main attraction. That said, there's plenty more to do and see, mostly in the surrounding countryside.

Patuna Farm Adventures HORSE RIDING, WALKING

(☎06-306 9966; www.patunafarm.co.nz; Ruakokoputuna Rd) This operator offers horse treks (from $50), a challenging pole-to-pole rope course (from $25), and a four-hour self-guided walk through native bush and a limestone chasm (adult/child $15/10). The chasm is open late October until Easter; other activities operate year-round (bookings essential). It's a pleasant 18km drive to get there.

Toratora Mountain Bike Park MOUNTAIN BIKING

(☎06-307 8151; www.toratora.co.nz; 460 Tora Rd; day pass adult/child $25/15, bike hire $45; ⏲open daily, call in advance) Half an hour's drive from Martinborough, this new, purpose-built mountain-bike track offers bike-fit visitors a classic NZ offroad experience. More than 25km of track loops through a native bush reserve, with accommodating climbs, huge views, and frightening but fun downhills. Farmstay accommodation is offered in a 100-year-old villa and a couple of small cabins (double $200 including track day pass), with the bonuses of a pool, tennis court and games room.

🛏 Sleeping

Martinborough

Top 10 Holiday Park HOLIDAY PARK $
(☏0800 780 909, 06-306 8946; www.martinbor oughholidaypark.com; cnr Princess & Dublin Sts; unpowered sites from $20, cabins $65-120; @🤶) An appealing campsite with grapevine views, just five minutes' walk to town. It has shady trees and the town pool over the back fence, making it a cooling oasis on sticky days. Cabins are basic but great value, freeing up your dollars for the cellar door. Bike hire available for $35 per day.

Aylstone Retreat BOUTIQUE HOTEL $$$
(☏06-306 9505; www.aylstone.co.nz; 19 Huangarua Rd; d incl breakfast $230-260; 🤶) Set among the vines on the edge of the village, this elegant retreat is a winning spot for the romantically inclined. Six en suite rooms exude a lightly floral, French-provincial charm, and share a pretty posh reading room. The on-site bistro does a magnificent croissant, and the whole shebang is surrounded by micro-mansion garden sporting lawns, boxed hedges and chichi furniture.

Claremont MOTEL $$
(☏06-306 9162, 0800 809 162; www.theclaremont. co.nz; 38 Regent St; d $130-158, 4-person apt $280; @) A classy accommodation enclave off Jellicoe St, the Claremont has two-storey, self-contained units in great nick, modern studios with spa baths, and sparkling two-bedroom apartments, all at reasonable rates (even cheaper in winter and/or midweek). Attractive gardens, barbecue areas and bike hire.

🍴 Eating & Drinking

Trio Café at
Coney Winery MODERN NZ $$
(☏06-306 8345; www.coneywines.co.nz; Dry River Rd; snacks $12, mains $22-24; ⊙noon-3pm Sat & Sun; 🍴) Wine and dine in a courtyard of gorgeous white roses or in the light and airy dining room. The great-value food is sophisticated, fresh and delicious, and all made from scratch. The atmosphere is relaxed and fun, a testament to your host Tim Coney, an affable character who makes a mighty syrah and may sing at random. Booking advisable.

Tirohana Estate MODERN NZ $$
(☏06-306 9933; www.tirohanaestate.com; 42 Puruatanga Rd; lunch mains $25-33, 3-course prix fixe dinner $59; ⊙lunch noon-3pm, dinner 6pm-late Tue-Sun) On sunny days, casual brunches and lunches are served on the terrace at this pretty vineyard, while evenings are set aside for finer dining in the elegant dining room with global decor and artwork. There's something for everyone on the good-value prix fixe menu; we'll vouch for the olive-crusted lamb with mint and tomato salad. Impeccable service; dinner booking essential.

Village Cafe CAFE $
(6 Kitchener St; mains $9-22; ⊙8am-4.30pm, dinner Fri; 🍴) In the barnlike back-end of the Wine Centre and opening out onto a sunny courtyard, this on-song cafe cranks out fine works: from a properly composed feijoa and ginger muffin, through a pallete of eggy brekkiness and smoothies, towards serious stuff like mince on toast and pizza.

Martinborough Hotel PUB
(Memorial Sq; mains $12-22) The Settlers Bar in the historic Martinborough Hotel is deservedly and perenially popular, welcoming to all and setting them up with some craft beers, local wines and honest grub. Best enjoyed outside on pavement tables on sunny days, or gathered inside with all the other out-of-towners and a clutch of down-to-earth locals.

☆ Entertainment

Circus CINEMA, CAFE
(☏06-306 9442; www.circus.net.nz; 34 Jellicoe St; adult/child $15/10; ⊙4pm-late Wed-Mon) The town's cultural hub is arguably Circus, a stylish art-house cinema (movieline 056-306 9434) where you can watch the cream of contemporary movies in a a modern, micro-size complex. There are two comfy studio theatres, as well as a stylish foyer and cafe that open out on to a rather Zen garden. Reasonably priced food (mains $20 to $28) includes bar snacks, pizza, mains with plenty of seasonal veg, and gelato.

ℹ Information

The **Martinborough i-SITE** (☏06-306 5010; www.wairarapanz.com; 18 Kitchener St; ⊙9am-5pm Mon-Fri, 10am-4pm Sat & Sun) is small, helpful and cheery. It stocks the Martinborough Wine Village Map, produced by the people behind the useful site www.martinboroughnz.com.

WAIRARAPA WINE COUNTRY

Wairarapa's world-renowned wine industry was nearly crushed in infancy. The region's first vines were planted in 1883, but the prohibition movement in 1908 soon put a cap on that corker idea. It wasn't until the 1980s that winemaking was revived, after Martinborough's *terroir* was discovered to be similar to Burgundy in France. A few vineyards soon sprang up, but the number has now ballooned to nearly 50 regionwide. Martinborough is the undisputed hub of the action, but vineyards around Gladstone and Masterton are also on the up.

Martinborough plays host to **Toast Martinborough** (☎06-306 9183; www.toastmartinborough.co.nz; tickets $70), held annually on the third Sunday in November. Enjoyable on many levels (standing up and quite possibly lying on the grass), this is a hugely popular wine, food and music event, and you'll have to be quick on the draw to get a ticket.

The **Wairarapa Wines Harvest Festival** (www.wairarapawines.co.nz; tickets $40) celebrates the beginning of the harvest with an extravaganza of wine, food and family fun. It's held at a remote riverbank setting 10 minutes from Carterton on a Saturday in mid-March.

Wairarapa's wineries thrive on visitors; Martinborough's 20-odd are particularly welcoming with well-oiled cellar doors and noteworthy food served in some gorgeous gardens and courtyards. The *Wairarapa Wine Trail Map* (available from the i-SITE and many other locations) will aid your navigations. Read all about it at www.winesfrommartinborough.com.

An excellent place to sample and purchase many wines, and for advice on local cellar doors, is the **Martinborough Wine Centre** (www.martinboroughwinecentre.co.nz; 6 Kitchener St; ☉10am-5pm), which also sells olive oils, books, clothing and art.

Recommended Wineries

Ata Rangi (www.atarangi.co.nz; 14 Puruatanga Rd; ☉1pm-3pm Mon-Fri, noon-4pm Sat & Sun) One of the region's pioneering winemakers. Great drops across the board and cute cellar door.

Coney (www.coneywines.co.nz; Dry River Rd; ☉11am-4pm Fri-Sun) Friendly, operatic tastings and lovely restaurant.

Margrain (www.margrainvineyard.co.nz; cnr Ponatahi & Huangarua Rds; ☉11am-5pm Fri-Sun) Pretty winery and site of the Taste Vin Café, a good pit stop overlooking the vines.

Palliser (www.palliser.co.nz; Kitchener St; ☉10.30am-4pm Mon-Fri, 10.30am-5pm Sat & Sun) Wines so good, even the Queen has some stashed away in her cellar. Slick outfit.

Cape Palliser

The Wairarapa coast south of Martinborough around Palliser Bay and Cape Palliser is remote and sparsely populated. The bendy road to the Cape is stupendously scenic: a big ocean and black-sand beaches on one side; barren hills and sheer cliffs on the other. Look for hints of the South Island, visible on a clear day.

Standing like giant organ pipes in the Putangirua Scenic Reserve are the **Putangirua Pinnacles**, formed by rain washing silt and sand away and exposing the underlying bedrock. Accessible by a track near the car park on Cape Palliser Rd, it's an easy three-hour return walk along a streambed to the pinnacles, or take the 3½-hour loop track past hills and coastal viewpoints. For some rugged tramping nearby, head to **Aorangi (Haurangi) Forest Park**. Maps and more information (including details on camping and a DOC cottage for rent) can be obtained from DOC in Masterton and Wellington.

Further south is the wind-worn fishing village **Ngawi**. The first things you'll notice here are the rusty bulldozers on the beach, used to drag fishing boats ashore. Next stop is the malodorous **seal colony**, the North Island's largest breeding area. Whatever you do in your quest for a photo, don't get between the seals and the sea. If you block their escape route they're likely to have a go at you!

Get your thighs thumping on the steep, 250-step (or is it 249?) climb to **Cape Palliser Lighthouse**, from where there are yet more amazing coastal views.

On the way there or back, take the short detour to the wind-blown settlement of **Lake Ferry**, overlooking Lake Onoke, where there's birdwatching to be enjoyed. This area is also good for exploration – discover the lake edge, the wild and woolly coastline

Vynfields (www.vynfields.com; 22 Omarere Rd; ⊙11am-4pm) Five-star, savoury pinot noir and a lush lawn on which to enjoy a platter. Organic/biodynamic wines.

Bicycle Tours

The best and most eco-friendly way to explore the Wairarapa's wines is by bicycle, as the flat landscape makes for puff-free cruising. Martinborough has four options:

Christina Estate Vineyard (☎06-306 8920; christinaestate@xtra.co.nz; 28 Puruatanga Rd; half-day $25-40, full day $35-50; ⊙8.30am-6pm) Bikes, plus tandems for the coordinated.

March Hare (☎021 668 970; www.march-hare.co.nz; 18 Kitchener St; $65) Two wheels and a picnic.

Martinborough Top 10 Holiday Park (☎0800 780 909, 06-306 8946; www.martin boroughholidaypark.com; cnr Princess & Dublin St; full day $40) Super-convenient if you're staying on-site.

Martinborough Wine Centre (☎06-306 9040; www.martinboroughwinecentre.co.nz; 6 Kitchener St; half-day $25, full day $35) Morning, afternoon or all-day rentals.

Guided Tours

The following companies will guide you round the vines:

Dynamic Tours (☎04-478 8533; www.dynamictours.co.nz; from $250) Customised wine tours, run from Wellington.

Hammond's Scenic Tours (☎04-472 0869; www.wellingtonsightseeingtours.com; full-day tour adult/child $200/100) Full-day winery tours including gourmet lunch.

Tour Wairarapa (☎06-372 7554; www.tourwairarapa.co.nz; $190) Wine tastings, chocolate and lunch at the historic Gladstone Inn.

Tranzit Tours (☎0800 471 227, 06-370 6600; www.tranzittours.co.nz; from $142) Four vineyards and a platter lunch at Martinborough's Village Café.

Zest Food Tours (☎04-801 9198; www.zestfoodtours.co.nz; $369) Small-group food and wine tours in Greytown and Martinborough.

(prime for surfing), and the cliffs behind. You'll also find the **Lake Ferry Hotel** (mains $12-28; ⊙from 11am) with its retro fitout (check out the formica), which has great views and fish and chips.

Martinborough i-SITE can help with accommodation options in the Lake Ferry and Cape Palliser area, which include campsites and holiday homes for rent.

Greytown

POP 2000

The most seductive of several small towns along SH2, Greytown has tarted itself up over recent years and is now full of Wellingtonians on the weekend. It has plenty of accommodation, some decent food, three high-street pubs and some swanky shopping. Check out www.greytown.co.nz for more information.

◉ Sights

Cobblestones Village Museum MUSEUM (www.cobblestonesmuseum.org.nz; 169 Main St; adult/child/family $5/2/10; ⊙10am-4.30pm) Greytown was the country's first planned inland town: intact Victorian architectural specimens line the main street. The quaint Cobblestones Village Museum is an enclave of period buildings and various historic objects, dotted around pretty grounds inviting a lie-down on a picnic blanket.

TOP CHOICE **Schoc Chocolates** FOOD (www.chocolatetherapy.com; 177 Main St) No picnic? No worries. Visit Schoc in its 1920s cottage beside Cobblestones Village Museumvillage. Sublime flavours, worth every single penny of 10 bucks a tablet. Truffles, rocky road and peanut brittle, too. Free tastings.

Stonehenge Aotearoa   MONUMENT

(☏06-377 1600; www.stonehenge-aotearoa.com; tours adult/child $16/8; ☉10am-4pm, tours 11am Sat & Sun & by appointment) About 10km south-east of Carterton, this full-scale adaptation of the UK's Stonehenge is orientated for its location on a grassy knoll overlooking the Wairarapa Plain. Its mission: to bring the night sky to life, even in daylight. The pre-tour talk and audiovisual presentation are excellent, and the henge itself a pretty sur-real sight – especially when interpreted by one of its tour guides, who are consummate storytellers. Self-guided 'Stone Trek' tours are also available for adult/child $6/3.

🛏 Sleeping & Eating

Greytown Campground   CAMPSITE $

(☏06-304 9837; Kuratawhiti St; unpowered/powered sites $18/22) A basic camping op-tion (with equally basic facilities) scenically spread through Greytown Park, 500m from town.

Greytown Hotel   HOTEL $

(☏06-304 9138; www.greytownhotel.co.nz; 33 Main St; s/d with shared bathroom $50/80) A serious contender for 'oldest hotel in New Zealand', the Top Pub (as it's known) is looking great for her age. Upstairs rooms are small and basic but comfortable, with no-frills furnish-ings and shared bathrooms. Downstairs is a chic dining room, alongside an ol' faithful lounge-bar (meals $12 to $20) and popular garden-courtyard.

Oak Estate Motor Lodge   MOTEL $$

(☏06-304 8188, 0800 843 625; www.oakestate. co.nz; cnr Main St & Hospital Rd; r $125-185) A stand of gracious roadside oaks and pretty gardens shield a smart complex of self-con-tained units: studios, one- and two-bedroom options.

Salute   TAPAS $$

(83 Main St; tapas $8-15, pizza $19; ☉noon-late Wed-Sat, 12.30-3.30pm Sun; 🖋) Heavy on the Med vibe but with a delicate touch on the food front, Salute will suit you down to the ground if you like saucy, succulent, crisp, charred and fried, along with lashings of olive oil and wedges of lemon. Food so colourful you'll for-get you're in grey-town.

Cuckoo Cafe   ITALIAN $$

(☏06-304 8992; 128 Main St; meals $15-25; ☉10am-late Wed-Sun; 🖋) Refreshingly unruly joint littered with mismatched retro furni-ture in a shocking-pink villa on the main street. Substantial pizzas are the mainstay, along with pasta and blackboard specials, with house-churned ice cream and cheese-cake for pud. Inexpensive local wines.

French Baker   BAKERY $

(81 Main St; snacks $4-7, mains $13-19) Buttery croissants, tempting tarts and authentic breads; artisan baker Moïse Cerson is le real McCoy. Great coffee too and a compact menu of suitably Gallic offerings, such as Roquefort salad and French toast.

Masterton & Around

POP 19,500

Masterton is the Wairarapa's utilitarian hub, an unselfconscious town getting on with its business. Its main claim to immortality is the 50-year-old sheep-shearing competi-tion, the international **Golden Shears** (www. goldenshears.co.nz), held annually in the first week of March.

Masterton spins the wool out a bit longer at the **Wool Shed** (www.thewoolshednz.com; Dixon St; adult/child/family $8/2/15; ☉10am-4pm), a baaaa-loody marvellous little museum dedicated to NZ's sheep-shearing and wool-production industries.

Next door is the region's foremost cultural institution, the small but rather splendid **Aratoi Wairarapa Museum of Art & His-tory** (www.aratoi.co.nz; cnr Bruce & Dixon Sts; admission by donation; ☉10am-4.30pm), which hosts an impressive program of exhibitions and events (and has a very nice shop!)

Opposite the Wool Shed and Aratoi is **Queen Elizabeth Park** (Dixon St), perfect for stretching your legs. Feed the ducks, dump someone on the see-saw, have a round of minigolf or practise your high catches on the cricket oval. You could also eat a magnificent meat pie, purchased from Masterton's nota-ble bakery, the **Ten O'Clock Cookie** (180 Queen St).

There are a few interesting sights fur-ther afield, one of which is , on the coast 68km east of Masterton. It's a truly awe-some, end-of-the-world place, with a reef, the lofty 162m-high Castle Rock, largely safe swimming and walking tracks. There's an easy (but sometimes ludicrously windy) 30-minute return walk across the reef to the lighthouse, where 70-plus shell species are fossilised in the cliffs. Another one-hour return walk runs to a huge limestone cave (take a torch), or take the 1½-hour return track from Deliverance Cove to Castle Rock.

Keep well away from the lower reef when there are heavy seas. Ask the staff at Masterton i-SITE about accommodation here.

Thirty kilometres north of Masterton on SH2, **Pukaha Mt Bruce National Wildlife Centre** (www.pukaha.org.nz; adult/child/family $20/6/50; ⊙9am-4.30pm) is not only one of NZ's most successful wildlife and captive breeding centres, it's also the most readily accessible bush experience off the highway. The visitor centre has various exhibits including an interactive gallery, while outside there's a new kiwi house with a nursery, aviaries, virgin forest and a scenic one-hour loop track taking in some great views. Huge eels, tuatara and other creatures also reside here. The daily visitor program allows you to see tuatara being fed (11.30am), attend the eel-feeding (1.30pm) and watch the kaka circus (3pm). There are also guided tours on weekends (adult/child $35/15). There's a cafe on-site.

The turn-off to the main eastern entrance of the **Tararua Forest Park** (www.doc.govt.nz) is just south of Masterton on SH2; follow Norfolk Rd about 15km to the gates. Mountain streams dart through virgin forest in this reserve, known as 'Holdsworth'. At the park entrance are swimming holes, picnic areas, campsites and a lodge. Walks include short, easy family tramps, excellent one- or two-day tramps, and longer, challenging tramps for experienced bush-bods (west through to Otaki Forks). The resident caretaker has maps and hut accommodation info. Check weather and track updates before setting off, and be prepared to be baked, battered and buffeted by fickle conditions.

As you've had the stamina to read this far, it's only fair that we share with you one final tip. If you've got your own wheels, and you like a good garden bar, head to the **Gladstone Inn** (51 Gladstone Rd, Gladstone). Cheers!

ℹ **Information**

The **Masterton i-SITE** (☑06-370 0900; www.wairarapanz.com; cnr Dixon & Bruce Sts; ⊙9am-5pm Mon-Fri, 10am-4pm Sat & Sun) can sort you out with oodles of information including a copy of the *Wairarapa Visitor Guide*, advice on accommodation, and directions to the Gladstone Inn.

Understand the
› North Island

population per sq km

NORTH ISLAND

SOUTH ISLAND

AUSTRALIA

♟ ≈ 3 people

The North Island Today

A Unified Country

Auckland vs Christchurch. North Island vs South Island. Like many nations, New Zealand suffers from friendly intra-country rivalries, and less helpful and often petty parochialism. And while some misguided South Islanders still think they pay for Auckland's roads and supposedly ostentatious lifestyles, events of the past two years have conspired to bring the country closer together than ever before.

A trifecta of tragedies – one natural and two man-made – were balanced by success in the sport most proud Kiwis regard as the only game in town. Sure, it's nice to occasionally beat the Aussies at cricket, league and netball, but reinforcing the All Blacks' rugby dominance on a global stage is what really matters. And after a tough year, especially for the South Island, New Zealand's victory in the 2011 Rugby World Cup was exactly what the country needed.

Shaky Isles

In September 2010, just as New Zealand was edging out of its worst recession in 30 years, a magnitude 7.1 earthquake struck near Christchurch on the South Island. The damage to the country's second-largest city was extensive, but miraculously no life was lost. While the clean up was continuing on the East Coast of the South Island, tragedy struck across the Southern Alps on the West Coast when an explosion occurred at the Pike River coalmine near Greymouth, sealing 29 men inside.

Then in the early afternoon of 22 February 2011, a magnitude 6.3 earthquake struck Christchurch. This time the city wasn't so lucky and 185 people lost their lives. In a society as compact and mobile as New Zealand, the earthquake's impact was felt profoundly across

You'll Need

» Travel insurance covering high-risk activities.

» Insect repellent to keep the sandflies away.

» Enthusiasm for the game of rugby.

» An appetite for Kiwi food and wine.

Faux Pas

» Don't refer to the fuzzy green fruit as kiwis, they're kiwifruit; kiwi is a bird or nationality.

» Don't insist that Phar Lap, pavlova and Crowded House are Australian icons.

» Sheep jokes just aren't funny.

Top Films

The Piano (1993) Dir: Jane Campion

Once Were Warriors (1994) Dir: Lee Tamahori

Whale Rider (2002) Dir: Niki Caro

Sione's Wedding (2006) Dir: Chris Graham

Boy (2010) Dir: Taika Waititi

Where they live
(% of New Zealanders)

North Island 64
South Island 20

10 — Australia
5 — Rest of the World
2 — Travelling

if the North Island were 100 people

66 would be European
15 would be Maori
10 would be Asian
8 would be Pacific Islanders
1 would be other

the entire nation. Many North Islanders have friends or family in Christchurch, know the city well, and quickly offered moral and financial support.

More than a year after the February 2011 earthquake, few can fully understand what the resilient people of Christchurch have experienced, but hopefully the nation's reinvigorated unity will last long into the future.

Rugby Success & Rena's Mess

Throughout September and October 2011, the influx of tourists for the Rugby World Cup provided a welcome distraction after a tough 12 months. Matches were held across the North and South Islands, with Auckland and Wellington hosting the bulk of the important games. Despite a few public transport hiccups, Auckland proudly displayed the city's Polynesian flair in a spectacular opening ceremony, and then six weeks later ignited nationwide celebrations when the All Blacks edged France 8–7 in the tournament's finale. A lasting legacy of the tournament is the expansion of the Wynyard Quarter and Britomart Precinct in Auckland, with new cafes, bars and restaurants taking advantage of the city's harbourfront location.

But while the All Blacks were marching to rugby success in early October 2011, yet more bad news hit the country. When the MV *Rena*, a fully loaded container ship, hit the Astrolabe Reef off the North Island's Bay of Plenty, the resulting fuel spill became NZ's worst maritime environmental disaster on record. Around 2000 seabirds were killed, and rotting food and debris from trashed containers washed up on the shores around Tauranga and Mt Maunganui.

» Population: 3.4 million

» Area: 113,729 sq km (smaller than Victoria, bigger than Tasmania)

» Total number of snakes: 0

» Distance between North and South Islands: 23km

» Auckland is NZ's most cosmopolitan, ethnically diverse city, with 43.5% of the population identifying as Maori, Polynesian or Asian.

Top Books

Sons for the Return Home (1973) Albert Wendt
Under the Mountain (1979) Maurice Gee
Potiki (1986) Patricia Grace
The House of Strife (1993) Maurice Shadbolt

Top Beers

Deception Schwarzbier Hallertau
Resurrection Belgian Trippel Galbraith's Brewing Company
Aotearoa Pale Ale Tuatara Brewery
Citra Imperial IPA Liberty Brewing

Pasifika Anthems

French Letter (1982) Herbs
In the Neighbourhood (1994) Sisters Underground
How Bizarre (1995) OMC
Chains (1997) Che Fu & DLT
Screems from tha Old Plantation (2001) King Kapisi

History

James Belich
One of New Zealand's foremost modern historians, James Belich has written a number of books on NZ history and hosted the TV documentary series *The New Zealand Wars*.

New Zealand's history is not long, but it is fast. In less than a thousand years these islands have produced two new peoples: the Polynesian Maori and European New Zealanders. The latter are often known by their Maori name, 'Pakeha' (though not all like the term). NZ shares some of its history with the rest of Polynesia, and with other European settler societies, but has unique features as well. It is the similarities that make the differences so interesting, and vice versa.

Making Maori

Despite persistent myths, there is no doubt that the first settlers of NZ were the Polynesian forebears of today's Maori. Beyond that, there are a lot of question marks. Exactly where in east Polynesia did they come from – the Cook Islands, Tahiti, the Marquesas? When did they arrive? Did the first settlers come in one group or several? Some evidence, such as the diverse DNA of the Polynesian rats that accompanied the first settlers, suggests multiple founding voyages. On the other hand, only rats and dogs brought by the founders have survived, not the more valuable pigs and chickens. The survival of these cherished animals would have had high priority, and their failure to be successfully introduced suggests fewer voyages.

NZ seems small compared with Australia, but it is bigger than Britain, and very much bigger than other Polynesian islands. Its regions vary wildly in environment and climate. Prime sites for first settlement were warm coastal gardens for the food plants brought from Polynesia (kumara or sweet potato, gourd, yam and taro); sources of workable stone

'Kaore e mau te rongo – ake, ake!' (Peace never shall be made – never, never!) War chief Rewi Maniapoto in response to government troops at the battle of Orakau, 1864

TIMELINE	AD 1000– 1200	1642	1769
	Possible date of the arrival of Maori in NZ. Solid archaeological evidence points to about AD 1200, but much earlier dates have been suggested for the first human impact on the environment.	First European contact: Abel Tasman arrives on an expedition from the Dutch East Indies (Indonesia) to find the 'Great South Land'. His party leaves without landing, after a sea skirmish with Maori.	European contact recommences with visits by James Cook and Jean de Surville. Despite some violence, both manage to communicate with Maori. This time NZ's link with the outside world proves permanent.

for knives and adzes; and areas with abundant big game. NZ has no native land mammals apart from a few species of bat, but 'big game' is no exaggeration: the islands were home to a dozen species of moa (a large flightless bird), the largest of which weighed up to 240kg, about twice the size of an ostrich. There were also other species of flightless birds and large sea mammals such as fur seals, all unaccustomed to being hunted. For people from small Pacific islands, this was like hitting the jackpot. The first settlers spread far and fast, from the top of the North Island to the bottom of the South Island within the first 100 years. High-protein diets are likely to have boosted population growth.

By about 1400, however, with big-game supply dwindling, Maori economics turned from big game to small game – forest birds and rats – and from hunting to gardening and fishing. A good living could still be made, but it required detailed local knowledge, steady effort and complex communal organisation, hence the rise of the Maori tribes. Competition for resources increased, conflict did likewise, and this led to the building of increasingly sophisticated fortifications, known as *pa*. Vestiges of *pa* earthworks can still be seen around the country (on the hilltops of Auckland, for example).

The Maori had no metals and no written language (and no alcoholic drinks or drugs). But their culture and spiritual life was rich and distinctive. Below Ranginui (sky father) and Papatuanuku (earth mother) were various gods of land, forest and sea, joined by deified ancestors over time. The mischievous demigod Maui was particularly important. In legend, he vanquished the sun and fished up the North Island before meeting his death between the thighs of the goddess Hine-nui-te-po in an attempt to conquer the human mortality embodied in her. Maori traditional performance art, the group singing and dancing known as *kapa haka,* has real power, even for modern audiences. Visual art, notably

For a thorough overview of NZ history from Gondwanaland to today, visit history-nz.org.

Rumours of late survivals of the giant moa bird abound, but none have been authenticated. So if you see a moa in your travels, photograph it – you have just made the greatest zoological discovery of the last 100 years.

THE MORIORI & THEIR MYTH

One of NZ's most persistent legends is that Maori found mainland NZ already occupied by a more peaceful and racially distinct Melanesian people, known as the Moriori, whom they exterminated. This myth has been regularly debunked by scholars since the 1920s, but somehow hangs on.

To complicate matters, there were real 'Moriori', and Maori did treat them badly. The real Moriori were the people of the Chatham Islands, a windswept group about 900km east of the mainland. They were, however, fully Polynesian, and descended from Maori – 'Moriori' was their version of the same word. Mainland Maori arrived in the Chathams in 1835, as a spin-off of the Musket Wars, killing some Moriori and enslaving the rest. But they did not exterminate them. The mainland Moriori remain a myth.

PAUL KENNEDY / LONELY PLANET IMAGES ©

» Statue of James Cook

1772
Marion du Fresne's French expedition arrives; it stays for some weeks at the Bay of Islands. Relations with Maori start well, but a breach of Maori *tapu* (sacred law) leads to violence.

1790s
Whaling ships and sealing gangs arrive in the country. Relations are established with Maori, with Europeans depending on the contact for essentials such as food, water and protection.

1818–36
Intertribal Maori 'Musket Wars' take place: tribes acquire muskets and win bloody victories against tribes without them. The war tapers off in 1836, probably due to the equal distribution of weapons.

woodcarving, is something special – 'like nothing but itself', in the words of 18th-century explorer-scientist Joseph Banks.

Enter Europe

NZ became an official British colony in 1840, but the first authenticated contact between Maori and the outside world took place almost two centuries earlier in 1642, in Golden Bay at the top of the South Island. Two Dutch ships sailed from Indonesia, to search for southern land and anything valuable it might contain. The commander, Abel Tasman, was instructed to pretend to any natives he might meet 'that you are by no means eager for precious metals, so as to leave them ignorant of the value of the same'.

When Tasman's ships anchored in the bay, local Maori came out in their canoes to make the traditional challenge: friends or foes? Misunderstanding this, the Dutch challenged back, by blowing trumpets. When a boat was lowered to take a party between the two ships, it was attacked. Four crewmen were killed. Tasman sailed away and did not come back; nor did any other European for 127 years. But the Dutch did leave a name: 'Nieuw Zeeland' or 'New Sealand'.

Contact between Maori and Europeans was renewed in 1769, when English and French explorers arrived, under James Cook and Jean de Surville. Relations were more sympathetic, and exploration continued, motivated by science, profit and great power rivalry. Cook made two more visits between 1773 and 1777, and there were further French expeditions.

Unofficial visits, by whaling ships in the north and sealing gangs in the south, began in the 1790s. The first mission station was founded in 1814, in the Bay of Islands, and was followed by dozens of others: Anglican, Methodist and Catholic. Trade in flax and timber generated small European–Maori settlements by the 1820s. Surprisingly, the most numerous category of European visitor was probably American. New England whaling ships favoured the Bay of Islands for rest and recreation; 271 called there between 1833 and 1839 alone. To whalers, 'rest and recreation' meant sex and drink. Their favourite haunt, the little town of Kororareka (now Russell) was known to the missionaries as 'the hellhole of the Pacific'. New England visitors today might well have distant relatives among the local Maori.

One or two dozen bloody clashes dot the history of Maori–European contact before 1840 but, given the number of visits, interracial conflict was modest. Europeans needed Maori protection, food and labour, and Maori came to need European articles, especially muskets. Whaling stations and mission stations were linked to local Maori groups by intermarriage, which helped keep the peace. Most warfare was between

Similarities in language between Maori and Tahitian indicate close contact in historical times. Maori is about as similar to Tahitian as Spanish is to French, despite the 4294km separating these island groups.

The Ministry for Culture & Heritage's history website (www. nzhistory.net.nz) is an excellent source of info on NZ history.

1837	1840	1844	1858
Possums are introduced to New Zealand from Australia. Brilliant.	Starting at Waitangi in the Bay of Islands on 6 February, around 500 chiefs countrywide sign the Treaty of Waitangi to 'settle' sovereignty once and for all. NZ becomes a nominal British colony.	Young Ngapuhi chief Hone Heke challenges British sovereignty, first by cutting down the British flag at Kororareka (now Russell), then by sacking the town itself. The ensuing Northland war continues until 1846.	The Waikato chief Te Wherowhero is installed as the first Maori King.

CAPTAIN JAMES COOK *TONY HORWITZ*

If aliens ever visit earth, they may wonder what to make of the countless obelisks, faded plaques and graffiti-covered statues of a stiff, wigged figure gazing out to sea from Alaska to Australia, from NZ to North Yorkshire, from Siberia to the South Pacific. James Cook (1728–79) explored more of the earth's surface than anyone in history, and it's impossible to travel the Pacific without encountering the captain's image and his controversial legacy in the lands he opened to the West.

For a man who travelled so widely, and rose to such fame, Cook came from an extremely pinched and provincial background. The son of a day labourer in rural Yorkshire, he was born in a mud cottage, had little schooling, and seemed destined for farm work – and for his family's grave plot in a village churchyard. Instead, Cook went to sea as a teenager, worked his way up from coal-ship servant to naval officer, and attracted notice for his exceptional charts of Canada. But Cook remained a little-known second lieutenant until, in 1768, the Royal Navy chose him to command a daring voyage to the South Seas.

In a converted coal ship called *Endeavour,* Cook sailed to Tahiti, and then became the first European to land at NZ and the east coast of Australia. Though the ship almost sank after striking the Great Barrier Reef, and 40% of the crew died from disease and accidents, the *Endeavour* limped home in 1771. On a return voyage (1772–75), Cook became the first navigator to pierce the Antarctic Circle and circle the globe near its southernmost latitude, demolishing the myth that a vast, populous and fertile continent surrounded the South Pole. Cook crisscrossed the Pacific from Easter Island to Melanesia, charting dozens of islands between. Though Maori killed and cooked 10 sailors, the captain remained sympathetic to islanders. 'Notwithstanding they are cannibals,' he wrote, 'they are naturally of a good disposition.'

On Cook's final voyage (1776–79), in search of a northwest passage between the Atlantic and Pacific, he became the first European to visit Hawaii, and coasted America from Oregon to Alaska. Forced back by Arctic pack ice, Cook returned to Hawaii, where he was killed during a skirmish with islanders who had initially greeted him as a Polynesian god. In a single decade of discovery, Cook had filled in the map of the Pacific and, as one French navigator put it, 'left his successors with little to do but admire his exploits'.

But Cook's travels also spurred colonisation of the Pacific, and within a few decades of his death, missionaries, whalers, traders and settlers began transforming (and often devastating) island cultures. As a result, many indigenous people now revile Cook as an imperialist villain who introduced disease, dispossession and other ills to the Pacific (hence the frequent vandalising of Cook monuments). However, as islanders revive traditional crafts and practices, from tattooing to *tapa* (traditional barkcloth), they have turned to the art and writing of Cook and his men as a resource for cultural renewal. For good and ill, a Yorkshire farm boy remains the single most significant figure in the shaping of the modern Pacific.

Tony Horwitz is a Pulitzer-winning reporter and nonfiction author. In researching Blue Latitudes (or Into the Blue), Tony travelled the Pacific – 'boldly going where Captain Cook has gone before'.

1860–69	1861	1863–64	1868–72
First and Second Taranaki wars, starting with the controversial swindling of Maori land by the government at Waitara, and continuing with outrage over the confiscation of more land as a result.	Gold discovered in Otago by Gabriel Read, an Australian prospector. As a result, the population of Otago climbs from less than 13,000 to over 30,000 in six months.	Waikato Land War. Up to 5000 Maori resist an invasion mounted by 20,000 imperial, colonial and 'friendly' Maori troops. Despite surprising successes, Maori are defeated and much land is confiscated.	East Coast war. Te Kooti, having led an escape from his prison on the Chatham Islands, leads a holy guerrilla war in the Urewera region. He finally retreats to establish the Ringatu Church.

Maori and Maori: the terrible intertribal 'Musket Wars' of 1818–36. Because Northland had the majority of early contact with Europe, its Ngapuhi tribe acquired muskets first. Under their great general Hongi Hika, Ngapuhi then raided south, winning bloody victories against tribes without muskets. Once they acquired muskets, these tribes saw off Ngapuhi, but also raided further south in their turn. The domino effect continued to the far south of the South Island in 1836. The missionaries claimed that the Musket Wars then tapered off through their influence, but the restoration of the balance of power through the equal distribution of muskets was probably more important.

Europe brought such things as pigs (at last) and potatoes, which benefited Maori, while muskets and diseases had the opposite effect. The negative effects have been exaggerated, however. Europeans expected peoples like the Maori to simply fade away at contact, and some early estimates of Maori population were overly high – up to one million. Current estimates are between 85,000 and 110,000 for 1769. The Musket Wars killed perhaps 20,000, and new diseases did considerable damage too (although NZ had the natural quarantine of distance: infected Europeans usually recovered or died during the long voyage, and smallpox, for example, which devastated native Americans, did not make it here). By 1840, the Maori had been reduced to about 70,000, a decline of at least 20%. Maori bent under the weight of European contact, but they certainly did not break.

Making Pakeha

By 1840, Maori tribes described local Europeans as 'their Pakeha', and valued the profit and prestige they brought. Maori wanted more of both, and concluded that accepting nominal British authority was the way to get them. At the same time, the British government was overcoming its reluctance to undertake potentially expensive intervention in NZ. It too was influenced by profit and prestige, but also by humanitarian considerations. It believed, wrongly but sincerely, that Maori could not handle the increasing scale of unofficial European contact. In 1840, the two peoples struck a deal, symbolised by the treaty first signed at Waitangi on 6 February that year. The Treaty of Waitangi now has a standing not dissimilar to that of the Constitution in the US, but is even more contested. The original problem was a discrepancy between British and Maori understandings of it. The English version promised Maori full equality as British subjects in return for complete rights of government. The Maori version also promised that Maori would retain their chieftainship, which implied local rights of government. The problem was not great at first, because the Maori version applied outside the small European settlements. But as those settlements grew, conflict brewed.

Abel Tasman named NZ Statenland, assuming it was connected to Staten Island near Argentina. It was subsequently named after the province of Zeeland in Tasman's Holland.

'God's own country, but the devil's own mess.' Prime Minister Richard (King Dick) Seddon, speaking on the source of NZ's self-proclaimed nickname 'Godzone'.

1886–87

Tuwharetoa tribe gifts the mountains of Ruapehu, Ngauruhoe and Tongariro to the government to establish the world's fourth national park.

1893

NZ becomes the first country in the world to grant the vote to women, following a campaign led by Kate Sheppard, who petitioned the government for years.

JOHN ELK III / LONELY PLANET IMAGES ©

» Mt Ngauruhoe (p260), Tongariro National Park

In 1840, there were only about 2000 Europeans in NZ, with the shanty town of Kororareka (now Russell) as the capital and biggest settlement. By 1850, six new settlements had been formed with 22,000 settlers between them. About half of these had arrived under the auspices of the New Zealand Company and its associates. The company was the brainchild of Edward Gibbon Wakefield, who also influenced the settlement of South Australia. Wakefield hoped to short-circuit the barbarous frontier phase of settlement with 'instant civilisation', but his success was limited. From the 1850s, his settlers, who included a high proportion of upper-middle-class gentlefolk, were swamped by succeeding waves of immigrants that continued to wash in until the 1880s. These people were part of the great British and Irish diaspora that also populated Australia and much of North America, but the NZ mix was distinctive. Lowland Scots settlers were more prominent in NZ than elsewhere, for example, with the possible exception of parts of Canada. NZ's Irish, even the Catholics, tended to come from the north of Ireland. NZ's English tended to come from the counties close to London. Small groups of Germans, Scandinavians and Chinese made their way in, though the last faced increasing racial prejudice from the 1880s, when the Pakeha population reached half a million.

Much of the mass immigration from the 1850s to the 1870s was assisted by the provincial and central governments, which also mounted large-scale public works schemes, especially in the 1870s under Julius Vogel. In 1876, Vogel abolished the provinces on the grounds that they were hampering his development efforts. The last imperial governor with substantial power was the talented but Machiavellian George Grey, who ended his second governorship in 1868. Thereafter, the governors (governors-general from 1917) were largely just nominal heads of state; the head of government, the premier or prime minister, had more power. The central government, originally weaker than the provincial governments, the imperial governor and the Maori tribes, eventually exceeded the power of all three.

The Maori tribes did not go down without a fight, however. Indeed, their resistance was one of the most formidable ever mounted against European expansion, comparable to that of the Sioux and Seminole in the US. The first clash took place in 1843 in the Wairau Valley, now a wine-growing district. A posse of settlers set out to enforce the myth of British control, but encountered the reality of Maori control. Twenty-two settlers were killed, including Wakefield's brother, Arthur, along with about six Maori. In 1845, more serious fighting broke out in the Bay of Islands, when Hone Heke sacked a British settlement. Heke and his ally Kawiti baffled three British punitive expeditions, using a modern variant of the traditional *pa* fortification. Vestiges of these innovative earthworks

Maurice Shadbolt's *Season of the Jew* (1987) is a semifictionalised story of bloody campaigns led by warrior Te Kooti against the British in Poverty Bay in the 1860s. Te Kooti and his followers compared themselves to the Israelites who were cast out of Egypt.

To find out more about the New Zealand Wars, visit www.newzealandwars.co.nz.

'I believe we were all glad to leave New Zealand. It is not a pleasant place. Amongst the natives there is absent that charming simplicity...and the greater part of the English are the very refuse of society.' Charles Darwin, referring to Kororareka (Russell), in 1860.

1901	1908	1914–18	1931
NZ politely declines the invitation to join the new Commonwealth of Australia.	NZ physicist Ernest Rutherford is awarded the Nobel Prize in chemistry for 'splitting the atom', investigating the disintegration of elements and the chemistry of radioactive substances.	NZ's contribution to WWI is staggering for a country of just over one million people: about 100,000 NZ men serve overseas. Some 60,000 become casualties, mostly on the Western Front in France.	Napier earthquake kills 131 people.

can still be seen at Ruapekapeka (south of Kawakawa). Governor Grey claimed victory in the north, but few were convinced at the time. Grey had more success in the south, where he arrested the formidable Ngati Toa chief Te Rauparaha, who until then wielded great influence on both sides of Cook Strait. Pakeha were able to swamp the few Maori living in the South Island, but the fighting of the 1840s confirmed that the North Island at that time comprised a European fringe around an independent Maori heartland.

In the 1850s, settler population and aspirations grew, and fighting broke out again in 1860. The wars burned on sporadically until 1872 over much of the North Island. In the early years, a Maori nationalist organisation, the King Movement, was the backbone of resistance. In later years, some remarkable prophet-generals, notably Titokowaru and Te Kooti, took over. Most wars were small-scale, but the Waikato war of 1863–64 was not. This conflict, fought at the same time as the American Civil War, involved armoured steamships, ultramodern heavy artillery, telegraph and 10 proud British regular regiments. Despite the odds, the Maori won several battles, such as that at Gate Pa, near Tauranga, in 1864. But in the end they were ground down by European numbers and resources. Maori political, though not cultural, independence ebbed away in the last decades of the 19th century. It finally expired when police invaded its last sanctuary, the Urewera Mountains, in 1916.

Welfare & Warfare

From the 1850s to the 1880s, despite conflict with Maori, the Pakeha economy boomed on the back of wool exports, gold rushes and massive overseas borrowing for development. The crash came in the 1880s, when NZ experienced its Long Depression. In 1890, the Liberals came to power, and stayed there until 1912, helped by a recovering economy. The Liberals were NZ's first organised political party, and the first of several governments to give NZ a reputation as 'the world's social laboratory'. NZ became the first country in the world to give women the vote in 1893, and introduced old-age pensions in 1898. The Liberals also introduced a long-lasting system of industrial arbitration, but this was not enough to prevent bitter industrial unrest in 1912–13. This happened under the conservative 'Reform' government, which had replaced the Liberals in 1912. Reform remained in power until 1928, and later transformed itself into the National Party. Renewed depression struck in 1929, and the NZ experience of it was as grim as any. The derelict little farmhouses still seen in rural areas often date from this era.

The Six o'clock Swill referred to the frantic after-work drinking at pubs when men tried to drink as much as possible from 5.05pm until strict closing time at 6pm.

Wellington-born Nancy Wake (codenamed 'The White Mouse') led a guerrilla attack against the Nazis with a 7000-strong army. She had the multiple honours of being the Gestapo's most-wanted person and being the most decorated Allied servicewoman of WWII.

1935–49	**1936**	**1939–45**	**1948**
First Labour government in power, under Michael Savage. This government creates NZ's pioneering version of the welfare state, and also takes some independent initiatives in foreign policy.	NZ aviatrix Jean Batten becomes the first aviator to fly solo from Britain to NZ.	NZ troops back Britain and the Allied war effort during WWII; from 1942 a hundred thousand or so Americans arrive to protect NZ from the Japanese.	Maurice Scheslinger invents the Buzzy Bee, NZ's most famous children's toy.

In 1935, a second reforming government took office: the First Labour government, led by Michael Joseph Savage, easily NZ's favourite Australian. For a time, the Labour government was considered the most socialist government outside Soviet Russia. But, when the chips were down in Europe in 1939, Labour had little hesitation in backing Britain.

NZ had also backed Britain in the Boer War (1899–1902) and WWI (1914–18), with dramatic losses in WWI in particular. You can count the cost in almost any little NZ town. A central square or park will contain a memorial lined with names – more for WWI than WWII. Even in WWII, however, NZ did its share of fighting: a hundred thousand or so New Zealanders fought in Europe and the Middle East. NZ, a peaceful-seeming country, has spent much of its history at war. In the 19th century it fought at home; in the 20th, overseas.

LAND WARS *ERROL HUNT*

Five separate major conflicts made up what are now collectively known as the New Zealand Wars (also referred to as the Land Wars or Maori Wars). Starting in Northland and moving throughout the North Island, the wars had many complex causes, but *whenua* (land) was the one common factor. In all five wars, Maori fought both for and against the government, on whose side stood the Imperial British Army, Australians and NZ's own Armed Constabulary. Land confiscations imposed on the Maori as punishment for involvement in these wars are still the source of conflict today, with the government struggling to finance compensation for what are now acknowledged to have been illegal seizures.

Northland war (1844–46) 'Hone Heke's War' began with the famous chopping of the flagpole at Kororareka (now Russell) and 'ended' at Ruapekapeka (south of Kawakawa). In many ways, this was almost a civil war between rival Ngapuhi factions, with the government taking one side against the other.

First Taranaki war (1860–61) Starting in Waitara, the first Taranaki war inflamed the passions of Maori across the North Island.

Waikato war (1863–64) The largest of the five wars. Predominantly involving Kingitanga, the Waikato war was caused in part by what the government saw as a challenge to sovereignty. However, it was land, again, that was the real reason for friction. Following defeats such as Rangiriri, the Waikato people were pushed entirely from their own lands, south into what became known as the King Country.

Second Taranaki war (1865–69) Caused by Maori resistance to land confiscations stemming from the first Taranaki war, this was perhaps the war in which the Maori came closest to victory, under the brilliant, one-eyed prophet-general Titokowaru. However, once he lost the respect of his warriors (probably through an indiscretion with the wife of one of his warriors), the war too was lost.

East Coast war (1868–72) Te Kooti's holy guerrilla war.

1953	1973	1974	1981
New Zealander Edmund Hillary, with Tenzing Norgay, 'knocks the bastard off'; the pair become the first men to reach the summit of Mt Everest.	Fledgling Kiwi prog-rockers Split Enz enter a TV talent quest... finishing second to last.	Pacific Island migrants who have outstayed visas ('overstayers') are subjected to Dawn Raids by immigration police under Robert Muldoon and the National government. These raids continue until the early 1980s.	Springbok rugby tour divides the nation. Many New Zealanders show a strong anti-apartheid stance by protesting the games. Others feel sport and politics shouldn't mix, and support the tour going ahead.

Better Britons?

British visitors have long found NZ hauntingly familiar. This is not simply a matter of the British and Irish origin of most Pakeha. It also stems from the tightening of NZ links with Britain from 1882, when refrigerated cargoes of food were first shipped to London. By the 1930s, giant ships carried frozen meat, cheese and butter, as well as wool, on regular voyages taking about five weeks one way. The NZ economy adapted to the feeding of London, and cultural links were also enhanced. NZ children studied British history and literature, not their own. NZ's leading scientists and writers, such as Ernest Rutherford and Katherine Mansfield, gravitated to Britain. This tight relationship has been described as 'recolonial', but it is a mistake to see NZ as an exploited colony. Average living standards in NZ were normally better than in Britain, as were the welfare and lower-level education systems. New Zealanders had access to British markets and culture, and they contributed their share to the latter as equals. The list of 'British' writers, academics, scientists, military leaders, publishers and the like who were actually New Zealanders is long. Indeed, New Zealanders, especially in war and sport, sometimes saw themselves as a superior version of the British – the Better Britons of the south. The NZ–London relationship was rather like that of the American Midwest and New York.

'Recolonial' NZ prided itself, with some justice, on its affluence, equality and social harmony. But it was also conformist, even puritanical. Until the 1950s, it was technically illegal for farmers to allow their cattle to mate in fields fronting public roads, for moral reasons. The 1953 American movie, *The Wild One,* was banned until 1977. Sunday newspapers were illegal until 1969, and full Sunday trading was not allowed until 1989. Licensed restaurants hardly existed in 1960, nor did supermarkets or TV. Notoriously, from 1917 to 1967, pubs were obliged to shut at 6pm. Yet the puritanical society of Better Britons was never the whole story. Opposition to Sunday trading stemmed, not so much from belief in the sanctity of the Sabbath, but from the belief that workers should have weekends too. Six o'clock closing was a standing joke in rural areas, notably the marvellously idiosyncratic region of the South Island's West Coast. There was always something of a Kiwi counterculture, even before imported countercultures took root from the 1960s.

There were also developments in cultural nationalism, beginning in the 1930s but really flowering from the 1970s. Writers, artists and filmmakers were by no means the only people who 'came out' in that era.

The Waitangi Treaty Grounds, where the Treaty of Waitangi was first signed in 1840, is now a tourist attraction for Kiwis and non-Kiwis alike. Each year on 6 February, Waitangi hosts treaty commemorations and protests

TREATY OF WAITANGI

1985

Rainbow Warrior is sunk in Auckland Harbour by French government agents to prevent the Greenpeace protest ship from making its intended voyage to Mororua, where the French are conducting nuclear tests.

1992

Government begins reparations for the Land Wars, and confirms Maori fishing rights in the 'Sealord deal'. Major settlements follow, including, in 1995, reparations for the Waikato land confiscations.

» Memorial to the sunken ship, *Rainbow Warrior* (p138)

Coming In, Coming Out

The 'recolonial' system was shaken several times after 1935, but managed to survive until 1973, when Mother England ran off and joined the Franco-German commune now known as the EU. NZ was beginning to develop alternative markets to Britain, and alternative exports to wool, meat and dairy products. Wide-bodied jet aircraft were allowing the world and NZ to visit each other on an increasing scale. NZ had only 36,000 tourists in 1960, compared with more than two million a year now. Women were beginning to penetrate first the upper reaches of the workforce and then the political sphere. Gay people came out of the closet, despite vigorous efforts by moral conservatives to push them back in. University-educated youths were becoming more numerous and more assertive.

From 1945, Maori experienced both a population explosion and massive urbanisation. In 1936, Maori were 17% urban and 83% rural. Fifty years later, these proportions had reversed. The immigration gates, which until 1960 were pretty much labelled 'whites only', widened, first to allow in Pacific Islanders for their labour, and then to allow in (East) Asians for their money. These transitions would have generated major socioeconomic change whatever happened in politics. But most New Zealanders associate the country's recent 'Big Shift' with the politics of 1984.

In 1984, NZ's third great reforming government was elected – the Fourth Labour government, led nominally by David Lange and in fact by Roger Douglas, the Minister of Finance. This government adopted an antinuclear foreign policy, delighting the left, and a more-market economic policy, delighting the right. NZ's numerous economic controls were dismantled with breakneck speed. Middle NZ was uneasy about the antinuclear policy, which threatened NZ's ANZUS alliance with Australia and the US. But in 1985, French spies sank the antinuclear protest ship *Rainbow Warrior* in Auckland Harbour, killing one crewman. The lukewarm American condemnation of the French act brought middle NZ in behind the antinuclear policy, which became associated with national independence. Other New Zealanders were uneasy about the more-market economic policy, but failed to come up with a convincing alternative. Revelling in their new freedom, NZ investors engaged in a frenzy of speculation, and suffered even more than the rest of the world from the economic crash of 1987.

The early 21st century is an interesting time for NZ. Food, wine, film and literature are flowering as never before, and the new ethnic mix is creating something very special in popular music. There are continuities, however – the pub, the sportsground, the quarter-acre section, the bush, the beach and the bach – and they too are part of the reason people like to come here. Realising that NZ has a great culture, and an intriguing history, as well as a great natural environment, will double the bang for your buck.

Scottish influence can still be felt in NZ, particularly in the south of the South Island. NZ has more Scottish pipe bands per capita than Scotland itself.

HISTORY

NZ's staunch antinuclear stance earned it the nickname 'The Mouse that Roared'.

1995	2004	2010	2011
Peter Blake and Russel Coutts win the Americas Cup for NZ, sailing *Black Magic*; red socks become a matter of national pride.	Maori TV begins broadcasting – for the first time, a channel committed to NZ content and the revitalisation of Maori language and culture hits the small screen.	A cave-in at Pike River coalmine on the South Island's West Coast kills 29 miners.	A severe earthquake strikes Christchurch, killing 185 people and badly damaging the central business district.\n\nNZ hosts (and wins!) the Rugby World Cup.

Environment

Vaughan Yarwood
Vaughan Yarwood is a historian and travel writer who is widely published in New Zealand and internationally. His most recent book is *The History Makers: Adventures in New Zealand Biography*.

The Land

New Zealand is a young country – its present shape is less than 10,000 years old. Having broken away from the supercontinent of Gondwanaland (which included Africa, Australia, Antarctica and South America) in a stately geological dance some 85 million years ago, it endured continual uplift and erosion, buckling and tearing, and the slow fall and rise of the sea as ice ages came and went. Straddling the boundary of two great colliding slabs of the earth's crust – the Pacific plate and the Indian/Australian plate – to this day NZ remains the plaything of nature's strongest forces.

The result is one of the most varied and spectacular series of landscapes in the world, ranging from snow-dusted mountains and drowned glacial valleys to rainforests, dunelands and an otherworldly volcanic plateau. It is a diversity of landforms you would expect to find across an entire continent rather than a small archipelago in the South Pacific.

Evidence of NZ's tumultuous past is everywhere. The South Island's mountainous spine – the 650km-long ranges of the Southern Alps – is a product of the clash of the two plates; the result of a process of rapid lifting that, if anything, is accelerating. Despite NZ's highest peak, Aoraki/Mt Cook, losing 10m from its summit overnight in a 1991 landslide, the Alps are on an express elevator that, without erosion and landslides, would see them 10 times their present height within a few million years.

On the North Island, the most impressive changes have been wrought by volcanoes. Auckland is built on an isthmus peppered by scoria cones, on many of which you can still see the earthworks of *pa* (fortified villages) built by early Maori. The city's biggest and most recent volcano, 600-year-old Rangitoto Island, is just a short ferry ride from the downtown wharves. Some 300km further south, the classically shaped cone of snowcapped Mt Taranaki/Egmont overlooks tranquil dairy pastures.

But the real volcanic heartland runs through the centre of the North Island, from the restless bulk of Mt Ruapehu in Tongariro National Park northeast through the Rotorua lake district out to NZ's most active volcano, White Island, in the Bay of Plenty. Called the Taupo Volcanic Zone, this great 250km-long rift valley – part of a volcano chain known as the 'Pacific Ring of Fire' – has been the seat of massive eruptions that have left their mark on the country physically and culturally.

Most spectacular were the eruptions that created Lake Taupo. Considered the world's most productive volcano in terms of the amount of material ejected, Taupo last erupted 1800 years ago in a display that was the most violent anywhere on the planet within the past 5000 years.

You can experience the aftermath of volcanic destruction on a smaller scale at Te Wairoa (the Buried Village), near Rotorua on the shores of Lake Tarawera. Here, partly excavated and open to the public, lie the remains of a 19th-century Maori village overwhelmed when nearby Mt Tarawera erupted without warning. The famous Pink and White Terraces (one of several claimants to the popular title 'eighth wonder of the world') were destroyed overnight by the same upheaval.

But when nature sweeps the board clean with one hand she often rebuilds with the other: Waimangu Valley, born of all that geothermal violence, is the place to go to experience the hot earth up close and personal amid geysers, silica pans, bubbling mud pools, and the world's biggest hot spring. Or you can wander around Rotorua's Whakarewarewa Thermal Village, where descendants of Maori displaced by the eruption live in the middle of steaming vents and prepare food for visitors in boiling pools.

A second by-product of movement along the tectonic plate boundary is seismic activity – earthquakes. Not for nothing has NZ been called 'the Shaky Isles'. Most quakes only rattle the glassware, but one was indirectly responsible for creating an internationally celebrated tourist attraction...

In 1931, an earthquake measuring 7.9 on the Richter scale levelled the Hawke's Bay city of Napier, causing huge damage and loss of life. Napier was rebuilt almost entirely in the then-fashionable art-deco architectural style, and walking its streets today you can relive its brash exuberance in what has become a mecca for lovers of art deco.

However, the North Island doesn't have a monopoly on earthquakes. In September 2010 Christchurch was rocked by a magnitude 7.1 earthquake. Less than six months later, in February 2011, a magnitude 6.3 quake destroyed much of the city's historic heart and claimed 185 lives, making it the country's second-deadliest natural disaster. NZ's second city continues to be jostled by aftershocks as it begins to build anew.

The South Island can also see some evidence of volcanism – if the remains of the old volcanoes of Banks Peninsula weren't there to repel the sea, the vast Canterbury Plains, built from alpine sediment washed down the rivers from the Alps, would have eroded away long ago.

But in the south it is the Southern Alps themselves that dominate, dictating settlement patterns, throwing down engineering challenges and offering outstanding recreational opportunities. The island's mountainous backbone also helps shape the weather, as it stands in the path of the prevailing westerly winds which roll in, moisture-laden, from the Tasman Sea. As a result bush-clad lower slopes of the western Southern Alps are among the wettest places on earth, with an annual precipitation of some 15,000mm. Having lost its moisture, the wind then blows dry across the eastern plains towards the Pacific coast.

The North Island has a more even rainfall and is spared the temperature extremes of the South – which can plunge when a wind blows in from Antarctica. The important thing to remember, especially if you are tramping at high altitude, is that NZ has a maritime climate. This means weather can change with lightning speed, catching out the unprepared.

Wildlife

NZ may be relatively young, geologically speaking, but its plants and animals go back a long way. The tuatara, for instance, an ancient reptile unique to these islands, is a Gondwanaland survivor closely related to the dinosaurs, while many of the distinctive flightless birds (ratites) have distant African and South American cousins.

Due to its long isolation, the country is a veritable warehouse of unique and varied plants, most of which are found nowhere else. And with separation of the landmass occurring before mammals appeared on the scene, birds and insects have evolved in spectacular ways to fill the gaps.

ENVIRONMENT

NZ is one of the most spectacular places in the world to see geysers. Rotorua's short-lived Waimangu geyser, formed after the Mt Tarawera eruption, was once the world's largest, often gushing to a dizzying height of 400m.

GEYSERS

ENVIRONMENTAL ISSUES IN AOTEAROA NEW ZEALAND
NANDOR TANCZOS

Aotearoa New Zealand likes to sell itself as clean and green. We have the NZ Forest Accord to protect native forests. National parks and reserves now cover a third of the country. Marine reserves continue to pop up around the coast. Our antinuclear legislation seems unassailable. A closer look, however, reveals a dirtier picture.

New Zealand is one of the highest per-capita emitters of greenhouse gases. We are one of the most inefficient users of energy in the developed world. Public transport is negligible in most places. Add the ongoing battle in many communities to stop the pumping of sewage and toxic waste into waterways, a conflict often spearheaded by *tangata whenua* (Maori), and the 'clean and green' label looks a bit tarnished.

One of our challenges is that our biggest polluting sector is also our biggest export earner. Pastoral farming causes half of our greenhouse-gas emissions. Clearing forests to grow cows and sheep has left many hillsides scoured by erosion. Grazing animals damage stream edges and lake margins and farm run-off has left many waterways unsafe for swimming or drinking. The worse culprit is dairy farming, and while regional councils and farming groups are fencing and planting stream banks to protect water quality, their efforts are outstripped by the sheer growth in dairying. Meanwhile governments are reluctant to take on the powerful farming lobby.

Our other major challenge is around mining and drilling. The state-owned company Solid Energy plans to expand coalmining on the West Coast and convert lignite (the dirtiest form of coal) into fertiliser and diesel. The government is also encouraging overseas companies to prospect for off-shore oil in what would be some of the deepest and most difficult waters for drilling in the world. Once again local *iwi* (tribes) such as Te Whanau a Apanui are in the front lines alongside environmental groups like Greenpeace, fighting to prevent the marine ecosystems of the East Coast being put at risk.

Despite these things, New Zealand has some good things going on. A high proportion of our energy is from renewable sources. Farm animals, except for pigs and chickens, are mostly grass fed and free range. We are getting better with waste minimisation and resource recovery. Like most countries, though, we need to make a stronger effort to develop not just sustainable, but regenerative economic systems.

Our biggest saving grace is our small population. As a result, Aotearoa is a place well worth visiting. This is a beautiful land with enormous geographical and ecological diversity. Our forests are unique and magnificent, and the bird species that evolved in response to an almost total lack of mammalian life are spectacular, although now reduced in numbers from introduced predators such as rats, stoats and hedgehogs.

Visitors who want to help protect our ecological integrity can make the biggest impact by asking questions of their hosts: every time you ask where the recycling centre is; every time you question wasteful energy use, car use and water use; every time you ask for organic or free-range food at a cafe or restaurant; you affect the person you talk to.

Aotearoa New Zealand has the potential to be a world leader in ecological wisdom. We have a strong tradition to draw from – the careful relationship of reciprocity that Maori developed with the natural world over the course of many, many generations. We live at the edge of the Pacific, on the Rim of Fire, a remnant of the ancient forests of Gondwanaland. We welcome conscious travellers.

Nandor Tanczos is a social ecologist based in Ngaruawahia. He was a Member of Parliament for the Green Party from 1999 to 2008.

The now extinct flightless moa, the largest of which grew to 3.5m tall and weighed over 200kg, browsed open grasslands much as cattle do today (skeletons can be seen at Auckland Museum), while the smaller kiwi still ekes out a nocturnal living rummaging among forest leaf litter for insects and worms much as small mammals do elsewhere. One of the country's most ferocious-looking insects, the mouse-sized giant weta, meanwhile, has taken on a scavenging role elsewhere filled by rodents.

As one of the last places on earth to be colonised by humans, NZ was for millennia a safe laboratory for such risky evolutionary strategies, but with the arrival first of Maori and soon after of Europeans, things went downhill fast.

Many endemic creatures, including moa and the huia, an exquisite songbird, were driven to extinction, and the vast forests were cleared for their timber and to make way for agriculture. Destruction of habitat and the introduction of exotic animals and plants have taken a terrible environmental toll and New Zealanders are now fighting a rearguard battle to save what remains.

Birds & Animals

The first Polynesian settlers found little in the way of land mammals – just two species of bat – but forests, plains and coasts alive with birds. Largely lacking the bright plumage found elsewhere, NZ's birds – like its endemic plants – have an understated beauty that does not shout for attention.

Among the most musical is the bellbird, common in both native and exotic forests everywhere except Northland, though like many birds it is more likely to be heard than seen. Its call is a series of liquid bell notes, most often sounded at dawn or dusk.

The tui, another nectar eater and the country's most beautiful songbird, is a great mimic, with an inventive repertoire that includes clicks, grunts and chuckles. Notable for the white throat feathers that stand out against its dark plumage, the tui often feeds on flax flowers in suburban gardens but is most at home in densely tangled forest ('bush' to New Zealanders).

Fantails are commonly encountered on forest trails, swooping and jinking to catch insects stirred up by passing hikers, while pukeko, elegant swamp-hens with blue plumage and bright-red beaks, are readily seen along wetland margins and even on the sides of roads nearby – be warned, they have little road sense.

If you spend any time in the South Island high country, you are likely to come up against the fearless and inquisitive kea – an uncharacteristically drab green parrot with bright-red underwings. Kea are common in the car parks of the Fox and Franz Josef Glaciers, where they hang out for food scraps or tear rubber from car windscreens.

Then there is the takahe, a rare flightless bird thought extinct until a small colony was discovered in 1948, and the equally flightless kiwi, NZ's national emblem and the nickname for New Zealanders themselves.

The kiwi has a round body covered in coarse feathers, strong legs and a long, distinctive bill with nostrils at the tip for sniffing out food. It is not easy to find them in the wild, but they can be seen in simulated environments at excellent nocturnal houses. One of the best is the Otorohanga Kiwi House, which also has other birds, including native falcons, moreporks (owls) and weka.

To get a feel for what the bush used to be like, take a trip to Tiritiri Matangi island. This regenerating island is an open sanctuary and one of the country's most successful exercises in community-assisted conservation.

BIRDWATCHING

The flightless kiwi is the species most sought after by birdwatchers. Sightings of the Stewart Island subspecies are common at all times of the year. Elsewhere, wild sightings of this increasingly rare nocturnal species are difficult, apart from in enclosures. Other birds that twitchers like to sight are the royal albatross, white heron, Fiordland crested penguin, yellow-eyed penguin, Australasian gannet and wrybill.

On the Coromandel Peninsula, the Firth of Thames (particularly Miranda) is a haven for migrating birds, while the Wharekawa Wildlife

B Heather and H Robertson's *Field Guide to the Birds of New Zealand* is a comprehensive guide for birdwatchers and a model of helpfulness for anyone even casually interested in the country's remarkable bird life.

ENVIRONMENT

KIWI SPOTTING

A threatened species, the kiwi is also nocturnal and difficult to see in the wild, although you can do this in Trounson Kauri Park in Northland, Okarito on the West Coast and on Stewart Island. They can, however, be observed in many artificially dark 'kiwi houses':

» Auckland Zoo (p57)
» Kiwi North (p115), Maunu
» Rainbow Springs Kiwi Wildlife Park (p288), Rotorua
» Otorohanga Kiwi House & Native Bird Park (p197)
» National Aquarium of New Zealand (p335), Napier
» Nga Manu Nature Reserve (p376), Waikanae
» Pukaha Mt Bruce National Wildlife Centre (p381), near Masterton
» Wellington Zoo (p357)

Refuge at Opoutere Beach is a breeding ground of the endangered NZ dotterel. There's also a very accessible Australasian gannet colony at Muriwai, west of Auckland, and one in Hawke's Bay. There are popular trips to observe pelagic birds out of Kaikoura, and royal albatross viewing on the Otago Peninsula.

Two good guides are the revised *Field Guide to the Birds of New Zealand,* by Barrie Heather and Hugh Robertson, and *Birds of New Zealand: Locality Guide* by Stuart Chambers.

MARINE MAMMAL-WATCHING

Kaikoura, on the northeast coast of the South Island, is NZ's nexus of marine mammal-watching. The main attraction here is whale-watching, but this is dependent on weather conditions, so don't expect to just be able to rock up and head straight out on a boat for a dream encounter. The sperm whale, the largest toothed whale, is pretty much a year-round resident, and depending on the season you may also see migrating humpback whales, pilot whales, blue whales and southern right whales. Other mammals – including fur seals and dusky dolphins – are seen year-round.

Kaikoura is also an outstanding place to swim with dolphins. Pods of up to 500 playful dusky dolphins can be seen on any given day. Dolphin swimming is common elsewhere in NZ, with the animals gathering off the North Island near Whakatane, Paihia, Tauranga, and in the Hauraki Gulf, and off Akaroa on the South Island's Banks Peninsula. Seal swimming is possible in Kaikoura and in the Abel Tasman National Park.

Swimming with sharks is also possible, though with a protective cage as a chaperone; you can do it in Gisborne.

Nature Guide to the New Zealand Forest, by J Dawson and R Lucas, is a beautifully photographed foray into the world of NZ's forests. Far from being drab and colourless, these lush treasure houses are home to ancient species dating from the time of the dinosaurs. This guidebook will have you reaching for your boots.

Trees

No visitor to NZ (particularly Australians!) will go for long without hearing about the damage done to the bush by that bad-mannered Australian import, the brush-tailed possum. The long list of mammal pests introduced to NZ accidentally or for a variety of misguided reasons includes deer, rabbits, stoats, pigs and goats. But the most destructive by far is the possum, 70 million of which now chew through millions of tonnes of foliage a year despite the best efforts of the Department of Conservation (DOC) to control them.

Among favoured possum food are NZ's most colourful trees: the kowhai, a small-leaved tree growing to 11m, that in spring has drooping clusters of bright-yellow flowers (NZ's national flower); the pohutukawa, a beautiful coastal tree of the northern North Island which bursts into vivid red flower in December, earning the nickname 'Christmas tree'; and a similar crimson-flowered tree, the rata. Rata species are found on both islands; the northern rata starts life as a climber on a host tree (that it eventually chokes).

The few remaining pockets of mature centuries-old kauri are stately emblems of former days. Their vast hammered trunks and towering, epiphyte-festooned limbs, which dwarf every other tree in the forest, are reminders of why they were sought after in colonial days for spars

National Parks

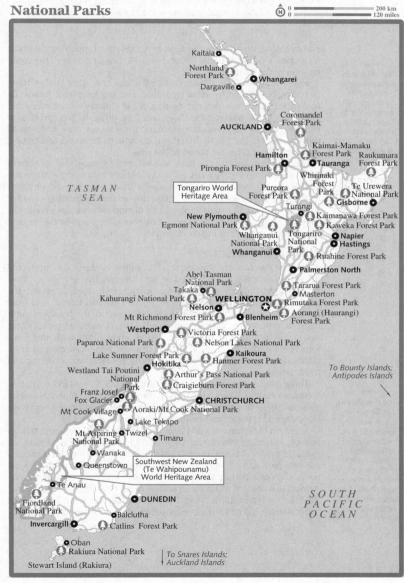

0 — 200 km
0 — 120 miles

Kaitaia

Northland Forest Park
Whangarei
Dargaville

Coromandel Forest Park

AUCKLAND

Kaimai-Mamaku Forest Park   Raukumara Forest Park
Hamilton
Tauranga
Pirongia Forest Park

Whirinaki Forest Park   Te Urewera National Park
Pureora Forest Park
Tongariro World Heritage Area
Gisborne
Turangi
Kaimanawa Forest Park

New Plymouth
Egmont National Park
Kaweka Forest Park
Whanganui National Park
Tongariro National Park
Napier
Hastings
Whanganui
Ruahine Forest Park

TASMAN SEA

Palmerston North

Abel Tasman National Park
Tararua Forest Park
Takaka
Masterton
Kahurangi National Park
WELLINGTON
Rimutaka Forest Park
Nelson
Aorangi (Haurangi) Forest Park
Mt Richmond Forest Park
Blenheim
Westport
Victoria Forest Park
Paparoa National Park
Nelson Lakes National Park
Kaikoura
Lake Sumner Forest Park
Hanmer Forest Park
Hokitika
Westland Tai Poutini National Park
Arthur's Pass National Park
Craigieburn Forest Park
Franz Josef
Fox Glacier
CHRISTCHURCH
Mt Cook Village
Aoraki/Mt Cook National Park
Lake Tekapo
Mt Aspiring National Park
Twizel
Timaru
Wanaka
Queenstown
Southwest New Zealand (Te Wahipounamu) World Heritage Area
Te Anau
DUNEDIN
Fiordland National Park
Balclutha
Invercargill
Catlins Forest Park
Oban
Rakiura National Park
Stewart Island (Rakiura)

To Bounty Islands; Antipodes Islands

SOUTH PACIFIC OCEAN

To Snares Islands; Auckland Islands

TOWERING KAURI

When Chaucer was born this was a sturdy young tree. When Shakespeare was born it was 300 years old. It predates most of the great cathedrals of Europe. Its trunk is sky-rocket straight and sky-rocket bulky, limbless for half its height. Ferns sprout from its crevices. Its crown is an asymmetric mess, like an inverted root system. I lean against it, give it a slap. It's like slapping a building. This is a tree out of Tolkien. It's a kauri.

Joe Bennett (A Land of Two Halves) referring to the McKinney kauri in Northland.

ENVIRONMENT

The 🖉 icon in this book marks places that demonstrate a commitment to sustainability. Travellers seeking other sustainable tourism operators should look for operators accredited with Qualmark Green (www.qualmark.co.nz) or listed at Organic Explorer (www.organicexplorer.co.nz).

and building timber. The best place to see the remaining giants is Northland's Waipoua Kauri Forest, home to three-quarters of the country's surviving kauri.

Now the pressure has been taken off kauri and other timber trees, including the distinctive rimu (red pine) and the long-lived totara (favoured for Maori war canoes), by one of the country's most successful imports – *Pinus radiata*. Pine was found to thrive in NZ, growing to maturity in just 35 years, and plantation forests are now widespread through the central North Island – the southern hemisphere's biggest, Kaingaroa Forest, lies southeast of Rotorua.

You won't get far into the bush without coming across one of its most prominent features – tree ferns. NZ is a land of ferns (more than 80 species) and most easily recognised are the mamaku (black tree fern) – which grows to 20m and can be seen in damp gullies throughout the country – and the 10m-high ponga (silver tree fern) with its distinctive white underside. The silver fern is equally at home as part of corporate logos and on the clothing of many of the country's top sportspeople.

National Parks

A third of the country – more than 5 million hectares – is protected in environmentally important parks and reserves that embrace almost every conceivable landscape: from mangrove-fringed inlets in the north to the snow-topped volcanoes of the Central Plateau, and from the forested fastness of the Ureweras in the east to the Southern Alps' majestic mountains, glaciers and fiords. The 14 national parks, three marine parks and more than 30 marine reserves, along with numerous forest parks, offer huge scope for wilderness experiences, ranging from climbing, snow skiing and mountain biking to tramping, kayaking and trout fishing.

Three places are World Heritage areas: NZ's Subantarctic Islands, Tongariro National Park and Te Wahipounamu, an amalgam of several national parks in southwest NZ that boast the world's finest surviving Gondwanaland plants and animals in their natural habitats.

The Department of Conservation website (www.doc.govt.nz) has useful information on the country's national parks, tracks and walkways. It also lists backcountry huts and campsites.

Access to the country's wild places is relatively straightforward, though huts on walking tracks require passes and may need to be booked in advance. In practical terms, there is little difference for travellers between a national park and a forest park, though dogs are not allowed in national parks without a permit. Camping is possible in all parks, but may be restricted to dedicated camping grounds – check first. Permits are required for hunting (game birds), and licences are needed for inland fishing (trout, salmon); both can be bought online at www.fishandgame.org.nz.

Maori Culture

John Huria

John Huria (Ngai Tahu, Muaupoko) has an editorial, research and writing background with a focus on Maori writing and culture. He was senior editor for Maori publishing company Huia (NZ) and now runs an editorial and publishing services company, Ahi Text Solutions Ltd (www.ahitextsolutions.co.nz).

'Maori' once just meant 'common' or 'everyday', but now it means...let's just begin by saying that there is a lot of 'then' and a lot of 'now' in the Maori world. Sometimes the cultural present follows on from the past quite seamlessly; sometimes things have changed hugely; sometimes we just want to look to the future.

Maori today are a diverse people. Some are engaged with traditional cultural networks and pursuits; others are occupied with adapting tradition and placing it into a dialogue with globalising culture. The Maori concept of *whanaungatanga* – family relationships – is important to the culture. And families spread out from the *whanau* (extended family) to the *hapu* (subtribe) and *iwi* (tribe) and even, in a sense, beyond the human world and into the natural and spiritual worlds.

Maori are New Zealand's *tangata whenua* (people of the land), and the Maori relationship with the land has developed over hundreds of years of occupation. Once a predominantly rural people, many Maori now live in urban centres, away from their traditional home base. But it's still common practice in formal settings to introduce oneself by referring to home: an ancestral mountain, river, sea or lake, or an ancestor. There's no place like home, but it's good to be away as well.

If you're looking for a Maori experience in NZ you'll find it – in performance, in conversation, in an art gallery, on a tour...

> The best way to learn about the relationship between the land and the *tangata whenua* is to get out there and start talking with Maori.

Maori Then

Some three millennia ago people began moving eastward into the Pacific, sailing against the prevailing winds and currents (hard to go out, easier to return safely). Some stopped at Tonga and Samoa, and others settled the small central East Polynesian tropical islands.

The Maori colonisation of Aotearoa began from an original homeland known to Maori as Hawaiki. Skilled navigators and sailors travelled across the Pacific, using many navigational tools – currents, winds, stars, birds and wave patterns – to guide their large, double-hulled ocean-going craft to a new land. The first of many was the great navigator Kupe, who arrived, the story goes, chasing an octopus named Muturangi. But the distinction of giving NZ its well-known Maori name – Aotearoa – goes to his wife, Kuramarotini, who cried out, '*He ao, he ao tea, he ao tea roa!*' (A cloud, a white cloud, a long white cloud!).

Kupe and his crew journeyed around the land, and many places around Cook Strait (between the North and South Islands), and the Hokianga in Northland still bear the names that they gave them and the marks of his passage. Kupe returned to Hawaiki, leaving from (and naming) Northland's Hokianga. He gave other seafarers valuable navigational information. And then the great *waka* (ocean-going craft) began to arrive.

The *waka* that the first setters arrived on, and their landing places, are immortalised in tribal histories. Well-known *waka* include *Takitimu, Kurahaupo, Te Arawa, Mataatua, Tainui, Aotea* and *Tokomaru*. There are many others. Maori trace their genealogies back to those who arrived on the *waka* (and further back as well).

What would it have been like making the transition from small tropical islands to a much larger, cooler land mass? Goodbye breadfruit, coconuts, paper mulberry; hello moa, fernroot, flax – and immense space (relatively speaking). NZ has over 15,000km of coastline. Rarotonga, by way of contrast, has a little over 30km. There was land, lots of it, and a flora and fauna that had developed more or less separately from the rest of the world for 80 million years. There was an untouched, massive fishery. There were great seaside mammalian convenience stores – seals and sea lions – as well as a fabulous array of birds.

The early settlers went on the move, pulled by love, by trade opportunities and greater resources; pushed by disputes and threats to security. When they settled, Maori established *mana whenua* (regional authority), whether by military campaigns, or by the peaceful methods of intermarriage and diplomacy. Looking over tribal history it's possible to see the many alliances, absorptions and extinctions that went on.

Histories were carried by the voice, in stories, songs and chants. Great stress was placed on accurate learning – after all, in an oral culture where people are the libraries, the past is always a generation or two away from oblivion.

Maori lived in *kainga,* small villages, which often had associated gardens. Housing was quite cosy by modern standards – often it was hard

Arriving for the first time in NZ, two crew members of *Tainui* saw the red flowers of the pohutukawa tree, and they cast away their prized red feather ornaments, thinking that there were plenty to be had on shore.

HOW THE WORLD BEGAN

In the Maori story of creation, first there was the void, then the night, then Rangi-nui (sky father) and Papa-tu-a-nuku (earth mother) came into being, embracing with their children nurtured between them. But nurturing became something else. Their children were stifled in the darkness of their embrace. Unable to stretch out to their full dimensions and struggling to see clearly in the darkness, their children tried to separate them. Tawhiri-matea, the god of winds, raged against them; Tu-mata-uenga, the god of war, assaulted them. Each god child in turn tried to separate them, but still Rangi and Papa pressed against each other. And then Tane-mahuta, god of the great forests and of humanity, placed his feet against his father and his back against his mother and slowly, inexorably, began to move them apart. Then came the world of light, of demigods and humanity.

In this world of light Maui, the demigod ancestor, was cast out to sea at birth and was found floating in his mother's topknot. He was a shape-shifter, becoming a pigeon or a dog or an eel if it suited his purposes. He stole fire from the gods. Using his grandmother's jawbone, he bashed the sun so that it could only limp slowly across the sky, so that people would have enough time during the day to get things done (if only he would do it again!). Using the South Island as a canoe, he used the jawbone as a hook to fish up Te Ika a Maui (the fish of Maui) – the North Island. And, finally, he met his end trying to defeat death itself. The goddess of death, Hine Nui Te Po, had obsidian teeth in her vagina (obsidian is a volcanic glass that takes a razor edge when chipped). Maui attempted to reverse birth (and hence defeat death) by crawling into her birth canal to reach her heart as she slept. A small bird – a fantail – laughed at the absurd sight. Hine Nui Te Po awoke, and crushed Maui between her thighs. Death one, humanity nil.

to stand upright while inside. From time to time people would leave their home base and go to harvest seasonal foods. When peaceful life was interrupted by conflict, the people would withdraw to *pa,* fortified dwelling places.

And then Europeans began to arrive.

Maori Today

Today's culture is marked by new developments in the arts, business, sport and politics. Many historical grievances still stand, but some *iwi* (Ngai Tahu and Tainui, for example) have settled historical grievances and are major forces in the NZ economy. Maori have also addressed the decline in Maori language use by establishing *kohanga reo, kura kaupapa Maori* and *wananga* (Maori-medium preschools, schools and universities). There is now a generation of people who speak Maori as a first language. There is a network of Maori radio stations, and Maori TV is attracting a committed viewership. A recently revived Maori event is becoming more and more prominent – Matariki, or Maori New Year. The constellation Matariki is also known as Pleiades. It begins to rise above the horizon in late May or early June and its appearance traditionally signals a time for learning, planning and preparing as well as singing, dancing and celebrating. Watch out for talks and lectures, concerts, dinners, and even formal balls.

Religion

Christian churches and denominations are important in the Maori world: televangelists, mainstream churches for regular and occasional worship, and two major Maori churches (Ringatu and Ratana) – we've got it all.

But in the (non–Judaeo Christian) beginning there were the *atua Maori,* the Maori gods, and for many Maori the gods are a vital and relevant force still. It is common to greet the earth mother and sky father when speaking formally at a *marae.* The gods are represented in art and carving, sung of in *waiata* (songs), invoked through *karakia* (prayer and incantation) when a meeting house is opened, when a *waka* is launched, even (more simply) when a meal is served. They are spoken of on the *marae* and in wider Maori contexts. The traditional Maori creation story is well known and widely celebrated.

The Arts

There are many collections of Maori *taonga* (treasures) around the country. Some of the largest and most comprehensive are at Wellington's Te Papa Museum and the Auckland Museum. Canterbury Museum in Christchurch also has a good collection, and Hokitika Museum has an exhibition showing the story of *pounamu* (nephrite jade, or greenstone).

You can stay up to date with what is happening in the Maori arts by reading *Mana* magazine (available from most newsagents), listening to *iwi* stations (www.irirangi.net) or weekly podcasts from Radio New Zealand (www.radionz.co.nz). Maori TV also has regular features on the Maori arts – check out www.maoritelevision.com.

Maori TV went to air in 2004, an emotional time for many Maori who could at last see their culture, their concerns and their language in a mass medium. Over 90% of content is NZ-made, and programs are in both Maori and English: they're subtitled and accessible to everyone. If you want to really get a feel for the rhythm and meter of spoken Maori from the comfort of your own chair, switch to Te Reo, a Maori-language-only channel.

IWI

You can check out a map that shows *iwi* distribution and a good list of *iwi* (tribe) websites on Wikipedia (www.wikipedia.org).

TA MOKO

Ta moko is the Maori art of tattoo, traditionally worn by men on their faces, thighs and buttocks, and by women on their chins and lips. *Moko* were permanent grooves tapped into the skin using pigment (made from burnt caterpillar or kauri gum soot), and bone chisels: fine, sharp combs for broad work, and straight blades for detailed work. Museums in the major centres – Auckland, Wellington and Christchurch – all display traditional implements for *ta moko*.

The modern tattooist's gun is common now, but bone chisels are coming back into use for Maori who want to reconnect with tradition. Since the general renaissance in Maori culture in the 1960s, many artists have taken up *ta moko* and now many Maori wear *moko* with quiet pride and humility.

Can visitors get involved, or even get some work done? The term *kirituhi* (skin inscriptions) has arisen to describe Maori motif–inspired modern tattoos that non-Maori can wear.

See Ngahuia Te Awekotuku's *Mau Moko: The World of Maori Tattoo* (2007) for the big picture, with powerful, beautiful images and an incisive commentary.

CARVING

Traditional Maori carving, with its intricate detailing and curved lines, can transport the viewer. It's quite amazing to consider that it was done with stone tools, themselves painstakingly made, until the advent of iron (nails suddenly became very popular).

Some major traditional forms are *waka* (canoes), *pataka* (storage buildings), and *wharenui* (meeting houses). You can see sublime examples of traditional carving at Te Papa in Wellington, and at the following:

» Auckland Museum (p51) Maori Court
» Hell's Gate (p288) Carver in action every day; near Rotorua
» Parihaka (p222) Historic site on Surf Highway 45, Taranaki
» Putiki Church (p226) Interior covered in carvings and *tukutuku* (wall panels), Whanganui
» Taupo Museum (p245) Carved meeting house
» Te Manawa (p236) Museum with a Maori focus, Palmerston North
» Waikato Museum (p180) Beautifully carved *waka taua* (war canoe), Hamilton
» Wairakei Terraces (p246) Carved meeting house, Taupo
» Waitangi Treaty Grounds (p130) *Whare runanga* and *waka taua*
» Whakarewarewa Thermal Village (p275) The 'living village' – carving, other arts, meeting house and performance, Rotorua
» Whanganui Regional Museum (p225) Wonderful carved *waka*, Whanganui

For information on Maori arts today, check out Toi Maori www.maoriart.org.nz.

The apex of carving today is the *whare whakairo* (carved meeting house). A commissioning group relates its history and ancestral stories to a carver, who then draws (sometimes quite loosely) on traditional motifs to interpret or embody the stories and ancestors in wood or composite fibreboard.

Rongomaraeroa Marae, by artist Cliff Whiting, at Te Papa in Wellington is a colourful example of a contemporary re-imagining of a traditional art form. The biggest change in carving (as with most traditional arts) has been in the use of new mediums and tools. Rangi Kipa uses a synthetic polymer called Corian to make his *hei tiki* (figure motif worn around the neck), the same stuff that is used to make kitchen benchtops. You can check out his gallery at www.rangikipa.com.

VISITING MARAE

As you travel around the North Island, you will see many *marae* complexes. Often *marae* are owned by a descent group. They are also owned by urban Maori groups, schools, universities and church groups, and they should only be visited by arrangement with the owners. Some *marae* that may be visited include Huria Marae (p293) in Tauranga; Koriniti
Marae (p235) on the Whanganui River Rd; Te Manuka Tutahi Marae (p306) in Wakatane; and Te Papa (p358) in Wellington.

Marae complexes include a *wharenui* (meeting house), which often embodies an ancestor. Its ridge is the backbone, the rafters are ribs, and it shelters the descendants. There is a clear space in front of the *wharenui* (ie the *marae atea*). Sometimes there are other buildings: a *wharekai* (dining hall); a toilet and shower block; perhaps even classrooms, play equipment and the like.

Hui (gatherings) are held at *marae*. Issues are discussed, classes conducted, milestones celebrated and the dead farewelled. *Te reo Maori* (the Maori language) is prominent, sometimes exclusively so.

Visitors sleep in the meeting house if a *hui* goes on for longer than a day. Mattresses are placed on the floor, someone may bring a guitar, and stories and jokes always go down well as the evening stretches out...

The Powhiri

If you visit a *marae* as part of an organised group, you'll be welcomed in a *powhiri* (formal welcome). The more common ones are outlined here.

There may be a *wero* (challenge). Using *taiaha* (quarter-staff) moves, a warrior will approach the visitors and place a baton on the ground for a visitor to pick up.

There is a *karanga* (ceremonial call). A woman from the host group calls to the visitors and a woman from the visitors responds. Their long, high, falling calls begin to overlap and interweave and the visiting group walks on to the *marae atea*.

It is then time for *whaikorero* (speechmaking). The hosts welcome the visitors, the visitors respond. Speeches are capped off by a *waiata* (song), and the visitors' speaker places *koha* (gift, usually an envelope of cash) on the *marae*. The hosts then invite the visitors to *hariru* (shake hands) and *hongi* (press foreheads together). Visitors and hosts are now united and will share light refreshments or a meal.

The Hongi

Press forehead and nose together firmly, shake hands, and perhaps offer a greeting such as *'Kia ora'* or *'Tena koe'*. Some prefer one press (for two or three seconds, or longer), others prefer two shorter (press, release, press). Men and women sometimes kiss on one cheek. Some people mistakenly think the *hongi* is a pressing of noses only (awkward to aim!) or the rubbing of noses (even more awkward).

Tapu

Tapu (spiritual restrictions) and *mana* (power and prestige) are taken seriously in the Maori world. Sit on chairs or seating provided (never on tables), and walk around people, not over them. The *powhiri* is *tapu*, and mixing food and *tapu* is right up there on the offence-o-meter. Do eat and drink when invited to do so by your hosts. You needn't worry about starvation: an important Maori value is *manaakitanga* (kindness).

Depending on the area, the *powhiri* has gender roles: women *karanga* (call), men *whaikorero* (orate); women lead the way on to the *marae,* men sit on the *paepae* (the speakers' bench at the front). In a modern context, the debate around these roles continues.

WEAVING

Weaving was an essential art that provided clothing, nets and cordage, footwear for rough country travel, mats to cover earthen floors, and *kete* (bags). Many woven items are beautiful as well as practical. Some were major works – *korowai* (cloaks) could take years to finish. Woven predominantly with flax and bird feathers, they are worn now on ceremonial occasions, a stunning sight.

Working with natural materials for the greater good of the people involved getting things right by maintaining the supply of raw material and ensuring that it worked as it was meant to. Protocols were necessary, and women were dedicated to weaving under the aegis of the gods. Today, tradition is greatly respected, but not all traditions are necessarily followed.

Flax was (and still is) the preferred medium for weaving. To get a strong fibre from flax leaves, weavers scraped away the leaves' flesh with a mussel shell, then pounded until it was soft, dyed it, then dried it. But contemporary weavers are using everything in their work: raffia, copper wire, rubber – even polar fleece and garden hoses!

The best place to experience weaving is to contact one of the many weavers running workshops. By learning the art, you'll appreciate the examples of weaving in museums even more. And if you want your own? Woven *kete* and backpacks have become fashion accessories and are on sale in most cities. Weaving is also found in dealer art galleries around the country.

HAKA

Experiencing *haka* can get the adrenaline flowing, as it did for one Pakeha observer in 1929 who thought of dark Satanic mills: 'They looked like fiends from hell wound up by machinery'. *Haka* can be awe-inspiring; they can also be uplifting. The *haka* is not only a war dance – it is used to welcome visitors, honour achievement, express identity or to put forth very strong opinions.

Haka involve chanted words, vigorous body movements, and *pukana* (when performers distort their faces, eyes bulging with the whites showing, perhaps with tongue extended).

The well-known *haka* 'Ka Mate', performed by the All Blacks before rugby test matches, is credited to the cunning fighting chief Te Rauparaha. It celebrates his escape from death. Chased by enemies, he hid himself in a food pit. After they had left, a friendly chief named Te Whareangi (the 'hairy man' referred to in the *haka*), let him out; he climbed out into the sunshine and performed 'Ka Mate'.

On the North Island, you can experience *haka* at various cultural performances in Rotorua, including at Mitai Maori Village (p278), Tamaki Maori Village (p278) and Whakarewarewa Thermal Village (p275). In the Bay of Islands, *haka* is performed at Culture North (p131) and the Waitangi Treaty Grounds (p130).

But the best displays of *haka* are at the national Te Matatini National Kapa Haka Festival when NZ's top groups compete. It is held every two years, with the next festival in February 2013 to take place in Rotorua.

CONTEMPORARY VISUAL ART

A distinctive feature of Maori visual art is the tension between traditional Maori ideas and modern artistic mediums and trends. Shane Cotton produced a series of works that conversed with 19th-century painted meeting houses, which themselves departed from Maori carved houses. Kelcy Taratoa uses toys, superheroes and pop urban imagery alongside weaving and carving design.

Kupe's passage is marked around NZ: he left his sails (Nga Ra o Kupe) near Cape Palliser as triangular landforms; he named the two islands in Wellington Harbour Matiu and Makoro after his daughters; his blood stains the red rocks of Wellington's south coast.

Maori legends are all around you as you tour NZ: Maui's *waka* became today's Southern Alps; a *taniwha* (aupernatural creature) formed Lake Waikaremoana in its death throes; and a rejected Mt Taranaki walked into exile from the central North Island mountain group, carving the Whanganui River.

Of course not all Maori artists use Maori motifs. Ralph Hotere is a major NZ artist who 'happens to be Maori' (his words), and his career-long exploration of black speaks more to modernism than the traditional *marae* context.

Contemporary Maori art is by no means only about painting. Many other artists use installations as the preferred medium – look out for work by Jacqueline Fraser and Peter Robinson.

There are some great permanent exhibitions of Maori visual arts in the major centres. Both the Auckland and Christchurch Art Galleries hold strong collections, as does Wellington's Te Papa.

CONTEMPORARY THEATRE

The 1970s saw the emergence of many Maori playwrights and plays, and theatre is a strong area of the Maori arts today. Maori theatre drew heavily on the traditions of the *marae*. Instead of dimming the lights and immediately beginning the performance, many Maori theatre groups began with a stylised *powhiri*, had space for audience members to respond to the play, and ended with a *karakia* or a farewell.

Taki Rua is an independent producer of Maori work for both children and adults and has been in existence for over 25 years. As well as staging its shows in the major centres, it tours most of its work – check out its website (www.takirua.co.nz) for the current offerings. Maori drama is also often showcased at the professional theatres in the main centres as well as the biennial New Zealand International Festival. Hone Kouka and Briar Grace-Smith (both have published playscripts available) have toured their works around NZ and to festivals in the UK.

CONTEMPORARY DANCE

Contemporary Maori dance often takes its inspiration from *kapa haka* and traditional Maori imagery. The exploration of pre-European life also provides inspiration. For example, a Maori choreographer, Moss Patterson, used *kokowai* (a body-adorning paste made from reddish clay and shark oil) as the basis of his most recent piece of the same name.

NZ's leading specifically Maori dance company is the Atamira Dance Collective (www.atamiradance.co.nz), which has been producing critically acclaimed, beautiful and challenging work since 2000. If that sounds too earnest, another choreographer to watch out for is Mika Torotoro, who happily blends *kapa haka* (cultural dance), drag, opera, ballet and disco into his work. You can check out clips of his work at www.mika.co.nz.

MAORI FILM-MAKING

Although there had already been successful Maori documentaries (*Patu!* and the *Tangata Whenua* series are brilliant, and available from some urban video stores), it wasn't until 1987 that NZ had its first fiction feature-length movie by a Maori director with Barry Barclay's *Ngati*. Mereta Mita was the first Maori woman to direct a fiction feature, with *Mauri* (1988). Both Mita and Barclay had highly political aims and ways of working, which involved a lengthy pre-production phase, during which they would consult with and seek direction from their *kaumatua* (elders). Films with significant Maori participation or control include the harrowing *Once Were Warriors* and the uplifting *Whale Rider*. Oscar-shortlisted Taika Waititi, of Te Whanau-a-Apanui descent, wrote and directed *Eagle vs Shark*.

The New Zealand Film Archive (www.filmarchive.org.nz) is a great place to experience Maori film, with most showings being either free or relatively inexpensive. It has offices in Auckland and Wellington.

See Hirini Moko Mead's *Tikanga Maori*, Pat and Hiwi Tauroa's *Visiting a Marae*, and Anne Salmond's *Hui* for detailed information on Maori customs.

Music plays an important role in traditional and contemporary Maori culture.

The first NZ hip-hop song to become a hit was Dalvanius Prime's 'Poi E', which was sung entirely in Maori by the Patea Maori Club. It was the highest-selling single of 1984 in NZ, outselling all international artists.

MAORI WRITING

There are many novels and collections of short stories by Maori writers, and personal taste will govern your choices. How about approaching Maori writing regionally? Read Patricia Grace *(Potiki, Cousins, Dogside Story, Tu)* around Wellington, and maybe Witi Ihimaera *(Pounamu, Pounamu, The Matriarch, Bulibasha, The Whale Rider)* on the North Island's East Coast. Keri Hulme *(The Bone People, Stonefish)* and the South Island go together like a mass of whitebait bound in a frying pan by a single egg (ie very well). Read Alan Duff *(Once Were Warriors)* anywhere, but only if you want to be saddened, even shocked. Definitely take James George *(Hummingbird, Ocean Roads)* with you to Auckland's West Coast beaches and Northland's Ninety Mile Beach. Paula Morris *(Queen of Beauty, Hibiscus Coast, Trendy but Casual)* and Kelly Ana Morey *(Bloom, Grace Is Gone)* – hmm, Auckland and beyond? If poetry appeals you can't go past the giant of Maori poetry in English, the late, lamented Hone Tuwhare *(Deep River Talk: Collected Poems)*. Famously sounding like he's at church and in the pub at the same time, you *can* take him anywhere.

The Kiwi Psyche

What Makes Kiwis Tick?

New Zealand is like that little guy at school when they're picking rugby teams – quietly waiting to be noticed, desperately wanting to be liked. Then, when he does get the nod, his sheer determination to prove himself propels him to score a completely unexpected try. When his teammates come to congratulate him he stares at the ground and mumbles, 'It was nothing, ay'.

While NZ is a proud little nation, Kiwis traditionally don't have time for show-offs. Jingoistic flag-waving is generally frowned upon. People who make an impression on the international stage are respected and admired, but flashy tall poppies have traditionally had their heads lopped off. This is perhaps a legacy of NZ's early egalitarian ideals – the ones that sought to avoid the worst injustices of the 'mother country' (Britain) by breaking up large land holdings and enthusiastically adopting a 'cradle to grave' welfare state. 'Just because someone's got a bigger car than me, or bigger guns, doesn't make them better' is the general Kiwi attitude.

NZ has rarely let its size get in the way of making a point on the international stage. A founding member of the League of Nations (the precursor to the UN), it ruffled feathers between the world wars by failing to blindly follow Britain's position. It was in the 1980s, however, that things got really interesting.

People born in other countries make up 23% of NZ residents. Of these, the main regions of origin are the UK and Ireland (29%), the Pacific Islands (15%), Northeast Asia (15%) and Australia (7%).

A Turbulent Decade

Modern Kiwi culture pivots on that decade. Firstly, the unquestioned primacy of rugby union as a source of social cohesion (which rivalled the country's commitment to the two world wars as a foundation of nation-building) was stripped away when tens of thousands of New Zealanders took to the streets to protest a tour by the South African rugby side in 1981. The protestors held that the politics of apartheid not only had a place in sport, they trumped it. The country was starkly divided; there were riots in paradise. The scar is still strong enough that most New Zealanders over the age of 40 will recognise the simple phrase 'The Tour' as referring to those events.

The tour protests both harnessed and nourished a political and cultural renaissance among Maori that had already been rolling for a decade. Three years later, that renaissance found its mark when a reforming Labour government gave statutory teeth to the Waitangi Tribunal, an agency that has since guided a process of land return, compensation for past wrongs and interpretation of the Treaty of Waitangi – the 1840 pact between Maori and the Crown – as a living document.

At the same time antinuclear protests that had been rumbling for years gained momentum, with mass blockades of visiting US naval ships. In 1984 Prime Minister David Lange barred nuclear-powered or armed ships from entering NZ waters. The mouse had roared. As a result the US

NZ is defined as a state in the Australian constitution. At the time of Australia's federation into one country it was hoped that NZ would join. On this side of the Tasman that idea proved as unpopular then as it does now.

'SO, WHAT DO YOU THINK OF NEW ZEALAND?' *RUSSELL BROWN*

That, by tradition, is the question that visitors are asked within an hour of disembarking in NZ. Sometimes they might be granted an entire day's research before being asked to pronounce, but asked they are. The question – composed equally of great pride and creeping doubt – is symbolic of the national consciousness.

When George Bernard Shaw visited for four weeks in 1934, he was deluged with what-do-you-think-of questions from newspaper reporters the length of the country. Although he never saw fit to write a word about NZ, his answers to those newspaper questions were collected and reprinted as *What I Saw in New Zealand: the Newspaper Utterances of George Bernard Shaw in New Zealand*. Yes, people really were that keen for vindication.

Other visitors were more willing to pronounce in print, including the British Liberal MP, David Goldblatt, who wrote an intriguing and prescient little book called *Democracy At Ease: a New Zealand Profile*. Goldblatt found New Zealanders a blithe people: kind, prosperous and fond of machines.

For the bon vivant Goldblatt, the attitude towards food and drink was all too telling. He found only 'the plain fare and even plainer fetch and carry of the normal feeding machine of this country' and shops catering 'in the same pedestrian fashion for a people never fastidious – the same again is the order of the day'.

Thus, a people with access to some of the best fresh ingredients on earth tended to boil everything to death. A nation strewn almost its entire length with excellent microclimates for viticulture produced only fortified plonk. Material comfort was valued, but was a plain thing indeed.

It took New Zealanders a quarter of a century more to shuck 'the same dull sandwiches', and embrace a national awareness – and, as Goldblatt correctly anticipated, it took 'hazards and misfortunes' to spur the 'divine discontent' for change.

But when it did happen, it really happened.

Russell Brown is a journalist and manager of the popular Public Address blog site (www.publicaddress.net).

threw NZ out of ANZUS, the country's main strategic military alliance, which also included Australia, declaring NZ 'a friend but not an ally'.

However, it was an event in the following year that completely changed the way NZ related to the world, when French government agents launched an attack in Auckland Harbour, sinking Greenpeace's antinuclear flagship *Rainbow Warrior* and killing one of its crew. Being bombed by a country that NZ had fought two world wars with – and the muted or nonexistent condemnation by other allies – left an indelible mark. It strengthened NZ's resolve to follow its own conscience in foreign policy, and in 1987 the New Zealand Nuclear Free Zone, Disarmament, and Arms Control Act became law.

From the Boer to Vietnam Wars, NZ had blithely trotted off at the behest of the UK or US. Not anymore, as is demonstrated by its lack of involvement in the invasion of Iraq. That's not to say that the country shirks its international obligations: NZ troops continue to be deployed in peacekeeping capacities throughout the world and are currently active in Afghanistan.

'...a sordid act of international state-backed terrorism...' – Prime Minister David Lange, describing the bombing of the *Rainbow Warrior* (1986)

If that wasn't enough upheaval for one decade, 1986 saw another bitter battle split the community – this time over the decriminalisation of homosexuality. The debate was particularly rancorous, but the law that previously incarcerated consenting gay adults was repealed, paving the way for the generally accepting society that NZ is today. In 1999 Georgina Beyer, an openly transsexual former prostitute, would win a once-safe rural seat off a conservative incumbent – an unthinkable achievement in most of the world, let alone in the NZ of 13 years earlier.

Yet while the 1980s saw the country jump to the left on social issues, simultaneously economic reforms were carried out that were an extreme step to the right (to paraphrase one-time Hamiltonian Richard O'Brien's song 'The Time Warp'). The bloated public sector was slashed, any state assets that weren't bolted to the floor were sold off, regulation was removed from many sectors, trade barriers dismantled and the power of the unions greatly diminished.

If there is broad agreement that the economy had to be restructured, the reforms carried a heavy price. The old social guarantees are not as sure. New Zealanders work long hours for lower wages than their Australian cousins would ever tolerate. Compared with other Organisation for Economic Co-operation and Development (OECD) nations, NZ family incomes are low, child poverty rates are high and the gap between rich and poor is widening.

Yet there is a dynamism about NZ that was rare in the 'golden weather' years before the reforms. NZ farmers take on the world without the massive subsidies of yore, and Wellington's inner city – once virtually closed after dark by oppressive licensing laws – now thrives with great bars and restaurants.

As with the economic reforms, the 'Treaty process' of redress and reconciliation with Maori makes some New Zealanders uneasy, more in their uncertainty about its extent than that it has happened at all. The Maori population sat somewhere between 85,000 and 110,000 at the time of first European contact 200 years ago. Disease and warfare subsequently decimated the population, but a high birth rate now sees about 15% of New Zealanders (565,000 people) identify as Maori, and that proportion is likely to grow.

The implication of the Treaty is one of partnership between Maori and the British Crown, together forging a bicultural nation. After decades of attempted cultural assimilation it's now accepted in most quarters that the indigenous culture has a special and separate status within the country's ethnic mix. For example, Maori is an official language and there is a separate electoral roll granting Maori guaranteed parliamentary seats.

Yet room has had to be found for the many New Zealanders of neither British nor Maori heritage. In each new wave of immigration there has been a tendency to demonise before gradually accepting and celebrating what the new cultures have to offer. This happened with the Chinese in the mid-19th century, Croatians at the beginning of the 20th, Pacific Islanders in the 1970s and, most recently, the Chinese again in the 1990s. That said, NZ society is more integrated and accepting than most. People of all races are represented in all levels of society and race isn't an obstacle to achievement.

THE KIWI PSYCHE

Ironically, the person responsible for the nuclear age was a New Zealander. In 1917 Ernest Rutherford was the first to split the nucleus of an atom. His face appears on the $100 note.

IT'S A WOMAN'S WORLD

New Zealand is justifiably proud of being the first country in the world to give women the vote (in 1893). Kate Sheppard, the hero of the women's suffrage movement, even features on the country's $10 bill. Despite that early achievement, the real role for women in public life was modest for many years. That can hardly be said now. Since 1997 the country has had two female prime ministers and for a time in 2000 every key constitutional position was held by a woman, including the prime minister, attorney general, chief justice, governor general and head of state – although New Zealanders can't take credit for choosing Betty Windsor for that last role. At the same time a Maori queen headed the Kingitanga (King Movement; see p197) and a woman led NZ's biggest listed corporation. Things have slipped a little since and only two of those roles are held by women – and, yes, one of those is filled by Queen Elizabeth II.

A SPORTING CHANCE

The arena where Kiwis have most sated their desperation for recognition on the world stage is sport. In 2011, NZ was ranked the third most successful sporting nation per capita in the world (behind only Jamaica and Norway). NZ's teams are the current world champions in Rugby Union and Rugby League, holding both the men's and women's world cup in each code.

For most of the 20th century, NZ's All Blacks dominated international rugby union, with one squad even dubbed 'The Invincibles'. Taking over this pastime of the British upper class did wonders for national identity and the game is now interwoven with NZ's history and culture. The 2011 Rugby World Cup victory did much to raise spirits after a year of tragedy and economic gloom.

For all rugby's influence on the culture, don't go to a game expecting to be caught up in an orgy of noise and cheering. Rugby crowds at Auckland's Eden Park are as restrained as their teams are cavalier, but they get noisier as you head south. In contrast, a home game for the NZ Warriors rugby league team at Auckland's Mt Smart Stadium is a thrilling spectacle, especially when the Polynesian drummers kick in.

Despite the everyman appeal of rugby union in NZ (unlike in the UK), rugby league retains the status of the working-class sport and support is strongest from Auckland's Maori, Polynesian and other immigrant communities. Still, taking the Rubgy League World Cup off the Australians – NZ's constant arch-rivals – brought a smile to the faces of even the staunchest supporters of the rival rugby code.

Netball is the leading sport for women and the one in which the national team, the Silver Ferns, perpetually vies for world supremacy with the Australians – one or other of the countries has taken the world championship at every contest (except for a three-way tie in 1979).

In 2010 the All Whites, NZ's national soccer (football) squad, competed in the FIFA World Cup for the second time ever, emerging with the totally unanticipated distinction of being the only unbeaten team in the competition. They didn't win any games either, but most Kiwis were overjoyed to have seen their first ever World Cup goals and three draws.

Other sports in which NZ punches above its weight include sailing, rowing, canoeing, equestrian, cycling and triathlon. The most Olympic medals NZ has won have been in athletics, particularly in track and field events. Cricket is the established summer team sport, although not one in which the Kiwis are currently setting the world alight.

If you truly want to discover the good, the bad and the ugly of the national psyche, the sporting field isn't a bad place to start.

For many, Sir Edmund Hillary, the first person to climb Mt Everest, was the consummate New Zealander: humble, practical and concerned for social justice. A public outpouring of grief followed his death in 2008.

For the younger generation, for whom the 1980s are prehistory, political apathy is the norm. Perhaps it's because a decade of progressive government has given them little to kick against – unlike those politicised by the anti–Iraq War movements elsewhere. Ironically, as NZ has finally achieved its own interesting, independent cultural sensibility, the country's youth seem more obsessed with US culture than ever. This is particularly true within the hip-hop scene, where a farcical identification with American gangsta culture has developed into a worrying youth gang problem.

A Long Way From Britain

Most Kiwis (except perhaps the farmers) would probably wish it rained a little less and they got paid a little more, but it sometimes takes a few years travelling on their 'Big OE' (Overseas Experience – a traditional rite of passage) before they realise how good they've got it. In a 2011 study of the quality of life in the world's major cities, Auckland was rated third and Wellington 13th.

Despite all the change, key elements of the NZ identity are an unbroken thread, and fortune is still a matter of economics rather than class. If you are well served in a restaurant or shop, it will be out of politeness or pride in the job, rather than servility.

In country areas and on bushwalks don't be surprised if you're given a cheery greeting from passers-by, especially in the South Island. In a legacy of the British past, politeness is generally regarded as one of the highest virtues. A 'please' and 'thank you' will get you a long way. The three great exceptions to this rule are: a) on the road, where genteel Dr Jekylls become raging Mr Hydes, especially if you have the misfortune of needing to change lanes in Auckland; b) if you don't speak English very well; and c) if you are Australian.

The latter two traits are the product of insularity and a smallness of world view that tends to disappear among Kiwis who have travelled (and luckily many do). The NZ/Australian rivalry is taken much more seriously on this side of the Tasman Sea. Although it's very unlikely that Kiwis will be rude outright, visiting Aussies must get pretty sick of the constant ribbing, much of it surprisingly ill-humoured. It's a sad truth that while most Australians would cheer on a NZ sports team if they were playing anyone other than their own, the opposite is true in NZ.

Number-Eight Wire

You might on your travels hear the phrase 'number-eight wire' and wonder what on earth it means. It's a catchphrase New Zealanders still repeat to themselves to encapsulate a national myth: that NZ's isolation and its pioneer stock created a culture in which ingenuity allowed problems to be solved and tools to be built from scratch. A NZ farmer, it was said, could solve pretty much any problem with a piece of number-eight wire (the gauge used for fencing on farms).

It's actually largely true – NZ farms are full of NZ inventions. One reason big offshore film and TV producers bring their projects here – apart from the low wages and huge variety of locations – is that they like the can-do attitude and ability to work to a goal of NZ technical crews. Many more New Zealanders have worked as managers, roadies or chefs for famous recording artists (everyone from Led Zeppelin and U2 to Madonna) than have enjoyed the spotlight themselves. Which just goes to show that New Zealanders operate best at the intersection of practicality and creativity, with an endearing (and sometimes infuriating) humility to boot.

THE KIWI PSYCHE

In 2009 and 2010 NZ topped the Global Peace Index, earning the distinction of being rated the world's most peaceful country. In 2011 it dropped to second place behind Iceland – something to do with all those *haka* performed during the Rugby World Cup, perhaps?

No matter where you are in NZ, you're never more than 128km from the sea.

Arts & Music

It took a hundred years for post-colonial New Zealand to develop its own distinctive artistic identity. In the first half of the 20th century it was writers and visual artists who led the charge. By the 1970s, NZ pub rockers had conquered Australia, while in the 1980s, indie-music obsessives the world over hooked into Dunedin's weird and wonderful alternative scene. However, it took the success of the film industry in the 1990s to catapult the nation's creativity into the global consciousness.

Literature

A nationalist movement first arose in NZ literature in the 1930s, striving for an independent identity and challenging the notion of NZ simply being an annexe of the 'mother country'.

Katherine Mansfield's work began a NZ tradition in short fiction, and for years the standard was carried by novelist Janet Frame, whose dramatic life was depicted in Jane Campion's film of her autobiography, *An Angel at My Table*. Frame's novel *The Carpathians* (1989) won the Commonwealth Writers' Prize. A new era of international recognition began in 1985 when Keri Hulme's haunting *The Bone People* won the Booker Prize (the world is still waiting for the follow-up, *Bait*).

It wasn't until 2007 that another Kiwi looked likely to snag the Booker. Lloyd Jones' *Mister Pip* was pipped at the post, but the nomination rocketed his book up literature charts the world over; a film version is due in 2012.

Less recognised internationally, Maurice 'gee-I've-won-a-lot-of-awards' Gee has gained the nation's annual top fiction gong six times, most recently with *Blindsight* (2005) and *Live Bodies* (1998). His much-loved children's novel *Under the Mountain* (1979) was made into a seminal NZ TV series in 1981 and then a major motion picture in 2009. In 2004 the adaptation of another of his novels, *In My Father's Den* (1972), won major awards at international film festivals and is one of the country's highest grossing films. His latest novel is *Access Road* (2009).

Maurice is an auspicious name for NZ writers, with the late Maurice Shadbolt achieving much acclaim for his many novels, particularly those set during the NZ Wars. Try *Season of the Jew* (1987) or *The House of Strife* (1993).

MAORI VOICES IN PRINT

Some of the most interesting and enjoyable NZ fiction voices belong to Maori writers, with Booker-winner Keri Hulme leading the way. Witi Ihimaera's novels give a wonderful insight into small-town Maori life on the East Coast – especially *Bulibasha* (1994) and *The Whale Rider* (1987), which was made into an acclaimed film – while *Nights in the Gardens of Spain* (1996) casts a similar light on Auckland's gay scene. Patricia Grace's work is similarly filled with exquisitely told stories of rural *marae*-centred life: try *Mutuwhenua* (1978), *Potiki* (1986), *Dogside Story* (2001) or *Tu* (2004).

MIDDLE-EARTH TOURISM

If you are one of those travellers inspired to come down under by the scenery of the *LOTR* movies, you won't be disappointed. Jackson's decision to film in NZ wasn't mere patriotism. Nowhere else on earth will you find such wildly varied, unspoiled landscapes – not to mention poorly paid actors.

You will doubtless recognise some places from the films. For example, Hobbiton (near Matamata), Mt Doom (instantly recognisable as towering Ngauruhoe) or the Misty Mountains (the South Island's Southern Alps). The visitor information centres in Wellington and Matamata should be able to direct you to local *LOTR* sites of interest. If you're serious about finding the exact spots where scenes were filmed, buy a copy of Ian Brodie's nerdtastic *The Lord of the Rings: Location Guidebook,* which includes instructions, and even GPS coordinates, for finding all the important places. Keep an eye out also for new tours visiting locations from *The Hobbit,* Peter Jackson's new Middle Earth opus, due to be released late in 2012.

Cinema & TV

If you first got interested in NZ by watching it on the silver screen, you're in good company. Sir Peter Jackson's NZ-made *Lord of the Rings* (*LOTR*) trilogy was the best thing to happen to NZ tourism since Captain Cook.

Yet NZ cinema is hardly ever easygoing. In his BBC-funded documentary, *Cinema of Unease,* NZ actor Sam Neill described the country's film industry as 'uniquely strange and dark', producing bleak, haunted work. One need only watch Lee Tamahore's harrowing *Once Were Warriors* (1994) to see what he means.

The *Listener*'s film critic, Philip Matthews, makes a slightly more upbeat observation: 'Between (Niki Caro's) *Whale Rider,* (Christine Jeffs') *Rain* and *Lord of the Rings,* you can extract the qualities that our best films possess. Beyond slick technical accomplishment, all share a kind of land-mysticism, an innately supernatural sensibility'.

You could add to this list Jane Campion's *The Piano* (1993), Brad McGann's *In My Father's Den* (2004) and Jackson's *Heavenly Creatures* (1994) – all of which use magically lush scenery to couch disturbing violence. It's a land-mysticism constantly bordering on the creepy.

Even when Kiwis do humour it's as resolutely black as their rugby jerseys; check out Jackson's early splatter-fests and Taika Waititi's *Boy* (2010). Exporting NZ comedy hasn't been easy, yet the HBO-produced TV musical parody *Flight of the Conchords* – featuring a mumbling, bumbling Kiwi folk-singing duo trying to get a break in New York – has found surprising international success.

It's the Polynesian giggle-factor that seems likeliest to break down the bleak house of NZ cinema, with feel-good-through-and-through *Sione's Wedding* (2006) netting the second-biggest local takings of any NZ film.

New Zealanders have gone from never seeing themselves in international cinema to having whole cloned armies of Temuera Morrisons invading the universe in *Star Wars.* Familiar faces such as Cliff Curtis and Karl Urban seem to constantly pop up playing Mexican or Russian gangsters in action movies. Many of them got their start in long-running soap opera *Shortland St* (7pm weekdays, TV2).

While the tourist industry waits for Jackson's *The Hobbit* (due late 2012), the NZ film industry has quietly continued producing well-crafted, affecting movies, such as *The Topp Twins: Untouchable Girls* (people's choice documentary winner at the Toronto and Melbourne film festivals, 2009).

Other than 2003's winner *Return of the King, The Piano* is the only NZ movie to be nominated for a Best Picture Oscar. Jane Campion was the first Kiwi nominated as Best Director and Peter Jackson the first to win it.

The TV show *Popstars* originated in New Zealand, though the resulting group, True Bliss, was short-lived. The series concept was then picked up in Australia, the UK, and the US, inspiring the *Idol* series.

Music

NZ music began with the *waiata* (singing) developed by Maori following their arrival in the country. The main musical instruments were wind instruments made of bone or wood, the most well known of which is the *nguru* (also known as the 'nose flute'), while percussion was provided by chest- and thigh-slapping. These days, the liveliest place to see Maori music being performed is at *kapa haka* competitions in which groups compete with their own routines of traditional song and dance. In a similar vein is the Pasifika Festival (p65) in Auckland, which has areas to represent each of the Pacific Islands. It is a great place to see both traditional and modern forms of Polynesian music, whether that means modern hip-hop beats or throbbing Cook Island drums, or island-style guitar, ukulele and slide guitar.

Early European immigrants brought their own styles of music and gave birth to local variants during the early 1900s. In the 1950s Douglas Lilburn became one of the first internationally recognised NZ classical composers. More recently the country has produced a number of world-renowned musicians in this field, including opera singer Dame Kiri Te Kanawa, million-selling pop diva Hayley Westenra, composer John Psathas (who created music for the 2004 Olympic Games) and composer/percussionist Gareth Farr (who also performs in drag under the name Lilith). Each of the main universities in NZ has its own music school and these often have free concerts, which visitors can attend. Larger-scale performances are held in the Edge conglomerate of venues in Auckland and the Town Hall/Michael Fowler Centre in Wellington.

NZ also has a strong rock-music scene, its most acclaimed exports being the revered indie label Flying Nun and the music of the Finn Brothers. In 1981 Flying Nun was started by Christchurch record store owner Roger Shepherd (who sold it in the '90s, but bought back partial ownership in 2009). Many of the early groups came from Dunedin, where local musicians took the DIY attitude of punk but used it to produce a lo-fi indie-pop that received rave reviews from the likes of *NME* in the UK and *Rolling Stone* magazine in the US. Billboard even claimed in 1989: 'There doesn't seem to be anything on Flying Nun Records that is less than excellent.'

Many of the musicians from the Flying Nun scene still perform live to this day, including David Kilgour (from The Clean), Martin Phillipps (from The Chills), and Shayne Carter (from the Straitjacket Fits, now fronting Dimmer and The Adults). These days, the spirit of the scene is kept alive at Chick's Hotel in Port Chalmers (near Dunedin). The indie scene in New Zealand is being kept fresh by newer labels such as Lil Chief Records and Arch Hill Recordings. For more adventurous listeners, Bruce Russell continues to play in influential underground group The Dead C, and releases music through his Corpus Hermeticum label.

Since the millennium, the NZ music scene has developed a new vitality after the government convinced commercial radio stations to adopt a voluntary quota of 20% local music. This enabled commercially oriented musicians to develop solid careers. Rock groups such as Shihad, The Feelers and Op-shop have thrived in this environment, as have a set of soulful female solo artists (who all happen to have Maori heritage): Bic Runga, Anika Moa, and Brooke Fraser (daughter of All Black Bernie Fraser).

However, the genres of music that have been adopted most enthusiastically by Maori and Polynesian New Zealanders have been reggae (in the 1970s) and hip-hop (in the 1980s), which has led to distinct local forms. In Wellington, a thriving jazz scene took on a reggae influence to create a host of groups that blend dub, roots, and funky jazz – most

---

Gareth Shute

Gareth Shute wrote this music section. He is the author of four books, including *Hip Hop Music in Aotearoa* and *NZ Rock 1987–2007.* He is also a musician and has toured the UK, Europe and Australia as a member of The Ruby Suns and The Brunettes. He now plays in indie soul group The Cosbys.

For indie rock fans, a great source of local information is www.cheeseon toast. co.nz, which lists gigs and has interviews/photographs of bands (both local and international). Local hip hop, pop, and rock is also discussed at www.thecorner. co.nz. One of the longest running local music websites is www. muzic.net.nz.

notably Fat Freddy's Drop. Most of Wellington's music venues are located on Cuba St and immediate surrounds. The national public holiday, Waitangi Day, on 6 February, also happens to fall on the birthday of Bob Marley and annual reggae concerts are held on this day in Auckland and Wellington.

The local hip-hop scene has its heart in the suburbs of South Auckland, which have a high concentration of Maori and Pacific Island residents. This area is home to one of NZ's foremost hip-hop labels, Dawn Raid, which takes its name from the infamous early-morning house raids of the 1970s that police performed on Pacific Islanders suspected of outstaying their visas.

Dawn Raid's most successful artist is Savage, who sold a million copies of his single 'Swing' after it was featured in the movie *Knocked Up*. Within NZ, the most well-known hip-hop acts are Scribe, Che Fu, and Smashproof (whose song 'Brother' held number one on the NZ singles charts longer than any other local act).

Early in the new millennium, NZ also produced two internationally acclaimed garage rock acts: the Datsuns and the D4. In Auckland the main venues for rock music are the Kings Arms Tavern (p79) and Cassette Nine (p79), though two joint venues in St Kevins Arcade (off Karangahape Rd) are also popular – the Wine Cellar & Whammy Bar (p78). Wellington is rife with live music venues from Mighty Mighty (p367) to the San Francisco Bath House (p369), to Bodega (p369).

Dance music had its strongest following in Christchurch in the 1990s, spawning dub/electronica outfit Salmonella Dub and its offshoot act, Tiki Taane. Drum 'n' bass remains popular locally and has spawned internationally renowned acts such as Concord Dawn and Shapeshifter.

An up-to-date list of gigs in the main centres is listed at www.grooveguide.co.nz. Tickets for most events can be bought at: www.ticketek.co.nz, www.ticketmaster.co.nz, or, for smaller gigs, www.undertheradar.co.nz.

THE BROTHERS FINN

There are certain tunes that all Kiwis can sing along to, given a beer and the opportunity. A surprising proportion of these were written by Tim and Neil Finn, and many of their songs have gone on to be international hits.

Tim Finn first came to prominence in the 1970s group Split Enz. When the original guitarist quit, Neil flew over to join the band in the UK despite being only 15 at the time. Split Enz amassed a solid following in Australia, New Zealand and Canada before disbanding in 1985.

Neil then formed Crowded House with two Australian musicians (Paul Hester and Nick Seymour) and one of their early singles, 'Don't Dream It's Over', hit number two on the US charts. Tim later did a brief spell in the band, during which the brothers wrote 'Weather With You' – a song that reached number seven on the UK charts, pushing their album *Woodface* to gold sales. The original line-up of Crowded House played their final show in 1996 in front of 100,000 people on the steps of the Sydney Opera House (though Finn and Seymour reformed the group in 2007 and continue to tour and record occasionally). Tim and Neil have both released a number of solo albums, as well as releasing material together as the Finn Brothers.

More recently, Neil has also remained busy, organising a set of shows/releases under the name Seven Worlds Collide, which is a collaboration with well-known overseas musicians, including Jeff Tweedy (Wilco), Johnny Marr (The Smiths) and members of Radiohead. His latest band is the Pajama Club, a collaboration with wife Sharon and Auckland musicians Sean Donnelly and Alana Skyring.

Neil's son Liam also has a burgeoning solo career, which has seen him tour the US with Eddie Vedder and The Black Keys, as well as appearing on the David Letterman show. Both Tim and Neil were born in the small Waikato town of Te Awamutu and the local museum has a collection that documents their work.

In summer, many of the beachfront towns throughout the country are visited by touring bands (winery shows are also popular).

A number of festivals take place around the North Island during the summer months, including new year's celebration Rhythm & Vines and the Christian-rock festival Parachute (www.parachutemusic.com), held near Hamilton in January. Also recommended is the underground festival held early each year by A Low Hum (www.alowhum.com). Lovers of world music may enjoy the local version of WOMAD, which is held in New Plymouth (www.taft.co.nz/womad) and features both local and overseas acts that draw from traditional music forms.

Visual Arts

The NZ 'can do' attitude extends to the visual arts. If you're visiting a local's home don't be surprised to find one of the owner's paintings on the wall or one of their mate's sculptures in the back garden, pieced together out of bits of shell, driftwood and a length of the magical 'number-eight wire'.

This is symptomatic of a flourishing local art and crafts scene cultivated by lively tertiary courses churning out traditional carvers and weavers, jewellery makers, multimedia boffins, and moulders of metal and glass. The larger cities have excellent dealer galleries representing interesting local artists working across all media.

Not all the best galleries are in Auckland or Wellington. The energetic Govett-Brewster Art Gallery (p211) – home to the legacy of sculptor and film-maker Len Lye – is worth a visit to New Plymouth in itself.

Traditional Maori art has a distinctive visual style with well-developed motifs that have been embraced by NZ artists of every race. In the painting medium, these include the cool modernism of the work of Gordon Walters and the more controversial pop-art approach of Dick Frizzell's *Tiki* series. Likewise, Pacific Island themes are common, particularly in Auckland. An example is the work of Niuean-born Auckland-raised John Pule.

It should not be surprising that in a nation so defined by its natural environment, landscape painting constituted the first post-European body of art. John Gully and Petrus van der Velden were among those to arrive and paint memorable (if sometimes overdramatised) depictions of the land.

A little later, Charles Frederick Goldie painted a series of compelling, realist portraits of Maori, who were feared to be a dying race. Debate over the political propriety of Goldie's work raged for years, but its value is widely accepted now: not least because Maori themselves generally acknowledge and value them as ancestral representations.

From the 1930s NZ art took a more modern direction and produced some of the country's most celebrated artists including Rita Angus, Toss Woollaston and Colin McCahon. McCahon is widely regarded to have been the country's most important artist. His paintings might seem inscrutable, even forbidding, but even where McCahon lurched into Catholic mysticism or quoted screeds from the Bible, his spirituality was rooted in geography. His bleak, brooding landscapes evoke the sheer power of NZ's terrain.

A wide range of cultural events is listed on www.eventfinder.co.nz. This is a good place to find out about concerts, classical music recitals and *kapa haka* performances. For more specific information on the NZ classical music scene, see www.sounz.org.nz.

Survival Guide

Directory A–Z

Accommodation

Across the North Island, you can bed down in historic guesthouses, facility-laden hotels, uniform motel units, beautifully situated camp-sites, and hostels that range in character from clean-living to tirelessly party-prone.

Accommodation listings are in order of authorial preference, based on our assessment of atmosphere, cleanliness, facilities, location and bang for your buck.

If you're travelling during peak tourist seasons, book your bed well in advance. Accommodation is most in demand (and at its priciest) during the summer holidays from Christmas to late January, and at Easter.

Visitor information centres provide reams of local accommodation information, often in the form of folders detailing facilities and up-to-date prices; many can also make bookings on your behalf.

For online listings, visit **Automobile Association** (AA; www.aa.co.nz) and **Jasons** (www.jasons.com).

B&Bs

Bed and breakfast (B&B) accommodation is a growth industry across NZ's North Island, popping up in the middle of cities, in rural hamlets and on stretches of isolated coastline, with rooms on offer in everything from suburban bungalows to stately manors owned by one family for generations.

Breakfast may be 'continental' (cereal, toast and tea or coffee), 'hearty continental' (add yoghurt, fruit, home-baked bread or muffins), or a stomach-loading cooked meal including eggs, bacon and sausages. Some B&B hosts may also cook dinner for guests and advertise dinner, bed and breakfast (DB&B) packages.

B&B tariffs are typically in the $120 to $180 bracket (per double), though some places charge upwards of $300 per double. Some hosts continue to be cheeky-as-a-kea, charging hefty prices for what is, in essence, a bedroom in their home.

Online resources:

Bed & Breakfast Book (www.bnb.co.nz)

Bed and Breakfast Directory (www.bed-and-breakfast.co.nz)

Camping & Holiday Parks

Campers and campervan drivers alike converge upon NZ's hugely popular 'holiday parks', slumbering peacefully in powered and unpowered sites, cheap bunk rooms (dorm rooms), cabins and self-contained units that are often called motels or tourist flats. Well-equipped communal kitchens, dining areas and games and TV rooms often feature. In cities, holiday parks are usually a fair way from the action, but in smaller towns they can be impressively central or near lakes, beaches, rivers and forests.

The nightly cost of holiday-park camping is usually between $15 and $20 per adult, with children charged half-price; powered sites are a couple of dollars more. Cabin/unit accommodation normally ranges from $60 to $120 per double. Unless noted otherwise, the prices we've listed for campsites, campervan sites, huts and cabins are for two people. The 'big three' holiday park operators around NZ – Top 10, Kiwi Parks and Family Parks – all offer discount cards for loyal slumberers.

DOC CAMPSITES & FREEDOM CAMPING

A fantastic option for those in campervans are NZ's 250-plus vehicle-accessible

SLEEPING PRICE RANGES

The following price ranges refer to a double with en suite.

» **$ Budget** Less than $100
» **$$ Midrange** $100-180
» **$$$ Top end** More than $180

Price ranges generally increase by 20% to 25% in Auckland and Wellington. Here you can still find budget accommodation at up to $100 per double, but midrange stretches from $100 to $200, with top-end rooms more than $200.

'Conservation Campsites' run by the **Department of Conservation** (DOC; www. doc.govt.nz), with fees ranging from free (basic toilets and fresh water) to $19 per adult (flush toilets and showers). DOC publishes free brochures with detailed descriptions and instructions to find every campsite (even GPS coordinates). Pick up copies from DOC offices before you hit the road, or visit the website.

DOC also looks after hundreds of 'Backcountry Huts', which can only be reached on foot. See the website for details.

Never just assume it's OK to camp somewhere. Always ask a local first. Check at the local i-SITE or DOC office, or with commercial camping grounds. If you are freedom camping (p441), treat the area with respect. Instant fines can be charged for camping in prohibited areas, or irresponsible disposal of waste. For more freedom camping info see, www. camping.org.nz.

Farmstays

Farmstays open the door on the agricultural side of North Island life, with visitors encouraged to get some dirt beneath their fingernails at orchards, and dairy, sheep and cattle farms. Costs can vary widely, with B&Bs generally ranging from $80 to $120. Some farms have separate cottages where you can fix your own food, while others offer low-cost, shared,

backpacker-style accommodation.

Farm Helpers in NZ (FHINZ; www.fhinz.co.nz) produces a booklet ($25) that lists around 350 NZ farms providing lodging in exchange for four to six hours' work per day. **Rural Holidays NZ** (www.ruralholidays. co.nz) lists farmstays and homestays throughout the country on its website.

Hostels

The North Island is packed to the rafters with backpacker hostels, both independent and part of large chains, ranging from small, homestay-style affairs with a handful of

beds to refurbished hotels and towering modern structures in the big cities. Hostel bed prices listed throughout this book are nonmember rates, usually between $25 and $35 per night.

If you're a Kiwi travelling in your own country, be warned that some hostels only admit overseas travellers, typically inner-city places. If you encounter such discrimination, either try another hostel or insist that you're a genuine traveller and not a bedless neighbour.

Online, www.hostelworld. com is useful for pre-trip planning.

HOSTEL ORGANISATIONS
Budget Backpacker Hostels (BBH; www.bbh.co.nz) NZ's biggest hostel group, with around 300 hostels on its books, including homestays and farmstays. Membership costs $45 and entitles you to stay at member hostels at rates listed in the annual (free) *BBH Backpacker Accommodation* booklet. Nonmembers pay an extra $3 per night, though not all hostel owners

PRACTICALITIES

» **News** Leaf through Auckland's *New Zealand Herald* or Wellington's *Dominion Post*. Online you can check out www.stuff.co.nz and www.nzherald.co.nz.

» **TV** Watch one of the national government-owned TV stations (TV One, TV2, TVNZ 6, TVNZ 7, Maori TV and the 100% Maori language Te Reo) or the subscriber-only Sky TV (www.skytv.co.nz).

» **Radio** Tune in to Radio National for current affairs and Concert FM for classical and jazz (see www. radionz.co.nz for frequencies). Kiwi FM (www.kiwifm. co.nz) showcases NZ music; Radio Hauraki (www. hauraki.co.nz) cranks out classic rock (the national appetite for Fleetwood Mac is insatiable...).

» **DVDs** Kiwi DVDs are encoded for Region 4, which includes Mexico, South America, Central America, Australia, the Pacific and the Caribbean.

» **Electrical** To plug yourself into the electricity supply (230V AC, 50Hz), use a three-pin adaptor (the same as in Australia; different from British three-pin adaptors).

» **Weights & measures** NZ uses the metric system.

WWOOFING

If you don't mind getting your hands dirty, an economical way of travelling around NZ involves doing some voluntary work as a member of **Willing Workers on Organic Farms** (WWOOF; ☎03-544 9890; www.wwoof.co.nz). Membership of this popular, well-established international organisation scores you access to hundreds of organic and permaculture farms, market gardens and other environmentally sound cottage industries across the country. Down on the farm, in exchange for a hard day's work, owners provide food, accommodation and some hands-on organic farming experience. Contact farm owners a week or two beforehand to arrange your stay, as you would for a hotel or hostel – don't turn up unannounced!

A one-year online membership costs $40; an online membership and a farm-listing book, which is mailed to you, costs $50. You should be part of a Working Holiday Scheme when you visit NZ, as the immigration department considers WWOOFers to be working.

charge the difference. Pick up a membership card from any member hostel, or have one mailed to you overseas for $50 (see the website for details).

YHA New Zealand (Youth Hostels Association; www.yha.co.nz) Has 23 hostels in prime North Island locations. The YHA is part of the **Hostelling International** (HI; www.hihostels.com) network, so if you're already an HI member in your own country, membership entitles you to use NZ hostels. If you don't already have a membership card from home, you can buy one at major NZ YHA hostels for $42 for 12 months, or book online and have your card mailed to you overseas for the same price. Hostels also take non-YHA members for an extra $3 per night. NZ YHA hostels also supply bed linen, so you don't need to bring a sleeping bag.

VIP Backpackers (www.vipbackpackers.com) International organisation affiliated with around 20 NZ hostels (not BBH or YHA), mainly in the cities and tourist hot-spots. For around $63 (including postage) you'll receive a 12-month

membership entitling you to a $1 discount off nightly accommodation. You can join online, at VIP hostels or at larger agencies dealing in backpacker travel.

Nomads Backpackers (www.nomadsworld.com) Five North Island hostels in Auckland, Paihia, Rotorua, Taupo and Wellington. Membership costs AUD$37 for 12 months and like VIP offers NZ$1 off the cost of nightly accommodation. Join at participating hostels, backpacker travel agencies or online.

Base Backpackers (www.stayatbase.com) Nationwide chain with five North Island locations. Expect clean dorms, girls-only areas and party opportunities aplenty. Offers a 10-night 'Base Jumping' accommodation card for $239, bookable online.

Pubs, Hotels & Motels

Pubs The least expensive form of North Island hotel accommodation is the humble pub. As is often the case elsewhere, some of the North Island's old pubs are full of character (and characters), while others are

grotty, ramshackle places that are best avoided, especially by women travelling solo. Also check whether there's a band cranking out the tunes the night you plan to be in town, as you could be in for a sleepless night. In the cheapest pubs, singles/doubles might cost as little as $30/60 (with a shared bathroom down the hall), though $50/80 is more common.

Hotels At the top end of the hotel scale are five-star international chains, resort complexes and architecturally splendorous boutique hotels, all of which charge a hefty premium for their mod cons, snappy service and/or historic opulence. We quote 'rack rates' (official advertised rates) for such places throughout this book, but discounts and special deals often mean you won't have to pay these prices.

Motels NZ's towns have a glut of nondescript, low-rise motels and 'motor lodges', charging between $80 and $180 for double rooms. These tend to be squat structures congregating just outside CBDs, or skulking by highways on the edge of towns. Most are modernish (though decor is often mired in the '90s) and have similar facilities, namely tea- and coffee-making equipment, fridge, and TV – prices vary with standard.

Rental Accommodation

The basic Kiwi holiday home is called a 'bach', which is short for 'bachelor', as they were often used by single men as hunting and fishing hideouts. These are simple self-contained cottages that can be rented in rural and coastal areas, often in isolated locations. Prices are typically $80 to $130 per night, which isn't bad for a whole house or self-contained bungalow.

For more upmarket holiday houses, the current

trend is to throw rusticity to the wind and erect luxurious cottages on beautiful nature-surrounded plots. Expect to pay anything from $130 to $400 per double.

Online resources:
» www.holidayhomes.co.nz
» www.bookabach.co.nz
» www.holidayhouses.co.nz
» www.nzapartments.co.nz

Business Hours

Note that most attractions close on Christmas Day and Good Friday.

Shops & businesses 9am to 5.30pm Monday to Friday, and 9am to 12.30pm or 5pm Saturday. Late-night shopping (until 9pm) in larger cities on Thursday and/or Friday nights. Sunday trading in most big towns and cities.

Supermarkets 8am to 7pm, often 9pm or later in cities.

Banks 9.30am to 4.30pm Monday to Friday; some city branches also open Saturday mornings.

Post offices 8.30am to 5pm Monday to Friday; larger branches also 9.30am to 1pm Saturday. Postal desks in newsagencies open later.

Restaurants Food until 9pm, often until 11pm on Fridays and Saturdays.

Cafes 7am to 4pm or 5pm.

Pubs Noon until late; food from noon to 2pm and from 6pm to 8pm.

Children

Accommodation Many motels and holiday parks have playgrounds, games and DVDs, and occasionally fenced swimming pools and trampolines. Cots and high-chairs aren't always available at budget and midrange accommodation, but top-end hotels supply them and often provide child-minding services. B&Bs aren't usually amenable to families – many promote themselves

Climate
Auckland

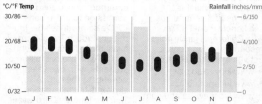

Rotorua

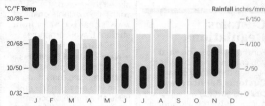

Wellington

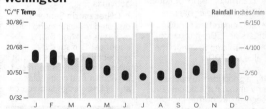

as kid-free. Hostels focusing on the backpacker demographic don't welcome kids either, but there are plenty of other hostels (including YHA hostels) that do.

Babysitting For specialised childcare, try www.rockmybaby.co.nz, or look under 'babysitters' and 'child care centres' in the *Yellow Pages* directory.

Car seats Some smaller car-hire companies don't provide baby seats – double-check that your company can supply the right-sized seat for your child, and that the seat will be properly fitted. Some companies may legally require you to fit the seat yourself.

Change rooms & breast-feeding Cities and most major towns have public rooms where parents can go

to nurse a baby or change a nappy (diaper); check with the local visitor info centre or council, or ask a local.

Concessions Kids' and family rates are often available for accommodation, tours, entry fees, and air, bus and train transport, with discounts of as much as 50% off the adult rate. The definition of 'child' can vary from under 12 to under 18 years; toddlers (under four years old) usually get free admission and transport.

Eating out There are plenty of family-friendly restaurants in NZ with highchairs and kids' menus. Pubs often serve kids' meals and most cafes and restaurants (with the exception of upmarket eateries) can handle the idea of child-sized portions.

Health NZ's medical services and facilities are world-class, with goods like formula and disposable nappies widely available.

For helpful general tips, see Lonely Planet's *Travel with Children*. Handy online resources for kid-centric activities and travel info:

» www.kidzgo.co.nz
» www.kidspot.co.nz
» www.kidsnewzealand.com
» www.kidsfriendlynz.com

Customs Regulations

For the low-down on what you can and can't bring into NZ, see the **New Zealand Customs Service** (www.customs.govt.nz) website. Per-person duty-free allowances:

» 1125mL of spirits or liqueur
» 4.5L of wine or beer
» 200 cigarettes (or 50 cigars or 250g of tobacco)
» dutiable goods up to the value of $700.

It's a good idea to declare any unusual medicines. Biosecurity is another customs buzzword – authorities are serious about keeping out any diseases that may harm NZ's agricultural industry. Tramping gear such as boots and tents will be checked and may need to be cleaned before being allowed in. You must declare any plant or animal products (including anything made of wood), and food of any kind. You'll also come under greater scrutiny if you've arrived via Africa, Southeast Asia or South America. Weapons and firearms are either prohibited or require a permit and safety testing.

Discount Cards

» **International Student Identity Card** The internationally recognised ISIC is produced by the **International Student Travel Con-** federation (ISTC; www.istc.org), and issued to full-time students aged 12 and over. It provides discounts on accommodation, transport and admission to attractions. The ISTC also produces the International Youth Travel Card, available to folks between 12 and 26 who are not full-time students, with equivalent benefits to the ISIC. Also similar is the International Teacher Identity Card, available to teaching professionals. All three cards (NZ$25 each) are available online at www.isiccard.co.nz, or from student travel companies like STA Travel.

» **New Zealand Card** This is a $35 discount **pass** (www.newzealandcard.com) that'll score you between 5% and 50% off a range of accommodation, tours, sights and activities.

» **Other cards** Senior and disabled travellers who live overseas will find that discount cards issued by their respective countries are not always 'officially' recognised in NZ, but that many places still acknowledge such cards.

Electricity

230V/50Hz

Embassies & Consulates

Most principal diplomatic representations to NZ are in Wellington, with a few in Auckland.

Remember that while in NZ you are bound by NZ laws. Your embassy will not be sympathetic if you end up in jail after committing a crime locally, even if such actions are legal in your own country.

In genuine emergencies you may get some assistance, but only if other channels have been exhausted. For example, if you need to get home urgently, a free ticket is unlikely as the embassy would expect you to have insurance. If you have all your money and documents stolen, it might assist with getting a new passport, but a loan for onward travel is out of the question.

Embassies, consulates and high commissions include the following:

Australia (☏04-473 6411; www.australia.org.nz; 72-76 Hobson St, Thorndon, Wellington)

Canada (☏04-473 9577; www.newzealand.gc.ca; L11, 125 The Terrace, Wellington)

China (☏04-472 1382; www.chinaembassy.org.nz; 2-6 Glenmore St, Kelburn, Wellington)

Fiji (☏04-473 5401; www.fiji.org.nz; 31 Pipitea St, Thorndon, Wellington)

France (☏04-384 2555; www.ambafrance-nz.org; 34-42 Manners St, Wellington)

Germany (☏04-473 6063; www.wellington.diplo.de; 90-92 Hobson St, Thorndon, Wellington)

Israel (☏04-439 9500; info@wellington.mfa.gov.il; L13, Bayley's Building, 36 Brandon St, Wellington)

Ireland (☏09-977 2252; www.ireland.co.nz; L7, Citigroup Bldg, 23 Customs St E, Auckland)

Japan (☏04-473 1540; www.nz.emb-japan.go.jp; L18, The Majestic Centre, 100 Willis St, Wellington)

Netherlands (✆04-471 6390; www.netherlands embassy.co.nz; L10, PSIS House, cnr Featherston & Ballance Sts, Wellington)
UK (✆04-924 2888; www. britain.org.nz; 44 Hill St, Thorndon, Wellington)
USA (✆04-462 6000; http:// wellington.usembassy.gov; 29 Fitzherbert Tce, Thorndon, Wellington)

Food & Drink

The NZ foodie scene once slavishly reflected Anglo-Saxon stodge, but nowadays the country's restaurants and cafes are adept at throwing together traditional staples (lamb, beef, venison, green-lipped mussels) with Asian, European and pan-Pacific flair.

Eateries themselves range from fry-'em-up fish-and-chip shops and pub bistros to cafes drowned in faux-European, grungy or retro stylings; to restaurant-bars with full à-la-carte service; to fine-dining establishments with linen so crisp you'll be afraid to prop your elbows on it. Listings are in order of authorial preference, based on our assessment of ambience, service, value and, of course, deliciousness. For online listings:

» www.dineout.co.nz
» www.menus.co.nz

EATING PRICE RANGES

The following price ranges refer to a main course.
» **$ Budget** Less than $15
» **$$ Midrange** $15 to $32
» **$$$ Top end** More than $35

On the liquid front, NZ wine is world class (especially sauvignon blanc and pinot noir), and you'll be hard-pressed to find a NZ town of any size without decent espresso. NZ microbrewed beers have also become mainstream.

Practicalities

Smoking Banned in all restaurants, pubs and bars.
Tipping Not mandatory, but feel free if you've had a happy culinary experience (about 10% of the bill).
Opening hours Restaurants to 9pm, often 11pm Friday and Saturday. Cafes 7am to 4pm or 5pm. Pub food noon to 2pm, and 6pm to 8pm.

Vegetarians & Vegans

Most large urban centres have at least one dedicated vegetarian cafe or restaurant. See the **New Zealand Vegetarian Society** (www. vegsoc.org.nz) restaurant guide for listings. Also look for the vegetarian icon in Eating listings in this book, as it indicates a good vegetarian selection.

Beyond this, almost all restaurants and cafes offer vegetarian menu choices (although sometimes only one or two). Many eateries also provide gluten-free and vegan options. Always check that stocks and sauces are vegetarian too.

Gay & Lesbian Travellers

The gay and lesbian tourism industry in NZ isn't as high-profile as it is in neighbouring Australia, but homosexual communities are prominent in the main cities of Auckland and Wellington, with myriad support organisations across both islands. NZ has relatively progressive laws protecting the rights of gays and lesbians; the legal minimum age for sex between consenting persons is 16. Generally speaking, Kiwis are fairly relaxed and accepting about homosexuality, but that's not to say that homophobia doesn't exist.

Resources

There are loads of websites dedicated to gay and lesbian travellers. **Gay Tourism New Zealand** (www.gaytourism newzealand.com) is a good starting point, with links to various sites. Other worthwhile queer websites include the following:

» www.gaynz.com
» www.gaynz.net.nz
» www.lesbian.net.nz
» www.gaystay.co.nz

Check out the nationwide magazine *express* (www. gayexpress.co.nz) every second Wednesday for the latest happenings, reviews and listings on the NZ gay scene.

TO MARKET, TO MARKET

There are more than 30 farmers markets held around the North Island. Most happen on weekends and are happy local affairs where visitors will meet local producers and find fresh regional produce. Mobile coffee is usually present, and tastings are offered by enterprising and innovative stall holders.

Always take a bag to carry purchases, as many of the sustainably minded markets ban the use of plastic bags. And arrive as early as possible – the best produce sells out quickly.

Check out www.farmersmarkets.org.nz for dates and times of farmers markets throughout the North Island.

Festivals & Events

Big Gay Out (www.biggayout. co.nz) Free festival (food, drink, entertainment) held every February in Auckland.

Out Takes (www.outtakes. org.nz) G&L film festival staged in Auckland, Wellington and Christchurch in June.

Health

New Zealand is one of the healthiest countries in the world in which to travel. Diseases such as malaria and typhoid are unheard of, and the absence of poisonous snakes or other dangerous animals makes this a very safe region to get off the beaten track and out into the beautiful countryside.

Before You Go
MEDICATIONS

Bring medications in their original, clearly labelled containers. A signed and dated letter from your physician describing your medical conditions and medications, including generic names, is also a good idea. If carrying syringes or needles, be sure to have a physician's letter documenting their medical necessity.

VACCINATIONS

NZ has no vaccination requirements for any traveller, but the World Health Organization recommends that all travellers should be covered for diphtheria, tetanus, measles, mumps, rubella, chickenpox and polio, as well as hepatitis B, regardless of their destination. Ask your doctor for an International Certificate of Vaccination (or 'the yellow booklet'), which will list all the vaccinations you've received.

INSURANCE

If your current health insurance doesn't cover you for medical expenses incurred overseas, you should think about getting extra insur-ance – check out www. lonelyplanet.com for more information. Find out in advance if your insurance plan will make payments directly to providers or reimburse you at a later date for overseas health expenditures. (In many countries doctors expect payment in cash.)

In New Zealand
AVAILABILITY & COST OF HEALTH CARE

Health insurance is essential for all travellers. While health care in NZ is of a high standard and not overly expensive by international standards, considerable costs can be built up and repatriation can be extremely expensive.

NZ does not have a government-funded system of public hospitals. All travellers are, however, covered for medical care resulting from accidents that occur while in NZ (eg motor-vehicle accidents, adventure-activity accidents) by the Accident Compensation Corporation (ACC). Costs incurred due to treatment of a medical illness that occurs while in NZ will only be covered by travel insurance. For more details, see www.moh.govt.nz and www.acc.co.nz.

The 24-hour, free-call **Healthline** (☑0800 611 116; www.healthline.govt.nz) offers health advice throughout NZ.

PHARMACEUTICAL SUPPLIES

Over-the-counter medications are widely available in NZ through private chemists. These include painkillers, antihistamines for allergies, and skin-care products.

Some medications that are available over the counter in other countries are only available by a prescription obtained from a general practitioner. These include the oral contraceptive pill, most medications for asthma and all antibiotics. If you take medication on a regular basis, bring an adequate supply and ensure you have details of the generic name, as brand names differ between countries. The majority of medications in use outside the region are available.

INFECTIOUS DISEASES

The giardia parasite is widespread in the waterways of NZ. Drinking untreated water from streams and lakes is not recommended. Using water filters and boiling or treating water with iodine are effective ways of preventing the disease. Symptoms consist of intermittent bad-smelling diarrhoea, abdominal bloating and wind. Effective treatment is available (tinidazole or metronidazole).

ENVIRONMENTAL HAZARDS

Hypothermia This is a significant risk, especially during the winter months or year-round in the mountains of the North Island and all of the South Island. Mountain ranges and/or strong winds produce a high chill factor, which can result in hypothermia, even in moderately cool temperatures. Early signs include the inability to perform fine movements (such as doing up buttons), shivering and a bad case of the 'umbles' (fumbles, mumbles, grumbles, stumbles). The key element of treatment are changing the environment to one where heat loss is minimised: changing out of wet clothing, adding dry clothes with wind- and waterproof layers, adding insulation and providing fuel (water and carbohydrates) to allow shivering to build the internal temperature. In severe hypothermia, shivering actually stops; this is a medical emergency requiring rapid evacuation in addition to the above measures.

Surf Beaches & Drowning NZ has exceptional surf beaches. The power of the surf can fluctuate as a result of the varying slope of the seabed at many beaches.

Check with local surf life-saving organisations before entering the surf and be aware of your own limitations and expertise.

Insurance

A watertight travel-insurance policy covering theft, loss and medical problems is essential. Some policies specifically exclude designated 'dangerous activities' such as scuba diving, parasailing, bungy jumping, white-water rafting, motorcycling, skiing and even tramping. If you plan on doing any of these things (a distinct possibility in NZ), make sure the policy you choose covers you fully.

You may prefer a policy that pays doctors or hospitals directly rather than you having to pay on the spot and claim later. If you have to claim later, make sure you keep all documentation. Some policies ask you to call back (reverse charges) to a centre in your home country where an immediate assessment of your problem is made. Check that the policy covers ambulances and emergency medical evacuations by air.

It's worth mentioning that under NZ law, you cannot sue for personal injury (other than exemplary damages). Instead, the country's **Accident Compensation Corporation** (ACC; www.acc.co.nz) administers an accident compensation scheme that provides accident insurance for NZ residents and visitors to the country, regardless of fault. This scheme, however, does not cancel out the necessity for your own comprehensive travel-insurance policy, as it doesn't cover you for such things as loss of income or treatment in your home country or ongoing illness.

Worldwide cover for travellers from over 44 countries is available online at www.

lonelyplanet.com/bookings/insurance.do.

Internet Access

Getting online in NZ is easy in all but the most remote locales.

Internet Cafes

Internet cafes in the bigger urban centres or tourist areas are usually brimming with high-speed terminals. Facilities are a lot more haphazard in small, out-of-the-way towns, where a so-called internet cafe could turn out to be a single terminal in the corner of a DVD store.

Most hostels make an effort to hook you up, with internet access sometimes free for guests. Many public libraries have free internet access too, but there can be a limited number of terminals.

Internet access at cafes ranges anywhere from $4 to $6 per hour. There's often a minimum period of access, usually 10 or 15 minutes.

Wireless Access & Internet Service Providers

Increasingly, you'll be able to find wi-fi access around the country, from hotel rooms to pub beer gardens to hostel dining rooms. Usually you have to be a guest or customer to access the internet at these locations – you'll be issued with a code, a wink and a secret handshake to enable you to get online. Sometimes it's free; sometimes there's a charge.

The country's main telecommunications company is **Telecom New Zealand** (www.telecom.co.nz), which has wireless hot spots around the country. If you have a wi-fi-enabled device, you can purchase a Telecom wireless prepaid card from participating hot spots. Alternatively, you can purchase

a prepaid number from the login page and any wireless hotspot using your credit card. See the website for hot spot listings.

If you've brought your palmtop or notebook computer, you might consider buying a prepay USB modem (aka a 'dongle') with a local SIM card: both Telecom and **Vodafone** (www.vodarent.co.nz) sell these from around $100. If you want to get connected via a local internet service provider (ISP), there are plenty of options, though some companies limit their dial-up areas to major cities or particular regions. ISPs include the following:

Clearnet (☎0508 888 800; www.clearnet.co.nz)
Earthlight (☎03-479 0303; www.earthlight.co.nz)
Freenet (☎0800 645 000; www.freenet.co.nz)
Slingshot (☎0800 892 000; www.slingshot.co.nz)

Maps

The **Automobile Association** (AA; ☎0800 500 444; www.aa.co.nz/travel) produces excellent city, town, regional, island and highway maps, available from its local offices. The AA also produces a detailed *New Zealand Road Atlas*. Other reliable countrywide atlases, available from visitor information centres and bookshops, are published by Hema, KiwiMaps and Wises.

Land Information New Zealand (LINZ; www.linz.govt.nz) publishes several exhaustive map series, including street, country and holiday maps, national park and forest park maps, and topographical trampers' maps. Scan the larger bookshops, or try the nearest DOC office or visitor information centre for topo maps.

Online, log onto **AA SmartMap** (www.aamaps.co.nz) or **Yellow Maps** (www.

maps.yellowpages.co.nz) to pinpoint exact addresses in NZ cities and towns.

Money

ATMs & Eftpos

Branches of the country's major banks, including the Bank of New Zealand, ANZ, Westpac and ASB, have 24-hour ATMs that accept cards from other banks and provide access to overseas accounts. You won't find ATMs everywhere, but they're widespread across both islands.

Many NZ businesses use electronic funds transfer at point of sale (Eftpos), a convenient service that allows you to use your bank card (credit or debit) to pay directly for services or purchases, and often withdraw cash as well. Eftpos is available practically everywhere, even in places where it's a long way between banks. Just like an ATM, you need to know your personal identification number (PIN) to use it.

Bank Accounts

We've heard mixed reports on how easy it is for non-residents to open a bank account in NZ. Some sources say it's as simple as flashing a few pieces of ID, providing a temporary postal address (or your permanent address) and then waiting a few days while your request is processed. Other sources say that many banks won't allow visitors to open an account with them unless they're planning to stay in NZ for at least six months, or unless the application is accompanied by some proof of employment. Bank websites are also rather vague on the services offered to short-term visitors. If you think you'll need to open an account, do your homework before you arrive in the country and be prepared to shop around to get the best deal.

Credit & Debit Cards

Perhaps the safest place to keep your NZ travelling money is inside a plastic card! The most flexible option is to carry both a credit and a debit card.

CREDIT CARDS

Credit cards (Visa, Master Card etc) are widely accepted for everything from a hostel bed to a bungy jump. Credit cards are pretty much essential if you want to hire a car. They can also be used for over-the-counter cash advances at banks and from ATMs, depending on the card, but be aware that such transactions incur charges. Charge cards such as Diners Club and Amex are not as widely accepted.

DEBIT CARDS

Apart from losing them, the obvious danger with credit cards is maxing out your limit and going home to a steaming pile of debt. A safer option is a debit card, with which you can draw money directly from your home bank account using ATMs, banks or Eftpos machines. Any card connected to the international banking network (Cirrus, Maestro, Visa Plus and Eurocard) should work, provided you know your PIN. Fees for using your card at a foreign bank or ATM vary depending on your home bank; ask before you leave. Companies such as Travelex offer debit cards (Travelex calls them Cash Passport cards) with set withdrawal fees and a balance you can top-up from your personal bank account while on the road – nice one!

Currency

NZ's currency is the NZ dollar, comprising 100 cents. There are 10c, 20c, 50c, $1 and $2 coins, and $5, $10, $20, $50 and $100 notes. Prices are often still marked in single cents and then rounded to the nearest 10c when you hand over your money.

Moneychangers

Changing foreign currency or travellers cheques is usually no problem at banks throughout NZ or at licensed moneychangers such as Travelex in the major cities. Moneychangers can be found in all major tourist areas, cities and airports.

Taxes & Refunds

The Goods and Services Tax (GST) is a flat 15% tax on all domestic goods and services. Prices in this book include GST. There's no GST refund available when you leave NZ.

Tipping

Tipping is completely optional in NZ – the total at the bottom of a restaurant bill is all you need to pay (note that sometimes there's an additional service charge). That said, it's totally acceptable to reward good service – between 5% and 10% of the bill is fine.

Travellers Cheques

Amex, Travelex and other international brands of travellers cheques are a bit old-fashioned these days, but they're easily exchanged at banks and moneychangers. Present your passport for identification when cashing them; shop around for the best rates/lowest fees.

Post

The services offered by **New Zealand Post** (☑0800 501 501; www.nzpost.co.nz) are reliable and reasonably inexpensive. Within NZ, standard postage is 60c for regular letters and postcards, and $1.20 for larger letters.

International destinations are divided into two zones: Australia and the South Pacific, and the rest of the world. The standard rate for postcards is $1.90 worldwide, and for regular letters $1.90 to Australia and the South Pacific and $2.40 elsewhere. Express rates are also available. Check out the incredibly precise calculator on the website for more details, including info on parcels.

Public Holidays

NZ's main public holidays:
New Year 1 and 2 January
Waitangi Day 6 February
Easter Good Friday and Easter Monday; March/April
Anzac Day 25 April
Queen's Birthday First Monday in June
Labour Day Fourth Monday in October
Christmas Day 25 December
Boxing Day 26 December

In addition, each NZ province has its own anniversary-day holiday. The dates of these provincial holidays vary – when these dates fall on Friday to Sunday, they're usually observed the following Monday; if they fall on Tuesday to Thursday, they're held on the preceding Monday.

North Island anniversary holidays:
Wellington 22 January
Auckland 29 January
Northland 29 January
Taranaki 31 March
Hawke's Bay 1 November

School holidays

The Christmas holiday season, from mid-December to late January, is part of the summer school vacation. It's the time you'll most likely to find transport and accommodation booked out, and long, grumpy queues at tourist attractions. There are three shorter school-holiday periods during the year: from mid- to late April, early to mid-July, and mid-September to early October. For exact dates see the **Ministry of Education** (www.minedu.govt.nz) website.

Safe Travel

Although it's no more dangerous than other developed countries, violent crime does happen in NZ, so it's worth taking sensible precautions on the streets at night or if staying in remote areas. Gang culture permeates some parts of the country; give any black-jacketed, insignia-wearing groups a wide berth.

Theft from cars is a problem around NZ – travellers are viewed as easy marks. Avoid leaving valuables in vehicles, no matter where they're parked; you're tempting fate at tourist parking areas and trailhead car parks.

Don't underestimate the dangers posed by NZ's unpredictable, ever-changing climate, especially in high-altitude areas. Hypothermia is a real risk.

NZ has been spared the proliferation of venomous creatures found in neighbouring Australia (spiders, snakes, jellyfish...). Sharks patrol NZ waters, but rarely nibble on humans. Much greater ocean hazards are rips and undertows, which can quickly drag swimmers out to sea: heed local warnings.

Kiwi roads are often made hazardous by speeding locals, wide-cornering campervans and traffic-ignorant sheep. Set yourself a reasonable itinerary and keep your eyes on the road. Cyclists take care: motorists can't always overtake easily on skinny roads.

In the annoyances category, NZ's sandflies are a royal pain. Lather yourself with insect repellent in coastal areas.

Shopping

NZ isn't one of those countries where it's necessary to buy a T-shirt to help you remember your visit, but

there are some unique locally crafted items you might consider.

Clothing

Auckland and Wellington boast fashion-conscious boutiques ablaze with the sartorial flair of NZ designers. Check out www.fashionz.co.nz for up-to-date information. Keep an eye out for labels such as Zambesi, Kate Sylvester, Karen Walker, Trelise Cooper, NOM D and Little Brother.

From the backs of NZ sheep come sheepskin products such as footwear (including the much-loved ugg boot) and beautiful woollen jumpers (jerseys or sweaters) made from hand-spun, hand-dyed wool. Other knitted knick-knacks include hats, gloves and scarves.

Long woollen Swanndri jackets, shirts and pullovers are so ridiculously practical, they're almost the national garment in country areas. Most common are the red-and-black or blue-and-black plaid ones; pick up 'Swannies' in outdoor-gear shops.

Maori Art

Maori *whakairo rakau* (woodcarving) features intricate forms like leaping dolphins, as well as highly detailed traditional carvings. You'll pay a premium for high-quality work; avoid the poor examples in Auckland souvenir shops.

Maori artisans have always made bone carvings in the shape of humans and animals, but nowadays they cater to the tourist industry. Bone fish-hook pendants, carved in traditional Maori and modernised styles, are most common, worn on a leather string around the neck.

Paua

Abalone shell, called paua in NZ, is carved into some beautiful ornaments and jewellery and is often used as an inlay in Maori carvings. Be aware that it's illegal to take natural paua shells out of the country – only processed ornaments can be taken with you.

Pounamu

Maoris consider *pounamu* (greenstone, or jade or nephrite) to be a culturally invaluable raw material. It's found predominantly on the west coast of the South Island – Maoris called the island Te Wahi Pounamu (The Place of Greenstone) or Te Wai Pounamu (The Water of Greenstone).

One of the most popular Maori *pounamu* motifs is the *hei tiki*, the name of which literally means 'hanging human form'. They are tiny, stylised Maori figures worn on a leather string or chain around the neck. They've got great *mana* (power), but they also serve as fertility symbols.

Check out the gift shops of Rotorua for *pounamu* crafts.

Traditionally, *pounamu* is bought as a gift for another person, not for yourself. Ask a few questions to ensure you're buying from a local operator who crafts local stone, not an offshore company selling imported (usually Chinese or European) jade.

Telephone

Telecom New Zealand (www.telecom.co.nz) The country's key domestic player, with a stake in the local mobile (cell) market.
Vodafone (www.vodafone. co.nz) Alternative mobile network option.

International Calls

Payphones allow international calls, but the cost and international dialling code for calls will vary depending on which provider you're using. International calls from NZ are relatively inexpensive and subject to specials that reduce the rates even more, so it's worth shopping around –

consult the Yellow Pages for providers.

To make international calls from NZ, you need to dial the international access code (☎00), the country code and the area code (without the initial 0). So for a London number, you'd dial ☎00-44-20, then the number.

If dialling NZ from overseas, the country code is ☎64, followed by the appropriate area code minus the initial zero.

Local Calls

Local calls from private phones are free! Local calls from payphones cost $1 for the first 15 minutes, and 20c per minute thereafter, though coin-operated payphones are scarce – you'll need a phonecard. Calls to mobile phones attract higher rates.

Long Distance Calls & Area Codes

NZ uses regional two-digit area codes for long-distance calls, which can be made from any payphone. If you're making a local call (ie to someone else in the same town), you don't need to dial the area code. But if you're dialling within a region (even if it's to a nearby town with the same area code), you do have to dial the area code.

Information & Toll-Free Calls

Numbers starting with ☎0900 are usually recorded information services, charging upwards of $1 per minute (more from mobiles); these numbers cannot be dialled from payphones.

Toll-free numbers in NZ have the prefix ☎0800 or ☎0508 and can be called free of charge from anywhere in the country, though they may not be accessible from certain areas or from mobile phones. Telephone numbers beginning with ☎0508, ☎0800 or ☎0900 cannot be dialled from outside NZ.

Mobile Phones

Local mobile phone numbers are preceded by the prefix ☎021, ☎022, ☎025 or ☎027. Mobile phone coverage is good in cities and towns and most parts of the North Island.

If you want to bring your own phone and use a prepaid service with a local SIM card, **Vodafone** (www.vodafone. co.nz) is a practical option. Any Vodafone shop (found in most major towns) will set you up with a SIM card and phone number (about $40); top-ups can be purchased at newsagencies, post offices and petrol stations practically anywhere.

Alternatively, if you don't bring your own phone from home, you can rent one from **Vodafone Rental** (www. vodarent.co.nz) priced from $5 per day (for which you'll also need a local SIM card), with pick-up and drop-off outlets at NZ's major airports. We've also had some positive feedback on **Phone Hire New Zealand** (www.phonehirenz. com), which hires out mobile phones, SIM cards, modems and GPS systems.

Phonecards

NZ has a wide range of phonecards available, which can be bought at hostels, newsagencies and post offices for a fixed dollar value (usually $5, $10, $20 and $50). These can be used with any public or private phone by dialling a toll-free access number and then the PIN number on the card. Shop around – rates vary from company to company.

Time

NZ is 12 hours ahead of GMT/UTC and two hours ahead of Australian Eastern Standard Time. The Chathams are 45 minutes ahead of NZ's main islands.

In summer, NZ observes daylight-saving time, where clocks are wound forward by one hour on the last Sunday in September; clocks are wound back on the first Sunday of the following April.

Tourist Information

Local Tourist Offices

Almost every North Island city or town seems to have a visitor information centre. The bigger centres stand united within the outstanding **i-SITE** (www.newzealand.com/travel/i-sites) network, affiliated with Tourism New Zealand (the official national tourism body). i-SITEs have trained staff, information on local activities and attractions, and free brochures and maps. Staff can also book activities, transport and accommodation.

Bear in mind that many information centres only promote accommodation and tour operators who are paying members of the local tourist association, and that sometimes staff aren't supposed to recommend one activity or accommodation provider over another.

There's also a network of **Department Of Conservation** (DOC; www.doc.govt.nz) visitor centres to help you plan activities and make bookings. Visitor centres – in national parks, regional centres and major cities – usually also have displays on local lore, flora, fauna and biodiversity.

Tourist Offices Abroad

Tourism New Zealand (www.newzealand.com) has representatives in various countries around the world. A good place for pretrip research is the official website (emblazoned with the hugely successful 100% Pure New Zealand branding), which has information in several languages, including German and Japanese. Overseas offices:

Australia (☑0415-123 362; L12, 61 York St, Sydney)
UK & Europe (☑020-7930 1662; L7, New Zealand House, 80 Haymarket, London, UK)
USA & Canada (☑310-395 7480; Suite 300, 501 Santa Monica Blvd, Santa Monica, USA)

Travellers with Disabilities

Kiwi accommodation generally caters fairly well for travellers with disabilities, with a significant number of hostels, hotels, motels and B&Bs equipped with wheelchair-accessible rooms. Many tourist attractions similarly provide wheelchair access, with wheelchairs often available.

Tour operators with accessible vehicles operate from most major centres. Key cities are also serviced by 'kneeling' buses (buses that hydraulically stoop down to kerb level to allow easy access); taxi companies offer wheelchair-accessible vans. Large car-hire firms (Avis, Hertz etc) provide cars with hand controls at no extra charge (advance notice required). Mobility parking permits are available from branches of **CCS Disability Action** (☑0800 227 200, 04-384 5677; www.ccsdisability action.org.nz) in the main centres.

For good general information, see NZ's disability information website **Weka** (www.weka.net.nz), which has categories including Transport and Travel.

If cold-weather activity is more your thing, see the **Adaptive Snow Sports NZ** (www.disabledsnowsports.org. nz) website.

Visas

Visa application forms are available from NZ diplomatic missions overseas, travel agents and **Immigration New Zealand** (☑0508 558 855, 09-914 4100; www.immi gration.govt.nz). Immigration New Zealand has over a dozen offices overseas; consult the website.

Visitor's Visa

Citizens of Australia don't need a visa to visit NZ and can stay indefinitely (provided they have no criminal convictions). UK citizens don't need a visa either and can stay in the country for up to six months.

Citizens of another 56 countries that have visa-waiver agreements with NZ don't need a visa for stays of up to three months, provided they have an onward ticket and sufficient funds to support their stay: see the website for details. Nations in this group include Canada, France, Germany, Ireland, Japan, the Netherlands and the USA.

Citizens of other countries must obtain a visa before entering NZ. Visas come with three months' standard validity and cost $110 if processed in Australia or certain South Pacific countries (eg Samoa, Fiji), or around $140 if processed elsewhere in the world.

A visitor's visa can be extended for stays of up to nine months within one 18-month period, or to a maximum of 12 months in the country. Applications are assessed on a case-by-case basis; visitors will need to meet criteria such as proof of ongoing financial self-support. Apply for extensions at any Immigration New Zealand office – see the website for locations.

Work Visa & Working Holiday Scheme
WORK VISA

It's illegal for foreign nationals to work in NZ on a visitor's visa, except for Australians who can legally gain work without a visa or permit. If you're visiting NZ to find work, or you already have an employment offer, you'll need to apply for a work visa, which translates into a work permit once you arrive and is valid for up to three years. You can apply for a work permit after you're in NZ, but its validity will be backdated to when you entered the country. The fee for a work visa ranges from NZ$200 to NZ$310, depending on where and how it's processed (paper or online) and the type of application.

WORKING HOLIDAY SCHEME

Eligible travellers who are only interested in short-term employment to supplement their travels can take part in one of NZ's working-holiday schemes (WHS). Under these schemes citizens aged 18 to 30 years from 36 countries – including Canada, France, Germany, Ireland, Japan, Malaysia, the Netherlands, Scandinavian countries, the UK and the USA – can apply for a visa. For most nationalities the visa is valid for 12 months. It's only issued to those seeking a genuine working holiday, not permanent work, so you're not supposed to work for one employer for more than three months.

Most WHS-eligible nationals must apply for this visa from within their own country; residents of some countries can apply online. Applicants must have an onward ticket, a passport valid for at least three months from the date they will leave NZ and evidence of at least NZ$4200 in accessible funds. The application fee is NZ$140 regardless of where you apply, and isn't refunded if your application is declined.

The rules vary for different nationalities, so make sure you read up on the specifics of your country's agreement with NZ at www.immigration. govt.nz/migrant/stream/ work/workingholiday.

Women Travellers

NZ is generally a very safe place for women travellers, although the usual sensible precautions apply: avoid walking alone late at night and never hitchhike alone. If you're out on the town, always keep enough money aside for a taxi back to your accommodation. Lone women should also be wary of staying in basic pub accommodation unless it looks safe and well managed. Sexual harassment is not a widely reported problem in NZ, but of course it does happen.

See www.womentravel. co.nz for more information.

Work

If you arrive in NZ on a visitor's visa, you're not allowed to work for pay. If you're caught breaching this (or any other) visa condition, you could be booted back to where you came from.

If you have been approved for a WHS visa, look into the possibilities for temporary employment. There's plenty of casual work around, mainly in agriculture (fruit picking, farming, wineries), hospitality or ski resorts. Office-based work can be found in IT, banking, finance and telemarketing. Register with a local office-work agency to get started.

Seasonal fruit picking, pruning and harvesting is prime short-term work for visitors. More than 300 sq km of apples, kiwifruit and other fruit and veg are harvested from December to May. Rates are around $10 to $15 an hour for physically taxing toil – turnover of workers is high. You're usually paid by how much you pick (per bin, bucket or kilogram). Prime North Island picking locations include the Bay of Islands (Kerikeri and Paihia), rural Auckland, Tauranga, Gisborne and Hawke's Bay (Napier and Hastings).

Winter work at ski resorts and their service towns includes bartending, waiting, cleaning, ski-tow operation and, if you're properly qualified, ski or snowboard instructing.

Resources

Backpacker publications, hostel managers and other travellers are the best sources of info on local work possibilities. **Base Backpackers** (www.stayatbase.com/work) runs an employment service via its website, while the Notice Boards page on **Budget Backpacker Hostels** (BBH; www.bbh.co.nz) lists job vacancies in BBH hostels and a few other possibilities.

Kiwi Careers (www.kiwi careers.govt.nz) lists professional opportunities in various fields (agriculture, creative, health, teaching,

---

VOLUNTOURISM

NZ presents a swathe of active, outdoorsy volunteer opportunities for travellers to get some dirt under their fingernails and participate in conservation programs. Programs can include anything from tree-planting and weed removal to track construction, habitat conservation and fencing. Ask about local opportunities at any regional i-SITE visitor information centre, or check out www.conservationvolunteers.org.nz and www.doc.govt. nz/getting-involved, both of which allow you to browse for opportunities by region.

volunteer work and recruitment), while **Seek** (www.seek.co.nz) is one of the biggest NZ job-search networks, with thousands of jobs listed.

Check ski-resort websites for work opportunities in the snow, and in the fruit-picking/horticultural realm, try the following websites:

» www.seasonalwork.co.nz
» www.seasonaljobs.co.nz
» www.picknz.co.nz
» www.pickingjobs.com

Income Tax

Death and taxes – no escape! For most travellers, Kiwi dollars earned in NZ will be subject to income tax, deducted from payments by employers – a proc-ess called Pay As You Earn (PAYE). Standard NZ income tax rates are 12.5% for annual salaries up to $14,000, then 19.5% up to $48,000, 32% up to $70,000, then 35% for higher incomes. A NZ Accident Compensation Corporation (ACC) scheme levy (2%) will also be deducted from your pay packet. Note that these rates tend to change slightly year to year.

If you visit NZ and work for a short time (eg on a working holiday scheme), you may qualify for a tax refund when you leave. Complete a *Refund Application – People Leaving New Zealand IR50* form and submit it with your tax return, along with proof of departure (eg air-ticket copies) to the **Inland Revenue Department** (www.ird.govt.nz). For more info, see the IRD website, or contact the **Inland Revenue Non-Resident Centre** (☎03-951 2020; nonres@ird.govt.nz; Private Bag 1932).

IRD Number

Travellers undertaking paid work in NZ must obtain an IRD number. Download the *IRD Number Application – Individual IR595* form from the **Inland Revenue Department** (www.ird.govt.nz) website. IRD numbers normally take eight to 10 working days to be issued.

Transport

GETTING THERE & AWAY

Flights, tours and rail tickets can be booked online at lonelyplanet.com/bookings.

Entering the Country

Disembarkation in New Zealand is generally a straightforward affair, with only the usual customs declarations to endure and the uncool scramble at the luggage carousel. Recent global instability has resulted in increased security in NZ airports, in both domestic and international terminals, and you may find customs procedures more time-consuming.

One procedure has the Orwellian title Advance Passenger Screening, a system whereby documents that used to be checked after you touched down in NZ (passport, visa etc) are now checked before you board your flight – make sure all your documentation is in order so that your check-in is stress-free.

Passport

There are no restrictions when it comes to foreign citizens entering NZ. If you have a current passport and visa (or don't require one), you should be fine.

Air

There's a number of competing airlines servicing NZ and a wide variety of fares to choose from if you're flying in from Asia, Europe or North America, though ultimately you'll still pay a lot for a flight unless you jet in from Australia. NZ's inordinate popularity and abundance of year-round activities mean that almost any time of year airports can be swarming with inbound tourists – if you want to fly at a particularly popular time of year (eg over the Christmas period), book well in advance.

High season for flights into NZ is summer (December to February), with slightly less of a premium on fares over the shoulder months (October/November and March/April). The low season generally tallies with the winter months (June to August), though this is still a busy time for airlines ferrying ski bunnies and powder hounds.

Airports & Airlines

Four North Island airports handle international flights, with Auckland receiving most traffic:

Auckland International Airport (AKL; ✆09-275 0789, 0800 247 767; www.auckland airport.co.nz; Ray Emery Dr)

Hamilton International Airport (HIA; ✆07-848 9027; www.hamiltonairport.co.nz; Airport Rd)

Rotorua International Airport (✆07-345 8800; www.rotorua-airport.co.nz)

Wellington Airport (WLG; ✆04-385 5100; www.wellington-airport.co.nz; Stewart Duff Dr)

AIRLINES FLYING TO & FROM NEW ZEALAND

Winging-in from Australia, Virgin Australia, Qantas and Air New Zealand are the key players. Air New Zealand

---

DEPARTURE TAX

An international departure tax of NZ$25 applies when leaving NZ at Wellington or Hamilton airports, payable by anyone aged 12 and over (NZ$10 for children aged two to 11, free for those under two years of age). The tax is not included in the price of airline tickets, but must be paid separately at the airport before you board your flight (via credit card or cash). If you are leaving NZ from Auckland airport, the departure tax is included in the cost of your airline ticket.

CLIMATE CHANGE & TRAVEL

Every form of transport that relies on carbon-based fuel generates CO_2, the main cause of human-induced climate change. Modern travel is dependent on aeroplanes, which might use less fuel per kilometre per person than most cars but travel much greater distances. The altitude at which aircraft emit gases (including CO_2) and particles also contributes to their climate change impact. Many websites offer 'carbon calculators' that allow people to estimate the carbon emissions generated by their journey and, for those who wish to do so, to offset the impact of the greenhouse gases emitted with contributions to portfolios of climate-friendly initiatives throughout the world. Lonely Planet offsets the carbon footprint of all staff and author travel.

also flies in from North America, but you can also head south with Air Canada and American Airlines. From Europe, the options are a little broader, with British Airways, Lufthansa and Virgin Atlantic entering the fray, and several others stopping in NZ on broader round-the-world routes.

NZ's own overseas carrier is Air New Zealand, which flies to runways across Europe, North America, eastern Asia and the Pacific. Airlines that connect NZ with international destinations include the following (note that 0800 and 0508 phone numbers mentioned here are for dialling from within NZ only):

Aerolineas Argentinas (AR; ☑09-379 3675; www.aerolineas.com.ar)

Aircalin (SB; ☑09-977 2238; www.aircalin.com)

Air Canada (AC; ☑09-969 7470; www.aircanada.com)

Air China (CA; ☑09-379 7696; www.airchina.com.cn)

Air New Zealand (NZ; ☑09-357 3000, 0800 737 000; www.airnewzealand.co.nz)

Air Pacific (FJ; ☑09-379 2404, 0800 800 178; www.airpacific.com)

Air Tahiti Nui (YN; ☑09-308 3360; www.airtahitinui.com.au)

Air Vanuatu (NF; ☑09-373 3435; www.airvanuatu.com)

American Airlines (AA; ☑09-912 8814, 0800 445 442; www.aa.com)

British Airways (BA; ☑09-966 9777; www.britishairways.com)

Cathay Pacific (CX; ☑09-379 0861, 0800 800 454; www.cathaypacific.com)

China Airlines (CI; ☑09-308 3364; www.china-airlines.com)

China Southern (CZ; ☑09-302 0666; www.flychinasouthern.com)

Emirates (EK; ☑09-968 2208, 0508 364 728; www.emirates.com)

Etihad Airways (EY; ☑09-977 2207; www.etihadairways.com)

Japan Airlines (JL; ☑0800 525 747; www.jal.com)

Jetstar (JQ; ☑0800 800 995; www.jetstar.com)

Korean Air (KE; ☑09-914 2000; www.koreanair.com)

LAN (LA; ☑09-308 3352; www.lan.com)

Lufthansa (LH; ☑09-303 1529; www.lufthansa.com)

Malaysia Airlines (MH; ☑09-379 3743, 0800 777 747; www.malaysiaairlines.com)

Qantas (QF; ☑09-357 8900, 0800 808 767; www.qantas.com.au)

Singapore Airlines (SQ; ☑09-379 3209, 0800 808 909; www.singaporeair.com)

South African Airways (SA; ☑09-977 2237; www.flysaa.com)

Thai Airways International (TG; ☑09-377 3886; www.thaiairways.com)

Virgin Atlantic (VS; ☑09-308 3377; www.virginatlantic.com)

Virgin Australia (DJ; ☑0800 670 000; www.virginaustralia.com)

Virgin Samoa (☑0800 670 000; www.virginaustralia.com)

Tickets

Automated online ticket sales work well if you're doing a simple one-way or return trip on specified dates, but are no substitute for a travel agent with the low-down on special deals, strategies for avoiding layovers and other useful advice.

ROUND-THE-WORLD (RTW) TICKETS

If you're flying to New Zealand from the other side of the world, RTW tickets can be bargains. They're generally put together by the big airline alliances, and give you a limited period (usually a year) in which to circumnavigate the globe. You can go anywhere the participating airlines go, as long as you stay within the prescribed kilometre extents or number of stops and don't backtrack when flying between continents.

Ticket providers include the following:

Oneworld (www.oneworld.com)

Skyteam (www.skyteam.com)

Star Alliance (www.staralliance.com)

CIRCLE PACIFIC TICKETS

A Circle Pacific ticket is similar to a RTW ticket but covers a more limited region, using a combination of airlines to connect Australia, NZ, North America and Asia, with stopover options in the Pacific islands. As with RTW tickets, there are restrictions on how many stopovers you can take.

ONLINE TICKET SALES
For online ticket bookings, including RTW fares, start with the following websites:

AirTreks (www.airtreks.com) A US company with some tasty round-the-world fares.

Cheap Flights (www.cheap flights.com) Global sites (US, Australia/NZ, Spain, Germany, UK/Ireland, France, Canada and Italy) with specials, destination information and flight searches.

Cheapest Flights (www. cheapestflights.co.uk) Cheap worldwide flights from the UK; get in early for the bargains.

Co-operative Travel (www. co-operativetravel.co.uk) International site for affordable holiday packages.

Expedia (www.expedia.com) Microsoft's travel site; good for USA-related flights.

Flight Centre International (www.flightcentre. com) Respected operator handling direct flights, with sites for NZ, Australia, the UK, the USA, Canada and South Africa.

Roundtheworldflights. com (www.roundtheworld flights.com) Build your own adventure from the UK with up to six stops, including Asia, Australia, NZ and the USA. Good rates in the NZ winter.

STA Travel (www.statravel. com) The full package: flights (including RTW), tours, accommodation and insurance.

Travel Online (www.travel online.co.nz) Good place to check worldwide flights from NZ.

Travel.com.au (www.travel. com.au) Solid Australian site; look up fares and flights to/ from the country.

Travelocity (www.travelocity. com) Global site that allows you to search fares from/to practically anywhere.

Sea

It's possible (though by no means easy or safe) to make your way between NZ and Australia, and some smaller Pacific islands, by hitching rides or crewing on yachts. Try asking around at harbours, marinas, and yacht and sailing clubs. Popular yachting harbours in NZ include the Bay of Islands and Whangarei (both in Northland), Auckland and Wellington. March and April are the best months to look for boats heading to Australia. From Fiji, October to November is a peak departure season to beat the cyclones that soon follow in that neck of the woods.

There are no passenger liners operating to/from NZ, and finding a berth on a cargo ship (much less enjoying the experience) is no easy task.

GETTING AROUND

Air

Those who have limited time to get between NZ's attractions can make the most of a widespread network of intra- and inter-island flights.

Airlines in New Zealand

The country's major domestic carrier, Air New Zealand, has an aerial network covering most of the country. Australia-based Jetstar also flies between main urban areas. Between them, these two airlines service the main routes and carry the vast majority of domestic passengers in NZ. Beyond this, several small-scale regional operators provide services, including between the North and South Islands, around the Bay of Islands and

Auckland, and in the Bay of Plenty and Hawke's Bay. Operators include the following:

Air New Zealand (NZ; ☎09-357 3000, 0800 737 000; www.airnewzealand.co.nz) Offers flights between 30-plus domestic destinations.

Air2there.com (☎04-904 5130, 0800 777 000; www. air2there.com) Connects destinations across Cook Strait, including Paraparaumu, Wellington, Nelson and Blenheim.

Fly My Sky (☎09-256 7025; www.flymysky.co.nz) At least three flights daily from Auckland to Great Barrier Island.

Golden Bay Air (☎03-525 8725, 0800 588 885; www. goldenbayair.co.nz) Flies regularly between Wellington and Takaka in Golden Bay. Also connects to Karamea for Heaphy Track trampers.

Great Barrier Airlines (☎09-275 9120, 0800 900 600; www.greatbarrierairlines. co.nz) Plies the skies over Great Barrier Island, Auckland and Whangarei.

Jetstar (JQ; ☎0800 800 995; www.jetstar.com) Joins the dots between key tourism centres: Auckland, Wellington, Christchurch, Dunedin and Queenstown (and flies Queenstown to Sydney).

Salt Air (☎09-402 8338, 0800 472 582; www.saltair. co.nz) Flies to Kerikeri from Whangarei and Auckland's North Shore.

Soundsair (☎0800 505 005, 03-520 3080; www. soundsair.co.nz) Numerous flights each day between Picton and Wellington, with connections to Blenheim and Nelson.

Sunair (☎07-575 7799, 0800 786 247; www.sunair.co.nz) Flies to Whitianga from Auckland, Great Barrier Island, Hamilton, Rotorua and Tauranga. Other North Island routes too.

Air Passes

With discounting being the norm these days, and a number of budget airlines now serving the trans-Tasman route as well as the Pacific islands, the value of air passes isn't as red-hot as in the past.

From Los Angeles return, **Air New Zealand** (NZ; ☑09-357 3000, 0800 737 000; www.airnewzealand.co.nz) offers the Explore New Zealand Airpass, which includes a stop in either Wellington, Queenstown or Christchurch plus three other domestic NZ destinations. Prices at the time of research started at around US$1150.

Star Alliance (www.star alliance.com) offers the coupon-based South Pacific Airpass, valid for selected journeys within NZ, and between NZ, Australia and several Pacific islands, including Fiji, New Caledonia, Tonga, the Cook Islands and Samoa. Passes are available to nonresidents of these countries, must be issued outside NZ in conjunction with Star Alliance international tickets, and are valid for three months. A typical Sydney–Christchurch–Wellington–Auckland–Nadi pass cost NZ$1050 at the time of research.

Bicycle

Touring cyclists proliferate in NZ, particularly over summer. NZ is clean, green and relatively uncrowded, and has lots of cheap accommodation (including camping) and abundant fresh water. The roads are generally in good nick, and the climate is generally not too hot or cold. Road traffic is the biggest danger: trucks overtaking too close to cyclists are a particular threat. Bikes and cycling gear (to rent or buy) are readily available in the main centres, as are bicycle repair shops.

By law all cyclists must wear an approved safety hel-

> ## NGA HAERENGA, NEW ZEALAND CYCLE TRAIL
>
> The **Nga Haerenga, New Zealand Cycle Trail** (www.nzcycletrail.com) is a major nationwide project that has been in motion since 2009, expanding and improving NZ's extant network of bike trails. Funded to the tune of around $46 million, the project currently has 18 'Great Rides' under construction across both islands, most of which are already open to cyclists in some capacity. See the website for info and updates.

met (or risk a fine); it's also vital to have good reflective safety clothing. Cyclists who use public transport will find that major bus lines and trains only take bicycles on a 'space available' basis and charge up to $10. Some of the smaller shuttle bus companies, on the other hand, make sure they have storage space for bikes, which they carry for a surcharge.

If importing your own bike or transporting it by plane within NZ, check with the relevant airline for costs and the degree of dismantling and packing required.

See www.nzta.govt.nz/traffic/ways/bike for more bike safety and legal tips.

Hire

The rates offered by most outfits for renting road or mountain bikes range from $10 to $20 per hour and $30 to $50 per day. Longer-term rentals are often available by negotiation.

Boat

NZ may be an island nation but there's virtually no long-distance water transport around the country.

Obvious exceptions include the boat services between Auckland and various islands in the Hauraki Gulf, the inter-island ferries that chug across Cook Strait between Wellington and Picton.

Bus

Bus travel in NZ is relatively easy and well organised, with services transporting you to the far reaches of both islands (including the start/end of various walking tracks), but it can be expensive, tedious and time-consuming.

NZ's dominant bus company is **InterCity** (☑09-583 5780; www.intercity.co.nz), which also has an extra-comfort travel and sightseeing arm called **Newmans Coach Lines** (☑09-583 5780; www.newmanscoach.co.nz). InterCity can drive you to just about anywhere on the North Island. **Naked Bus** (☑0900 625 33; www.nakedbus.com) is the main competition, a budget operator with fares as low as $1 (!).

Seat Classes

There are no allocated economy or luxury classes on NZ buses; smoking is a no-no.

Reservations

Over summer, school holidays and public holidays, book well in advance on popular routes. At other times a day or two ahead is usually fine. The best prices are generally available online, booked a few weeks in advance.

Bus Passes

If you're covering a lot of ground, both **InterCity** (☑09-583 5780, 0800 222

146; www.intercity.co.nz) and **Naked Bus** (☎0900 625 33; www.nakedbus.com) offer bus passes that can be cheaper than paying as you go, but they do of course lock you into using their respective networks. InterCity also offers a 15% discount for YHA, BBH and VIP backpacker members. All the following passes are valid for 12 months.

Backpacker Buses also offers fixed-itinerary bus-pass options for dorm dwellers.

NATIONWIDE PASSES

Flexipass A hop-on, hop-off InterCity pass, allowing travel to pretty much anywhere in NZ, in any direction. The pass is purchased in blocks of travel time: minimum 15 hours ($117), maximum 60 hours ($449). The average cost of each block becomes cheaper the more hours you buy. You can top up the pass if you need more time.

Flexitrips An InterCity bus-pass system whereby you purchase a specific number of bus trips (eg Auckland to Tauranga would count as one trip) in blocks of five, with or without the north–south ferry trip included. Five/15/30 trips including the ferry cost $210/383/550 (subtract $54 if you don't need the ferry).

Naked Passport A Naked Bus **pass** (www.nakedpass port.com) that allows you to buy trips in blocks of five, which you can add to any time, and book each trip as needed. Five/15/30 trips cost $157/330/497. An unlimited pass costs $597 – great value if you're travelling NZ for many moons.

NORTH ISLAND PASSES

InterCity also offers 13 hop-on, hop-off, fixed-itinerary North Island bus passes, ranging from short $43 runs between Rotorua and Taupo, to $249 trips from Auckland

to Wellington via the big sights in between. See www.travelpass.co.nz for details.

Shuttle Buses

Other than InterCity and Naked Bus, North Island regional shuttle-bus operators include the following:

Alpine Scenic Tours (☎07-378 7412; www.alpine scenictours.co.nz) Has services around Taupo and into Tongariro National Park, plus the ski fields around Mt Ruapehu and Mt Tongariro.

Atomic Shuttles (☎03-349 0697; www.atomic travel.co.nz) Has services throughout the South Island, including to Christchurch, Dunedin, Invercargill, Picton, Nelson, Greymouth/Hokitika, Te Anau and Queenstown/Wanaka

Dalroy Express (☎06-759-0197, 0508 465 622; www.dalroytours.co.nz) Operates a daily service between Auckland and New Plymouth via Hamilton, extending to Hawera Monday to Friday. Also runs from Auckland to Pahia, and from Hamilton to Rotorua and Taupo.

Go Kiwi Shuttles (☎07-866 0336; www.go-kiwi.co.nz) Links Auckland with Whitianga on the Coromandel Peninsula daily, with extensions to Rotorua in summer.

Waitomo Wanderer (☎03-477 9083, 0800 000 4321; www.travelheadfirst.com) Does a loop from Rotorua or Taupo to Waitomo.

Backpacker Buses

If you feel like clocking up some kilometres with like-minded fellow travellers, the following operators run fixed-itinerary bus tours, nationwide or on the North or South Islands. Accommodation and hop-on/hop-off flexibility are often included.

Adventure Tours New Zealand (☎09-526 2149; www.adventuretours.com.au)

Flying Kiwi (☎03-547 0171, 0800 693 296; www.flyingkiwi.com)

Kiwi Experience (☎09-336 4286; www.kiwi experience.com)

Haka Tours (☎03-980 4252; www.hakatours.com)

Magic Travellers Network (☎09-358 5600; www.magicbus.co.nz)

Stray Travel (☎09-526 2140; www.straytravel.com)

Car & Motorcycle

The best way to explore New Zealand in depth is to have your own wheels. It's easy to hire cars and campervans at good rates; alternatively, consider buying your own vehicle.

Automobile Association (AA)

NZ's **Automobile Association** (AA; ☎0800 500 444; www.aa.co.nz/travel) provides emergency breakdown services, maps and accommodation guides (from holiday parks to motels and B&Bs).

Members of overseas automobile associations should bring their membership cards – many of these bodies have reciprocal agreements with the AA.

Driving Licences

International visitors to New Zealand can use their home country's driving licence – if your licence isn't in English, it's a good idea to carry a certified translation with you.

Alternatively, use an International Driving Permit (IDP), which will usually be issued on the spot (valid for 12 months) by your home country's automobile association.

Fuel

Fuel (petrol, aka gasoline) is available from service stations across New Zealand. LPG (gas) is not always stocked by rural suppliers; if you're on gas, it's safer to have dual-fuel capability. Aside from remote locations like Milford Sound and Mt Cook, petrol prices don't vary much from place to place (very democratic): per-litre costs at the time of research were around $2.10.

Hire

CAMPERVAN

Check your rear-view mirror on any far-flung NZ road and you'll probably see a shiny white campervan (aka mobile home, motor home, RV) packed with liberated travellers, mountain bikes and portable barbecues cruising along behind you.

Most towns of any size have a campground or holiday park with powered sites for around $35 per night. There are also 250-plus vehicle-accessible **Department of Conservation** (DOC; www.doc.govt.nz) campsites around NZ, ranging in price from free to $19 per adult: check the website.

You can hire campervans from dozens of companies, prices varying with season, vehicle size and length of rental.

A small van for two people typically has a minikitchen and foldout dining table, the latter transforming into a double bed when dinner is done and dusted. Larger 'superior' two-berth vans include shower and toilet. Four- to six-berth campervans are the size of trucks (and similarly sluggish) and, besides the extra space, usually contain a toilet and shower.

Over summer, rates offered by the main rental firms for two-/four-/six-berth vans start at around $160/260/300 per day, dropping to as low as $45/60/90 in winter for month-long rentals.

Major operators include the following:

Apollo (☑09-889 2976, 0800 113 131; www.apollocamperco.nz)

Britz (☑09-255 3910, 0800 831 900; www.britz.co.nz)

Kea (☑09-448 8800, 0800 520 052; www.keacampers.com)

Maui (☑09-255 3910, 0800 651 080; www.maui.co.nz)

Pacific Horizon (☑09-257 4331; www.pacifichorizon.co.nz)

United Campervans (☑09-275 9919; www.unitedcampervans.co.nz)

BACKPACKER VAN RENTALS

Budget players in the campervan industry offer slick deals and funky, well-kitted-out vehicles for backpackers. Rates are competitive (from $35 per day May to September; from $80 per day December to February). Operators include the following:

Backpacker Campervans (☑0800 422 267; www.backpackercampervans.co.nz) Reliable operator, affiliated with Britz and Maui.

Backpacker Sleeper Vans (☑03-359 4731, 0800 325 939; www.sleepervans.co.nz) The name says it all.

Escape Rentals (☑0800 216 171; www.escaperentals.co.nz) Loud, original paintwork, plus DVDs, TVs and outdoor barbecues for hire.

Hippie Camper (☑0800 113 131; www.hippiecamper.co.nz) Think Combi vans for the new millennium.

Jucy (☑0800 399 736; www.jucy.co.nz)

Spaceships (☑09-526 2130, 0800 772 237; www.spaceshipsrentals.co.nz) The customised 'Swiss Army Knife of campervans', with extras including DVD and CD players, roof racks and solar showers.

Wicked Campers (☑09-634 2994, 0800 246 870; www.wicked-campers.co.nz) Spray-painted vans bedecked with everything/everyone from Mr Spock to Sly Stone.

CAR

Competition between car-rental companies in NZ is torrid, particularly in the big cities and Picton. Remember that if you want to travel far, you need unlimited kilometres. Some (but not all) companies require drivers to be at least 21 years old – ask around.

Most car-hire firms suggest (or insist) that you don't take their vehicles between islands on the Cook Strait ferries. Instead, you leave your car at either Wellington or Picton terminal and pick up another car once you've crossed the strait. This saves you paying to transport a vehicle on the ferries, and is a pain-free exercise.

INTERNATIONAL RENTAL COMPANIES

The big multinational companies have offices in most major cities, towns and airports. Firms sometimes offer one-way rentals (eg collect a car in Auckland, leave it in Wellington), but there are often restrictions and fees. On the other hand, an operator in Christchurch may need to

TRANSPORT CAR & MOTORCYCLE

ROAD DISTANCES (KM)

	Auckland	Cape Reinga	Dargaville	Gisborne	Hamilton	Hicks Bay	Kaitaia	Napier	New Plymouth	Paihia	Palmerston North	Rotorua	Taupo	Tauranga	Thames	Waitomo Caves	Whanganui	Wellington	Whakatane
Cape Reinga	430																		
Dargaville	175	280																	
Gisborne	490	920	675																
Hamilton	125	555	300	390															
Hicks Bay	510	945	690	180	400														
Kaitaia	325	115	170	820	440	800													
Napier	420	860	590	215	300	395	735												
New Plymouth	360	790	530	570	240	580	680	410											
Paihia	225	220	130	720	340	720	120	645	590										
Palmerston North	520	950	690	395	400	570	840	180	230	750									
Rotorua	235	670	405	295	110	285	550	220	300	460	325								
Taupo	280	720	450	330	155	365	600	140	300	505	250	80							
Tauranga	210	635	385	290	110	290	525	300	330	435	400	85	155						
Thames	115	540	280	410	110	400	430	360	340	345	470	170	210	115					
Waitomo Caves	200	620	360	440	75	440	515	300	180	420	340	165	170	150	175				
Whanganui	455	880	615	465	330	645	770	250	160	670	75	310	225	375	430	270			
Wellington	640	1080	805	530	520	730	960	320	350	860	140	450	375	530	590	460	190		
Whakatane	300	740	470	200	190	204	620	300	380	525	410	85	160	95	210	240	380	540	
Whangarei	160	280	55	640	280	650	165	580	515	70	680	390	430	350	265	345	600	790	450

get a vehicle back to Auckland and will offer an amazing one-way deal (sometimes free!).

The major companies offer a choice of either unlimited kilometres, or 100km (or so) per day free, plus so many cents per subsequent kilometre. Daily rates in main cities typically start at around $40 per day for a compact, late-model, Japanese car, and around $75 for medium-sized cars (including GST, unlimited kilometres and insurance).

Avis (☑09-526-2847, 0800 655 111; www.avis.co.nz)

Budget (☑09-529 7784, 0800 283 438; www.budget.co.nz)

Europcar (☑03-357 0920, 0800 800 115; www.europcar.co.nz)

Hertz (☑03-520 3044, 0800 654 321; www.hertz.co.nz)

Thrifty (☑03-359 2720, 0800 737 070; www.thrifty.co.nz)

LOCAL RENTAL COMPANIES

Local rental firms dapple the *Yellow Pages*. These are almost always cheaper than the big boys – sometimes half the price – but the cheap rates may come with serious restrictions: vehicles are often older, and with less formality sometimes comes a less protective legal structure for renters.

Rentals from local firms start at around $30 per day for the smallest option. It's obviously cheaper if you rent for a week or more, and there are often low-season and weekend discounts.

Affordable and independent operators with national networks include the following:

a2b Car Rentals (☑0800 666 703; www.a2b-carrentals.co.nz)

Ace Rental Cars (☑09-303 3112, 0800 502 277; www.acerentalcars.co.nz)

Apex Rentals (☑03-379 6897, 0800 939 597; www.apexrentals.co.nz)

Ezy Rentals (☑09-374 4360, 0800 399 736; www.ezy.co.nz)

Go Rentals (☑09-525 7321, 0800 467 368; www.gorentals.co.nz)

Omega Rental Cars (☑09-377 5573, 0800 525 210; www.omegarentalcars.com)

Pegasus Rental Cars (☑03-548 2852, 0800 803 580; www.rentalcars.co.nz)

MOTORCYCLE

Born to be wild? New Zealand has great terrain for

motorcycle touring, despite the fickle weather in some regions. Most of the North Island's motorcycle-hire shops are in Auckland, where you can hire anything from a little 50cc moped (aka nifty-fifty) to a throbbing 750cc touring motorcycle and beyond.

Recommended operators (who also run guided tours) with rates from $80 to $345 per day:

New Zealand Motorcycle Rentals & Tours (☎09-486 2472; www.nzbike.com)

Te Waipounamu Motorcycle Tours (☎03-377 3211; www.motorcycle-hire.co.nz)

Insurance

Rather than risk paying out wads of cash if you have an accident, you can take out your own comprehensive insurance policy, or (the usual option) pay an additional fee per day to the rental company to reduce your excess. This brings the amount you must pay in the event of an accident down from around $1500 or $2000 to around $200 or $300. Smaller operators offering cheap rates often have a compulsory insurance excess, taken as a credit-card bond, of around $900.

Most insurance agreements won't cover the cost of damage to glass (including the windscreen) or tyres, and insurance coverage is often invalidated on beaches and certain rough (4WD) unsealed roads – read the fine print.

Purchase

Buying a car then selling it at the end of your travels can be one of the cheapest and best ways to see NZ. On the North Island, Auckland is the easiest place to buy a car: scour the hostel notice boards. **Turners Auctions** (☎03-343 9850, 09-525 1920; www.turners.co.nz) is NZ's biggest car-auction operator, with 10 locations.

LEGALITIES

Make sure your prospective vehicle has a Warrant of Fitness (WoF) and registration valid for a reasonable period: see the **Land Transport New Zealand** (www.landtransport.govt.nz) website for details.

Buyers should also take out third-party insurance, covering the cost of repairs to another vehicle in an accident that is your fault: try the **Automobile Association** (AA; ☎0800 500 444; www.aa.co.nz/travel). NZ's no-fault Accident Compensation Corporation scheme covers personal injury, but make sure you have travel insurance too.

Various car-inspection companies inspect cars for around $150; find them at car auctions, or they will come to you. Try **Vehicle Inspection New Zealand** (VINZ; ☎09-573 3230, 0800 468 469; www.vinz.co.nz) or the AA.

Before you buy it's wise to confirm ownership of the vehicle, and find out if there's anything dodgy about the car (eg stolen, or outstanding debts). The AA's **Lemon-Check** (☎09-414 6665, 0800 536 662; www.lemoncheck.co.nz) offers this service.

BUY-BACK DEALS

You can avoid the hassle of buying/selling a vehicle privately by entering into a buy-back arrangement with a dealer. Predictably, dealers often find sneaky ways of knocking down the return-sale price, which may be 50% less than what you paid.

Hiring or buying and selling a vehicle yourself (if you have the time) is usually a better bet.

Road Hazards

Kiwi traffic is usually pretty light, but it's easy to get stuck behind a slow-moving truck or campervan – pack plenty of patience. There are also lots of slow wiggly roads, one-way bridges and

plenty of gravel roads, all of which require a more cautious driving approach. And watch out for sheep!

Road Rules

Kiwis drive on the left-hand side of the road; cars are right-hand drive. Give way to the right at intersections.

At single-lane bridges (of which there are a surprisingly large number), a smaller red arrow pointing in your direction of travel means that *you* give way.

Speed limits on the open road are generally 100km/h; in built-up areas the limit is usually 50km/h. Speed cameras and radars are used extensively.

All vehicle occupants must wear a seatbelt or risk a fine. Small children must be belted into approved safety seats.

Always carry your licence when driving. Drink-driving is a serious offence and remains a significant problem in NZ, despite widespread campaigns and severe penalties. The legal blood alcohol limit is 0.08% for drivers over 20, and 0% (zero!) for those under 20.

Hitching & Ride-Sharing

NZ is no longer immune from the perils of solo hitching (especially for women). Those who decide to hitch are taking a small but potentially serious risk. That said, it's not unusual to see hitch-hikers along country roads.

Alternatively, check hostel notice boards for ride-share opportunities, or have a look at www.carpoolnz.org or www.nationalcarshare.co.nz.

Local Transport

Bus, Train & Tram

NZ's larger cities have extensive bus services but, with a few honourable exceptions, they are mainly daytime, weekday operations;

weekend services can be infrequent or nonexistent.

Negotiating inner-city Auckland is made easier by the Link and free City Circuit buses. Hamilton also has a free city-centre loop bus; Christchurch has a free city shuttle service and the historic tramway (closed post-earthquake at the time of research). The larger North Island cities also have late-night buses on boozy Friday and Saturday nights.

The only city with a decent train service is Wellington, which has five suburban routes.

Taxi

The main cities have plenty of taxis and even small towns may have a local service.

Train

NZ train travel is about the journey, not about getting anywhere in a hurry. **KiwiRail Scenic Journeys** (☏04-495 0775, 0800 872 467; www.tranzscenic.co.nz) operates two routes in the North Island:

Overlander Between Auckland and Wellington.
Capital Connection Weekday commuter service

between Palmerston North and Wellington.

Reservations can be made through KiwiRail Scenic Journeys directly, or at most train stations (notably *not* at Palmerston North or Hamilton), travel agents and visitor info centres.

Train Passes

KiwiRail Scenic Journeys' **Scenic Rail Pass** (www. tranzscenic.co.nz) allows unlimited travel on all of its rail services, including passage on the Wellington–Picton Interislander ferry. A two-week pass costs $528/402 per adult/child.

Language

WANT MORE?

For in-depth language information and handy phrases, check out Lonely Planet's *South Pacific Phrasebook*. You'll find it at **shop.lonelyplanet.com**, or you can buy Lonely Planet's iPhone phrasebooks at the Apple App Store.

New Zealand has three official languages: English, Maori and NZ sign language. Although English is what you'll usually hear, Maori has been making a comeback. You can use English to speak to anyone in New Zealand, but there are some occasions when knowing a small amount of Maori is useful, such as when visiting a *marae,* where often only Maori is spoken. Some knowledge of Maori will also help you interpret the many Maori place names you'll come across.

KIWI ENGLISH

Like the people of other English-speaking countries in the world, New Zealanders have their own, unique way of speaking the language. The flattening of vowels is the most distinctive feature of Kiwi pronunciation. For example, in Kiwi English, 'fish and chips' sounds more like 'fush and chups'. On the North Island sentences often have 'eh!' attached to the end. In the far south a rolled 'r' is common, which is a holdover from that region's Scottish heritage – it's especially noticeable in Southland.

MAORI

The Maori have a vividly chronicled history, recorded in songs and chants that dramatically recall the migration to New Zealand from Polynesia as well as other important events. Early missionaries were the first to record the language in a written form using only 15 letters of the English alphabet.

Maori is closely related to other Polynesian languages such as Hawaiian, Tahitian and Cook Islands Maori. In fact, New Zealand

Maori and Hawaiian are quite similar, even though more than 7000km separates Honolulu and Auckland.

The Maori language was never dead – it was always used in Maori ceremonies – but over time familiarity with it was definitely on the decline. Fortunately, recent years have seen a revival of interest in it, and this forms an integral part of the renaissance of *Maoritanga* (Maori culture). Many Maori people who had heard the language spoken on the *marae* for years but had not used it in their day-to-day lives, are now studying it and speaking it fluently. Maori is taught in schools throughout New Zealand, some TV programs and news reports are broadcast in it, and many English place names are being renamed in Maori. Even government departments have been given Maori names: for example, the Inland Revenue Department is also known as Te Tari Taake (the last word is actually *take,* which means 'levy', but the department has chosen to stress the long 'a' by spelling it 'aa').

In many places, Maori have come together to provide instruction in their language and culture to young children; the idea is for them to grow up speaking both Maori and English, and to develop a familiarity with Maori tradition. It's a matter of some pride to have fluency in the language. On some *marae* only Maori can be spoken.

Pronunciation

Maori is a fluid, poetic language and surprisingly easy to pronounce once you remember to split each word (some can be amazingly long) into separate syllables. Each syllable ends in a vowel. There are no 'silent' letters.

Most consonants in Maori – h, k, m, n, p, t and w – are pronounced much the same as in English. The Maori r is a flapped sound (not rolled) with the tongue near the front of the mouth. It's closer to the English 'l' in pronunciation.

The ng is pronounced as in the English words 'singing' or 'running', and can be used at the beginning of words as well as at the end. To practise, just say 'ing' over and over, then isolate the 'ng' part of it.

The letters wh, when occuring together, are generally pronounced as a soft English 'f'. This pronunciation is used in many place names in New Zealand, such as Whakatane, Whangaroa and Whakapapa (all pronounced as if they begin with a soft 'f'). There is some local variation: in the region around the Whanganui River, for example, wh is pronounced as in the English word 'when'.

The correct pronunciation of the vowels is very important. The examples below are a rough guideline – it helps to listen carefully to someone who speaks the language well. Each vowel has both a long and a short sound, with long vowels often denoted by a line over the letter or a double vowel. We have not indicated long and short vowel forms in this book.

Vowels

a	as in 'large', with no 'r' sound
e	as in 'get'
i	as in 'marine'
o	as in 'pork'
u	as the 'oo' in 'moon'

Vowel Combinations

ae, ai	as the 'y' in 'sky'
ao, au	as the 'ow' in 'how'
ea	as in 'bear'
ei	as in 'vein'
eo	as 'eh-oh'
eu	as 'eh-oo'
ia	as in the name 'Ian'
ie	as the 'ye' in 'yet'
io	as the 'ye o' in 'ye old'
iu	as the 'ue' in 'cue'
oa	as in 'roar'
oe	as in 'toe'
oi	as in 'toil'
ou	as the 'ow' in 'how'
ua	as the 'ewe' in 'fewer'

Greetings & Small Talk

Maori greetings are becoming increasingly popular – don't be surprised if you're greeted with Kia ora.

Welcome!	Haere mai!
Hello./Good luck./ Good health.	Kia ora.
Hello. (to one person)	Tena koe.
Hello. (to two people)	Tena korua.
Hello. (to three or more people)	Tena koutou.
Goodbye. (to person staying)	E noho ra.
Goodbye. (to person leaving)	Haere ra.
How are you? (to one person)	Kei te pehea koe?
How are you? (to two people)	Kei te pehea korua?
How are you? (to three or more people)	Kei te pehea koutou?
Very well, thanks./ That's fine.	Kei te pai.

Maori Geographical Terms

The following words form part of many Maori place names in New Zealand, and help you understand the meaning of these place names. For example: Waikaremoana is the Sea (moana) of Rippling (kare) Waters (wai), and Rotorua means the Second (rua) Lake (roto).

a – of
ana – cave
ara – way, path or road
awa – river or valley
heke – descend
hiku – end; tail
hine – girl; daughter
ika – fish
iti – small
kahurangi – treasured possession; special greenstone
kai – food
kainga – village
kaka – parrot
kare – rippling
kati – shut or close
koura – crayfish
makariri – cold
manga – stream or tributary
manu – bird

maunga – mountain
moana – sea or lake
moko – tattoo
motu – island
mutu – finished; ended; over
nga – the (plural)
noa – ordinary; not *tapu*
nui – big or great
nuku – distance
o – of, place of...
one – beach, sand or mud
pa – fortified village
papa – large blue-grey mudstone
pipi – common edible bivalve
pohatu – stone
poto – short
pouri – sad; dark; gloomy
puke – hill
puna – spring; hole; fountain
rangi – sky; heavens
raro – north
rei – cherished possession
roa – long
roto – lake
rua – hole in the ground; two
runga – above
tahuna – beach; sandbank
tane – man
tangata – people
tapu – sacred, forbidden or taboo
tata – close to; dash against; twin islands
tawaha – entrance or opening
tawahi – the other side (of a river or lake)
te – the (singular)

tonga – south
ure – male genitals
uru – west
waha – broken
wahine – woman
wai – water
waingaro – lost; waters that disappear in certain seasons
waka – canoe
wera – burnt or warm; floating
wero – challenge
whaka... – to act as ...
whanau – family
whanga – harbour, bay or inlet
whare – house
whenua – land or country
whiti – east

Here are some more place names composed of words in the list:

Aramoana – Sea (*moana*) Path (*ara*)
Awaroa – Long (*roa*) River (*awa*)
Kaitangata – Eat (*kai*) People (*tangata*)
Maunganui – Great (*nui*) Mountain (*maunga*)
Opouri – Place of (*o*) Sadness (*pouri*)
Te Araroa – The (*te*) Long (*roa*) Path (*ara*)
Te Puke – The (*te*) Hill (*puke*)
Urewera – Burnt (*wera*) Penis (*ure*)
Waimakariri – Cold (*makariri*) Water (*wai*)
Wainui – Great (*nui*) Waters (*wai*)
Whakatane – To Act (*whaka*) as a Man (*tane*)
Whangarei – Cherished (*rei*) Harbour (*whanga*)

GLOSSARY

Following is a list of abbreviations, 'Kiwi English', Maori, and slang terms used in this book and which you may hear in New Zealand.

All Blacks – NZ's revered national rugby union team
ANZAC – Australia and New Zealand Army Corps
Aoraki – *Maori* name for Mt Cook, meaning 'Cloud Piercer'
Aotearoa – *Maori* name for NZ, most often translated as 'Land of the Long White Cloud'

aroha – love

B&B – 'bed and breakfast' accommodation
bach – holiday home (pronounced 'batch'); see also crib
black-water rafting – rafting or tubing underground in a cave
boozer – public bar
bro – literally 'brother'; usually meaning mate
BYO – 'bring your own' (usually applies to alcohol at a restaurant or cafe)

choice/chur – fantastic; great
crib – the name for a bach in Otago and Southland

DB&B – 'dinner, bed and breakfast' accommodation
DOC – Department of Conservation (or Te Papa Atawhai); government department that administers national parks, tracks and huts

eh? – roughly translates as 'don't you agree?'

farmstay – accommodation on a Kiwi farm

football – rugby, either union or league; occasionally socce7

Great Walks – a set of nine popular tramping tracks within NZ

greenstone – jade; *pounamu*

gumboots – rubber boots or Wellingtons; originated from diggers on the gum-fields

Hawaiki –an original homeland of the *Maori*

haka – any dance, but usually a war dance

hangi – oven whereby food is steamed in baskets over embers in a hole; a *Maori* feast

hapu – subtribe or smaller tribal grouping

hei tiki – carved, stylised human figure worn around the neck; also called a *tiki*

homestay – accommodation in a family house

hongi – *Maori* greeting; the pressing of foreheads and noses, and sharing of life breath

hui – gathering; meeting

i-SITE – information centre

iwi – large tribal grouping with common lineage back to the original migration from Hawaiki; people; tribe

jandals – a contraction of Japanese sandals; flip-flops; thongs; usually rubber footwear

jersey – jumper, usually woollen; the shirt worn by rugby players

kauri – native pine

kia ora – hello

Kiwi – A New Zealander; an adjective to mean anything relating to NZ

kiwi – flightless, nocturnal brown bird with a long beak

Kiwiana – things uniquely connected to NZ life and culture, especially from bygone years

kiwifruit – small, succulent fruit with fuzzy brown skin and juicy green flesh; aka Chinese gooseberry or zespri

kumara – Polynesian sweet potato, a *Maori* staple food

Kupe – early Polynesian navigator from *Hawaiki*, credited with the discovery of the islands that are now NZ

mana – spiritual quality of a person or object; authority or prestige

Maori – indigenous people of NZ

Maoritanga – things *Maori*, ie *Maori* culture

marae – the sacred ground in front of the *Maori* meeting house; more commonly used to refer to the entire complex of buildings

Maui – a figure in *Maori* (Polynesian) mythology

mauri – life force/principle

moa – large, extinct flightless bird

moko – tattoo; usually refers to facial tattoos

munted – damaged or destroyed

nga – the (plural); see also *te*

ngai/ngati – literally, 'the people of' or 'the descendants of'; tribe (pronounced 'kai' on the South Island)

NZ – the universal term for New Zealand; pronounced 'en zed'

pa – fortified *Maori* village, usually on a hilltop

Pacific Rim – modern NZ cuisine; local produce cooked with imported styles

Pakeha – *Maori* for a white or European person

Pasifika – Pacific Island culture

paua – abalone; iridescent paua shell is often used in jewellery

pavlova – meringue cake topped with cream and kiwifruit

PI – Pacific Islander

poi – ball of woven flax

pounamu – *Maori* name for *greenstone*

powhiri – traditional *Maori* welcome onto a marae

rip – dangerously strong current running away from the shore at a beach

Roaring Forties – the ocean between 40° and 50° south, known for very strong winds

silver fern – the symbol worn by the *All Blacks* and other national sportsfolk on their jerseys; the national netball team is called the Silver Ferns

sweet, sweet as – all-purpose term like choice; fantastic, great

tapu – a strong force in *Maori* life, with numerous meanings; in its simplest form it means sacred, forbidden, taboo

te – the (singular); see also *nga*

te reo – literally 'the language'; the *Maori* language

tiki – short for *hei tiki*

tiki tour – scenic tour

tramp – bushwalk; trek; hike

tuatara – prehistoric reptile dating back to the age of dinosaurs

tui – native parson bird

wahine – woman

wai – water

wairua – spirit

Waitangi – short way of referring to the Treaty of Waitangi

waka – canoe

Warriors – NZ's popular rugby league club, affiliated with Australia's NRL

Wellywood – Wellington, because of its thriving film industry

zorbing – rolling down a hill inside an inflatable plastic ball

behind the scenes

SEND US YOUR FEEDBACK

We love to hear from travellers – your comments keep us on our toes and help make our books better. Our well-travelled team reads every word on what you loved or loathed about this book. Although we cannot reply individually to postal submissions, we always guarantee that your feedback goes straight to the appropriate authors, in time for the next edition. Each person who sends us information is thanked in the next edition – the most useful submissions are rewarded with a selection of digital PDF chapters.

Visit **lonelyplanet.com/contact** to submit your updates and suggestions or to ask for help. Our award-winning website also features inspirational travel stories, news and discussions.

Note: We may edit, reproduce and incorporate your comments in Lonely Planet products such as guidebooks, websites and digital products, so let us know if you don't want your comments reproduced or your name acknowledged. For a copy of our privacy policy visit lonelyplanet.com/privacy.

OUR READERS

Many thanks to the travellers who used the last edition and wrote to us with helpful hints, useful advice and interesting anecdotes: George & Maureen Aungle, M Byrnes, Leanne Logan

AUTHOR THANKS
Brett Aktinson

Thanks to all the i-SITE and DOC staff I tapped for vital information. At Lonely Planet, it's always great to work with Errol Hunt and the NZ author crew. Final thanks to Carol back at Casa Loma in Auckland.

Sarah Bennett & Lee Slater

Thanks to everyone who helped us on the road, including RTO, DOC and i-SITE staff, tourism operators and travellers. Big ups to everyone in-house at Lonely Planet and to Team NZ, including Errol, Peter, Brett, Charles, Sarah Ewing and, by proxy, Arnott Potter at CPP. To all who provided a park for our camper, a fridge for the flagon and even turkey for thanksgiving: *arohanui, e hoa ma*.

Peter Dragicevich

If I were to thank everyone who helped me eat and drink my way around Auckland it would be a very long list indeed. Particular thanks go to Shenita Prasad and Tania Wong for their

help in the Coromandel, and to Joanne Cole in Northland. Extra special thanks are due to my trusty Bay of Islands sidekick Matt Swaine, Taupo font-of-all-knowledge Donna Jarden, and to Tony Dragicevich and Debbie Debono for the writing retreat.

Charles Rawlings-Way

Thanks to the many generous, knowledgeable and quietly self-assured Kiwis I met on the road, especially the i-SITE staff in Palmerston North, Hamilton, Waitomo and New Plymouth. Thanks to Errol Hunt for the gig, and the ever-impressive LP production staff (including the Lords of SPP). Humongous gratitude to my tireless, witty and professional co-authors: Sarah, Brett, Peter and Lee. Thanks also to Warren for Wellington, and to Meg, Ione and Remy for holding the fort while I was away.

ACKNOWLEDGMENTS

Climate map data adapted from Peel MC, Finlayson BL & McMahon TA (2007) 'Updated World Map of the Köppen-Geiger Climate Classification', *Hydrology and Earth System Sciences*, 11, 163344.

Cover photograph: Surf at Piha beach, Massimo Ripano/Corbis. Many of the images in this guide are available for licensing from Lonely Planet Images: www.lonelyplanet images.com.

This Book

This 2nd edition of Lonely Planet's *New Zealand's North Island* guidebook was coordinated by Brett Atkinson, and researched and written by Brett, Sarah Bennett, Peter Dragicevich, Charles Rawlings-Way and Lee Slater. It includes content from the 16th edition of the *New Zealand* guide, coordinated by Charles Rawlings-Way. This guidebook was commissioned in Lonely Planet's Melbourne office, and produced by the following:

Commissioning Editor
Errol Hunt

Coordinating Editor
Amanda Williamson
Coordinating Cartographer Laura Matthewman
Coordinating Layout Designer Jacqui Saunders
Managing Editors Barbara Delissen, Martine Power
Managing Cartographers Shahara Ahmed, Corey Hutchison
Managing Layout Designer Jane Hart
Assisting Layout Designer Wibowo Rusli
Cover Research
Naomi Parker

Internal Image Research
Rebecca Skinner
Language Content
Branislava Vladisavljevic
Thanks to

Anita Banh, Imogen Bannister, David Carroll, David Connolly, Daniel Corbett, Laura Crawford, Ryan Evans, Larissa Frost, Chris Girdler, Paul Iacono, Alison Lyall, Ross Macaw, Erin McManus, Anna Metcalfe, Jane Nethercote, Susan Paterson, Trent Paton, Anthony Phelan, Kirsten Rawlings, Jessica Rose, Dianne Schallmeiner, Amanda Sierp, Gina Tsarouhas, Diana Von Holdt, Gerard Walker

452

index

how to use this book

These symbols will help you find the listings you want:

👁	Sights	👉	Tours	🍷	Drinking
🏄	Beaches	🎉	Festivals & Events	☆	Entertainment
🏃	Activities	🛏	Sleeping	🛍	Shopping
🎓	Courses	✖	Eating	ℹ	Information/Transport

Look out for these icons:

TOP CHOICE — Our author's recommendation

FREE — No payment required

🍃 — A green or sustainable option

Our authors have nominated these places as demonstrating a strong commitment to sustainability – for example by supporting local communities and producers, operating in an environmentally friendly way, or supporting conservation projects.

These symbols give you the vital information for each listing:

☏	Telephone Numbers	🛜	Wi-Fi Access	🚌	Bus
⊙	Opening Hours	🏊	Swimming Pool	⛴	Ferry
P	Parking	✅	Vegetarian Selection	M	Metro
⊖	Nonsmoking	📖	English-Language Menu	S	Subway
✳	Air-Conditioning	👪	Family-Friendly	🚋	Tram
@	Internet Access	🐾	Pet-Friendly	🚆	Train

Reviews are organised by author preference.

Map Legend

Sights
- 🏖 Beach
- 🛕 Buddhist
- 🏯 Castle
- ✝ Christian
- 🕉 Hindu
- ☪ Islamic
- ✡ Jewish
- 🏛 Monument
- 🏛 Museum/Gallery
- 🏚 Ruin
- 🍇 Winery/Vineyard
- 🦁 Zoo
- ⊙ Other Sight

Activities, Courses & Tours
- 🤿 Diving/Snorkelling
- 🛶 Canoeing/Kayaking
- 🎿 Skiing
- 🏄 Surfing
- 🏊 Swimming/Pool
- 🚶 Walking
- 🏄 Windsurfing
- ➕ Other Activity/Course/Tour

Sleeping
- 🛏 Sleeping
- ⛺ Camping

Eating
- ✖ Eating

Drinking
- ☕ Drinking
- ☕ Cafe

Entertainment
- ✪ Entertainment

Shopping
- 🛍 Shopping

Information
- ✉ Post Office
- ℹ Tourist Information

Transport
- ✈ Airport
- ⊗ Border Crossing
- 🚌 Bus
- Cable Car/Funicular
- Cycling
- Ferry
- M Metro
- Monorail
- P Parking
- S S-Bahn
- Taxi
- Train/Railway
- Tram
- Tube Station
- U U-Bahn
- • Other Transport

Routes
- Tollway
- Freeway
- Primary
- Secondary
- Tertiary
- Lane
- Unsealed Road
- Plaza/Mall
- Steps
- Tunnel
- Pedestrian Overpass
- Walking Tour
- Walking Tour Detour
- Path

Boundaries
- International
- State/Province
- Disputed
- Regional/Suburb
- Marine Park
- Cliff
- Wall

Population
- 🔴 Capital (National)
- ◉ Capital (State/Province)
- ● City/Large Town
- • Town/Village

Geographic
- 🏠 Hut/Shelter
- 🗼 Lighthouse
- Lookout
- ▲ Mountain/Volcano
- Oasis
- 🌳 Park
-)(Pass
- Picnic Area
- Waterfall

Hydrography
- River/Creek
- Intermittent River
- Swamp/Mangrove
- Reef
- Canal
- Water
- Dry/Salt/Intermittent Lake
- Glacier

Areas
- Beach/Desert
- +++ Cemetery (Christian)
- ××× Cemetery (Other)
- Park/Forest
- Sportsground
- Sight (Building)
- Top Sight (Building)

Contributing Authors

Professor James Belich wrote the History chapter (p386). James is one of NZ's pre-eminent historians and the award-winning author of *The New Zealand Wars, Making Peoples* and *Paradise Reforged*. He has also worked in TV – *New Zealand Wars* was screened in NZ in 1998.

Tony Horwitz wrote the Captain James Cook boxed text (p389) in the History chapter. Tony is a Pulitzer-winning reporter and nonfiction author. His fascination with James Cook, and with travel, took him around NZ, Australia and the Pacific while researching *Blue Latitudes* (alternatively titled *Into the Blue*), part biography of Cook and part travelogue.

John Huria (Ngai Tahu, Muaupoko) wrote the Maori Culture chapter (p403). John has an editorial, research and writing background with a focus on Maori writing and culture. He was senior editor for Maori publishing company, Huia and now runs an editorial and publishing services company, Ahi Text Solutions Ltd (www.ahitextsolutions.co.nz).

Josh Kronfeld wrote the Surfing in New Zealand boxed text (p38) in the Active North Island chapter. Josh is an ex–All Blacks flanker, whose passion for surfing NZ's beaches is legendary and who found travelling for rugby a way to surf other great breaks around the world.

Gareth Shute wrote the Music section (p418) in the Arts & Music chapter. Gareth is the author of four books, including *Hip Hop Music in Aotearoa* and *NZ Rock 1987–2007*. He is also a musician and has toured the UK, Europe and Australia as a member of the Ruby Suns and the Brunettes. He now plays in indie soul group the Cosbys.

Nandor Tanczos wrote the Environmental Issues in Aotearoa New Zealand boxed text (p398) in the Environment chapter. NZ's first Rastafarian Member of Parliament (NZ Greens Party), and the first to enter parliament in dreadlocks and a hemp suit, he was also the Green Party's spokesperson on constitutional issues and the environment from 1999 to 2008.

Vaughan Yarwood wrote the Environment chapter (p396). Vaughan is an Auckland-based writer whose most recent book is *The History Makers: Adventures in New Zealand Biography*. Earlier work includes *The Best of New Zealand, a Collection of Essays on NZ Life and Culture by Prominent Kiwis*, which he edited, and the regional history *Between Coasts: from Kaipara to Kawau*. He has written widely for NZ and international publications and is the former associate editor of *New Zealand Geographic*, for which he continues to write.

Thanks to Dr David Millar for his help with the Health content, Grace Hoet for her contribution to the Maori Culture chapter, and all the NZ regional tourism organisations for their help with preresearch briefings.

OUR STORY

A beat-up old car, a few dollars in the pocket and a sense of adventure. In 1972 that's all Tony and Maureen Wheeler needed for the trip of a lifetime – across Europe and Asia overland to Australia. It took several months, and at the end – broke but inspired – they sat at their kitchen table writing and stapling together their first travel guide, *Across Asia on the Cheap*. Within a week they'd sold 1500 copies. Lonely Planet was born.

Today, Lonely Planet has offices in Melbourne, London and Oakland, with more than 600 staff and writers. We share Tony's belief that 'a great guidebook should do three things: inform, educate and amuse'.

OUR WRITERS

Brett Atkinson

Coordinating Author, Plan Your Trip, North Island Today On his third research trip to the 'mainland', Brett explored Maori rock art, stayed in a historic cottage in the Gibbston Valley and negotiated a penny-farthing bicycle around Oamaru. Two weeks researching earthquake-damaged Christchurch left him even more impressed with the resilience and determination of the people of Canterbury. Brett has covered 10 countries for Lonely Planet, and more than 40 countries as a freelance travel and food writer. See also www.brett-atkinson.net.

Sarah Bennett & Lee Slater

East Coast, Wellington Region Raised at the top of the South, Sarah migrated to Wellington at 16 and has lived there ever since, except for various travels and a stint in London working at Lonely Planet's UK office. During research, she strives to find fault, particularly in relation to baked goods and beer selection. Sarah is joined in this endless quest by her husband and co-writer, Lee. English by birth and now a naturalised New Zealander, Lee's first career as an engineer has seen him travel extensively around Europe, the Middle East, North Africa and the Caucasus. Sarah and Lee are co-authors of *Let's Go Camping* and *The New Zealand Tramper's Handbook*. They are also freelance feature writers for newspapers and magazines, including the *Dominion Post* and *Wilderness*.

Peter Dragicevich

Auckland, Bay of Islands & Northland, Coromandel Peninsula, Taupo & the Central Plateau, The Kiwi Psyche, Arts & Music After nearly a decade working for off-shore publishing companies, Peter's life has come full circle, returning to West Auckland where he was raised. As managing editor of Auckland-based *Express* newspaper he spent much of the '90s writing about the local arts, club and bar scenes. Peter has worked on several of Lonely Planet's New Zealand guides and, after dozens of Lonely Planet assignments, it remains his favourite gig.

Charles Rawlings-Way

Waikato & the King Country, Taranaki & Whanganui, Rotorua & the Bay of Plenty, Survival Guide English by birth, Australian by chance, All Blacks fan by choice: Charles' early understanding of Aotearoa was less than comprehensive (sheep, mountains, sheep on mountains...). He realised there was more to it when a wandering uncle returned with a faux-jade *tiki* in 1981. Mt Taranaki's snowy summit, Raglan's point breaks and Whanganui's raffish charm have enthralled. He's once again smitten with NZ's phantasmal landscapes, disarming locals and determination to sculpt its own political and indigenous destiny.

OVER MORE
PAGE WRITERS

Published by Lonely Planet Publications Pty Ltd
ABN 36 005 607 983
2nd edition – October 2012
ISBN 978 1 74220 213 6
© Lonely Planet 2012   Photographs © as indicated 2012
10 9 8 7 6 5 4 3 2 1
Printed in Singapore